GET THE MOST FROM YOUR BOOK

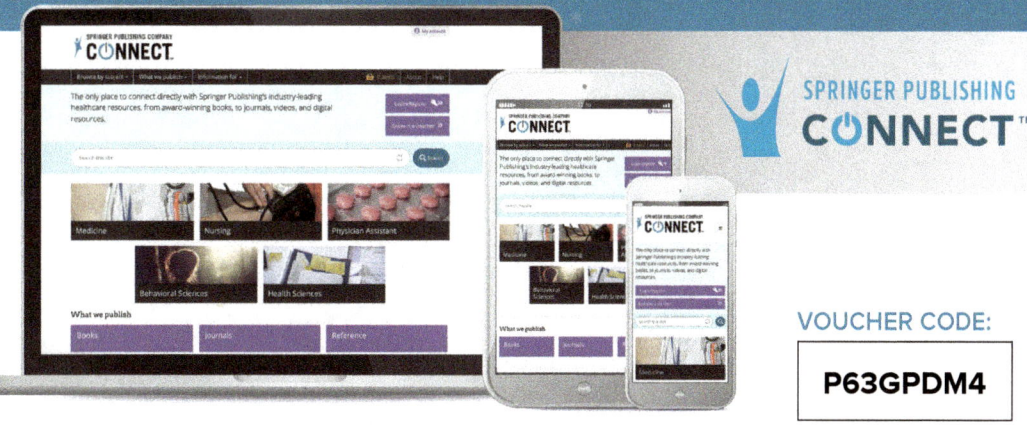

VOUCHER CODE:

P63GPDM4

Online Access

Your print purchase of *Psychology of Aging: A Biopsychosocial Perspective,* Second Edition, includes **online access via Springer Publishing Connect**™ to increase accessibility, portability, and searchability.

Insert the code at http://connect.springerpub.com/content/book/978-0-8261-6617-3 or scan the QR code and insert the voucher code today!

Having trouble? Contact our customer service department at ***cs@springerpub.com***

Instructor Resource Access for Adopters

Let us do some of the heavy lifting to create an engaging classroom experience with a variety of instructor resources included in most textbooks SUCH AS:

Visit **https://connect.springerpub.com/** and look for the **"Show Supplementary"** button on your **book homepage** to see what is available to instructors! First time using Springer Publishing Connect?

Email **textbook@springerpub.com** to create an account and start unlocking valuable resources.

Psychology of Aging

Erin L. Woodhead, PhD, is a professor in the Department of Psychology at San José State University. She completed her undergraduate degree in human development and family studies at Pennsylvania State University. She completed her master's and doctoral degrees in clinical psychology at West Virginia University. Dr. Woodhead completed postdoctoral fellowships in geropsychology at Rush University Medical Center and at the Geriatric, Research, Education, and Clinical Center (GRECC) at the VA Palo Alto Health Care System. She teaches graduate and undergraduate classes in the areas of clinical psychology, psychology of aging, and addictions. Dr. Woodhead's research is in the areas of mental health and substance use disorders among adults and older adults.

Brian P. Yochim, PhD, ABPP, is a board-certified neuropsychologist at the San Francisco VA Health Care System and a health sciences clinical professor at the University of California, San Francisco (UCSF). Prior to this, he worked at the VA Saint Louis Health Care System, VA Palo Alto Health Care System, and University of Colorado at Colorado Springs. He is a fellow of the Society for Clinical Neuropsychology (Division 40 of the American Psychological Association) and past president of the Society of Clinical Geropsychology. He has performed various service roles in the Society for Clinical Neuropsychology, Society of Clinical Geropsychology, and American Academy of Clinical Neuropsychology. He created the Verbal Naming Test for the assessment of word-finding in older adults, and his clinical work, teaching, and publications have centered on the neuropsychological assessment of older adults.

Psychology of Aging

A Biopsychosocial Perspective

SECOND EDITION

Erin L. Woodhead, PhD
Brian P. Yochim, PhD, ABPP

Editors

Copyright © 2025 Springer Publishing Company, LLC
All rights reserved.
First Springer Publishing edition 978-0-8261-3728-9 (2018)

No part of this publication may be reproduced, stored in a retrieval system, or transmitted in any form or by any means, electronic, mechanical, photocopying, recording, or otherwise, without the prior permission of Springer Publishing Company, LLC, or authorization through payment of the appropriate fees to the Copyright Clearance Center, Inc., 222 Rosewood Drive, Danvers, MA 01923, 978-750-8400, fax 978-646-8600, info@copyright.com or at www.copyright.com.

Springer Publishing Company, LLC
902 Carnegie Center/Suite 140, Princeton, NJ 08540
www.springerpub.com
connect.springerpub.com

Acquisitions Editor: Mindy Okura-Marszycki
Compositor: Thomson Digital
Production Editor: Diana Osborne

ISBN: 978-0-8261-6616-6
e-book ISBN: 978-0-8261-6617-3
DOI: 10.1891/9780826166173

SUPPLEMENTS:

 A robust set of instructor resources designed to supplement this text is located at http://connect.springerpub.com/content/book/978-0-8261-6617-3. Qualifying instructors may request access by emailing textbook@springerpub.com.

Instructor Materials:
LMS Common Cartridge–All Instructor Resources ISBN: 978-0-8261-6039-3
Instructor Manual ISBN: 978-0-8261-6618-0
Instructor Chapter PowerPoint Slides ISBN: 978-0-8261-6619-7
Sample Syllabi ISBN: 978-0-8261-6809-2
Transition Guide ISBN: 978-0-8261-8998-1

24 25 26 27 / 5 4 3 2 1

The author and the publisher of this Work have made every effort to use sources believed to be reliable to provide information that is accurate and compatible with the standards generally accepted at the time of publication. Because medical science is continually advancing, our knowledge base continues to expand. Therefore, as new information becomes available, changes in procedures become necessary. We recommend that the reader always consult current research and specific institutional policies before performing any clinical procedure or delivering any medication. The author and publisher shall not be liable for any special, consequential, or exemplary damages resulting, in whole or in part, from the readers' use of, or reliance on, the information contained in this book. The publisher has no responsibility for the persistence or accuracy of URLs for external or third-party Internet websites referred to in this publication and does not guarantee that any content on such websites is, or will remain, accurate or appropriate.

Library of Congress Control Number: 2024945692

Contact sales@springerpub.com to receive discount rates on bulk purchases.

Publisher's Note: New and used products purchased from third-party sellers are not guaranteed for quality, authenticity, or access to any included digital components.

Printed in the United States of America.

Contents

Contributors xii
Foreword Brian D. Carpenter, PhD xv
Preface xvii
Acknowledgments xx
Instructor Resources xxii

1 Introduction to the Psychology of Aging   1
Brian P. Yochim and Erin L. Woodhead

Defining Older Adults   3
Aging Internationally   5
Meeting the Needs of an Aging Population   9
Generational Influences   10
Research Methods in the Psychology of Aging   11
Conclusion   14
References   14

2 Cultural Variations in Aging Experiences of Ethnically and Sexually Diverse Older Adults   16
Kimberly E. Hiroto, Jennifer S. Ho, and Sarah J. Yarry

Ethnically Minoritized Older Adults   17
    Cohort Effects   17
    Health Disparities and Cultural Stressors   19
    Resilience and Growth   20
Sexually and Gender-Diverse Older Adults   21
    Cohort Effects   23
    Health Disparities and Cultural Stressors   25
    Resilience and Growth   27
Intersectionality   27
Conclusion   30
References   30

3   Models of Aging   35
Erin L. Woodhead and Brian P. Yochim

Biological Models of Aging   36
  Telomeres   36
  Free Radicals and Aging   39
  Caloric Restriction   40
  Genetics of Aging   41
Psychological Models of Aging   43
  Erikson's Stages of Psychosocial Development   44
  Selective Optimization With Compensation   44
  Socioemotional Selectivity Theory   46
  Life Course Perspective   47
Social Models of Aging   47
  Role Theory   48
  Activity Theory   48
  Disengagement Theory   49
  Continuity Theory   49
  Critical Gerontology   49
  Social Determinants of Health and the Weathering Hypothesis   50
Conclusion   50
References   51

4   The Aging Body   55
Adriana Savettiere and J. Kaci Fairchild

The Integumentary System   56
  Age-Related Changes to the Physiology of the Integumentary System   56
The Musculoskeletal System   57
  Age-Related Changes to the Physiology of the Musculoskeletal System   58
The Nervous System   59
  Age-Related Changes to the Physiology of the Nervous System   59
The Cardiovascular System   62
  Age-Related Changes to the Physiology of the Cardiovascular System   62
The Immune System   63
  Age-Related Changes to the Physiology of the Immune System   63
The Respiratory System   64
  Age-Related Changes to the Physiology of the Respiratory System   64
The Endocrine System   65
  Age-Related Changes to the Physiology of the Endocrine System   65
The Urinary System   66
  Age-Related Changes to the Physiology of the Urinary System   67
The Reproductive System   68
  Age-Related Changes to the Physiology of the Reproductive System   68
The Digestive System   69
  Age-Related Changes to the Physiology of the Digestive System   69
Conclusion   70
References   70

CONTENTS vii

5 Age-Related Illnesses 74
Eliza Morgan, Devon Delaney, and J. Kaci Fairchild

Common Disorders of the Integumentary System 74
    Dermatitis and Pruritus 75
    Shingles 75
    Skin Cancer 75
Common Disorders of the Musculoskeletal System 75
    Osteoporosis 76
    Sarcopenia 76
    Osteoarthritis 76
Common Disorders of the Nervous System 76
    Cataracts, Macular Degeneration, and Glaucoma 77
    Tinnitus and Presbycusis 77
    Peripheral Neuropathy 78
Common Disorders of the Cardiovascular System 78
    Hypertension 79
    Congestive Heart Failure 79
    Cerebral Arteriosclerosis and Strokes 79
Common Disorders of the Respiratory System 80
    Coronavirus Disease-19 80
    Pneumonia 80
    Chronic Obstructive Pulmonary Disease 81
    Asthma 81
    Lung Cancer 81
Common Disorders of the Endocrine System 82
    Diabetes 82
    Hyperthyroidism 82
    Hypothyroidism 84
    Thyroid Cancer 84
Common Disorders of the Urinary System 84
    Urinary Tract Infections 84
    Chronic Kidney Disease 85
Common Disorders of the Reproductive System 85
    Uterine and Ovarian Cancer 85
    Prostate Cancer 86
Common Disorders of the Digestive System 86
    Constipation 86
    Gastritis 87
Conclusion 87
References 87

6 Changes to the Brain: Methods of Investigation, Aging, and Neuroplasticity 92
Tyler A. Rickards, Emily E. Smith, Juliana Baldo, and Brian P. Yochim

Part 1: Methods of Investigating Age-Related Changes in the Brain 93
Part 2: Changes That Occur to the Brain With Typical Aging 100
Part 3: Neuroplasticity 103
    A Brief History of Neuroplasticity 103
    On Naming: The Plasticity of the Term "Neuroplasticity" 104
    Novel Methods to Enhance Neuroplasticity 109

Conclusion 110
References 110

7 Personality and Emotional Development 117
Erin L. Woodhead

Personality Development 117
  Overview of Personality Theories 118
Emotional Functioning in Late Life 125
  Age and Emotional Well-Being 126
  Models of Emotional Functioning in Late Life 126
  Changes in Emotional Functioning in Older Adulthood 128
  Attention to Positive and Negative Stimuli 131
  Age-Related Differences in Emotion Regulation 133
  Keys to Happy Aging 135
Conclusion 135
References 136

8 Mental Health and Aging 141
Erin L. Woodhead

Use of Mental Health Services by Older Adults 142
Beliefs and Stigma Around Mental Healthcare 142
  Beliefs About Mental Healthcare 142
  Mental Health Stigma 143
Diagnosing Mental Health Conditions Among Older Adults 144
  Mood Disorders 144
  Anxiety Disorders 145
  Posttraumatic Stress Disorder 147
  Personality Disorders 147
  Suicidality 148
  Substance Use Disorders 148
  Schizophrenia 150
Assessment of Mental Health Conditions Among Older Adults 151
  The Center for Epidemiologic Studies Depression Scale 151
  The Geriatric Depression Scale 151
  The Patient Health Questionnaire-9 152
  The Cornell Scale for Depression in Dementia 152
Empirically Supported Treatments for Older Adults 154
  Mood Disorders and Suicidality 154
  Anxiety Disorders and Posttraumatic Stress Disorder 156
  Personality Disorders 156
  Substance Use Disorders 157
  Schizophrenia 157
Conclusion 158
References 159

9 Cognition and Aging 166
Kathrine Whitman, Talia Barrett, Jennifer H. Coane, and Sharda Umanath

Aging: Changes in Cognitive Functioning 166
Primary Cognitive Functions Affected in Aging 167
  Sensation and Perception 167
  Attention 168

      Memory   169
      Intelligence and Executive Functioning   170
      Language   171
      Emotional Processing   172
      Wisdom   172
   Theories of Cognitive Aging   173
      Top-Down and Bottom-Up Processing   173
      Controlled and Automatic Processing   173
      Speed of Processing   174
      Sensory Deficit and Common Cause Hypotheses   174
      Inhibitory Deficit Hypothesis   174
      Other Theories of Cognitive Aging   175
   Methodological Considerations in Cognitive Aging Research   176
   Impacts of Cognitive Aging on Everyday Living   177
      Activities of Daily Living   177
      Cognitive Training and Rehabilitation   178
      Factors That Promote Healthy Cognitive Aging   178
   Conclusion   178
   References   179

10   Neurocognitive Disorders in Late Life   185
Brian P. Yochim

Delirium   186
Neurocognitive Disorders: Diagnostic Terminology   187
Prevalence of Dementia   189
Causes of Neurocognitive Disorders   189
Traumatic Brain Injuries   190
Alzheimer Disease   191
   Treatments for Alzheimer Disease   191
   Neuropathological Ratings of Alzheimer Disease   192
   Genetics of Alzheimer Disease   192
   Biomarkers of Alzheimer Disease   193
   Progression of Alzheimer Disease   193
Lewy Body Disease   195
Parkinson Disease   197
Vascular Disease   197
Frontotemporal Dementia   198
Limbic-Predominant Age-Related TDP-43 Encephalopathy   200
Alcohol-Related Dementia   200
Other Causes of Neurocognitive Disorders   201
Conclusion   201
References   203

11   Death and the Dying Process, Bereavement, and Widowhood   209
Andrea June and Meghan A. Marty

Dying in America   210
   Definition and Causes of Death   210
   Institutionalization of Death   211
   Death Trajectories   211
Attitudes Toward Death   211
Advance Care Planning   212

Palliative and Hospice Care   213
Mental Health at the End of Life   214
Medical Aid in Dying   215
Bereavement   216
   Definitions of Bereavement, Grief, and Mourning   216
   Common Reactions to Bereavement   217
   Bereavement and Mental Health Disorders   217
   Prolonged Grief Disorder   219
   Theoretical Models of Adjustment to Bereavement   220
   Intervention for Bereaved Individuals   222
Late-Life Spousal Loss   223
   General Characteristics   223
   Impact of Spousal Loss on Partner Mortality   224
   Bereavement After Caregiving   224
Conclusion   224
References   225

12 Relationships, Families, and Aging: Changes in Roles With Aging   230
Rachel L. Rodriguez, J. W. Terri Huh, and Susan Ryan

Nuptial and Relationship Status: Prevalence and Demographics   231
Effects of Nuptial and Relationship Status on Physical and Psychological Health   232
   Marital Quality and the Effects of Marriage on Physical and Psychological Health   233
   When Marriage Ends: Impact on Health and Psychological Outcomes   234
   Cohabitation   235
   Other Significant Relationships in Late Life   235
Caregiving Relationships   237
   General Trends in Caregiving   238
   Physical, Psychological, and Emotional Impacts of Caregiving   239
   Adult Children as Caregivers   240
   Older Adults as Caregivers   242
Impact of the COVID-19 Pandemic on Older Adult Relationships   242
Conclusion   243
References   244

13 Aging, Work, and Retirement   251
Christina Matz and Jacquelyn James

The Intersection of Aging, Work, and Retirement   252
Ageism and Marginalization   253
Who Is an Older Worker?   255
The Aging Workforce   257
   Historical and Demographic Changes   257
   Job Performance and Age   259
Changing Nature of Retirement   261
   Historical Changes   261
   Retirement Patterns and Options   261
   Factors Related to Retirement Transitions   262
   Retirement Planning   265
Conclusion   266
Acknowledgments   267
References   267

14 Aging and the Legal System   274
Sheri Gibson and Rachel Weiskittle

Ethical Competencies in Geropsychology   274
Advance Care Planning for Older Adults   275
Ethics in Long-Term Care   277
Foundational Ethics of Decision-Making   279
Autonomy and Surrogate Decision-Making   280
   Clinical Decisional Capacity   280
   Guardianship, Conservatorship, and Other Protective Arrangements   281
   Assessing Financial Capacity   283
   Assessing Sexual Consent Capacity   284
   Assessing Driving Capacity   284
Elder Mistreatment, Neglect, and Exploitation   285
   Risk and Protective Factors for Elder Abuse   286
   Ethical Considerations in Cases of Elder Abuse   286
   Respecting Cultural Differences in Cases of Elder Abuse   288
Ethics in Research   291
Conclusion   292
Acknowledgments   293
References   293

15 The Social Context of Aging   298
Nancy A. Pachana and Sophie Griffiths

Models of Healthy Aging   299
   The Pathway to Optimize Functional Ability   299
Social Determinants of Health in Later Life   302
   The Social Determinants of Health   302
   The Importance of Social Relationships and Group Membership   303
Strategies to Maintain Physical and Mental Well-Being in Later Life   303
   Physical Activity   304
   Mental Stimulation   305
   Social Engagement   307
   Loneliness   308
Stereotypes and Ageism   309
   The Stereotype Content Model   310
   Stereotype Embodiment   310
Ageism   311
   Hostile and Benevolent Ageism   311
   The Financial and Social Costs of Ageism and Negative Age Stereotypes   312
   WHO Framework for Action Against Ageism   312
   An Age-Friendly World   313
Conclusion   315
References   316

Index   321

Contributors

Juliana Baldo, PhD
Research Neuropsychologist, Research Service, VA Northern California Health Care System, Martinez, California, and Clinical Associate, Department of Neurology, University of California, Davis, California

Talia Barrett, BA
Clinical Research Coordinator, Colby College, Waterville, Maine

Jennifer H. Coane, PhD
Professor, Psychology Department, Colby College, Waterville, Maine

Devon Delaney, MA, MS
Doctoral Candidate, Department of Clinical Psychology, PGSP-Stanford PsyD Consortium, Palo Alto, California

J. Kaci Fairchild, PhD, ABPP-Gero
Deputy Director, Clinical Professor (affiliated), Psychiatry and Behavioral Sciences, Stanford University School of Medicine, Stanford, California

Sheri Gibson, PhD
Faculty Affiliation, Gerontology Center, University of Colorado Colorado Springs, Colorado Springs, Colorado

Sophie Griffiths, BPsycSc (Hons)
Postgraduate Scholar, School of Psychology, The University of Queensland, Brisbane, Australia

Kimberly E. Hiroto, PhD
Clinical Psychologist, VA Palo Alto Health Care System, Palo Alto, California

Jennifer S. Ho, PsyD
Clinical Psychologist, Durham VA Health Care System, Durham, North Carolina

J. W. Terri Huh, PhD, ABPP
Program Director, Wright Institute Cognitive Behavioral Therapy Program and Older Adult Counseling and Psychological Services, Wright Institute Clinical Services, Berkeley, California

Jacquelyn James, PhD
Founder, Sloan Research Network on Aging & Work, Boston College School of Social Work, Chestnut Hill, Massachusetts

Andrea June, PhD
Professor and Gerontology Program Coordinator, Department of Psychological Science, Central Connecticut State University, New Britain, Connecticut

Meghan A. Marty, PhD
Clinical Psychologist, Home-Based Primary Care, Western North Carolina Veterans Affairs Health Care System, Asheville, North Carolina

Christina Matz, MSW, PhD
Associate Professor and Director, Center on Aging & Work, Boston College School of Social Work, Chestnut Hill, Massachusetts

Eliza Morgan, MS
Doctoral Candidate, Department of Clinical Psychology, Palo Alto University, Palo Alto, California

Nancy A. Pachana, PhD
Professor of Clinical Geropsychology, School of Psychology, The University of Queensland, Brisbane, Australia

Tyler A. Rickards, PhD, ABPP
Neuropsychologist, Department of Psychiatry and Neuropsychology, University of Maryland Rehabilitation & Orthopaedic Institute, Baltimore, Maryland

Rachel L. Rodriguez, PhD, MPH, ABPP
Clinical Psychologist, Mental and Behavioral Health Service Line, Durham VA Health Care System, Durham, North Carolina

Susan Ryan, PsyD
Associate Director, Wright Institute Older Adult Counseling Program, Wright Institute Clinical Services, Berkeley, California

Adriana Savettiere, BS
Doctoral Candidate, Palo Alto University, Palo Alto, California

Emily E. Smith, PhD
Rehabilitation Neuropsychologist, Division of Medical Psychology, Department of Neurology, The Sandra and Malcolm Berman Brain & Spine Institute, LifeBridge Health, Baltimore, Maryland

Sharda Umanath, PhD
Associate Professor, Psychological Science Department, Claremont McKenna College, Claremont, California

Rachel Weiskittle, PhD
Assistant Professor, Department of Psychology, University of Colorado Colorado Springs, Colorado Springs, Colorado

Kathrine Whitman, BA
Lab Manager, Psychological Science Department, Claremont McKenna College, Claremont, California

Erin L. Woodhead, PhD
Professor, Department of Psychology, San José State University, San José, California

Sarah J. Yarry, PhD
Licensed Clinical Psychologist, Albany, New York

Brian P. Yochim, PhD, ABPP
Clinical Neuropsychologist, San Francisco VA Health Care System, and Health Sciences Clinical Professor, Department of Psychiatry and Behavioral Sciences, University of California San Francisco, San Francisco, California

Foreword

Everyone needs to know something about aging. Of course we all hope to experience it firsthand in our personal lives, in the long lives of our family members, friends, and, ultimately, ourselves. Likewise, we'll all encounter issues related to aging in our work, regardless of what type of work that is. To be effective in that work requires knowledge about the aging experience, and *Psychology and Aging* is a superb resource for professionals across disciplines and specialties and anyone who wants to expand their familiarity with what it means to grow older.

The editors, Drs. Woodhead and Yochim, have assembled an exceptional group of contributors, each of whom shares their expertise across essential topics related to aging, bringing both breadth and depth where it's needed. Throughout these pages, chapters cover foundational knowledge about aging, ranging from biological underpinnings of the aging process, to psychological theory and applications related to well-being, to social aspects about what it means to be an older adult living in contemporary society. Readers at all levels could choose any one chapter and obtain a solid introduction to a topic, but taken altogether, the book provides a comprehensive summary of current issues and empirically informed facts about aging. Embedded within its biopsychosocial perspective is particularly welcome coverage of cognitive health and mental health in later life and their critical intersections to physical health and social well-being. Aging is a grand, multifaceted experience, and the variety of the chapters in this book acknowledge the richness of growing older, its challenges and opportunities, and its relevance across disciplines and professions.

Psychology of Aging will be a valuable resource for students, instructors, and professionals alike. Students in different areas of study will get a thorough primer on aging, one that prepares them for their career ahead and might even encourage some students to pursue more in-depth training related to aging, where opportunities continue to expand and the need is great. Instructors will find in this book a well-organized, clear, and concise set of readings and accompanying resources to guide course construction and implementation. Finally, professionals across fields and settings can turn to the text for informative, contemporary summaries of key topics relevant to clinical practice, research, and public policy.

Readers are in good hands with these editors, both of whom have superlative training in geropsychology themselves and have been immersed in scholarship, training, and leadership roles throughout their long, distinguished careers. Likewise, the contributors reflect a broad range of perspectives, each an expert in their area and knowledgeable about current issues and trends and the necessity of attention to sociodemographic diversity, cultural variation, and the social determinants that influence health and human experience.

People who are knowledgeable about aging will be well equipped to help shape a society that cares for older adults expertly, supports older adults expansively, and values older adults enthusiastically. *Psychology and Aging* is an important text that advances that cause.

Brian D. Carpenter, PhD
Professor of Psychological and Brain Sciences
Professor of Medicine, Division of Palliative Medicine
Co-Director, Harvey A. Friedman Center for Aging
Washington University in St. Louis
St. Louis, Missouri

Preface

OVERALL GOAL OF THE BOOK

An instructor for a graduate course on the psychology of aging has the challenge of finding a textbook for this area that is tailored to graduate students. In addition, the book has to be relevant to multiple fields since many types of disciplines are involved in the study of aging. When we undertook writing the first edition, it was in response to the need for such a book in our courses. A search of available textbooks did not arrive at a choice that would fit well with a graduate-level course. There were books about gerontology in general, handbooks that went into depth on specific topics but did not have the same breadth of coverage as a typical textbook, books focused on certain aspects of aging (e.g., mental health), or books on adult development and aging that included coverage of early and middle adulthood that was beyond the scope of this class. Like most graduate-level instructors, at the time we cobbled together a series of articles for the class to read and opted not to have any textbook. This book was written to fill the gap in the options available to graduate-level instructors of aging-related courses.

The current book can serve as a primer for any graduate student who is going to work with older adults in any significant capacity, ranging from clinical work, to research lab work, to other allied health professions. In reading any of the chapters, students are provided with the requisite foundational knowledge in a given area and are introduced to specific areas in greater depth. For example, a reader of Chapter 6 will be prepared to enter a neuroimaging lab that explores neuroplasticity in older adults. Readers of Chapter 10 will have a solid foundation on neurocognitive disorders that they may encounter in their future work. The level of depth provided in these chapters is typically not available in undergraduate textbooks on aging, as textbooks aimed at undergraduates tend to target breadth rather than depth. This book is unique in that it quickly introduces students to the background knowledge needed in order to understand some of the more complex concepts in the psychology of aging. Additionally, this book provides clear explanations of concepts (e.g., genetics of aging research, neuroimaging techniques, understanding of important legal documents for older adults, neurocognitive disorders) that, in our experience as instructors for psychology of aging classes, prove to be stumbling blocks for students wanting to learn about aging.

DISTINGUISHING FEATURES

While other textbooks include coverage of adults of all ages, this text is unique in that it focuses solely on older adults, providing in-depth coverage of this growing population. The two editors, Brian P. Yochim and Erin L. Woodhead, work in full-time clinical and academic positions, and the content of the book is applicable to students who plan to work in academic or allied health fields. Both editors have taught psychology of aging courses at the graduate and undergraduate levels and are familiar with the textbooks available to instructors in this area.

The second edition provides several new features. First, a new chapter was added on the social context of aging. This chapter acknowledges the large roles that society and culture play in aging and introduces students to models of ageism as well as age-friendly initiatives. Second, the chapter "The Aging Body and Age-Related Health Conditions" from the first edition was split into two chapters: "The Aging Body" and "Age-Related Illnesses." This represents an increased need to separate "typical" aging from diseases of aging, since typical age-related changes are not synonymous with disease, and this is a common assumption that students make. Third, the first edition chapter "Biological Theories of Aging" was expanded to include models of aging from across the fields of biology, psychology, and sociology. Additionally, learning objectives are now incorporated into the start of each chapter so that the goals of the chapter are clear to students. Finally, references were updated throughout the second edition with a stronger overall focus on diversity in each chapter.

The second edition continues to have a unique focus on biological aspects of aging, written in such a manner as to be easily comprehensible to graduate students who are not specializing in this area. When students need important biological concepts explained to them, this book can serve as a useful and user-friendly resource. At the same time, students specializing in biological aspects of aging will find the book to be a useful introduction to the psychology of aging, and research methods and findings from psychology will enhance their research in the biology of aging. The book also provides more coverage on cognitive reserve and neurocognitive disorders than other textbooks in the area. This is balanced by coverage of social aspects of aging that one would not find in books on the biology of aging, such as legal aspects of aging or the aging experience for LGBTQ+ older adults and intersectionality as it applies to older adults.

Instructors can teach a class with this book as the sole collection of readings or can supplement this text with additional articles. Each chapter ends with discussion questions that can be used for discussion in class or essay questions for exams in graduate classes. In support of the text, an Instructor Manual, PowerPoints, and Syllabi are available at http://connect.springerpub.com/content/book/978-0-8261-6617-3. Qualified instructors can request these ancillaries by emailing textbook@springerpub.com.

INTENDED AUDIENCE

This book is intended for graduate students or upper-level undergraduate students in psychology, biology, public health, nursing, counseling, social work, gerontology, speech pathology, psychiatry, and other disciplines who provide services for, or perform research with, older adults. Unlike undergraduate textbooks, this text provides a foundation for graduate students across disciplines who want to embark on research, clinical, or healthcare careers with older adults. After reading this book, it will serve as a reference that is frequently consulted to provide explanations of many concepts in the field.

THE BOOK'S ORGANIZATION AND CONTENT

Each chapter in this text was authored by experts in the field to ensure appropriate coverage of the area. An introduction to the field is presented in Chapter 1, which also covers common research methods in the area. Following this, Chapter 2 discusses diversity in the aging experience, including risk and resilience factors among racial and ethnic minority older adults as well as LGBTQ+ older adults. Chapters then provide foundational knowledge on theories of aging, biological aspects of aging, and psychological and social aspects of aging. An understanding of the psychological aspects of aging must begin with a core foundation in biological aspects of aging, age-related health changes, and chronic illnesses common among older adults, which are covered in Chapters 3 to 5. This section includes a chapter on general theories of aging across multiple disciplines, such as the free radical theory of aging from a biological perspective. Chapters 4 and 5 provide a detailed overview of typical age-related health changes and common physical health problems in older adults, as well as how these conditions impact the quality of life of older adults. This will help any professional understand the health problems that older adults are facing. Chapter 6 provides an overview of normal changes that occur to the brain with aging, starting with an overview of neuroimaging methods and ending with an introduction to the exciting area of neuroplasticity.

The book then moves into psychological aspects of aging. Changes in personality and emotional development are covered in Chapter 7. A discussion of the unique mental health aspects of aging is presented in Chapter 8. Typical changes in cognitive functioning are presented in Chapter 9. Chapter 10 consists of an up-to-date presentation of neurocognitive disorders in aging, including timely topics such as Alzheimer disease, delirium, Lewy body disease, frontotemporal dementia, and traumatic brain injuries in older adults.

Social aspects of aging are covered in the last chapters. Death, bereavement, and widowhood are covered in Chapter 11. Aging's impact on relationships and families is discussed in Chapter 12. Working in late life and retirement are covered in Chapter 13, with a focus on helping students understand the complexities of medical coverage and retirement options in the current economic climate. The intersection of aging and the legal system is covered in Chapter 14, with explanations of concepts such as durable power of attorney, advance directives, capacity assessment, and elder abuse. Finally, the closing chapter (Chapter 15) focuses on the social context of aging in the United States and internationally, specifically around the role of ageism and updated work on age-friendly communities.

Thank you for your interest in the psychology of aging. We hope you find this learning journey as fascinating as all the authors of this book have. May this book serve as a solid foundation for a career serving older adults wherever you are.

Erin L. Woodhead, PhD
Brian P. Yochim, PhD, ABPP

Acknowledgments

FROM ERIN L. WOODHEAD

Thank you to my coeditor, Brian P. Yochim, for taking on this revision together. We helped each other through the process, and I look forward to more projects together in the future! We also benefited greatly from the guidance provided by our editors at Springer Publishing Company, who helped us meet our deadlines and shape our materials into a book.

I would also like to thank the mentors I have had over the years at the Pennsylvania State University, West Virginia University, Rush University Medical Center, and the VA Palo Alto Health Care System. I value their mentorship and their assistance with my career path more than I can describe in this section. I am also grateful to my coworkers at San José State University, who have created an environment where balancing work and family life is the norm rather than the exception. They continue to inspire me with their dedication to their research, their students, and their lives outside of academia.

Brian and I also owe a debt of gratitude to all of the clinicians, researchers, and trainees who contributed to this book. They put up with a lot of emails from us and produced excellent work to help train the future generation of professionals working in the field of aging.

Finally, I would like to thank my family for supporting my work on this book and my career in higher education and academia.

FROM BRIAN P. YOCHIM

I want to thank my friend and colleague Erin L. Woodhead, PhD, for coediting this book with me. Without you, this book would not have been completed. I hope you are willing to work on future projects with me. I am grateful to Kirsten Elmer, associate content strategist, and Mindy Okura-Marszycki, senior content strategist and acquisitions editor in behavioral sciences, at Springer Publishing Company for all your help along the way. Thank you for your guidance and immediate responses whenever we needed assistance.

The broad field of gerontology owes its existence to the thousands of older adults who have donated their time to participate in research. We also are indebted to the researchers who have spent their careers tirelessly performing studies to add to our knowledge base and to the agencies that fund them. This book is a result of your work. Without you, books such as this would not exist.

Thank you to my friends and colleagues who contributed chapters to this book. I want to thank my friends and colleagues at the University of Colorado at Colorado Springs, at the VA Palo Alto Health Care System, the VA Saint Louis Health Care System, and the VA San Francisco Health Care System. I have learned a great deal from you about aging, how to be a great colleague, and many other things. Thank you to my mentor, Peter Lichtenberg, who has been everything I could ask for in a mentor throughout my career.

Most of all, I thank my dear wife Jill and our son Ellis, who supported me spending my weekends and evenings working on this book. I look forward to seeing the contributions you will make to the world throughout your lives.

Instructor Resources

 A robust set of instructor resources designed to supplement this text is located at http://connect.springerpub.com/content/book/978-0-8261-6617-3. Qualifying instructors may request access by emailing textbook@springerpub.com.

- LMS Common Cartridge–All Instructor Resources
- Instructor Manual
    - Chapter Overview
    - Learning Objectives
    - Classroom Discussion Prompts with possible discussion points
    - Case Studies with accompanying discussion questions and suggested responses
- Instructor Chapter PowerPoint Slides
- Sample Syllabi
- Transition Guide: First Edition to Second Edition

Introduction to the Psychology of Aging

Brian P. Yochim and Erin L. Woodhead

LEARNING OBJECTIVES

- Describe approximate proportions of older adults residing at home, in assisted living environments, or in long-term care facilities.
- Summarize trends in the older adult population internationally.
- Distinguish between life expectancy at birth and life expectancy at 65 and older.
- Describe some of the limitations in meeting the healthcare needs of an aging population
- Compare the strengths and limitations of cross-sectional and longitudinal research designs.

In 2021, at age 100, Betty Reid Soskin was the oldest ranger in the National Park System. Born on September 22, 1921, she has lived through racial discrimination, gender discrimination, and World War II and other wars and worked until age 100 to tell her story at Rosie the Riveter/World War II Home Front National Historical Park in Richmond, California. Her great-grandmother had been held in slavery, and Betty carried a picture of her when she attended President Barack Obama's inauguration in 2009, before meeting him in 2015. She has been interviewed on National Public Radio (NPR), the Public Broadcasting Service (PBS), the *Today Show*, *Newsweek*, and other news outlets, and multiple films have been made about her life (National Park Service, 2023; see Box 1.1).

BOX 1.1 Betty Reid Soskin

One of the authors of this chapter met with Betty Reid Soskin in April 2017, when she was 95. She gave a talk three times a week at Rosie the Riveter/World War II Homefront National Historical Park in Richmond, California, and the auditorium was usually filled to capacity. Betty spoke for 40 minutes, without notes or slides, about her experiences as a young African American woman working in World War II.

Afterward, Betty agreed to answer several questions about her life (B. R. Soskin, personal communication, April 29, 2017).

On continuing to work at age 95:

"It's never been a conscious choice. . . . I never really stopped working . . . but then I never had a job that I sought. I've never had a job because I wanted it; I've always been invited in. I've just never been invited out!"

On looking toward the future:

"As long as I have first experiences, a sense of life continually unfolding, I still wake up every morning, expecting newness. There is so much that's novel, that I have a sense that life is continually opening up, so I don't have a sense of completion."

On the mental health needs of women in their 90s:

"There are days when I have a sense that I'm living my life out of context. I've outlived all my peers, and it gives me a sense of being in uncharted waters, because I don't have role models anymore. If I didn't have work that was significant, I'd get lost. People visit from nursing homes, 10 years younger than I am, and that's when I feel out of context. I'm 10 years their senior. But I'm not threatened by the unfamiliar. I have a feeling that I'm in control."

On political activism:

"I went through the 1960s as a political activist. I was fighting for my personal rights and the rights of my children, granted by the Constitution. The Constitution and Bill of Rights are only blueprints . . . each generation has to re-create democracy. By participating in it or by not doing so, we determine the outcome."

How is the aging experience different for her as an African American woman? Why was she able to be healthy enough to work into her 90s, whereas other people develop neurocognitive disorders or physical disabilities at a much younger age that prevent them from working? What is her physical health like? How does past and present racism affect her life now? Are her cognitive abilities similar to how they were in her 50s? Is she more or less likely to develop mental health problems at her age? Is her personality more likely to be similar or different than how it was in her younger years? In her 90s, was it necessary for her to be working to support herself? How have her relationships changed in the past several decades? These questions are explored in this textbook.

DEFINING OLDER ADULTS

Discussions around aging always bring up the question about what is considered older adulthood. Many factors go into who we consider older, and chronological age reflects only one of those components. We might also consider social age, which considers the types of roles the person occupies. We typically think of grandparents as older adults, but what about people who become grandparents in their 30s or 40s? Are these individuals "older adults"? What about functional age? This refers to the idea that some older adults may have "the heart of a 25-year-old" in terms of their physiological functioning. Another metric of age might be how old you feel, often termed "subjective age" or "felt age." Research finds that there is often a discrepancy between "felt age" and chronological age, with a trend starting in younger adulthood showing that many people feel and act younger than their chronological age (Ambrosi-Randić et al., 2018). In a sample of adults age 60 to 95, the subjective age reported by participants was, on average, 59.5 years old, which was 10 years younger than the average chronological age of the sample (Ambrosi-Randić et al., 2018). Within the sample, 52.9% of participants reported feeling younger than their chronological age, 35.5% felt the same age, and 11.6% reported feeling older than their chronological age. Perhaps not unexpectedly, those with a younger subjective age tended to report good self-rated physical and mental health and higher levels of optimism, life satisfaction, and sense of a meaningful life.

Typically, the chronological age of 65 is used as the cutoff between middle age and old age. This criterion may have originated in Germany, which was the first country to create a social insurance program for older adults, in 1889. The retirement age was first designated as 70 and was lowered to 65 in 1916. When Social Security was created in the United States in 1935, age 65 was chosen as the retirement age for two main reasons. First, at that time, approximately half of the existing state pension systems used age 65 as the retirement age and half used age 70. The federal Railroad Retirement System was newly created in 1934 and used age 65 as its retirement age. Second, actuarial studies found that a self-sustaining system could be created with small levels of payroll taxation using age 65 (Social Security Administration, 2015).

Some countries, such as Japan, have suggested moving the definition of older adulthood to age 75 (Ouchi et al., 2017). As noted by the Japan Geriatrics Society, many adults between the ages of 65 to 74 are still active and engaged. In addition, as noted by measures such as grip strength and gait speed, many older adults have maintained physical functioning into late life more so than older adults in prior generations (see Figure 1.1).

In thinking about the current definition of older adulthood starting at age 65, you might also consider the difference between a 65-year-old and a 90-year-old. These individuals likely have vastly different abilities and daily experiences, yet we technically consider both of them "older adults." Researchers have historically delineated

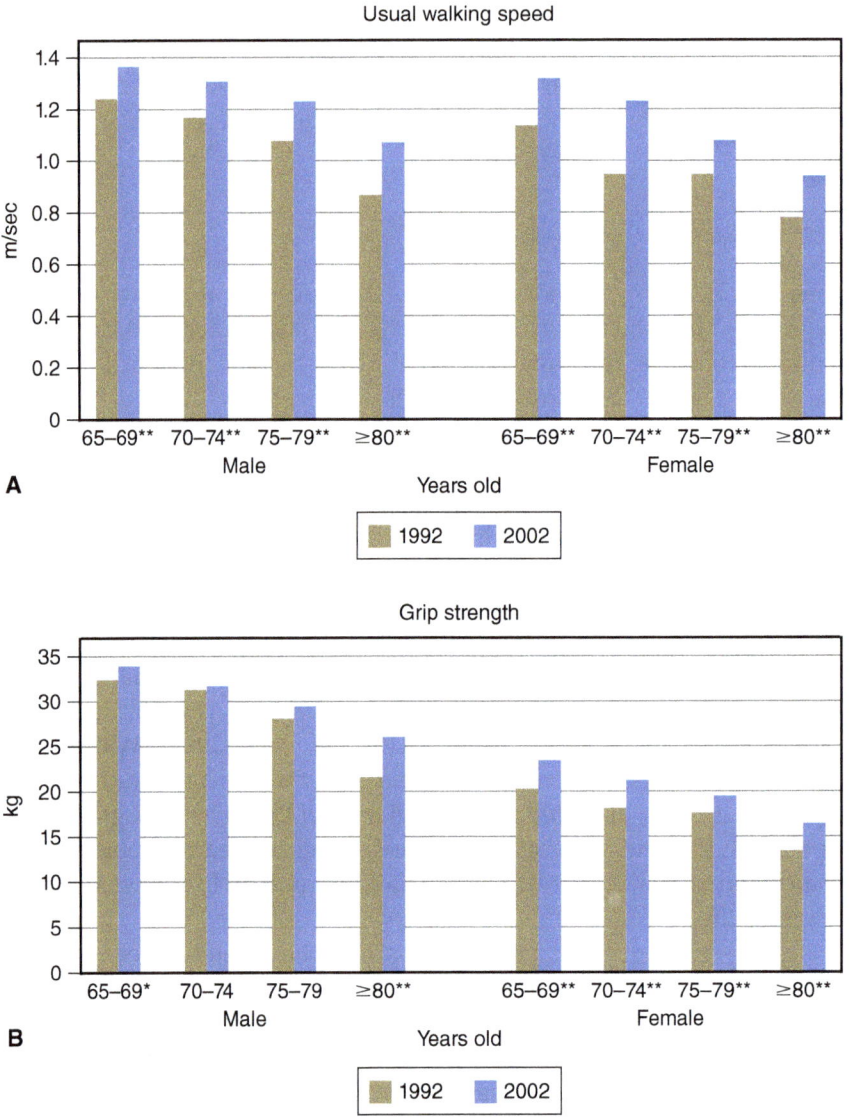

Figure 1.1 (**A**) Gait speed and (**B**) grip strength improvements between 1992 and 2022, as recorded from older adult participants in Japan.

*p < .05. **p < .01.

Source: Ouchi, Y., Rakugi, H., Arai, H., Akishita, M., Ito, H., Toba, K., Kai, I., & on behalf of the Joint Committee of Japan Gerontological Society & Japan Geriatrics Society. (2017). Redefining the elderly as aged 75 years and older: Proposal from the Joint Committee of Japan Gerontological Society and the Japan Geriatrics Society. *Geriatrics and Gerontology International*, 17, 1045–1047. https://doi.org/10.1111/ggi.13118.

older adults into three groups based on chronological age: young-old (65–74 years old), old-old (75–84 years old), and the oldest-old (age 85 and older; Neugarten, 1974). This helps counteract the idea that all older adults are alike and have similar concerns or needs. The proposal from Japan suggests that adults ages 65 to 74 be classified into a group known as "pre–old age" followed by adults ages 75 and older classified as "old age," and those over age 90 as the "oldest old" or "super old" (Ouchi et al., 2017).

Who is the typical older adult? First, it's important to note that there is much heterogeneity among older adults, and it is difficult to articulate one pattern that represents aging. However, even within this wide age range of older adulthood, you may have certain beliefs about where older adults live, how they spend their time, and other ideas about this population. Around the world, the most common living arrangement for older adults is living with an extended circle of family members (Pew Research Center, 2020). According to this survey, approximately 4 in 10 older adults around the world live with extended family members. In the United States, this living arrangement is far less common, with approximately 60% of U.S. older adults living with a spouse or partner and 27% living alone (Administration for Community Living, 2022). Household size also differs by country. In the United States, older adults have an average household size of 2.1 people, compared with 3.4 people as the worldwide average. Older women are more likely than older men to live by themselves (20% vs. 11%).

A relatively small percentage of older adults live in long-term care facilities (e.g., nursing homes) and assisted living facilities. The percentage of older adults living in long-term care facilities increases with age, with about 1% of those 65 to 74 living in long-term care, compared with 2% for those 75 to 84, and 8% of those age 85 and older (Administration for Community Living, 2022). The majority of older adults live in their own homes or apartments and do not live in assisted living facilities, nursing homes, or senior communities. We refer to this group of older adults who live in their own homes as "community dwelling." Around 6.6% of older adults report being part of the U.S. workforce in either a part- or full-time capacity (Administration for Community Living, 2022). In terms of functioning, 82% of older adults reported little to no difficulty with areas of functioning including hearing, vision, cognition, self-care, mobility, or communication. Of the 18% of older adults who did report significant difficulties in this area, the most common difficulties were in the area of mobility (39%), hearing (29%), and cognition (28%).

In terms of daily activities, survey data suggest that screen time has increased for older adults in the past decade, with relatively less time spent on other types of leisure activities (Pew Research Center, 2019). Approximately 73% of older adults report themselves as internet users and 53% are smartphone owners. Estimates suggest that older adults spend about half of their daily leisure time on screens, mostly spent on TV and videos, with relatively less time spent socializing and reading compared with older adults in prior years (Pew Research Center, 2019).

AGING INTERNATIONALLY

In 2019 there were 1 billion adults over age 60 in the world. Projections indicate that the number of adults over age 60 will increase to 1.4 billion by 2030 and 2.1 billion by 2050 (World Health Organization, 2023). In countries such as Japan and South Korea, the majority of the population is projected to be over age 50 by 2050 (see Figure 1.2).

Given the increasing numbers of older adults worldwide, some countries have become concerned about meeting the needs of an aging population. As shown in Figure 1.3, East Asian countries report the most concern about an aging population, whereas the U.S. reports relatively less concern in comparison to other countries. This may be because the United States, as well as other individualistic countries such as

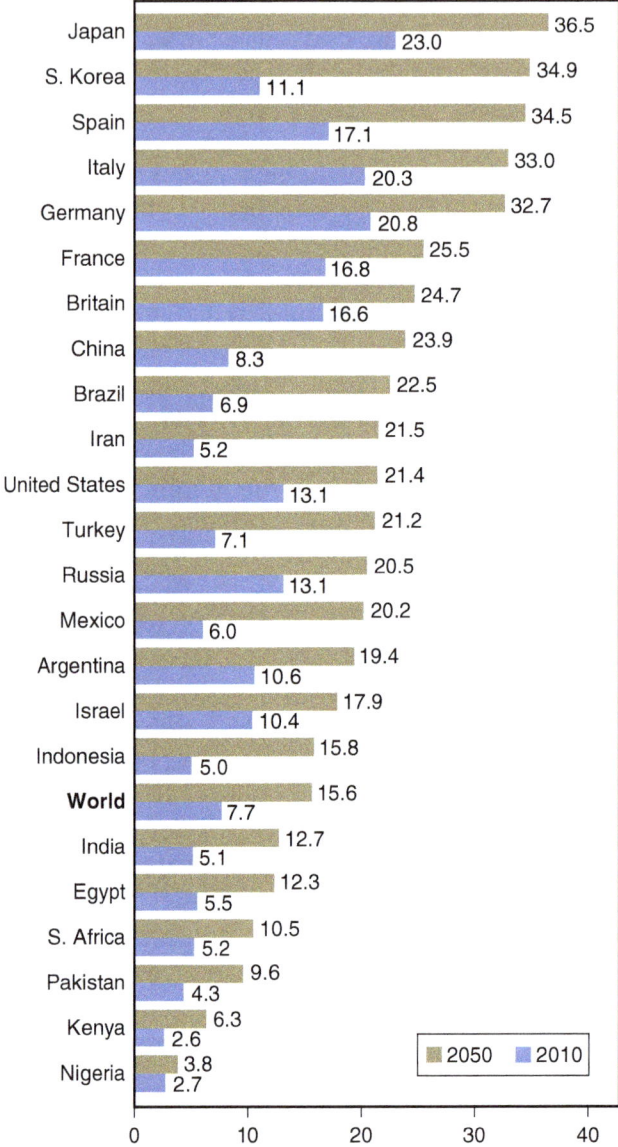

Figure 1.2 Proportion of older adults in a country's population, 2010 versus 2050.

Source: Pew Research Center. (2014). *Attitudes about aging: A global perspective: In a rapidly graying world, Japanese are worried, Americans aren't*. https://www.pewresearch.org/global/2014/01/30/attitudes-about-aging-a-global-perspective/

Britain and Germany, tend to hold a belief that individuals are responsible for their own well-being in older adulthood and that it should not fall on the government or society to support older adults. This is in sharp contrast to countries who view the government as primarily responsible for supporting older adults (Pew Research Center, 2014). As a response to the aging population, some countries have started to implement cost-saving reforms, such as increasing the retirement age. For example, in 2023 there were multiple protests after the government of France raised the retirement age from 62 to 64 to save on pension costs.

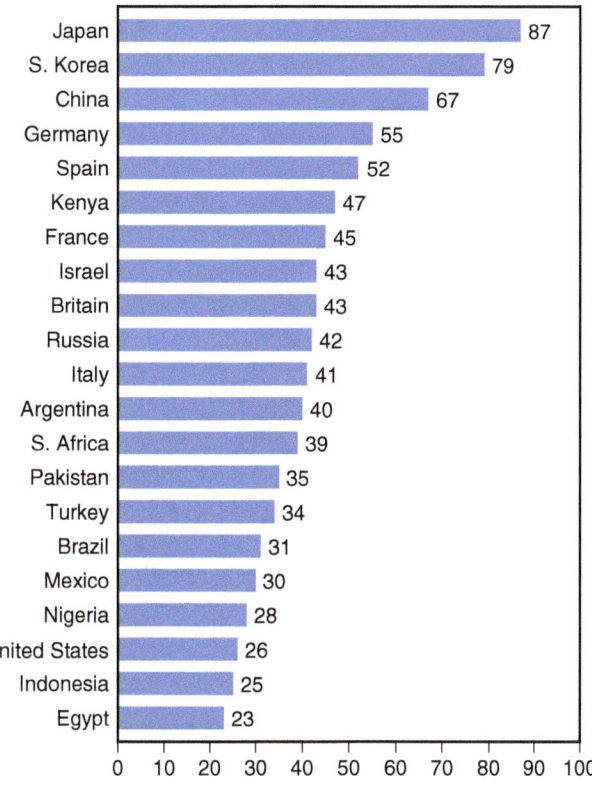

Figure 1.3 Percentage of participants from each country who report that the growing number of older people in their country is a "major problem."

Source: Pew Research Center. (2014). *Attitudes about aging: A global perspective: In a rapidly graying world, Japanese are worried, Americans aren't*. https://www.pewresearch.org/global/2014/01/30/attitudes-about-aging-a-global-perspective/

Although growth in the older population is happening internationally, some regions are experiencing more growth than others. By 2050, older adults will account for 20% of the population in developing regions. Approximately two thirds of the world's older adults currently live in developing regions (United Nations, 2017), and the number of older adults living in developing regions is growing faster than those in developed regions. Population aging is related to fertility rates, which are declining globally, leading to a larger proportion of older adults in the population relative to younger adults and children. Developing regions are also experiencing a decline in younger populations, with the population of children and teens under age 15 dropping from 42% in 2005 to 29% in 2050. This means that developing regions will not have as many younger people moving into the job market, leading to a large older population with few resources for support. There are some regions that are experiencing a "youth bulge," which stems from declining childhood mortality rates primarily in the least developed regions. This means that some countries have a much larger proportion of younger adults in their population compared with older adults. This pattern is particularly notable in countries such as Zimbabwe, Afghanistan, the Palestinian Territories, Yemen, and Syria, among others.

In the United States, older adults are one of the fastest-growing and increasingly diverse segments of the population. The population of Americans age 65 and over grew five times faster than the entire population in the century leading up to 2020, and in 2020, 16.8% (approximately one in six) of Americans were age 65 and over (Caplan, 2023; see Figure 1.4). In 2009, 20% of older Americans were from racial and ethnic minority groups. In 2019, this percentage rose to 24%; by 2040, it is projected that 34% of older Americans will be from racial and ethnic minority groups (Administration for Community Living, 2022). Between 2019 and 2040, the population of White, non-Hispanic older adults is projected to increase by 29%, compared with a 115% expected increase for racial and ethnic minority older adults. In 2019 in the United States, the four states with the highest percentage of adults aged 65 and older were Maine, Florida, West Virginia, and Vermont (Administration for Community Living, 2022). The population of adults living to be 100 or older, termed centenarians, is also growing rapidly. Between 1980 and 2019, the population of centenarians more than tripled from around 32,000 in the United States in 1980 to around 100,000 in 2019. In fact, the population of centenarians experienced a larger percentage increase during that time than did the total population (Administration for Community Living, 2022). There are fewer men compared with women at higher ages when considering both international and U.S. statistics. In 2019 in the United States, there were 125 women for every 100 men age 65 and over. When considering only those 85 and over, there were 178 women for every 100 men (Administration for Community Living, 2022). In 2022, 8.7% of the men in the world were 65 and older, compared with 11.1% for women. Men aged 80 and over comprised 1.5% of the population in the world, whereas women age 80 and over represented 2.5%.

As mentioned previously, one of the reasons people are living longer is decreased adult mortality, potentially related to improved healthcare. These changes are reflected in the dramatic changes in life expectancy across the past century. Life expectancy is the mean number of additional years a person can expect to live, assuming that current

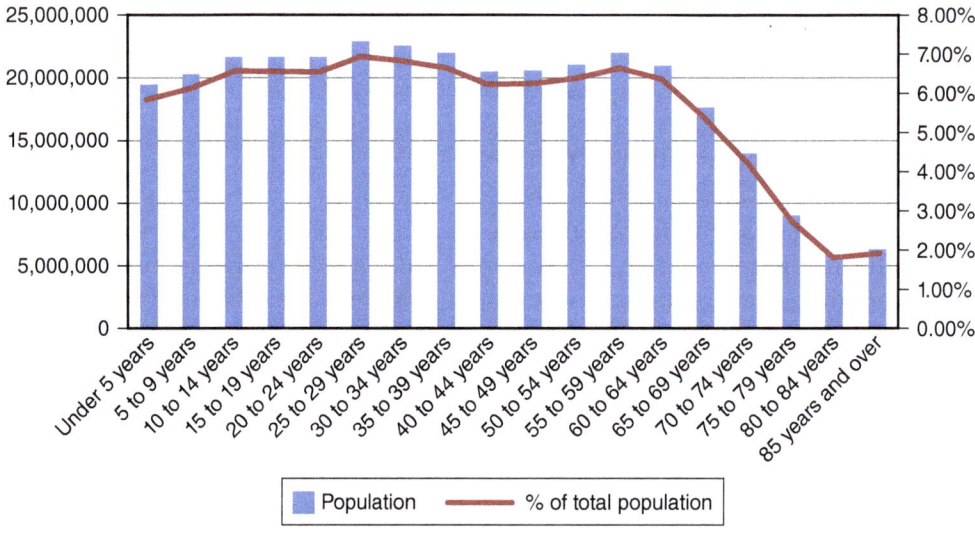

Figure 1.4 U.S. population by age group, as of 2023.

Source: Data from Neilsberg Research (2023). *United States population by age.* https://www.neilsberg.com/insights/united-states-population-by-age/

mortality rates for ages above the person's age were to stay constant for the remainder of that person's life. Life expectancy at birth was 65 years in 1950 in more developed areas of the world and now is estimated to be 75 years for men and 82 for women in developed areas, compared with 63 for men and 67 for women in less developed regions. Gaps in life expectancy exist between men and women and across different races and ethnicities. For example, women born in 2019 have an average life expectancy of 81.4 years compared with 76.3 years for men (Centers for Disease Control and Prevention [CDC], 2022). African American individuals born in 2019 have an average life expectancy of 74.8 years, compared with 78.8 years for White individuals, 81.9 years for Hispanic individuals, and 85.6 for Asian individuals (CDC, 2022). These differences in life expectancy between groups are often tied to access to healthcare and social resources.

The previous paragraph describes life expectancy at birth. One can also look at life expectancy once a person reaches older adulthood. This number depicts the average number of years the person has left to live. A person who is age 65 in 2019 can expect to live for 19.6 more years, on average. If a person is age 75 in 2019, they can expect to live for 12.4 more years on average (CDC, 2022). This highlights the idea that older adults are already a select group of individuals who have survived various hardships and illnesses in order to reach older adulthood. Individuals who engaged in risky behaviors or faced multiple illnesses may have died before reaching older adulthood. Therefore, from a statistical perspective, the longer you live, the more likely you are to keep living.

MEETING THE NEEDS OF AN AGING POPULATION

Considering the rapidly increasing numbers of older Americans, there is concern about meeting the healthcare needs of an aging population. A 2018 survey found that there were approximately 1.07 geriatricians per 10,000 older adult patients, with estimates that around 30,000 geriatricians will be needed by 2030 to provide care to older adults (Geriatrics Workforce by the Numbers, 2018). In terms of medical training, less than 3% of medical students enroll in geriatric electives even though 75% of schools offered electives in geriatrics. This is also seen across other health professions, with less than 1% of nurses having certifications related to gerontology. Even though a survey found that 63% of newly licensed nurses anticipated having older adults as clients, more than 85% of nursing programs did not require any coursework related to gerontology (Bardach & Rowles, 2012). Similarly, less than 1% of pharmacists have certifications related to gerontology, despite older adults taking many medications with risks of interactions. These trends are similar across other health professions that frequently serve older adults, including physical therapy, dentistry, physician assistants, and communication disorder specialists. Although many of these professions have required competencies related to older adults, they are differentially developed and evaluated at each institution.

In terms of mental health specialists, only 3% of psychologists in the United States identify geropsychology as their primary or secondary specialty (American Psychological Association, 2015). In contrast, 30% of psychologists identify child or adolescent psychology as their specialty. Unless psychology trainees enter a specialized geropsychology program, of which there are few, it is unlikely that trainees will have access to classes on aging and be able to acquire practicum hours with older adult clients (Woodhead et al., 2013). There is also concern about a low number of geriatric psychiatrists, with about 57 programs providing this specialization in the United States, offering about 60 to 65 training spots each year, approximately half of which are not filled (Juul et al., 2017).

GENERATIONAL INFLUENCES

Cohorts are groups of people who have similar cultural experiences and values. In the psychology of aging, cohorts are typically defined by the year of birth, which determines the generation to which they belong (Schaie, 1965). Different birth cohorts are often given names that reflect their core traits. For example, Generation Z, defined as individuals born between 1997 and 2012, are often characterized as the first generation who never knew the world without the internet. Early characterizations of Gen Z portrayed them as "soft" and overly coddled. Some media used terms such as "snowflakes" to describe this generation. Additional research into this cohort has found that they are pragmatic and value authentic communication. Each birth cohort often has many positive and negative labels attached to it, even though many individuals within that cohort may not fit those labels. Being aware of the overall experiences of each cohort can be helpful in working with current and future populations of older adults.

Most of today's older adults are a part of the "Baby Boom" generation. This generation is notable for being the largest, wealthiest, and best-educated generation ever produced in America (Jones, 1980). While the birth rate had declined for 200 years, and continues to decline, a major exception to this occurred after World War II. Births started increasing during World War II, from 1940 to 1943. In 1946, twice as many couples married than in any year before the war. Couples were marrying at younger ages than before the war; the median age of marriage declined from 1940 to 1956 (Jones, 1980). Rather than the increasing birth rate being a temporary increase as soldiers returned home after the war, it continued into the early 1960s, peaking in 1957, when over 4.3 million babies were born. From 1946 to 1964, 76,441,000 babies were born in the United States, and these citizens range from age 60 to 78 as of 2024 (see Figure 1.5). The Baby Boom was unique among developed countries such as the United States, Canada, Australia, and New Zealand. While European countries saw increases in numbers of births after the war ended, their birthrates decreased by the end of the 1940s (Jones, 1980; Owram, 1996).

The next generation who will enter older adulthood is Generation X, typically defined as individuals born between 1965 and 1980. This generation will begin turning 65 in 2030. There has been some discussion around whether individuals in Gen X are prepared for retirement. These individuals were entering their peak years of earning potential during the 2008 financial crisis, resulting in stops or gaps in retirement savings. This generation is also less likely to benefit from pension plans, with 33% reporting that they plan to receive pensions from defined benefit plans, compared with 50% of the Baby Boom generation. In support of this, Qi et al. (2022) found that Gen X was the least-prepared generation in terms of retirement planning.

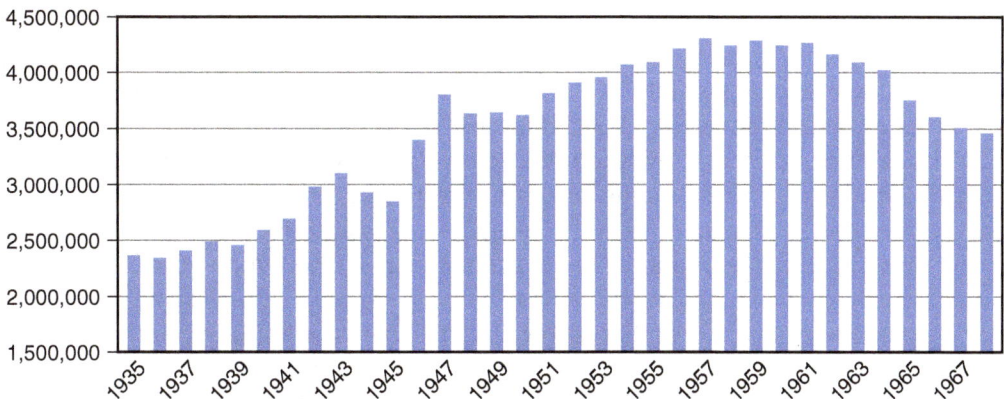

Figure 1.5 Number of reported births in the United States, 1935–1968.

RESEARCH METHODS IN THE PSYCHOLOGY OF AGING

An exploration of the psychology of aging requires an understanding of how knowledge is acquired in this field. Three variables of interest to researchers in psychology of aging include *age effects, cohort effects,* and *time-of-measurement* effects (Cavanaugh & Blanchard-Fields, 2024). Age effects refer to changes within the person including biological and psychological changes that occur with time, such as changes to the body's structures and functions or changes to traits over time. Cohort effects refer to differences caused by experiences and circumstances particular to one's generation. For example, the Baby Boom generation was the first to experience television within the home. Lastly, time of measurement effects refer to differences caused by sociocultural or environmental conditions at the time data are obtained from participants. For instance, research on marital relationships may have produced different results before and after the 2015 Supreme Court ruling on same-sex marriage. Data from longitudinal research were likely acquired over the telephone or video teleconference during the COVID-19 pandemic. Developmental researchers strive to isolate these three effects, but this is rarely straightforward and often involves the use of complex research designs, some of which are described in the next few paragraphs. Researchers must also distinguish between *age change* and *age difference.* Age change refers to fluctuations in people's behavior over time. People must be observed over time in order to determine age change. Age differences, on the other hand, are found when different people at different ages are compared with each other, typically at one time point.

There are several common methods that researchers in aging use to conduct research: longitudinal, cross-sectional, time lag, and sequential designs. *Longitudinal* research involves gathering data from the same participants at two or more time points. For example, the Nun Study has gathered data from Catholic Nuns at multiple time points until death, when brain autopsies were performed. This method is the clearest way to measure change as it occurs and is often considered the "gold standard" of developmental research. Approximately 35% of research studies published between 2000 and 2008 that examined some aspect of the psychology of aging were longitudinal in nature (Bleszner & Sanford, 2010). Longitudinal studies account for the effects of age and time of measurement but not for cohort effects. That is, following one cohort over time allows us to comment on age changes and presents multiple time points to control for time of measurement. However, by following only one cohort, the results that are obtained may be due to cohort effects that would not be seen if we were to follow a different cohort at a different point in time.

Although longitudinal studies are often thought of as the gold standard, there are limitations to longitudinal designs. Practice effects can occur, in which participants improve their performance on various measures (e.g., cognitive tests) simply by taking the measure more than once. This may manifest as improvement on test scores, stable test scores when a decline has actually occurred in the ability being measured, or even a decline in test scores that is lower in proportion than the decline occurring in real life. In neuropsychological research, practice effects can be quantified and controlled for (e.g., Duff et al., 2017), but the degree of improvement with practice for many measures is not known.

There is also the need for *measurement invariance*. Measurement invariance implies that each measure relates to the underlying construct in the same way over time, so that the latent construct is defined similarly over time. This also implies that scores on the measure are on the same measurement scale at different points in time. One way to increase the likelihood of measurement invariance is to choose measures that have high reliability and validity for the sample you are using. In many complex longitudinal studies, techniques such as factor analysis, structural equation modeling, or item response theory are used to ensure measurement invariance. This highlights another potential problem with longitudinal designs, which is that measures can be outdated by the time the study is complete. If a researcher chooses a specific measure and uses the same measure for each time point, a new version of the measure may become available during the course of the study. Opting to use the new measure may lead to problems with measurement invariance, as noted earlier.

Another limitation to longitudinal research is participant dropout, or attrition (Ferrer & Ghisletta, 2011). Reasons for attrition include participants moving and becoming unreachable, participants declining follow-up sessions, participants becoming incapacitated, or death. This can result in lower external validity because the remaining participants may not be representative of the population that was initially sampled. For instance, participants who remain in studies may be healthier than the population from which they are sampled (Ferrer & Ghisletta, 2011). Attrition is a central problem in longitudinal research and must be addressed in any such study. Participants may drop out because of reasons unrelated to the study, with the data considered *missing completely at random* (MCAR). For example, a person may move to a new location and be unable to participate in the study. This reason for dropping out is unrelated to the outcomes of the study or the variables in the study. Another option is that the data may be missing because of reasons related to the variables that have been measured, which would enable the researchers to account for them in analyses. This is commonly called *missing at random* (MAR). An example of this is that you may find that women were more likely to complete your study than men. In this case, you can control for gender in your analyses. Unfortunately, often the missing data are related to outcomes of the study but without enough information to explain the reasons for it; these data are considered *not missing at random* (NMAR). An example of this might be that in a longitudinal study of physical health, the participants who drop out are the ones who are experiencing the worst health outcomes.

Researchers have used several methods to address the problems posed by missing data. One method has been to simply delete the cases that have missing data and perform analyses only on the participants with complete data. However, this practice causes the omission of large amounts of valuable data. Another approach is to compare the characteristics of participants who did and did not complete the study. This would allow you to see whether participants with certain characteristics were less likely to complete the study. In this situation, you could control for those variables in your analyses, as mentioned earlier.

In addition to the challenge of handling missing data, there are other limitations to longitudinal research. Findings obtained in one cohort in a longitudinal investigation may not generalize to other cohorts. Another practical limitation of longitudinal research is the time and expense required to perform this research. By definition, these studies may take years to complete and may require collaboration among several study sites. Nonetheless, longitudinal studies such as the Berlin Aging Study, Seattle Longitudinal Study, and Nun Study have yielded a tremendous amount of knowledge for the field.

Cross-sectional research involves gathering data from participants of various ages at one point in time. With this design, researchers can detect age *differences* but not age *change*. This is because different ages are compared, allowing the possibility that the results are age related; however, participants are not followed over time, which means that other variables may be responsible for the age differences. Therefore, this type of design does not account for time of measurement or cohort effects because only one time point is used and the age differences that are detected may be related to the cohorts that are sampled. For example, differences found between 60- and 80-year-olds may simply represent differences in cohorts rather than changes that occur with age. This design has the advantages of lower cost and increased convenience of being performed, and researchers use this design more than any other. It can generate hypotheses to further explore in longitudinal or sequential studies. However, it has significant limitations, a chief one being the lack of information learned about change over time.

One type of cross-sectional study is the extreme age groups design, which involves adults at young and old extremes. Most commonly, these studies recruit students at universities and older adults from community centers like senior centers or churches. These convenience samples are obviously not representative of the larger populations, so findings from these studies are less likely to generalize to people not represented by these samples. Another limitation frequently encountered in these studies is that age is represented by categorical variables ("young" and "old"), and this gross classification may decrease the power to detect smaller changes that occur with aging. This design also carries the assumption that measures used in one group assess the same variable in other groups. Measures need to have similar reliability and validity in each age group being examined.

In order to address the limitations inherent in both longitudinal and cross-sectional studies, *sequential* designs involve combinations of both of these types. For example, a *time-sequential* study involves cross-sectional data collected at two separate time points. In a study like this, multiple cohorts could be studied at two or more points in time, which allows researchers to examine whether results are due to time of measurement. This design does not rule out the influence of cohort effects since only a limited number of cohorts are studied. In a *cohort-sequential* design, two or more cohorts are followed longitudinally. This design can assess whether effects found in one cohort are specific to that cohort or due to the aging process. Sequential studies provide the most information in developmental psychology, but are also the most difficult and costly.

CONCLUSION

The goal of this chapter was to introduce some of the concepts that are important in the psychology of aging. We started by discussing definitions of older adulthood and some characteristics of older adults. We then reviewed the data on the projected increase in older adults in the United States and internationally and how healthcare is working to meet the needs of an aging population. The importance of birth cohort was discussed in this chapter and continues to be an important theme throughout this book. We ended with a discussion of research methods that attempt to untangle the effects of age, cohort, and time of measurement.

DISCUSSION QUESTIONS

1. Describe how older adulthood is defined in terms of age and some typical characteristics of older adults.
2. Summarize the information on the projected increase in the aging population both in the United States and internationally.
3. Define what a cohort is, and describe some features of the Baby Boom cohort.
4. Describe the difference between age changes and age effects. How can researchers determine whether results are due to age changes or age effects?
5. Summarize the strengths and weaknesses of cross-sectional and longitudinal research in the study of aging. Describe other research designs that can account for the weaknesses of these two designs.

A robust set of instructor resources designed to supplement this text is located at http://connect.springerpub.com/content/book/978-0-8261-6617-3. Qualifying instructors may request access by emailing textbook@springerpub.com.

REFERENCES

Administration for Community Living. (2022). *2021 profile of older Americans*. https://acl.gov/aging-and-disability-in-america/data-and-research/profile-older-americans

Ambrosi-Randić, N., Nekić, M., & Tucak Junaković, I. (2018). Felt age, desired, and expected lifetime in the context of health, well-being, and successful aging. *The International Journal of Aging and Human Development, 87*(1), 33–51. https://doi.org/10.1177/0091415017720881

American Psychological Association. (2015). *Survey of psychology health service providers* (Unpublished special analysis).

Bardach, S. H., & Rowles, G. D. (2012). Geriatric education in the health professions: Are we making progress? *The Gerontologist, 52*(5), 607–618. https://doi.org/10.1093/geront/gns006

Bleszner, R., & Sanford, N. (2010). Looking back and looking ahead as *Journal of Gerontology: Psychological Sciences* turns 65. *Journals of Gerontology: Psychological Sciences, 65B*, 3–4. https://doi.org/10.1093/geronb/gbp097

Caplan, Z. (2023, May 25). *U.S. older population grew from 2010 to 2020 at fastest rate since 1880 to 1890.* United States Census Bureau. https://www.census.gov/library/stories/2023/05/2020-census-united-states-older-population-grew.html

Cavanaugh, J. C., & Blanchard-Fields, F. (2024). *Adult development and aging* (9th ed.). Cengage.

Centers for Disease Control and Prevention. (2022). *United States life tables, 2019.* https://www.cdc.gov/nchs/products/life_tables.htm#life

Duff, K., Atkinson, T. J., Suhrie, K. R., Dalley, B. C., Schaefer, S. Y., & Hammers, D. B. (2017). Short-term practice effects in mild cognitive impairment: Evaluating different methods of change. *Journal of Clinical and Experimental Neuropsychology, 39*(4), 396–407. https://doi-org.ucsf.idm.oclc.org/10.1080/13803395.2016.1230596

Ferrer, E., & Ghisletta, P. (2011). Methodological and analytical issues in the psychology of aging. In K. W. Schaie & S. L. Willis (Eds.), *Handbook of the psychology of aging* (pp. 25–39). Academic Press.

Geriatrics Workforce by the Numbers. (2018). *Geriatrics workforce numbers.* https://www.americangeriatrics.org/geriatrics-profession/about-geriatrics/geriatrics-workforce-numbers

Jones, L. Y. (1980). *Great expectations: America and the baby boom generation.* Coward, McCann, & Geoghegan.

Juul, D., Colenda, C. C., Lyness, J. M., Dunn, L. B., Hargrave, R., & Faulkner, L. R. (2017). Subspecialty training and certification in geriatric psychiatry: A 25-year overview. *The American Journal of Geriatric Psychiatry, 25*(5), 445–453. https://doi.org/10.1016/j.jagp.2016.12.018

National Park Service. (2023). *Rosie the Riveter National Historical Park, Richmond, California: Betty Reid Soskin.* https://www.nps.gov/rori/learn/historyculture/betty-reid-soskin.htm

Neugarten, B. L. (1974). Age groups in American society and the rise of the young-old. *Annals of the American Academy of Political and Social Science, 415*(1), 187–198. https://doi.org/10.1177/000271627441500114

Ouchi, Y., Rakugi, H., Arai, H., Akishita, M., Ito, H., Toba, K., Kai, I., & on behalf of the Joint Committee of Japan Gerontological Society & Japan Geriatrics Society. (2017). Redefining the elderly as aged 75 years and older: Proposal from the Joint Committee of Japan Gerontological Society and the Japan Geriatrics Society. *Geriatrics and Gerontology International, 17*(7), 1045–1047. https://doi.org/10.1111/ggi.13118

Owram, D. (1996). *Born at the right time: A history of the baby-boom generation.* University of Toronto Press.

Pew Research Center. (2014). *Global public opinion on aging* (Chapter 1). https://www.pewresearch.org/global/2014/01/30/chapter-1-global-public-opinion-on-aging/

Pew Research Center. (2019). *Americans 60 and older are spending more time in front of their screens than a decade ago.* https://www.pewresearch.org/short-reads/2019/06/18/americans-60-and-older-are-spending-more-time-in-front-of-their-screens-than-a-decade-ago/

Pew Research Center. (2020). *Older people are more likely to live alone in the U.S. than elsewhere in the world.* https://www.pewresearch.org/short-reads/2020/03/10/older-people-are-more-likely-to-live-alone-in-the-u-s-than-elsewhere-in-the-world/

Qi, J., Chatterjee, S., & Liu, Y. (2022). Retirement preparedness of Generation X compared to other cohorts in the United States. *International Journal of Financial Studies, 10*(2), 45. https://doi.org/10.3390/ijfs10020045

Schaie, K. W. (1965). A general model for the study of developmental problems. *Psychological Bulletin, 64,* 92–107. https://doi.org/10.1037/h0022371

Social Security Administration. (2015). *Age 65 retirement.* http://www.ssa.gov/history/age65.html.

United Nations, Department of Economic and Social Affairs, Population Division (2017). *World population ageing 2017* (ST/ESA/SER.A/408).

Woodhead, E. L., Emery, E. E., Pachana, N. A., Scott, T. L., Konnert, C. A., & Edelstein, B. A. (2013). Graduate students' geropsychology training opportunities and perceived competence in working with older adults. *Professional Psychology: Research and Practice, 44,* 355–362. https://doi.org/10.1037/a0034632

World Health Organization. (2023). *Aging.* https://www.who.int/health-topics/ageing#tab=tab_1

2

Cultural Variations in Aging Experiences of Ethnically and Sexually Diverse Older Adults

Kimberly E. Hiroto, Jennifer S. Ho, and Sarah J. Yarry

> **LEARNING OBJECTIVES**
>
> - Demonstrate increased awareness of systemic and sociocultural-historical factors impacting the intersectional experiences of racially/ethnically minoritized older adults.
> - Learn strategies to identify and counter ageism.
> - Apply resilience models to working with racially/ethnically minoritized and/or LGBTQ+ older adults.
> - Develop ways to improve the healthcare of older LGBTQ+ adults.
> - Apply the concept of intersectionality to better understand older adults with whom they may work.

Working with older adults involves developing an appreciation for the sociohistorical context within which older adults live. This includes understanding the zeitgeist of the times, the social mores, and the watershed events that shaped a cohort's experiences. It also involves exploring individual and collective cultures and traditions that shaped the person's or the group's life experiences. Finally, this work requires a dose of humility to learn about one's unique and shared experiences, including the regional, local, and personal experiences that affected their lives.

Like any other population, the aging population is heterogeneous, consisting of multiple cultural, cohort, and age groups. Individuals present with varying life experiences, cultural backgrounds, living conditions, physical and cognitive abilities, differential access to socioeconomic resources, and diverse ways of expressing their gender and sexual orientation (Ayalon et al., 2021). In this chapter, we discuss the wealth of diversity within older adults, focusing specifically on ethnic diversity, sexual orientation, and gender expression. Our aim is to provide a general overview of the themes that may arise when working with diverse older adults, knowing that each person and group has their own story and collection of life experiences that may or may not be captured here. Specifically, we focus on three major themes: cohort effects, health disparities and cultural stressors, and factors contributing to resilience and growth.

ETHNICALLY MINORITIZED OLDER ADULTS

By 2050, older adults are projected to comprise 22% of the total population, outnumbering children for the first time in U.S. history (Vespa et al., 2020). Nearly half aged 60 and older are expected to be from racially/ethnically minoritized populations, with a projected increase of 105% in the next 20 years compared with 26% among non-Hispanic White peers (Association for Community Living, 2022).

Multiple factors explain these anticipated shifts in population demographics, including changes in immigration trends, increased life expectancies across groups, and the general increase in racial and ethnic minorities in the United States (Ortman et al., 2014; Vespa et al., 2020). Similar changes in aging demographics are anticipated globally as well (Department of Economic and Social Affairs Population Division, 2015). These anticipated shifts in the coming decades will increase the need for services catering to older adults including, for example, medical and mental healthcare, housing options, retirement and financial resources, in-home support services, and a host of bilingual or polylingual service providers who can accommodate the linguistic and cultural needs of older adults.

Cohort Effects

As defined elsewhere, cohorts are groups of people (not necessarily the same age) with shared cultural experiences and values (e.g., Sinnott & Shifren, 2001). Importantly, cohorts within specific time periods differ depending on their own cultural experiences. For example, the cohorts who lived through the COVID-19 pandemic differed in experiences depending on multiple factors: regional location, racial/ethnic identity, household makeup (e.g., living alone vs. living with multiple generations), health status, age, ability to work from home, availability of infection control precautions, and so forth. Within-group differences add to the complexity, highlighting the importance of understanding and appreciating an individual's or cohort's experiences as they intersect with other aspects of identity.

Take a moment and consider your own cohort's experiences to date. Which of these watershed moments have affected your experiences and outlook on life: the terrorist attacks on September 11, 2001; the election of Barack Obama as the first African American president; the Black Lives Matter movement; the 2020 COVID-19 pandemic; and the ongoing tensions around race, religion, sexual orientation, and gender identity? How have these experiences shaped your cohort, your culture, and you as a person? How might you have experienced these events differently compared with someone of a different racial or ethnic background? Part of working with older adults involves being curious about their lived experiences and understanding how your own experiences, and theirs, may shape your interactions.

VIEWS OF AGING

Exposure to ageist stereotypes in early childhood often continues into later adulthood and can affect older adults' views of aging and themselves (Gordon & Gonzales, 2022; Levy, 2009; North & Fiske, 2012). Within our youth-oriented culture lie deeply embedded anti-aging sentiments further reified by institutional policies and practices (Levy, 2003; Levy et al., 2022). Ageism can occur on three levels: institutional, interpersonal, and individual (Centre for Ageing Better, 2023).

Institutional practices create policies resulting in structural ageism, rendering such stereotypes and practices nearly invisible (Levy et al., 2022). As noted by the World Health Organization (WHO) report on ageism, "Often people fail to recognize the existence of such institutional ageism because the rules, norms and practices of the institution are long-standing, have become ritualized and are seen as normal" (WHO, 2021, p. 5). Resulting policies then legitimize the status quo and can shape interpersonal encounters via benevolent ("compassionate") ageism or hostile ageism, either of which can lead to harm, neglect, or disenfranchisement (Gans et al., 2023; North & Fiske, 2012). Aging occurs within broader contexts of one's identity. The intersection of aging and minoritized racial/ethnic groups amplifies the complexity of navigating structural inequities and individual experiences.

Challenging the *culture hypothesis* that Asian countries are less prone to ageism than Eurocentric societies, Vauclair et al.'s study (2017) found nuanced results comparing ageist attitudes between generally more individualistic and interdependent communities. While societal perceptions of older adults tend to be slightly more positive in collectivistic cultures than in individualistic ones, studies show shifting trends in aging attitudes across the globe (Löckenhoff et al., 2009). For instance, belief that older age naturally imbues wisdom is declining in Eastern cultures but rising in Western societies (Löckenhoff et al., 2009). Traditionally collectivistic cultures report mixed attitudes of aging regarding respect, obligation, contempt, envy, and perceptions of older adults' affective and behavioral traits (Vauclair et al., 2017). Societal views of aging appear to be ever-evolving, informed by the existing sociopolitical climate, intergenerational contact, modernization, education opportunities, immigration, and perceived availability of resources (Löckenhoff et al., 2009; Vauclair et al., 2017). Working with older adults involves a flexible understanding of broad cultural frameworks and a culturally sensitive approach that adopts openness, humility, and curiosity about each person's lived experience.

STRATEGIES TO COUNTERACT AGEISM

Debiasing ageism is part of culturally attuned care involving humble intention, purposeful attention, and adequate time (Hammond, 2015). Drawing from Hammond's culturally responsive teachings (2015), here are suggested approaches to counter ageism:

- Reassociating, or stereotype replacement, involves awareness and effortful reframing of negative associations. For instance, instead of thinking "I don't want to get old because it is bad," a reframe would be, "It would be such a privilege to age."

- Refuting, or counter-stereotyping, finds counter-examples that refute the initial bias. For example, remembering instances of older adults who are physically active and involved in the community can fight against stereotypes of older adults as frail and useless.
- Remember that the older adult has gone through multiple life transitions that you may have gone through or will eventually go through, accruing decades of experiences. Taking the perspective of the other person and honoring their personhood can help mitigate microaggressions (e.g., "would I want to be talked to like a child?").
- Increasing positive contact with older adults dismantles single narratives and enriches appreciation for the heterogeneity of the older population.
- Education can facilitate staff awareness and decrease microaggression and elderspeak (Williams, 2004).

Health Disparities and Cultural Stressors

Health disparities in care refer to "racial or ethnic differences in the quality of healthcare that are not due to access-related factors or clinical needs, preferences, or appropriateness of interventions" (Smedley et al., 2003, pp. 3-4). Factors including socioeconomic status (SES), access to healthcare, health literacy, and minoritized ethnic/racial identities contribute to health inequalities. Indeed, racially and ethnically minoritized adults in general have premature morbidity rates across the life span suggesting complex, multifactorial contributions to health disparities. Often SES, race, and ethnicity are related to factors including residential segregation with differential access to resources (e.g., medical care, senior centers, healthy food options, transportation, education) and differential exposure to risk (e.g., crime, poor-quality housing, pollution). Exploring the intersection of structural racism and ageism, Farrell et al. (2022) argue that racism and ageism act synergistically to determine one's ability to obtain intergenerational wealth, earn power, and pursue social mobility, educational opportunity, and housing and transportation accessibility. Minoritized older adults face social and structural inequities that can lead to delayed care, exclusion from research, adverse health outcomes, and increased morbidity and mortality. Peeling back the layers of artificial hierarchies reveals a caste infrastructure using metrics (e.g., race, class, religion, gender, sexuality) to determine an individual's place in society (Wilkerson, 2020). These metrics may change or dissolve, but the systemic factors remain intact. These factors may manifest as structural and legalized discriminatory policies and practices, contributing to disparities in health, finances, and general well-being (Alexander, 2012).

Minoritized social status and systemic inequities interact to cause significant and often intergenerational impact that affects the lives of individuals and communities across the life span. Ongoing discussion about reparations for African Americans speaks to the intergenerational trauma incurred since slavery and its consequent effect on the lives of individuals and the community at large (Pew Research Center, 2022). Historic events targeting minoritized populations (e.g., the disenfranchisement and cultural genocide of indigenous peoples; the Chinese Exclusion Act; the sterilization of people based on race, intellectual and developmental disabilities, and incarceration status; the Holocaust; the incarceration of Japanese Americans) create ripple effects across generations. Overtly discriminatory policies and practices often evolve as societal awareness increases but only undergo cosmetic changes, while the biased attitudes and practices remain intact to maintain the status quo (Hatzenbuehler et al., 2013). Consequently, disparities in health, housing, finances, and so forth persist across generations in the same minoritized communities, despite advances in technology, because the policies and practices that discriminated against them have only changed in name. Such practices affect minoritized communities, including rural and impoverished ones, regardless of race or ethnicity. For example, rural communities often lack critical infrastructure and resources necessary to access care. Understanding the larger socio-historical-cultural and political influences and intergenerational challenges (and resilience) contextualizes how an older individual may be presenting, reducing the risk of holding one accountable for behaviors beyond their control (e.g., blaming an individual for excess alcohol use when treatment services were inaccessible or not yet developed for their particular problem).

Many minoritized communities face chronic stressors experienced from societies that stigmatize and disenfranchise them. This phenomenon is termed minority stress (Meyer, 2003). Minority stress highlights how this type of stress can accumulate across generations with lasting effects. A lifetime of segregation and minority stress may contribute to the development of chronic health problems among minoritized older adults, reflecting the effect of psychological stress on important health factors. For example, research evaluating the role of social location demonstrated higher probability of hypertension among African American males living and working in segregated locations compared with those who did not (Gilbert et al., 2015). Furthermore, research demonstrates the effect of chronic stress on physical and cognitive health (Juster et al., 2009), placing disadvantaged and lower-SES older adults at greater risk for health problems and potentially less access to care compared with peers with more resources. However, other research proposes that health literacy (i.e., general understanding of health information to guide medical decisions) helps explain the relationship between race and health disparities (Bennett et al., 2009). Such findings reflect the complexity of this issue when considering the intersection of multiple demographic factors (e.g., race, age, SES, cohort).

Resilience and Growth

Multiple factors contribute to the resilience and growth experienced by minoritized older adults. The formal definition of resilience remains nebulous among researchers, although common themes relate to one's ability to overcome and cope with adversity. The word itself connotes positive adaptation to manage hardship (Infurna, 2021), although the type, frequency, and intensity of adversity can vary by age. This is especially true for older adults given the increased prevalence of hardship and challenges faced with aging (e.g., illness, functional change, retirement, loss of family/loved ones). Having additional marginalized identities can further magnify these hardships. Resilience often relates to concepts of flourishing and growth, reflecting themes of finding meaning, and even wisdom, amid adversity. Coping strategies, cultural factors (e.g., religion, spirituality, values), and age-related processes (e.g., focusing on time remaining) are often credited for fostering individual and collective resilience and growth. Examples of specific cultural groups exceed the scope of this chapter, but it remains important to consider cultural practices that promote interpersonal connectedness, belonging, meaning-making, and hope.

Often resilience gets conflated with "healthy aging," although researchers advocate for these concepts to remain separate (Kim et al., 2021). Some propose that resilience embodies both the hope for improvement and an acceptance of reality, clarifying that one can be ill yet still be aging well. Indeed, the concept of aging well is itself culturally determined and dependent on one's cultural values and expectations. Some propose a movement toward "meaningful aging" to highlight the importance of cultivating meaning in life as part of aging well. Importantly, broader social and political contexts also factor into individual and collective resilience given one's access to resources and infrastructures (e.g., access to health insurance and care). In the absence of such critical support, many lean on their faith, spirituality, and/or social networks that support their values and functioning.

The ability to seek meaning and purpose through hardship also contributes to one's fortitude and ability to persevere through adversity. Researchers often relate well-being in late life to the concept of *generativity*, or the process of giving back to the next generation (Keyes & Ryff, 1998). Relatedly, many view well-being as comprising six overarching themes: purpose in life, autonomy (e.g., living in alignment with one's values), personal growth (e.g., reaching one's potential), environmental mastery (e.g., management of life situations), depth of interpersonal relationships, and self-awareness (e.g., knowing one's self, including strengths and limitations; Ryff, 2014). International studies have found variations on these themes based on cultural values, with collectivist cultures highlighting interdependence over independence, the latter often being emphasized in more individualistic cultures (e.g., United States). The motivation to live by one's values, find meaning, and support the next generation can enhance one's willingness to push through adversity. At the end of our lives, many of us want to be remembered, and these normative late-life processes are ways of doing that. How this manifests varies by cultural values, practices, and beliefs, but the underlying drive to survive and find meaning in hardship often persists, even if one is survived through legacy, memories, or storytelling.

SEXUALLY AND GENDER-DIVERSE OLDER ADULTS

The LGBTQ+ aging community is growing in numbers and prominence, although it remains highly disenfranchised and underrepresented (e.g., Fredriksen-Goldsen et al., 2015, 2019). As terminology evolves to accurately reflect and include diverse identities, for the purposes of this chapter, we use the term LGBTQ+ with the plus (+) sign to signal inclusion of the wide diversity of sexual and gender identities. Research on this heterogeneous group is growing, although their health needs are often collapsed together. A number of identities are associated with sexual orientation and gender diversity, some of which are defined in Table 2.1. While attention to these populations is growing, there are still not nearly enough studies to do justice to the lived experiences of LGBTQ+ individuals. The politicization of LGBTQ+ identities contributes to the ongoing systemic and institutional discriminatory practices and policies. LGBTQ+ adults face cumulative effects of lifelong exposure to discrimination, prejudice, and criminalization, resulting in higher rates of mental illness, substance use, suicide,

TABLE 2.1 DEFINITIONS OF SEXUAL ORIENTATION AND GENDER-DIVERSE TERMS

Term	Definition
Asexual	Individuals who experience little to no sexual attraction to other people
Biological sex	The unique biological makeup of an individual including sexual hormones, genetics, chromosomes, and genitals
Bisexual	A person who experiences sexual and emotional attachments to both women and men
Cisgender	A person whose binary gender assigned at birth is concordant with his or her sense of identity
Gay	Men who experience their primary sexual/emotional attachments to other men
Gender identity	The extent to which a person identifies on a spectrum of masculine and feminine traits
Lesbian	Women who experience their primary sexual and emotional attachments to other women
Queer	A sociopolitical umbrella term that may be associated with all levels of exploring one's nonbinary sexuality and gender identity
Sexual orientation	How one identifies themselves and to whom they are sexually attracted and with whom they are sexually active
Intersex	Individuals who have sex characteristics (e.g., genitals, chromosomes, or reproductive organs) that do not fit into the medical or social male/female binary
Two spirit	An umbrella term used by Indigenous people to describe their sexual, gender, and/or spiritual identity encompassing both masculine and feminine spirits
Transgender	An umbrella term to describe an array of identities that do not conform to the pervasive binary gender system of most cultures
Gender diverse	An increasingly popular term describing individuals whose gender identity, role, or expression differs from the cultural norms prescribed for people of a particular sex

poverty, abuse, and violence (Substance Abuse and Mental Health Services Administration, 2023; Truman & Morgan, 2022). In spite of these challenges, LGBTQ+ older adults also display varied strengths and resilience to age successfully, including finding acceptance and support among their (chosen) families and friends, adopting positive personal qualities and identity, and engaging in health-promoting behaviors (Fredriksen-Goldsen et al., 2015).

By 2060, LGBTQ+ older adults are expected to comprise over 20 million in the nation (Fredriksen-Goldsen & Kim, 2017). The U.S. Census first started collecting data on same-sex households in 1990, but not until 2021 did the U.S. Census include questions about sexual orientation and gender identity (U.S. Census Bureau, 2021). This marks the first year that researchers have access to nationally representative samples to examine the overall health of LGBTQ+ older adults. The census estimates that 4.4% of adults aged 50 to 64 years and 2.4% of adults over 65 identify as LGBTQ+ in the United States. More specifically, 95% of these populations identified as LGB, while 5% identified as transgender. Variations in race also exist, with the majority of U.S. Census LGBTQ+ respondents identifying as White, although few statistically significant racial differences emerged between cisgender straight and LGBTQ+ respondents. Researchers expect that by 2030 the LGBTQ+ population will double to 5 million (Fredriksen-Goldsen et al., 2015). Additionally, one of the largest studies of transgender adults across the life span found that the overwhelming majority (97%) of those age 65 years and older reported transitioning at age 55 or older (Cook-Daniels, 2015; Grant et al., 2011). These statistics suggest that, for various reasons, older adults transition later in their lives after having established decades of life as their assigned sex.

Cohort Effects

Many of today's older adults identifying as LGBTQ+ grew up prior to the 1969 Stonewall Inn Riots, often considered the start of the Gay Liberation Movement (Choi & Meyer, 2016; Fredriksen-Goldsen & Muraco, 2010). The pre-Stonewall era criminalized homosexuality and considered it a mental illness, resulting in many families rejecting their kin. Whether forced or voluntary, upon disclosing their sexual orientation, adults from this cohort often faced consequences, including psychiatric institutionalization, electric shock therapy, ostracism from their families of origin and communities, homelessness, and religious conversion therapy or individual therapy to change their sexual orientation. A review of the LGBTQ+ rights movement exceeds the scope of this chapter; however, some of the lesser known but equally critical moments in history are described here to provide some sociopolitical context. Executive Order 10450, signed into law by President Eisenhower in 1953, required dismissal of government employees deemed to be threats to national security. Such groups included those with mental illness whose judgment may be adversely affected (at the time, homosexuality was deemed a mental disorder) and those who engaged in "any criminal, infamous, dishonest, immoral, or notoriously disgraceful conduct, habitual use of intoxicants to excess, drug addiction, or sexual perversion" (National Archives, 2016). Identifying mental illness and "sexual perversion" as threats to national security resulted in hundreds of LGBTQ+ adults losing their jobs.

Sociohistorical and political structures play significant roles in how marginalized populations navigate and survive in society. This is especially true for transgender and gender-diverse (TGGD) older adults. Frederikson-Goldsen et al. (2019) developed the Iridescent Life Course to capture the intersectionality and ways structural inequity operate across socioeconomic and political spheres. The framework identified three distinct cohorts of TGGD older adults (Fredriksen-Goldsen, 2016): the Invisible generation (those born 1934 and earlier), the Silenced generation (born 1935–1949), and the Pride generation (born 1950–1964). The Invisible generation, so named because TGGD individuals were excluded from public discussion in the United States and other nations, survived the Great Depression, and many served in World War II. Between these two periods, TGGD individuals began gaining some attention due to medical procedures (primarily in Germany) to transform one's birth sex to their psychological gender (Fredriksen-Goldsen et al., 2022). The Silenced generation reflects the growing recognition of TGGD identities and increasing antagonism toward these communities. This period witnessed the politicization of LGTBQ+ identities and pathologizing of TGGD identities as a psychiatric disorder. A few medical providers in the United States emerged as advocates for hormone replacement therapy, some of whom recommended surgeons abroad given the controversy of such affirming surgeries in the United States.

On the heels of these developments, the Pride generation arose. Children of this generation grew up amid the Civil Rights era (1958–1964), during which social uprisings and protests arose demanding equitable rights for communities minoritized by race and ethnicity (especially Black communities), sexual orientation, and gender identity (Fredriksen-Goldsen et al., 2022). Much of the righteous anger arose from national policies that strategically excluded and criminalized individuals for their identities, such as the 1953 executive order described earlier. In 1956, Evelyn Hooker's research demonstrated no differences in the mental health of heterosexual and homosexual adults. This research played a critical role in the removal of homosexuality as a mental health diagnosis *nearly 20 years later*. Illinois was the first state in 1962 to repeal its sodomy laws to decriminalize private same-sex activity with another consenting adult. However, not until 1973 in Michigan was there any substantial law protecting LGB adults from discrimination (Fitzgerald, 2013). Oppressive policies, along with growing hope for change, likely contributed to LGBTQ+ communities demanding basic human rights. Events included the 1959 police raid on Coopers Doughnuts in Los Angeles and the 1966 Compton Cafeteria Riots, both of which involved transgender, drag queens, and sex workers fighting against police. These and other events preceded and likely set the stage for the well-known Stonewall Riots of June 1969.

We encourage you to consider how LGBTQ+ communities are viewed today. While homophobia and transphobia still exist, think of the openly gay or transgender celebrities embraced by the public; the stories of LGBTQ+ protagonists portrayed with complexity, respect, and dignity; and celebrity advocates who celebrate sexual and gender diversity. National mental health associations such as the American Psychological Association (APA) have endorsed guidelines to provide compassionate, inclusive care for sexual minority persons (Nakamura et al., 2022) and for transgender and gender nonconforming people (APA, 2015). While much progress is still needed, these advances would not be possible without the current aging cohort who courageously raised their voices and sacrificed their safety, and sometimes their lives, to create a more equitable and accepting society.

The changing landscape of federal and state laws has impacted the current cohort of LGBTQ+ older adults. The 21st century witnessed improved regulations protecting LGBTQ+ communities. From *Lawrence v. Texas*, a 2003 U.S. Supreme Court decision striking down the Texas sodomy law and, by extension, sodomy laws in 13 other states, to the 2012 challenge to Section 3 of the Defense of Marriage Act in *United States v. Windsor*, the LGBTQ+ community has had a windfall of legal rights in recent years. Like a pendulum swing, however, we also witness the reduction of rights for LGBTQ+ communities and oppression of such identities. Many states are limiting access to care for TGGD individuals and families, and the plethora of material reflecting LGBTQ+ identities, especially for youth, are also being banned. Older adults who grew up during various points in history may remain wary of progress given continued political and social tensions that determine their civil rights. Recognizing and honoring their experiences, regardless of personal beliefs, are the first steps toward seeing them as a full person, respecting their lived experiences, and understanding how these factors affect their aging process.

Health Disparities and Cultural Stressors

Chronic exposure to adversity and discrimination contributes to depressive symptomatology, medical comorbidities (e.g., stress-related diseases), and overall poor physical health in middle-aged and older LGBTQ+ adults (Fredriksen-Goldsen et al., 2023). During the pandemic, LGBTQ+ older adults reported increased depressive and anxious symptoms, with higher rates seen among multiracial adults, compared with straight and cisgender older adults (Bouton et al., 2023). While causation for this finding remains unclear, it occurred within the larger social context of heightened overt discrimination and violence against minoritized communities and social uprisings. Furthermore, as noted by the National Gay and Lesbian Task Force, "Health disparities and economic insecurity are compounded over the course of a lifetime and have devastating effects on LGBTQ+ older adults" (Fitzgerald, 2013, p. 1). A study of midlife and older adults identifying as LGBTQ+ found that 75% of respondents reported lifetime experiences of violence, discrimination, and microaggressions (Fredriksen-Goldsen et al., 2023). Of the 2,450 adults in this study, 60% reported being verbally insulted, 41% reported being threatened with physical violence, 19.5% were physically beaten, 15.6% were threatened with a weapon, and 15.7% were sexually assaulted. Additionally, over 25% reported having property damaged and 15.5% reported being denied care or receiving inferior care. Indeed, older LGBTQ+ adults face more limitations accessing care than their cisgender heterosexual peers (Bouton et al., 2023; Institute of Medicine [IOM], 2011). Many LGBTQ+ older adults subsequently avoid seeking healthcare services, partly contributing to significant health disparities today. Minority stress, described earlier, can further account for the disproportionate rates of health disparities in LGBTQ+ populations (IOM, 2011; Meyer, 2003).

The accumulation of minority stress over decades has compounding effects on the mental and physical health status of LGBTQ+ older adults (Foglia & Fredriksen-Goldsen, 2014; Fredriksen-Goldsen, Hoy-Ellis, et al., 2014).

Over 30% of LGBTQ+ older adults reported clinically significant depressive symptoms, which is two to three times higher than the generational population, with relatively higher rates in transgender older adults than lesbian, gay, or bisexual peers (Fredriksen-Goldsen et al., 2011). Furthermore, older LGBTQ+ adults report higher rates of attempted suicide than non-LGBTQ+ peers, with higher risk associated with histories of abuse and trauma (IOM, 2011). Nearly 40% of older LGBTQ+ adults reported seriously considering suicide at some point in their lives, and over 70% of older transgender adults seriously considered suicide at some point in their lives (Fredriksen-Goldsen et al., 2011). Other studies note that over 50% of transgender older adults have reported a lifetime prevalence of thinking, planning, and attempting suicide (IOM, 2011). Within these groups, higher rates of depression (and suicidality) were linked to psychological and physical abuse. Additional factors affecting the mental health of older LGBTQ+ participants in Fredriksen-Goldsen et al.'s (2011) study included loneliness and neglect, reflecting the degree of perceived and actual emotional, social, and instrumental support.

Regarding physical health, older LGBTQ+ adults generally have higher rates of chronic health conditions compared with non-LGBTQ+ adults (Fredriksen-Goldsen et al., 2011, 2013; IOM, 2011). For example, gay, bisexual, and transfemale older adults have higher rates of prostate cancer than heterosexual and/or cisgender men for various reasons, some of which are hypothesized to relate to issues of minority stress (IOM, 2011). Indeed, transgender women who fully transitioned often maintain their prostate. Additionally, men who have sex with men (MSM) tend to have higher rates of anal human papillomavirus (HPV) infections, a significant risk factor for anal cancer. Moreover, partly due to poor health behaviors (e.g., obesity, tobacco use, lower frequency of Pap smears and mammograms), lesbian women tend to have higher rates of breast cancer than heterosexual women (Dean, et al., 2000; IOM, 2011). Some literature finds higher rates of chronic heart failure, diabetes, asthma, and obesity within the transgender aging community than the LGB community, often related to the direct (e.g., discrimination) and indirect (e.g., tobacco and alcohol use to cope with stressors) effects of minority stress (Dean et al., 2000; IOM, 2011). LGBTQ+ older adults with dementia can face greater stigma and marginalization due to heterosexist policies in institutions, which can exacerbate social isolation, anxiety, confusion, and distress (Westwood, 2016). More research is needed on lesbian, gay, bisexual, and especially transgender older adults to understand their unique health needs and interventions.

Utilization patterns of LGBTQ+ older adults demonstrate a tendency to delay or avoid use of formal healthcare services, often due to fear of discrimination (e.g., Choi & Meyer, 2016; Dean et al., 2000; Fitzgerald, 2013). Fredriksen-Goldsen et al. (2011) examined factors contributing to health disparities in older transgender adults. They found that transgender older adults reported on average 11 lifetime experiences of discrimination and/or victimization, with denial of or inferior healthcare being among the top forms (40%), compared with an average of 6 experiences for cisgender LGB older adults. Furthermore, LGBTQ+ older adults are less likely to have health insurance and have greater likelihood of facing financial barriers to healthcare services relative to their cisgender, heterosexual peers (Fredriksen-Goldsen et al., 2011). Not surprisingly, researchers also noted that healthy coping mechanisms facilitate healthcare utilization patterns (Loeb et al., 2021). These include good-quality social support, the size of one's social support network, provider competence (e.g., sensitivity to LGBTQ+ needs, providing affirming practices), and one's ability to manage disclosure of identity; these all contributed to improved healthcare utilization patterns.

Only recently has the health of LGBTQ+ populations garnered more attention. The landmark report by the IOM (2011) addressed the overall health of LGBTQ+ populations. Their recommendations involved supporting the National Institutes of Health to develop a research agenda focusing on LGBTQ+ health (demographics, social supports, health inequities and interventions, transgender health needs). This includes adding sexual orientation and gender identity to federally funded surveys through the Department of Health and Human Services, including such identifiers in electronic health records, and developing research training and protocols focused on LGBTQ+ health. In response to the IOM recommendations, in late 2016 the National Institute on Minority Health and Health Disparities (NIMHD) identified "sexual and gender minorities as a health disparity population for research purposes" (NIMHD, 2016). Similarly, the American Geriatrics Society Ethics Committee (2015) issued a position statement on LGBTQ+ older adults. Their vision for the care of LGBTQ+ older adults included the creation and evaluation of policies to offset health inequalities, education for healthcare providers on age-related LGBTQ+ health concerns and the effect of minority stress on health, emphasis on cultural considerations when working with LGBTQ+ older adults, and increased research funding on LGBTQ+ health and the effect of discrimination on health.

Resilience and Growth

While the majority of research on LGBTQ+ older adults focuses on health disparities, only a paucity of research examines factors contributing to resilience and growth (e.g., Fredriksen-Goldsen et al., 2011). Existing research in this area largely addresses the health behaviors and social support networks that help LGBTQ+ older adults cope with the compounding effects of minority stress and aging. Some studies describe the importance of belonging to a larger LGBTQ+ community to increase their sense of empowerment and offset the history of discrimination and victimization experienced (Fredriksen-Goldsen et al., 2011, 2015; Van Wagenen et al., 2013). However, the degree of social support may differ by age group (Fredriksen-Goldsen et al., 2015) and gender identity (Fredriksen-Goldsen, et al., 2013), with some of the oldest adults and transgender adults reporting the least sense of community.

A qualitative study focusing on the resilience of transgender older adults identified various themes that facilitated the aging process (McFadden et al., 2013). Emerging themes included nurturing one's spiritual self, exercising one's sense of agency (e.g., determining when and how to transition, managing finances for a secure future, engaging in healthy coping to prevent illness), practicing self-acceptance, maintaining caring relationships, engaging in advocacy and activism, and enjoying an active and healthy life. Similar themes of self-acceptance, life engagement, and financial planning surfaced in another survey of transgender-bisexual older adults (Witten, 2016). Some respondents reflected on the personal growth experienced by overcoming adversity, while still acknowledging the fears of increased vulnerability to institutional and interpersonal discrimination that often comes with age for LGBTQ+ older adults (e.g., worries about receiving respectful care in nursing homes). Other studies found that personal mastery, social support, access to socialization, physical activity, and LGBTQ+ community engagement aided in supporting one's health-related quality of life (Frederikson-Goldsen et al., 2023). The paucity of research in these areas suggests that further research is needed to understand factors contributing to the resilience evidenced within many LGBTQ+ older adults.

INTERSECTIONALITY

Earlier models of successful aging are couched within Eurocentric, capitalistic values that do not adequately account for the structural determinants and systemic barriers that minoritized LGBTQ+ older adults have to traverse (Fabbre, 2015). Moving beyond heteronormative frameworks, intersectionality examines an individual's lived experience within sociocultural, historical, and economic power structures

(Oswald et al., 2023). In addition to traditional life-span milestones (e.g., family and child rearing), there are unique critical events that LGBTQ+ individuals experience such as timing of disclosure or coming out experiences and gender transitions (Oswald et al., 2023).

The Health Equity Promotion Model (Fredriksen-Goldsen, Simoni et al., 2014) takes a life span developmental perspective to examine how intersectionality influences health equity. As delineated in subsequent paragraphs, this model focuses on how "(a) *social positions* (socio-economic status, age, race/ethnicity) and (b) *individual and structural environmental context* (social exclusion, discrimination, and victimization), intersect with (c) *health-promoting and adverse pathways* (behavioral, social, psychological, and biological processes) to influence the continuum of health outcomes in LGBTQ+ communities" (p. 6, emphasis in original). These factors shape both health equity and resiliency within the aging population of racial, sexual, and gender minorities. Building on this existing model, the updated Iridescent Life Course framework (Fredriksen-Goldsen et al., 2019) supports the incorporation of *queering* and *trans-forming* approaches to capture the intersectionality, fluidity, and biopsychosocial dimensions of LGBTQ aging.

Social positions refer to the multiple layers of one's cultural identity and how these intersect to create further health disparities as well as resilience (Fredriksen-Goldsen, Simoni, et al., 2014). Individual aspects of identity (e.g., SES, age, race, sexual and gender identity) carry various burdens and privileges; however, their intersection can contribute to increased marginalization and disenfranchisement while also possibly strengthening a group's resolve to persevere. The whole is greater than the sum of its parts, and these aspects of one's identity provide context for other environmental factors described here. For example, studies of aging African American LGB women find increased isolation, discrimination, and invisibility compared with heterosexual peers (e.g., Woody, 2015). Qualitative research by Woody (2015) suggests that in African American culture the term *lesbian* holds negative connotations, leading to a sense of otherness. Instead, many African American women report preference for other terms including *same gender loving*. Relatedly, ethnic and racial minoritized LGBTQ+ older adults reported less willingness to disclose hidden identities (sexual/gender identities) given the added stressor of holding multiple stigmatizing identities (Chen et al., 2022). Individual and structural environmental contexts refer to the effect of both individual and systemic discrimination, prejudice, and exclusion on the health of LGBTQ+ individuals. Not surprisingly, studies consistently find that experiences of interpersonal microaggressions, overt discrimination, and physical assaults at the individual level adversely affect the physical and mental health of sexual and gender minorities (Chen et al., 2022; Fredriksen-Goldsen, Emlet, et al., 2013; Meyer, 2003). At the systemic level, policies that exclude LGBTQ+ individuals or place barriers to accessing care (e.g., hospital visitation rights restricted to family/spouses) create further health inequity and at times even reduce the likelihood that some LGBTQ+ individuals seek care (Fredriksen-Goldsen, Simoni, et al., 2014). As Fredriksen-Goldsen, Simoni, and colleagues (2014) explain, "Structural and contextual factors create a context of marginalization and oppression, including laws and policies that unfairly treat sexual and gender minorities as well as cultural and institutional oppressions, widespread societal stigma, and religious intolerance and persecution" (p. 8). Such factors can directly affect the mental and physical health of LGBTQ+ adults (e.g., Fredriksen-Goldsen et al., 2011; Fredriksen-Goldsen, Emlet, et al., 2013).

A study of transgender bisexual adults across the life span found a preponderance of respondents sharing their fears of growing older and the potential for institutional discrimination and interpersonal prejudice and violence (Witten, 2016). Many shared their concerns for systemic discrimination in institutional settings (e.g., nursing homes) and their fears that their gender identities would not be respected should they lose their abilities to communicate healthcare needs. However, some also reflected on the resiliencies they developed by overcoming adversity, processes aided by social and intrapersonal factors including long-term partnership and psychological health (Williams & Fredriksen-Goldsen, 2014). Furthermore, institutional factors promoting inclusion can also affect general health status, including the recent legalization of gay marriage (Goldsen et al., 2017).

Social processes can also affect health outcomes, with relative emphasis on the quality over quantity of social networks (Antonucci, 2001; Fredriksen-Goldsen, Simoni, et al., 2014). Among aging LGBTQ+ adults, a sense of belonging within the larger community can serve as a protective factor against adversity (Chen et al., 2022; Fredriksen-Goldsen et al., 2011; Fredriksen-Goldsen, Kim, et al., 2014; Van Wagenen et al., 2013). However, some old-old adults (85+ years old) and transgender older adults more broadly report less sense of community, placing them at higher risk for adverse health outcomes (Fredriksen-Goldsen, Cook-Daniels, et al., 2013; Fredriksen-Goldsen, Kim, et al., 2014). Many older adults identifying as transgender bisexual shared concerns about being unable to care for themselves in old age, with uncertainty for who may serve as a caregiver (Witten, 2016). Indeed, the support network of many LGBTQ+ older adults consists of similar-aged peers (Witten, 2009). While this affords unique opportunities for shared experiences, this also creates the challenge of lateral caregiving (peer caregivers) compared with the more traditional vertical caregiving (e.g., adult children caring for aging parents; Witten, 2009). As LGBTQ+ adults age with their support networks, there may come a time when their respective needs prohibit mutual caregiving, raising their concerns for who will care for them and fears for the type of treatment they may receive (Witten, 2016).

Psychological, cognitive, and biological factors, as influenced by social positions and environmental contexts, also affect health outcomes (Chen et al., 2022; Fredriksen-Goldsen, Simoni, et al., 2014). Basic factors including cognitive health and adaptive approaches to coping influence health outcomes in general (e.g., Rowe & Kahn, 1998). However, when considering the complexity of intersectionality, factors including internalized stigma (ageism, racism, homophobia, and transphobia) and victimization increase in salience (Fredriksen-Goldsen, Emlet, et al., 2013). The impact of internalized stigma and externalized discrimination can lead to greater rates of anxiety, depression, suicidality, and substance use, which further exacerbate health conditions (e.g., Fredriksen-Goldsen, Emlet, et al., 2013; IOM, 2011; Witten, 2016). More broadly, the biological response to chronic stress adversely affects health outcomes, including cognition (e.g., Juster et al., 2009). Considering the prevalence of lifetime discrimination and victimization among older LGBTQ+ adults (e.g., Fredriksen-Goldsen, Emlet, et al., 2013; IOM, 2011), these factors must be considered when discussing the overall health of diverse ethnic, sexual, and gender minority older adults.

CONCLUSION

This chapter aimed to discuss the cohort effects, health disparities and cultural stressors, and factors contributing to the resiliency and growth of ethnic, sexual, and gender minority older adults. The intersectionality of these factors makes for complex, inspiring, and sometimes distressing stories about overcoming adversity, achieving new heights, and at times sitting with the pain and frustration of discrimination and prejudice. The diversity within older adult populations also affords invaluable research opportunities to improve our knowledge of aging and enhance our provision of care. Moreover, developing a greater appreciation for older adults, including their strengths and hard-fought battles, can help us appreciate the privileges and civil rights we often take for granted. We stand on the shoulders of giants, and it can be humbling and empowering to acknowledge the experiences and advocacy of those who came before.

DISCUSSION QUESTIONS

1. How might race and cohort factors affect your work with older adults (e.g., language use, historical events)?
2. What are common ageist microaggressions? What types of communication patterns can you keep watch for and try to avoid when working with older adults?
3. What are common factors to consider when working with an older adult identifying as LGBTQ+?
4. What resiliencies might you look for when working with older adults?

A robust set of instructor resources designed to supplement this text is located at http://connect.springerpub.com/content/book/978-0-8261-6617-3. Qualifying instructors may request access by emailing textbook@springerpub.com.

REFERENCES

Alexander, M. (2012). *The new Jim Crow: Mass incarceration in the age of colorblindness.* The New Press.

American Psychological Association. (2015). Guidelines for psychological practice with transgender and gender nonconforming people. *American Psychologist, 70*(9), 832–864. https://doi.org/10.1037/a0039906

Antonucci, T. C. (2001). Social relations an examination of social networks, social support. In J. E. Birren & K. W. Schaie (Eds.), *Handbook of the psychology of aging* (pp. 427–453). Academic Press.

Association for Community Living. (2022). *2021 profile of older Americans.* https://acl.gov/sites/default/files/Profile%20of%20OA/2021%20Profile%20of%20OA/2021ProfileOlderAmericans_508.pdf

Ayalon, L., Chasteen, A., Diehl, M., Levy, B. R., Neupert, S. D., Rothermund, K., Tesch-Römer, C., & Wahl., H. (2021). Aging in times of the COVID-19 pandemic: Avoiding ageism and fostering intergenerational solidarity. *The Journals of Gerontology. Series B, Psychological Sciences and Social Sciences, 76*(2), e49–e52. https://doi.org/10.1093/geronb/gbaa051

Bennett, I. M., Chen, J., Soroui, J. S., & White, S. (2009). The contribution of health literacy to disparities in self-rated health status and preventive health behaviors in older adults. *Annals of Family Medicine, 7*(3), 204–2011. https://doi.org/10.1370/amf.940.

Bouton, L. J., Brush, A. M., & Meyer, I. H. (2023). *LGBT adults aged 50 and older in the US during the COVID-19 pandemic*. SAGE.

Centre for Ageing Better. (2023). *Ageism: What's the harm?* https://ageing-better.org.uk/resources/ageism-whats-harm

Chen, J., McLaren, H., Jones, M., & Shams, L. (2022). The aging experiences of LGBTQ ethnic minority older adults: A systematic review. *The Gerontologist, 62*(3), e162–e177. https://doi.org/10.1093/geront/gnaa134.

Choi, S. K., & Meyer, I. H. (2016). *LGBT aging: A review of research findings, needs, and policy implications*. eScholarship, University of California.

Cook-Daniels, L. (2015). Transgender aging: What practitioners should know. In N. A. Orel & C. A. Fruhauf (Eds.), *The lives of LGBT older adults: Understanding challenges and resilience* (pp. 193–215). American Psychological Association.

Dean, L., Meyer, I. H., Robinson, K., Sell, R. L., Sember, R., Silenzio, V., . . ., Tierney, R. (2000). Lesbian, gay, bisexual, and transgender health: Findings and concerns. *Journal of the Gay and Lesbian Medical Association, 4*, 101–151. https://doi.org/10.1023/A:1009573800168

Department of Economic and Social Affairs Population Division. (2015). *World population ageing 2015*. http://www.un.org/en/development/desa/population/publications/pdf/ageing/WPA2015_Report.pdf

Fabbre, V. D. (2015). Gender transitions in later life: A queer perspective on successful aging. *The Gerontologist, 55*(1), 144–153. https://doi.org/10.1093/geront/gnu079

Farrell, T. W., Hung, W. W., Unroe, K. T., Brown, T. R., Furman, C. D., Jih, J., Karani, R. K., Mulhausen, P., Nápoles, A. M., Nnodim, J. O., Upchurch, G., Wittaker, C. F., Kim, A., Lundebjerg, N. E., & Rhodes, R. L. (2022). Exploring the intersection of structural racism and ageism in healthcare. *Journal of the American Geriatrics Society, 70*(12), 3366–3377. https://doi.org/10.1111/jgs.18105

Fitzgerald, D. (2013). *No golden years at the end of the rainbow: How a lifetime of discrimination compounds economic and health disparities for LGBT older adults*. http://www.thetaskforce.org/static_html/downloads/reports/reports/no_golden_years.pdf

Foglia, M. B., & Fredriksen-Goldsen, K. I. (2014). Health disparities among LGBT older adults and the role of nonconscious bias. *Hastings Center Report, 44*(04), S40–S44. https://doi.org/10.1002/hast.369.

Fredriksen-Goldsen, K. I. (2016). The future of LGBT+ aging: a blueprint for action in services, policies, and research. *Generations, 40*(2), 6–15. PMID: 28366980; PMCID: PMC5375167.

Fredriksen-Goldsen, K. I., & Kim, H. J. (2017). The science of conducting research with LGBT older adults-an introduction to aging with pride: National health, aging, and sexuality/gender study (NHAS). *The Gerontologist, 57*(Suppl 1), S1–S14. https://doi.org/10.1093/geront/gnw212

Fredriksen-Goldsen, K. I., & Muraco, A. (2010). Aging and sexual orientation: A 25-year review of literature. *Research on Aging, 32*(3), 372–413. https://doi.org/10.1177/0164027509360355

Fredriksen-Goldsen, K. I., Cook-Daniels, L., Kim, H.-J., Erosheva, E. A., Emlet, C. A., Hoy-Ellis, C. P., . . ., Muraco, A. (2013). Physical and mental health of transgender older adults: An at-risk and underserved population. *The Gerontologist, 54*(3), 488–500. https://doi.org/10.1093/geront/gnt021.

Fredriksen-Goldsen, K., Emlet, C. A., Fabbre, V. D., Kim, H. J., Lerner, J., Jung, H. H., ..., Goldsen, J. (2022). Historical and social forces in the Iridescent Life Course: Key life events and experiences of transgender older adults. *Ageing & Society*, 1–23. https://doi.org/10.1017/S0144686X22000563

Fredriksen-Goldsen, K. I., Emlet, C. A., Kim, H-J., Muraco, A., Erosheva, E. A., Goldsen, J., & Hoy-Ellis, C. P. (2013). The physical and mental health of lesbian, gay male, and bisexual (LGB) older adults: The role of key health indicators and risk and protective factors. *The Gerontologist, 53*(4), 664–675. https://doi.org/10.1093/geront/gns123

Fredriksen-Goldsen, K. I., Hoy-Ellis, C. P., Goldsen, J., Emlet, C. A., & Hooyman, N. R. (2014). Creating a vision for the future: Key competencies and strategies for culturally competent practice with lesbian, gay, bisexual, and transgender (LGBT) older adults in the health and human services. *Journal of Gerontology Social Work, 57*(0), 80–107. https://doi.org/10.1080/01634372.2014.890690.

Fredriksen-Goldsen, K. I., Jen, S., & Muraco, A. (2019). Iridescent life course: LGBTQ aging research and blueprint for the future–A systematic review. *Gerontology, 65*(3), 253–274. https://doi.org/10.1159/000493559

Fredriksen-Goldsen, K. I., Kim, H.-J., Emlet, C. A., Muraco, A., Erosheva, E. A., Hoy-Ellis, C. P., . . ., Petry, H. (2011). *The aging and health report: Disparities and Resilience among lesbian, gay, bisexual and transgender older adults*. http://depts.washington.edu/agepride/wordpress/wp-content/uploads/2012/10/Full-report10-25-12.pdf

Fredriksen-Goldsen, K. I., Kim, H-J., Shiu, C., Goldsen, J., & Emlet, C. A. (2015). Successful aging among LGBT older adults: Physical and mental health-related quality of life by age group. *The Gerontologist, 55*(1), 154–68. https://doi.org/10.1093/geront/gnu081

Fredriksen-Goldsen, K., Prasad, A., Kim, H., & Jung, H. (2023). Lifetime violence, lifetime discrimination, and microaggressions in the Lives of LGBT midlife and older adults: Findings from aging with pride: National health, aging, and sexuality/gender study. *LGBT Health, 10*(Suppl 1), S49–S60. http://doi.org/10.1089/lgbt.2023.0139

Fredriksen-Goldsen, K. I., Simoni, J. M., Kim, H.-J., Lehavot, K., Walters, K. L., Yang, J., Hoy Ellis, C. P. (2014). The health equity promotion model: Reconceptualization of lesbian, gay, bisexual, and transgender (LGBT) health disparities. *American Journal of Orthopsychiatry, 84*(6), 653–663. https://doi.org/10.1037/ort0000030.

Gans, H. M., Horhota, M., & Chasteen, A. L. (2023). Ageism against older adults: How do intersecting identities influence perceptions of ageist behaviors?. *Journal of Applied Gerontology, 42*(6), 1191–1199. https://doi.org/10.1177/07334648231161937

Gilbert, K. L., Elder, K., Lyons, S., Kaphingst, K., Blanchard, M., & Goodman, M. (2015). Racial composition over the life course: Examining separate and unequal environments and the risk for heart disease for African American men. *Ethnicity & Disease, 25*(3), 295–304. https://doi.org/10.18865/ed.25.3.295

Gordon, S., & Gonzales, E. (2022). *Ageism in the family*. The Center for Health and Aging Innovation Working Paper Series, No. 20222. http://hdl.handle.net/2451/63896

Grant, J. M., Mottet, L. A., Tanis, J., Harrison, J., Herman, J. L., & Keisling, M. (2011). *Injustice at every turn: A report of the national transgender discrimination survey*. http://www.thetaskforce.org/static_html/downloads/reports/reports/ntds_full.pdf

Hammond, Z. (2015). *Culturally responsive teaching & the brain: Promoting authentic engagement and rigor among culturally and linguistically diverse students*. Corwin.

Hatzenbuehler, M. L., Phelan, J. C., & Link, B. G. (2013). Stigma as a fundamental cause of population health inequalities. *American Journal of Public Health, 103*(5), 813–821. https://doi.org/10.2105/AJPH.2012.301069

Infurna, F. J. (2021). Utilizing principles of life-span developmental psychology to study the complexities of resilience across the adult life span. *The Gerontologist, 61*(6), 807–818. https://doi.org/10.1093/geront/gnab086

Institute of Medicine. (2011). *The health of lesbian, gay, bisexual and transgender people: Building a foundation for better understanding*. National Academies Press.

Juster, R. P., McEwen, B. S., & Lupien, S. J. (2009). Allostatic load biomarkers of chronic stress and impact on health and cognition. *Neuroscience & Behavioral Reviews, 35*(1), 2–16. https://doi.org/10.1016/j.neubiorev.2009.10.002

Keyes, C. L. M., & Ryff, C. D. (1998). Generativity in adult lives: Social structural contours and quality of life consequences. In D. P. McAdams & E. de St. Aubin (Eds.), *Generativity and adult development: How and why we care for the next generation* (pp. 227–263). American Psychological Association. https://doi.org/10.1037/10288-007

Kim, E. S., Tkatch, R., Martin, D., MacLeod, S., Sandy, L., & Yeh, C. (2021). Resilient aging: Psychological well-being and social well-being as targets for the promotion of healthy aging. *Gerontology & Geriatric Medicine, 7*, 1–12. https://doi.org/10.1177/23337214211002951.

Levy, B. R. (2003). Mind matters: Cognitive and physical effects of aging self-stereotypes. *Journal of Gerontology, 58*(4), P203–P211. https://doi.org/10.1093/geronb/58.4.P203

Levy, B. (2009). Stereotype embodiment: A psychosocial approach to aging. *Current Directions in Psychological Science, 18*(6), 332–336. https://doi.org/10.1111/j.1467-8721.2009.01662.x

Levy, B. R., Chang, E.-S., Lowe, S. R., Provolo, N., & Slade, M. D. (2022). Impact of media-based negative and positive age stereotypes on older individuals' mental health. *Journal of Gerontology: Series B Psychological and Social Sciences, 77*(4), e70–e75. https://doi.org/10.1093/geronb/gba085.

Löckenhoff, C. E., De Fruyt, F., Terracciano, A., McCrae, R. R., De Bolle, M., Costa Jr., P. T., Aguilar-Vafaie, M. E, ..., Yik, M. (2009). Perceptions of aging across 26 cultures and their culture-level associates. *Psychology and Aging, 24*(4), 941–954. https://doi.org/10.1037/a0016901

Loeb, A. J., Wardell, D. W., & Johnson, C. M. (2021). Coping and health care utilization in LGBTQ older adults: A systematic review. *Geriatric Nursing, 42*(4), 833–842. https://doi.org/10.1016/j.gerinurse.2021.04.016.

McFadden, S. H., Frankowski, S., Flick, H., & Witten, T. M. (2013). Resilience and multiple stigmatized identities: Lessons from transgender persons' reflections on aging. In J. D. Sinnott (Ed.), *Positive psychology: Advances in understanding adult motivation* (pp. 247–268). Springer.

Meyer, I. H. (2003). Prejudice, social stress, and mental health in lesbian, gay, and bisexual populations: Conceptual issues and research evidence. *Psychological Bulletin, 129*(5), 674–697. https://doi.org/10.1037/0033-2909.129.5.674

Nakamura, N., Dispenza, F., Abreu, R. L., Ollen, E. W., Pantalone, D. W., Canillas, G., ..., Vencill, J. A. (2022). The APA guidelines for psychological practice with sexual minority persons: An executive summary of the 2021 revision. *American Psychologist, 77*(8), 953–962. https://doi.org/10.1037/amp0000939

National Archives. (2016). *Executive orders.* https://www.archives.gov/federal-register/codification/executive-order/10450.html

National Institute on Minority Health and Health Disparities. (2016). *Sexual and gender minorities formally designated as a health disparity population for research purposes.* https://www.nimhd.nih.gov/about/directors-corner/message.html

North, M. S., & Fiske, S. T. (2012). An inconvenienced youth? Ageism and its potential intergenerational roots. *Psychological Bulletin, 138*(5), 982–997. https://doi.org/10.1037/a0027843

Ortman, J. M., Velkoff, V. A., & Hogan, H. (2014). *An aging nation: The older population in the United States.* Current Population Report No. P25-1140. https://www.census.gov/prod/2014pubs/p25-1140.pdf

Oswald, A. G., Cooper, L., & Guess, A. (2023). Intersectional epistemic tensions associated with building knowledge with LGBTQ+ older adults of color. *Journal of Aging Studies, 66,* 101161. https://doi.org/10.1016/j.jaging.2023.101161

Pew Research Center. (2022). *Black Americans have a clear vision for reducing racism but little hope it will happen.* https://www.pewresearch.org/race-ethnicity/wp-content/uploads/sites/18/2022/08/RE_2022.08.30_Black-Voices-Politics_REPORT.pdf

Rowe, J. W., & Kahn, R. L. (1998). *Successful aging.* Pantheon.

Ryff, C. D. (2014). Self-realisation and meaning making in the face of adversity: A eudaimonic approach to human resilience. *Journal of psychology in Africa, 24*(1), 1–12. https://doi.org/10.1080/14330237.2014.904098

Sinnott, J. D., & Shifren, K. (2001). Gender and aging. Gender differences and gender roles. In J. E. Birren & K. W. Schaie (Eds.), *Handbook of psychology and aging* (5th ed., pp. 454–476). Academic Press.

Smedley, B. D., Stith, A. Y., & Nelson, A. R. (2003). *Unequal treatment. Confronting racial and ethnic disparities in health care.* The National Academies Press.

Substance Abuse and Mental Health Services Administration. (2023). *Lesbian, gay, and bisexual behavioral health: Results from the 2021 and 2022 National Surveys on Drug Use and Health* (SAMHSA Publication No. PEP23-07-01-001). Center for Behavioral Health Statistics and Quality, Substance Abuse and Mental Health Services Administration. https://www.samhsa.gov/data/report/LGB-Behavioral-Health-Report-2021-2022

Truman, J. L., & Morgan, R. E. (2022). *Violent victimization by sexual orientation and gender identity, 2017-2020.* U.S. Dept of Justice. https://bjs.ojp.gov/content/pub/pdf/vvsogi1720.pdf

U.S. Census Bureau. (2021). *Sexual orientation and gender identity in household pulse survey.* https://www.census.gov/library/visualizations/interactive/sexual-orientation-and-gender-identity.html

Van Wagenen, A., Driskell, J., & Bradford, J. (2013). "I'm still raring to go": Successful aging among lesbian, bisexual, and transgender older adults. *Journal of Aging Studies, 27*(1), 1–14. https://doi.org/10.1016/j.jaging.2012.09.001

Vauclair, C. M., Hanke, K., Huang, L. L., & Abrams, D. (2017). Are Asian cultures really less ageist than Western ones? It depends on the questions asked. *International Journal of Psychology, 52*(2), 136–144. https://doi.org/10.1002/ijop.12292

Vespa, J., Medina, L., & Armstrong, D. M. (2020). *Demographic turning points for the United States: Population projections 2020–2060.* https://www.census.gov/content/dam/Census/library/publications/2020/demo/p25-1144.pdf

Westwood, S. (2016). Dementia, women and sexuality: How the intersection of ageing, gender and sexuality magnify dementia concerns among lesbian and bisexual women. *Dementia (London), 15*(6), 1494–1514. https://doi.org/10.1177/1471301214564446

World Health Organization. (2021). *Global report on ageism.* https://iris.who.int/bitstream/handle/10665/340208/9789240016866-eng.pdf?sequence=1

Wilkerson, I. (2020). *Caste: The origins of our discontents.* Random House.

Williams, K. N. (2004). Elderspeak: Impact on geriatric care. *Geriatrics and Aging, 7*(1), 57–60.

Williams, M. E., & Fredriksen-Goldsen, K. I. (2014). Same-sex partnerships and the health of older adults. *Journal of Community Psychology, 42*(5), 558–570. https://doi.org/10.1002/Jcop.21637

Witten, T. M. (2009). Graceful exits: Intersection of aging, transgender identities, and the family/community. *Journal of GLBT Family Studies, 5*(1–2), 35–61. https://doi.org/10.1080/15504280802595378

Witten, T. M. (2016). Aging and transgender bisexuals: Exploring the intersection of age, bisexual sexual identity, and transgender identity. *Journal of Bisexuality, 16*(1), 58–80. https://doi.org/10.1080/15299716.2015.1025939

Woody, I. (2015). Lift every voice: Voices of African-American lesbian elders. *Journal of Lesbian Studies, 19*(1), 50–58. https://doi.org/10.1080/10894160.2015.972755

3

Models of Aging

Erin L. Woodhead and Brian P. Yochim

> **LEARNING OBJECTIVES**
>
> - Explain what telomeres are and their relevance to the aging process.
> - Illustrate the relationship between free radicals and antioxidants and their relationships with longevity.
> - Compare and contrast the presented psychological theories of aging.
> - Describe how social factors contribute to the aging process.

Aging can be viewed from multiple perspectives, including what happens within the body's cells during aging, what happens interpersonally and intrapersonally with aging, and how the social context impacts aging. This chapter reviews biological models of aging as well as psychological and social models. Each of the models reviewed in this chapter offers different perspectives on what happens during the aging process.

The topic of human aging is certainly not new to the current era. In 44 BCE the famous Roman orator Cicero wrote one of the earliest known pieces on human aging, "De Senectitute." This work is notable for addressing many of the same topics we are exploring today in the field and in this book, such as losing sensory acuity, staying actively employed in old age, and being "freed from the bondage of passion." The reader is encouraged to review this work of Cicero to view how conceptualizations of aging in the time of the ancient Romans were strikingly similar to the current era.

One of the earliest modern-era works devoted to the psychology of aging was G. Stanley Hall's *Senescence, the Last Half of Life* (1922). In this text, he proposed five stages of life, which included the last two stages, "senescence, which begins in the early forties, or before in women, and . . . senectitude, the post-climacteric or old age proper" (p. vii). Chapters in this text included "The History of Old Age," "Literature by and on the Aged," "Statistics of Old Age and Its Care," "Medical Views and Treatment of Old Age" (which included a "Protest Against the Prepotence of Heredity in Determining Longevity," an early exploration of genetics versus environment in determining longevity), "The Contributions of Biology and Physiology," "Some Conclusions" (which includes a summary of what was known about psychosocial issues at the time [e.g., "superior powers of the old in perspective and larger views"]), and "The Psychology of Death." A case against differentiating between "presenile dementia" and "senile dementia" was made when he wrote, "As to premature senility, in general its symptoms are identical with those of mature senility" (p. 207). Experts would arrive at this same conclusion in later editions of the *Diagnostic and Statistical Manual of Mental Disorders* and discard the differentiation between "presenile" and "senile." His reference to "memory, the loss of which comes as an advance guard of many symptoms" (p. 206), remains true, as decline in memory often precipitates the cascade of decline that occurs with dementia.

BIOLOGICAL MODELS OF AGING

The media is full of references to antioxidants and various antiaging treatments. What are antioxidants? What do they have to do with the aging process? Why does the human body experience conditions involving excessive growth (e.g., cancer) and excessive destruction (e.g., Alzheimer disease)? This section explores these general concepts and more.

While aging is typically associated with an increased prevalence of disease in humans and other species, other organisms seem to avoid the development of disease. Sequoia and redwood trees, for instance, live hundreds of years while avoiding disease (Sillett et al., 2015). The longest-living organism on Earth is the bristlecone pine tree, which can live more than 4,000 years; one tree is believed to be at least 4,713 years old (Lanner & Connor, 2001). These species are mostly free of internal disease processes. When they die, it tends to be due to external factors such as lightning strikes, fire, pest outbreaks, soil erosion, or damage inflicted by humans. Bristlecone pines, sequoias, redwoods, and other tree species do not seem to show symptoms of senescence (Lanner, 2002), a topic described in the following section on telomeres. One can ponder a time far into the future in which the prevalence of mortal disease is so low that humans only die from external forces. How is it that these species have evolved to be so resistant to disease, and can we learn from that? A comprehensive account of the psychology of human aging begins at the cellular or genetic level.

Telomeres

An important variable that determines how long humans live is the length of telomeres (Chakravarti et al., 2021). Telomeres lie at the ends of chromosomes and protect the ends, similar to the plastic coverings on the ends of shoelaces (see Figure 3.1). The function of telomeres is to maintain the integrity of chromosomes. As you will learn in this section, telomere dysfunction can lead to premature aging, cancer, and other types of degenerative disease (Chakravarti et al., 2021).

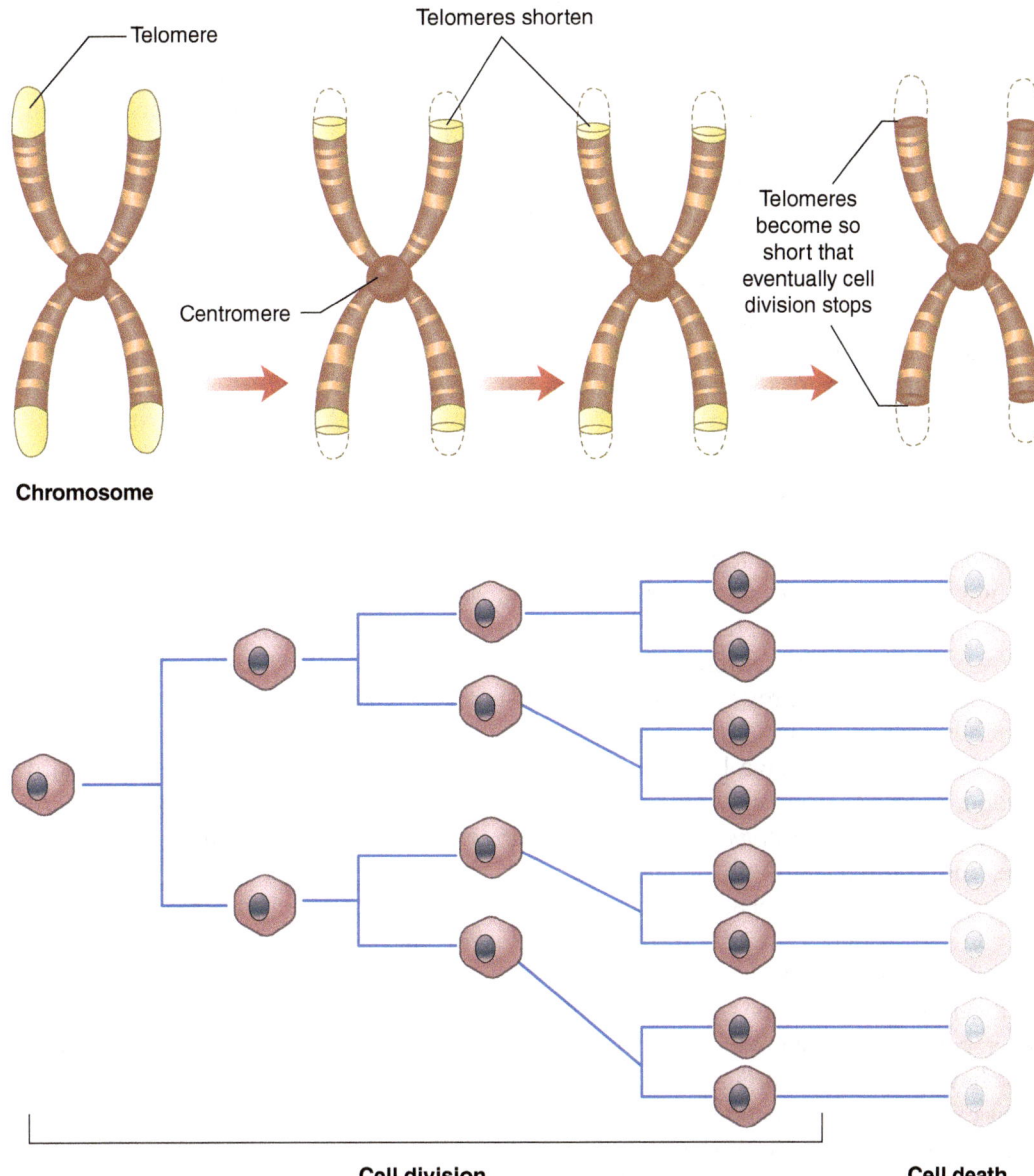

Figure 3.1 Telomeres.

Telomeres serve at least three important functions (Yang et al., 2016): (a) they prevent chromosome ends from degrading; (b) they prevent chromosome ends from being perceived as broken and in need of cessation of division or programmed cell death, and (c) they prevent DNA repair mechanisms that could mistakenly cause problems, such as chromosome fusions. Cells reproduce by dividing multiple times over the life span, most predominantly from birth to adulthood. Prior research indicates that there is a limit on how often cells can divide, termed the *Hayflick limit* (Hayflick, 1965). Prior to this groundbreaking work, researchers assumed that human cells could replicate endlessly. Each time a cell divides, the DNA at the very end of the chromosome, contained in the telomeres, cannot be copied accurately during each division, leading to a shortening of the chromosome after every division. This is termed the *end replication problem.* With each cell division, telomeres become shorter and shorter until a point at which cells are no longer able to divide. This point is termed *replicative senescence* or *replicative aging* (Shay & Wright, 2011; Yang et al., 2016). The end replication problem, resulting in replicative senescence, is not the only way in which telomeres shorten over time, and some researchers propose that replicative senescence is the exception rather than the rule (von Zglinicki, 2021). Mild oxidative stress, leading to accumulation of DNA damage, can also contribute to telomere shortening by causing a repair deficiency (von Zglinicki, 2021).

After reaching the replication limit or experiencing oxidative stress, two situations can occur with telomeres. First, the cell can enter *senescence,* which means that the cell stops multiplying but does not go through the process of cell death. Second, cell death, termed *apoptosis,* can occur due to chromosomal instability. Apoptosis is most common in cell types for which disposal is easy, such as skin or intestine cells. Once a cell can no longer divide, it can remain in a state of *cell senescence* for years. If a cell remains in senescence for prolonged periods (e.g., as in skin moles), it can undergo major changes in its physiology. The accumulation of senescent cells is an ongoing area of interest in biological aging research, particularly around ways in which to remove senescent cells from the body. In a pilot study, Justice et al. (2019) used senolytics, which are drugs that clear out senescent cells, to demonstrate that certain physical markers of idiopathic pulmonary fibrosis were improved with 3 weeks of senolytic use.

Cell senescence influences age-related pathology by at least two mechanisms. First, senescent cells have limited ability to create new cells needed for tissue health. Second, senescent cells may also affect their surrounding cells by releasing *senescence-associated secretory phenotype* (SASP), which can lead to inflammation, alter tissue structure, and stimulate growth of malignant cells in old age (Tchkonia et al., 2013). It is important to note that not all senescent cells have a negative impact on surrounding cells. Senescent cells play a positive and important role in embryonic development, childbirth, and wound healing (National Institute on Aging, 2021). Due to its beneficial effects in younger people, SASP may exhibit *antagonistic pleiotropy.* Antagonistic pleiotropy occurs when genes that may have harmful effects in late life are favored by natural selection if they have beneficial effects earlier in life (Gavrilov & Gavrilova, 2006). Natural selection leads to increased production of genes that benefit an organism during reproductive years even if the gene can cause detrimental effects after the reproductive years. Therefore, although SASP may be harmful in older adults, it may lead to tissue healing in younger people, promoting immune clearance of damaged cells such as in skin wounds.

Shortened telomere length is associated with increased overall mortality as well as mortality related to diseases of the cardiovascular, respiratory, digestive, and musculoskeletal systems, and COVID-19 (Schneider et al., 2022). Telomere length has also been linked to diabetes mellitus (Cheng et al., 2021). Radiation can induce cell senescence and shorten telomeres, inhibiting cell growth (Tchkonia et al., 2013), which has led to it being used to prevent the growth of cancer, a form of uncontrolled cell growth (Yang et al., 2016). Although telomere length has been discussed up to this point as a biological aspect of aging, there are psychological and social mechanisms by which individuals can influence their telomere length. In a comprehensive review of telomere length and psychosocial stressors, Rentscher et al. (2020) found that early life adversity and in utero adversity were most closely associated with shortened telomere length, as well as the absence of close social relationships in adulthood. Taken together, the researchers conclude that there is a window of vulnerability early in life, as well as an additional impact in adulthood of social isolation on decreased telomere length.

The enzyme *telomerase* makes telomeres longer and adds new DNA onto them. In human embryonic development, telomerase is active but dissipates in brain and bone tissue after 16 weeks and declines in other tissue during fetal development (Yang et al., 2016). Regenerative tissues in the esophagus, intestines, hair, skin, uterus, sperm, and other tissues show some telomerase activity, but most human tissue contains insufficient levels of telomerase to stop the loss of telomeres that occurs with age (Yang et al., 2016).

Cancer cells have evolved to have the ability to circumvent replicative senescence by preserving telomere lengths, allowing cancer cells to reproduce without limit. Cancer cells often avoid cell death, or apoptosis, by producing more telomerase, which limits the shortening of telomeres during cell division. Telomerase is found in 85% to 95% of malignant tumors (Okamoto & Seimaya, 2019) and enables cancer cells to reproduce indefinitely (Shay & Wright, 2011). Because of its presence in almost all cancer cells, and because it facilitates the growth of cancer, measuring the presence of telomerase may be a way to detect cancer. Stopping the production of telomerase may be one way to limit cancer cell reproduction and lead to cell death. Treatments that inhibit telomerase are in various stages of development for pancreatic cancer, breast cancer, lung cancer, and multiple myeloma (Shay & Wright, 2011). However, there are risks of blocking telomerase, since it remains active in some cells related to fertility, wound healing, and production of certain types of cells.

Free Radicals and Aging

One of the longest-lasting theories of aging has been the free radical theory of aging, put forth by Harman (1956). The free radical theory of aging proposes that cellular aging is due to the accumulation of oxidative cellular damage in the mitochondrial DNA, leading to an updated naming of this theory to "mitochondrial free radical theory" (Ludovico & Burhans, 2014). *Free radicals* are atoms or molecules that have at least one unpaired electron, making them volatile and destabilizing molecules near them. These effects on nearby molecules lead to the formation of more free radicals, causing further instability and cellular damage. Free radicals can be produced through typical biological processes such as aerobic metabolism and pathogenic defense mechanisms. They can also be produced from environmental toxins such as cigarette smoke, various types of pollutants, and radiation. The predominant type of free radical related to human aging is generated during cellular metabolism involving mitochondria. Damage and mutations to the mitochondrial DNA are associated with aging-related disorders (Someya & Ikeda, 2021) and are therefore of interest to researchers studying the biology of aging.

Mitochondria generate energy within cells. Oxygen is necessary for energy production, but this process also leads to the production of reactive oxygen species (ROS) as by-products. ROS are free radicals that contain oxygen molecules, such as OH and HO_2 molecules (Harman, 1956). Mitochondria are the main creators of ROS and a common site for oxidative damage due to ROS, with as many of 90% of intracellular ROS generated by mitochondrial reactions and processes that require oxygen (Someya & Ikeda, 2021). In healthy cells, ROS generation occurs at controlled rates, and mitochondria have a complex system of antioxidant enzymes in place to protect themselves from ROS damage (Someya & Ikeda, 2021). However, with increasing age, researchers propose that the mitochondrial defense systems are unable to keep up with ROS production. The balance between these two processes, ROS production and the mitochondrial antioxidant defense systems, is associated with the extent of cell damage seen due to ROS. ROS lead to many consequences including altered gene expression, genomic instability, genetic mutations, loss of ability to engage in mitosis (cellular reproduction), impaired communication between cells, disorganized tissue, organ dysfunction, and increased vulnerability to stress (Rattan, 2006). ROS lead to cumulative damage to cells, eventually leading to cell death (Scheibye-Knudsen et al., 2015) and death of an organism.

Antioxidants are chemicals that inhibit or eliminate oxidation and therefore may protect against free radicals. The antioxidant *resveratrol* has inherent antioxidant characteristics and prompts the activity of other antioxidant enzymes (Salehi et al., 2018). Resveratrol is a polyphenol (nutrient) found in plants, particularly plants going through environmental stresses. These plants include grapes, raspberries, blueberries, peanuts, and some pine trees. However, resveratrol has low bioavailability, meaning that it is not easily absorbed and used by the body, and can have negative side effects in higher doses.

While excessive ROS may harm cells, there can be an adaptive response to low levels, such that the cell is protected when it experiences higher levels of ROS. This process is known as *hormesis* (Ludovico & Burhans, 2014). This idea has stemmed from research showing that (a) ROS may increase life span in yeast and worms (Mesquita et al., 2010; Van Raamsdonk & Hekimi, 2009), (b) increasing mitochondrial ROS do not always decrease life span in mice (Zhang et al., 2009), and (c) ROS do have important biological roles (Ramis et al., 2015). Small levels of ROS may be implicated in caloric restriction, described next.

Caloric Restriction

One of the most consistent findings in the biology of aging is that decreasing rats' food intake slows growth and increases their life span, reported as early as 1917 by Osborne, Mendel, and Ferry. During the Great Depression, there were concerns that chronic hunger might shorten the human life span (Kenyon, 2010), but McCay and colleagues (1935, 1939) showed that decreased food intake lengthened the life span of rats. Additionally, reduced caloric intake has been associated with slower progression of age-related cancers and other chronic illnesses in short-lived organisms (López-Lluch & Navas, 2016). This reduction in calories has been shown to increase life span in yeast, fruit flies, nematodes, fish, rats, mice, hamsters, and dogs (Ramis et al., 2015). In two seminal studies of rhesus monkeys, one study found that a 30% caloric reduction improved mortality and delayed the onset of age-related conditions, whereas the second study found that there was no influence of caloric restriction on mortality, though there was a positive impact on the monkeys' lipid profile and susceptibility to diseases such as cancer and type 2 diabetes (Colman et al., 2014; Mattison et al., 2012, 2017).

Research on caloric restriction in humans is difficult to perform, primarily because humans have a relatively long life span and it is difficult to maintain caloric restriction across the adult life span. In early trials of 25% to 30% caloric restriction over the course of 1 year, obese and nonobese individuals showed reductions in some markers of oxidative stress, as well as improvements in lipid profile and decreases in insulin resistance (Kobara et al., 2020). Research on caloric restriction in humans has found that a 25% or less calorically restricted diet is safe and feasible for long-term maintenance (Kobara et al., 2020).

There are several proposed mechanisms by which caloric restriction improves longevity. One mechanism is that caloric restriction reduces the buildup of ROS, thereby preserving the function of the mitochondrial DNA and increasing antioxidant capacity (Kobara et al., 2020). Another proposed mechanism of caloric restriction is by increasing the expression of *sirtuins*. Sirtuins are mammalian homologues of the yeast *silent information regulator 2* (Sir2). There are seven homologues of the Sir2 protein, which are sirtuins 1 to 7 (SIRT1, SIRT2, SIRT3, SIRT4, SIRT5, SIRT6, and SIRT7), and they regulate systems associated with energy metabolism and cell longevity (Kobara et al., 2020). Sirtuins are important contributors to the life span of animals (Ramis et al., 2015). Sirtuins have many beneficial effects related to aging, and caloric restriction increases the activity of sirtuins. Overall, the proposed mechanisms by which caloric restriction increases longevity tend to center on mitochondrial maintenance. Caloric restriction introduces mitochondrial reprogramming through multiple pathways (i.e., ROS reduction, increased sirtuin production), reducing oxidative stress and improving the longevity of cells.

If caloric restriction could lengthen the human life span, the feasibility or desirability of engaging in such a restricted dietary regimen throughout life is questionable. Researchers have therefore sought to identify ways to mimic the effects of caloric restriction, or to find *mimetics* for caloric restriction. Current research suggests three areas of inquiry around mimetics: intermittent fasting, specific component restriction, and ingestion. An 8-week program of alternate-day fasting, where 25% of caloric needs were consumed on one day with unrestricted eating on the next day, led to reductions in oxidative and inflammatory indicators as well as decreases in blood pressure and improvements in lipid profile (Johnson et al., 2007). Specific component restriction focuses on reduced consumption of carbohydrates and, in some studies, reduced protein intake, both of which were associated with more favorable health and mortality outcomes (Kobara et al., 2020). Ingestion of the antioxidant resveratrol (discussed previously), a chemical in various foods, can mimic the benefits of caloric restriction (Mansur et al., 2017). Resveratrol increases activation of SIRT1. Sirtuins may be instrumental in creating strategies to mimic the beneficial effects of caloric restriction.

Melatonin is another chemical found in plants that may increase SIRT1 activity. It has antioxidant properties and decreases free radicals. In humans it is released from the pineal gland at night (Ramis et al., 2015). This cycle weakens with age but tends to be preserved in animals undergoing caloric restriction (Reiter, 1992). Melatonin may be involved in cancer reduction by inhibiting SIRT1, which is overexpressed in prostate cancer (Jung-Hynes et al., 2011). Research in the coming decades will continue to explore mimetics of caloric restriction. Next, we review genes pertinent to aging.

Genetics of Aging

Approximately 20% to 40% of longevity in humans is explained by genetic factors, with longevity typically clustered within families (Bin-Jumah et al., 2022). Hundreds of genes are associated with longevity or with other phenotypes related to aging, and researchers have focused on some of the common "longevity" genes discussed in this section.

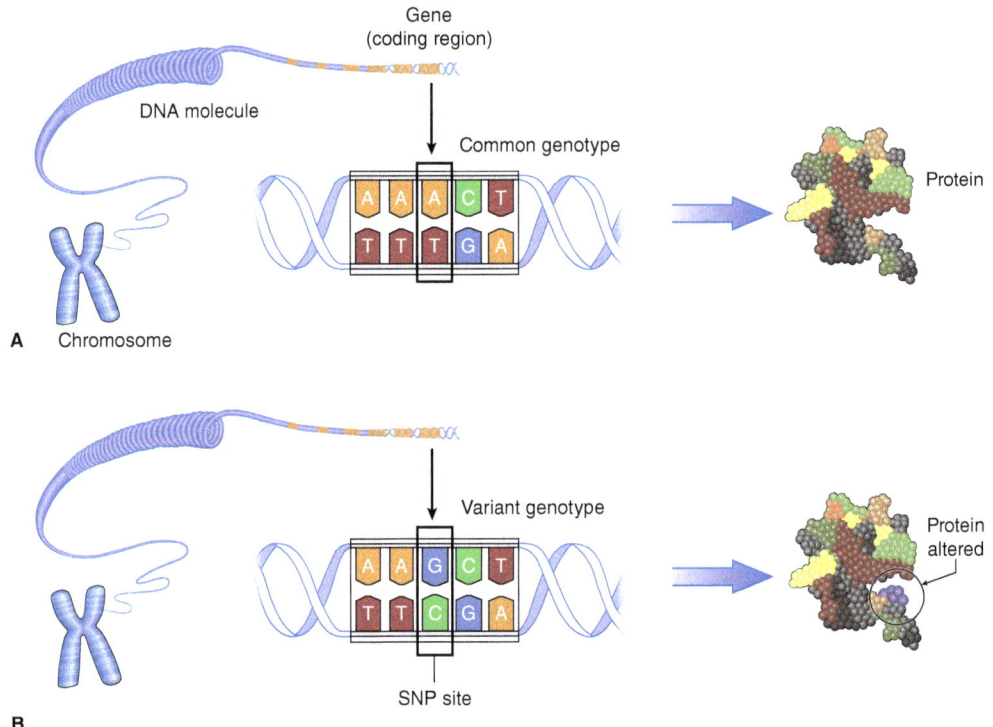

Figure 3.2 A single nucleotide polymorphism. (**A**) a depiction of a chromosome and gene that encode the formation of a protein, (**B**) a single nucleotide polymorphism that alters the formation of that protein.
SNP, single nucleotide polymorphism.
Source: From Camp, K. M., & Trujillo, E. (2014). Position of the academy of nutrition and dietetics: Nutritional genomics. *Journal of the Academy of Nutrition and Dietetics*, *114*(2), 299–312. https://doi.org/10.1016/j.jand.2013.12.001

There are different ways to study how genes are related to aging. *Molecular* studies primarily consist of genetic association studies. These studies investigate whether specific polymorphisms are related to phenotypes, or the observable traits that are encoded by genes (e.g., one's hair color). A polymorphism is a variation of a DNA sequence inherited by an individual. When a single nucleotide varies across individuals at a certain place on a gene, this is called a *single nucleotide polymorphism* (SNP; see Figure 3.2). An SNP consists of one of the four bases (A, C, G, or T), a sugar, and a phosphate molecule. Such genetic variants must typically exist in at least 1% of the population to be considered an SNP (Kremen & Lyons, 2011). SNPs can consist of substitutions, deletions, or insertions. Approximately 1% to 2% of SNPs are found to be *functional* (i.e., to lead to amino acid changes in *translation*). *Translation* is the production of proteins from DNA and essentially is how genetic alterations are manifest.

Researchers explore as much of the human genome as possible to find candidate genes in *genome-wide association studies* (GWAS). This approach brings forth the problem, however, of hundreds of thousands of statistical tests and the accompanying need to change the alpha level to avoid Type 1 statistical errors. That is, when performing a large number of statistical tests, a researcher is bound to find effects by chance and might conclude a relationship exists when it in fact does not (i.e., a Type 1 error). Thus, large effect sizes are required to determine the presence of significant effects. To complicate this further, most traits related to the psychology of aging are *polygenic*. That is, the majority of psychological traits are associated with multiple genetic and environmental factors, each likely with a small effect size. Researchers attempt as much as possible to specify a priori hypotheses in a candidate gene approach to guide their analyses and give them support for conclusions that may be drawn from small effect sizes.

When studying genes related to aging, it is important to consider how the genome interacts with environmental conditions. Nongenetic factors (e.g., exposure to carcinogens, diet, degree of stress) can turn the expression of a gene on or off without changing the underlying DNA structure. These differences are known as *epigenetics*. In relation to aging, an individual might have one of the relevant genes for longevity, but the expression of that gene is turned off due to a lifetime exposure to environmental toxins or a stressful environment. These epigenetic modifications, or "tags," on each gene can be passed onto the next generation, even though those individuals did not experience the original stressor that led to the gene expression being switched off (Handy et al., 2011).

APOLIPOPROTEIN E (APOE), P53, AND SIRTUIN

The gene for APOE, located on chromosome 19, has consistently been related to longer human life spans, with some estimates that APOE contributes 3.5% to the variance in human longevity (Bin-Jumah et al., 2022). The APOE gene has three possible alleles, ε2, ε3, and ε4, thus leading to six genotypes that one can inherit: ε2/ε2, ε2/ε3, ε2/ε4, ε3/ε3, ε3/ε4, and ε4/ε4. This gene encodes an apolipoprotein that is a large component of very low-density lipoproteins (VLDLs), which remove excess cholesterol from blood. Allelic variants of APOE are related to Alzheimer disease, atherosclerosis, and other pathologies related to aging. Because of its role in metabolizing triglycerides and cholesterol, the ε3/ε4 and ε4/ε4 genotypes have been found to be associated with increased risk of myocardial infarction, whereas the ε2/ε3 genotype is associated with decreased risk (Wang et al., 2015). That is, the ε4 allele may lead to increased cholesterol levels, whereas the ε2 allele may lower cholesterol levels. Apolipoprotein is expressed in many organs and is expressed the most in the liver followed by the brain (Verghese et al., 2011). High frequency of the ε4 allele is associated with a 4.2-year reduction in life span and is also associated with shorter telomeres (Bin-Jumah et al., 2022). In relation to epigenetics, aerobic exercise can improve the longevity of individuals who have the ε4 allele, and there is an interaction between diet and genotype that influences human longevity. This research suggests that environmental factors, such as regular exercise and a healthy diet, can offset the presence of the ε4 allele for many individuals.

p53 is a gene that is partially responsible for maintaining the health of DNA and may also reduce the risk of cancer. Mutations in p53 have commonly been linked to cancerous tumors in humans; around 50% of all tumors involve disruption in p53 (Bin-Jumah et al., 2022). As discussed in the "Caloric Restriction" section, sirtuin gene activity is thought to improve longevity by delaying cellular senescence. The sirtuin gene family promotes the repair of DNA and its resistance to oxidative stress (Bin-Jumah et al., 2022).

PSYCHOLOGICAL MODELS OF AGING

Psychological models of aging consider how emotions, attitudes, mental processes, personality factors, and motivation influence the aging process. Several theorists have proposed models of aging that influence our knowledge and research into typical aging from a psychological perspective. Jean Piaget's work (1972) is typically included in texts of human development. His work focused on cognitive changes throughout childhood, adolescence, and early adulthood. He did not explore development in adulthood or older adulthood. His cognitive stages were later expanded to include postformal thought, though this stage is typically applied to emerging adults (individuals between ages 18 and 25). In this section we focus on theories that have contributed substantially to our knowledge of the aging process.

Erikson's Stages of Psychosocial Development

Erik Erikson (1902–1994) was a prominent developmental theorist. He generated a comprehensive theory of human development and created the term *identity crisis*. He was heavily influenced by psychoanalytic theory and the work of Anna Freud. He proposed that humans progress through various stages in life, characterized by specific conflicts (Erikson, 1997). For example, most of adulthood was thought to be characterized by a conflict between "generativity" and "stagnation." Generativity is characterized by procreation, productivity, and creativity. Adults develop an interest in caring for others during this stage, and in the development of the next generation. He proposed that the very last stage of life involves a crisis between "integrity" and "despair." From this conflict humans develop wisdom, which he defined as "informed and detached concern with life itself in the face of death itself" (p. 61). When older adults experience despair, it is often due to a sense of stagnation in life. The despair may also involve mourning for lost time, decreased independence, decreased initiative, lost opportunities for intimacy, and missed opportunities for generativity. He proposed that the last stage of life involves a psychosexual "generalization of sensual modes" (p. 64) that enriches physical and psychological experiences even if sexual functioning declines. The primary trait involved in this stage is "integrity," or a sense of coherence and wholeness in the face of losses of physical, cognitive, and generative functioning. He concluded his discussion of old age by pointing out: "For individual life is the coincidence of but one life cycle with but one segment of history" (pp. 65–66).

In 1997, Joan Erikson published an expanded version of her husband's *The Life Cycle Completed*, which added a discussion about the "ninth stage" of human development, which occurs in one's 80s and 90s. Erik Erikson noted: "Lacking a culturally viable ideal of old age, our civilization does not really harbor a concept of the whole of life" (p. 114). Paul Baltes (1997) expressed this same notion, discussed in the next section.

Selective Optimization With Compensation

Paul Baltes (1939–2006) offered a comprehensive theory of human development that included more of a focus on late life. He proposed three principles of human development and aging (Baltes, 1997). First, because natural selection leads to evolution of characteristics that increase the chances of human reproduction, and traits that lengthen the life span into old age are less needed for this purpose, human genes are less likely to protect against diseases and other health problems that can arise in aging. As Baltes notes, throughout most of human history, people died before problematic genes were activated or their negative effects could occur. Baltes terms this the "unfinished architecture" of the human life span.

TABLE 3.1 BALTES'S MODEL OF HUMAN DEVELOPMENT: EXAMPLES OF SELECTION, OPTIMIZATION, AND COMPENSATION

Selection	Optimization	Compensation
Elective selection	Attentional focus	Increased time allocation
Specification of goals	Effort/energy	Increased attentional focus
Goal commitment	Time allocation	Increased effort/energy
Loss-based selection	Practice of skills	Activation of unused skills/resources
Focusing on most important goals	Acquiring new skills/resources	Use of external aids/help of others
Search for new goals	Modeling successful others	Therapeutic intervention

Source: From Baltes, P. B. (1979). Life-span developmental psychology: Some converging observations on history and theory. In P. B. Baltes & J. O. G. Brim (Eds.), *Life-span development and behavior* (Vol. 2, pp. 255–279). New York, NY: Academic Press.

The second principle of Baltes's (1997) theory is that with age, our need for culture increases, with "culture" defined as the psychological, social, economic, and knowledge resources that humanity has generated throughout our existence. These resources have been transmitted across generations, enable human development, and are needed in increasing amounts as we age. Unfortunately, as the third principle spells out, as we need culture more, the effectiveness of culture simultaneously declines with age. Baltes (1997) proposed that humans assign resources to three areas across the life span: growth, maintenance, and managing losses. Early life development predominantly involves *gains*, and as we develop into middle and old age, we experience increasingly higher proportions of *losses*. Thus, as we enter old age, we experience less growth and more maintenance and loss management.

Baltes (1997) proposed a model of human development that is particularly relevant to aging: selective optimization with compensation (SOC), outlined in Table 3.1. Selection involves the specification of goals, commitment to goals, and adapting the goal hierarchy when needed. Optimization refers to how one allocates time and resources to the goals that have been selected and the acquisition and practice of skills necessary for self-development. We engage in compensation when a particular resource is no longer available. Compensation can include increased attentional allocation, increased effort and time, activating unused skills and resources, use of external aids, and help from others.

The SOC model emphasizes the adaptiveness of older adults in the face of possible declines. Examples of the SOC model are typically applied to age-related health changes. For example, an older adult may reduce time spent in vigorous exercise and instead apply their time to studying yoga or another form of less strenuous activity. In this example, the older adult selects physical activity as an important goal and compensates for declines in physical functioning by optimizing their performance in other physical activities. Another example of the SOC model could be an older adult who selects driving as an important goal but realizes some of the age-related limitations experienced in driving ability. To compensate for declines in this area, one could optimize driving skills such that they only make right turns and avoid left turns, because accidents are more common when making left rather than right turns.

Baltes also proposed a way to conceptualize social aging, that is, changes that take place in our environment that may influence our aging process. Baltes (1979) proposed that social influences can include normative history-graded influences, normative age-graded influences, and nonnormative influences. Normative history-graded influences include cultural, political, and social events that impacted a specific generation. For example, the COVID-19 pandemic impacted the lives of each cohort in unique ways, such as causing academic delays in schoolchildren or causing the loss of loved ones among older adults. The lives of members of Generation X were changed when the World Trade Center was destroyed on September 11, 2001. Members of the Baby Bfoomer generation can likely tell you where they were when John F. Kennedy was assassinated or when Neil Armstrong walked on the moon. Cultural shifts are also captured in the concept of normative history-graded influences, such as the rise in the use of technology and social media. Normative age-graded influences include events that are expected to take place at certain ages, such as obtaining a driver's license, getting married, having children, retiring, and so on. These events typically have socially accepted age norms attached to them, such as marrying in your 20s and having kids in your 30s. Even if these ages are not made explicit, most individuals have a general sense of when these events "should" happen and may experience questions from others if they have not met these milestones. Nonnormative influences are specific to each individual and include unique events that shape development, such as losing a parent, obtaining a new job, or acquiring an illness. Each of these three types of influences shapes developmental trajectories in different ways and is often tied to cultural factors, as well as one's birth cohort.

Baltes (1997) proposed that the time of life from age 80 onward be called the "fourth age" and considered this a major area of growth for research and theory development. He challenged developmental scientists to strive to "complete the biological and cultural architecture of the life span" so that the maximization of development (i.e., a positive balance of gains versus losses) could be extended further into the life span (p. 377). With evolution's lack of focus on old age, however, this challenge will be increasingly difficult into advanced ages.

Socioemotional Selectivity Theory

Socioemotional selectivity theory (SST) is a theory of late-life emotional development (Carstensen et al., 1999). SST hypothesizes that older adults begin to prioritize emotionally meaningful goals as their time perspective changes. That is, upon realizing that time horizons are limited (time is running out), there is a motivated shift in goals away from seeking knowledge and new experiences and toward more emotionally meaningful goals. It was originally thought that older adults focused on positive goals and stimuli because they lacked the cognitive capacity to process negative stimuli. In contrast, SST has shown that prioritization of positive information and emotionally meaningful goals is a motivated shift due to a change in goals, as opposed to a compensation mechanism due to reduced processing capacity. SST provides psychologists with a broader understanding of typical emotional changes that occur with age, outside of the context of clinical problems.

Life Course Perspective

The life course perspective is a developmental psychology model that views individual development through the lens of the historical time period, culture, and social location of the individual (Elder, 1974). In the context of aging, the life course perspective is used to better understand how aging is influenced by events that happened earlier in the person's life. Research using the life course perspective aims to understand stability and change in behavior over time based on the key concepts of cohorts, transitions, trajectories, life events, and turning points. Cohorts are groups of people born around the same time who experience various social, cultural, and historical events at around the same age. Although cohorts are similar to generations, some researchers have proposed that the term "generation" tends to cover a larger time period (20 years or so) than the term "cohort." The cohort to which an individual belongs provides details on the historical context they experienced when they were coming of age and making the transition to adulthood.

Transitions are also an important concept in the life course perspective. Transitions refer to a change in role or status that can occur within families, small groups, communities, and other organizations to which the individual belongs. Transitions signal a change in the development of an individual through the start of a new phase; transitions are often considered discrete events with a beginning and an end. In contrast, trajectories represent multiple transitions across distinct developmental periods that often lead to longer-term patterns of stability or change for the individual. As an example, a transition to retirement may lead to a longer term trajectory that involves changes in relationships with one's family and community through increased involvement and engagement.

In the life course perspective, life events typically precede transitions, which can lead to a new or shifting trajectory. For an older adult, a life event might include the death of a spouse or partner, which leads to a transition from a married person to a widow and may alter one's developmental trajectory across several years. A life event is typically viewed as a significant event that involves an abrupt change, leading to a transition and perhaps a shifting trajectory for an individual. Finally, the life course perspective considers turning points as life events or transitions that lead to a permanent shift in one's developmental trajectory. Hser et al. (2007) has used the life course perspective to study substance use across the life span, identifying specific drug use trajectories as well as turning points and transitions that can lead to a decrease in substance use, such as death of a loved one, meaningful employment, or the need to provide childcare.

SOCIAL MODELS OF AGING

Social models of aging consider that age is primarily a social construct and that aging occurs within a social context. These models reflect the field of social gerontology, which studies social relationships in older adulthood and the participation of older adults in our social world (Biggs et al., 2020). Early social models of aging include role theory, continuity theory, activity theory, and disengagement theory. A criticism of these early theories is that they were formulated based on the aging experience in the United States and therefore do not reflect the aging experience of many older adults. More modern social theories of aging include critical gerontology and social determinants of health.

Role Theory

Role theory proposes that each person holds various social roles at one time and that these roles vary across adulthood (Biddle, 1986). As a society, we often have expectations about what a person should be doing if they occupy a certain role. For example, as a student, there are often expectations or norms about what you should be doing and how you should be spending your time. For many of us, the roles that we hold in life define much of what we spend our time doing throughout the day. Throughout adulthood and moving into older adulthood, roles may shift such that some remain relatively the same (role continuity), some roles are lost (role loss), and some roles become less clear with age (role ambiguity). An example of role continuity might be the role of parent or sibling. Even though it may shift throughout adulthood, the expectations remain similar. An example of role loss is when a spouse or long-term partner passes away. The individual changes roles from "married/partnered" to "widower," taking on a new role and losing an old role. Role ambiguity might occur during retirement. Older adults may transition from a job that had clear expectations to retirement, which has relatively unclear expectations regarding what one should do on a daily basis as a retired individual. In general, role theory posits that, with age, role continuity declines and both role loss and role ambiguity increase. These changes may affect self-esteem and ultimately affect overall well-being. A controversial proposition of role theory is that, due to role changes, life satisfaction generally declines with age. Research is generally mixed on this topic, with some cross-sectional studies showing an increase in life satisfaction with age and longitudinal studies showing a decline (Hudomiet et al., 2021). You likely know some older adults who have gone through role changes and not experienced a decline in life satisfaction. To explain this, social gerontologists proposed activity theory.

Activity Theory

One way of explaining differences in life satisfaction following role theory was to propose that some older adults maintained high life satisfaction due to continued engagement in society despite role changes. Specifically, activity theory proposes that older adults who pursue more activities and remain involved in society have a more positive aging experience. According to activity theory, older adults who lose roles will retain high life satisfaction if they find new and meaningful roles to replace the lost roles. Therefore, activity theory proposes that older adults engage in the process of "role replacement" in order to maintain high life satisfaction. The content of meaningful roles may vary by individual and cultural factors and could include volunteer work, providing childcare and support within one's family, or giving back to the community in various ways. There is evidence for this theory, in that higher involvement in everyday and leisure activities among older adults predicts higher self-esteem and greater life satisfaction (Reitzes et al., 1995). The primary criticism of activity theory is that older adults may not have access to leisure activities that they would like to pursue. This may be due to mobility or functional limitations but could also be related to financial status, neighborhood location, and other factors that are beyond the control of the individual. Another concern about activity theory was that it could not account for older adults who reduced their overall activity level with increasing age yet reported high life satisfaction. Although now outdated, disengagement theory attempted to account for these individuals.

Disengagement Theory

Activity theory proposes that high life satisfaction in older adulthood is due to engagement in society and maintenance of new and meaningful roles. In contrast, disengagement theory proposes that life satisfaction in older adulthood is related to an acceptance of role loss in a "mutual withdrawal," whereby older adults and society both disengage from each other. Disengagement theory proposes that as older adults lose roles with age, society also moves forward toward more modernization, creating a need for workers with new skills and knowledge. Therefore, life satisfaction in older adulthood results from this mutual disengagement process—many older adults want to do less as they get older and there is a need to make room for younger individuals, along with their new skills. There are many criticisms of this theory and it has largely fallen out of favor as more older adults remain actively engaged in life as they move into retirement (Cornwell et al., 2008).

Continuity Theory

Continuity theory proposes that older adults maintain many of their original interests and traits into older adulthood (Atchley, 1989). That is, older adults do not become "more" or "less" of something simply because they have entered into older adulthood. Rather, these traits and interests are likely an extension of traits and interests from earlier in life. Continuity theory has been applied to interests, hobbies, activities, personality traits, and other intra- and interpersonal behaviors. Even when facing major life transitions, such as retirement, continuity theory posits that there is a consistency in traits and overall behavior, even if daily activities may change significantly. Criticisms of continuity theory focus on how it only applies to relatively healthy older adults (Birren & Schroots, 2001). Older adults who have limitations due to chronic medical conditions may not have a choice with regard to maintaining continuity in goals and activities. These limitations in goals and activities, due to health or other factors, may have a negative impact on intra- and interpersonal behaviors that were previously consistent across the life span.

Critical Gerontology

Critical gerontology is a multidisciplinary approach to understanding aging that includes consideration of the sociology of aging, demography, anthropology, and the politics of aging. As noted by Estes and Grossman (2007), there are five basic tenets of critical gerontology: (a) placing a stronger emphasis on the role of social and behavioral processes in aging while criticizing the biomedical model of aging; (b) highlighting the forces that shape an individual's aging, including sociocultural, economic, and political factors; (c) applying multiple levels of analysis to the study of aging, including micro, meso, and macro levels; (d) recognizing the role of the media in portraying social constructions of aging and establishing norms around the aging process; and (e) determining how aging issues can be linked with social and political action. Ultimately the goal of critical gerontology is to change the social construction of aging. For example, critical gerontology examines the role of health disparities in aging by socioeconomic status, ageism in the family and workplace, and the aging experience among older women and older adults who identify as part of a minority group. Additionally, critical gerontology promotes the development of age-friendly cities and communities and examines the globalization of aging. In sum, critical gerontology incorporates the perspective of multiple disciplines and aims to move beyond the biomedical model of aging and the ageism that exists in social policies (Chong & Gu, 2022).

Social Determinants of Health and the Weathering Hypothesis

Social determinants of health are typically defined as any nonmedical factors that influence health. These factors can be further divided into downstream and upstream factors (Braveman et al., 2011). Upstream factors focus on social policies relevant to the issue, such as access to healthy food and community centers in one's neighborhood. Downstream factors are typically focused on the individual's behavior and attitudes, for example, the attitudes that an individual might hold toward eating healthy food and exercising.

The weathering hypothesis is one approach to understanding health disparities that considers social determinants of health. It also provides an explanation for the health disparities seen across the life span between Black and White individuals. Specifically, Black individuals have worse physical and mental health, lower life expectancy, more psychological distress, and greater health declines over time as compared with White individuals (Forde et al., 2019). For many years, the differences in health outcomes between White older adults and minority older adults were attributed to lifestyle differences that led to a worse health profile in older adulthood (Simons et al., 2021). The weathering hypothesis counteracts this idea by hypothesizing that health disparities between White and minority adults are due to the effects of racism and social inequality, resulting in a cumulative disadvantage (Ferraro et al., 2009). As an example of the weathering hypothesis, Simons et al. (2021) found that education, income, neighborhood disadvantage, and discrimination predicted accelerated aging (as measured by epigenetic biomarkers) among older Black men and women even when controlling for individual health factors such as diet, exercise, and alcohol consumption.

CONCLUSION

This chapter introduced current models and theories in the areas of biological, psychological, and social aging. In the biological models, telomeres, free radicals, caloric restriction, and the genetics of longevity were reviewed. Psychological models consider aging from the perspective of individual development and inter- and intrapersonal processes. The relevant models reviewed in this chapter include Erikson's stages of psychosocial development, selective optimization with compensation, socioemotional selectivity theory, and the life course perspective. Social models of aging consider how society constructs and influences the aging process, which removes some of the focus on individual behavior in the aging process. Social models reviewed in this chapter include role theory, activity theory, disengagement theory, continuity theory, critical gerontology, and social determinants of health. An understanding of the aging process requires consideration of aspects of all of these models in order to better understand aging from multiple perspectives.

DISCUSSION QUESTIONS

1. What are telomeres and telomerase, and how are they involved in determining longevity?
2. What are antioxidants, and how do they impact our biological health?
3. Explain caloric restriction and how it may lead to longer life spans.
4. Explain the relationship between APOE and Alzheimer disease.
5. Apply Baltes's SOC model to a challenge someone might face in late life.
6. Apply role theory to a change that you or a loved one has recently undergone.
7. Describe social determinants of health that are relevant to your community.

A robust set of instructor resources designed to supplement this text is located at http://connect.springerpub.com/content/book/978-0-8261-6617-3. Qualifying instructors may request access by emailing textbook@springerpub.com.

REFERENCES

Atchley, R. C. (1989). A continuity theory of normal aging. *The Gerontologist*, 29(2), 183–190. https://doi.org/10.1093/geront/29.2.183

Baltes, P. B. (1979). Life-span developmental psychology: Some converging observations on history and theory. In P. B. Baltes & J. O. G. Brim (Eds.), *Life-span development and behavior* (Vol. 2, pp. 255–279). Academic Press.

Baltes, P. B. (1997). On the incomplete architecture of human ontogeny: Selection, optimization, and compensation as foundation of developmental theory. *American Psychologist*, 52(4), 366–380. https://doi.org/10.1037//0003-066x.52.4.366

Biddle, B. J. (1986). Recent developments in role theory. *Annual Review of Sociology*, 12(1), 67–92. https://doi.org/10.1146/annurev.so.12.080186.000435

Biggs, S., Hendricks, J., & Lowenstein, A. (2020). *The need for theory: Critical approaches to social gerontology*. Routledge.

Bin-Jumah, M. N., Nadeem, M. S., Gilani, S. J., Al-Abbasi, F. A., Ullah, I., Alzarea, S. I., ..., Kazmi, I. (2022). Genes and longevity of lifespan. *International Journal of Molecular Sciences*, 23(3), 1499. https://doi.org/10.3390/ijms23031499

Birren, J. E., & Schroots, J. J. F. (2001). History of geropsychology. In J. E. Birren & K. W. Schaie (Eds.), *Handbook of the psychology of aging* (5th ed., pp. 3–28). Academic Press.

Braveman, P., Egerter, S., & Williams, D. R. (2011). The social determinants of health: Coming of age. *Annual Review of Public Health*, 32, 381–398. https://doi.org/10.1146/annurev-publhealth-031210-101218

Carstensen, L. L., Isaacowitz, D. M., & Charles, S. T. (1999). Taking time seriously: A theory of socioemotional selectivity. *American Psychologist, 54*(3), 165–181. https://doi.org/10.1037/0003-066X.54.3.165

Chakravarti, D., LaBella, K. A., & DePinho, R. A. (2021). Telomeres: History, health, and hallmarks of aging. *Cell, 184*(2), 306–322. https://doi.org/10.1016/j.cell.2020.12.028

Cheng, F., Carroll, L., Joglekar, M. V., Januszewski, A. S., Wong, K. K., Hardikar, A. A., …, Ma, R. C. (2021). Diabetes, metabolic disease, and telomere length. *The Lancet Diabetes & Endocrinology, 9*(2), 117–126. https://doi.org/10.1016/S2213-8587(20)30365-X

Chong, W. F. W., & Gu, D. (2022). Critical gerontology. In D. Gu, & M. E. Dupre (Eds.), *Encyclopedia of gerontology and population aging*. Springer. https://doi.org/10.1007/978-3-319-69892-2_951-2

Colman, R. J., Beasley, T. M., Kemnitz, J. W., Johnson, S. C., Weindruch, R., & Anderson, R. M. (2014). Caloric restriction reduces age-related and all-cause mortality in rhesus monkeys. *Nature Communications, 5*, 3557. https://doi.org/10.1038/ncomms4557

Cornwell, B., Laumann, E. O., & Schumm, L. P. (2008). The social connectedness of older adults: A national profile. *American Sociological Review, 73*(2), 185–203. https://doi.org/10.1177/000312240807300201

Elder, G. H. (1974). *Children of the great depression*. Routledge.

Erikson, E. H. (1997). *The life cycle completed* (Extended version with new chapters on the ninth stage of development by J. M. Erikson.) W. W. Norton.

Estes, C. L., & Grossman, B. R. (2007) Critical perspectives in gerontology. In K. Markides (Ed.), *Encyclopedia of health & aging* (pp 130–133). SAGE.

Ferraro, K. F., Shippee, T. P., & Schafer, M. H. (2009). Cumulative inequality theory for research on aging and the life course. In V. L. Bengston, D. Gans, N. M. Pulney, & M. Silverstein (Eds.), *Handbook of theories of aging* (pp. 413–433). Springer Publishing Company.

Forde, A. T., Crookes, D. M., Suglia, S. F., & Demmer, R. T. (2019). The weathering hypothesis as an explanation for racial disparities in health: A systematic review. *Annals of Epidemiology, 33*, 1–18.e3. https://doi.org/10.1016/j.annepidem.2019.02.011

Gavrilov, L. A., & Gavrilova, N. S. (2006). Reliability theory of aging and longevity. In E. J. Masoro & S. N. Austad (Eds.), *Handbook of the biology of aging* (6th ed., pp. 3–42). Academic Press.

Hall, G. S. (1922). *Senescence: The last half of life*. D. Appleton. https://archive.org/details/senescencelastha00halliala

Handy, D. E., Castro, R., & Loscalzo, J. (2011). Epigenetic modifications: basic mechanisms and role in cardiovascular disease. *Circulation, 123*(19), 2145–2156. https://doi.org/10.1161/CIRCULATIONAHA.110.956839

Harman, D. H. (1956). Aging: A theory based on free radical and radiation chemistry. *Journal of Gerontology, 11*(3), 298–300. https://doi.org/10.1093/geronj/11.3.298

Hayflick, L. (1965). The limited in vitro lifetime of human diploid cell strains. *Experimental Cell Research, 37*(3), 614–636. https://doi.org/10.1016/0014-4827(65)90211-9

Hser, Y. I., Longshore, D., & Anglin, M. D. (2007). The life course perspective on drug use: A conceptual framework for understanding drug use trajectories. *Evaluation Review, 31*(6), 515–547. https://doi.org/10.1177/0193841X07307316

Hudomiet, P., Hurd, M. D., & Rohwedder, S. (2021). The age profile of life satisfaction after age 65 in the US. *Journal of Economic Behavior & Organization, 189*, 431–442. https://doi.org/10.1016/j.jebo.2021.07.002

Johnson, J. B., Summer, W., Cutler, R. G., Martin, B., Hyun, D. H., Dixit, V. D., …, Mattson, M. P. (2007). Alternate day calorie restriction improves clinical findings and reduces markers of oxidative stress and inflammation in overweight adults with moderate asthma. *Free Radical Biology and Medicine, 42*(5), 665–674. https://doi.org/10.1016/j.freeradbiomed.2006.12.005

Jung-Hynes, B., Schmit, T. L., Reagan-Shaw, S. R., Siddiqui, I. A., Mukhtar, H., & Ahmad, N. (2011). Melatonin, a novel Sirt1 inhibitor, imparts antiproliferative effects against prostate cancer in vitro in culture and in vivo in TRAMP model. *Journal of Pineal Research, 50*(2), 140–149. https://doi.org/10.1111/j.1600-079X.2010.00823.x

Justice, J. N., Nambiar, A. M., Tchkonia, T., LeBrasseur, N. K., Pascual, R., Hashmi, S. K., …, Kirkland, J. L. (2019). Senolytics in idiopathic pulmonary fibrosis: Results from a first-in-human, open-label, pilot study. *EBioMedicine, 40*, 554–563. https://doi.org/10.1016/j.ebiom.2018.12.052

Kenyon, C. J. (2010). The genetics of ageing. *Nature, 464*, 504–512. https://doi.org/10.1038/nature08980

Kobara, M., Toba, H., & Nakata, T. (2020). Caloric restriction, reactive oxygen species, and longevity. In V. R. Preedy & V. B. Patel (Eds.), *Aging* (2nd ed., pp. 11–18). Academic Press. https://doi.org/10.1016/B978-0-12-818698-5.00002-X

Kremen, W. S., & Lyons, M. J. (2011). Behavior genetics of aging. In K. W. Schaie & S. L. Willis (Eds.), *Handbook of the psychology of aging* (7th ed., pp. 93–107). Elsevier.

Lanner, R. M. (2002). Why do trees live so long? *Ageing Research Reviews, 1*(4), 653–671. https://doi.org/10.1016/S1568-1637(02)00025-9

Lanner, R. M., & Connor, K. F. (2001). Does bristlecone pine senesce? *Experimental Gerontology, 36*(4–6), 675–685. https://doi.org/10.1016/s0531-5565(00)00234-5

López-Lluch, G., & Navas, P. (2016). Calorie restriction as an intervention in ageing. *The Journal of Physiology, 594*(8), 2043–2060. https://doi.org/10.1113/JP270543

Ludovico, P., & Burhans, W. C. (2014). Reactive oxygen species, ageing and the hormesis police. *FEMS Yeast Research, 14*(1), 33–39. https://doi.org/10.1111/1567-1364.12070

Mansur, A. P., Roggerio, A., Goes, M. F., Avakian, S. D., Leal, D. P., Maranhão, R. C., & Strunz, C. M. (2017). Serum concentrations and gene expression of sirtuin 1 in healthy and slightly overweight subjects after caloric restriction or resveratrol supplementation: A randomized trial. *International Journal of Cardiology, 227*, 788–794. https://doi.org/10.1016/j.ijcard.2016.10.058

Mattison, J. A., Colman, R. J., Beasley, T. M., Allison, D. B., Kemnitz, J. W., Roth, G. S., ..., Anderson, R. M. (2017). Caloric restriction improves health and survival of rhesus monkeys. *Nature Communications, 8*(1), 14063. https://doi.org/10.1038/ncomms14063

Mattison, J. A., Roth, G. S., Beasley, T. M., Tilmont, E. M., Handy, A. M., Herbert, R. L., . . ., de Cabo, R. (2012). Impact of caloric restriction on health and survival in rhesus monkeys from the NIA study. *Nature, 489*(7415), 318–321. https://doi.org/10.1038/nature11432

McCay, C. M., Crowell, M. F., & Maynard, L. A. (1935). The effect of retarded growth upon the length of life and upon the ultimate body size. *Journal of Nutrition, 10*(1), 63–79. https://doi.org/10.1093/jn/10.1.63

McCay, C. M., Maynard, L. A., Sperling, G., & Barnes, L. L. (1939). Retarded growth, lifespan, ultimate body size, and age changes in the albino rat after feeding diets restricted in calories. *Journal of Nutrition, 18*(1), 1–13. https://doi.org/10.1093/jn/18.1.1

Mesquita, A., Weinberger, M., Silva, A., Sampaio-Marques, B., Almeida, B., Leão, C., . . ., Ludovico, P. (2010). Caloric restriction or catalase inactivation extends yeast chronological lifespan by inducing H_2O_2 and superoxide dismutase activity. *Proceedings of the National Academy of Sciences United States of America, 107*(34), 15123–15128. https://doi.org/10.1073/pnas.1004432107

National Institute on Aging. (2021). *Does cellular senescence hold secrets for healthier aging?* https://www.nia.nih.gov/news/does-cellular-senescence-hold-secrets-healthier-aging

Okamoto, K., & Seimiya, H. (2019). Revisiting telomere shortening in cancer. *Cells, 8*(2), 107. https://doi.org/10.3390/cells8020107

Osborne, T. B., Mendel, L. B., & Ferry, E. L. (1917). The effect of retardation of growth upon the breeding period and duration of life in rats. *Science, 45*(1160), 294–295. https://doi.org/10.1126/science.45.1160.294

Piaget, J. (1972). Intellectual evolution from adolescence to adulthood. *Human Development, 15*(1), 1–12. https://doi.org/10.1159/000271225

Ramis, M. R., Esteban, S., Miralles, A., Tan, D.-X., & Reiter, R. J. (2015). Caloric restriction, resveratrol and melatonin: Role of SIRT1 and implications for aging and related-diseases. *Mechanisms of Ageing and Development, 146–148*, 28–41. https://doi.org/10.1016/j.mad.2015.03.008

Rattan, S. I. (2006). Theories of biological aging: Genes, proteins, and free radicals. *Free Radical Research, 40*(12), 1230–1238. https://doi.org/10.1080/10715760600911303

Reiter, R. J. (1992). The ageing pineal gland and its physiological consequences. *Bioessays, 14*(3), 169–175. https://doi.org/10.1002/bies.950140307

Reitzes, D. C., Mutran, E. J., & Verrill, L. A. (1995). Activities and self-esteem: Continuing the development of activity theory. *Research on Aging, 17*(3), 260–277. https://doi.org/10.1177/0164027595173002

Rentscher, K. E., Carroll, J. E., & Mitchell, C. (2020). Psychosocial stressors and telomere length: A current review of the science. *Annual Review of Public Health, 41*, 223–245. https://doi.org/10.1146/annurev-publhealth-040119-094239

Salehi, B., Mishra, A. P., Nigam, M., Sener, B., Kilic, M., Sharifi-Rad, M., ..., Sharifi-Rad, J. (2018). Resveratrol: A double-edged sword in health benefits. *Biomedicines, 6*(3), 91. https://doi.org/10.3390/biomedicines6030091

Scheibye-Knudsen, M., Fang, E. F., Croteau, D. L., Wilson, D. M., & Bohr, V. A. (2015). Protecting the mitochondrial powerhouse. *Trends in Cell Biology, 25*(3), 158–170. https://doi.org/10.1016/j.tcb.2014.11.002

Schneider, C. V., Schneider, K. M., Teumer, A., Rudolph, K. L., Hartmann, D., Rader, D. J., & Strnad, P. (2022). Association of telomere length with risk of disease and mortality. *JAMA Internal Medicine, 182*(3), 291–300. https://doi.org/10.1001/jamainternmed.2021.7804

Shay, J. W., & Wright, W. E. (2011). Role of telomeres and telomerase in cancer. *Seminars in Cancer Biology, 21*(6), 349–353. https://doi.org/10.1016/j.semcancer.2011.10.001

Sillett, S. C., Van Pelt, R., Carroll, A. L., Kramer, R. D., Ambrose, A. R., & Trask, D. (2015). How do tree structure and old age affect growth potential of California redwoods? *Ecological Monographs, 85*(2), 181–212. https://doi.org/10.1890/14-1016.1

Simons, R. L., Lei, M.-K., Klopack, E., Beach, S. R. H., Gibbons, F. X., & Philibert, R. A. (2021). The effects of social adversity, discrimination, and health risk behaviors on the accelerated aging of African Americans: Further support for the weathering hypothesis. *Social Science & Medicine, 282*, 113169. https://doi.org/10.1016/j.socscimed.2020.113169

Someya, S., & Ikeda, A. (2021). Aging of the sensory systems: Hearing and vision disorders. *Handbook of the biology of aging* (9th ed., pp. 297–321). https://doi.org/10.1016/B978-0-12-815962-0.00014-7

Tchkonia, T., Zhu, Y., Deursen, J. V., Campisi, J., & Kirkland, J. L. (2013). Cellular senescence and the senescent secretory phenotype: Therapeutic opportunities. *Journal of Clinical Investigation, 123*(3), 966–972. https://doi.org/10.1172/JCI64098

Van Raamsdonk, J. M., & Hekimi, S. (2009). Deletion of the mitochondrial superoxide dismutase sod-2 extends lifespan in Caenorhabditis elegans. *Public Library of Science Genetics, 5*(2), e1000361. https://doi.org/10.1371/journal.pgen.1000361

Verghese, P. B., Castellano, J. M., & Holtzman, D. M. (2011). Apolipoprotein E in Alzheimer's disease and other neurological disorders. *Lancet Neurology, 10*(3), 241–252. https://doi.org/10.1016/S14744422(10)70325-2

von Zglinicki, T. (2021). Mechanisms of cell senescence in aging. In N. Musi & P. J. Hornsby (Eds.), *Handbook of the biology of aging* (pp. 53–67). Academic Press.

Wang, Y.-L., Sun, L.-M., Zhang, L., Xu, H.-T., Dong, Z., Wang, L.-Q., & Wang, M.-L. (2015). Association between Apolipoprotein E polymorphism and myocardial infarction risk: A systematic review and meta-analysis. *FEBS Open Bio, 5*, 852–858. https://doi.org/10.1016/j.fob.2015.10.006

Yang, T.-L. B., Song, S., & Johnson, F. B. (2016). Contributions of telomere biology to human age-related disease. In M. R. Kaeberlein & G. M. Martin (Eds.), *Handbook of the biology of aging* (8th ed., pp. 205–239). Elsevier.

Zhang, Y., Ikeno, Y., Qi, W., Chaudhuri, A., Li, Y., Bokov, A., . . ., Van Remmen, H. (2009). Mice deficient in both Mn superoxide dismutase and glutathione peroxidase-1 have increased oxidative damage and a greater incidence of pathology but no reduction in longevity. *Journal of Gerontology: Biological Sciences, 64*(12), 1212–1220. https://doi.org/10.1093/gerona/glp132

4

The Aging Body

Adriana Savettiere and J. Kaci Fairchild

> **LEARNING OBJECTIVES**
>
> - Articulate why it is critical to distinguish between normative and non-normative aging (Bloom's level 3).
> - Describe some of the common age-related changes experienced by older adults (Bloom's level 2).
> - Understand how common age-related changes impact older adults' overall health and daily functioning.

Older adults are one of the most diverse segments of the population, yet there are universal physical changes that everyone experiences as part of the normative aging process. This is also termed primary aging, which refers to the intrinsic biological process of aging that is universally experienced. On the other hand, secondary aging refers to external factors such as environment or disease that can exacerbate and change the trajectory of age-related changes. Differentiating between normative and non-normative aging and age-related pathophysiology is essential to the care of older adults. Providers must avoid dismissing clinically significant complaints as "old age" while not overtreating age-associated physical changes as pathophysiology.

The purpose of this chapter is to present a general overview of the structural and physiological changes that occur with normative aging. The ensuing sections are organized around the body's 11 organ systems including the integumentary, muscular, skeletal, nervous, circulatory, lymphatic, respiratory, endocrine, urinary/excretory, reproductive, and digestive systems. We recognize the ambitious nature of this chapter;

thus, much of the information provided herein should serve as an overview of this topic. Readers are encouraged to explore the listed references for a more in-depth discussion of this field.

THE INTEGUMENTARY SYSTEM

The integumentary system is the largest organ system as it comprises the skin and associated structures (e.g., hair, nails, sweat glands, and sebaceous glands). The integumentary system acts as the body's exoskeleton to provide a protective physical barrier against the outside world. The integumentary system also interacts with other organ systems to guard against disease, regulate body temperature, retain bodily fluids, and eliminate waste. The skin has three layers: the epidermis, dermis, and subcutis. The skin's outermost layer is the epidermis, a thin yet tough and relatively waterproof layer of the skin. The epidermis is composed of keratinocytes, Langerhans cells, melanocytes, and Merkel cells. Most cells in the epidermis are keratinocytes, which serve as a barrier against foreign organisms including bacteria, parasites, and viruses (McGrath & Uitto, 2016). Langerhans cells defend against infection, thus playing a role in immune health. Merkel and melanocyte cells are in the deepest (i.e., basal) layer of the epidermis. Merkel cells are believed to be involved in tactile sensory perception. Melanocytes produce the pigment melanin (a main contributor to skin color) that filters harmful ultraviolet B (UVB) radiation out of sunlight.

Below the epidermis is the dermis, a dense, fibrous, elastic layer of tissue that provides strength and flexibility while also cushioning the body from stress and strain. The dermis includes nerve endings, sweat glands, sebaceous oil glands, hair follicles, and blood vessels. These nerve endings sense pain, touch, pressure, and temperature. When the body is exposed to heat or stress, sweat glands regulate temperature by producing sweat that cools the body as it evaporates on the skin. Hair, produced by hair follicles found in the dermis, assists with regulating body temperature and also acts as a sensitive touch receptor. Sebaceous oil glands secrete sebum into hair follicles to condition the hair while keeping the surrounding skin moist and soft. The blood vessels in the dermis respond to changes in temperature by expanding to release heat and contracting to preserve heat. The deepest layer of the integumentary system is the subcutis. This subcutaneous tissue is a connective layer of fat, which insulates the body from extreme temperatures, provides protective padding, and serves as an energy repository.

Age-Related Changes to the Physiology of the Integumentary System

As a person ages, structural and functional changes occur throughout the layers and associated structures of the skin (see Box 4.1). The epidermis and dermis layers of the skin grow thinner, which decreases the skin's resilience to injury. In the epidermis, keratinocytes shrink, reducing skin elasticity. Langerhans, Merkel cells, and melanocytes lessen in number as we age. Reduction in Langerhans cells weakens the skin's immune system (Nagaratnam et al., 2016). Fewer Merkel cells cause decreased tactile

BOX 4.1 Integumentary System: Key Points

Age-Associated Physiological Changes	
▪ Thinning of epidermis, dermis, and subcutis	▪ Reduced ability to filter UV radiation
▪ Reduced elasticity	▪ Weakened skin immune system
▪ Reduced ability to regulate temperature	▪ Reduced sensation

sensory perception. Specifically, a reduction in Merkel cells contributes to difficulty detecting light touch, including skin indentation and pressure detection, which increases older adults' vulnerability to external injuries and pressure sores (Bataille et al., 2022). Additionally, reducing melanocytes lowers the ability to filter UVB radiation from sunlight.

Age-related changes also affect associated structures of the dermis. For example, the sebaceous oil glands secrete less sebum, leading to drier skin. Fewer nerve endings reduce sensation, and a reduction in blood vessels decreases the skin's ability to respond to temperature change effectively. This contributes to an increased risk of developing hypothermia or heat stroke when older adults are exposed to high or low temperatures (Alba et al., 2019). Furthermore, in the subcutis, the proportion of the subcutaneous layers of fat changes in different body areas (e.g., decrease in hands and face and increase in thighs and abdomen; Farage et al., 2013).

Overall, these cumulative changes cause the skin to be more easily damaged and slower to heal. While structural and functional age-related changes to the skin are predetermined by intrinsic factors (e.g., age, time, genetics), environmental factors (e.g., sunlight, pollution, and cigarette smoking) often result in premature aging (Csekes & Rackova, 2021). Sun exposure (UV light) is the most significant environmental factor of aging. UV radiation causes visible signs of skin aging (e.g., wrinkles, irregular pigmentation, sagging skin) by increasing the production of metalloproteinases that break down collagen and elastin, which are proteins in the skin (Gromkowska-Kępka et al., 2021). Furthermore, DNA damage is one of the most deleterious effects of UV light, as UV light can alter base pairs and nucleic acid sequence, thereby changing the genetic code of DNA. This can alter gene expression and, in turn, cellular function, and contribute to an increased risk for skin cancer.

THE MUSCULOSKELETAL SYSTEM

While the integumentary system acts as the body's exoskeleton, the musculoskeletal system serves as its endoskeleton. This system provides the body with movement and mechanical support and protection of soft tissues and serves as a calcium repository (Fillit et al., 2017). Components of this system include the body's bones, muscles, joints, and connective tissues (e.g., ligaments, tendons, and cartilage) that support and bind tissues and organs.

Age-Related Changes to the Physiology of the Musculoskeletal System

Beginning in middle age, the musculoskeletal system undergoes widespread changes, which become more pronounced in older adulthood (see Box 4.2). For instance, calcium levels in the skeleton begin to decline in middle age, decreasing bone mass, a process that is greatly accelerated in postmenopausal women (Gregson, 2017). Alterations in hormone levels drive this accelerated change (i.e., estradiol and follicle-stimulating hormone) as the body is less able to retain calcium from food (Karlamangla et al., 2018). This calcium reduction creates an imbalance where bone resorption (destruction of bone tissue) exceeds bone formation, thereby reducing bone mass and strength. Furthermore, this imbalance reduces the body's ability to break down and repair micro-fractures that accumulate over time, increasing fracture susceptibility (Sözen et al., 2017).

Muscle tissue is also greatly affected by the aging process. After age 50, muscle mass loss occurs at about 1% annually (Wilkinson et al., 2018). In adults aged 75 and older, muscle strength is lost two to five times more rapidly than muscle loss, at an annual rate of 0.6% to 0.98% and 2.5% to 4%, respectively (Mitchell et al., 2012). Reductions in muscle mass and strength are attributable to muscle fiber atrophy. This atrophy occurs when muscle protein breakdown exceeds muscle protein creation (Wilkinson et al., 2018). In younger adults, environmental factors such as exercise and nutrition can aid in muscle protein creation, while in older adulthood, our bodies are less responsive to these stimuli. This phenomenon is called anabolic resistance. While the body may be less responsive to these stimuli, these interventions are not ineffective; therefore, maintaining consistent aerobic exercise and adequate nutrition as one ages is recommended. The overall loss of muscle mass and strength places increased stress on a person's joints, subsequently increasing the risk for certain illnesses (e.g., arthritis) and injuries (e.g., falls).

While the body's bone density and muscle mass decrease with age, the percentage of body fat increases until around age 80, at which point it levels off. In fact, by age 75, a person's muscle mass will be reduced by up to half, while the amount of body fat will double (Nagaratnam et al., 2016). People also lose height as they age due to changes in skeleton, muscle mass, and connective tissues. This age-related height loss, coupled with changing body composition, can lead to an increase in body mass index (BMI), even in a weight-stable individual (Ponti et al., 2020). Older adults also have less total body water due to reduced kidney functioning, reduced thirst, and lower muscle mass

BOX 4.2 Musculoskeletal System: Key Points

Age-Associated Physiological Changes

- Reduced bone density
- Increased fat–to–muscle mass ratio
- Reduced height
- Thinning of cartilage
- Increased rigidity of ligaments and tendons
- Stiff joints with reduced range of motion

(as muscles contain a high percentage of water), which increases the risk of dehydration (Hooper et al., 2014). Furthermore, older adults' changing body composition increases their sensitivity to the adverse effects of alcohol, drugs, and medications.

Joints are complex structures that are composed of bones, muscles, and connective tissues. Muscles are connected to the body's bones via tendons, which are tough, fibrous connective tissues. Ligaments, another connective tissue, join the ends of two bones to form a joint. The ends of the two bones are then covered with cartilage, a tissue that reduces friction to promote movement in a joint. Age-related changes to the connective tissues can compromise the overall integrity of the joint. Cartilage grows thinner, and ligaments and tendons become more rigid and brittle. These changes reduce the joint's resiliency, making it more vulnerable to damage (Brodkey, 2022). With age and disuse, joints become stiffer with a reduced range of motion, greatly limiting a person's mobility.

THE NERVOUS SYSTEM

While the integumentary and musculoskeletal systems protect the body, the nervous system is the medium through which the body communicates with the outside world. This system also controls many of the body's inner workings. It comprises two separate systems: (a) the central nervous system, which includes the brain, cranial nerves, and spinal cord, and (b) the peripheral nervous system, which includes all other nerves in the body. The nervous system is further divided into the voluntary, or somatic, nervous system, comprising consciously controlled functions (e.g., moving arms and legs), and the involuntary, or autonomic, nervous system, comprising unconsciously controlled functions (e.g., heart rate and breathing). The central and peripheral nervous systems each have voluntary and involuntary components. The involuntary nervous system is further divided into three parts: the sympathetic nervous system, the parasympathetic nervous system, and the enteric (i.e., gastrointestinal) nervous system.

Age-Related Changes to the Physiology of the Nervous System

As the body ages, the brain and spinal cord lose neurons and begin to atrophy. Neurons become less responsive and may transmit information more slowly. The impact of these age-related changes can be easily seen through changes in the five senses. The nervous system processes information from the body's sensory organs. The structure and function of all sensory organs change with age, though with some variability in the attributes and extent of the decline. This age-related decline in sensory ability may be due to decrements in the sensory receptors themselves but can also be caused by differences in the peripheral and central nerve pathways that support these functions (Völter et al., 2021). Ongoing research explores two competing theories: the common factor theory (sensory decline as a globally affected process) and the specific factor theory (each sensory system has an individualized mechanism and timeline of decline). Recent evidence highlights that a combination of these theories may be the most likely, whereby there may be interrelated mechanisms of some senses, but the decline of one sense does not ultimately imply global decline (O'Dowd et al., 2022). Overall, in older adults ages 70 to 79, 25% have functional impairment in multiple senses and 40% have impairment in a single sensory modality (Völter et al., 2021). The following sections discuss age-related sensory changes (see also Box 4.3).

VISION

Several age-related changes contribute to visual difficulties. Decreased muscle ability to control pupil size reduces visual acuity and light's ability to reach the retina, making it difficult to read in lower light (Dev et al., 2022). Change in muscle functioning also results in slower constricting and dilating of the iris, which impacts the eye's ability to adjust to brightness.

Aging also affects the lens of the eye, as it hardens and yellows over time. The hardening of the lens causes the muscles in the eye to have more difficulty expanding or contracting to focus on objects or small print close-up (Mayo Clinic, 2021). The yellowing of the lens causes colors to appear less vibrant and can lead to difficulties distinguishing between colors (Salvi et al., 2006). The blue spectrum is especially impacted, causing added difficulty when reading letters in blue ink or text appearing on a blue background. Perception of color is further impacted due to a reduction in the density of cone cells in an area of the eye called the fovea. Cones are a photoreceptor that is specialized to detect color. While this impact varies from person to person, using contrasting warm colors (e.g., red, yellow, and orange) in older adults' homes can improve the ability to find objects. The change in the transparency of the lens also causes a scattering of light within the eye, thereby creating additional glare. The combination of increased glare and poorer reactivity to changes in light has significant implications for night driving, which can become hazardous.

HEARING

Disabling hearing loss affects 25% of adults ages 65 to 74 and 50% of adults who are 75 and older (National Institute on Deafness and Other Communication Disorders [NIDCD], 2021). Age-related hearing loss (i.e., presbycusis) can occur for a multitude of reasons (e.g., genetic, sensory, neural, and structural atrophy of the ear; Jayakody et al., 2018). For example, the atrophy of hair follicles, which bend to transform sound waves into chemical messengers (i.e., neurotransmitters), can result in hearing loss (Fettiplace, 2017). This atrophy is especially prevalent in hair follicles related to the higher frequency range. Men tend to experience hearing loss at higher rates than women, at an earlier age, and at a higher severity (NIDCD, 2021). This difference has been shown to persist even

BOX 4.3 Nervous System: Key Points

Age-Associated Physiological Changes	
■ Fewer neurons in brain and spinal cord ■ Reduced visual acuity ■ Reduced hearing acuity, particularly higher frequencies ■ Changes in smell	■ Reduced number of taste receptors ■ Reduced accuracy in touch sensitivity ■ Reduced balance ■ Overall brain atrophy and reduced volume

when controlling for potential occupational noise differences (e.g., military, construction). While the reasons underlying this difference are not fully known, some research suggests genetics and hormonal differences may play a role (Nolan, 2020).

When communicating with older adults with hearing loss, people may speak louder or overarticulate words; however, this approach should be avoided, as it can create great distortion in speech sounds, making it even more difficult to be understood (National Institute on Aging [NIA], 2023). Instead, communication can be enhanced by speaking in a lower or deeper tone and eliminating background noises.

SMELL

Olfactory impairment risk increases with age, with up to one in three adults aged 80 and older self-reporting smell alterations (Rawal, 2016). Age-related olfactory changes can include decreased sensitivity to smells. This can result in decreased awareness of unpleasant smells such as gas leakage or spoiled food, putting older adults at greater risk for adverse events (Kondo et al., 2020). While increased age is related to greater olfaction impairment, research suggests these changes may be more related to chronic diseases, sinus problems, and medications than age per se (Rawson, 2006).

TASTE

Significant age-related changes in taste can, in part, be linked to decreases in the functioning and number of taste receptors. By age 70, the typical male has less than half the number of taste buds as he had in his early 20s (Aiken, 2001). While changes can be present for all taste modalities (e.g., sweet, salt, sour, and bitter), there is greater loss of the sensitivity to sweet and salt. This loss can lead to older adults using greater amounts of seasoning (e.g., salt), which may need to be monitored to avoid worsening health problems (e.g., diabetes and hypertension). Additionally, age-related change in taste (in addition to smell and vision) can lead to a decreased appetite and increase the risk of nutritional deficits. Age-related declines in appetite occur in up to one in three older adults (Pilgrim et al., 2015).

CUTANEOUS/SKIN

The four traditional cutaneous senses are touch, pain, temperature (warm and cold), and pruritic (itch). As discussed previously, age-related changes in touch sensitivity can increase older adults' vulnerability to external injury (Bataille et al., 2022). Changes in pain sensitivity are not uniform across the entire body. For example, there is greater loss of pain sensitivity within the hands, feet, and face than within the legs (Wickremaratchi & Llewelyn, 2006). Change in temperature sensitivity can reduce one's ability to adapt to or tolerate temperature extremes, especially when coupled with age-related decreased sweat output (Dufour & Candas, 2007). Such changes in the skin have important implications for morbidity and mortality since impairment in temperature sensitivity and decreased ability to regulate the body's core temperature can cause death due to hyperthermia or hypothermia when in extreme environmental conditions (e.g., cold snaps and heat waves).

BALANCE/GAIT

Receptors for the vestibular senses evidence age-related changes beginning around age 50. Vestibular receptors contribute to our sense of balance and posture, both of which are critically important across the life span, but especially so in late life (Arshad et al., 2016). Vestibular receptors are located on cells found in the semicircular and otolith organs of the inner ear. In addition to these age-related changes in the vestibular receptors, normative cognitive decline in the frontal regions of the brain can impact planning and motor coordination required for proper gait (Cohen et al., 2016). Age-related changes in gait and balance increase fall risk (Dickin et al., 2006), which has implications for quality of life, independent living, and mortality. In 2018, 35.6 million falls were reported in the United States, resulting in 32,000 deaths, making falls the leading cause of injury in older adults (Moreland, 2020).

THE CARDIOVASCULAR SYSTEM

The cardiovascular system undergoes progressive, cumulative decline with advancing age, although not all people, nor all systems, are uniformly affected. Aging of the cardiovascular system is a complex, multifactorial process that is not dependent on a single etiological pathway, process, or genetic contribution. With age the cardiovascular system undergoes many physiological changes including alterations in ventricular function, heart rate, cardiac electrophysiology, vascular compliance, and endothelial function.

Age-Related Changes to the Physiology of the Cardiovascular System

As we age, the left ventricle of the heart becomes less efficient, contributing to deleterious changes to the entire cardiovascular system (see Box 4.4). The left ventricle pumps oxygenated blood out of the heart and into the arteries. With age, the left ventricle wall thickens as myocardial cells are lost over time, which causes the remaining cells to enlarge. The thickening of the left ventricle wall makes the heart larger and less capable of contracting (Akasheva et al., 2015). This effectively reduces diastolic functioning (i.e., less blood exiting from the aorta with each contraction of the heart; Parikh et al., 2016). When coupled with decreased vascular compliance (i.e., the arteries' ability to adjust to changes in blood flow), the arteries are less able to accommodate the flow of blood that the ventricle ejects.

Aging causes fewer and more irregular heartbeats (also known as an arrhythmia, or an abnormal heart rhythm; Minaker, 2011). This results in a reduction of the blood

BOX 4.4 Cardiovascular System: Key Points

Age-Associated Physiological Changes
<ul><li>Thickened left ventricle wall resulting in larger, less efficient heart</li><li>Number of heartbeats is reduced and becomes more irregular</li><li>Reduced resting heart rate variability</li></ul> <ul><li>Arteries lose elasticity (i.e., become stiffer)</li><li>Reduced body water</li><li>Reduced red blood cells and certain white blood cells (e.g., neutrophils)</li></ul>

output volume. After age 65, resting heart rate variability also decreases (Umetani et al., 1998). The heart also takes longer to return to its normal pumping and beating levels after excitement or exercise (Ogawa et al., 1992).

In addition to these changes of the heart, the arteries within the vascular system undergo age-related changes. Age-related arterial changes include reduced distensibility and compliance of the large artery walls (Vatner et al., 2021). Distensibility reflects the elasticity of the artery, while compliance refers to the buffering capacity, or the ability of the vessel to change in area, diameter, or volume in response to a given change in pressure.

As mentioned, as the body ages there is an overall reduction in total body water, resulting in less fluid in the bloodstream. With decreases in blood volume, the number of red blood cells declines. As such, older adults do not recover as quickly from blood loss and are at risk for anemia. The blood also has less of certain types of white blood cells, called neutrophils, which reduces one's ability to fight off infection (Minaker, 2011).

THE IMMUNE SYSTEM

The immune system protects the body from infection and disease through a complex system of cells that circulate through the body and reside in specific organs. These cells detect problems, interact with other cells, and perform cell-specific functions. The lymphatic system is part of the body's immune system and comprises a network of vessels consisting of lymph, extracellular fluid, and lymphoid organs. Lymph is a watery fluid that carries nutrients to cells and waste away from cells. Lymph travels through the lymph nodes, which contain both immune cells that help fight infection and filters that remove waste from the lymph before directing it back into the bloodstream. While the spleen is not part of the lymphatic system per se, it functions similarly. The spleen acts as a filter for blood by recycling iron from damaged red blood cells. The spleen also stores platelets and red blood cells (Kapila et al., 2023). The thymus, a gland located in the upper center of the chest under the breastplate, is essential to the immune system as it produces thymosin, a hormone that stimulates the production of T cells. Matured T cells are released from the thymus and travel to the lymph nodes where they fight infections and antigens. The function of the thymus is only active until puberty after which time it shrinks and is replaced with fatty tissue. Antibodies are proteins that are produced by specialized white blood cells known as B cells, or B lymphocytes, located in the plasma. These important proteins identify and remove antigens or target viruses and bacteria (Kale et al., 2012).

Age-Related Changes to the Physiology of the Immune System

Age-related changes to the immune system reduce its ability to fight infection, a process known as immunosenescence (Kale et al., 2012; see also Box 4.5). With age, the immune system becomes less accurate in distinguishing foreign substances from itself, resulting in it battling its own tissues and cells (i.e., autoimmune response). Macrophages, a type of white blood cell that consumes bacteria and other foreign bodies, respond more slowly to infections. With age, the thymus's remaining T cells also respond more slowly, thus inhibiting the body's immune response. Bone marrow produces fewer white blood cells, further weakening the body's immune response. An important part of the immune system is the complement system, which

> **BOX 4.5** Immune System: Key Points
>
> | Age-Associated Physiological Changes |
> | --- |
> | ▪ Reduced ability to fight infection
▪ Increased autoimmune responses
▪ Reduced response to vaccinations |

is comprises proteins that enhance the immune system by augmenting the work of antibodies. Older adults produce fewer complement proteins when faced with infection than younger adults. In addition to fewer complement proteins, older adults produce fewer antibodies that are then less able to effectively attach to invading antigens. Immunosenescence can also impact the body's receptiveness to vaccinations (Allen et al., 2020). With advanced age, the ratio of naïve T cells to memory T cells decreases (Zhang et al., 2021). When naïve T cells encounter a pathogen, they become memory T cells that remember and respond to a pathogen more effectively when encountered the second time. Vaccines capitalize on this biological process by introducing a weakened or inactive pathogen to the body that causes naïve T cells to mount an immune response and produce antibodies to respond to that pathogen when re-encountered. As we age, the number and functionality of naïve T cells decrease, which lessens the body's ability to respond and react to new pathogens. For example, aged naïve T cells have reduced cytokine secretion, receptor types, and increased activation thresholds that lessen overall immune response. Overall, this decreases the effectiveness of vaccines for older adults due to lowered immune resistance to a new type of pathogen.

THE RESPIRATORY SYSTEM

The respiratory system is a group of tissues and organs that work together to facilitate breathing. The main function of the respiratory system is to bring fresh air into the body (i.e., oxygen) and expel waste gases (i.e., carbon dioxide). This system consists of three main parts: the airway, the lungs, and the muscles of respiration. These parts are further divided into their subparts. The airway consists of the nose and nasal cavities; the mouth, larynx, and trachea; and the bronchi and their branches. The airway is responsible for moving air into the lungs and carrying carbon dioxide out of the lungs. The lungs and associated blood vessels transmit oxygen to the blood as well as remove carbon dioxide from the body. The muscles surrounding the lungs work with the lungs to contract and expand to promote breathing. These muscles include the diaphragm, intercostal muscles, abdominal muscles, and muscles in the neck and collarbone area.

Age-Related Changes to the Physiology of the Respiratory System

Normative age-related changes reduce the efficiency of the respiratory system (see Box 4.6). Environmental exposures accumulated across a person's lifetime also result in structural and functional changes throughout the respiratory system. For

BOX 4.6 Respiratory System: Key Points

Age-Associated Physiological Changes

- Aging and the cumulative environmental exposures result in structural and functional changes.
- Reduced peak airflow
- Increased susceptibility to infections
- Reduced gas exchange
- Weakened respiratory muscles

example, environmental exposures can damage the endothelial cells that line the alveoli, which are the part of the lungs that are largely responsible for gas exchange (Eckhardt & Wu, 2021). As we age, the functionality of type II alveolar cells that repair environmental damage decreases due to cellular senescence (i.e., halting of cellular growth and functioning). Furthermore, the lungs experience a decrease in peak airflow and gas exchange, as well as a decrease in vital capacity, which is defined as the greatest amount of air that can be expelled from the lungs after the biggest breath. The overall weakening of the respiratory muscles reduces their strength and endurance. As some of the respiratory muscles grow weaker, this creates an imbalance in the respiratory muscles, resulting in feelings of breathlessness. As the immune system weakens, the lungs are less able to effectively combat pathogens, resulting in more frequent and severe respiratory infections (Davies & Bolton, 2010).

THE ENDOCRINE SYSTEM

The endocrine system plays an important role in regulating the body's organs through hormone secretion. The endocrine system consists of the major endocrine glands, which are the hypothalamus, pituitary gland, thyroid gland, parathyroid gland, adrenal gland, and pineal body, as well as the reproductive organs, which will be discussed in a subsequent section. These glands and organs work together to regulate and control bodily functions through the production and secretion of hormones. Hormones control the functions of certain organs and impact vital processes such as growth and development, reproduction, and expression of sexual characteristics. Hormones also influence how the body uses and stores energy.

Age-Related Changes to the Physiology of the Endocrine System

As with many other physical functions, certain endocrine functions are more vulnerable to dysfunction or disease with age. This vulnerability is due to changes in the functions of the endocrine system (see Box 4.7). For example, there are age-related changes in the responsiveness of tissues, levels of hormone secretion, and hormone release rhythms (Pataky et al., 2021). Hormones serve a variety of functions, including promotion of tissue growth, muscle mass production, and regulation of sex drives. Examples of common hormones in our body include testosterone, growth hormone, and dehydroepiandrosterone (DHEA). Age-related decreases in hormone levels can

> **BOX 4.7** Endocrine System: Key Points
>
> **Age-Associated Physiological Changes**
> - Changes in body composition impact metabolism and circulation of hormones.
> - Reproductive hormones decrease.
> - Insulin resistance can increase.
> - Thyroid hormone synthesis and secretion decline.

cause physical and metabolic problems, including increased risk for obesity, reduced muscle mass, high blood pressure, and decreased bone density.

In healthy individuals, the pancreas (more specifically, beta cells within the pancreas) produces and releases insulin into the bloodstream in response to rising blood glucose levels. Insulin helps absorb, store, and use glucose for energy. Yet as part of the aging process, the body can develop *insulin resistance*, which creates a situation in which the body is unable to use insulin effectively and therefore requires more insulin to maintain normal blood sugar levels (National Institute of Diabetes and Digestive and Kidney Diseases [NIDDK], 2018). While the mechanisms underlying age-related insulin resistance are not yet fully clear, altered age-related alteration in beta-cell function has been identified as a contributor (Zhu et al., 2021). Beta-cells in the pancreas are responsible for secreting insulin in response to higher levels of glucose. The pancreas must then produce more insulin to accommodate for the insulin resistance. In some instances, the pancreas cannot produce enough insulin to overcome the insulin resistance, leading to glucose buildup in the blood and eventually prediabetes and diabetes (NIDDK, 2018).

The thyroid also undergoes age-related changes. Human and animal studies have shown that both thyroid hormone synthesis and secretion decrease with age. Additionally, of the two thyroid hormones (triiodothyronine or T_3, and thyroxine, or T_4), T_3 declines with age. The metabolism and action of thyroid hormones in the body also change with age. T_4 secretion is reduced in older adults, yet the concentrations of T_4 remain stable due to decreases in degradation of T_4 (Peeters, 2008). In other words, the ability of T_4 to catalyze into T_3 is reduced. Thyroid-stimulating hormone (TSH) is also known to decrease over the course of healthy aging (Bahri, 2019). These changes and other factors, such as chronic illness or medications, can lead to thyroid problems.

THE URINARY SYSTEM

The urinary system filters waste and fluid from the bloodstream and then removes it from the body. The urinary system includes the kidneys and the urinary tract, which consists of the ureters, bladder, and urethra. Inside the kidneys are filtering units, called nephrons, that filter waste from the blood. The kidneys are capable of filtering 120 to 150 quarts of blood a day, resulting in 1 to 2 quarts of urine. Each kidney is connected to the bladder by a ureter, which is a thin muscular tube through which urine flows from the kidney to the bladder. The bladder acts as a reservoir and can hold up to 2 cups of urine. A trio of muscles work together to hold the urine in the bladder.

These muscles include the urethra, the internal sphincter, and the pelvic floor muscles. Unlike tkidney function, a person has control over bladder function. When a person urinates, the brain signals the muscles of the bladder wall to contract and the sphincter to relax, which has the sum effect of pushing urine out of the bladder through the urethra (Malykhina, 2017).

Age-Related Changes to the Physiology of the Urinary System

As the arteries that supply the kidneys with blood narrow with age, the kidneys become smaller. There is also an accompanying decline in the ability of the glomerulus, located in the nephrons, to filter waste from the blood (Wiggins, 2012). The basement membrane of the glomerulus, which is the bottom cell wall that separates the capillaries from the urinary space, is composed of epithelial cells called podocytes. In normal aging, the glomerulus will grow larger, causing the podocyte cells to grow in size but not in number. These structural changes decrease the function of the podocytes and the overall functionality of the glomerulus, which in turn slows the filtering process. While these structural changes do not alter the filtering process to a degree that prevents the kidneys from functioning adequately, they do make the kidneys vulnerable to injury or illness that would further impair kidney function (Minaker, 2011; see also Box 4.8).

While the ureters are fairly immune to the aging process, the bladder and urethra do exhibit age-associated change. The wall of the bladder becomes more rigid, causing the bladder to be less elastic, which limits the amount of urine it can store. Bladder muscles also weaken with age, which affects the rate at which urine flows out of the bladder. There may be sporadic contractions of the bladder, which result in instances of urinary incontinence. Older adults may need to urinate more often as the bladder becomes less efficient as it empties, resulting in some urine remaining in the bladder. These age-related changes to the bladder increase the risk for urinary tract infections (UTIs).

There are gender differences in age-related urinary system changes. After menopause, a woman's urethra shortens as its lining grows thinner. The urinary sphincter is less able to close tightly, thus increasing the risk for urinary incontinence. Men may experience an enlargement of the prostate gland, which may block the urethra. This results in men having the urge to urinate while being unable to effectively void. An

BOX 4.8 Urinary System: Key Points

Age-Associated Physiological Changes

- Kidneys grow smaller.
- Bladder grows more rigid.
- Urinary incontinence may occur due to bladder spasms.
- Women are at greater risk of urinary incontinence.
- Men may have increased urge to urinate though be unable to due to enlarged prostate.

untreated enlarged prostate can result in the retention of urine and eventually kidney damage (Smith & Kuche, 2017).

THE REPRODUCTIVE SYSTEM

The primary function of the reproductive system is to produce sex cells and hormones. The female reproductive system consists of the ovaries, fallopian tubes, uterus, cervix, and vagina. The male reproductive system consists of the penis, scrotum, testes, epididymis, vas deferens, urethra, prostate, and seminal vesicles. Other parts of the body, such as the hypothalamus, pituitary gland, and adrenal glands, also affect the function of the female and male reproductive system.

Age-Related Changes to the Physiology of the Reproductive System

Age-associated changes occur in both the female and male reproductive systems (see Box 4.9). Women have a finite number of usable eggs. As the usable eggs are depleted, the ovaries stop producing estrogen and progesterone. Menopause in women occurs when the ovaries cease production of estrogen. This typically occurs around age 51. This results in less frequent menstruation and ovulation. Once a woman has been without a menstrual cycle for a year, she is in menopause.

Symptoms of menopause include irregular menstrual periods, hot flashes, mood changes, irritability, sleep disturbances, night sweats, and difficulty concentrating. These symptoms become less frequent and less severe after menopause, although the reduced estrogen can negatively impact a woman's health. Other physical changes associated with menopause include vaginal atrophy, shrinking sex organs, and reduced libido. The urinary tract also experiences changes as the urethra becomes thinner and shorter, which in turn increases a woman's risk for UTI and urinary incontinence. As the body produces less estrogen, the skin becomes thinner, drier, and vulnerable to injury. Reduced estrogen contributes to reduced bone density, which increases the risk of osteoporosis and hip fractures. Breast tissue also changes with age as the connective tissue in the breast decreases and fibrous tissue is replaced with fat, leading to sagging and less firm breasts. Finally, women may experience increased low-density lipoprotein (LDL) cholesterol, which places them at risk of atherosclerosis and coronary artery disease (Nagaratnam et al., 2016).

BOX 4.9   Reproductive System: Key Points

Age-Associated Physiological Changes
- Menopause occurs in women around age 51.
- Reduced estrogen increases risk of osteoporosis.
- Women experience increases in LDL cholesterol.
- Testosterone declines in men with age, as does libido.

Men experience gradual age-related changes in sexual functioning, including declines in the frequency, duration, and rigidity of an erection. Older males experience a loss of total testosterone at a rate of 1% a year, which reduces libido. Interestingly, it is estimated that half of the decline is due to increased body fat, which occurs as the muscle–to–body fat ratio shifts with age. Additional changes include reduced sensitivity in the penis, reduced volume of ejaculation, reduced forewarning of ejaculation, orgasms without ejaculation, more rapid detumescence, and longer refractory periods (Nagaratnam et al., 2016).

THE DIGESTIVE SYSTEM

The digestive system is responsible for ingestion and digestion of food, absorption of nutrients, and discharge of residual waste. The digestive system consists of the digestive tract as well as several organs outside of the digestive tract. The digestive tract comprises the mouth, throat and esophagus, stomach, small intestine, large intestine (or colon), rectum, and anus. Other key organs of the digestive system that lie outside of the digestive tract include the pancreas, the liver, and the gallbladder. The digestive system is also responsible for other functions beyond those listed previously. For instance, organs in the digestive tract produce blood clotting factors and hormones, remove harmful substances from the bloodstream, and metabolize medications.

Age-Related Changes to the Physiology of the Digestive System

While there are age-related structural changes in the digestive tract and the organs of the digestive system, many of these changes do not result in functional impairment. Esophageal contractions weaken, as does the esophageal sphincter. The lining of the stomach is more susceptible to damage, which increases a person's risk for peptic ulcers. As the stomach becomes less elastic, the amount of food that it can accommodate decreases, as does the rate at which the stomach passes food to the small intestine. While the structure of the small intestine undergoes minimal change with aging, changes inside the intestine result in older adults being more vulnerable to lactose intolerance. While the colon is resistant to the effects of age, the rectum can enlarge, resulting in decreased contractions when filled with stool (Bartell, 2022). This can result in increased constipation for older adults. Organs associated with the digestive system also undergo some age-related changes (see Box 4.10). Both the liver and the

BOX 4.10   Digestive System: Key Points

Age-Associated Physiological Changes
■ Weakened esophageal contractions and sphincter ■ Less elastic stomach, which can accommodate less food ■ Increased vulnerability to lactose intolerance ■ Enlarged rectum ■ Lighter liver and pancreas

pancreas decrease in weight. In the liver, hepatocytes that are responsible for most liver functions, including detoxification and metabolism, begin to decline in function because of oxidative stress, changes in DNA that occur with aging, and changes in mitochondria, which generate energy (Hunt et al., 2019).

CONCLUSION

Older adults experience a myriad of age-related physiological changes. While some of these physiological changes are benign, other changes increase the risk of age-associated pathophysiological changes, which can result in significant functional impairment or morbidity. Therefore, understanding how the normative process of aging works can help us understand when pathology may begin and intervention may be needed.

DISCUSSION QUESTIONS

1. State the 11 organ systems that make up the body.
2. Describe age-related changes to three organ systems.
3. Describe the problems that can result when providers fail to differentiate between normative and non-normative aging.

A robust set of instructor resources designed to supplement this text is located at http://connect.springerpub.com/content/book/978-0-8261-6617-3. Qualifying instructors may request access by emailing textbook@springerpub.com.

REFERENCES

Aiken, L. R. (2001). *Aging and later life: Growing old in modern society*. Charles C Thomas Publisher.

Akasheva, D. U., Plokhova, E. V., Tkacheva, O. N., Strazhesko, I. D., Dudinskaya, E. N., Kruglikova, A. S., Pykhtina, V. S., Brailova, N. V., Pokshubina, I. A., Sharashkina, N. V., Agaltsov, M. V., Skvortsov, D., & Boytsov, S. A. (2015). Age-related left ventricular changes and their association with leukocyte telomere length in healthy people. *PLoS One, 10*(8), e0135883. https://doi.org/10.1371/journal.pone.0135883

Alba, B. K., Castellani, J. W., & Charkoudian, N. (2019). Cold-induced cutaneous vasoconstriction in humans: Function, dysfunction and the distinctly counterproductive. *Experimental Physiology, 104*(8), 1202–1214. https://doi.org/10.1113/EP087718

Allen, J. C., Toapanta, F. R., Chen, W., & Tennant, S. M. (2020). Understanding immunosenescence and its impact on vaccination of older adults. *Vaccine, 38*(52), 8264–8272. https://doi.org/10.1016/j.vaccine.2020.11.002

Arshad, Q., & Seemungal, B. M. (2016). Age-related vestibular loss: Current understanding and future research directions. *Frontiers in Neurology, 7*, 231. https://doi.org/10.3389/fneur.2016.00231

Bahri, S., Tehrani, F. R., Amouzgar, A., Rahmati, M., Tohidi, M., Vasheghani, M., & Azizi, F. (2019). Overtime trend of thyroid hormones and thyroid autoimmunity and ovarian reserve: A longitudinal population study with a 12-year follow up. *BMC Endocrine Disorders, 19*(1), 47. https://doi.org/10.1186/s12902-019-0370-7

Bartell, M. (2022). Digestive disorders: Effects of aging on the digestive system. *Merck Manuals Consumer Version.* https://www.merckmanuals.com/home/digestive-disorders/biology-of-the-digestive-system/effects-of-aging-on-the-digestive-system

Bataille, A., Le Gall, C., Misery, L., & Talagas, M. (2022). Merkel cells are multimodal sensory cells: A review of study methods. *Cells, 11*(23), 3827. https://doi.org/10.3390/cells11233827

Brodkey, F. (2022, July). *Aging changes in the bones, muscles, joints.* Medline Plus, National Library of Medicine. https://medlineplus.gov/ency/article/004015.htm

Cohen, J. A., Verghese, J., & Zwerling, J. L. (2016). Cognition and gait in older people. *Maturitas, 93*, 73–77. https://doi.org/10.1016/j.maturitas.2016.05.005

Csekes, E., & Račková, L. (2021). Skin aging, cellular senescence and natural polyphenols. *International Journal of Molecular Sciences, 22*(23), 12641. https://doi.org/10.3390/ijms222312641

Davies, G. A., & Bolton, C. E. (2010). Age-related changes in the respiratory system. In H. M. Fillit, K. Rockwood, & K. Woodhouse (Eds.), *Brocklehurst's textbook of geriatric medicine and gerontology* (7th ed., Chapter 17). Elsevier Saunders.

Dev, M. K., Black, A. A., Cuda, D., & Wood, J. M. (2022). Low light exposure and physical activity in older adults with and without age-related macular degeneration. *Translational Vision Science and Technology, 11*(3), 21. https://doi.org/10.1167/tvst.11.3.21

Dickin, D. C., Brown, L. A., & Doan, J. B. (2006). Age-dependent differences in the time course of postural control during sensory perturbations. *Aging and Clinical Experimental Research, 18*(2), 94–99. https://doi.org/10.1007/BF03327423

Dufour, A., & Candas, V. (2007). Ageing and thermal responses during passive heat exposure: Sweating and sensory aspects. *European Journal of Applied Physiology, 100*(1), 19–26. https://doi.org/10.1007/s00421-007-0396-9

Eckhardt, C. M., & Wu, H. (2021). Environmental exposures and lung aging: Molecular mechanisms and implications for improving respiratory health. *Current Environmental Health Reports, 8*(4), 281–293. https://doi.org/10.1007/s40572-021-00328-2

Farage, M. A., Miller, K. W., Elsner, P., & Maibach, H. I. (2013). Characteristics of the aging skin. *Advances in Wound Care, 2*(1), 5–10. https://doi.org/10.1089/wound.2011.0356

Fettiplace, R. (2017). Hair cell transduction, tuning, and synaptic transmission in the mammalian cochlea. *Comprehensive Physiology, 7*(4), 1197–1227. https://doi.org/10.1002/cphy.c160049

Fillit, H. M., Rockwood, K., & Young, J. (2017). *Brocklehurst's textbook of geriatric medicine and gerontology* (8th ed.). Elsevier.

Gregson, C. (2017). Bone and joint aging. In H. M. Fillit, K. Rockwood, & J. Young (Eds.), *Brocklehurst's textbook of geriatric medicine and gerontology* (8th ed., pp. 120–126.e2). Elsevier.

Gromkowska-Kępka, K. J., Puścion-Jakubik, A., Markiewicz-Żukowska, R., & Socha, K. (2021). The impact of ultraviolet radiation on skin photoaging: Review of in vitro studies. *Journal of Cosmetic Dermatology, 20*(11), 3427–3431. https://doi.org/10.1111/jocd.14033

Hooper, L., Bunn, D., Jimoh, F. O., & Fairweather-Tait, S. J. (2014). Water-loss dehydration and aging. *Mechanisms of Ageing and Development, 136–137*, 50–58. https://doi.org/10.1016/j.mad.2013.11.009

Hunt, N. J., Kang, S. W. S., Lockwood, G. P., Le Couteur, D. G., & Cogger, V. C. (2019). Hallmarks of aging in the liver. *Computational and Structural Biotechnology Journal, 17*, 1151–1161. https://doi.org/10.1016/j.csbj.2019.07.021

Jayakody, D. M. P., Friedland, P. L., Martins, R. N., & Sohrabi, H. R. (2018). Impact of aging on the auditory system and related cognitive functions: A narrative review. *Frontiers in Neuroscience, 12.* 125. https://doi.org/10.3389/fnins.2018.00125

Kale, S. S., Namita, A., & Yende, S. (2012). Aging, infection, and immunity. In A. B. Newman & J. A. Cauley (Eds.), *The epidemiology of aging* (pp. 237–253). Springer.

Kapila, V., Wehrle, C. J., & Tuma, F. (2023, May). Physiology, spleen. In *StatPearls.* StatPearls Publishing. https://www.ncbi.nlm.nih.gov/books/NBK537307/

Karlamangla, A. S., Burnett-Bowie, S. M., & Crandall, C. J. (2018). Bone health during the menopause transition and beyond. *Obstetrics and Gynecology Clinics of North America, 45*(4), 695–708. https://doi.org/10.1016/j.ogc.2018.07.012

Kondo, K., Kikuta, S., Ueha, R., Suzukawa, K., & Yamasoba, T. (2020). Age-related olfactory dysfunction: Epidemiology, pathophysiology, and clinical management. *Frontiers in Aging Neuroscience, 12*, 208. https://doi.org/10.3389/fnagi.2020.00208

Malykhina, A. P. (2017). How the brain controls urination. *eLife, 6*, e33219. https://doi.org/10.7554/eLife.33219

Mayo Clinic. (2021, November). *Presboypia*. https://www.mayoclinic.org/diseases-conditions/presbyopia/symptoms-causes/

McGrath, J. A., & Uitto, J. (2016). Structure and function of the skin. In C. Griffiths, J. Barker, T. Bleiker, R. Chalmers, & D. Creamer (Eds.), *Rook's textbook of dermatology* (9th ed.). John Wiley.

Minaker, K. L. (2011). Common clinical sequelae of aging. In L. Goldman & A. I. Schafer (Eds.), *Goldman's Cecil medicine* (24th ed., pp. 104–110). Elsevier Saunders.

Moreland, B., Kakara, R., & Henry, A. (2020). Trends in nonfatal falls and fall-related injuries among adults aged ≥65 years—United States, 2012–2018. *MMWR. Morbidity and Mortality Weekly Report, 69*(27), 875–881. https://doi.org/10.15585/mmwr.mm6927a5

Mitchell, W. K., Williams, J., Atherton, P., Larvin, M., Lund, J., & Narici, M. (2012). Sarcopenia, dynapenia, and the impact of advancing age on human skeletal muscle size and strength; a quantitative review. *Frontiers in Physiology, 3*, 260. https://doi.org/10.3389/fphys.2012.00260

Nagaratnam, N., Nagaratnam, K., & Cheuk, G. (2016). *Diseases in the elderly: Age-related changes and pathophysiology*. Springer.

National Institute on Aging. (2023, January). *Talking with your older patients*. U.S. Department of Health and Human Services, National Institutes of Health. https://www.nia.nih.gov/health/talking-your-older-patients

National Institute on Deafness and Other Communication Disorders. (2021, March). *Statistics and epidemiology*. U.S. Department of Health and Human Services, National Institutes of Health. https://www.nia.nih.gov/health/talking-your-older-patients

National Institute of Diabetes and Digestive and Kidney Diseases. (2018, May). *Insulin resistance and pre-diabetes*. U.S Department of Health and Human Services, National Institutes of Health.

Nolan, L. S. (2020). Age-related hearing loss: Why we need to think about sex as a biological variable. *Journal of Neuroscience Research, 98*(9), 1705–1720. https://doi.org/10.1002/jnr.24647

O'Dowd, A., Hirst, R. J., Setti, A., Kenny, R. A., & Newell, F. N. (2022). Self-reported sensory decline in older adults is longitudinally associated with both modality-general and modality-specific factors. *Innovation in Aging, 6*(7), igac069. https://doi.org/10.1093/geroni/igac069

Ogawa, T., Spina, R. J., Martin, W. H., 3rd, Kohrt, W. M., Schechtman, K. B., Holloszy, J. O., & Ehsani, A. A. (1992). Effects of aging, sex, and physical training on cardiovascular responses to exercise. *Circulation, 86*(2), 494–503. https://doi.org/10.1161/01.cir.86.2.494

Parikh, J. D., Hollingsworth, K. G., Wallace, D., Blamire, A. M., & MacGowan, G. A. (2016). Normal age-related changes in left ventricular function: Role of afterload and subendocardial dysfunction. *Internation Journal of Cardiology, 223*, 306–312. https://doi.org/10.1016/j.ijcard.2016.07.25

Pataky, M. W., Young, W. F., & Nair, K. S. (2021). Hormonal and metabolic changes of aging and the influence of lifestyle modifications. *Mayo Clinic Proceedings, 96*(3), 788–814. https://doi.org/10.1016/j.mayocp.2020.07.033

Peeters, R. P. (2008). Thyroid hormones and aging. *Hormones, 7*(1), 28–35. https://doi.org/10.14310/horm.2002.1111035

Pilgrim, A. L., Robinson, S. M., Sayer, A. A., & Roberts, H. C. (2015). An overview of appetite decline in older people. *Nursing Older People, 27*(5), 29–35. https://doi.org/10.7748/nop.27.5.29.e697

Ponti, F., Santoro, A., Mercatelli, D., Gasperini, C., Conte, M., Martucci, M., Sangiorgi, L., Franceschi, C., Bazzochi, A. (2020). Aging and imaging assessment of body composition: From fat to facts. *Frontiers in Endocrinology, 10*, 861. https://doi.org/10.3389/fendo.2019.00861

Rawal, S., Hoffman, H.J., Bainbridge, K.E., Huedo-Medina, T.B., Duffy, V.B. (2016). Prevalence and risk factors of self-reported smell and taste alterations: Results from the 2011–2012 US National Health and Nutrition Examination Survey (NHANES). *Chemical Senses 41*(1), 69–76. https://doi.org/10.1093/chemse/bjv057

Rawson, N. E. (2006). Olfactory loss in aging. *Science of Aging Knowledge Environment: SAGE KE, 2006*(5). https://doi.org/10.1126/sageke.2006.5.pe6

Salvi, S. M., Akhtar, S., & Currie, Z. (2006). Ageing changes in the eye. *Postgraduate Medical Journal, 82*(971), 581–587. https://doi.org/10.1136/pgmj.2005.040857

Smith, P. P., & Kuche, G. A. (2017). Aging of the urinary tract. In H. M. Fillit, K. Rockwood, & J. Young (Eds.), *Brocklehurst's textbook of geriatric medicine and gerontology* (8th ed., pp. 133–137). Elsevier.

Sözen, T., Özışık, L., & Başaran, N. Ç. (2017). An overview and management of osteoporosis. *European Journal of Rheumatology, 4*(1), 46–56. https://doi.org/10.5152/eurjrheum.2016.048

Umetani, K., Singer, D. H., McCraty, R., & Atkinson, M. (1998). Twenty-four hour time domain heart rate variability and heart rate: Relations to age and gender over nine decades. *Journal of the American College of Cardiology, 31(3)*, 593–601. https://doi.org/10.1016/s0735-1097(97)00554-8

Vatner, S. F., Zhang, J., Vyzas, C., Mishra, K., Graham, R. M., & Vatner, D. E. (2021). Vascular stiffness in aging and disease. *Frontiers in Physiology, 12*, 762437. https://doi.org/10.3389/fphys.2021.762437

Völter, C., Thomas, J. P., Maetzler, W., Guthoff, R., Grunwald, M., & Hummel, T. (2021). Sensory dysfunction in old age. *Deutsches Arzteblatt International, 118*(29–30), 512–520. https://doi.org/10.3238/arztebl.m2021.0212

Wickremaratchi, M., & Llewelyn, J. (2006). Effects of ageing on touch. *Postgraduate Medical Journal, 82*(967), 301–304. https://doi.org/10.1136/pgmj.2005.039651

Wiggins, J. E. (2012). Aging in the glomerulus. *The Journals of Gerontology. Series A, Biological Sciences and Medical Sciences, 67*(12), 1358–1364. https://doi.org/10.1093/gerona/gls157

Wilkinson, D. J., Piasecki, M., & Atherton, P. J. (2018). The age-related loss of skeletal muscle mass and function: Measurement and physiology of muscle fibre atrophy and muscle fibre loss in humans. *Ageing Research Reviews, 47*, 123–132. https://doi.org/10.1016/j.arr.2018.07.005

Zhang, H., Weyand. C., & Gorony, J. J. (2021). Hallmarks of aging T-cell system. *The FEBS Journal, 288*(24), 7123–7141. https://doi.org/10.1111/febs.15770

Zhu, M., Liu, X., Liu, W., Lu, Y., Cheng, J., & Chen, Y. (2021). β cell aging and age-related diabetes. *Aging, 13*(5), 7691–7706. https://doi.org/10.18632/aging.202593

5

Age-Related Illnesses

Eliza Morgan, Devon Delaney, and J. Kaci Fairchild

LEARNING OBJECTIVES

- Describe three causes of visual impairment in older adults.
- Explain what congestive heart failure is and why it leads to shortness of breath and edema in one's feet.
- Connect the effects of diabetes mellitus to two or more organ systems.

Although there are normative age-related changes in physical health, only some changes result in diagnosable illnesses. Three out of four older adults have at least one diagnosed chronic health condition. Over 60% of those aged 65 to 74 and over 80% of those aged 85 or older have at least two or more diagnosed chronic health conditions (Quiñones et al., 2016). These statistics highlight the concept of *multimorbidity*, which is defined as the co-occurrence of two or more chronic health conditions in one person. These multiple physical conditions often interact to create adverse outcomes in this population.

The aim of this chapter is to explore prevalent age-related illnesses and their symptoms, risk factors, and treatments. The following sections are categorized by major organ system with an overview of common conditions pertaining to each system. The reader is invited to explore the listed references for a more extensive discussion of this topic.

COMMON DISORDERS OF THE INTEGUMENTARY SYSTEM

Age-related structural and functional changes to our skin reduce its resilience and make it more vulnerable to damage. Some of the most common skin disorders include dermatitis and pruritus, shingles, and skin cancer.

Dermatitis and Pruritus

Dermatitis and pruritus are two of the most common disorders in older adults. Dermatitis is a collection of disorders that includes xerosis and seborrheic dermatitis. Xerosis, which is rough or dry skin, results from reduced production of sebum and age-related changes in the surface of the epidermis. Left untreated, xerosis can progress from scales to fissures, inflammation, and infection. Seborrheic dermatitis is a chronic condition that causes red, scaly patches and inflamed skin, usually on the scalp, although it can occur in any area with abundant sebaceous oil glands (Fillit et al., 2017). Pruritus is severe skin itching in the absence of an obvious skin lesion. It is often a symptom of other ailments including diabetes, anemia, thyroid disease, and drug sensitivity. While not life threatening, dermatitis and pruritus are physically uncomfortable and may negatively impact psychosocial functioning (Chung et al., 2020). Treatment often focuses on symptom relief via a combination of topical and oral anti-inflammatory and antihistamine medications (Kahremany et al., 2021).

Shingles

Shingles (i.e., herpes zoster) is a reactivation of the varicella-zoster virus (i.e., the virus that causes chickenpox). The Centers for Disease Control and Prevention (CDC) estimates that over 99% of people aged 40 and older have had chickenpox, which places virtually all older adults at risk for shingles. Shingles is prevalent in late life, with one in three older adults developing shingles during their lifetime. Symptoms of shingles include a painful, itchy, red rash, which most commonly appears on a person's trunk. Older adults are also at risk for postherpetic neuralgia (PHN), which is persistent pain at the site of the rash. While there is no cure for shingles, antiviral medications may shorten its duration, and medication may be used to manage pain (Pierwola et al., 2017). The shingles vaccine reduces the risk of shingles by 51% and the risk of PHN by 67% (CDC, 2017).

Skin Cancer

Chronic ultraviolet radiation from sun exposure coupled with skin's age-related diminished resiliency increases the risk of skin cancer in older adults. In fact, most skin cancers occur in older adults. Basal cell and squamous cell carcinomas are two of the most common types of skin cancer, and both are highly curable with low mortality rates. On the other hand, melanoma represents only 4% of skin cancers yet has the highest mortality rate. Men aged 80 and older have a threefold greater risk for developing melanoma than women (American Cancer Society [ACS], 2016). Treatment includes surgery, radiation therapy, chemotherapy, photodynamic therapy, biologic therapy, and targeted therapy.

COMMON DISORDERS OF THE MUSCULOSKELETAL SYSTEM

Musculoskeletal problems are a significant concern for older adults, as they can result in substantial pain and functional impairment. The most common disorders of the musculoskeletal system in older adults are osteoporosis, sarcopenia, and osteoarthritis.

Osteoporosis

Osteoporosis is responsible for 70% of fractures in late life, making it a leading cause of disability for older adults (Glowacki & Vokes, 2016). The risk for osteoporotic fractures, which most frequently occur in the hip, wrist, and vertebra, increases with age as the body's bones become less dense and more brittle. Women are more likely to develop osteoporosis, likely due to their thinner bones and menopause-associated estrogen loss. After the age of 50, one in two women will experience an osteoporotic fracture. In a national study of older women, osteoporotic fractures accounted for 4.9 million hospitalizations over a 12-year period. To put that in perspective, 2.9 million adults were hospitalized for myocardial infarction, 3 million for stroke, and roughly 700,000 for breast cancer. Thus, osteoporotic fractures accounted for 40% of the hospital admissions in this nationwide sample (Singer et al., 2015). As the effects of osteoporosis are difficult to reverse, treatments and interventions are typically focused on prevention. These include exercise, hormone replacement therapy, medication, and a diet rich in calcium and vitamin D (Gregson et al., 2022).

Sarcopenia

Sarcopenia is the insidious loss of skeletal muscle mass and function. It impacts one in three older adults and leads to increased fall risk. Sarcopenia has multiple etiological determinants including reduced neuronal communication between the brain and muscles, hormone reduction (e.g., growth factor, testosterone, estrogen), slowed protein synthesis, and reduced caloric intake to support muscle mass (Pascual-Fernández et al., 2020). The primary treatment for sarcopenia is exercise, with a focus on resistance training (Hurst et al., 2022).

Osteoarthritis

The World Health Organization (WHO) estimates that 130 million people will develop osteoarthritis by 2050 and 30% of those will be severely disabled (Mobasheri, 2019). Joints in the hips, knees, and hands are most frequently afflicted. Like osteoporosis, the disorder is most common in women. Osteoarthritis occurs when the cartilage inside a joint wears down, leading to inflammation, pain, and eventual cartilage loss. The causes of osteoarthritis are multifactorial and include aging, overuse, past injury or trauma, and metabolic abnormalities (Fillit et al., 2017), with some suggestion of a genetic component (Butterfield et al., 2021). Treatment focuses on symptom management via physical activity, weight management, stretching and range of motion exercises, occupational and physical therapy, assistive devices, pain or anti-inflammatory medications, and in severe cases, surgery.

COMMON DISORDERS OF THE NERVOUS SYSTEM

Given the widespread age-related changes in the nervous system, it can be difficult to differentiate normative aging from age-related pathophysiology. Common age-related disorders affecting sensory organs, the brain, and the peripheral nervous system are described next.

Cataracts, Macular Degeneration, and Glaucoma

Globally, cataracts are the leading cause of blindness. The National Eye Institute (NEI) projects that 50 million people will have cataracts in the United States by the year 2050 (NEI, 2015). Cataracts occur when proteins aggregate on the lens of the eye, resulting in visual impairment. This aggregation is often gradual; thus, the initial changes may escape notice. As the proteins build and the cataract grows, vision blurs and reduces visual acuity. Risk factors include age, diabetes, smoking, alcohol use, and prolonged exposure to sunlight. Treatment options for cataracts vary based on the size of the cataract and degree of functional impairment. While vision changes due to small cataracts may be helped with assistive devices (e.g., glasses or magnification tools), once the cataract reaches a certain size or vision becomes further impaired, surgical removal of the cloudy lens and replacement with an artificial lens is warranted (NEI, 2015).

Macular degeneration is the leading cause of vision loss in persons aged 50 and older. As the name implies, macular degeneration involves the deterioration of the macula. The macula is part of the retina that focuses central vision and transmits visual information from the eye via the optic nerve to the brain. There are two types of macular degeneration: dry (atrophic) and wet (exudative). The dry type is most common, as it comprises 85% to 90% of cases. While age is the biggest risk factor for macular degeneration, other risk factors include heredity and European American race. Smoking also effectively doubles a person's susceptibility to macular degeneration. Macular degeneration is incurable, though physical exercise, avoiding smoking, and eating a balanced, nutrient-rich diet reduce the risk of onset (NEI, 2021).

Glaucoma refers to a group of disorders that damage the optic nerve and result in visual impairment and blindness. The most common type of glaucoma is known as *open-angle glaucoma*. In this type of glaucoma, a naturally occurring fluid builds up inside the eye, creating excessive pressure that damages the optic nerve. While eye pressure is a leading cause of optic nerve damage in glaucoma, not all persons who have elevated pressure in the eye will develop glaucoma, and not all cases of glaucoma are due to elevated pressure in the eye (e.g., normal-tension glaucoma). Initially, a person may not realize they have glaucoma, as there is no pain or visual changes. As the disease progresses, a person will experience peripheral vision loss, producing tunnel vision. If untreated, blindness can occur. Risk factors for glaucoma include heredity, increased age, and African American race. Treatments for glaucoma include medications, laser, and conventional surgery or a combination of these. Early intervention is essential, as the treatments may stop the progression of glaucoma, though it cannot correct premorbid visual impairments (NEI, 2015).

Tinnitus and Presbycusis

Tinnitus is persistent abnormal noise in the absence of sound and afflicts up to 20% of people, many of whom are older adults. Tinnitus may present as a ringing, buzzing, roaring, clicking, or hissing sound that can vary in pitch and occur in one or both ears (Mayo, 2022). There are two types of tinnitus: subjective (i.e., audible to only the affected person) and objective (i.e., audible to others in addition to the affected person). Subjective tinnitus results from damage in the ear, auditory nerve, or the auditory pathways in the brain. This type of tinnitus is likened to "phantom hearing," as it is the brain's response to a lack of auditory stimulation and is associated with neuronal hyperactivity along the auditory pathway. Objective tinnitus, which is rare, results from sound being created by vascular or muscular etiology occurring somewhere in the body (Moller, 2016). There are no approved pharmacological interventions for tinnitus, though some medications may improve comorbid symptoms (i.e., depression, anxiety, insomnia). Some recommended nonpharmacological interventions for tinnitus include assistive devices like hearing aids, sound therapy, cognitive behavioral therapy, tinnitus retraining therapy, and repetitive transcranial magnetic stimulation (Maldonado Fernández et al., 2017; Noh et al., 2020).

Presbycusis, gradual age-related hearing loss, affects about two thirds of adults aged 70 or older (Tu & Friedman, 2018). Hearing loss is typically specific to frequencies, including the frequencies of sibilants (i.e., *s, sh,* and *ch),* which are carried over speech frequencies above 3,500 hertz. Older adults may have difficulty hearing conversations against loud background noise (e.g., in a restaurant), hearing high-pitched sounds, or may perceive other's speech as slurred. Presbycusis is often sensorineural in nature. The associated damage or impairment in the inner ear can be caused by repeated exposure to loud sounds, such as construction, loud music, or any equipment that causes loud noises. It can also occur with aging or health conditions such as heart disease, hypertension, or diabetes. Interventions for presbycusis often focus on prevention of damage via the use of ear protection. Once hearing impairment occurs, assistive devices such as hearing aids or assistive listening devices may be helpful (Roth, 2015), and in more severe cases, cochlear implants can be used to directly stimulate the auditory nerve (Löhler et al., 2019).

Peripheral Neuropathy

Peripheral neuropathy results from damage to the peripheral nervous system and affects over 20 million people in the United States. Symptoms include burning, numbness, tingling, paresthesia (i.e., prickling sensation), allodynia (i.e., pain resulting from stimuli that would not normally provoke it), muscle weakness and wasting, and, in severe cases, paralysis. Damage to the peripheral nervous system may also result in organ or gland dysfunction, which can impact digestion, sexual function, urination, and sweating. There are over 100 types of peripheral neuropathy, and each has its own symptom presentation and prognosis. The most common causes of peripheral neuropathy are injury (e.g., physical trauma or repetitive movements), disease (e.g., endocrine, metabolic, or autoimmune disorders; infections; small vessel disease; cancer; kidney dysfunction; or neuromas), or toxic exposure (e.g., medication, environmental, heavy alcohol use). Treatment of peripheral neuropathy requires treating the underlying cause and offering symptom management. The latter is often focused on relief from neuropathic pain through pharmacological (e.g., medications, topical ointments, or creams) or nonpharmacological means (e.g., transcutaneous electrical nerve stimulation [TENS]), acupuncture, psychotherapy, plasmapheresis, surgery, physical therapy, or assistive devices (U.S. Department of Health and Human Services, 2023).

COMMON DISORDERS OF THE CARDIOVASCULAR SYSTEM

Cardiovascular disorders (CVDs) are highly pervasive in older adults, as up to 70% of people over the age of 70 will develop CVD (Aïdoud et al., 2023).

Hypertension

Essential hypertension is a chronic, age-related condition with no clear underlying cause (Montecucco et al., 2011). A diagnosis of hypertension is defined as an average systolic blood pressure (BP) above 140 to 160 mmHg and/or diastolic BP above 90 mm Hg with measurements taken over the course of days to months (Bergler-Klein, 2019). While no single etiological factor causes hypertension, numerous factors are associated with it including diminished compliance of the aorta and large arteries, changes in heart rate, narrowed vessel walls, long-term high sodium intake, obesity, and changes in blood volume (see Oparil et al., 2003 for a comprehensive review). Hypertension is the most prevalent vascular disease in older adults, occurring in over 55% of adults aged 70 years and older (Ong et al., 2007). The prevalence increases with age, as more than 90% of individuals who are free of hypertension at 65 years of age will go on to develop hypertension in their remaining lifetime (Mosley & Lloyd-Jones, 2009).

Congestive Heart Failure

Worldwide, there are over 64 million cases of congestive heart failure (CHF; National Institutes of Health, 2022). CHF is caused by inadequate blood flow from the heart to other organs in the body. Slowed blood flow through the heart results in abnormal pressure inside of the heart. As the heart works to accommodate this pressure, the walls of the heart weaken, further compromising the heart's ability to pump blood. Eventually, the tissues being supplied with blood from the heart become congested with fluid.

Fluid builds up in the arms, legs, ankles, feet, lungs, and other organs causing edema (i.e., swelling). Symptoms of CHF include shortness of breath (due to the collection of fluid within the lungs), chest pain, weakness, and swelling. While many disorders can impact the pumping efficiency of the heart, the most common are coronary artery disease, hypertension, chronic heavy alcohol use, and underlying heart disease (i.e., a range of conditions affecting the heart including narrowing of blood vessels, arrhythmia, and congenital heart defects). The incidence of developing CHF increases from approximately 1.9% in middle age to 14.7% between the ages of 80 and 89 (Azad & Lemay, 2014). Treatment for CHF is often dictated by the underlying cause of the disorder. Common treatments include fluid restriction, reduced sodium intake, diuretics, and medications that improve cardiac performance like angiotensin-converting enzyme (ACE) inhibitors and beta blockers. Other interventions include physical exercise, quitting tobacco use, and management of chronic health conditions that may cause CHF (i.e., hypertension, hyperlipidemia, and diabetes; Inamdar & Inamdar, 2016).

Cerebral Arteriosclerosis and Strokes

In addition to the changes noted within the vasculature of the body, there are also diseases related to vascular changes in the brain. Cerebral arteriosclerosis is the hardening of the arteries within the brain (National Institute of Neurological Disorders and Stroke [NINDS], 2023). Additionally, age-related thickening of the artery walls, along with reductions in diameter of the vessels due to accumulation of fatty tissues and calcification, can interfere with blood circulation to the brain. This interference results in the brain being deprived of vital nutrients, vitamins, and oxygen and can lead to a stroke (i.e., the blockage or rupture of the blood vessels).

COMMON DISORDERS OF THE RESPIRATORY SYSTEM

The respiratory system undergoes age-related structural changes that increase the risk for lung infections (e.g., pneumonia and bronchitis) and compound the effects of pre-existing cardiovascular or respiratory diseases.

Coronavirus Disease-19

First infecting people in 2019, coronavirus disease-19 (COVID-19) is a respiratory infectious disease caused by severe acute respiratory syndrome coronavirus 2, or SARS-CoV-2, that typically causes mild to moderate flulike symptoms. Older adults are more susceptible to severe illness, hospitalization, and fatality from COVID-19 infection due to immunosenescence, or age-related immune dysfunction, and the high prevalence of multimorbidity within the population (Abul et al., 2023). Compared with adults aged 18 to 29 years, COVID-19 fatalities are 60 times higher in those aged 65 to 74 years and 360 times higher in those aged 85 years or older (CDC, 2023b). About 9% of older adults experience "long COVID" (i.e., post-acute sequelae of COVID-19), which can entail fatigue, shortness of breath, coughing, cognitive impacts (frequently termed "brain fog"), joint pain, and olfactory and gustatory changes (Mansell et al., 2022). The primary method of preventing severe illness and mortality from COVID-19 infection is via vaccination. Upon infection, over-the-counter medicines (i.e., acetaminophen or ibuprofen) may alleviate mild symptoms, and more severe infection may be prevented with antiviral mediations.

Pneumonia

Pneumonia, the second most common infection in older adults, produces painful labored breathing and reduced oxygen intake. It is an infection or inflammation of one or both lungs that causes the small sacs (e.g., alveoli) in the lungs to fill with pus and fluid. Older adults have a higher prevalence of pneumonia due to their weakened immune system. Cases of bacterial pneumonia can be effectively treated with antibiotics; in contrast, treatment of viral pneumonia focuses on ameliorating the symptoms rather than the cause of the virus itself. Risk factors for the onset of pneumonia include age greater than 65, exposure to infectious environments (i.e., childcare facilities), comorbid chronic illness, alcohol use disorder, malnutrition, and immune suppression (Regunath & Oba, 2021). Post-recovery, older adults often experience long-term sequelae like reduced exercise capacity, worsened CVD, cognitive decline, and reduced quality of life. Pneumococcal vaccines are recommended for older adults, as they are 60% to 80% effective in significantly lowering the risk of serious pneumococcal disease (Shah et al., 2020).

Chronic Obstructive Pulmonary Disease

Chronic obstructive pulmonary disease (COPD) is the progressive restriction of airflow due to inflammation that causes the lungs to thicken and destroy tissue responsible for the exchange of oxygen. Reduced air flow results in less oxygen transmitted to bodily tissues and increased difficulty removing carbon dioxide from the body. Over time, the affected person develops shortness of breath, wheezing, chest tightness, and productive cough. COPD is the third leading cause of death globally (Jarhyan et al., 2022). While smoking tobacco causes up to 70% of COPD cases, other risk factors include age, exposure to air pollution, secondhand smoke, genetic predisposition, and smoke exposure in utero (Lõpez-Campos et al., 2016). COPD can lead to reduced activity and more fatigue as well as have downstream effects including increased vulnerability to CVD, other chronic health conditions, depression, and anxiety (WHO, 2023). Current treatments focus on symptom management. Such treatments include smoking cessation, avoidance of lung irritants, dietary intervention, vitamins or nutritional supplements, physical activity, pulmonary rehabilitation, oxygen therapy, medications (e.g., bronchodilators, inhaled glucocorticosteroids), and vaccination to prevent respiratory infections. In severe cases, surgical interventions such as a bullectomy, lung volume reduction, and a lung transplant may be beneficial.

Asthma

Asthma is a chronic lung disease that causes inflammation and narrowing of the airways. Symptoms of asthma include recurrent wheezing, chest tightness, shortness of breath, and coughing. Older age increases the likelihood of more severe airflow obstruction and asthma presentation overall (Zein et al., 2015). Approximately 10% of older adults experience asthma, yet more than 50% of fatalities related to asthma annually are in older adults (Baptist et al., 2018). The most common causes of late-onset asthma are respiratory infection or virus, exercise, allergens, and air pollution or irritants. Quick-relief medications focus on alleviation of symptom flare-ups. Long-term control medications work to reduce airway inflammation and prevent chronic symptoms like coughing and shortness of breath. Older adults often take other medications (e.g., beta blockers, aspirin, nonsteroidal anti-inflammatory drugs [NSAIDs]) that may reduce the effectiveness of asthma medications or worsen asthma symptoms; thus, it is important for doctors to be aware of all the medications an affected person takes (Hanania & Busse, 2016).

Lung Cancer

Lung cancer is the second most common type of cancer and accounts for more deaths annually than colon, breast, and prostate cancers combined. Two out of three new lung cancer cases are diagnosed in persons aged 65 or older (ACS, 2016). Lung cancer can metastasize to the liver, bone, brain, and adrenal glands. Of note, older adults often present with bony metastases. The primary risk factor for lung cancer is smoking, although 10% to 20% of cases in the United States occur in nonsmokers (Zhang et al., 2021). Additional risk factors include heredity; exposure to radon; history of radiation therapy; secondhand smoke; environmental exposures; and diseases such as COPD, pulmonary fibrosis, and HIV. Precision oncology protocols recommend using a patient's genetics, genome mapping, imaging results, vital signs, metabolic information, lifestyle, living environment, stage of disease, and more to develop an individualized treatment plan. Combinations of treatments may include surgery, chemotherapy, radiation therapy, targeted therapy, and immunotherapy (Guan et al., 2022).

COMMON DISORDERS OF THE ENDOCRINE SYSTEM

Two common endocrine system diseases that can occur with age include diabetes and thyroid dysfunction. These conditions exemplify how dysfunction in one system can create a host of problems throughout the body.

Diabetes

Diabetes, or diabetes mellitus (DM), is described as a group of metabolic diseases caused by either a lack of insulin production by the pancreas or a reduced ability to use insulin, which results in high blood sugar levels, or hyperglycemia (WHO, 2016). Diabetes is divided into two primary categories: type 1 and type 2. As type 1 is an autoimmune response typically diagnosed before young adulthood and accounts for only 5% to 10% of cases (CDC, 2023a), this section will focus primarily on type 2 DM (Figure 5.1). Type 2 DM, accounting for 90% to 95% of cases, is characterized by insulin resistance, or an abnormal cell response to insulin. Approximately 20% to 30% of older adults have type 2 DM, while an estimated 16% are undiagnosed (Laiteerapong & Elbert, 2018). Up to one in two older adults are estimated to have prediabetes, a state in which blood sugar levels are above normal but still below the range classified as diabetic (CDC, 2022).

Acute symptoms of type 2 DM include polyuria (increased urine production), polydipsia (excessive thirst), weight loss, and blurred vision (Cloete, 2022). While these short-term symptoms may seem innocuous, early intervention is critical, as the long-term symptoms are severe and often irreversible. Over time, high blood glucose levels damage blood vessels in the brain, heart, eyes, kidneys, and nerves through the body. This damage leads to reduced neuronal connectivity, cognitive decline, renal failure, peripheral neuropathy, peripheral artery disease, and increased risk for blindness, stroke, heart attack, and mortality (Laiteerapong & Elbert, 2018; Moheet et al., 2015). Risks for the onset of type 2 DM include age, obesity, physical inactivity, diet, education level, family history, race/ethnicity, high blood pressure, abnormal cholesterol levels, and a prior diagnosis of gestational diabetes (American Diabetes Association, 2022; Forouhi & Wareham, 2019).

Early detection and management of risk factors (i.e., lifestyle, weight, blood pressure, and cholesterol) are the first steps to preventing or delaying the onset of DM. Pharmaceutical treatment protocols for type 2 DM often target cholesterol, blood pressure, and blood sugar, and more severe cases of type 2 DM will require insulin injections (Laiteerapong & Elbert, 2018).

Hyperthyroidism

Hyperthyroidism is a condition where the thyroid synthesizes and secretes too much thyroid hormone (Bahn et al., 2011). The prevalence of hyperthyroidism increases among older adults (frequencies range from 1%–3%; Samuels, 2021). Toxic

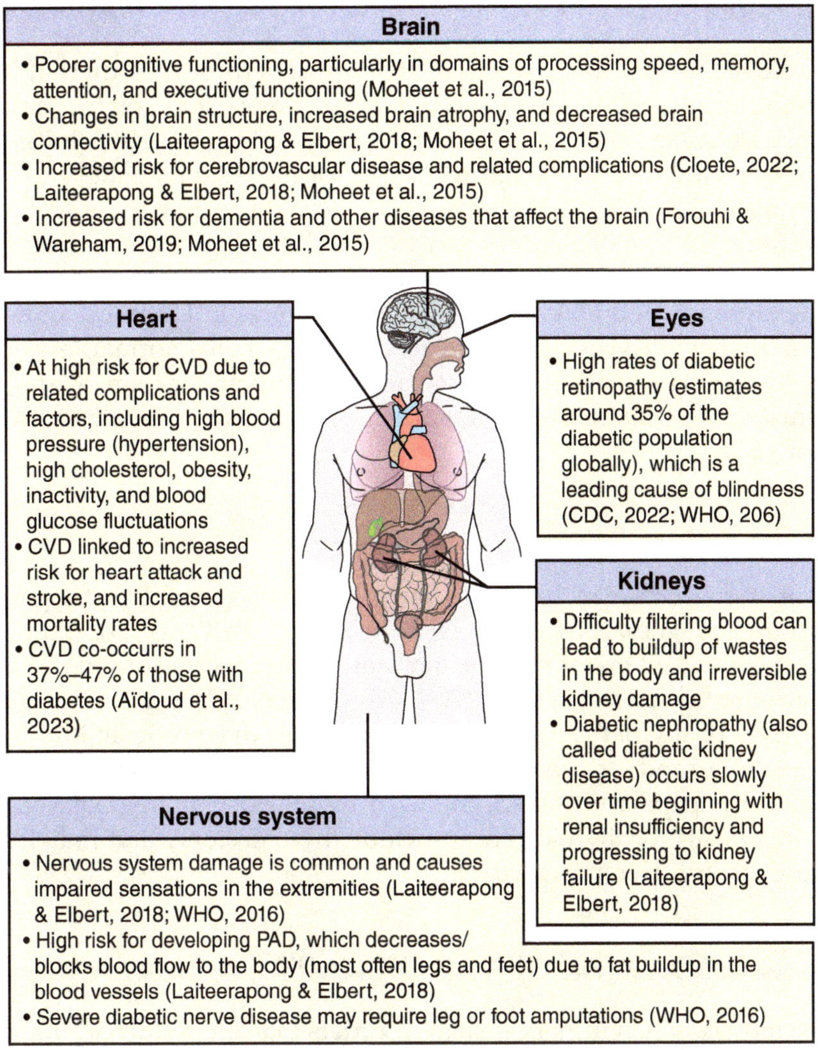

Brain
- Poorer cognitive functioning, particularly in domains of processing speed, memory, attention, and executive functioning (Moheet et al., 2015)
- Changes in brain structure, increased brain atrophy, and decreased brain connectivity (Laiteerapong & Elbert, 2018; Moheet et al., 2015)
- Increased risk for cerebrovascular disease and related complications (Cloete, 2022; Laiteerapong & Elbert, 2018; Moheet et al., 2015)
- Increased risk for dementia and other diseases that affect the brain (Forouhi & Wareham, 2019; Moheet et al., 2015)

Heart
- At high risk for CVD due to related complications and factors, including high blood pressure (hypertension), high cholesterol, obesity, inactivity, and blood glucose fluctuations
- CVD linked to increased risk for heart attack and stroke, and increased mortality rates
- CVD co-occurrs in 37%–47% of those with diabetes (Aïdoud et al., 2023)

Eyes
- High rates of diabetic retinopathy (estimates around 35% of the diabetic population globally), which is a leading cause of blindness (CDC, 2022; WHO, 206)

Kidneys
- Difficulty filtering blood can lead to buildup of wastes in the body and irreversible kidney damage
- Diabetic nephropathy (also called diabetic kidney disease) occurs slowly over time beginning with renal insufficiency and progressing to kidney failure (Laiteerapong & Elbert, 2018)

Nervous system
- Nervous system damage is common and causes impaired sensations in the extremities (Laiteerapong & Elbert, 2018; WHO, 2016)
- High risk for developing PAD, which decreases/blocks blood flow to the body (most often legs and feet) due to fat buildup in the blood vessels (Laiteerapong & Elbert, 2018)
- Severe diabetic nerve disease may require leg or foot amputations (WHO, 2016)

Figure 5.1 Long-term problems associated with diabetes mellitus.

multinodular goiter and Graves disease are common causes of hyperthyroidism in older adults. Symptoms of hyperthyroidism include appetite or weight loss and muscle weakness or wasting. Older adults have fewer signs and symptoms compared with their younger counterparts, which may make it more difficult to detect (Samuels, 2021). If untreated, hyperthyroidism can lead to cardiovascular complications, gastrointestinal symptoms (e.g., diarrhea or constipation), insulin resistance, osteoporosis, and neurological symptoms or cognitive decline (Samuels, 2021). Subclinical hyperthyroidism, which is diagnosed when thyroid-stimulating hormone (TSH) levels are low but triiodothyronine (T_3) and thyroxine (T_4) are within the normal range, is also prevalent among older adults (ranging from 0.8% to 2%; Ross et al., 2016; Samuels, 2021). Depending on the cause and severity of the hyperthyroidism, treatment may involve radioactive iodine, antithyroid or beta-blocking medications, or thyroidectomy (Bahn et al., 2011).

Hypothyroidism

Hypothyroidism, a condition when the thyroid underproduces thyroid hormones, affects up to 17% of adults aged 65 and older and is more common in women than in men (Kim, 2020). Over half of the cases of hypothyroidism in older adults are caused by autoimmune thyroiditis, though treatment for hyperthyroidism can also lead to hypothyroidism (Kim, 2020). As with hyperthyroidism, hypothyroidism presents slightly differently in older adults and can be difficult to detect. Symptoms may include fatigue, weakness, cold intolerance, CHF, dry skin, depression, neurological symptoms, dyspnea, and wheezing (Kim, 2020). Subclinical hypothyroidism, which is diagnosed when TSH levels are elevated but T_4 remains normal, is important to detect, as it is correlated with cardiovascular risk factors and insulin resistance. Hypothyroidism is commonly treated with the drug levothyroxine, a synthetic thyroid hormone (Kim, 2020).

Thyroid Cancer

The rates of thyroid cancer in the United States have risen threefold in the past 40 years; the risk of onset is highest between the ages of 40 and 75 (Williams, 2015). Yet despite the increased prevalence of thyroid cancer, mortality rates (reported around 0.5 deaths per 100,000) have remained stable since the 1970s (National Cancer Institute, 2024). The increased rates of thyroid cancer could reflect better diagnostic abilities (i.e., ultrasound availability) and/or overdiagnosis (Williams, 2015). The most common type of thyroid cancer is papillary thyroid, followed by follicular thyroid cancer. The most common treatments for thyroid cancer include thyroidectomy and radioiodine ablation (Sajid-Crokett & Hershman, 2015).

COMMON DISORDERS OF THE URINARY SYSTEM

Two of the most common urinary system disorders that affect older adults are urinary tract infections (UTIs) and chronic kidney disease (CKD).

Urinary Tract Infections

A UTI is an infection of the urinary system that may involve only the lower urinary tract or both the upper and lower tracts. UTIs are highly prevalent in older adults and are recognized as the most common type of infection in long-term care (LTC) facilities (Herzig et al., 2017). UTIs are more common in older women; roughly 10% of women older than age 65 have experienced a UTI in the past year. The prevalence rate increases threefold in women aged 85 and older (Rowe & Juthani-Mehta, 2013). Risk factors in older adults include reduced immune response, exposure to hospital-associated pathogens, increased rates of urinary incontinence and retention, urinary catheterizations, vaginal atrophy, prostatic hyperplasia, and higher rates of comorbidity (Cortes-Penfield et al., 2017). Accurate and early diagnosis of UTIs in older adults with cognitive impairment can be challenging due to difficulty expressing the nature of their symptoms to providers. Use of antibiotics is the most common treatment for UTIs.

Chronic Kidney Disease

CKD affects about 50% of adults aged 70 or older and broadly includes any condition that damages the kidneys over a period of months to years (Levey et al., 2015). The two most common causes of CKD are diabetes and hypertension. As the kidneys grow more impaired, a buildup of waste and fluid accumulates in the body, which then affects most organ systems. Symptoms of CKD vary by the disease state. In the early stages, symptoms are nonspecific and include loss of appetite, general malaise, headaches, pruritus, and nausea. With greater kidney damage, symptoms include skin discoloration, bone pain, drowsiness, problems concentrating, numbness and swelling in the extremities, muscle twitching or cramps, bruising, blood in the stool, dehydration, thirst, hiccups, amenorrhea, shortness of breath, sleep problems, and vomiting. Slow symptom progression leads many to not recognize the symptoms until the kidneys have minimal function. The final stage of CKD (i.e., end-stage renal disease) often requires the life-sustaining treatment of chronic dialysis, as the kidneys are unable to process waste or excess fluid (Kalantar-Zadeh et al., 2021). Other CKD treatments include management of hypertension and hyperlipidemia, as well as lifestyle changes like smoking cessation; increased physical exercise; and dietary changes to limit salt, potassium, phosphorous, protein, and fluids (Fogarty & Tall, 2012).

COMMON DISORDERS OF THE REPRODUCTIVE SYSTEM

Older men and women experience higher rates of cancer in the reproductive system. The most common cancers of the reproductive system are uterine and ovarian cancer (in females) and prostate cancer (in males).

Uterine and Ovarian Cancer

Uterine cancer is a gynecologic cancer that begins when cells in the uterus proliferate, change, and form a malignant tumor. Uterine cancer is the most common gynecologic cancer, as it affects over 60,000 women annually (ACS, 2023a). Endometrial cancer, a subtype of uterine cancer, is more common in older women, with the median age of onset being 62 years (Duska et al., 2016). While uterine cancer is more common in European American women, African Americans are more likely to die from the disease (Mukerji et al., 2018). Symptoms of uterine cancer include unusual vaginal bleeding, difficulty or pain when urinating, pain during intercourse, and pain in the pelvic area. The 5-year survival rate for localized uterine cancer is 96% (ACS, 2023c). The 10-year survival rate is around 79%. Uterine cancer treatments include surgery, radiation, chemotherapy, and hormone therapy (ACS, 2016).

Ovarian cancer is a gynecologic cancer that originates in cells in the ovaries, fallopian tube, or peritoneum. Over 22,000 women in the United States are diagnosed with ovarian cancer annually. Survival rates of ovarian cancer are lower than uterine cancer; the 5-year survival rate for women aged 65 and older is 28%. Women with a family history of breast or ovarian cancer and with certain genetic conditions (e.g., Lynch syndrome, Peutz–Jeghers syndrome, nevoid basal cell carcinoma, and ataxia-telangiectasia) develop ovarian cancer at higher rates. Women who are obese have a 50% greater risk of developing ovarian cancer and have a higher mortality risk from the disease. Women of North American, Northern European, and Ashkenazi Jewish heritage have a greater risk of developing ovarian cancer, as do women who have not had children or have not taken birth control. Recommended treatments include surgery, chemotherapy, hormone therapy, targeted therapy to attack specific cancer cells, and radiation therapy (ACS, 2016).

Prostate Cancer

Prostate cancer is one of the most common cancer types that can affect adult men. Men between the ages of 60 to 69 years have a 1 in 19 chance of developing the disease, while men over 70 have a 1 in 8 chance (Siegel et al., 2022). Prostate cancer is the second leading cause of cancer death in men, accounting for approximately 11% of all cancer deaths in men in 2022. The average age of diagnosis is 66 (ACS, 2023b), and prostate cancer is more common in men who have African American and Caribbean African ancestry. Having an affected immediate relative (i.e., father or brother) doubles a person's risk for developing prostate cancer. Persons may be symptom free in the early stages, but with disease progression, they may experience problems urinating, blood in the urine, erectile dysfunction, bone pain, or weakness or numbness in the lower extremities. Treatments for prostate cancer include active surveillance, surgery, radiation therapy, chemotherapy, cryotherapy, hormone therapy, vaccine treatment, and bone-directed treatment. The 5-year relative survival rate for prostate cancer is almost 100% (ACS, 2016) and remains largely stable at the 15-year mark regardless of treatment modality (Hamdy et al., 2023).

COMMON DISORDERS OF THE DIGESTIVE SYSTEM

Despite the digestive system being resistant to age-related changes, aging does influence the development of some digestive system disorders, like constipation and gastritis.

Constipation

Constipation is a condition where a person has fewer than three bowel movements a week; has small, dry, hard, painful stool; or has bowel movements that are difficult to pass. Constipation is considered chronic when it occurs over several weeks. Risk factors for constipation in older adults include reduced physical activity, reduced fluid intake, dietary changes, reduced motility in the large intestine, and medication side effects. Up to 40% of older adults report symptoms of constipation, and the prevalence increases to approximately 80% of LTC residents (Gustafsson et al., 2019). Treatments include lifestyle changes (e.g., increased fiber intake and physical activity) and medication (e.g., laxatives and medication that increases water in the intestine). Surgery is an option for more severe cases of chronic constipation or if the constipation is due to posterior prolapse, anal fissure, or anal stenosis.

Gastritis

Gastritis, or the inflammation of the stomach lining, can cause symptoms of indigestion, nausea, vomiting, and feelings of fullness in the upper abdomen. Older adults have a heightened risk for gastritis due to stomach lining thinning, reduced immune function, greater incidence of bacterial infection (e.g., *Helicobacter pylori*), and greater use of NSAIDs. Other risk factors include chronic heavy alcohol use, stress, and autoimmune disorders. Treatment choice for gastritis is often predicated on the cause. Possible treatments include antibiotics used to kill bacteria like *H pylori,* medications that block acid production and promote healing of the gut, medications that reduce acid production, and antacids that neutralize stomach acid (Feldstein et al., 2017).

CONCLUSION

Most older adults are diagnosed with at least one chronic health condition in late life, and many experience comorbid conditions that impact multiple organ systems simultaneously. While the common diseases affecting older adults range in severity, many are treatable and/or preventable with appropriate lifestyle changes and pharmacological intervention. Therefore, older adults and their care teams should be familiar with symptoms often associated with common age-related illnesses to ensure swift intervention and symptom management.

DISCUSSION QUESTIONS

1. Describe why it is important to understand the various physical health conditions that may impact older adults.
2. Offer an example of how dysfunction in one organ system can impact another.
3. Describe common age-related disorders in three of the systems.
4. Describe lifestyle practices that reduce the risk of some age-related illnesses.

A robust set of instructor resources designed to supplement this text is located at http://connect.springerpub.com/content/book/978-0-8261-6617-3. Qualifying instructors may request access by emailing textbook@springerpub.com.

REFERENCES

Abul, Y., Leeder, C., & Gravenstein, S. (2023). Epidemiology and clinical presentation of COVID-19 in older adults. *Infectious Disease Clinics of North America, 37*(1), 1–26. https://doi.org/10.1016/j.idc.2022.11.001

Aïdoud, A., Gana, W., Poitau, F., Debacq, C., Leroy, V., Nkodo, J., Poupin, P., Angoulvant, D., & Fougère, B. (2023). High prevalence of geriatric conditions among older adults with cardiovascular disease. *Journal of the American Heart Association, 12*(2), e026850. https://doi.org/10.1161/jaha.122.026850

American Cancer Society. (2016). *Cancer facts & figures 2016.* American Cancer Society.

American Cancer Society. (2023a). *Key statistics for endometrial cancer.* https://www.cancer.org/content/dam/CRC/PDF/Public/8609.00.pdf

American Cancer Society. (2023b). *Key statistics for prostate cancer.* https://www.cancer.org/content/dam/CRC/PDF/Public/8793.00.pdf

American Cancer Society. (2023c). *Survival rates for endometrial cancer.* https://www.cancer.org/cancer/types/endometrial-cancer/detection-diagnosis-staging/survival-rates.html

American Diabetes Association. (2022). *Statistics about diabetes.* https://diabetes.org/about-us/statistics/about-diabetes

Azad, N., & Lemay, G. (2014). Management of chronic heart failure in the older population. *Journal of Geriatric Cardiology, 11*(4), 329–337. https://doi.org/10.11909/j.issn.1671-5411.2014.04.008

Bahn, R. S., Burch, H. B., Cooper, D. S., Garber, J. R., Greenlee, M. C., Klein, I., Laurberg, P., McDougall, I. R., Montori, V. M., Rivkees, S. A., Ross, D. S., Sosa, J. A., & Stan, M. N. (2011). Hyperthyroidism and other causes of thyrotoxicosis: Management guidelines of the American Thyroid Association and American Association of Clinical Endocrinologists. *Thyroid, 21*(6), 593–646. https://doi.org/10.1089/thy.2010.0417

Baptist, A. P., Hao, W., Karamched, K. R., Kaur, B., Carpenter, L., & Song, P. X. K. (2018). Distinct asthma phenotypes among older adults with asthma. *Journal of Allergy and Clinical Immunology: In Practice, 6*(1), 244–249.e2. https://doi.org/10.1016/j.jaip.2017.06.010

Bergler-Klein, J. (2019). What's new in the ESC 2018 guidelines for arterial hypertension. *Wiener Klinische Wochenschrift, 131*(7–8), 180–185. https://doi.org/10.1007/s00508-018-1435-8

Butterfield, N. C., Curry, K. F., Steinberg, J., Dewhurst, H., Komla-Ebri, D., Mannan, N. S., Adoum, A.-T., Leitch, V. D., Logan, J. G., Waung, J. A., Ghirardello, E., Southam, L., Youlten, S. E., Mark Wilkinson, J., McAninch, E. A., Vancollie, V. E., Kussy, F., White, J. K., Lelliott, C. J., …, Duncan Bassett, J. H. (2021). *Accelerating functional gene discovery in osteoarthritis.* https://doi.org/10.1101/836221

Centers for Disease Control and Prevention. (2017). *What everyone should know about shingles vaccine.* https://www.cdc.gov/vaccines/vpd/shingles/public/index.html

Centers for Disease Control and Prevention. (2022). *Prevalence of prediabetes among adults.* https://www.cdc.gov/diabetes/data/statistics-report/prevalence-of-prediabetes.html

Centers for Disease Control and Prevention. (2023a). *Diabetes in the US: A snapshot.* https://www.cdc.gov/diabetes/images/library/socialmedia/DiabetesInTheUS_Print.pdf

Centers for Disease Control and Prevention. (2023b). *Risk for COVID-19 infection, hospitalization, and death by age group.* https://www.cdc.gov/coronavirus/2019-ncov/covid-data/investigations-discovery/hospitalization-death-by-age.html

Chung, B. Y., Um, J. Y., Kim, J. C., Kang, S. Y., Park, C. W., & Kim, H. O. (2020). Pathophysiology and treatment of pruritus in elderly. *International Journal of Molecular Sciences, 22*(1), 174. https://doi.org/10.3390/ijms22010174

Cloete, L. (2022). Diabetes mellitus: An overview of the types, symptoms, complications and management. *Nursing Standard, 37*(1), 61–66. https://doi.org/10.7748/ns.2021.e11709

Cortes-Penfield, N. W., Trautner, B. W., & Jump, R. L. P. (2017). Urinary tract infection and asymptomatic bacteriuria in older adults. *Infectious Disease Clinics, 31*(4), 673–688. https://doi.org/10.1016/j.idc.2017.07.002

Duska, L., Shahrokni, A., & Powell, M. (2016). Treatment of older women with endometrial cancer: Improving outcomes with personalized care. *American Society of Clinical Oncology Educational Book, 35,* 164–174. https://doi.org/10.1200/edbk_158668

Feldstein, R., Beyda, D. J., & Katz, S. (2017). Aging and the gastrointestinal system. In H. M. Fillit, K. Rockwood, & J. Young (Eds.), *Brocklehurst's textbook of geriatric medicine and gerontology* (8th ed., pp. 127–132). Elsevier.

Fillit, H. M., Rockwood, K., & Young, J. (2017). *Brocklehurst's textbook of geriatric medicine and gerontology* (8th ed.). Elsevier.

Fogarty, D. G., & Tall, M. W. (2012). A stepped care approach to the management of chronic kidney disease. In M. W. Taal, G. M. Chertow, P. A. Marsden, A. Skorecki, A. S. L. Yu, & B. M. Brenner, (Eds.), *Brenner and Rector's the kidney* (9th ed., pp. 2205–2239). Elsevier Saunders.

Forouhi, N. G., & Wareham, N. J. (2019). Epidemiology of diabetes. In *Medicine (United Kingdom)* (Vol. 47, Issue 1, pp. 22–27). Elsevier Ltd. https://doi.org/10.1016/j.mpmed.2018.10.004

Glowacki, J., & Vokes, T. (2016). Osteoporosis and mechanisms of skeletal aging. In F. Sierra & R. Kohanski (Eds.), *Advances in geroscience* (pp. 277–308). Springer.

Gregson, C. L., Armstrong, D. J., Bowden, J., Cooper, C., Edwards, J., Gittoes, N. J., Harvey, N., Kanis, J., Leyland, S., Low, R., McCloskey, E., Moss, K., Parker, J., Paskins, Z., Poole, K., Reid, D. M., Stone, M., Thomson, J., Vine, N., & Compston, J. (2022). UK clinical guideline for the prevention and treatment of osteoporosis. *Archives of Osteoporosis, 17*(1), 58. https://doi.org/10.1007/s11657-022-01061-5

Gustafsson, M., Lämås, K., Isaksson, U., Sandman, P.-O., & Lövheim, H. (2019). Constipation and laxative use among people living in nursing homes in 2007 and 2013. *BMC Geriatrics, 19*(1), 38. https://doi.org/10.1186/s12877-019-1054-x

Guan, X., Qin, T., & Qi, T. (2022). Precision medicine in lung cancer theranostics: Paving the way from traditional technology to advance era. *Cancer Control, 29*. https://doi.org/10.1177/10732748221077351

Hamdy, F. C., Donovan, J. L., Lane, J. A., Metcalfe, C., Davis, M., Turner, E. L., Martin, R. M., Young, G. J., Walsh, E. I., Bryant, R. J., Bollina, P., Doble, A., Doherty, A., Gillatt, D., Gnanapragasam, V., Hughes, O., Kockelbergh, R., Kynaston, H., Paul, A., …, Neal, D. E. (2023). Fifteen-year outcomes after monitoring, surgery, or radiotherapy for prostate cancer. *New England Journal of Medicine, 388*(17), 1547–1558. https://doi.org/10.1056/NEJMoa2214122

Hanania, N. A., & Busse, P. (2016). Asthma and aging. In F. Sierra & R. Kohanski (Eds.), *Advances in geroscience* (pp. 397–429). Springer.

Herzig, C. T. A., Dick, A. W., Sorbero, M., Pogorzelska-Maziarz, M., Cohen, C. C., Larson, E. L., & Stone, P. W. (2017). Infection trends in US nursing homes, 2006–2013. *Journal of the American Medical Directors Association, 18*(7), 635.e9–635.e20. https://doi.org/10.1016/j.jamda.2017.04.003

Hurst, C., Robinson, S. M., Witham, M. D., Dodds, R. M., Granic, A., Buckland, C., De Biase, S., Finnegan, S., Rochester, L., Skelton, D. A., & Sayer, A. A. (2022). Resistance exercise as a treatment for sarcopenia: Prescription and delivery. *Age and Ageing, 51*(2), afac003. https://doi.org/10.1093/ageing/afac003

Inamdar, A., & Inamdar, A. (2016). Heart failure: Diagnosis, management and utilization. *Journal of Clinical Medicine, 5*(7), 62. https://doi.org/10.3390/jcm5070062

Jarhyan, P., Hutchinson, A., Khaw, D., Prabhakaran, D., & Mohan, S. (2022). Prevalence of chronic obstructive pulmonary disease and chronic bronchitis in eight countries: A systematic review and meta-analysis. *Bulletin of the World Health Organization, 100*(03), 216–230. https://doi.org/10.2471/BLT.21.286870

Kahremany, S., Hofmann, L., Harari, M., Gruzman, A., & Cohen, G. (2021). Pruritus in psoriasis and atopic dermatitis: current treatments and new perspectives. *Pharmacological Reports, 73*(2), 443–453). https://doi.org/10.1007/s43440-020-00206-y

Kalantar-Zadeh, K., Jafar, T. H., Nitsch, D., Neuen, B. L., & Perkovic, V. (2021). Chronic kidney disease. *The Lancet, 398*(10302), 786–802. https://doi.org/10.1016/S0140-6736(21)00519-5

Kim, M. I. (2020). Hypothyroidism in older adults. In K. R. Feingold, B. Anawalt, M. R. Blackman, et al. (Eds.), *Endotext [Internet]*. MDText.com, Inc.

Laiteerapong, N., & Elbert S. H. (2018). Diabetes in older adults. In C. C. Cowie, S. S. Casagrande, A. Menke, et al. (Eds), *Diabetes in America* (3rd ed., Chapter 16). National Institute of Diabetes and Digestive and Kidney Diseases.

Levey, A. S., Inker, L. A., & Coresh, J. (2015). Chronic kidney disease in older people. *Journal of the American Medical Association, 314*(6), 557–558. https://doi.org/10.1001/jama.2015.6753

Löhler, J., Cebulla, M., Shehata-Dieler, W., Volkenstein, S., Völter, C., & Walther, L. E. (2019). Hearing impairment in old age. *Deutsches Ärzteblatt International, 116*, 301–310. https://doi.org/10.3238/arztebl.2019.0301

López-Campos, J. L., Tan, W., & Soriano, J. B. (2016). Global burden of COPD. *Respirology, 21*(1), 14–23. https://doi.org/10.1111/resp.12660

Maldonado Fernández, M., Shin, J., Scherer, R. W., & Murdin, L. (2017). Interventions for tinnitus in adults: an overview of systematic reviews. *Cochrane Database of Systematic Reviews, 2017*(1), CD011795. https://doi.org/10.1002/14651858.CD011795.pub2

Mansell, V., Hall Dykgraaf, S., Kidd, M., & Goodyear-Smith, F. (2022). Long COVID and older people. *The Lancet Healthy Longevity, 3*(12), e849–e854. https://doi.org/10.1016/S2666-7568(22)00245-8

Mayo Clinic. (2022). *Tinnitus*. https://www.mayoclinic.org/diseases-conditions/tinnitus/symptoms-causes/syc-20350156

Mobasheri, A., Saarakkala, S., Finnilä, M., Karsdal, M. A., Bay-Jensen, A.-C., & van Spil, W. E. (2019). Recent advances in understanding the phenotypes of osteoarthritis. *F1000Research, 8*, 2091. https://doi.org/10.12688/f1000research.20575.1

Moheet, A., Mangia, S., & Seaquist, E. R. (2015). Impact of diabetes on cognitive function and brain structure. *Annals of the New York Academy of Sciences, 1353*, 60–71. https://doi.org/10.1111/nyas.12807

Moller, A. R. (2016). Sensorineural tinnitus: Its pathology and probable therapies. *International Journal of Otolaryngology, 2016*, 2830157. https://doi.org/10.1155/2016/2830157

Montecucco, F., Pende, A., Quercioli, A., & Mach, F. (2011). Inflammation in the pathophysiology of essential hypertension. *Journal of Nephrology, 24*(1), 23–34. https://doi.org/10.5301/jn.2010.4729

Mosley, W. J., & Lloyd-Jones, D. M. (2009). Epidemiology of hypertension in the elderly. *Clinics in Geriatric Medicine, 25*(2), 179–189. https://doi.org/10.1016/j.cger.2009.01.002

Mukerji, B., Baptiste, C., Chen, L., Tergas, A. I., Hou, J. Y., Ananth, C. V., Neugut, A. I., Hershman, D. L., & Wright, J. D. (2018). Racial disparities in young women with endometrial cancer. *Gynecologic Oncology, 148*(3), 527–534. https://doi.org/10.1016/j.ygyno.2017.12.032

National Cancer Institute. (2024). *Cancer stat facts: Thyroid cancer*. https://seer.cancer.gov/statfacts/html/thyro.html

National Eye Institute. (2015). *Facts about cataracts*. https://nei.nih.gov/health/cataract

National Eye Institute (2021). *Age-related macular degeneration (AMD)*. https://www.nei.nih.gov/learn-about-eye-health/eye-conditions-and-diseases/age-related-macular-degeneration

National Institutes of Health. (2022). *Congestive heart failure*. https://www.ncbi.nlm.nih.gov/books/NBK430873/

National Institute of Neurological Disorders and Stroke. (2023). *Cerebral arteriosclerosis*. https://www.ninds.nih.gov/health-information/disorders/cerebral-arteriosclerosis#toc-how-can-i-or-my-loved-one-help-improve-care-for-people-with-cerebral-arteriosclerosis-

Noh, T.-S., Kyong, J.-S., Park, M. K., Lee, J. H., Oh, S. H., & Suh, M.-W. (2020). Dual-site rTMS is more effective than single-site rTMS in tinnitus patients: A blinded randomized controlled trial. *Brain Topography, 33*(6), 767–775. https://doi.org/10.1007/s10548-020-00797-y

Ong, K. L., Cheung, B. M. Y., Man, Y. B., Lau, C. P., & Lam, K. S. L. (2007). Prevalence, awareness, treatment, and control of hypertension among United States adults 1999–2004. *Hypertension, 49*(1), 69–75. https://doi.org/10.1161/01.HYP.0000252676.46043.18

Oparil, S., Zaman, M. A., & Calhoun, D. A. (2003). Pathogenesis of hypertension. *Annals of Internal Medicine, 139*(9), 761. https://doi.org/10.7326/0003-4819-139-9-200311040-00011

Pascual-Fernández, J., Fernández-Montero, A., Córdova-Martínez, A., Pastor, D., Martínez-Rodríguez, A., & Roche, E. (2020). Sarcopenia: Molecular pathways and potential targets for intervention. *International Journal of Molecular Sciences, 21*(22), 1–16. https://doi.org/10.3390/ijms21228844

Pierwola, K. K., Patel, G. A., Lambert, W. C., & Schwarz, R. A. (2017). Skin disease and old age. In H. M. Fillit, K. Rockwood, & J. Young (Eds.), *Brocklehurst's textbook of geriatric medicine and gerontology* (8th ed., pp. 789–798). Elsevier.

Quiñones, A. R., Markwardt, S., & Botoseneanu, A. (2016). Multimorbidity combinations and disability in older adults. *The Journals of Gerontology: Series A, 71*(6), 823–830. https://doi.org/10.1093/GERONA/GLW035

Regunath, H., & Oba, Y. (2021). Community-acquired pneumonia. In *StatPearls [Internet]*. StatPearls Publishing.

Ross, D. S., Burch, H. B., Cooper, D. S., Greenlee, M. C., Laurberg, P., Maia, A. L., Rivkees, S. A., Samuels, M., Sosa, J. A., Stan, M. N., & Walter, M. A. (2016). 2016 American Thyroid Association guidelines for diagnosis and management of hyperthyroidism and other causes of thyrotoxicosis. *Thyroid, 26*(10), 1343–1421. https://doi.org/10.1089/thy.2016.0229

Roth, T. N. (2015). *Aging of the auditory system* (pp. 357–373). https://doi.org/10.1016/B978-0-444-62630-1.00020-2

Rowe, T. A., & Juthani-Mehta, M. (2013). Urinary tract infection in older adults. *Aging Health, 9*(5), 519–528. https://doi.org/10.2217/ahe.13.38

Sajid-Crokett, S., & Hershman, J. (2015). Thyroid nodules and cancer in the elderly. In L. J. De Groot, G. Chrousos, K. Dungan, A. Grossman, J. M. Hershman, C. Koch, M. Korbonits, R. McLachlan, M. New, J. Purnell, R. Rebar, F. Singer, & A. Vinik (Eds.), *Endotext*. MDText.com, Inc. https://www.ncbi.nlm.nih.gov/books/NBK278969

Samuels, M. H. (2021). Hyperthyroidism in aging. In K. R. Feingold, B. Anawalt, M. R. Blackman, et al. (Eds.), *Endotext*. MDText.com, Inc.

Shah, P., Woytanowski, J. R., Hadeh, A., Sockrider, M., Reviewers, D., & dela Cruz, C. S. (2020). *Pneumococcal (pneumonia) vaccines*. American Thoracic Society. https://www.thoracic.org/patients/patient-resources/resources/pneumonia-vaccines.pdf

Siegel, R. L., Miller, K. D., Fuchs, H. E., & Jemal, A. (2022). Cancer statistics, 2022. *CA: A Cancer Journal for Clinicians, 72*(1), 7–33. https://doi.org/10.3322/caac.21708

Singer, A., Exuzides, A., Spangler, L., O'Malley, C., Colby, C., Johnston, K., Agodoa, I., Baker, J., & Kagan, R. (2015). Burden of illness for osteoporotic fractures compared with other serious diseases among postmenopausal women in the United States. *Mayo Clinic Proceedings, 90*(1), 53–62. https://doi.org/10.1016/j.mayocp.2014.09.011

Tu, N. C., & Friedman, R. A. (2018). Age-related hearing loss: Unraveling the pieces. *Laryngoscope Investigative Otolaryngology, 3*(2), 68–72. https://doi.org/10.1002/lio2.134

U.S. Department of Health and Human Services. (2023, March 13). *Peripheral neuropathy*. National Institute of Neurological Disorders and Stroke. https://www.ninds.nih.gov/health-information/disorders/peripheral-neuropathy

Williams, D. (2015). Thyroid growth and cancer. *European Thyroid Journal, 4*(3), 164–173. https://doi.org/10.1159/000437263

World Health Organization. (2016). *Global report on diabetes*. WHO Press. https://www.who.int/publications/i/item/9789241565257

World Health Organization. (2023). *Chronic obstructive pulmonary disease (COPD)*. WHO. https://www.who.int/news-room/fact-sheets/detail/chronic-obstructive-pulmonary-disease-(copd)

Zhang, T., Joubert, P., Ansari-Pour, N., Zhao, W., Hoang, P. H., Lokanga, R., Moye, A. L., Rosenbaum, J., Gonzalez-Perez, A., Martínez-Jiménez, F., Castro, A., Muscarella, L. A., Hofman, P., Consonni, D., Pesatori, A. C., Kebede, M., Li, M., Gould Rothberg, B. E., Peneva, I., . . . Landi, M. T. (2021). Genomic and evolutionary classification of lung cancer in never smokers. *Nature Genetics, 53*(9), 1348–1359. https://doi.org/10.1038/s41588-021-00920-0

Zein, J. G., Dweik, R. A., Comhair, S. A., Bleecker, E. R., Moore, W. C., Peters, S. P., Busse, W. W., Jarjour, N. N., Calhoun, W. J., Castro, M., Chung, K. F., Fitzpatrick, A., Israel, E., Teague, W. G., Wenzel, S. E., Love, T. E., Gaston, B. M., & Erzurum, S. C. (2015). Asthma is more severe in older adults. *PLoS ONE, 10*(7), e0133490. https://doi.org/10.1371/journal.pone.0133490

6

Changes to the Brain: Methods of Investigation, Aging, and Neuroplasticity

Tyler A. Rickards, Emily E. Smith, Juliana Baldo, and Brian P. Yochim

LEARNING OBJECTIVES

- Discriminate among CT, MRI, fMRI, PET, SPECT, and EEG neuroimaging methods in the information they can provide and their level of burden to patients or research participants.
- Propose a cognitive subtraction study for a cognitive process of interest.
- Describe the "last in, first out" conceptualization of human brain aging and the neurobiological basis of this and apply this to research findings of differential aging of areas of the brain.
- Define "neuroplasticity," especially as it applies to the human brain.
- Apply Kleim and Jones's principles of neural plasticity to learning a new skill (e.g., learning to play an instrument; using one's nondominant hand for daily living activities after suffering a broken arm).
- Discuss behavioral factors that have been found to enhance neuroplasticity.

The goal of this chapter is to explore changes that occur to the brain, beginning with an overview of modern technologies that are used to answer questions about brain structure and function in older adults. Thereafter, a brief summary of changes that occur to the brain with normal aging is provided, followed by an overview of neuroplasticity.

PART 1: METHODS OF INVESTIGATING AGE-RELATED CHANGES IN THE BRAIN

Neuroimaging techniques are used to visualize and measure neurologic changes associated with brain aging, both for clinical purposes and research purposes. Early investigations of brain changes associated with aging were limited to postmortem data. In the 1970s, a revolution in brain imaging began with CT (computed tomography), which allowed an individual's brain to be visualized in vivo (Hounsfield, 1980). This major advance greatly facilitated brain-behavior research in all areas of neurology because a patient's symptoms or deficits could be assessed and related directly to the presence of current brain changes. CT scanning relies on x-rays to visualize brain tissue and then reconstructs a series of slices to allow for a 3D visualization of the brain. Early CT scans had relatively poor spatial resolution, producing fuzzy or grainy-looking pictures of the brain that lacked detail, and thus MRI (magnetic resonance imaging; described later) soon became the chosen method for assessing changes associated with aging. CT is still a preferred method of brain imaging in certain instances, however, such as when cost is a concern (as CT scans are much cheaper than MRI scans), if rapid scanning is needed, and in cases where MRI is contraindicated (such as when an individual has a pacemaker, metal fragment, or any other implant that is susceptible to magnetic forces).

By the 1980s, MRI technology was developed, which allowed for a much better spatial resolution and crisper brain images than CT imaging (see Figure 6.1; Sijbers et al., 1996). In addition, MRI does not expose individuals to the potentially harmful effects of ionizing radiation as in CT scanning. MRI works by placing an individual on a table that slides into a large, powerful magnet. This magnet has the effect of lining up all the protons in the brain and other parts of the body within the imaging field or

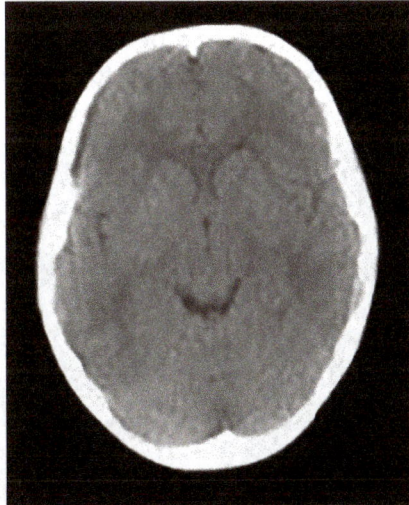 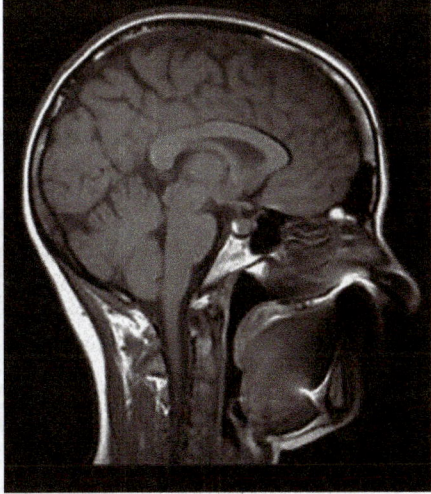

Figure 6.1 CT image shown on the left. On the right, MRI image of a mid-sagittal slice in a healthy individual, facing right. Prominent features include the gyri and sulci of the cerebral hemisphere, the cerebellum tucked underneath, the corpus callosum (the white, curved band across the middle), and the brainstem and spinal cord extending from the midbrain down into the neck.
Source: Image courtesy of Brian Curran.

targeted area. Next, a radio frequency pulse is emitted from the scanner, which causes all of the protons to get out of alignment. After the radio frequency pulse stops, the protons start to realign themselves within the field of the magnet, which is always "on." A computer in the scanner records two important bits of information: (a) the time it takes for the protons to get back into alignment and (b) the amount of energy they release to do so. Based on these two pieces of information, it is possible to deduce the type of tissue or fluid a proton is part of (e.g., bone, blood, cerebrospinal fluid, gray matter). The computer then "reconstructs" brain images based on this information, producing a series of brain slice images. MRI imaging is used clinically to follow patients' neurologic changes over time and also to conduct research studies to better understand the basis of dementia and related diseases (Chandra et al., 2019).

Modern MRI scanners have a spatial resolution on the order of millimeters, which means that the brain images look more like actual brain tissue and are much less fuzzy than CT or early MRI images. Typical MRI scanners used today for clinical purposes (e.g., in a hospital) have a field-strength of 1.5 to 3 tesla (T), and MRI scanners used for research are typically 3T but may have a field-strength up to 7T. The "T" refers to tesla, or the strength of the magnetic field. A higher magnetic field allows for better spatial resolution and thus a sharper brain image showing more detail. Such resolution and detail are critical when attempting to identify subtle or statistical changes in brain tissue. The standard of medical care with memory and cognitive complaints in aging often includes acquisition of brain MRI images to establish a baseline measurement that can be repeated over time to monitor changes such as atrophy and also to differentiate between different causes of cognitive and memory changes (e.g., atrophy vs. vascular changes).

Characterizing brain anatomy with MRI typically involves collecting multiple sequences, including T1-weighted, T2-weighted ("T" refers to a "time" constant), and fluid-attenuated inversion recovery (FLAIR) imaging, among others (see Figure 6.2). Each of these MR sequences emphasizes a different aspect of brain anatomy, depending on the tissue characteristics. For example, T1 and T2 images differ with respect to scanner parameters that vary the relaxation times for protons to return to equilibrium

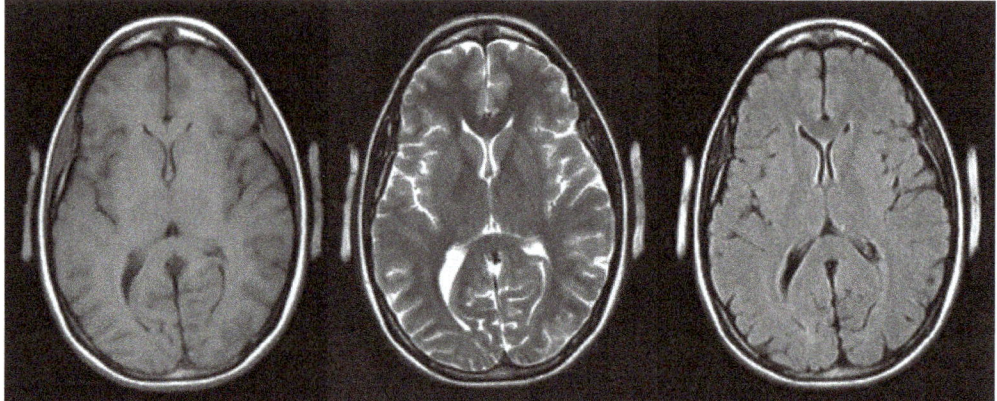

Figure 6.2 MRI slices in the axial plane (i.e., parallel to the ground), showing the distinction in images produced with T1-weighted (left), T2-weighted (middle), and FLAIR (right) sequences.

FLAIR, fluid-attenuated inversion recovery.

Source: Image courtesy of Tyler A. Rickards et al.

after being perturbed by the radio frequency pulse. These distinct relaxation time parameters result in brain images that vary with respect to signal intensity (e.g., fluid appears dark on T1 images but appears bright on T2 images). With FLAIR sequences, the signal from cerebrospinal fluid is suppressed to allow for more sensitivity to smaller changes or lesions in brain tissue that might otherwise be missed.

Diffusion-weighted imaging (DWI) is an additional MR sequence that provides indirect estimates of white matter in the brain (Kruggel et al., 2017; Moody et al., 2022). White matter refers to the brain's bundles of axons (where an axon is the tree trunk–like extension that emanates from the nerve cell body). White matter appears white in the brain because it is covered in a fatty substance, myelin, that helps propagate electrical signals along the axon of the nerve cell. If various brain structures are conceptualized as destinations or cities, the white matter tracts are like the highways or train lines that connect the different cities. Because recent research has shown that the connections between brain regions are important in understanding brain function, the development of imaging methods such as these that can distinguish these white matter tracts has been invaluable.

Diffusion MRI makes use of the fact that the rate of diffusion of water molecules across axon membranes is not random, but rather is constrained by the structure of these axon bundles. When a brain is injured or undergoes changes due to aging, DWI can highlight areas of abnormal diffusion. The information provided by DWI can also be used to reconstruct directional information of the diffusion pattern as a proxy for the underlying white matter pathways. This directional information can then be used to generate white matter maps that show colorized reconstructions of distinct white matter pathways in the brain (known as diffusion tractography). These maps can then be compared across different groups to identify neural changes associated with healthy aging and cognitive decline (Moody et al., 2022; see Figure 6.3).

Another MRI technique that is used in aging research to identify brain changes is magnetic resonance spectroscopy (MRS). MRS does not produce a brain image like T1 or T2 scans, but rather provides numeric information about metabolic activity, structural changes, and general health of the brain tissue as indexed by the amount of several different molecules in a given brain region (Hone-Blancheta et al., 2022; Jett et al., 2023). These MRS-derived levels are compared between an experimental group of interest (e.g., individuals with mild cognitive impairment or individuals with dementia) and a control group (e.g., age-matched, healthy individuals) and can also be used to track brain changes over time.

After an MRI scan is complete, a series of processing steps are undertaken in order to quantify and statistically compare brain images across individuals and groups. Early studies in aging and aging-related diseases made use of volumetric analyses, in which brain regions of interest (ROIs) were manually traced on every brain slice (Ikeda et al., 1994; Murphy et al., 1993). These studies showed a clear reduction in cortical volume in normal aging, and even more so in Alzheimer disease. For such volumetric studies, tracing was typically done on T1 MRI scans, as they provide good definition of the various cortical and subcortical structures in the brain. By the 1990s, computerized software was readily available that made it possible to directly trace brain structures on an MRI image to facilitate this type of analysis. For example, many aging studies have focused on the size of medial temporal lobe structures such as the hippocampus, and the ROI is traced on every brain slice where the hippocampus appears. Next, the number of pixels contained in each ROI on each slice is calculated and then multiplied

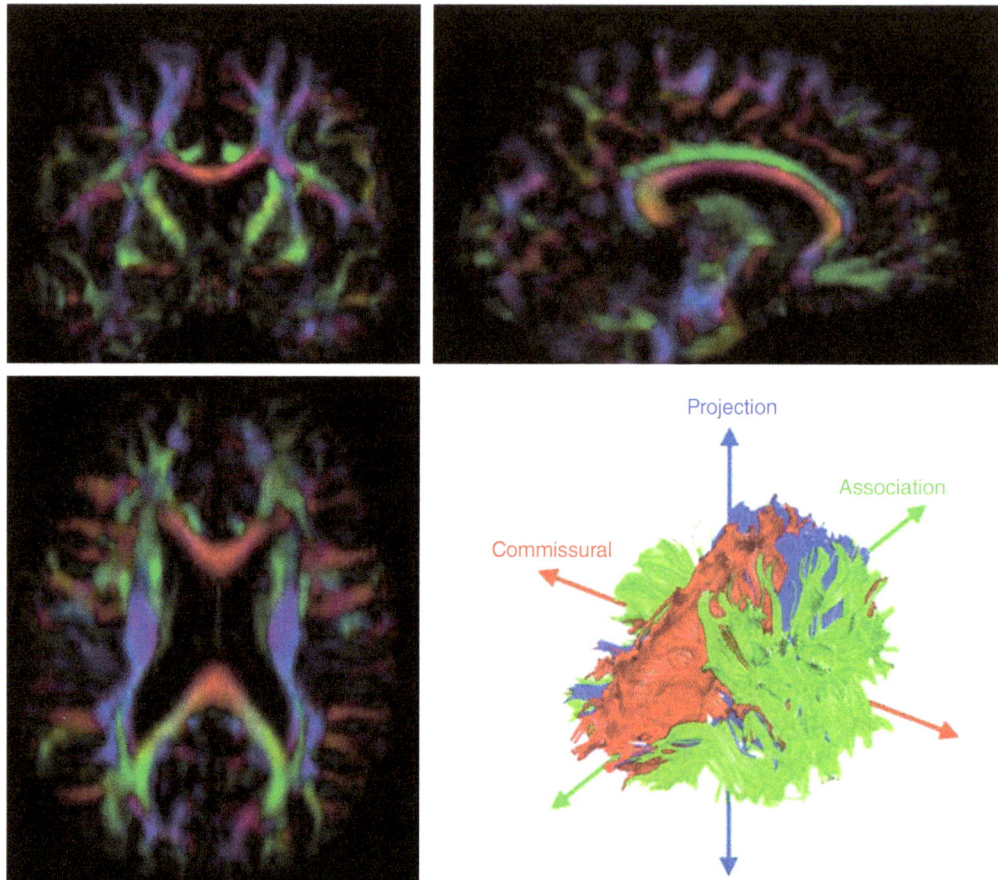

Figure 6.3 Diffusion imaging–derived maps used to reconstruct white matter pathways in the brain.
Source: Image courtesy of Stephanie Forkel.

by the slice thickness to obtain the ROI volume (where slice thickness is the number of millimeters captured in each MRI image). Variables such as a patient's overall cranial volume are also calculated and used as corrections in the analyses. Then, the average volume of the ROI (e.g., the hippocampus) can be compared between groups, such as younger versus older individuals, or healthy older adults versus individuals with dementia. These volumetric results can also then be correlated with behavioral measures (e.g., memory scores) in order to relate behavioral performance to the quantified MRI data (Golomb et al., 1994).

By the beginning of the 21st century, these slice-by-slice volumetric approaches were updated with automated, computerized methods that were more objective and did not require the painstaking work of manually tracing every ROI on every brain slice (Ashburner & Friston, 2000; Khagi et al., 2021; Knudsen et al., 2022). These voxel-based morphometry (VBM) techniques involve comparing the volume of gray and white matter structures across two groups (e.g., healthy older individuals and those with mild cognitive impairment) on a voxel-by-voxel basis (a voxel is a 3D pixel). That is, rather than selecting and manually tracing a particular ROI, VBM allows for a statistical, whole-brain comparison. To run VBM analyses, individuals' MRIs are first

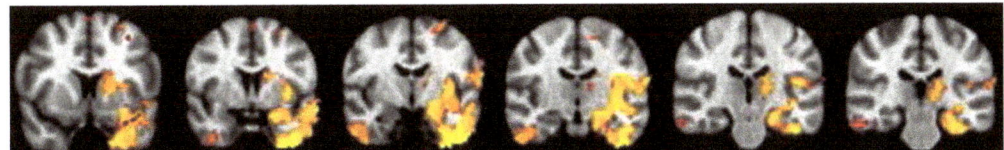

Figure 6.4 Voxel-based morphometry (VBM) map showing significant reductions in temporal lobe gray matter in patients with dementia relative to people without dementia.
Source: From Dalton, M. A., Weickert, T. W., Hodges, J. R., Piguet, O., & Hornberger, M. (2012). Impaired acquisition rates of probabilistic associative learning in frontotemporal dementia is associated with fronto-striatal atrophy. *NeuroImage: Clinical, 2,* 56–62. https://doi.org/10.1016/j.nicl.2012.11.001

"normalized," or warped to fit a representative brain template, so that all individuals' brains can be directly compared in the same reference frame. A spatial smoothing procedure is also applied in order to blur out small individual differences; this process reduces the spatial resolution of an individual image but facilitates the aggregation of data across a very large number of individuals that is not possible with manual data analyses. After normalization, each individual brain is then segmented into gray matter, white matter, and cerebrospinal fluid. The resultant VBM map is displayed on an average or standard MRI image, with a scale indicating those regions in which there are statistical differences in volume between the two groups (see Figure 6.4). One can also correlate voxel-wise measures with a variable such as age in order to study within-group, interindividual differences or to study longitudinal changes within the same individual. For example, VBM studies have been used to show the linear relationship between cognitive decline and reductions in gray matter in normal aging, as well as the neural progression of diseases such as Alzheimer disease over time. More recent VBM studies also make use of advanced statistical techniques and machine learning to help identify patterns associated with distinct dementia-related patterns in the brain (Nemoto et al., 2021; Rossini et al., 2022).

While the development of *structural* brain imaging techniques such as CT and MRI provide scientists with a snapshot of an individual's brain at a given point in time (analogous to a photograph), newer *functional* brain imaging methods allow scientists to measure ongoing regional brain activity. The earliest of these techniques, electroencephalography (EEG), is a relatively inexpensive and noninvasive technique that measures electrical brain activity by placing recording electrodes on the scalp. Differences in EEG patterns can be discerned between different patient groups (e.g., people with dementia vs. mild cognitive impairment) or different age groups (e.g., younger vs. older; Doan et al., 2021; Torres-Simón et al., 2022). One particular measure that can be derived from the EEG are event-related potentials (ERPs), which measure electrical brain activity that is time-locked to a given event or stimulus (e.g., the pattern of electrical activity produced every time a participant hears an unexpected word or sound; Choi et al., 2023). EEG data, and thus ERP data, provide very high temporal resolution of brain activity (i.e., they can measure electrical brain changes on the order of milliseconds), although they do not afford good spatial resolution like MRI (see Figure 6.5).

A similar, though not widely used, technique is magnetoencephalography (MEG), which measures small magnetic field changes produced by electrical activity in the brain. Like EEG, MEG offers excellent temporal resolution, on the order of milliseconds; however, given the way that magnetic fields interact with each other and with other layers of tissue, MEG provides better spatial estimates for the location of brain

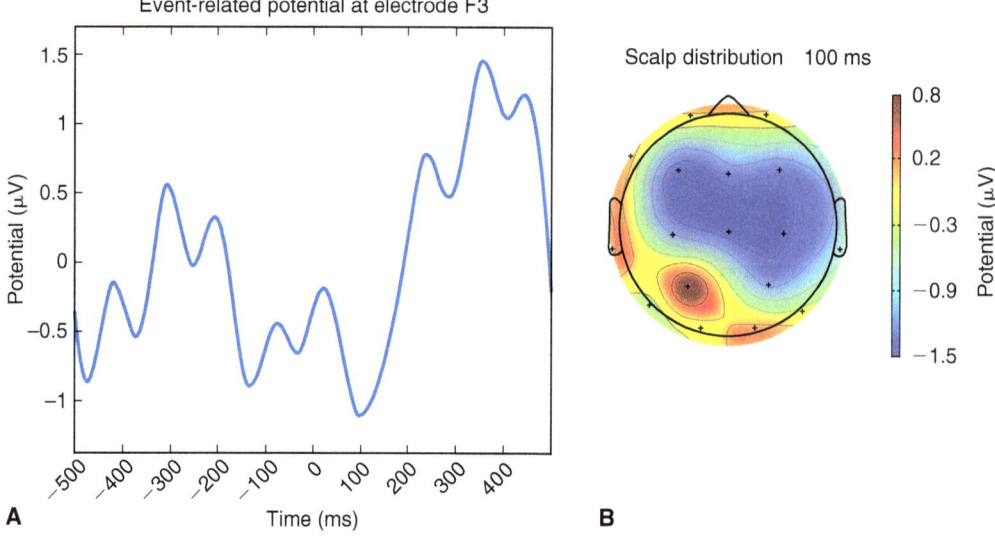

Figure 6.5 (**A**) Event-related brain potential (ERP) time-locked to hearing a drum beat and (**B**) scalp distribution of brain potentials at 100 ms after the drum beat.
ms, millisecond.
Source: Image courtesy of Matt Schalles.

activity than EEG. MEG has been used to identify biomarkers of aging and changes associated with Alzheimer disease and other causes of dementia (Torres-Simón et al., 2022). The drawbacks of MEG are its very high cost and the paucity of MEG centers.

Another set of important functional brain imaging techniques developed in the second half of the 20th century is PET and a related lower-spatial resolution technique, single-photon emission computed tomography (SPECT; Villemagne et al., 2021). For both of these techniques, a radioactively labeled tracer (a molecule that can be "traced") is introduced into the body (e.g., via injection), and the tracer is taken up by active brain regions. In this way, these techniques reflect ongoing, online brain activity that can be recorded while an individual is at rest in the scanner (e.g., lying quietly) or while the individual is engaged in a task (e.g., reading words on a computer screen). Early on, researchers using these functional imaging methods made use of the "subtraction" technique whereby brain activation patterns generated by a baseline task (e.g., reading a series of words) could be "subtracted" from a more complex task (e.g., generating a semantic associate for the same words) in order to identify brain regions specifically "activated" in the cognitive process of interest while controlling for baseline brain activity (Corbetta et al., 1993).

The most common PET and SPECT tracers track glucose metabolism (a reflection of synaptic activity) and regional blood flow (an indirect measure of neuronal activity). PET and SPECT have been used to identify differences between groups of individuals (e.g., the finding that older adults show reduced blood flow in limbic and association cortices), as well as differences between different brain regions within a particular patient group (e.g., the finding that glucose metabolism in the temporal lobe is very reduced in Alzheimer disease relative to other brain regions). The most commonly used tracer in PET scanning is [^{18}F]–fluorodeoxyglucose (FDG for short); the accumulation of FDG reflects the amount of synaptic or neuronal activity in a particular brain region. These methods have been used to aid diagnosis as well as track the progression of aging and disease (Minoshima et al., 2021).

PET and SPECT have also been used to study the regional uptake of specific molecules that provide information as to the functioning of particular neurotransmitters and other systems in the aging brain. For example, radioligands (radioactive tracers attached to a molecule) that preferentially bind to cholinergic or dopamine receptors can provide an indication of the integrity of these systems and how they are affected in healthy and diseased aging processes. Perhaps the most important of these for aging research is Pittsburgh Compound-B or PIB (Klunk et al., 2004). PIB was developed in the early 2000s as a PET radioligand that reflects the amount of beta-amyloid deposition in the brain. Beta-amyloid deposition is a hallmark symptom of Alzheimer disease that previously could only be visualized in postmortem brain tissue. PIB has been used not only as an important diagnostic tool in aging and Alzheimer research (e.g., differentiating between different types of dementia such as Alzheimer vs. Lewy body disease) but also to identify early changes in aging that predict later development of Alzheimer disease (Mayblyum et al., 2021).

Another functional brain imaging technique was developed in the early 1990s when it was shown that signals from a standard MRI scanner could be obtained that reflected changes in regional blood oxygenation (blood oxygenation level–dependent imaging or BOLD), a proxy for regional neuronal activity. This technique, known as functional MRI (fMRI), has been used widely to study brain activation patterns in both healthy and neurologically impaired individuals (Saykin et al., 1999). Similar to PET, fMRI studies of aging typically made use of the "subtraction" technique to uncover the neural basis of distinct cognitive processes underlying higher-level tasks and how these processes break down in aging and disease. Unlike PET, fMRI does not require a radioactive tracer and thus does not expose individuals to ionizing radiation. MRI scanners are also more readily available and less expensive to operate than PET scanners.

fMRI studies of aging have reported both underactivity and overactivity in various parts of the brain (McDonough et al., 2020). A number of reasons for these seemingly contradictory findings have been offered. Depending on the demands of the fMRI task, older participants may not make use of a strategy utilized by younger participants and thus may show underactivity in particular brain regions. On the other hand, overactivity in other brain regions may reflect the fact that the aging brain has to work harder to recruit additional brain regions to do the same thing (i.e., the aging brain becomes less efficient over time; see the HAROLD and CRUNCH models discussed in the following section.) It has also been suggested that apparent overactivity is actually due to a degradation of inhibitory pathways in the brain, which then appears as excess excitation during task-based fMRI.

A more recent development in fMRI research is the analysis of functional connectivity in brain networks when the brain is "at rest" (Fox & Raichle, 2007; Gusnard & Raichle, 2001). Unlike task-based fMRI that requires an individual to actively engage in a task while in the scanner, resting-state fMRI (rs-fMRI) simply requires individuals to lie quietly in the scanner. These so-called "resting-state networks" represent tightly interconnected brain regions that show highly correlated activity in the absence of a task. One of these networks, the default-mode network (DMN), is made up of a number of brain regions including medial prefrontal cortex, posterior cingulate, and medial temporal lobe regions. Altered activity in the DMN has been reported in aging and Alzheimer disease and may be useful as an early biomarker of progressive brain changes (Ibrahim et al., 2021).

In short, a wide variety of structural and functional brain imaging techniques is available for both clinical and research purposes in the area of aging and disease. Depending on the types of brain changes being studied and the type of information that is needed, clinicians or researchers focus their investigation on data from the technique that best highlights those changes. Structural brain imaging such as MRI is often used clinically to measure and monitor atrophy over time and also to rule out other causes of dementia, while functional imaging techniques such as fMRI are used by clinical researchers to better understand the functional basis of dementia. Newer "multimodal" imaging approaches are often used in research by combining different imaging modalities to capitalize, for example, on the temporal resolution of MEG and the spatial resolution of MRI (Vaghari et al., 2022). Such approaches require additional statistical analysis and machine learning techniques to combine information from multiple modalities. Research using multimodal imaging approaches, combined with advances in genetic and physiological biomarker technology, promises to provide an increasingly clearer picture of the brain in aging and ultimately will lead to improvements in diagnosis and treatment of age-related disorders.

PART 2: CHANGES THAT OCCUR TO THE BRAIN WITH TYPICAL AGING

All the methods described earlier have been used to determine what happens to the brain with age in the absence of neurological diseases. This section will present research findings on what happens to a typical brain with age. One obvious question that is difficult to answer is "What is a typical brain?" Most would agree that a brain that has experienced a large stroke is not typical, and a person with this history would not be included in a research study on this. The brains of most people, however, undergo some amount of ischemic damage in old age, and if a study excluded anyone with any evidence of ischemic damage, it would not be representative of most people. Cerebrovascular disease and cardiovascular disease are common among older adults. Likewise, it would be difficult to find someone who has not sustained any injury to the head, however mild, whether from a car accident, assault, falling, or playing a sport. Is the goal of the research to determine what happens to the brains of most people or to determine what happens to a brain if it does not undergo any damage in life? Therefore the choice of whom to include in studies on age-related changes to the brain can be difficult. This has led to differentiation between "typical brain aging," "healthy brain aging," and even "SuperAging." *Healthy* brain aging is thought to refer to structural and functional preservation of the brain in the absence of pathology and is less common than *typical* brain aging (Lockhart & DeCarli, 2014). SuperAging is a growing field of research investigating the cognitive profiles and pathological biomarkers of individuals 80 or older whose episodic memory capacity is at least as good as that of cognitively average individuals in their 50s and 60s (Gefen et al., 2021; Rogalski et al., 2019).

One factor that must be considered in this line of research is whether studies are cross-sectional or longitudinal. In this vein, Fotenos et al. (2005) found that in late life, cross-sectional and longitudinal estimates of rates of decline with age were similar. In contrast, Raz et al. (2005) found that longitudinal measures of atrophy surpassed cross-sectional estimates. Another consideration is the age range of the sample. If a researcher were to only include older adults, they might conclude that the brain continues a long-term trajectory of volume loss in old age. However, studies examining the life span find a more complicated picture characterized by growth, mild volume loss, and then an increase in the pace of volume loss. Raz et al. (2005) point out the importance of sampling a wide age range of participants in studies in this area in order to ensure nonlinear patterns of change can be found.

One leading theory of what happens to the brain with age is the premise of "last in, first out." This theory of brain aging proposes that areas of the brain that develop later than other areas are the first to be affected by advanced age. That is, the areas that are late to mature and have thinner myelinated fibers are more vulnerable to age-related declines (Raz et al., 2005). A graphical depiction of the volume of the brain over time shows an inverted-U shape throughout the life span, with increasing volume during young adulthood, stability in middle age, and decline in old age. The mid-50s (Raz et al., 2005) or age 60 (Pfefferbaum et al., 2013) may represent a time point at which the rate of volume loss begins to increase. Although the brain in general shrinks with age, the magnitude and rate of change vary across regions of the brain. In tandem with these losses of tissue volume, the ventricles increase in volume gradually until about 40 to 50 years of age, after which they increase sharply in size (Narvacan et al., 2017).

Gray matter includes neural tissue that is dominated by cell bodies, whereas the parts that are enclosed in myelin, which makes the tissue appear white, are known as white matter. White matter volume tends to decline more rapidly with age than gray matter (Lockhart & DeCarli, 2014). White matter grows in volume with increased myelination throughout early adulthood. At the same time, neurons also undergo pruning or elimination if they do not develop connections with other neurons, likely because of lack of environmental need or stimulation. This occurs until approximately age 30, and mild reduction of volume continues to occur until age 60, when volume decrease becomes more rapid (Pfefferbaum et al., 2013). Narvacan et al. (2017) found total brain, gray matter, and white matter volume decreased linearly as a function of age, accompanied by corresponding linear increases of bilateral ventricular volumes from 46 to 86 years.

Changes to the vascular supply of the brain can occur, with the arteries in the brain becoming thicker and stiffer, which can interfere with the removal of waste from cells and decrease the supply of oxygen and nutrients (Wardlaw et al., 2019). These changes can cause parts of the brain to appear bright, or "hyperintense," on the MRI scans of older adults. These occur in white matter and are known as white matter hyperintensities (WMHs). In typical aging they are often found in the deep white matter or near the ventricles, as in *periventricular* WMHs (Griffanti et al., 2018), particularly the anterior periventricular areas. WMHs may appear brighter because of increased water content and degeneration in damaged white matter. WMHs are associated with age and with vascular risk factors such as hypertension, diabetes, and smoking (Wardlaw et al., 2019), and periventricular WMHs are associated with reduced cognitive functioning (Griffanti et al., 2018). Pathological studies have shown them to be caused by demyelination, gliosis, and axonal atrophy, and they are generally thought to be caused by ischemic damage of small blood vessels, or "small vessel disease" (Wardlaw et al., 2019). Smoking cessation is critically important for patients with small vessel disease, and regular exercise and a healthy diet can also slow the rate of cognitive decline in patients with WMHs (Wardlaw et al., 2019). WMHs are often surrounded by a "penumbra" of reduced white matter functioning. WMHs are associated with reduced frontal lobe metabolism, possibly because they occur most often near the ventricles, which may disrupt axons connecting the frontal and posterior areas of the brain (Lockhart & DeCarli, 2014). They are associated with decreased attention, processing speed, memory, and executive functioning, likely due to slowing of the transmission of information across cortical networks. It is also typical to have very small brain infarctions found on MRI that are not associated with any discrete clinical event, and their prevalence increases with age. These are known as "lacunar" infarcts. Vascular risk factors are associated with increased rates of atrophy (Debette et al., 2011), even when blood pressure lies in the higher range of normal (Seshadri et al., 2004).

Researchers have investigated cortical thickness, surface area, and volume as measures of size of parts of the brain. Although some research has found the cerebellum to show the greatest rates of change in old age (Raz et al., 2005), the frontal lobes, responsible for much of our higher-level cognitive abilities, have consistently been found to show the greatest rates of atrophy (Lockhart & DeCarli, 2014; Pfefferbaum et al., 2013; Toepper, 2017). This rate of change increases with advanced age (Raz et al., 2005). The frontal lobes may show two phases of change, with a slow rate of reduction from age 20 to 60 and then accelerated decline after age 60 (Pfefferbaum et al., 2013). Hypertension is associated with a greater rate of volume loss in the orbitofrontal cortex (Raz et al., 2005).

After the frontal lobes, the hippocampus, which is highly involved with learning and memory, shows the second largest reduction in size with age (DeCarli et al., 2005), with the rate of shrinkage increasing in late life (Raz et al., 2005). It is unique in that its rate of decline is more rapid than its rate of growth earlier in life and was found to be the only structure to experience accelerated declines in volume with increasing age in the latter portion of the life span (Narvacan et al., 2017). While neurogenesis occurs throughout the life span, it decreases with age; when neurogenesis declines in the hippocampus, there is a corresponding decline in learning and memory (Isaev et al., 2019). The rate of atrophy in the hippocampus may stay stable until age 60 (Pfefferbaum et al., 2013) or the mid-50s (Raz et al., 2005), when the rate of atrophy increases. The rate of volume loss in the hippocampus is greater in older adults if they have hypertension (Raz et al., 2005). This indicates that age alone may not be the cause of volume loss, but time spent with hypertension may be the determining factor. The negative impact of hypertension increases with years of having this condition. The hippocampus shows a greater rate of volume decline than the nearby entorhinal cortex, which shows minimal change with typical aging (Raz et al., 2005), and a greater rate of decline than the basal ganglia (Narvacan et al., 2017), which does not change significantly with age.

The parietal lobes, involved in sensory processing such as hearing and vision, show less atrophy with age. The occipital lobes include the primary visual cortex and show the fewest changes with age, although they too become smaller with age, starting around age 60 (Lockhart & DeCarli, 2014; Pfefferbaum et al., 2013). In a 5-year follow-up study, Raz et al. (2005) also found no change in the volume of the primary visual cortex. The corpus callosum may be the only structure that does not show change with age (Pfefferbaum et al., 2013).

As can be seen, the areas of the brain that change the most with advancing age, such as the hippocampus, are also the areas most susceptible to Alzheimer disease. That is, they show a *normalcy–pathology homology* (Fjell et al., 2014). The vulnerability of these areas to typical age changes, even in the absence of disease, corresponds to their vulnerability to diseases such as Alzheimer disease. The common underlying factor may be that areas such as the hippocampus show a large degree of plasticity, or changing in response to external influence, throughout life. This property, which enables the hippocampus to engage in learning and memory, requiring high levels of plasticity throughout life, may also make it more vulnerable to decline with age. The decline in hippocampal integrity in age may then make these areas more vulnerable to insults such as Alzheimer disease. That is, the changes observed with typical aging are not thought to simply represent early signs of Alzheimer disease. Rather, these areas of the brain change with age, and their loss of integrity makes them more susceptible to Alzheimer disease. Alzheimer disease shows separate, qualitatively different processes than typical aging (Toepper, 2017). Qualitatively, Alzheimer disease involves more gray matter than white matter volume loss and more volume loss in the inferior parietal areas compared with superior parietal areas, whereas typical aging is characterized by opposite patterns. The frontal lobes show a decline with typical aging, whereas Alzheimer disease is characterized more by mediotemporal and parietal atrophy.

Given the consistent findings of brain volume loss with age, how does our brain continue to function well? Several models have emerged to explain how the brain reacts to reduced integrity in order to keep functioning. The HAROLD model (**H**emispheric **A**symmetry **R**eduction in **OLD**er adults; Cabeza, 2002) proposes that latent frontal areas contralateral to the areas involved in a task are increasingly recruited as we age in order to continue to complete cognitive tasks effectively. For example, completion of a task that involved the left frontal lobe throughout life now involves additional recruitment of the right frontal lobe. The compensation-related utilization of neural circuits hypothesis (CRUNCH; Reuter-Lorenz & Cappell, 2008) expands on this and proposes that compensation occurs by both increased activation of already-specialized brain regions and through selective recruitment of alternative regions that may or may not reside in the contralateral hemisphere. For example, an activity that involves the left temporal lobe involves increased activation of this same area in late life, as well as additional recruitment of left parietal areas. The scaffolding theory of aging and cognition (STAC; Goh & Park, 2009; Park & Reuter-Lorenz, 2009) proposes that the aging brain maintains the potential for positive neuroplasticity with new stimulation and learning and that increased compensatory frontal activation develops from engagement. The STAC highlights how more involvement of the frontal lobes with increasing age shows how the brain "scaffolds" as it changes in size with age. We turn now to a review of neuroplasticity and aging.

PART 3: NEUROPLASTICITY

A Brief History of Neuroplasticity

Ioan Minea is credited with being the first to use the term "plasticity" as it relates to the central nervous system (Jones, 2000; Minea, 1909). However, the modern conceptualization of brain plasticity may be traced to William James, who suggested that plasticity occurs gradually and is related to "habit" or acts that we repeatedly do. James went on to describe how these brain changes are not simply modifications of existing networks but also include the establishment of *new* networks or pathways (Berlucchi & Buchtel, 2009).

> Plasticity, then, in the wide sense of the word means the possession of a structure weak enough to yield to an influence, but strong enough not to yield all at once. . . . Organic matter, especially nervous tissue, seems endowed with a very ordinary degree of plasticity of this sort. (James, 1890, p. 105)

On Naming: The Plasticity of the Term "Neuroplasticity"

"Plasticity" and "neuroplasticity" have become ubiquitous in contemporary research findings and when describing observed phenomenon thought to reflect brain change (Jones, 2000). However, loose applications of these terms have been cautioned against (Berlucci & Buchtel, 2009; Paillard, 1976). Specifically, observed "changes" at a given cellular level may actually result from alterations at a lower (molecular) or higher (systems) level. More recent concepts stress the importance of systems-level, macro-structural, and microstructural changes and their interactions (Zatorre et al., 2012). Paillard suggested that "plasticity" can only be demonstrated if a new function is achieved by alterations in underlying internal connectivity or constituent elements (1976). Therefore, the morphologic change—in and of itself—is not sufficient to demonstrate plasticity.

More contemporary conceptualizations of neuroplasticity include changes in neuronal connectivity, generation of new neurons, and neurochemical changes (Fuchs & Flügge, 2014). Such neuroplastic changes are described by Roberto Cano-de-la-Cuerda in various proverbs and aphorisms, which borrow from the work of Hebb and others (Cano-de-la-Cuerda, 2021). The neuroimaging techniques described earlier in this chapter allow the increasingly accurate delineation of the "level" of change more related to the accompanying alteration in function or behavior. In addition to different types or "levels" of structural change, location and timing of change are important to consider (Valkanova et al., 2014). For example, stem cells may require up to 3 months to develop and differentiate (Cummings et al., 2005). Zatorre et al. (2012) describe how these observed plastic phenomena can be organized as being of gray matter or white matter or as extra-neuronal, as illustrated in Figure 6.6. Gray matter changes include the creation of new neurons (neurogenesis), new synapses (synaptogenesis), and changes in neuronal structure. White matter changes include myelination; packing density of fibers; and qualities of axons including their trajectories, quantity, diameter, and branching. Extra-neuronal changes include the formation of new blood vessels (angiogenesis) and increases in glial cell size and quantity.

Kleim and Jones (2008) suggested 10 "principles of experience-dependent plasticity" (p. S227), which highlight evidence-based behavioral dictums that drive neural plasticity (Table 6.1).

In Kleim and Jones's (2008) initial concept of the 10 principles, Principle 1, "use it or lose it," recognizes that, in the absence of use, neural circuits can actually deteriorate and/or become subsumed by another circuit. Consistent with this principle, fMRI

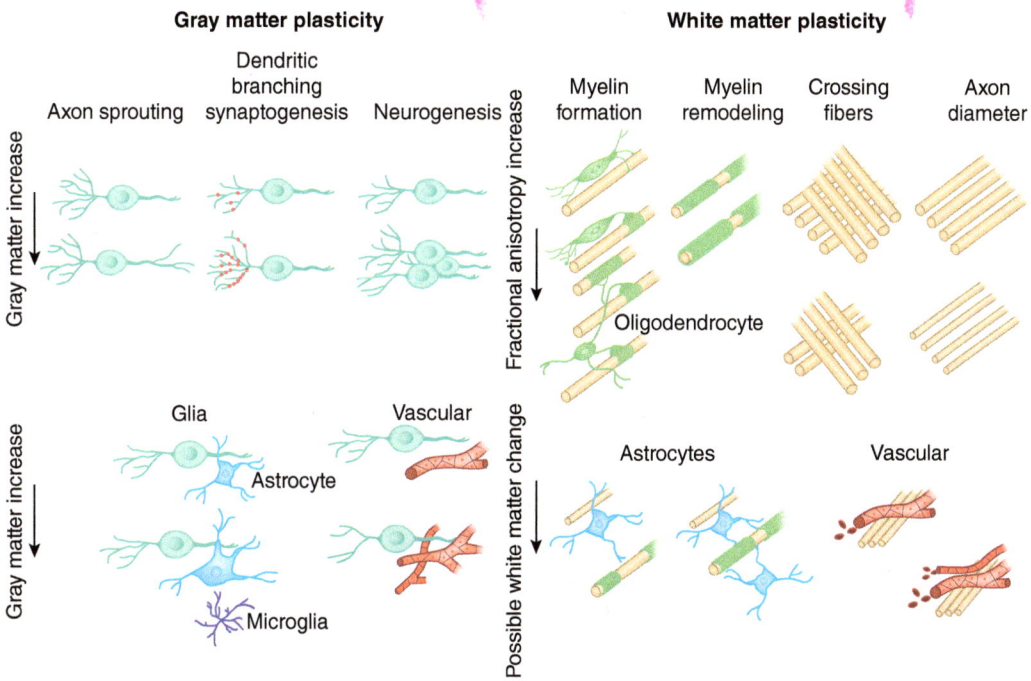

Figure 6.6 Drivers of neuroplasticity.
Source: Adapted from Zatorre, R. J., Fields, R. D., & Johansen-Berg, H. (2012). Plasticity in gray and white: Neuroimaging changes in brain structure during learning. *Nature Neuroscience, 15*(4), 531.

research has demonstrated that individuals with visual impairment show activation of their cortical areas typically dedicated to vision during tactile tasks (Sadato et al., 1996), and individuals who are deaf show activation of auditory cortical areas during visual tasks (Finney et al., 2001). Structural neuroplastic change has been demonstrated following skill training (increased "use") in healthy adults learning how to juggle (Boyke et al., 2008; Draganski et al., 2004) and in adults post-stroke (Gauthier et al., 2008), consistent with the idea of Principle 2, "use it and improve it." In the Gauthier et al. (2008) study, adults with stroke and upper extremity hemiparesis (between 38 and 87 years of age) who participated in upper extremity rehabilitation therapy showed improved functioning, which correlated with gray matter volume increases in the hippocampus, as well as sensory and motor areas of both sides of the brain. Importantly, age did not correlate with increases in gray matter volume, suggesting that age was not a factor in driving the observed volumetric change or clinical improvement. Also, these individuals were 3.6 years post stroke on average, and most had participated in some type of physical therapy for their hemiparesis prior to the experimental treatment, suggesting that improvement (and brain plasticity) can occur years following an injury and after previous attempts at improvement.

Simple repetition or "use" may not be sufficient in all cases to elicit neural change: Principle 3, the *specificity* of a task, must be considered. Perez et al. (2004) demonstrated that skilled ankle movements increased corticospinal excitability, whereas simple repeated movement of the ankle did not. Repetition, intensity, and salience are each relevant when evaluating drivers of neuroplastic change. Considering

TABLE 6.1 PRINCIPLES OF NEURAL PLASTICITY

1. Use It or Lose It	
Not using a specific brain function can lead to functional loss and structural atrophy.	
2. Use It and Improve It	
Training that drives a specific brain function can lead to an improvement of that function.	
3. Specificity	
The nature of a training experience influences the nature of the plasticity.	
4. Repetition	
Sufficient repetition is necessary for plasticity to occur.	
5. Intensity	
Sufficient training intensity is necessary for plasticity.	
6. Time	
Different forms of plasticity (e.g., different "levels") occur at different times during training.	
7. Salience	
The training experience must be sufficiently salient to induce plasticity.	
8. Age	
Training-induced plasticity occurs more readily in younger brains, as a general rule.	
9. Transference	
Current training can enhance subsequent plastic change.	
10. Interference	
Current training can hinder subsequent plastic change.	

Source: Adapted from Kleim, J. A., & Jones, T. A. (2008). Principles of experience-dependent neural plasticity: Implications for rehabilitation after brain damage. *Journal of Speech, Language, and Hearing Research, 51*(1), S227.

repetition (Principle 4), several days of training have been demonstrated to be necessary to increase synaptic strength (Monfils & Teskey, 2004) and number of synapses or cortical map reorganization (Kleim et al., 2002) in some cases. It follows, then, that a task may require sufficient *intensity* (Principle 5) to drive neuroplastic change as well: Raymer et al. (2007) echoed this sentiment in their review of aphasia rehabilitation. Relatedly, adaptive training paradigms—where intensity must be increased as the "difficulty of the task is adjusted according to individual performance"—may be influential in inducing plasticity as well (Valkanova et al., 2014, p. 905). In Gauthier et al.'s (2008) study in adults post stroke administered an upper extremity rehabilitation program, gray matter volume increase was related to improvement in real-world arm use, not improvement on a laboratory-based measure of maximum ability. This finding further substantiates the theory that neuroplastic change is driven by and is related to tasks of sufficient *salience* (Principle 7; e.g., tasks of real-world arm use), not simply performance on a laboratory-based measure of dexterity and motor speed. Similarly, in a group of patients with aphasia from strokes who underwent various types of language intervention (i.e., sentence comprehension/production, naming, or spelling), results suggested sentence-level treatment may promote greater neuroplasticity on naturalistic, language comprehension skills compared with word-level treatment (Barbieri et al., 2023). This highlights a criticism given in response to negative outcomes or lack of finding neuroplastic change in such research: It is speculated that insufficient importance or ecological validity is often the culprit of the limited or nonexistent observed change (Valkanova et al., 2014).

When considering Principle 6, how "time matters," it has been posited that *critical windows* for learning and development exist (Adams et al., 2000), and these periods may create times of high opportunity and vulnerability. In addition to "windows" of chronological age and development, there may be optimal "windows" of time following nervous system insult to capitalize upon neuroplastic potential (Kleim & Jones, 2008). Some research finds rehabilitation to be more efficacious post-stroke when initiated early thereafter (at day 5 vs. day 30; Biernaskie et al., 2004). However, animal models suggest that starting physical activity too quickly following an ischemic infarction can actually *increase* the lesion volume, possibly due to unique characteristics of the recovering brain tissue immediately surrounding the lesion (e.g., cortical hyperexcitability; Risedal et al., 1999). Following a traumatic brain injury (TBI), advanced rates of neurodegeneration ("negative neuroplasticity") may occur, and these changes correlate with poorer cognition and other functions (Tomaszczyk et al., 2014). Possible mechanisms of this negative neuroplasticity may include gliotic scar formation, inflammation, cell death, or other mechanisms (Su et al., 2016). New therapies with preliminary evidence of effectiveness from animal studies include interventions targeting neurogenesis, vascular development (angiogenesis), synaptic remodeling and formation, and reducing inflammation (Su et al., 2016). While time (and timing) may indeed matter when it comes to neuroplasticity, there is also evidence that timing of the intervention is less critical. Studies in adults with upper extremity hemiparesis following brain insult (e.g., TBI, stroke) have shown changes in gray matter, white matter, and functional brain activity in those *greater than 1 year* following *the insult* with an upper extremity rehabilitation therapy (Shaw et al., 2005; Taub & Uswatte, 2015).

In considering Principle 8, how "age matters," plastic change in the adult nervous system was long believed to be impossible, or nearly so, due to both a passing of "windows" of possible change and advancing age in general. However, neuroplastic change has been observed in adult humans (Gauthier et al., 2008; Valkanova et al., 2014). Boyke et al. (2008) demonstrated that while only 23% of their older adult sample mastered a juggling skill compared with 100% of younger samples in previous studies (Draganski et al., 2004; Driemeyer et al., 2008), older adults who did acquire the new skill showed neuroplastic gray matter volume increases. This illustrates that, while possibly more difficult to elicit, neuroplastic processes do occur even in older populations.

Principles 9 "transference" and 10 "interference" refer to the ability of a given circuit to enhance (transference) or disrupt (interference) subsequent plastic change (Kleim & Jones, 2008). Types of transference can include use of electrical brain stimulation (Hummel & Cohen, 2006), use of selective serotonin reuptake inhibitors (SSRIs; D'Sa & Durman, 2002), use of neuroprosthetics (Patil & Turner, 2008), and lifestyle factors including diet, exercise, and sleep (Figure 6.7).

Lifestyle Factors ⭐

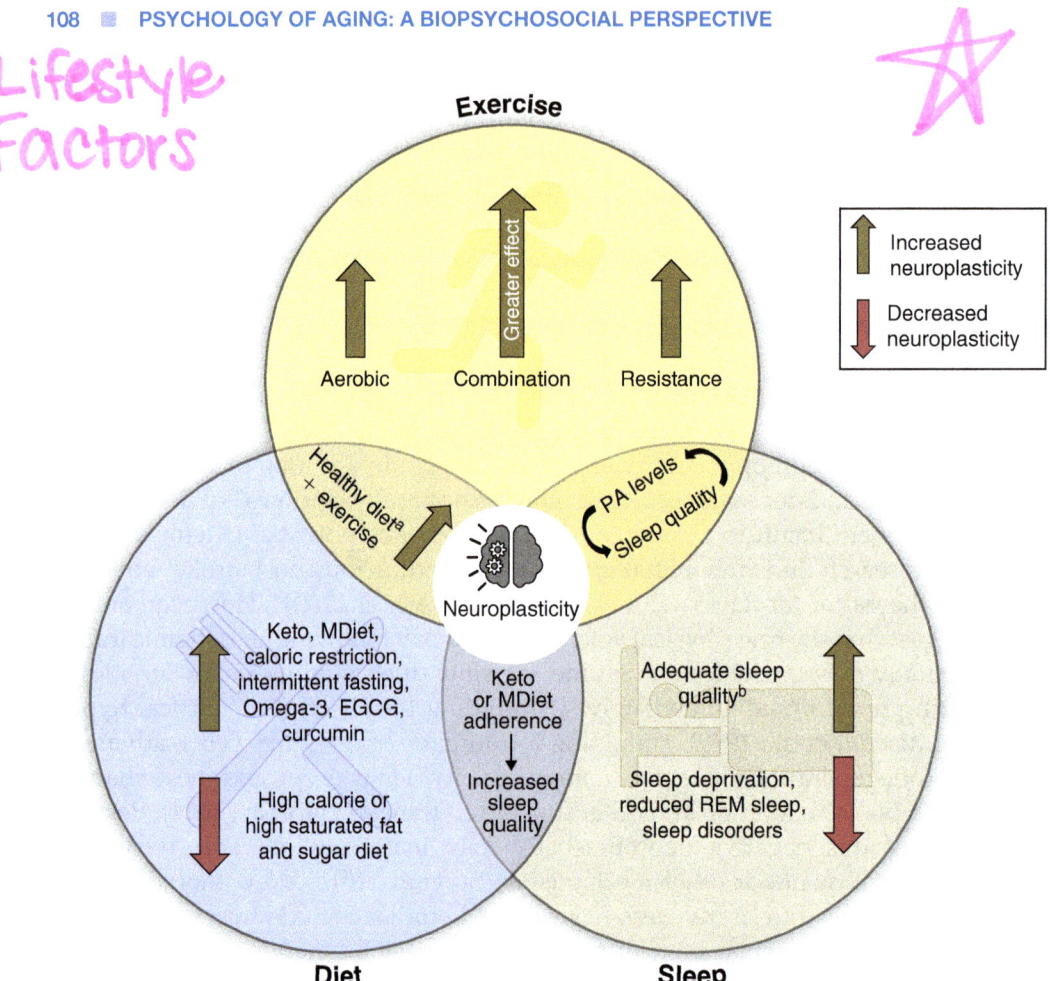

Figure 6.7 Individual and combined influences of exercise, diet, and sleep on neuroplasticity. This figure summarizes the key points from Pickersgill et al. (2022), which visually depicts how lifestyle factors are interrelated.

Note: Green upward arrows represent factors associated with increased neuroplasticity, whereas red downward arrows represent factors associated with decreased neuroplasticity.

[a]Healthy diet refers to evidence from the ketogenic diet, Mediterranean diet, and nutritional supplements.
[b]Adequate sleep quality is specific to individuals depending on age and other health factors.

keto, ketogenic diet; MDiet, Mediterranean diet; EGCG, (–)epigallocatechin-3-gallate; REM sleep, rapid eye movement sleep; PA levels, physical activity levels.

Source: From Pickersgill, J. W., Turco, C. V., Ramdeo, K., Rehsi, R. S., Foglia, S. D., Nelson, A. J. (2022). The combined influences of exercise, diet and sleep on neuroplasticity. *Frontiers in Psychology, 13*, 831819. https://doi.org/10.3389/fpsyg.2022.831819

Aerobic activity, resistance training, and a combination of both types of exercise have been shown to influence biomarkers of neuroplasticity, such as brain-derived neurotrophic factor (BDNF), insulin-like growth factor 1 (IGF-1), and vascular endothelial growth factor (VEGF; for a review see Pickersgill et al., 2022). White matter improvements have been linked to aerobic exercise (Mendez Colmenares et al., 2021), and 6 months of high-intensity resistance exercise resulted in better cognition in those with mild cognitive impairment (MCI), in addition to protecting Alzheimer disease–vulnerable hippocampal subfields from degeneration for at least 12 months postintervention (Broadhouse et al., 2020). Aspects of diet have also been found to modulate markers of neuroplasticity, including the Mediterranean diet (Pelletier et al., 2015), ketogenic diet (Cantello et al., 2007), and gluten-free diet (Bella et al., 2015), as well as caloric restriction (Maswood et al., 2004); intermittent fasting (Baik et al., 2020); and diet supplementation with omega-3 (Wu et al., 2004, 2007), catechin polyphenol (Haque et al., 2006), and curcumin (Sharma et al., 2010). Proposed mechanisms of action include interaction via the "gut-brain axis" and the saprophytic microorganismal communities inhabiting the intestinal ecosystem, collectively referred to as the gut microbiota (Sarubbo et al., 2022). Lastly, sleep is another lifestyle factor that may increase the propensity for neuroplasticity in the brain, both during sleep and while awake. During sleep, neuroplasticity is facilitated by the adequate delivery of cerebral blood flow to supply active neurons with oxygen while simultaneously removing waste products, as well as regulating neurotrophic factors such as growth hormone, IGF-1 axis, and BDNF levels (Pickersgill et al., 2022). The authors note that sleep deprivation, reduced REM sleep duration, or the presence of a sleep disorder may result in a disrupted neuroplastic process that negatively impacts cognition during waking hours (Pickersgill et al., 2022). Future directions will explore additional lifestyle factors such as mood, motivation, mindfulness, stress, socioeconomic status, intelligence, education level, and substance use (Pickersgill et al., 2022).

Contrary to *transference*, Principle 10, *interference*, includes activities that disrupt subsequent plastic change. Learning to complete a task in a different way following an injury—such as writing with a nondominant hand after a stroke impairing one's dominant hand—may be considered an example of interference. In this way, such compensatory strategies may lead to "bad habits," or the learned disuse or nonuse of an otherwise available capacity (Mark & Taub, 2004). Additionally, factors such as acute and chronic pain can similarly interfere with neuroplasticity. In a review paper exploring a motor learning paradigm in acute and chronic pain, results revealed both acute and chronic pain may impede training-induced neuroplasticity (Stanisic et al., 2022)

Novel Methods to Enhance Neuroplasticity

In addition to the recent focus on health behaviors to optimize neuroplasticity, various novel methods have been trialed focused on optimizing technology, pharmacology, and improved access. Gamification and virtual reality have demonstrated clinical improvement in post-stroke upper and lower extremity rehabilitation, for example (Karamians et al., 2020; Kim & Kaneko, 2023), but with some results being equivocal to traditional methods (Stockbridge et al., 2022) and without robust demonstration(s) of clinical gains to neoplastic change. Transcranial direct current stimulation (tDCS), a neuromodulatory technique that delivers low-intensity direct current to cortical areas that facilitates or inhibits cortical spontaneous neuronal activity, has received recent interest, as it has been shown to promote neuroplasticity in various clinical populations including frontotemporal dementia (Ferrucci et al., 2018), Parkinson disease (Brak et al., 2022), and chronic stroke (Vlotinou et al., 2022). Use of substances has been explored to enhance neuroplasticity. Similar to studies examining the use of SSRIs (mentioned earlier), psychedelics are increasingly being investigated due to their propensity to promote synapse and dendrite growth in the neocortex (Calder & Hasler, 2023). Finally, administering neurorehabilitation protocols virtually has been found to enhance participation and subsequently impact neuroplasticity in similar ways as in-person interventions (Matamala-Gomez et al., 2020). Overall, efforts to enhance neuroplasticity through lifestyle factors as well as technology continue to grow in interest and importance as research supports improved neuroplasticity above and beyond traditional methods.

CONCLUSION

This chapter explored changes that occur to the brain, beginning with an overview of modern technologies that are used to answer questions about brain functioning in older adults. A brief summary of changes that occur to the brain with typical aging was presented next. Last, an overview of neuroplasticity was presented, including its history, basic principles, and novel areas of research. Although the human brain clearly loses volume with age, the brain also shows plasticity that can be used to maintain functioning in old age. Research in the coming decades can use the principles of neuroplasticity described earlier to enhance the functioning of older adults, whether they are experiencing typical age-related change or damage to the brain following strokes or other neurological events. Neuroimaging methods will continue to be developed that allow us to determine what happens to the brain with age and in response to neurological events and how neuroplasticity enables the brain to adjust to such changes.

DISCUSSION QUESTIONS:

1. Explain how fMRI works.
2. Explain the differences between spatial and temporal resolution in neuroimaging techniques and which methods are strong in each category.
3. Describe the inclusion and exclusion criteria you would use for a study on age-related changes to a typical human brain and why.
4. Explain an overall theory to describe which areas of the brain experience the most volume loss with age and identify areas that show the most loss in old age.
5. Describe five principles of neuroplasticity and explain how they might apply to an older adult who experiences loss of language ability and use of the right hand in response to a stroke.

A robust set of instructor resources designed to supplement this text is located at http://connect.springerpub.com/content/book/978-0-8261-6617-3. Qualifying instructors may request access by emailing textbook@springerpub.com.

REFERENCES

Adams, J., Barone Jr., S., LaMantia, A., Philen, R., Rice, D. C., Spear, L., & Susser, E. (2000). Workshop to identify critical windows of exposure for children's health: Neurobehavioral work group summary. *Environmental Health Perspectives*, *108*(Suppl. 3), 535.

Ashburner, J., & Friston, K. J. (2000). Voxel-based morphometry—the methods. *Neuroimage, 11*(6), 805–821.

Baik, S. H., Rajeev, V., Fann, D. Y., Jo, D. G., & Arumugam, T. V. (2020). Intermittent fasting increases adult hippocampal neurogenesis. *Brain and Behavior, 10*(1), e01444. https://doi.org/10.1002/brb3.1444

Barbieri, E., Thompson, C. K., Higgins, J., Caplan, D., Kiran, S., Rapp, B., & Parrish, T. (2023). Treatment-induced neural reorganization in aphasia is language-domain specific: Evidence from a large-scale fMRI study. *Cortex, 159,* 75–100. https://doi.org/10.1016/j.cortex.2022.11.008

Bella, R., Lanza, G., Cantone, M., Giuffrida, S., Puglisi, V., Vinciguerra, L., Pennisi, M., Ricceri, R., D'Agate, C. C., Malaguarnera, G., Ferri, R., & Pennisi, G. (2015). Effect of a gluten-free diet on cortical excitability in adults with celiac disease. *PLoS One, 10*(6), e0129218. https://doi.org/10.1371/journal.pone.0129218

Berlucchi, G., & Buchtel, H. A. (2009). Neuronal plasticity: Historical roots and evolution of meaning. *Experimental Brain Research, 192*(3), 307–319. https://doi.org/10.1007/s00221-008-1611-6

Biernaskie, J., Chernenko, G., & Corbett, D. (2004). Efficacy of rehabilitative experience declines with time after focal ischemic brain injury. *The Journal of Neuroscience, 24*(5), 1245–1254. https://doi.org/10.1523/JNEUROSCI.3834-03.2004.

Boyke, J., Driemeyer, J., Gaser, C., Büchel, C., & May, A. (2008). Training-induced brain structure changes in the elderly. *The Journal of Neuroscience, 28*(28), 7031–7035. https://doi.org/10.1523/JNEUROSCI.0742-08.2008

Brak, I. V., Filimonova, E., Zakhariya, O., Khasanov, R., & Stepanyan, I. (2022). Transcranial current stimulation as a tool of neuromodulation of cognitive functions in Parkinson's disease. *Frontiers in Neuroscience, 16,* 781488. https://doi.org/10.3389/fnins.2022.781488

Broadhouse, K. M., Singh, M. F., Suo, C., Gates, N., Wen, W., Brodaty, H., Jain, N., Wilson, G. C., Meiklejohn, J., Singh, N., Baune, B. T., Baker, M., Foroughi, N., Wang, Y., Kochan, N., Ashton, K., Brown, M., Li, Z., Mavros, Y., Sachdev, P. S., …, Valenzuela, M. J. (2020). Hippocampal plasticity underpins long-term cognitive gains from resistance exercise in MCI. *NeuroImage. Clinical, 25,* 102182. https://doi.org/10.1016/j.nicl.2020.102182

Cabeza, R. (2002). Hemispheric asymmetry reduction in older adults: The HAROLD model. *Psychology and Aging, 17,* 85–100. https://doi.org/10.1037//0882-7974.17.1.85

Calder, A. E., & Hasler, G. (2023). Towards an understanding of psychedelic-induced neuroplasticity. *Neuropsychopharmacology: Official Publication of the American College of Neuropsychopharmacology, 48*(1), 104–112. https://doi.org/10.1038/s41386-022-01389-z

Cano-de-la-Cuerda R. (2021). Proverbs and aphorisms in neurorehabilitation: A literature review. *International Journal of Environmental Research and Public Health, 18*(17), 9240. https://doi.org/10.3390/ijerph18179240

Cantello, R., Varrasi, C., Tarletti, R., Cecchin, M., D'Andrea, F., Veggiotti, P., Bellomo, G., & Monaco, F. (2007). Ketogenic diet: Electrophysiological effects on the normal human cortex. *Epilepsia, 48*(9), 1756–1763. https://doi.org/10.1111/j.1528-1167.2007.01156.x

Chandra, A., Dervenoulas, G., Politis, M., & Alzheimer's Disease Neuroimaging Initiative. (2019). Magnetic resonance imaging in Alzheimer's disease and mild cognitive impairment. *Journal of Neurology, 266,* 1293–1302. https://doi.org/10.1007/s00415-018-9016-3

Choi, J., Ku, B., Doan, D. N. T., Park, J., Cha, W., Kim, J. U., & Lee, K. H. (2023). Prefrontal EEG slowing, synchronization, and ERP peak latency in association with predementia stages of Alzheimer's disease. *Frontiers in Aging Neuroscience, 15,* 1131857. https://doi.org/10.3389/fnagi.2023.1131857

Corbetta, M., Miezin, F. M., Shulman, G. L., & Petersen, S. E. (1993). A PET study of visuospatial attention. *Journal of Neuroscience, 13*(3), 1202–1226. https://doi.org/10.1523/JNEUROSCI.13-03-01202.1993

Cummings, B. J., Uchida, N., Tamaki, S. J., Salazar, D. L., Hooshmand, M., Summers, R., …, & Anderson, A. J. (2005). Human neural stem cells differentiate and promote locomotor recovery in spinal cord-injured mice. *Proceedings of the National Academy of Sciences of the United States of America, 102*(39), 14069–14074. https://doi.org/10.1371/journal.pone.0012272

Debette, S., Seshadri, S., Beiser, A., Au, R., Himali, J. J., Palumbo, C., & DeCarli, C. (2011). Midlife vascular risk factor exposure accelerates structural brain aging and cognitive decline. *Neurology, 77*(5), 461–468. https://doi.org/10.1212/WNL.0b013e318227b227

DeCarli, C., Massaro, J., Harvey, D., Hald, J., Tullberg, M., Au, R., & Wolf, P. A. (2005). Measures of brain morphology and infarction in the Framingham Heart Study: Establishing what is normal. *Neurobiology of Aging, 26*(4), 491–510. https://doi.org/10.1016/j.neurobiolaging.2004.05.004

Doan, D. N. T., Ku, B., Choi, J., Oh, M., Kim, K., Cha, W., & Kim, J. U. (2021). Predicting dementia with prefrontal electroencephalography and event-related potential. *Frontiers in Aging Neuroscience, 13*, 659817. https://doi.org/10.3389/fnagi.2021.659817

Draganski, B., Gaser, C., Busch, V., Schuierer, G., Bogdahn, U., & May, A. (2004). Neuroplasticity: Changes in grey matter induced by training. *Nature, 427*(6972), 311–312. https://doi.ucsf.idm.oclc.org/10.1038/427311a

Driemeyer, J., Boyke, J., Gaser, C., Büchel, C., & May, A. (2008). Changes in gray matter induced by learning—revisited. *PLoS One, 3*(7), e2669. https://doi.org/10.1371/journal.pone.0002669

D'Sa, C., & Duman, R. S. (2002). Antidepressants and neuroplasticity. *Bipolar Disorders, 4*(3), 183–194. https://doi.org/10.1034/j.1399-5618.2002.01203.x

Ferrucci, R., Mrakic-Sposta, S., Gardini, S., Ruggiero, F., Vergari, M., Mameli, F., Arighi, A., Spallazzi, M., Barocco, F., Michelini, G., Pietroboni, A. M., Ghezzi, L., Fumagalli, G. G., D'Urso, G., Caffarra, P., Scarpini, E., Priori, A., & Marceglia, S. (2018). Behavioral and neurophysiological effects of transcranial direct current stimulation (tDCS) in fronto-temporal dementia. *Frontiers in Behavioral Neuroscience, 12*, 235. https://doi.org/10.3389/fnbeh.2018.00235

Finney, E. M., Fine, I., & Dobkins, K. R. (2001). Visual stimuli activate auditory cortex in the deaf. *Nature Neuroscience, 4*(12), 1171–1173. https://doi.org/10.1038/nn763

Fjell, A. M., McEvoy, L., Holland, D., Dale, A. M., & Walhovd, K. B. (2014). What is normal in normal aging? Effects of aging, amyloid and Alzheimer's disease on the cerebral cortex and the hippocampus. *Progress in Neurobiology, 117*, 20–40. https://doi.org/10.1016/j.pneurobio.2014.02.004

Fotenos, A. F., Snyder, A. Z., Girton, L. E., Morris, J. C., & Buckner, R. L. (2005). Normative estimates of cross-sectional and longitudinal brain volume decline in aging and AD. *Neurology, 64*(6), 1032–1039. https://doi.org/10.1212/01.WNL.0000154530.72969.11

Fox, M. D., & Raichle, M. E. (2007). Spontaneous fluctuations in brain activity observed with functional magnetic resonance imaging. *Nature Reviews Neuroscience, 8*(9), 700–711. https://doi.org/10.1038/nrn2201

Fuchs, E., & Flügge, G. (2014). Adult neuroplasticity: More than 40 years of research. *Neural Plasticity, 2014*, 541870. https://doi.org/10.1155/2014/541870

Gauthier, L. V., Taub, E., Perkins, C., Ortmann, M., Mark, V. W., & Uswatte, G. (2008). Remodeling the brain plastic structural brain changes produced by different motor therapies after stroke. *Stroke, 39*(5), 1520–1525. https://doi.org/10.1161/STROKEAHA.107.502229

Gefen, T., Kawles, A., Makowski-Woidan, B., Engelmeyer, J., Ayala, I., Abbassian, P., Zhang, H., Weintraub, S., Flanagan, M. E., Mao, Q., Bigio, E. H., Rogalski, E., Mesulam, M. M., & Geula, C. (2021). Paucity of entorhinal cortex pathology of the Alzheimer's type in SuperAgers with superior memory performance. *Cerebral Cortex, 31*(7), 3177–3183. https://doi.org/10.1093/cercor/bhaa409

Goh, J. O., & Park, D. C. (2009). Neuroplasticity and cognitive aging: The scaffolding theory of aging and cognition. *Restorative Neurology and Neuroscience, 27*(5), 391–403. https://doi.org/10.3233/RNN-2009-0493

Golomb, J., Kluger, A., de Leon, M. J., Ferris, S. H., Convit, A., Mittelman, M. S., ..., George, A. E. (1994). Hippocampal formation size in normal human aging: A correlate of delayed secondary memory performance. *Learning & Memory, 1*(1), 45–54.

Griffanti, L., Jenkinson, M., Suri, S., Zsoldos, E., Mahmood, A., Filippini, N., Sexton, C. E., Topiwala, A., Allan, C., Kivimäki, M., Singh-Manoux, A., Ebmeier, K. P., Mackay, C. E., & Zamboni, G. (2018). Classification and characterization of periventricular and deep white matter hyperintensities on MRI: A study in older adults. *NeuroImage, 170*, 174–181. https://doi.org/10.1016/j.neuroimage.2017.03.024

Gusnard, D. A., & Raichle, M. E. (2001). Searching for a baseline: Functional imaging and the resting human brain. *Nature Reviews Neuroscience, 2*(10), 685–694. https://doi.org/10.1038/35094500

Haque, M., Hashimoto, M., Katakura, M., Tanabe, Y., Hara, Y., & Shido, O. (2006). Long-term administration of green tea catechins improves spatial cognition learning ability in rats. *The Journal of Nutrition, 136*(4), 1043–1047. https://doi.org/10.1093/jn/136.4.1043

Hone-Blancheta, A., Bohsalia, A., Krishnamurthyb, L. C., Shahida, S., Lina, Q., Zhaoe, L., ..., Crossona, B. (2022). Relationships between frontal metabolites and Alzheimer's disease biomarkers in cognitively normal older adults. *Neurobiol Aging, 109*, 22–30. https://doi.org/10.1016/j.neurobiolaging.2021.09.016

Hounsfield, G. N. (1980). Computed medical imaging. *Medical Physics, 7*(4), 283–290. https://doi.org/10.1118/1.594709

Hummel, F. C., & Cohen, L. G. (2006). Non-invasive brain stimulation: A new strategy to improve neurorehabilitation after stroke? *Lancet Neurology, 5*, 708–712. https://doi.org/10.1016/S1474-4422(06)70525-7

Ibrahim, B., Suppiah, S., Ibrahim, N., Mohamad, M., Hassan, H. A., Nasser, N. S., & Saripan, M. I. (2021). Diagnostic power of resting-state fMRI for detection of network connectivity in Alzheimer's disease and mild cognitive impairment: A systematic review. *Human Brain Mapping, 42*(9), 2941–2968. https://doi.org/10.1002/hbm.25369

Ikeda, M., Tanabe, H., Nakagawa, Y., Kazui, H., Oi, H., Yamazaki, H., ..., Nishimura, T. (1994). MRI-based quantitative assessment of the hippocampal region in very mild to moderate Alzheimer's disease. *Neuroradiology, 36*(1), 7–10. https://doi.org/10.1007/BF00599184

Isaev, N. K., Stelmashook, E. V., & Genrikhs, E. E. (2019). Neurogenesis and brain aging. *Reviews in the Neurosciences, 30*(6), 573–580. https://doi.org/10.1515/revneuro-2018-0084

James, W. (1890). *Principles of psychology*. MacMillan.

Jett, S., Boneu, C., Zarate, C., Carlton, C., Kodancha, V., Nerattini, M., ..., Mosconi, L. (2023). Systematic review of 31P-magnetic resonance spectroscopy studies of brain high energy phosphates and membrane phospholipids in aging and Alzheimer's disease. *Frontiers in Aging Neuroscience, 15*, 1183228. https://doi.org/10.3389/fnagi.2023.1183228

Jones, E. G. (2000). NEUROwords 8 Plasticity and neuroplasticity. *Journal of the History of the Neurosciences, 9*(1), 37–39. https://doi.org/10.1076/0964-704X(200004)9:1;1-2;FT037

Karamians, R., Proffitt, R., Kline, D., & Gauthier, L. V. (2020). Effectiveness of virtual reality-and gaming-based interventions for upper extremity rehabilitation poststroke: A meta-analysis. *Archives of Physical Medicine and Rehabilitation, 101*(5), 885–896. https://doi.org/10.1016/j.apmr.2019.10.195

Khagi, B., Lee, K. H., Choi, K. Y., Lee, J. J., Kwon, G. R., & Yang, H. D. (2021). VBM-based Alzheimer's disease detection from the region of interest of T1 MRI with supportive Gaussian smoothing and a Bayesian regularized neural network. *Applied Sciences, 11*(13), 6175. https://doi.org/10.3390/app11136175

Kim, M., & Kaneko, F. (2023). Virtual reality-based gait rehabilitation intervention for stroke individuals: A scoping review. *Journal of Exercise Rehabilitation, 19*(2), 95–104. https://doi.org/10.12965/jer.2346114.057

Kleim, J. A., & Jones, T. A. (2008). Principles of experience-dependent neural plasticity: Implications for rehabilitation after brain damage. *Journal of Speech, Language, and Hearing Research, 51*(1), S225–S239. https://doi.org/10.1044/1092-4388(2008/018

Kleim, J. A., Barbay, S., Cooper, N. R., Hogg, T. M., Reidel, C. N., Remple, M. S., & Nudo, R. J. (2002). Motor learning-dependent synaptogenesis is localized to functionally reorganized motor cortex. *Neurobiology of Learning and Memory, 77*(1), 63–77. https://doi-org.ucsf.idm.oclc.org/10.1006/nlme.2000.4004

Klunk, W. E., Engler, H., Nordberg, A., Wang, Y., Blomqvist, G., Holt, D. P., ..., Ausén, B. (2004). Imaging brain amyloid in Alzheimer's disease with Pittsburgh Compound-B. *Annals of Neurology, 55*(3), 306–319. https://doi.org/10.1002/ana.20009

Knudsen, L. V., Gazerani, P., Duan, Y., Michel, T. M., & Vafaee, M. S. (2022). The role of multimodal MRI in mild cognitive impairment and Alzheimer's disease. *Journal of Neuroimaging, 32*(1), 148–157. https://doi.org/10.1111/jon.12940

Kruggel, F., Masaki, F., Solodkin, A., & Alzheimer's Disease Neuroimaging Initiative. (2017). Analysis of longitudinal diffusion-weighted images in healthy and pathological aging: An ADNI study. *Journal of Neuroscience Methods, 278*, 101–115. https://doi-org.ucsf.idm.oclc.org/10.1016/j.jneumeth.2016.12.020

Lockhart, S. N., & DeCarli, C. (2014). Structural imaging measures of brain aging. *Neuropsychology Review, 24*, 271–289. https://doi.org/10.1007/s11065-014-9268-3

Mark, V. W., & Taub, E. (2004). Constraint-induced movement therapy for chronic stroke hemiparesis and other disabilities. *Restorative Neurology and Neuroscience, 22*(3–5), 317–336.

Maswood, N., Young, J., Tilmont, E., Zhang, Z., Gash, D. M., Gerhardt, G. A., Grondin, R., Roth, G. S., Mattison, J., Lane, M. A., Carson, R. E., Cohen, R. M., Mouton, P. R., Quigley, C., Mattson, M. P., & Ingram, D. K. (2004). Caloric restriction increases neurotrophic factor levels and attenuates neurochemical and behavioral deficits in a primate model of Parkinson's disease. *Proceedings of the National Academy of Sciences of the United States of America, 101*(52), 18171–18176. https://doi.org/10.1073/pnas.0405831102

Matamala-Gomez, M., Maisto, M., Montana, J. I., Mavrodiev, P. A., Baglio, F., Rossetto, F., Mantovani, F., Riva, G., & Realdon, O. (2020). The role of engagement in teleneurorehabilitation: A systematic review. *Frontiers in Neurology, 11*, 354. https://doi.org/10.3389/fneur.2020.00354

Mayblyum, D. V., Becker, J. A., Jacobs, H. I., Buckley, R. F., Schultz, A. P., Sepulcre, J., ..., Hanseeuw, B. J. (2021). Comparing PET and MRI biomarkers predicting cognitive decline in preclinical Alzheimer disease. *Neurology, 96*(24), e2933–e2943. https://doi.org/10.1212/WNL.0000000000012108

McDonough, I. M., Festini, S. B., & Wood, M. M. (2020). Risk for Alzheimer's disease: A review of long-term episodic memory encoding and retrieval fMRI studies. *Ageing Research Reviews, 62*, 101133. https://doi.org/10.1016/j.arr.2020.101133

Mendez Colmenares, A., Voss, M. W., Fanning, J., Salerno, E. A., Gothe, N. P., Thomas, M. L., McAuley, E., Kramer, A. F., & Burzynska, A. Z. (2021). White matter plasticity in healthy older adults: The effects of aerobic exercise. *NeuroImage, 239*, 118305. https://doi.org/10.1016/j.neuroimage.2021.118305

Minea, I. (1909). *Cercetäri experimentale asupra variatiunilor morfologice ale neuronului lervosale (studiul 'reactiunii plastice')*. Brozer and Parzer.

Minoshima, S., Mosci, K., Cross, D., & Thientunyakit, T. (2021, May). Brain [F-18] FDG PET for clinical dementia workup: Differential diagnosis of Alzheimer's disease and other types of dementing disorders. *Seminars in Nuclear Medicine, 51*(3), 230–240. https://doi.org/10.1053/j.semnuclmed.2021.01.002

Monfils, M. H., & Teskey, G. C. (2004). Skilled-learning-induced potentiation in rat sensorimotor cortex: A transient form of behavioural long-term potentiation. *Neuroscience, 125*(2), 329–336. https://doi.org/10.1016/j.neuroscience.2004.01.048.

Moody, J. F., Dean III, D. C., Kecskemeti, S. R., Blennow, K., Zetterberg, H., Kollmorgen, G., ..., Bendlin, B. B. (2022). Associations between diffusion MRI microstructure and cerebrospinal fluid markers of Alzheimer's disease pathology and neurodegeneration along the Alzheimer's disease continuum. *Alzheimer's & Dementia: Diagnosis, Assessment & Disease Monitoring, 14*(1), e12381. https://doi.org/10.1002/dad2.12381

Murphy, D. G. M., DeCarli, C. D., Daly, E., Gillette, J. A., McIntosh, A. R., Haxby, J. V., ..., Horwitz, B. (1993). Volumetric magnetic resonance imaging in men with dementia of the Alzheimer type: Correlations with disease severity. *Biological Psychiatry, 34*(9), 612–621. https://doi.org/10.1016/0006-3223(93)90153-5

Narvacan, K., Treit, S., Camicioli, R., Martin, W., & Beaulieu, C. (2017). Evolution of deep gray matter volume across the human lifespan. *Human Brain Mapping, 38*(8), 3771–3790. https://doi.org/10.1002/hbm.23604

Nemoto, K., Sakaguchi, H., Kasai, W., Hotta, M., Kamei, R., Noguchi, T., ..., Asada, T. (2021). Differentiating dementia with Lewy bodies and Alzheimer's disease by deep learning to structural MRI. *Journal of Neuroimaging, 31*(3), 579–587. https://doi.org/10.1111/jon.12835

Paillard, J. (1976). Réflexions sur l'usage du concept de plasticité en neurobiology. *Journal de Psychologie, 73*(1), 33–47.

Park, D. C., & Reuter-Lorenz, P. (2009). The adaptive brain: Aging and neurocognitive scaffolding. *Annual Review of Psychology, 60*, 173–196. https://doi.org/10.1146/annurev.psych.59.103006.093656

Patil, P. G., & Turner, D. A. (2008). The development of brain–machine interface neuroprosthetic devices. *Neurotherapeutics, 5*(1), 137–146. https://doi.org/10.1016/j.nurt.2007.11.002

Pelletier, A., Barul, C., Féart, C., Helmer, C., Bernard, C., Periot, O., Dilharreguy, B., Dartigues, J. F., Allard, M., Barberger-Gateau, P., Catheline, G., & Samieri, C. (2015). Mediterranean diet and preserved brain structural connectivity in older subjects. *Alzheimer's & Dementia: the journal of the Alzheimer's Association, 11*(9), 1023–1031. https://doi.org/10.1016/j.jalz.2015.06.1888

Perez, M. A., Lungholt, B. K., Nyborg, K., & Nielsen, J. B. (2004). Motor skill training induces changes in the excitability of the leg cortical area in healthy humans. *Experimental Brain Research, 159*(2), 197–205. https://doi.org/10.1007/s00221-004-1947-5.

Pfefferbaum, A., Rohlfing, T., Rosenbloom, M. J., Chu, W., Colrain, I. M., & Sullivan, E. V. Variation in longitudinal trajectories of regional brain volumes of healthy men and women (ages 10 to 85 years) measured with atlas-based parcellation of MRI. *NeuroImage, 65*, 176–193. https://doi.org/10.1016/j.neuroimage.2012.10.008

Pickersgill, J. W., Turco, C. V., Ramdeo, K., Rehsi, R. S., Foglia, S. D., & Nelson, A. J. (2022). The combined influences of exercise, diet and sleep on neuroplasticity. *Frontiers in Psychology, 13*, 831819. https://doi.org/10.3389/fpsyg.2022.831819

Raymer, A. M., Beeson, P., Holland, A., Kendall, D., Maher, L. M., Martin, N., Murray, L., Rose, M., Thompson, C. K., Turkstra, L., Altmann, L., Boyle, M., Conway, T., Hula, W., Kearns, K., Rapp, B., Simmons-Mackie, N., & Gonzalez Rothi, L. J. (2008). Translational research in aphasia: From neuroscience to neurorehabilitation. *Journal of Speech, Language, and Hearing Research: JSLHR, 51*(1), S259–S275. https://doi-org.ucsf.idm.oclc.org/10.1044/1092-4388(2008/020)

Raz, N., Lindenberger, U., Rodrigue, K. M., Kennedy, K. M., Head, D., Williamson, A., . . ., Acker, J. D. (2005). Regional brain changes in aging healthy adults: General trends, individual differences and modifiers. *Cerebral Cortex, 15*, 1676–1689. https://doi.org/10.1093/cercor/bhi044

Reuter-Lorenz, P. A., & Cappell, K. A. (2008). Neurocognitive aging and the compensation hypothesis. *Current Directions in Psychological Science, 17*, 177–182. https://doi.org/10.1111/j.1467-8721.2008.005

Risedal, A., Zeng, J., & Johansson, B. B. (1999). Early training may exacerbate brain damage after focal brain ischemia in the rat. *Journal of Cerebral Blood Flow & Metabolism, 19*(9), 997–1003. https://doi.org/10.1097/00004647-199909000-00007

Rogalski, E., Gefen, T., Mao, Q., Connelly, M., Weintraub, S., Geula, C., Bigio, E. H., & Mesulam, M. M. (2019). Cognitive trajectories and spectrum of neuropathology in SuperAgers: The first 10 cases. *Hippocampus, 29*(5), 458–467. https://doi.org/10.1002/hipo.22828

Rossini, P. M., Miraglia, F., & Vecchio, F. (2022). Early dementia diagnosis, MCI-to-dementia risk prediction, and the role of machine learning methods for feature extraction from integrated biomarkers, in particular for EEG signal analysis. *Alzheimer's & Dementia, 18*(12), 2699–2706.

Sadato, N., Pascual-Leone, A., Grafman, J., Ibañez, V., Deiber, M. P., Dold, G., & Hallett, M. (1996). Activation of the primary visual cortex by Braille reading in blind subjects. *Nature, 380*(6574), 526–528.

Sarubbo, F., Cavallucci, V., & Pani, G. (2022). The influence of gut microbiota on neurogenesis: Evidence and hopes. *Cells, 11*(3), 382. https://doi.org/10.3390/cells11030382

Saykin, A. J., Flashman, L. A., Frutiger, S. A., Johnson, S. C., Mamourian, A. C., Moritz, C. H., ..., Weaver, J. B. (1999). Neuroanatomic substrates of semantic memory impairment in Alzheimer's disease: Patterns of functional MRI activation. *Journal of the International Neuropsychological Society, 5*(05), 377–392. https://doi.org/10.1017/s135561779955501x

Seshadri, S., Wolf, P. A., Beiser, A., Elias, M. F., Au, R., Kase, C. S., & DeCarli, C. (2004). Stroke risk profile, brain volume, and cognitive function: The Framingham Offspring Study. *Neurology, 63*(9), 1591–1599. https://doi.org/10.1212/01.wnl.0000142968.22691.70

Sharma, S., Ying, Z., & Gomez-Pinilla, F. (2010). A pyrazole curcumin derivative restores membrane homeostasis disrupted after brain trauma. *Experimental Neurology, 226*(1), 191–199. https://doi.org/10.1016/j.expneurol.2010.08.027

Shaw, S. E., Morris, D. M., Uswatte, G., McKay, S., Meythaler, J. M., & Taub, E. (2005). Constraint-induced movement therapy for recovery of upper-limb function following traumatic brain injury. *Journal of Rehabilitation Research and Development, 42*(6), 769. https://doi.org/10.1111/1440-1630.12567

Sijbers, J., Scheunders, P., Bonnet, N., Van Dyck, D., & Raman, E. (1996). Quantification and improvement of the signal-to-noise ratio in a magnetic resonance image acquisition procedure. *Magnetic Resonance Imaging, 14*(10), 1157–1163. https://doi.org/10.1016/S0730-725X(96)00219-6

Stanisic, N., Häggman-Henrikson, B., Kothari, M., Costa, Y. M., Avivi-Arber, L., & Svensson, P. (2022). Pain's adverse impact on training-induced performance and neuroplasticity: A systematic review. *Brain Imaging and Behavior, 16*(5), 2281–2306. https://doi.org/10.1007/s11682-021-00621-6

Stockbridge, M. D., Bunker, L. D., & Hillis, A. E. (2022). Reversing the ruin: Rehabilitation, recovery, and restoration after stroke. *Current Neurology and Neuroscience Reports, 22*(11), 745–755. https://doi.org/10.1007/s11910-022-01231-5

Su, Y. S., Veeravagu, A., & Grant, G. (2016). Neuroplasticity after traumatic brain injury. In D. Laskowitz & G. Grant (Eds.), *Transnational research in traumatic brain injury* (Chapter 8). CRC Press/Taylor and Francis Group.

Taub, E., & Uswatte, G. (2015). *Harnessing neuroplasticity to promote rehabilitation: CI therapy for TBI*. Alabama University in Birmingham.

Toepper, M. (2017). Dissociating normal aging from Alzheimer's disease: A view from cognitive neuroscience. *Journal of Alzheimer's Disease, 57*(2), 331–352. https://doi.org/10.3233/JAD-161099

Tomaszczyk, J. C., Green, N. L., Frasca, D., Colella, B., Turner, G. R., Christensen, B. K., & Green, R. E. (2014). Negative neuroplasticity in chronic traumatic brain injury and implications for neurorehabilitation. *Neuropsychology Review, 24*(4), 409-427. https://doi.org/10.1007/s11065-014-9273-6

Torres-Simón, L., Doval, S., Nebreda, A., Llinas, S. J., Marsh, E. B., & Maestú, F. (2022). Understanding brain function in vascular cognitive impairment and dementia with EEG and MEG: A systematic review. *NeuroImage: Clinical, 35*, 103040. https://doi.org/10.1016/j.nicl.2022.103040

Vaghari, D., Kabir, E., & Henson, R. N. (2022). Late combination shows that MEG adds to MRI in classifying MCI versus controls. *Neuroimage, 252*, 119054. https://doi.org/10.1016/j.neuroimage.2022.119054

Valkanova, V., Rodriguez, R., & Ebmeier, K. P. (2014). Mind over matter—What do we know about neuroplasticity in adults. *International Psychogeriatrics, 26*, 891–909. https://doi.org/10.1017/S1041610213002482

Villemagne, V. L., Barkhof, F., Garibotto, V., Landau, S. M., Nordberg, A., & van Berckel, B. N. (2021). Molecular imaging approaches in dementia. *Radiology, 298*(3), 517–530. https://doi.org/10.1148/radiol.2020200028

Vlotinou, P., Tsiptsios, D., Karatzetzou, S., Kalogirou, G., Stefas, E., Aggelousis, N., & Vadikolias, K. (2022). Transcranial direct current stimulation in conjunction with mirror therapy for upper extremity rehabilitation in chronic stroke patients. *Maedica, 17*(1), 169–176. https://doi.org/10.26574/maedica.2022.17.1.169

Wardlaw, J. M., Smith, C., & Dichgans, M. (2019). Small vessel disease: Mechanisms and clinical implications. *The Lancet. Neurology, 18*(7), 684–696. https://doi.org/10.1016/S1474-4422(19)30079-1

Wu, A., Ying, Z., & Gomez-Pinilla, F. (2004). Dietary omega-3 fatty acids normalize BDNF levels, reduce oxidative damage, and counteract learning disability after traumatic brain injury in rats. *Journal of Neurotrauma, 21*(10), 1457–1467. https://doi.org/10.1089/neu.2004.21.1457

Wu, A., Ying, Z. H. E., & Gomez-Pinilla, F. (2007). Omega-3 fatty acids supplementation restores mechanisms that maintain brain homeostasis in traumatic brain injury. *Journal of Neurotrauma, 24*(10), 1587–1595. https://doi.org/10.1089/neu.2007.0313

Zatorre, R. J., Fields, R. D., & Johansen-Berg, H. (2012). Plasticity in gray and white: Neuroimaging changes in brain structure during learning. *Nature Neuroscience, 15*(4), 528–536. https://doi.org/10.1038/nn.3045

7

Personality and Emotional Development

Erin L. Woodhead

LEARNING OBJECTIVES

- Apply findings of attachment theory to the aging process and to caregiving.
- Differentiate between mean-level stability and rank-order stability of personality traits and how they are measured.
- Evaluate the research regarding whether personality (as measured by the five-factor model) changes or remains stable into late life.
- Differentiate between various ways of measuring happiness and describe its variability with age.
- Evaluate the evidence for the age-related positivity effect and describe a possible reason for it.

PERSONALITY DEVELOPMENT

In your undergraduate psychology courses, you may remember learning about different ways that personality is conceptualized. In this section of the chapter, we review the major perspectives on personality development with a focus on the trait approach (commonly called the "Big 5"), as well as the coping perspective, which emphasizes how people come to interpret and understand the situations they face. We also present research on the stability of personality traits across the life span.

Overview of Personality Theories

PSYCHODYNAMIC PERSPECTIVES

For most people, the name Sigmund Freud comes to mind when considering any type of psychodynamic theory. Most of Freud's work on personality development focused on changes occurring in childhood and adolescence. He believed that older adults had personalities that were so rigid that therapy was likely to be useless. Modern psychodynamic perspectives on personality development focus on ego psychology and Erik Erikson's theory of psychosocial development, adult attachment theory, and theories of defense mechanisms. We review each of these in turn.

Erik Erikson's theory of psychosocial development focuses on the successful resolution of eight developmental stages that occur throughout the life span. According to Erikson's theory, individuals have to successfully resolve each crisis before moving on to the next. In middle and older adulthood, the crises are generativity versus stagnation and ego integrity versus despair. Generativity focuses on achieving a legacy through making a positive impact in one's community, whereas stagnation results when an individual is lacking a sense of positive impact and legacy. Ego integrity focuses on finding meaning in one's life, as well as accepting shortcomings and failures of one's own in addition to the shortcomings and failures of others in one's life. According to Erikson, accepting this leads to ego integrity, whereas despair happens when an individual is unable to achieve this acceptance. It is presumed from Erikson's writings that individuals will face the ego integrity versus despair phase around age 60 or 65 and that individuals need to resolve the earlier stage-related crises in order to contemplate the concepts of ego integrity versus despair (Hannah et al., 1996). In his late life, Erikson started to revise his view on this, proposing that the outcome of the eighth stage (ego integrity vs. despair) is not necessarily determined by the successful resolution of the prior stages (Erikson et al., 1986). Erikson's wife, Joan Erikson, added to her husband's work by reconceptualizing the eighth stage as "disgust and despair versus integrity" (Erikson & Erikson, 1998). Erikson proposed that the eighth stage was characterized by reflection and reminiscence. Some authors have proposed that while navigating the eighth Erikson stage, older adults go through a process of acceptance versus denial. Denial is associated with late life depression and can lead to the experience of despair in the eighth stage (Jeffers et al., 2020)

Joan Erikson also proposed a ninth stage experienced by adults in their 80s and 90s (Erikson & Erikson, 1998). This stage focuses on "gerotranscendence." Further elaborated by Tornstam (1996), successful resolution of the gerotranscendence stage may result in a new and qualitatively different perspective on life (Jeffers et al., 2020). Gerotranscendence focuses on growth and reconciliation and is proposed to start around 80 years old. This stage is theorized to focus on three domains: cosmic relations (feeling connected to prior generations), a sense of coherence in life including a strong sense of self, and a focus on solitude and close interpersonal relationships (Jeffers et al., 2020).

Research on the eighth and ninth stages in Erikson's model suggests that the level of ego integrity achieved in the 60s is stable into later life, as measured by a 30-item questionnaire about ego integrity (Brown & Lowis, 2003). Example items from this scale include "I can accept the ups and downs of my past life" and "My life has been a growth process right up to the present" (Lowis & Raubenheimer, 1997). Attempts to measure levels of ego integrity using the Lowis and Raubenheimer (1997) scale prior to age 60 result in very low scores, suggesting that an individual needs to have lived a significant period of time before being able to reflect on their life. The finding that scores on the ego integrity measure did not increase with advancing age after age 60 implies that ego integrity stabilizes after it is successfully resolved. In contrast, scores on a measure designed to assess one's level of gerotranscendence, a prominent construct in the proposed ninth stage, continued to increase with increasing age, suggesting that "gerotranscendence" continues to increase into the 80s and 90s. Example items from the measure of gerotranscendence include: "Later life has given me a release from the stresses of life" and "The meaning of life seems more clear to me now" (Brown & Lowis, 2003).

Generativity is typically defined as some activity that supports the next generation, such as parenting and grandparenting, involvement in communities, political participation, civic engagement, and environmental advocacy (Newton et al., 2020). Generativity is often connected to the idea of leaving a legacy, which may include a personal legacy (making a lasting contribution within one's immediate social circle) and/or a broader legacy (making a lasting contribution for the greater good). Stagnation is typically characterized as low levels of caring interactions with the world and low levels of self-satisfaction. Newton et al. (2020) found that in a study of older women aged 60 to 75, higher scores on a measure of stagnation were related to a decreased likelihood of expressing a legacy of any type. Additionally, higher stagnation scores were associated with lower scores on a measure related to life satisfaction. This research suggests that generativity and stagnation are present in the age range that Erikson proposed and may be related to overall life satisfaction.

Generativity is often viewed as relating to interactions between older and younger generations. Although generativity is one of the major developmental tasks of middle and older adulthood, some level of generativity is present in younger individuals, and overall levels of generativity can be traced throughout the adult life span (McAdams et al., 1993). Generativity is thought to reach its peak in middle and older adulthood, when generative concerns become focused on taking action. Some researchers have proposed that levels of generativity may be transmitted intergenerationally, such as from adult parents to adult children. This may be due to similar personality traits between parents and offspring, as generativity is linked to some of the Big 5 personality traits discussed later in this chapter, including openness and extraversion (Cox et al., 2010). It could also be related to social learning theory and the role of parental modeling of generative actions. In a study of university students and their parents, Millová et al. (2023) found that maternal reports of generative action were significantly associated with offspring reports of generative action. Additionally, maternal reports of stagnation were significantly related to offspring reports of stagnation. The authors conclude that there is support for intergenerational transmission of generativity, particularly the behavioral components of generative action.

Significant criticisms of Erikson's work have emerged over the years. Erikson's theory assumes that the proposed developmental tasks are universal and apply to all individuals. Additionally, Erikson assumes that progression through the stages is linear and unidirectional and that resolution of each stage results in "healthy" adult development (Jordan & Tseris, 2018). When the stages are discussed as universal, some researchers have argued that the "universal" adult in this case is someone who identifies as a White, middle class, nondisabled male from a Western industrialized country. Therefore, Erikson's model can be seen as excluding women, racial and ethnic minorities, and those from a lower socioeconomic background (Jordan & Tseris, 2018). Some also argue that Erikson's theory is ableist, in the sense that disabilities are viewed as deficits that may limit progression through the proposed developmental stages. Although Erikson's stages are often presented in psychology courses as applying to all adults, readers should consider how the stages were developed without incorporating individuals from diverse backgrounds.

The second personality theory rooted in the psychodynamic perspective is adult attachment theory. John Bowlby studied infants' attachment to their primary caregiver and proposed that, through our early experiences with caregivers, we develop internal working models of how relationships should function, which may be carried into romantic relationships in adulthood. If infants feel safe and well-cared for by their primary caregivers, they will display a secure attachment style, with adult relationships characterized by confidence in themselves and the belief that others will treat them well. Inconsistent parenting in terms of physical and emotional availability is associated with an anxious attachment style in early childhood, with adult relationships characterized by clinging to romantic partners due to a fear of abandonment. A lack of responsiveness and emotional support from parents is associated with an avoidant attachment style, with adult relationships characterized by an avoidance of closeness.

In a study of attachment styles among older women between ages 50 and 83, Spence et al. (2020) found that 63% had an insecure attachment style. Insecure attachment styles were significantly associated with poor support, social isolation, and loneliness. This study replicates findings from Magai et al. (2001), which found that, among African American and White older adults, 22% of the sample was classified as securely attached and 78% of the sample was classified as dismissing, which is a variation of the avoidant attachment style. The researchers propose that the adverse events that are often faced by older adults, particularly older adults that are part of an ethnic minority group, may change attachment style over the course of the life span from secure to insecure due to adverse events that the adults faced in their emerging adulthood years (Magai et al., 2001).

Longitudinal studies suggest that attachment is moderately stable over time and becomes less stable the further apart the assessment points become. Over a 59-year period, Chopik et al. (2019) found that the average test–retest reliability for attachment anxiety (concerns about the availability of close others) was .40 and for attachment avoidance (discomfort with physical and emotional intimacy) was .44. Generally, both attachment anxiety and attachment avoidance decreased with age, and attachment security was highest among those in a relationship. Attachment in infancy is also associated with personality traits in adulthood (Young et al., 2019). In a 30-year study, individuals with a secure attachment in infancy scored higher on the personality traits of agreeableness and conscientiousness and lower on the trait of neuroticism compared with those with an insecure attachment. This research suggests that early attachment continues to have an impact on development into older adulthood.

Early attachment style may have long-lasting effects on cognitive development, including symptoms related to dementia and cognitive decline. In a scoping review, Walsh et al. (2019) hypothesized that early attachment style may impact late life cognition through a few mechanisms. First, early attachment style impacts the type of support that is available to adults as they age and how likely they are to benefit from such support. Individuals with insecure attachment styles may have more difficulty obtaining and benefiting from social support. There is evidence that having a fuller social support system is protective against cognitive decline in older adults, suggesting one mechanism by which early attachment style may affect the development of dementia and cognitive decline. Additionally, brain structures and systems may be impacted by early attachment style. For example, early insecure attachment can have a negative impact on some of the same areas of the brain that are impacted by dementia, namely the hippocampus, amygdala, and dysregulation of the hypothalamic-pituitary-adrenal (HPA) axis. Therefore, the presence of a secure, supportive, and responsive social environment early in life has long-lasting effects on development at multiple levels (see Figure 7.1).

The third personality theory rooted in the psychodynamic perspective is around the use of defense mechanisms and how the use of certain mechanisms may change with age. Based on psychodynamic theory, defense mechanisms are used by the ego to protect individuals from unacceptable urges and desires that develop in the id. Defense mechanisms are conceptualized as stable over time, unconscious, and related to personality structure. This conceptualization contrasts with coping mechanisms, discussed in the next section, which are viewed as dependent on the situation, flexibly applied, and conscious (Silverman & Aafjes-van Doorn, 2023). Defense mechanisms and coping are

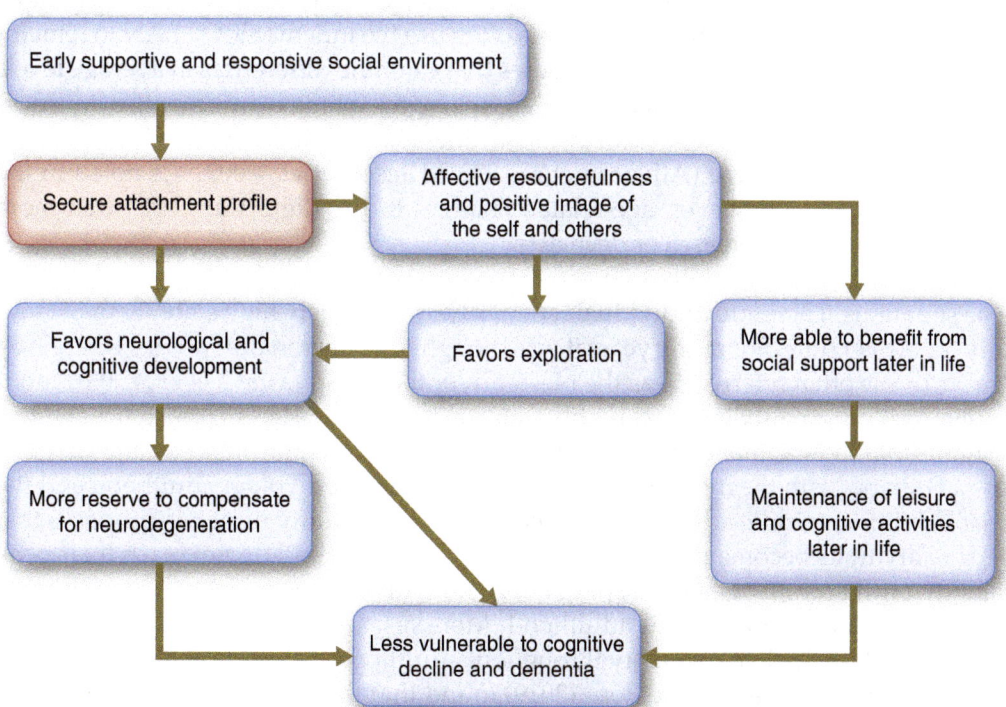

Figure 7.1 Proposed model of how early secure attachment is associated with reduced vulnerability to cognitive decline and dementia in later life.

Source: From Walsh, E., Blake, Y., Donati, A., Stoop, R., & Von Gunten, A. (2019). Early secure attachment as a protective factor against later cognitive decline and dementia. *Frontiers in Aging Neuroscience, 11*, 161. https://doi.org/10.3389/fnagi.2019.00161

correlated, with research suggesting that use of maladaptive coping strategies is associated with immature defense mechanisms, while adaptive coping strategies are associated with the use of mature defense mechanisms (Silverman & Aafjes-van Doorn, 2023).

More recent research supports the idea that defense mechanisms are tied to developmental period and that older adults tend to use more adaptive defense mechanisms. Diehl et al. (2014) found that the defense mechanisms of intellectualization (thinking about stressful events in a detached way), sublimation (converting impulses into more acceptable outlets), and suppression (keeping unpleasant information from one's conscious mind) increased from younger to middle adulthood with a decrease in older adulthood. The use of ego regression (reverting to earlier behaviors), isolation (avoiding the experience of an emotion), and rationalization (justifying an unacceptable behavior with logic) also showed steady decline with increasing age. Regression and displacement (taking feelings out on others) declined until about age 65 and then increased in older adulthood.

TRAIT PERSPECTIVES

Trait theories of personality are typically based on descriptions of an individual based on certain psychological characteristics, often thought to be tied to genetic predispositions. Trait theories assume that personality traits are enduring and stable. The most well-known trait approach is the five-factor model (McCrae & Costa, 2003). The five-factor model proposes that personality is made up of variations on five major traits, also known as the Big 5: **O**penness to experience, **C**onscientiousness, **E**xtraversion, **A**greeableness, and **N**euroticism. Students often use the mnemonic OCEAN to remember all five factors. In cross-sectional studies that examine differences in average levels of the Big 5 personality traits across age groups, agreeableness and conscientiousness tend to increase with age, while extraversion, openness to experience, and neuroticism tend to decrease with age (Atherton et al., 2021; Helson et al., 2002). As noted in the upcoming sections, however, age-related changes in the Big 5 traits are often more complex than linear increases or decreases.

Personality traits, by definition, are thought to be stable and enduring across multiple situations. Therefore, individuals should show relatively high stability in personality traits over time. For many years it was thought that personality was set in stone by age 30; this is often referred to as the plaster hypothesis (Srivastava et al., 2003), and it implies that personality traits are highly stable in adulthood. Recent research, however, suggests that the stability of personality traits changes across the life span and may follow a U shape, with the most stability in early adulthood and older adulthood and the least stability in middle adulthood. The cumulative continuity principle proposes that personality traits become more stable with increasing age and do not reach their peak stability until around age 60 (Caspi et al., 2005). This suggests that personality traits continue to change throughout adulthood. More research is emerging that supports the idea of plasticity in personality throughout adulthood (Schwaba & Bleidorn, 2018). For example, Schwaba and Bleidorn (2019) found that there were changes in the five-factor personality traits around the transition to retirement. Notably, there were sharp increases in openness to experience and agreeableness following retirement, with gradual declines in the 5 years after retirement. However, other research has found that personality is best characterized by stability rather than change throughout adulthood (Wagner et al., 2019). Overall, personality across adulthood is complex and not easily described by change or stability. Rather, personality change is likely a picture of both stability and change, with changes happening in systematic ways, and some individuals experiencing more change than others (Graham et al., 2020)

The extent to which individuals endorse certain personality characteristics is associated with physical and mental health. Most of the research in this area focuses on the personality traits of neuroticism and conscientiousness. For example, in a study of different dimensions of conscientiousness, Stephan et al. (2019) found that high scores on five of six dimensions of conscientiousness (order, traditionalism, virtue, responsibility, and industriousness) were associated with a 10% to 25% reduction in mortality risk. High levels of conscientiousness are also related to better cognitive performance among older adults, as well as more engagement in cognitively stimulating activities (Sutin et al., 2022). The proposed mechanism between conscientiousness and health is that individuals who are high on conscientiousness tend to engage in more health-promoting behaviors, such as regular physical activity and regular medical appointments. Older adults who report high levels of neuroticism also tend to report higher levels of depressive symptoms as well as higher levels of subjective cognitive impairment (Jenkins et al., 2019; Turunen et al., 2022). In a study of falls among older adults, higher levels of neuroticism were linked to more indoor and outdoor falls, even when controlling for other risk factors associated with falls among older adults (Turunen et al., 2022). The proposed mechanism is that a higher level of baseline neuroticism increases concern about perceived threats, including falls, and is associated with higher depressive symptoms, increasing the likelihood of falling. These findings are consistent with a large body of research suggesting that individuals high in conscientiousness tend to be in better health, potentially due to a tendency to engage in more preventive care throughout life. In contrast, individuals high in neuroticism tend to experience more physical and mental health difficulties.

Longitudinal Studies of Personality Change in Adulthood

There are two primary ways to examine change or stability in personality across adulthood: change across groups and change within individuals. When considering change over time, researchers have to consider both mean-level stability and rank-order stability (Schwaba & Bleidorn, 2018). *Mean-level stability* refers to stability in the overall mean of a trait across a period of time for the whole sample, also thought of as change across groups. Studies of mean-level stability examine changes in the mean level of a personality trait over the course of adulthood. *Rank-order stability* focuses on change within an individual and is typically measured by the correlation between personality scores across two time points. High levels of rank-order stability imply that an individual who scores high on a trait in comparison to others in the group will continue to score high on that trait over time compared with others, even if the group average increases or decreases (mean-level stability). Therefore, even if mean-level stability is low, indicated by significant mean differences across age groups, rank-order stability may be high if everyone maintains their same position in the group. This is often represented by the statement, "the highs stay high and the lows stay low." Stated another way, the most agreeable person in a group is likely to stay the most agreeable person, even if the overall levels of agreeableness decline in the group. While rank-order stability indicates the relative ordering of individuals on a specific trait, researchers can also examine individual differences in a trait, which is related to rank-order stability but is calculated slightly differently.

In a study of mean-level and individual differences, Graham et al. (2020) combined data from 16 longitudinal studies with participants ranging in age from adolescence to older adulthood. With regard to mean-level stability, Graham et al. (2020) found overall declines in neuroticism until around age 60, with a flattening of the slope after age 60. The pattern for extraversion showed decline for younger and middle-aged adults, with a steeper pattern of decline for adults over age 60. There was a similar pattern for openness, with a decline in younger and middle adulthood and a steeper decline in older adulthood. Conscientiousness increased slightly for younger and middle-aged adults and then declined in adults over age 60. Finally, the pattern for agreeableness indicated increases throughout younger and middle adulthood and then stability or a slight decrease in older adulthood. Graham et al. (2020) also found that there were significant individual differences in change patterns for all five factors, meaning that individuals deviated significantly from the mean trend for all five traits. As expected, individuals did not change at the same rate or in the same direction, suggesting plasticity within individuals over time. In a study of individual differences, Schwaba and Bleidorn (2018) found that, among individuals ages 16 to 84, individual differences in personality change were significant for all five factors. Changes within individuals were noted until late life, with individual differences no longer significant for conscientiousness after age 75, openness after age 70, agreeableness after age 65, and extraversion from ages 70 to 74. The pattern of individual differences followed a similar trend for all five factors, with the most change within individuals occurring during the emerging adulthood period, some change occurring in younger and middle adulthood, and the least change occurring in older adulthood. In contrast, individual differences for emotional stability were relatively constant from adolescence to older adulthood. Although the individual differences found in this study were small, the results suggest that individual change in personality throughout adulthood is present, which counteracts the idea of personality being set in stone by age 30.

COPING PERSPECTIVES

The coping perspective posits that the ways in which an individual copes with a stressful situation is based on a complex interaction between the person, their environment, and their resources. Although coping styles are distinct from personality traits, coping styles play an important role in daily functioning and well-being. Personality represents traits that are stable across time and situations, whereas coping styles may change depending on the type of stressor an individual faces (Connor-Smith & Flachsbart, 2007).

Coping styles are typically delineated into three major domains or approaches: (a) problem-focused versus emotion-focused strategies, (b) approach versus avoidance strategies, and (c) behavioral versus cognitive strategies (Nieto et al., 2020). Problem-focused coping strategies focus on efforts to manage the problem, as opposed to emotion-focused strategies, which emphasize regulating one's emotional response to the stressor. Similar to problem-focused strategies, approach strategies emphasize directly managing the problem versus managing the problem through avoidance. Avoidance coping tends to be characterized by strategies such as avoiding others and engaging in unhealthy behaviors to manage the stressor such as drugs and alcohol. Behavioral coping strategies focus on specific steps one can take to manage the stressor, whereas cognitive strategies focus on self-talk and other mental strategies to reduce the impact of the stressor. Coping strategies are deployed in response to a specific situation. Therefore, many people use different types of coping depending on the situation. Even certain types of avoidance coping can be helpful based on the context, particularly the use of positive distraction (Waugh et al., 2020). Generally, avoidance coping is typically thought of as less adaptive compared with the other types of coping strategies. In longitudinal studies, avoidance coping has been associated with negative outcomes such as problem drinking and suicidal ideation (Brennan et al., 2012; Woodhead et al., 2014).

Research on age-related differences in coping suggests that older adults engage in fewer avoidance coping strategies than younger adults (Nieto et al., 2020; Woodhead et al., 2014). There are a few proposed mechanisms for why older adults tend to engage in less avoidance coping. One of the primary mechanisms is that older adults become more effective at managing emotions with age and therefore are more adept at deploying adaptive coping strategies (Carstensen, 2006). This is consistent with socioemotional selectivity theory, which is discussed later in this chapter. Another possible mechanism is that older adults are less likely to engage in avoidance coping strategies because they have learned that avoidance coping strategies are unlikely to solve the problem (Yancura & Aldwin, 2008). A third possible mechanism is that older adults are more adept at managing stressors before they happen so that they have fewer stressful situations overall than younger adults who require use of distinct coping strategies. Later in this chapter we discuss this issue more when we review research on age-related differences in emotion regulation strategies.

The COVID-19 pandemic was a significant stressor for many older adults and required use of multiple types of coping strategies. Common coping strategies reported by older adults during the pandemic included exercising and being in the outdoors, creating daily routines, engaging in COVID-19 precautions like wearing masks and washing hands, shifting one's attitude and outlook, and relying on social connections (Finlay et al., 2021). Results of other studies suggest that older adults demonstrated a high level of resilience during the pandemic. Vannini et al. (2021) found that high levels of resilience among older adults during the pandemic were associated with more use of adaptive coping strategies and less use of maladaptive strategies. In another study of coping among older adults during the pandemic, more use of avoidant coping strategies was associated with higher reports of depression, anxiety, and loneliness, whereas more use of approach coping strategies was associated with lower reports of depression and loneliness (Minahan et al., 2021). Taken together, research on coping during the pandemic supports the idea that older adults may be better equipped than younger age groups to engage in adaptive coping strategies in the face of stress.

EMOTIONAL FUNCTIONING IN LATE LIFE

Think about a typical day for you and describe the types of emotions you experienced during that day. This task might seem straightforward, but with further thought you may notice that your emotional experience can vary on multiple dimensions, including the intensity of the emotions (i.e., strength of the emotions), their duration (i.e., how long they lasted), and their frequency (i.e., how often you experienced an emotion). You might also consider how well you were able to regulate your emotions that day, whether there was anything in your day that produced a strong emotion, and how you would describe your overall emotional well-being on that particular day. The goal of this section is to understand how the emotional experiences of older adults compare to other age groups, according to the aforementioned dimensions, as well as whether the structure or function of emotions changes with age.

Age and Emotional Well-Being

Early research on emotional development proposed that there were increases in emotional well-being through the 20s and then a steady decline through middle and older adulthood (Banham, 1951).

However, modern research suggests that the emotional experience of middle-aged and older adults is not as negative as outlined by Banham (1951). Researchers have long proposed a U-shaped curve to happiness, such that happiness ratings are highest in younger and older adulthood and lowest in middle age. However, the data in support of the U-shaped curve are primarily based on cross-sectional studies, which often conflate age differences with age change. A review of cross-sectional and longitudinal studies on the U-shaped curve suggests that happiness across adulthood is not easily represented by one trajectory and that data from both cross-sectional and longitudinal studies on the U-shaped curve are mixed (Galambos et al., 2020). Some longitudinal studies indicate that happiness ratings may be the lowest in adolescence with steady increases throughout younger adulthood and middle age. Other data suggest that happiness is highly stable until older adulthood, followed by declines in late life. The primary finding from longitudinal studies is diversity in happiness ratings, rather than a clear trajectory. Interestingly, when older individuals are asked about the best decade of their lives, they often report that the 30s and 40s were the best decades, with many participants reporting that their teenage years were the lowest point in terms of life satisfaction (Galambos et al., 2020).

These results might make you wonder how happiness is measured. Is happiness the same as life satisfaction? These types of questions about how to define and measure happiness have been discussed extensively in the literature (Oishi et al., 2013). In a study of the concept of happiness across cultures, Oishi et al. (2013) found that happiness was often defined as good luck and favorable external conditions. American English definitions of happiness tend to focus on positive internal feeling states. The term happiness is often used interchangeably with subjective well-being (Galambos et al., 2020). Subjective well-being includes ratings of life satisfaction, the subjective experience of positive emotional states over time, and low levels of negative affect such as sadness. Other ways of assessing happiness focus more on ratings of the meaningfulness of life (Ryff, 2014). Questions to assess happiness may focus on a single rating with a scale from not at all happy to very happy, or very dissatisfied to very satisfied. These questions often ask the individual to consider their life overall, across time and situations. A different approach is to ask participants to rate their happiness at different points throughout the day, often known as experience sampling studies, rather than assessing global reports of happiness (Stone et al., 2010).

Models of Emotional Functioning in Late Life

Theories of emotional development in older adulthood attempt to explain older adults' emotional experiences. Socioemotional selectivity theory (SST; Carstensen et al., 2003) posits that perceived limitations on the time that an individual has left to live leads to a motivational shift such that emotionally meaningful goals are pursued. The theory posits that goals are always set within a temporal context. When an individual is younger, time is seen as open ended. This leads a younger individual to pursue goals that emphasize the acquisition of knowledge and new experience (expansive goals). These goals may lead to the experience of negative emotions and feeling-states, such as anxiety, failure, and disappointment. As an individual ages, there is a shift in perception about time (termed *future time perspective*). Time horizons become shorter with age, which leads to a shift in goals. Whereas younger adulthood is characterized by information-seeking goals, older adulthood is characterized by emotionally meaningful goals. For example, the immediate positive feelings of connecting with a close friend or family member are prioritized over the desire to try something new such as traveling in order to gain knowledge, which may involve future payoffs (i.e., more knowledge about other cultures) at the expense of current emotional state (i.e., interacting with people you may or may not like, the stress of traveling, the inconvenience of being away from familiar friends and routines). In sum, SST posits that older adults experience a more positive and complex emotional life because their perception that time is "running out" leads them to prioritize emotionally meaningful goals, which limits their exposure to negative emotional states.

A second model that accounts for age-related differences in emotional functioning is the strength and vulnerability integration (SAVI) model (Charles, 2010). This model accounts for the strengths that older adults bring to emotional regulation and well-being, as well as the potential weaknesses. First we'll consider the strengths that older adults bring to the area of emotional well-being. The SAVI model considers that the limited time perspective of older adults increases emotional well-being because it leads to prioritization of emotionally meaningful goals and a focus on the present as opposed to the future, as discussed earlier with regard to SST. A second strength that is considered in the SAVI model is that the passage of time leads older adults to have a better understanding of how to keep themselves content and avoid situations that lead to high levels of distress in their daily lives. Therefore, older adults have at least two strengths that contribute to improved emotional well-being.

Older adults also have strengths that lead to improved ability to regulate emotions. First, the age-related positivity effect, discussed later in this chapter, leads to an improved ability to shift focus away from negative stimuli. Second, older adults are more likely to quickly disengage from a negative situation than younger adults. This is done by using the strategies discussed in the section on emotion regulation, such as doing nothing or walking away. These types of strategies should not be mistaken for passive–aggressive strategies, as the goal is typically to downplay the negative experience rather than deny that it has happened. This relates to the third strength that older adults have with emotion regulation, which is that they typically downplay the potentially negative sides of an event after it has passed.

The vulnerabilities that are discussed by the SAVI model focus on times when older adults are unable to escape negative situations, such as when they are unable to extricate themselves from a situation by not entering the situation in the first place, downplaying it, distracting attention away from the negative aspects, or engaging in passive regulation strategies. When older adults are exposed to inescapable negative situations, the vulnerabilities that they face include physiological impacts of sustained emotional arousal, such as reduced physiological flexibility in the cardiovascular system (seen in the decrease in heart rate variability) and neuroendocrine system (seen in the reduced ability to downregulate the activity of the HPA axis). These are all normal age-related physiological changes. However, in the context of prolonged exposure to a negative situation, these physiological changes lead to a more difficult time recovering from a stressful event, both emotionally and physiologically. These changes are not observed in younger adults and are therefore considered vulnerabilities in the context of the SAVI model. Taken together, the SAVI model seeks to combine the literature on age-related differences in emotional well-being and emotion regulation in order to understand a broader picture of emotional development across the life span. The SAVI model is summarized in Figure 7.2.

Changes in Emotional Functioning in Older Adulthood

In support of these two theories of emotional development, there is a large body of evidence suggesting that everyday emotional experience shifts during adulthood in favor of older adults. This is known as the paradox of aging. Specifically, although there are losses that occur with age, including losses to one's social network, health, and social status, emotional experience seems to stabilize or even improve in older adulthood (Carstensen, 2019). This realization led to a large body of research examining why older adults maintain positive emotional experiences in the face of other declines. As noted earlier, SST accounts for the emotional experience of older adulthood by emphasizing that future time horizons shift among older adults, such that they invest in emotional goals more deeply with age due to a perception of limited

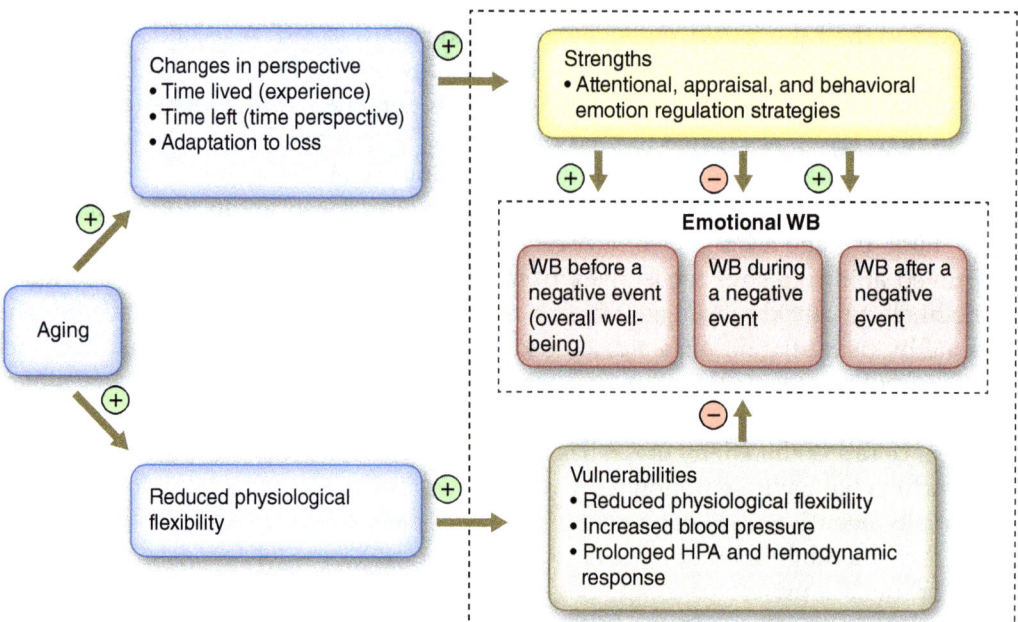

Figure 7.2 Summary of the strength and vulnerability integration (SAVI) model.
HPA, hypothalamic-pituitary-adrenal; WB, well-being.
Source: From Charles, S. T. (2010). Strength and vulnerability integration (SAVI): A model of emotional well-being across adulthood. *Psychological Bulletin, 136*(6), 1068–1091. https://doi.org/10.1037/a0021232

time left (Carstensen, 2021). Related to this line of research, a 20-year study of stress ratings among individuals aged 22 to 77 years old (Almeida et al., 2023) found that younger adults had the highest levels of stress compared with middle-aged and older adults. However, stress reactivity remained the same for participants ages 50 and older, despite an overall decrease in stressors over time. Stress reactivity decreased until around age 54 and then stabilized, whereas stressor occurrence continued to decrease with age (see Figure 7.3).

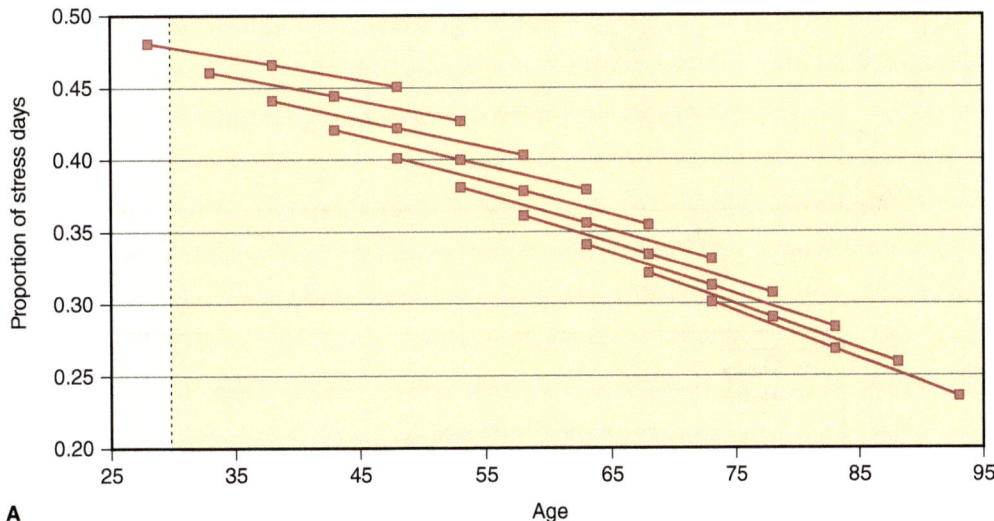

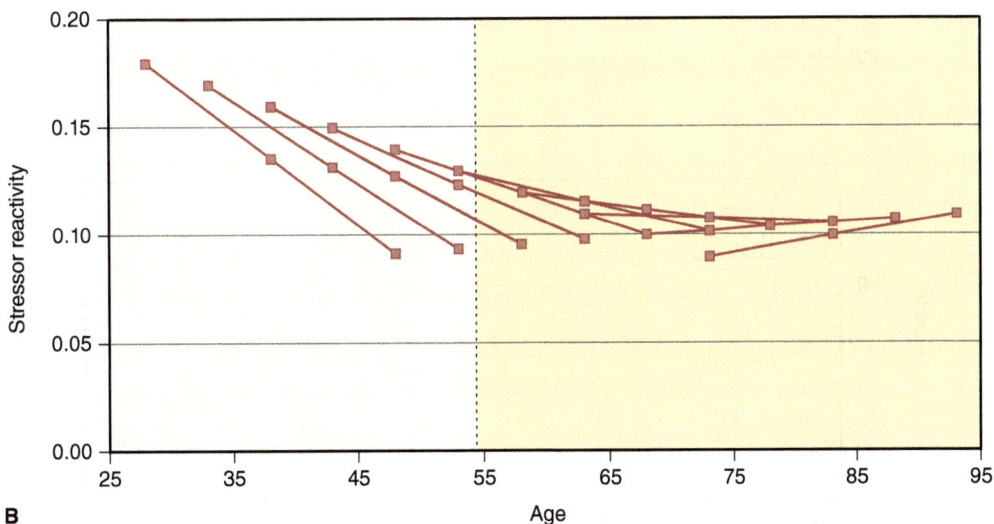

Figure 7.3 (**A**) Reduction in proportion of self-reported stressful days from younger to older adulthood. (**B**) Decrease in stress reactivity until middle adulthood, followed by stability throughout older adulthood.

Source: From Almeida, D. M., Rush, J., Mogle, J., Piazza, J. R., Cerino, E., & Charles, S. T. (2023). Longitudinal change in daily stress across 20 years of adulthood: Results from the national study of daily experiences. *Developmental Psychology, 59*(3), 515–523. https://doi.org/10.1037/dev0001469

With regard to daily emotional experiences, SST proposes a linear upward trend with age in preference for emotionally meaningful goals and in emotional experiences. Recent research examining daily emotional experiences of younger, middle-aged, and older adults presents a more complex picture (Wirth et al., 2023; see Figure 7.4). In

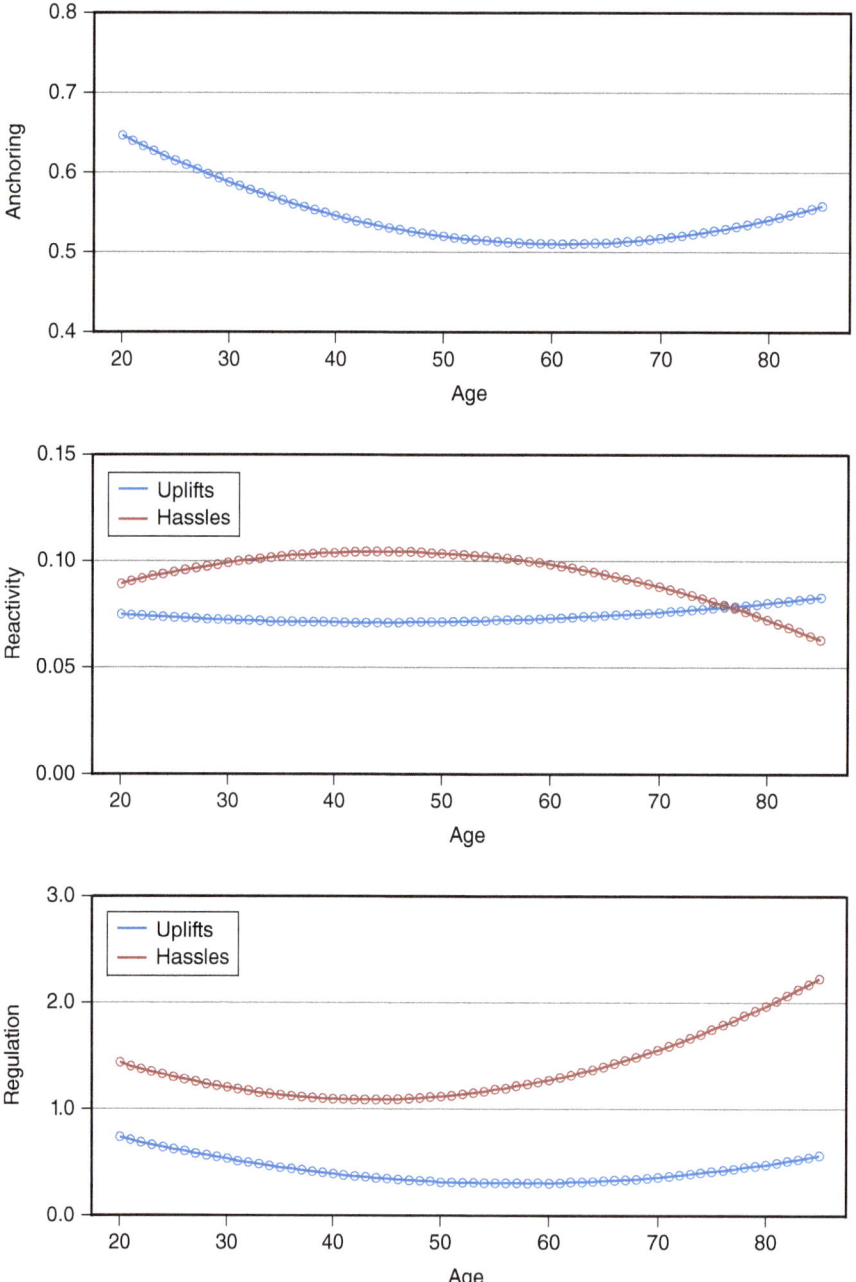

Figure 7.4 Age differences in daily positive affect (anchoring), emotional reactivity, and emotion regulation skills for daily uplifts and hassles.

Source: From Wirth, M., Voss, A., & Rothermund, K. (2023). Age differences in everyday emotional experience: Testing core predictions of socioemotional selectivity theory with the MIVA model. *The Journals of Gerontology: Series B, 78*(7), 1152–1162. https://doi.org/10.1093/geronb/gbad033

a sample ranging in age from 14 to 86, younger adults had the highest daily positive affect (termed "anchoring" in this study), followed by older adults, with middle-aged adults reporting the lowest daily positive affect. There was no effect of age on emotional reactivity to daily uplifts, whereas emotional reactivity to daily hassles was highest among middle-aged adults and similar between younger and older adults. Emotion regulation around the impact of uplift events was highest among younger adults compared with both middle-aged and older adults. In contrast, emotion regulation around daily hassles was highest among older adults, followed by younger adults and then middle-aged adults. Therefore, the picture of daily emotional experience in adulthood is potentially not as clear-cut as originally thought and is characterized by notable shifts throughout younger, middle age, and older adulthood.

The daily emotional experience of many people, including older adults, was impacted by the COVID-19 pandemic. In light of the information presented in this chapter on the emotional experience of older adults, some researchers hypothesized that older adults would fare better during COVID-19 in terms of their daily emotional experiences, even in light of COVID-19 posing a higher risk to older adults. In support of this, Carstensen et al. (2020) found that older adults reported experiencing negative emotions less frequently and positive emotions more frequently during the pandemic compared with younger age groups. Older adults also reported experiencing a lower intensity of negative emotions and a higher intensity of positive emotions compared with younger age groups.

It is possible that happiness ratings and the experience of positive and negative affect with increasing age are different among older adults who are coping with chronic illnesses. Much of the research on happiness and life satisfaction tends to be done with community-dwelling older adults who are relatively healthy compared with their peers. Some research suggests that older adults maintain similar happiness ratings as younger adults even in the face of declining physical and mental health (Vestergaard et al., 2015). However, specific chronic illnesses may impact daily well-being. In a study of adults over age 50, individuals with chronic illnesses reported significantly lower quality-of-life and happiness ratings than those older adults without chronic illnesses (Wikman et al., 2011). In this sample, approximately half of the participants had a chronic illness. Older adults who had a stroke reported the lowest level of happiness and quality of life as well as the most elevated reports of depressed mood. This is consistent with the "vascular depression" hypothesis of late-life depression (Alexopoulos, 2019), namely that cerebrovascular disease may predispose older adults to the development of depression. Reporting two or more chronic illnesses was associated with lower happiness ratings than having only one chronic illness.

Attention to Positive and Negative Stimuli

The research reviewed in the prior section suggests that older adults tend to report either greater or similar emotional well-being than other age groups and an overall decrease in the experience of negative emotion and psychological distress. Why do we see these findings? Evidence is accumulating that older adults may differentially attend to positive and negative stimuli, leading to a phenomenon known as the *age-related positivity effect* (Reed et al., 2014). We first consider evidence for the age-related positivity effect from laboratory studies and then consider evidence from cross-cultural studies of the positivity effect.

Laboratory-based studies of the age-related positivity effect typically ask participants to view a series of emotional (positive and negative) and neutral images involving both social and nonsocial material. The images are typically presented for a couple of seconds. After about a 15-minute delay, participants are asked to write down as much as they can remember about all of the images. In a study of younger, middle-aged, and older adults, Charles et al. (2003) found that middle-aged and older adults recalled a greater number of positive than negative images compared with younger adults, who recalled similar numbers of positive and negative images. This suggests that, with age, relatively more positive than negative information was recalled, which may partially explain why older adults show decreases in negative emotions compared with other age groups.

Another strategy for assessing age-related differences in attention to emotional stimuli is by studying how long participants look at emotional images, as opposed to what type of information is recalled. Two methods for assessing attention to emotional images are the dot-probe task and eye tracking. In the dot-probe task, two images are presented (one neutral and one emotional) for a short period of time. Once the images disappear, a dot is presented in place of one of the images, which remains until the participant presses a key to indicate the location of the dot. This produces a bias score, which can tell the researcher whether there were longer reaction times when the dot was in place of the emotional or nonemotional image. A positive bias score indicates a preference for emotional images (Isaacowitz et al., 2006). The eye-tracking paradigm involves tracking the movement of the left eye during presentation of the images. Relative looking times for the two images are compared and calculated into a fixation ratio score. Similar to the dot-probe paradigm, a positive ratio score indicates a preference for the emotional images. Isaacowitz et al. (2006), using both the dot-probe task and eye-tracking, found that older adults demonstrated an eye-tracking pattern whereby their gaze was more toward happy faces and away from sad faces. In contrast, younger adults also gazed away from sad faces but did not show a preference toward happy faces like the older adult participants. When considering the data from the dot-probe task, older adults responded more quickly to the location of the dot when it replaced positive stimuli (i.e., happy faces).

DiGirolamo et al. (2023) examined whether a similar pattern was present when eye-tracking experiments were done in the older adult's home rather than in a research lab. In the lab setting, the positivity effect was found, with older adults attending more to positive than to negative stimuli. However, in the home environment the reverse effect was found, with older adults attending more to negative than to positive stimuli. Similar to the research cited previously about everyday emotional experience, this finding suggests that the positivity effect is more complex than previously thought and should be examined in different contexts.

One criticism of the research on the age-related positivity effect is that it has been done primarily on U.S. participants. Some researchers suggest that the high value that Americans place on independence and autonomy may lead individuals to seek positive emotional experiences to maintain their sense of optimism and self-esteem (Fung et al., 2008). In contrast, other cultures that are more interdependent (i.e., East Asian cultures) may attune more to negative emotions in order to avoid social mistakes and therefore fit in better with one's social unit. Some researchers have replicated the age-related positivity effect in other countries, whereas others have not (Fung et al., 2019). For example, in a study of younger and older adults in Hong Kong (Fung et al., 2008), the older adults in the study gazed longer at fearful than at happy faces or sad faces, whereas the younger participants did not show attentional preferences toward any of the stimuli. This result was replicated by Fung et al. (2019), who found that U.S. older adults showed an age-related positivity effect with regard to gaze preference compared with U.S. younger adults, whereas no positivity effect was observed in a Hong Kong sample. The researchers concluded that the value placed on interpersonal harmony among some Asian cultures may lead individuals to attend more to negative cues. This suggests that there may not be an age-related positivity effect, per se, but instead a preference for emotionally meaningful information, which may vary across cultures.

Some researchers have posited that the age-related positivity effect may be an unintended consequence of aging, such that cognitive changes that occur with aging make it more difficult to process negative information (Foster et al., 2013). In a study of cognitive status and the positivity effect, Foster et al. (2013) found that older adults with stronger performance on cognitive tests devoted more attentional time to negative over positive images, whereas weaker performance on cognitive tests was associated with reduced processing of negative images. The authors propose that there may be multiple routes to a positivity effect among older adults: an involuntary one associated with cognitive difficulty in processing negative images and a voluntary process where older adults allocate more attention to positive images and information to improve daily emotional experience.

You might be able to think of situations in which turning your attention away from negative information may have caused problems. For example, in decisions related to your health, you may have to attend to negative information in order to make an informed choice about treatments for a serious health condition. Research on the positivity effect in the context of healthcare decision-making suggests that when older and younger adults are asked to make health decisions in a laboratory setting, older adults showed a positivity effect (English & Carstensen, 2015; Löckenhoff & Carstensen, 2007). However, in further analyses, English and Carstensen (2015) found that the positivity effect was present for older adults in relatively good health but not for those in poor health, who considered all the information in a more balanced manner. Additionally, the positivity effect was present for the same older adults when considering nonhealth decisions. This research suggests that older adults can consider both positive and negative health information in order to make a more informed choice when needed.

Age-Related Differences in Emotion Regulation

In light of the research on older adults' improved emotional experience compared with younger adults, some researchers propose that the mechanism underlying improved emotional experience is greater skills at emotion regulation (Charles & Carstensen, 2010). That is, older adults may be more effective at emotion regulation, thereby leading to an overall improvement in daily emotional experience compared with younger adults. For example, consider strategies that you use to regulate your emotions immediately during and after a negative event. You might talk to yourself to try to calm down or manage strong emotions. Are older adults better able to control their emotions in the moment when faced with a negative event? Additionally, consider your physiological reactivity during an emotional event. You may experience a racing heart, flushed face, and other signs that your body is under stress. How do older adults compare when we examine their emotional reactivity?

First, we have to consider what the various types of emotion regulation strategies are and then consider how they may be differentially used according to age. One well-known model of emotion regulation is the process model (Gross, 1998). The process model proposes five specific emotion-regulation strategies. *Situation selection* allows individuals to control their emotions by selecting the types of situations in which they find themselves. *Situation modification* involves changing the situation. *Attentional deployment* involves attending to other aspects of the situation or redirecting attention to something else. *Cognitive change* is when individuals try to reframe the situation or reappraise it so that the emotional impact is modified. Finally, *response modulation* refers to managing and changing emotions and behavior once the situation is happening, such as through suppressing emotions or displaying a different emotion than is felt internally by the individual.

The selection, optimization, and compensation with emotion regulation model (SOC-ER; Urry & Gross, 2010) suggests that the use of effective emotion regulation strategies throughout the life span depends on choosing strategies that draw on available resources (selection), engaging in efforts to ensure that the selected strategies work successfully (optimization), and being ready to deploy alternative strategies as needed when declines limit the use of certain emotion regulation strategies (compensation).

There is mixed research supporting the idea that older adults are more effective at emotion regulation compared with other age groups. Livingstone and Isaacowitz (2021) found that among younger, middle-aged, and older adults, the strategies of situation selection and situation modification were used most frequently, followed by attentional deployment, cognitive change, and response modulation. In this study, there were no age-related differences in strategy use. Older adults were more likely to endorse specific emotion regulation tactics of making situations more positive, attending to positive information, and seeking positive situations and were less likely to endorse tactics around avoiding or decreasing negative situations. In a review of emotion regulation studies, Allen and Windsor (2019) found that older adults preferred situation selection and attentional deployment strategies; however, context and individual differences mattered significantly in terms of which strategy was used.

In a review of age-related differences in emotion regulation, Isaacowitz (2022) highlights that there is no consistent evidence that older adults are more effective at emotion regulation than younger age groups. Therefore, it is not the case that a more positive affective experience in older adulthood implies that older adults are better, more effective, or notably different at how they regulate their emotions. Although the use of more adaptive emotion regulation strategies in older adulthood is consistent with some of the theories reviewed in this chapter, there is not consistent empirical support for different use of emotion regulation strategies with age (Eldesouky & English, 2018). Researchers have concluded that the way in which emotion regulation strategies change with age is more complex than can be seen through direct comparisons of different age groups. Instead, individual and contextual variables may play a larger role than expected in relation to how older adults deploy specific types of emotion regulation strategies.

Keys to Happy Aging

The age-related positivity effect suggests that older adults are motivated to attend to positive stimuli and avoid attention to negative stimuli. Socioemotional selectivity theory suggests that older adults prioritize emotionally meaningful goals as they realize that time is running out. Therefore, older adults may not have to "do" anything per se to experience a better emotional life with age. However, there may be daily activities that increase or decrease happiness ratings among older adults. Jarosz (2022) found that activities older adults reported as bringing the greatest enjoyment involved some type of social connectedness, such as religious activities, socializing, or childcare. Taking walks and caring for pets were also high on the list of most enjoyable activities. Least enjoyable activities included adultcare, shopping, and obtaining medical services. All activities were reported as more enjoyable if a friend or acquaintance were present, whereas the presence of family or a household member had no effect on the reported enjoyment of an activity. Older adults reporting poor health were also more likely to report low levels of enjoyment in all activities. A combination of low-effort and high-effort activities led to the most enjoyment, which is supported by other research suggesting that a mix of activities in late life is beneficial to overall well-being (Oerlemans et al., 2011). Other research suggests that regular interaction with friends has more of a positive impact on happiness and well-being among older adults than interactions with relatives, potentially due to the ability to confide in a friend, as well as less of a sense of obligation among friends than family members (Blieszner, 2014).

CONCLUSION

In this chapter we reviewed age-related changes in personality and emotional functioning. There are several theoretical approaches to studying personality, with the trait approaches having the most research related to aging. Although personality function within the Big 5 model was initially proposed to be fairly stable across the life span, recent longitudinal studies suggest that there is plasticity in personality throughout older adulthood. Additionally, the extent to which the Big 5 personality traits change with age is complex, with some traits increasing throughout young adulthood and middle age and then stabilizing or decreasing in older adulthood.

The second section of the chapter focused on emotional functioning in late life. Overall happiness and life satisfaction tend to increase with age. The experience of negative emotions tends to decrease with age, with a relative increase in attention to positive stimuli, termed the age-related positivity effect. Research is mixed regarding whether the improved emotional experience of older adults is due to improved emotion regulation strategies. Some of the changes seen in emotional functioning in older adulthood are accounted for through two theoretical models: SST and the SAVI model. SST posits that the changes seen in the emotional life of older adults are due to a shift in goals toward more emotionally meaningful interactions. The SAVI model integrates the research on emotional development and posits that older adults bring strengths and weaknesses to this process.

DISCUSSION QUESTIONS

1. Summarize the major theories of personality development.
2. Describe age-related changes seen in personality traits, as suggested by results of longitudinal studies.
3. Describe what is meant by the U-shaped curve for happiness across the life span and studies that are either consistent or inconsistent with the U-shaped curve.
4. How does socioemotional selectivity theory account for age-related differences in emotional functioning?
5. Explain the age-related positivity effect and discuss the cross-cultural findings on this effect.
6. Describe some of the emotion regulation strategies that older adults use and how they fit within Gross's process model of emotion regulation.

A robust set of instructor resources designed to supplement this text is located at http://connect.springerpub.com/content/book/978-0-8261-6617-3. Qualifying instructors may request access by emailing textbook@springerpub.com.

REFERENCES

Alexopoulos, G. S. (2019). Mechanisms and treatment of late-life depression. *Translational Psychiatry, 9*(1), 188. https://doi.org/10.1038/s41398-019-0514-6

Allen, V. C., & Windsor, T. D. (2019). Age differences in the use of emotion regulation strategies derived from the process model of emotion regulation: A systematic review. *Aging & Mental Health, 23*(1), 1–14. https://doi.org/10.1080/13607863.2017.1396575

Almeida, D. M., Rush, J., Mogle, J., Piazza, J. R., Cerino, E., & Charles, S. T. (2023). Longitudinal change in daily stress across 20 years of adulthood: Results from the national study of daily experiences. *Developmental Psychology, 59*(3), 515–523. https://doi.org/10.1037/dev0001469

Atherton, O. E., Grijalva, E., Roberts, B. W., & Robins, R. W. (2021). Stability and change in personality traits and major life goals from college to midlife. *Personality and Social Psychology Bulletin, 47*(5), 841–858. https://doi.org/10.1177/0146167220949362

Banham, K. M. (1951). Senescence and the emotions: A genetic theory. *The Pedagogical Seminary and Journal of Genetic Psychology, 78*, 175–183. https://doi.org/10.1080/08856559.1951.10533576

Blieszner, R. (2014). The worth of friendship: Can friends keep us healthy and happy? *Generations, 38*(1), 24–30. https://link.gale.com/apps/doc/A362781259/AONE?u=nysl_oweb&sid=googleScholar&xid=c08023f3

Brennan, P. L., Holland, J. M., Schutte, K. K., & Moos, R. H. (2012). Coping trajectories in later life: A 20-year predictive study. *Aging and Mental Health, 16*(3), 305–316. https://doi.org/10.1080/13607863.2011.628975

Brown, C., & Lewis, M. J. (2003). Psychosocial development in the elderly: An investigation into Erikson's ninth stage. *Journal of Aging Studies, 17*(4), 415–426. https://doi.org/10.1016/S0890-4065(03)00061-6

Carstensen, L. L. (2006). The influence of a sense of time on human development. *Science, 312*(5782), 1913–1915. https://doi.org/10.1126/science.112748

Carstensen, L. L. (2019). Integrating cognitive and emotion paradigms to address the paradox of aging. *Cognition and Emotion, 33*(1), 119–125. https://doi.org/10.1080/02699931.2018.1543181

Carstensen, L. L. (2021). Socioemotional selectivity theory: The role of perceived endings in human motivation. *The Gerontologist, 61*(8), 1188–1196. https://doi.org/10.1093/geront/gnab116

Carstensen, L. L., Fung, H., & Charles, S. T. (2003). Socioemotional selectivity theory and the regulation of emotion in the second half of life. *Motivation and Emotion, 27*, 103–123. https://doi.org/0146-7239/03/0600-0103/0

Carstensen, L. L., Shavit, Y. Z., & Barnes, J. T. (2020). Age advantages in emotional experience persist even under threat from the COVID-19 pandemic. *Psychological Science, 31*(11), 1374–1385. https://doi.org/10.1177/0956797620967261

Caspi, A., Roberts, B. W., & Shiner, R. L. (2005). Personality development: Stability and change. *Annual Review of Psychology, 56*, 453–484. https://doi.org/10.1146/annurev.psych.55.090902.141913

Charles, S. T. (2010). Strength and vulnerability integration (SAVI): A model of emotional well-being across adulthood. *Psychological Bulletin, 136*(6), 1068–1091. https://doi.org/10.1037/a0021232

Charles, S. T., & Carstensen, L. L. (2010). Social and emotional aging. *Annual Review of Psychology, 61*, 383–409. https://doi.org/10.1146/annurev.psych.093008.100448

Charles, S. T., Mather, M., & Carstensen, L. L. (2003). Aging and emotional memory: The forgettable nature of negative images for older adults. *Journal of Experimental Psychology: General, 132*(2), 310–324. https://doi.org/10.1037/0096-3445.132.2.310

Chopik, W. J., Edelstein, R. S., & Grimm, K. J. (2019). Longitudinal changes in attachment orientation over a 59-year period. *Journal of Personality and Social Psychology, 116*(4), 598–611. https://doi.org/10.1037/pspp0000167

Connor-Smith, J. K., & Flachsbart, C. (2007). Relations between personality and coping: A meta-analysis. *Journal of Personality and Social Psychology, 93*(6), 1080–1107. https://doi.org/10.1037/0022-3514.93.6.1080

Cox, K. S., Wilt, J., Olson, B., & McAdams, D. P. (2010). Generativity, the Big Five, and psychosocial adaptation in midlife adults. *Journal of personality, 78*(4), 1185–1208. https://doi.org/10.1111/j.1467-6494.2010.00647.x

Diehl, M., Chui, H., Hay, E. L., Lumley, M. A., Grühn, D., & Labouvie-Vief, G. (2014). Change in coping and defense mechanisms across adulthood: Longitudinal findings in a European American sample. *Developmental psychology, 50*(2), 634–648. https://doi.org/10.1037/a0033619

DiGirolamo, M. A., McCall, E. C., Kibrislioglu Uysal, N., Wan Ho, Y., Lind, M., & Isaacowitz, D. M. (2023). Attention to emotional stimuli across adulthood and older age: A novel application of eye-tracking within the home. *Journal of Experimental Psychology: General, 152*(5), 1439–1453. https://doi.org/10.1037/xge0001343

Eldesouky, L., & English, T. (2018). Another year older, another year wiser? Emotion regulation strategy selection and flexibility across adulthood. *Psychology and Aging, 33*(4), 572–585. https://doi.org/10.1037/pag0000251

English, T., & Carstensen, L. L. (2015). Does positivity operate when the stakes are high? Health status and decision making among older adults. *Psychology and Aging, 30*(2), 348–355. https://doi.org/10.1037/a0039121

Erikson, E. H., & Erikson, J. M. (1998). *The life cycle completed* (extended version). W. W. Norton.

Erikson, E. H., Erikson, J. M., & Kivnick, H. Q. (1986). *Vital involvement in old age: The experience of old age in our time.* W. W. Norton.

Finlay, J. M., Kler, J. S., O'Shea, B. Q., Eastman, M. R., Vinson, Y. R., & Kobayashi, L. C. (2021). Coping during the COVID-19 pandemic: A qualitative study of older adults across the United States. *Frontiers in Public Health, 9*, 643807. https://doi.org/10.3389/fpubh.2021.643807

Foster, S. M., Davis, H. P., & Kisley, M. A. (2013). Brain responses to emotional images related to cognitive ability in older adults. *Psychology and Aging, 28*(1), 179–190. https://doi.org/10.1037/a0030928

Fung, H. H., Gong, X., Ngo, N., & Isaacowitz, D. M. (2019). Cultural differences in the age-related positivity effect: Distinguishing between preference and effectiveness. *Emotion, 19*(8), 1414–1424. https://doi.org/10.1037/emo0000529

Fung, H. H., Isaacowitz, D. M., Lu, A. Y., Wadlinger, H. A., Goren, D., & Wilson, H. R. (2008). Age-related positivity enhancement is not universal: Older Chinese look away from positive stimuli. *Psychology and Aging*, *23*(2), 440–446. https://doi.org/10.1037/0882-7974.23.2.440

Galambos, N. L., Krahn, H. J., Johnson, M. D., & Lachman, M. E. (2020). The U shape of happiness across the life course: Expanding the discussion. *Perspectives on Psychological Science*, *15*(4), 898–912. https://doi.org/10.1177/1745691620902428

Graham, E. K., Weston, S. J., Gerstorf, D., Yoneda, T. B., Booth, T. O. M., Beam, C. R., ..., Mroczek, D. K. (2020). Trajectories of big five personality traits: A coordinated analysis of 16 longitudinal samples. *European Journal of Personality*, *34*(3), 301–321. https://doi.org/10.1002/per.2259

Gross, J. J. (1998). Antecedent- and response-focused emotion regulation: Divergent consequences for experience, expression, and physiology. *Journal of Personality and Social Psychology*, *74*(1), 224–237. https://doi.org/10.1037/0022-3514.74.1.224

Hannah, M. T., Domino, G., Figueredo, A. J., & Hendrickson, R. (1996). The prediction of ego integrity in older persons. *Educational and Psychological Measurement*, *56*(6), 930–950. https://doi.org/10.1177/0013164496056006002

Helson, R., Kwan, V. S., John, O. P., & Jones, C. (2002). The growing evidence for personality change in adulthood: Findings from research with personality inventories. *Journal of Research in Personality*, *36*(4), 287–306. https://doi.org/10.1016/S0092-6566(02)00010-7

Isaacowitz, D. M. (2022). What do we know about aging and emotion regulation? *Perspectives on Psychological Science*, *17*(6), 1541–1555. https://doi.org/10.1177/17456916211059819

Isaacowitz, D. M., Wadlinger, H. A., Goren, D., & Wilson, H. R. (2006). Is there an age-related positivity effect in visual attention? A comparison of two methodologies. *Emotion*, *6*(3), 511–516. https://doi.org/10.1037/1528-3542.6.3.511

Jarosz, E. (2022). What makes life enjoyable at an older age? Experiential wellbeing, daily activities, and satisfaction with life in general. *Aging & Mental Health*, *26*(6), 1242–1252. https://doi.org/10.1080/13607863.2021.1916879

Jeffers, S. L., Hill, R., Krumholz, M. F., & Winston-Proctor, C. (2020). Themes of gerotranscendence in narrative identity within structured life review. *GeroPsych: The Journal of Gerontopsychology and Geriatric Psychiatry*, *33*(2), 77–84. https://doi.org/10.1024/1662-9647/a000235

Jenkins, A., Tree, J. J., Thornton, I. M., & Tales, A. (2019). Subjective cognitive impairment in 55–65-year-old adults is associated with negative affective symptoms, neuroticism, and poor quality of life. *Journal of Alzheimer's Disease*, *67*(4), 1367–1378. https://doi.org/10.3233/JAD-180810

Jordan, K., & Tseris, E. (2018). Locating, understanding and celebrating disability: Revisiting Erikson's "stages." *Feminism & Psychology*, *28*(3), 427–444. https://doi.org/10.1177/0959353517705400

Livingstone, K. M., & Isaacowitz, D. M. (2021). Age and emotion regulation in daily life: Frequency, strategies, tactics, and effectiveness. *Emotion*, *21*(1), 39–51. https://doi.org/10.1037/emo0000672

Löckenhoff, C. E., & Carstensen, L. L. (2007). Aging, emotion, and health-related decision strategies: Motivational manipulations can reduce age differences. *Psychology and Aging*, *22*(1), 134–146. https://doi.org/10.1037/0882-7974.22.1.134

Lowis, M. J., & Raubenheimer, J. R. (1997). Ego integrity and life satisfaction in retired males. *Counseling Psychology in Africa*, *2*, 12–23.

Magai, C., Cohen, C., Milburn, N., Thorpe, B., McPherson, R., & Peralta, D. (2001). Attachment styles in older European American and African American adults. *The Journals of Gerontology*, *56B*(1), S28–S35. https://doi.org/10.1093/geronb/56.1.S28

McAdams, D. P., de St. Aubin, E., & Logan, R. L. (1993). Generativity among young, midlife, and older adults. *Psychology and Aging*, *8*(2), 221–230. https://doi.org/10.1037/0882-7974.8.2.221

McCrae, R. R., & Costa, Jr., P. T. (2003). *Personality in adulthood: A five-factor theory perspective* (2nd ed.). Guilford Press.

Millová, K., Malatincová, T., & Blatný, M. (2023). Intergenerational transmission of generativity and stagnation within families in a society after a macrosocial change: A two-generation study. *Current Psychology*, *42*, 3061–3075. https://doi.org/10.1007/s12144-021-01688-6

Minahan, J., Falzarano, F., Yazdani, N., & Siedlecki, K. L. (2021). The COVID-19 pandemic and psychosocial outcomes across age through the stress and coping framework. *The Gerontologist*, *61*(2), 228–239. https://doi.org/10.1093/geront/gnaa205

Newton, N. J., Chauhan, P. K., & Pates, J. L. (2020). Facing the future: Generativity, stagnation, intended legacies, and well-being in later life. *Journal of Adult Development, 27*, 70–80. https://doi.org/10.1007/s10804-019-09330-3

Nieto, M., Romero, D., Ros, L., Zabala, C., Martinez, M., Ricarte, J. J., Serrano, J. P., & Latorre, J. M. (2020). Differences in coping strategies between young and older adults: The role of executive functions. *The International Journal of Aging and Human Development, 90*(1), 28–49. https://doi.org/10.1177/0091415018822040

Oerlemans, W. G. M., Bakker, A. B., & Veenhoven, R. (2011). Finding the key to happy aging: A day reconstruction study of happiness. *The Journals of Gerontology, 66B*(6), 665–674. https://doi.org/10.1093/geronb/gbr040

Oishi, S., Graham, J., Kesebir, S., & Galinha, I. C. (2013). Concepts of happiness across time and cultures. *Personality and Social Psychology Bulletin, 39*(5), 559–577. https://doi.org/10.1177/0146167213480042

Reed, A. E., Chan, L., & Mikels, J. A. (2014). Meta-analysis of the age-related positivity effect: Age differences in preferences for positive over negative information. *Psychology and Aging, 29*(1), 1–15. https://doi.org/10.1037/a0035194

Ryff, C. D. (2014). Psychological well-being revisited: Advances in the science and practice of eudaimonia. *Psychotherapy and Psychosomatics, 83*, 10–28. https://doi.org/10.1159/000353263

Schwaba, T., & Bleidorn, W. (2018). Individual differences in personality change across the adult life span. *Journal of Personality, 86*(3), 450–464. https://doi.org/10.1111/jopy.12327

Schwaba, T., & Bleidorn, W. (2019). Personality trait development across the transition to retirement. *Journal of Personality and Social Psychology, 116*(4), 651–665. https://doi.org/10.1037/pspp0000179

Silverman, J., & Aafjes-van Doorn, K. (2023). Coping and defense mechanisms: A scoping review. *Clinical Psychology: Science and Practice, 30*(4), 381–392. https://doi.org/10.1037/cps0000139

Spence, R., Jacobs, C., & Bifulco, A. (2020). Attachment style, loneliness and depression in older age women. *Aging & Mental Health, 24*(5), 837–839. https://doi.org/10.1080/13607863.2018.1553141

Srivastava, S., John, O. P., Gosling, S. D., & Potter, J. (2003). Development of personality in early and middle adulthood: Set like plaster or persistent change?. *Journal of Personality and Social Psychology, 84*(5), 1041–1053. https://doi.org/10.1037/0022-3514.84.5.1041

Stephan, Y., Sutin, A. R., Luchetti, M., & Terracciano, A. (2019). Facets of conscientiousness and longevity: Findings from the Health and Retirement Study. *Journal of Psychosomatic Research, 116*, 1–5. https://doi.org/10.1016/j.jpsychores.2018.11.002

Stone, A. A., Schwartz, J. E., Broderick, J. E., & Deaton, A. (2010). A snapshot of the age distribution of psychological well-being in the United States. *Proceedings of the National Academy of Sciences of the United States of America, 107*(22), 9985–9990. https://doi.org/10.1073/pnas.1003744107

Sutin, A. R., Aschwanden, D., Stephan, Y., & Terracciano, A. (2022). The association between facets of conscientiousness and performance-based and informant-rated cognition, affect, and activities in older adults. *Journal of Personality, 90*(2), 121–132. https://doi.org/10.1111/jopy.12657

Tornstam, L. (1996). Gerotranscendence—A theory about maturing into old age. *Journal of Aging and Identity, 1*, 37–50.

Turunen, K. M., Kokko, K., Kekäläinen, T., Alén, M., Hänninen, T., Pynnönen, K., ..., Sipilä, S. (2022). Associations of neuroticism with falls in older adults: Do psychological factors mediate the association?. *Aging & Mental Health, 26*(1), 77–85. https://doi.org/10.1080/13607863.2020.1841735

Urry, H. L., & Gross, J. J. (2010). Emotion regulation in older age. *Current Directions in Psychological Science, 19*(6), 352–357. https://doi.org/10.1177/0963721410388395

Vannini, P., Gagliardi, G. P., Kuppe, M., Dossett, M. L., Donovan, N. J., Gatchel, J. R., ..., Marshall, G. A. (2021). Stress, resilience, and coping strategies in a sample of community-dwelling older adults during COVID-19. *Journal of Psychiatric Research, 138*, 176–185. https://doi.org/10.1016/j.jpsychires.2021.03.050

Vestergaard, S., Thinggaard, M., Jeune, B., Vaupel, J. W., McGue, M., & Christensen, K. (2015). Physical and mental decline yet rather happy: A study of Danes aged 45 and older. *Aging and Mental Health, 19*(5), 400–408. https://doi.org/10.1080/13607863.2014.944089

Wagner, J., Lüdtke, O., & Robitzsch, A. (2019). Does personality become more stable with age? Disentangling state and trait effects for the big five across the life span using local structural equation modeling. *Journal of Personality and Social Psychology, 116*(4), 666–680. https://doi.org/10.1037/pspp0000203

Walsh, E., Blake, Y., Donati, A., Stoop, R., & Von Gunten, A. (2019). Early secure attachment as a protective factor against later cognitive decline and dementia. *Frontiers in Aging Neuroscience, 11*, 161. https://doi.org/10.3389/fnagi.2019.00161

Waugh, C. E., Shing, E. Z., & Furr, R. M. (2020). Not all disengagement coping strategies are created equal: Positive distraction, but not avoidance, can be an adaptive coping strategy for chronic life stressors. *Anxiety, Stress, & Coping, 33*(5), 511–529. https://doi.org/10.1080/10615806.2020.1755820

Wikman, A., Wardle, A., & Steptoe, A. (2011). Quality of life and affective well-being in -aged and older people with chronic medical conditions: A cross-sectional population based study. *Public Library of Science One, 6*, e18952. https://doi.org/10.1371/journal.pone.0018952

Wirth, M., Voss, A., & Rothermund, K. (2023). Age differences in everyday emotional experience: Testing core predictions of socioemotional selectivity theory with the MIVA model. *The Journals of Gerontology: Series B, 78*(7), 1152–1162. https://doi.org/10.1093/geronb/gbad033

Woodhead, E. L., Cronkite, R. C., Moos, R. H., & Timko, C. (2014). Coping strategies predictive of adverse outcomes among community adults. *Journal of Clinical Psychology, 70*(12), 1183–1195. https://doi.org/10.1002/jclp.21924

Yancura, L. A., & Aldwin, C. M. (2008). Coping and health in older adults. *Current Psychiatry Reports, 10*(1), 10–15. https://doi.org/10.1007/s11920-008-0004-7

Young, E. S., Simpson, J. A., Griskevicius, V., Huelsnitz, C. O., & Fleck, C. (2019). Childhood attachment and adult personality: A life history perspective. *Self and Identity, 18*(1), 22–38. https://doi.org/10.1080/15298868.2017.1353540

8

Mental Health and Aging

Erin L. Woodhead

> **LEARNING OBJECTIVES**
> - Compare the prevalence rates among various mental health conditions between older and younger adults.
> - Describe the presentation of depression and other mental health conditions among older adults and how it compares to younger adults.
> - Compare various assessment measures for mental health conditions among older adults.
> - Compare types of interventions for mental health conditions among older adults.

The Institute of Medicine (IOM) estimates that by 2030, the number of Americans over age 65 who have mental health or substance use disorders will range between 10.1 million and 14.4 million (Institute of Medicine, 2012). The increase in mental health and substance use conditions is thought to be due to the increasing population of older adults in the United States and internationally (Administration on Aging, 2012; Karel et al., 2012; National Institute on Aging, 2011).

Although the overall prevalence of certain mental health conditions, such as major depressive disorder, declines with age (Jacobs & Bamonti, 2022), these disorders are still common among older adults and are often underdiagnosed and undertreated. In a review of mental health conditions in late life, Jacobs and Bamonti (2022) note that depressive disorders, anxiety disorders, personality disorders, bipolar disorder, and schizophrenia spectrum disorders are all less prevalent among older adults compared with younger adults, whereas substance use disorders, sleep disorders, neurocognitive disorders, and hoarding are more prevalent. The goal of the current chapter is to review use of mental health services among older adults, as well as diagnosis and treatment for common mental health conditions among older adults. Finally, assessment options for mental health conditions among older adults are reviewed.

USE OF MENTAL HEALTH SERVICES BY OLDER ADULTS

Older adults have particularly low use of mental health services. In a study of adults in England with a diagnosed mental health condition, primarily depression or anxiety, individuals between ages 18 and 24 were most likely to access mental health services and those aged 65 and older were least likely (Sharland et al., 2023). Similar studies have found that older adults are underrepresented in mental health services, despite having good outcomes when they do access services. For example, in a study of German adults, Gellert et al. (2021) found that rates of non-utilization of psychotherapy in two cohorts of participants were higher among adults age 75 and older compared with adults age 18 to 25. Specifically, non-utilization rates among those 75+ were 59.3% in 2014 and 52.5% in 2016, compared with non-utilization rates among those 18 to 25 of 29.1% in 2014 and 10.7% in 2016. Non-utilization was defined as the percentage of participants who reported a perceived need for mental health treatment but did not access any mental health services in the past 3 years.

Cultural background may have an influence on use of mental health services, leading to disparities in mental healthcare. Across all age groups, racial and ethnic minority individuals are less likely to access mental health services compared with White individuals (Babitsch et al., 2012); however, there is limited research on mental health services use among racial and ethnic minority older adults. Among older Chinese immigrants ranging in age from 60 to 97, those who were relatively older were 9.4% less likely to use mental health services for depression compared with those who were relatively younger (Chao et al., 2020). In a study of mental health services use among Native American older adults compared with White older adults, American Indian older adults were significantly more likely to report adverse childhood experiences (ACEs), previous negative experiences related to mental health services, and a lower level of knowledge about depression (Moon et al., 2018). Better perceived physical health and higher levels of depressive symptoms were associated with more use of mental health services among American Indian older adults but not White older adults. The authors suggest that American Indian older adults with poor health may experience a burden around physical illness that limits their ability to seek care for mental health conditions.

BELIEFS AND STIGMA AROUND MENTAL HEALTHCARE

As noted previously, older adults tend to not access needed mental healthcare. This has led some researchers to posit that older adults' use of mental health services is lower than that of other age groups due to differences in beliefs about mental health conditions as compared with younger adults, as well as stigma around obtaining mental healthcare.

Beliefs About Mental Healthcare

In a systematic review of beliefs and attitudes toward depression among older adults aged 60 to 90, Nair et al. (2020) found that beliefs about depression reflected a social explanatory model. Specifically, older adults believed that depression was a consequence of life stressors and was therefore less amenable to professional mental health services. Within this model of understanding depression, older adults were less likely to view it as a medical illness that required a specific treatment. Older adults also expressed a preference for nonmedical vocabulary to describe the depression, including terms such as sad mood rather than depression. Racial and ethnic minority older adults were particularly likely to view depression as rooted in social problems such as racism and immigration experiences.

As a consequence of these types of beliefs around depression, Nair et al. (2020) also found that older adults viewed the cure for depression as coming from within, such as through use of specific coping strategies or a certain level of resilience. Although prior studies have found that older adults tend to have positive views about mental healthcare (Byers et al., 2012), Nair et al. (2020) found that mental health services were viewed as being potentially more disruptive than self-management strategies, as well as having a higher chance of causing harm if therapy was delivered by a less experienced therapist.

This systematic review supports prior research suggesting that beliefs held by older adults about depression are more likely to reflect a social model rather than a medical model (e.g., Lawrence et al., 2006). Additionally, older adults may believe that they can handle their problems on their own (Mackenzie et al., 2010). Taken together, the research on beliefs about mental health conditions among older adults may serve to partially explain why older adults are less likely to utilize mental health services compared with younger adults. Nair et al. (2020) concludes that older adults should be supported in utilizing self-management strategies for low levels of depressive symptoms, which may be seen as a more acceptable intervention. When professional mental health services are needed, there should be a focus on accessible treatment options that are adapted to the needs of older adults.

Mental Health Stigma

Mental health stigma can be conceptualized in a few different ways. Some individuals may experience stigma around having a mental health condition, whereas others may experience stigma around seeking help for a mental health condition. Within the concept of stigma around help-seeking, individuals may experience self-stigma around seeking help, defined by negative views of oneself for seeking help, and/or public stigma around help-seeking, defined by the perceptions of how others view their help-seeking behavior (Murphy et al., 2024). One model of mental health stigma, the internalized model of mental health service use, proposes that public help-seeking stigma becomes internalized as self-stigma around help-seeking, thereby reducing the likelihood of accessing needed mental health services through both attitudes and behaviors (Vogel et al., 2013).

Overall, more research is emerging that suggests older adults have less stigma around mental health services than other age groups. Mackenzie et al. (2019) found that older adults reported significantly less public stigma and self-stigma around mental health services and better help-seeking attitudes as compared with both middle-aged and younger adults. In a test of the internalized model of mental health service use, Mackenzie et al. (2019) found that public stigma was associated with self-stigma for all age groups, and self-stigma was associated with help-seeking attitudes for all age groups. Additionally, these associations were strongest for older adults and weakest for younger adults. The researchers conclude that although older adults were the least likely to report public stigma, those who did report it were particularly likely to internalize the public stigma as self-stigma, more so than the other age groups.

In light of these findings and others (Mackenzie & Pankratz, 2022), stigma may not be as much of a barrier to mental health services among older adults as it is among younger age groups. Instead, other factors may influence use of mental health services including poor detection of mental health conditions, structural barriers in accessing care, lower levels of mental health literacy, and lower perceived need for help. This is consistent with the earlier research on beliefs (Nair et al., 2020), specifically that older adults may not perceive a need for help until they experience a more severe level of depression symptoms.

DIAGNOSING MENTAL HEALTH CONDITIONS AMONG OLDER ADULTS

Mood Disorders

Mood disorders are among the most common mental health conditions that appear in the United States. These disorders include major depressive disorder, persistent depressive disorder, bipolar disorder, and cyclothymia (American Psychiatric Association, 2022). Among older adults, subclinical depressive symptoms are also important to assess, as older adults may not meet full criteria for a major depressive disorder yet still experience symptoms that have a significant impact on their daily life and well-being. Although mood disorders are less common overall among older adults compared with younger adults, Yang et al. (2022) found that the prevalence of major depressive episodes among older adults (65+) in the last year increased from 2.0% in the 2010/2011 survey to 3.2% in the 2018/2019 National Survey on Drug Use and Health, which represented a 60% increase. With regard to demographic factors, there was an increase in major depressive episodes among men but not women and among non-Hispanic White individuals but not non-White individuals. Despite the increase in major depressive episodes, there was no increase in past-year mental health treatment (inpatient, outpatient, or pharmacological treatment) or alternative mental health treatments (self-help group, acupuncture, religious advisor, etc). When considering international data, a study of depression among adults age 50 and older living in European countries found that 29% of adults over age 50 met criteria for late-life depression (Horackova et al., 2019). Depression was more common among those with more chronic diseases, lower grip strength, more cognitive impairment, and more limitations in independent activities of daily living.

Depression among older adults can be divided into early onset and late onset. Early-onset depression indicates that an individual has experienced depressive episodes earlier in life and is now aging, whereas late-life depression indicates that an individual experienced their first depressive episode as an older adult with no prior episodes. About half of older adults presenting with depression are classified as late onset (Jacobs & Bamonti, 2022). Additionally, rates of significant depressive symptoms may vary by setting. Older adults who are medical outpatients, medical inpatients, or residents of long-term care facilities are more likely to express symptoms of major depressive disorder than those living in the community (Fiske et al., 2009).

Aging does seem to affect some symptoms related to major depressive disorder. While older adults with depression do not experience higher levels of sadness, they do suffer from increased anhedonia in comparison to younger adults (Wuthrich et al., 2015). However, older adults also tend to endorse somatic symptoms, such as psychomotor retardation, and cognitive symptoms, such as executive dysfunction. This differential symptom presentation may impact how likely it is that older adults meet *Diagnostic and Statistical Manual of Mental Disorders* (DSM) criteria for major depressive disorder (Fiske et al., 2009). For example, the somatic symptoms reported by older adults may be attributed to normal aging, which may cause practitioners to not consider a depression diagnosis among older patients.

Similar to depression, the prevalence of bipolar disorder decreases with age, with prevalence rates of 0.5% to 1.0% among older adults (Ljubic et al., 2021). Bipolar disorder among older adults can also be classified into early onset or late onset. The majority of individuals with bipolar disorder have an onset in adolescence or early adulthood, with a minority reporting their first episode in older adulthood (Sajatovic et al., 2015). Careful evaluation of older adults with late-onset bipolar disorder is needed, as prior episodes of depression or mania may not be accurately recalled, making it more likely that late-onset bipolar disorder represents a condition that was present but undiagnosed at younger ages. Diagnosing a manic or hypomanic episode among older adults is complex, as mania could be caused by a medical condition, a medication, or a medication interaction. Also, a new onset of some symptoms of mania (e.g., spending money excessively) may represent symptoms of a neurocognitive disorder rather than bipolar disorder. There is some indication that older adults may experience fewer manic or hypomanic episodes compared with younger ages and more depressive episodes (Ljubic et al., 2021). Older adults with bipolar disorder are more likely to have cognitive impairment compared with younger adults with bipolar disorder.

Anxiety Disorders

Like mood disorders, there are many types of anxiety disorders, such as specific phobias, panic disorder, agoraphobia, social anxiety disorder, and generalized anxiety disorder (GAD; American Psychiatric Association, 2022). The past-year prevalence of any type of anxiety disorder among older adults ranges from 5.6% to 17.2% (Jacobs & Bamonti, 2022; see Table 8.1). GAD is the most common type of anxiety disorder among older adults (Lenze & Wetherell, 2011). Subclinical anxiety symptoms are important to assess and address in older adults, typically defined as clinically significant symptoms that do not meet full criteria for an anxiety disorder diagnosis. Approximately half of older adults with GAD or agoraphobia developed the condition in older adulthood. A large proportion of older adults diagnosed with a depressive disorder also suffer from an anxiety disorder. Among patients older than 60 diagnosed with major depressive disorder, nearly 40% also met criteria for a comorbid anxiety disorder (van der Veen et al., 2015).

Diagnosis of anxiety disorders among older adults is complicated by overlap of symptoms with common medical conditions in older adulthood, particularly those that cause cardiac, respiratory, or vestibular symptoms. Older adults and providers may

TABLE 8.1 PREVALENCE OF MENTAL HEALTH CONDITIONS AMONG ADULTS AGE 65 AND OLDER

Diagnosis	12-Month Prevalence
Any anxiety disorder[a]	5.6%–17.2%
Generalized anxiety disorder[a]	0.8%–3.1%
Specific phobia[b]	3.1%–5.1%
Social phobia[b,d]	0.9%–3.5%
Panic disorder[b]	0.5%–3.8%
Obsessive-compulsive disorder	0.8%
Agoraphobia[d]	0.2%–4.9%
Posttraumatic stress disorder[a,d]	0.1%–2.8%
Any mood disorder[c,d]	1.4%–5.7%
Major depressive disorder[a,d]	1.1%–4.6%
Dysthymia	0.5%–1.6%
Bipolar disorder[c,e]	0%–0.7%
Any substance use disorder	0%–2.6%
Alcohol abuse/dependence	0%–1.7%
Any drug abuse/dependence	0%–0.2%
Any personality disorder	10.4%–13.2%
Any cluster A	2.8%–4.4%
Any cluster B	3.9%–6.6%
Any cluster C	5.3%–6.9%

Note: Prevalence rates are based on nationally representative studies and are grouped according to the *Diagnostic and Statistical Manual of Mental Disorders IV*, as this was the manual being used during the time of these epidemiological studies (Byers et al., 2012; Canuto et al., 2018; Gum et al., 2009; IOM, 2012; Reynolds et al., 2015).
[a]Lower rate is based on prevalence among individuals 75 to 84 years of age.
[b]Lower rate is based on prevalence among individuals ages 85 and older.
[c]Lower rate is based on prevalence among individuals ages 75 and older.
[d]Higher rate is based on prevalence among individuals 65 to 74 years of age.
[e]Higher rate is based on prevalence among individuals 75 to 84 years of age.
Source: From Jacobs, M. L., & Bamonti, P. M. (2022). Clinical practice: A foundational geropsychology knowledge competency. *Clinical Psychology: Science and Practice*, 29(1), 28–42. https://doi.org/10.1037/cps0000046.

attribute anxiety symptoms to medical conditions or other health problems, increasing the likelihood of underdiagnosis and undertreatment of anxiety disorders in older adults (Jacobs & Bamonti, 2022). In early adulthood, anxiety disorders are more common among women than men; however, this gender disparity may decrease in older adulthood, with older adults reporting similar levels of anxiety across genders (Granier et al., 2020).

Older and younger adults also report different types of worries (Gould et al., 2018). Older adults are more likely to worry about community and world affairs, whereas younger adults are more likely to worry about school-related concerns. One specific type of fear that is more common among older adults is fear of falling (Lenze & Wetherell, 2011). Fear of falling among older adults can lead to agoraphobia if the individual limits their outings and other activities due to the fear. Although these behaviors represent avoidance, which is counterproductive to anxiety and fears, providers may interpret it as adaptive for older adults, leading to underdiagnosis and undertreatment of agoraphobia in this population.

Posttraumatic Stress Disorder

Posttraumatic stress disorder (PTSD) can develop after an individual is exposed to actual or threatened death, serious injury, or sexual violence. PTSD is characterized by intrusive symptoms, such as episodic flashbacks or nightmares, avoidance of stimuli associated with the event, negative alterations in mood and cognition, and alterations in arousal and reactivity. The prevalence of PTSD among older adults ranges from 0.4% to 4.5% (Pless Kaiser et al., 2019). Not everyone exposed to a traumatic event will develop PTSD. Research suggests that certain characteristics, such as resilience and use of adaptive coping strategies following trauma exposure, may reduce the likelihood that trauma exposure will lead to a PTSD diagnosis (Thompson et al., 2018). Among older adults, PTSD can be a result of either early life or late life trauma. Early life trauma can include physical or sexual violence, combat exposure, war experiences, and prisoner of war (POW) experiences, among others. Late life trauma can include violence, motor vehicle accidents, and natural disasters (Böttche et al., 2012).

The history of a formal definition of PTSD has its origins dating back as early as World War I when the term "shell shock" sparked the initial interest in the psychological effects of combat (Crocq & Crocq, 2000). During World War II, the term evolved into "combat neurosis," which has a high degree of overlap with our modern symptom criteria for PTSD. PTSD first appeared in the *DSM* as a formal diagnosis in 1980. Therefore, older adults who experience PTSD symptoms may not realize that their symptoms are related to a traumatic event, may not have a way to describe and understand their symptoms, and may not be aware of current treatment options (Pless Kaiser et al., 2019). The presentation of specific symptoms of PTSD can change across the life span. Stressors that often accompany aging can worsen PTSD symptoms, such as bereavement, retirement, and medical conditions (Pless Kaiser et al., 2019). For example, loss of a spouse may trigger memories of prior losses that were connected to the traumatic event. Older adults with PTSD also tend to have more medical conditions compared with younger adults with PTSD (Thomas et al., 2017), which may lead to a greater degree of functional impairment and reduced quality of life among older adults with PTSD.

Personality Disorders

Personality disorders involve profound patterns of thought and behavior that lead to distress or impairment. These include borderline, obsessive compulsive, avoidant, schizotypal, antisocial, and narcissistic personality disorders (American Psychiatric

Association, 2022). Research on the prevalence of personality disorders among older adults shows that they are more common than expected, with prevalence rates for any type of personality disorder ranging from 10.7% to 14.5% (Penders et al., 2020). The most common types of personality disorders among older adults are obsessive-compulsive personality disorder, paranoid personality disorder, and narcissistic personality disorder. The least common types are dependent personality disorder and histrionic personality disorder. Personality disorders are more common among older men than older women and are also more common among older adults living in a long-term care setting compared with community-dwelling older adults.

The expression of certain types of personality disorders changes with age. For example, as adults with borderline personality disorder age, the externalizing symptoms tend to decrease while the other types of symptoms (fear of abandonment, manipulation, lack of empathy, and selfishness) stay constant (Videler et al., 2019). Some symptoms of borderline personality disorder can become worse depending on the context, for example, death of a partner or the transition to a new living situation. There are situations where a personality disorder is first diagnosed in older adulthood, similar to the other conditions described in this chapter. Late-onset personality disorders can occur when loss of social support reveals personality problems that were compensated for by individuals in the person's life or when new symptoms emerge in late life (Videler et al., 2019). Personality disorders were previously considered stable over time but the most recent *International Classification of Disease*, 11th Revision (*ICD*-11) indicates that personality disorders are only relatively stable after younger adulthood, with some younger adults no longer meeting criteria for a personality disorder in middle age (Bach & First, 2018).

Suicidality

Suicide is a severe and pervasive issue among older adults. Men over age 85 have the highest suicide rate of any group in the United States (Centers for Disease Control and Prevention, 2014). Suicide attempts among older adults are more fatal than younger adults, leading to a smaller attempt-to-completion ratio among older adults. Whereas younger adults are more likely to have multiple attempts without completion, older adults are more likely to die by suicide in fewer attempts. Compounding this problem is research suggesting that older adults are less likely to be discovered and rescued during a suicide attempt and that the additional medical conditions that older adults have make it less likely that older adults will recover from a suicide attempt (Conwell, 1997). Mental health conditions such as depression and social factors such as family discord are important when considering risk factors for suicide among older adults. Additional risk factors for suicide among older adults include social isolation, substance use, physical illness, disability, and pain (Conwell et al., 2002; Legarreta et al., 2015). Social connectedness, adaptive coping skills, and receiving treatment for mental health conditions are protective factors for suicide among older adults.

Substance Use Disorders

Although the general pattern of substance use across the life span suggests that rates of substance use disorder diagnoses tend to decrease with age (Barry & Blow, 2016), older adults are increasingly becoming a group of concern with regard to substance use, particularly with steady increases seen in drinking among older women and men (Breslow et al., 2017; Han et al., 2017). For example, Han et al. (2017) found that participants between the ages of 50 and 64 had a 23% relative increase between the years of 2005 and 2014 in binge drinking (defined as five or more drinks on one occasion), and adults age 65 and older had an 11% relative increase during the same time frame. Alcohol is the most commonly used substance among older adults followed by cannabis. Use of cannabis in the past month among adults age 50 and older increased from 3.9% in 2015 to 6.4% in 2019 (Kepner et al., 2023). Use of both alcohol and cannabis also increased significantly in the same time frame (see Figure 8.1). Although many states have legalized cannabis, concerns remain about the safety of cannabis use among older adults. In an analysis of data from California, Han et al. (2023) found that there were 366 cannabis-related emergency department visits among adults age 65 and older in 2015, increasing to 12,167 visits in 2019. Within the sample of older adults, those aged 65 to 74, older males, Black individuals, and those with more medical comorbidities experienced the highest rates of cannabis-related emergency department visits. The reason behind higher emergency department visits includes increased likelihood of falls and injury among older adults using cannabis (Han et al., 2023).

There is concern that older adults are uniquely vulnerable to substance use problems due to reduced tolerance for alcohol and other substances, as well as comorbid medical conditions and the impact of life stressors common to older adults including retirement and bereavement. Decreases in muscle mass and a longer time to digest alcohol and other substances mean that older adults can experience problems from a relatively small amount of a substance. Therefore, consuming the same amount of a substance as when one was younger may lead to problems

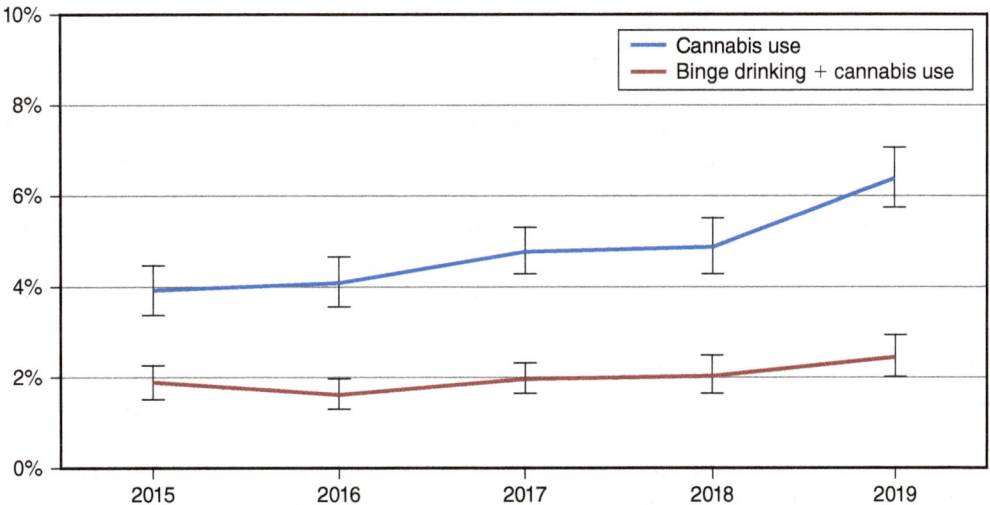

Figure 8.1 Trends in past-month cannabis use and both past-month cannabis use and binge drinking among adults aged ≥50, United States, 2015–2019.

Source: From Kepner, W. E., Han, B. H., Nguyen, D., Han, S. S., Lopez, F. A., & Palamar, J. J. (2023). Past-month binge drinking and cannabis use among middle-aged and older adults in the United States, 2015–2019. *Alcohol, 107*, 32–37. https://doi.org/10.1016/j.alcohol.2022.07.006

in older adulthood that were not present in younger adulthood. Additionally, new stressors associated with aging can lead to the onset of a new substance use problem in late life.

Although older adults report a high rate of physician visits, individuals with substance use disorders can be commonly misdiagnosed. Providers may not assess for substance use problems among older adults, assuming that symptoms are indicative of health problems rather than substance use. There is also concern that the current *DSM* criteria for substance use disorders do not adequately capture older adults, with many older adults being "diagnostic orphans," meaning that they meet one criterion for a substance use disorder but not enough criteria to receive a diagnosis (Kuerbis, 2020). Given the increase in use of both alcohol and cannabis among older adults, providers should routinely screen older adults for multiple substances.

Schizophrenia

Schizophrenia is characterized by delusions, hallucinations, disorganized speech, disorganized behavior, and/or negative symptoms such as diminished emotional expression or lack of engagement in goal-directed behavior (i.e., avolition). The majority of research on individuals with schizophrenia examines adults younger than age 65. Among nationally representative samples of older adults, the prevalence rate for schizophrenia is around 0.7% (Lacey et al., 2019). In the current version of the *DSM*, the schizophrenia diagnosis does not distinguish between subtypes (paranoid schizophrenia, etc.) like in prior years. Among individuals with schizophrenia worldwide, approximately 25% are age 55 and older (Cohen et al., 2015). The majority of individuals with schizophrenia are diagnosed prior to older adulthood, though approximately 20% to 25% of people with schizophrenia are diagnosed after age 40. Older adults with schizophrenia tend to have significant clinical needs, particularly because schizophrenia in older adulthood tends to include impaired quality of life, ongoing psychotic symptoms, comorbid mental health conditions, comorbid health conditions, and negative effects of long-term use of antipsychotics (Lacey et al., 2019). Common comorbid mental health conditions among older adults with schizophrenia include anxiety, depression, and bipolar disorder (Lacey et al., 2019). In terms of symptom presentation, the presence and severity of positive symptoms may decrease with age (delusions and hallucinations), while negative symptoms may fluctuate more over time (Cohen et al., 2015).

Cognitive impairment is a core feature of schizophrenia and may be exacerbated with age. Stroup et al. (2021) found that at age 66, the prevalence of dementia was 27.9% among individuals with schizophrenia, compared with 1.3% among those without schizophrenia. By age 80, the prevalence had increased to 70.2% among those with schizophrenia compared with 11.3% in the group without schizophrenia. In this study, individuals with schizophrenia received dementia diagnoses at younger ages compared with those without schizophrenia, and increased dementia prevalence rates were seen across gender and ethnicity groups. The mechanism behind increased dementia may be related to a higher rate of health conditions among those with schizophrenia that can lead to dementia, such as substance use disorders, cardiovascular disease, smoking, and hyperlipidemia (Stroup et al., 2021).

ASSESSMENT OF MENTAL HEALTH CONDITIONS AMONG OLDER ADULTS

When selecting an assessment instrument for use with older adults, it is important to examine the reliability and validity of the instrument with an older adult population. Many assessment instruments were developed and normed on a younger adult sample. Assessment instruments that were developed with younger adults may not be psychometrically valid with older adults. For example, older adults may experience different types of symptoms, or the diagnosis may be complicated by the presence of chronic medical conditions, leading to the possibility of misdiagnosis. Additionally, normative data may not be available for older adults, which may impact the interpretation of scores. In the following section, we review common self-report instruments for assessing depressive symptoms among older adults since this is one of the most common presenting clinical concerns among older adults.

The Center for Epidemiologic Studies Depression Scale

The Center for Epidemiologic Studies Depression Scale, or CES-D, is a common and widely used self-report measure for assessing depression in the general population (Radloff, 1977). The primary components of depression symptomology that the CES-D assesses are depressed mood, feelings of guilt and worthlessness, feelings of helplessness and hopelessness, psychomotor retardation, loss of appetite, and disturbances with sleep (Radloff, 1977).

The original CES-D includes 20 items. There is also a 10-item version and an 8-item version. The CES-D-8 has adequate internal consistency and criterion validity among nonclinical samples of older adults, suggesting that it is an effective screening measure for depression (Karim et al., 2014). The various versions of the CES-D (20 items, 10 items, and 8 items) are validated across multiple cultures and languages (Haringsma et al., 2004; Malakouti et al., 2015) as well as among older adults with chronic medical conditions (Zhang et al., 2015).

The Geriatric Depression Scale

The Geriatric Depression Scale (GDS) was developed by Yesavage et al. (1983) to address the lack of adequate depression assessment tools for older adult populations. The GDS is one of the most commonly used self-report instruments for depression screening among older adults. The scale consists of 30 items specifically tailored toward older adult populations. Each question is responded to in a yes/no format. There are also shorter versions, such as the GDS-15, GDS-10, and GDS-4. The 15-item version of the GDS is displayed in Figure 8.2. In a study of the different versions of the GDS, all versions had adequate sensitivity and specificity, whereas the shorter versions (GDS-15, GDS-10, and GDS-4) had improved diagnostic performance compared with the full version (GDS-30; Krishnamoorthy et al., 2020).

The GDS has been translated into multiple languages and validated with international samples of older adults (e.g., Bae & Cho, 2004; Sugishita et al., 2017). In an updated review and meta-analysis of the GDS-15, Park and Kwak (2021) found that diagnostic accuracy was lower among cognitively impaired older adults compared with those with

No.	Question	Answer	Score
1.	Are you basically satisfied with your life?	Yes/**No**	
2.	Have you dropped many of your activities and interests?	**Yes**/No	
3.	Do you feel that your life is empty?	**Yes**/No	
4.	Do you often get bored?	**Yes**/No	
5.	Are you in good spirits most of the time?	Yes/**No**	
6.	Are you afraid that something bad is going to happen to you?	**Yes**/No	
7.	Do you feel happy most of the time?	Yes/**No**	
8.	Do you often feel helpless?	**Yes**/No	
9.	Do you prefer to stay at home, rather than going out and doing new things?	**Yes**/No	
10.	Do you feel you have more problems with memory than most people?	**Yes**/No	
11.	Do you think it is wonderful to be alive?	Yes/**No**	
12.	Do you feel pretty worthless the way you are now?	**Yes**/No	
13.	Do you feel full of energy?	Yes/**No**	
14.	Do you feel that your situation is hopeless?	**Yes**/No	
15.	Do you think that most people are better off than you are?	**Yes**/No	
		Total	

Figure 8.2 15-item Geriatric Depression Scale.
Note: Positive responses are in bold.
Source: From Stanford University. (2017). *Geriatric depression scale.* https://web.stanford.edu/~yesavage/GDS.english.short.score.html

intact cognitive functioning, suggesting that a different assessment instrument may need to be considered for detecting depression among older adults with cognitive impairment.

The Patient Health Questionnaire-9

The Patient Health Questionnaire-9 (PHQ-9) is a commonly used depression assessment tool, particularly in primary care settings (Kroenke et al., 2001). Although the PHQ-9 was not developed specifically for older adults, there are many studies demonstrating adequate reliability and validity in older adult samples (Kroenke & Spitzer, 2002; Lamers et al., 2008; Phelan et al., 2010). Scores on the PHQ-9 range from 0 to 27. The cutoff thresholds of 5, 10, 15, and 20 are representative of mild, moderate, moderately severe, and severe depression, respectively (Kroenke et al., 2001). The PHQ-9 has been translated into multiple languages and assessed for use across multiple cultures, including among Brazilian older adults (Moreno-Agostino et al., 2022) and Chinese older adults in a primary care setting (Chen et al., 2010). The PHQ-9 is freely available in multiple languages at www.phqscreeners.com.

The Cornell Scale for Depression in Dementia

The Cornell Scale for Depression in Dementia (CSDD) was developed in order to effectively detect and assess symptoms of major depression in individuals afflicted with dementia (Alexopoulos et al., 1988). This measure was created in order to enable clinicians to accurately assess depression among patients with dementia, who may not be able to provide reliable responses. To effectively assess the individual, the CSDD utilizes two semistructured interviews with the patient and an informant. If there are any discrepancies between the informant and the patient, then the clinician performs an additional interview to effectively resolve the differences in information being provided. The CSDD takes approximately 20 minutes to complete.

The CSDD has been administered and validated in older adults from the United States and other countries. For example, Kook Lim et al. (2012) found acceptable reliability and validity of a Korean version of the CSDD, while Lin and Wang (2008) validated the CSDD in a Chinese sample. Additionally, Williams and Marsh (2009) found support for the CSDD in a sample of patients with Parkinson disease who had a range of levels of cognitive impairment. In short, the CSDD is a good choice for detecting depression in people with dementia from a variety of backgrounds. Table 8.2 presents

TABLE 8.2 ASSESSMENT INSTRUMENTS FOR MENTAL HEALTH CONDITIONS OTHER THAN DEPRESSION

Mental Health Condition	Assessment Instruments for Use With Older Adults
Anxiety disorders	Geriatric Anxiety Inventory (GAI; Pachana et al., 2007)
	Geriatric Anxiety Scale (Segal et al., 2010)
	Penn State Worry Questionnaire (PSWQ; Meyer et al., 1990)
Posttraumatic stress disorder (PTSD)	PTSD Checklist (PCL; Weathers et al., 2013)
Personality disorders	Gerontological Personality Disorders Scale (GPS; van Alphen et al., 2006)
	Severity Indices of Personality Problems Short Form (SIPP-SF; Verheul et al., 2008)
	Personality Inventory for Diagnostic and Statistical Manual of Mental Disorders, Fifth Edition, Brief Form (PID-5-BF; Debast et al., 2018)
Suicidality	Reasons for Living—Older Adults (RFL-OA; Edelstein et al., 2009)
	Brief Geriatric Suicide Ideation Scale (BGSIS; Heisel & Flett, 2022)
	Geriatric Hopelessness Scale (GHS; Heisel & Flett, 2005)
	Columbia Suicide Severity Risk Scale (C-SSRS; Posner et al., 2011)
Substance use disorders	Michigan Alcoholism Screen Test—Geriatric Version (MAST-G; Blow et al., 1992)
	Short Michigan Alcoholism Screen Test—Geriatric Version (SMAST-G; Blow et al., 1998)
	Alcohol Use Disorders Identification Test—Consumption Questions (AUDIT-C; Bush et al., 1998)
Schizophrenia	Brief Psychiatric Rating Scale—Expanded Version (BPRS-E; Dingemans et al., 1995)

common self-report instruments for other mental health conditions that are validated for use with older adults.

EMPIRICALLY SUPPORTED TREATMENTS FOR OLDER ADULTS

Older adults are typically underrepresented in settings where mental health services are provided; however, they benefit as much or more from psychological treatment for mental health conditions (Saunders et al., 2021). In a study comparing treatment outcomes of older adults compared with working-age adults, the likelihood of recovery was higher among older adults compared with working-age adults. Additionally, the likelihood of discontinuing treatment or experiencing a worsening of symptoms was lower for older adults compared with working-age adults (Saunders et al., 2021). These associations held even among older adults with chronic health conditions.

The majority of evidence-based treatments for mental health conditions are based on cognitive behavioral models. Broadly, cognitive behavioral models consider the ways in which thoughts, feelings, and behavior are connected and influence each other in maintaining symptoms of mental health conditions. In this section we review empirically supported treatments for the mental health conditions presented in the prior section. Table 8.3 summarizes this section by listing empirically supported psychological treatments by diagnosis.

Mood Disorders and Suicidality

Regardless of what type of treatment is selected (psychotherapy or medication), depression among older adults remains undertreated, with many older adults receiving either no treatment, doses of medication that are too low, or courses of treatment that are too short to effect significant change (Kok & Reynolds, 2017). Depression is unlikely to improve without treatment, with data suggesting that after a 2-year follow-up, only 33% of older adults with depression were in remission (Cole et al., 1999). Current treatment recommendations include psychotherapy for mild to moderate depression and

TABLE 8.3 OVERVIEW OF PSYCHOLOGICAL TREATMENT OPTIONS BY DIAGNOSIS

Diagnosis	Empirically Supported Psychological Treatments
Mood disorders and suicidality	Cognitive behavioral therapy (CBT), interpersonal psychotherapy (IPT), problem-solving therapy (PST), reminiscence therapy
Anxiety disorders and posttraumatic stress disorders (PTSD)	CBT, exposure treatment (anxiety disorders and PTSD)
Personality disorders	Dialectical behavior therapy (DBT), schema therapy
Substance use disorders	Brief motivational interventions, CBT
Schizophrenia	CBT with social skills training

inclusion of medication for severe depression among older adults. However, the efficacy of antidepressants appears to decrease with age, with some researchers proposing that antidepressants may be less effective because of other medical conditions that older adults often have along with depression, as well as prescribing practices that lead to lower doses than are needed (Kok & Reynolds, 2017). Older adults are also more likely to experience side effects from antidepressant medication and to have harmful drug-drug interactions with other medications they are prescribed.

Cognitive behavioral therapy (CBT) for depression has comparable outcomes to antidepressants in terms of overall effectiveness. The goal of CBT is to modify unhelpful thoughts and behaviors that contribute to the symptoms of depression. CBT involves examining how thoughts, feelings, and behaviors are connected. For example, restructuring one's thoughts to be more accurate and helpful may assist in modifying appraisals of situations and behavior, thereby reducing symptoms of depression. A large body of research suggests that CBT is effective for older adults with depression (Jayasekara et al., 2015).

Another intervention that can be used for treatment of mood disorders is interpersonal psychotherapy (IPT), which has been adapted for use with older adults (Hinrichsen, 2008). IPT uses a biopsychosocial model to explain depression and focuses on the role of interpersonal problems in maintaining depression symptoms. IPT explains depression as a medical illness that is affecting the client's ability to function. In part, this approach is taken to give the client the "sick role" so as to reduce self-blame and stigma around seeking treatment. IPT involves examining and addressing the interpersonal relationships of the patient. There are four focus areas in treatment, including grief, role disputes, role transitions, and interpersonal deficits. Therapists employ a number of techniques in IPT, such as clarification and communication analyses, which attempt to reduce symptoms of depression. IPT has been successfully adapted to treat suicidality among older adults (Heisel et al., 2015). In general, IPT is a highly effective treatment for depression as shown in meta-analyses of studies including adults of all ages (Cuijpers et al., 2011).

A third intervention for mood disorders is reminiscence therapy, also called life review therapy. In reminiscence therapy, therapists employ a structured approach where specific topics are the source of reminiscence for each session. The goal of reminiscence therapy is to develop alternative views of one's life that center the older adults as an active agent in their lives. This process can help older adults cope with negative experiences and conflicts while also giving a positive meaning to prior life experiences (Korte et al., 2012). In a randomized clinical trial comparing reminiscence therapy to treatment as usual, reminiscence therapy was more effective in reducing depressive symptoms than treatment as usual, and these gains were maintained at a 3- and 9-month follow-up (Korte et al., 2012).

Problem-solving therapy assumes that depression is maintained by inadequate social problem-solving skills and ineffective coping strategies (Nezu et al., 2015). Treatment is skills-based and focuses on teaching clients how to define problems, set realistic goals, brainstorm and identify solutions, and evaluate the effectiveness of the chosen solution. Problem-solving therapy has been successfully used among older adults with depression (Kirkham et al., 2016), and was part of the large IMPACT (**I**mproving **M**ood-**P**romoting **A**ccess to **C**ollaborative **T**reatment) trial (Unützer et al., 2002), which was one of the first clinical trials that integrated depression treatment into primary care for older adults.

Anxiety Disorders and Posttraumatic Stress Disorder

CBT is an effective treatment for GAD, which is one of the most common anxiety disorders among older adults (Lenze & Wetherell, 2011). Treatment focuses on psychoeducation about anxiety, relaxation training, problem-solving skills training, cognitive techniques, and exposure to anxiety-provoking stimuli. Among older adults, relaxation training appears to be particularly effective for GAD (Thorp et al., 2009). Brief treatment models, including the use of self-help workbooks and other forms of bibliotherapy, are also promising treatment options for older adults. Brief treatment models are typically based on the concept of stepped care, which means that the least intrusive option that is effective should be offered first. In an examination of a stepped care approach for anxiety among older adults, the first intervention was bibliotherapy, which was effective at preventing future anxiety and depressive episodes (van't Veer-Tazelaar et al., 2009).

Pharmacotherapy interventions for anxiety disorders typically involve the use of benzodiazepines, which are contraindicated for older adults because they increase the risk of falls, disability, and cognitive decline (Lenze & Wetherell, 2011). There are some promising data around using selective serotonin reuptake inhibitors (SSRIs) to treat anxiety among older adults (Lenze et al., 2009). In the early phases of treatment, some studies suggest that medication is more effective than CBT for anxiety disorders among older adults. The use of both psychotherapy and medication may be particularly effective for late-life anxiety, although it is unclear whether the treatment should occur simultaneously or be sequenced such that medication is taken initially during the acute phase, with CBT offered for maintenance (Lenze & Wetherell, 2011).

Typical treatments used for adult populations with PTSD include cognitive approaches, exposure approaches, and narrative/writing approaches (Böttche et al., 2012). Overall, there are very limited clinical trial data on treatments for PTSD among older adults, as older adults are often not included in treatment trials. In a review of treatment approaches for PTSD among older adults, Pless Kaiser et al. (2019) found that all treatments included some form of exposure, either through imaginal exercises, in vivo exercises, or written accounts of the trauma. There was previously some concern that exposure-based approaches may be contraindicated for older patients with cardiovascular disease due to the strong physiological reactions that may occur during treatment (Böttche et al., 2012). However, many published case studies and a small number of clinical trials indicate that exposure therapies are safe and effective among older adults. As a precaution, practitioners can work with the older adult's medical provider to ensure that any comorbid health conditions are safe for exposure therapy.

Personality Disorders

There are limited studies on psychological interventions for personality disorders among older adults. Two treatment options that have been studied among older adults include dialectical behavior therapy (DBT) and schema therapy (Lynch et al., 2007; Videler et al., 2018). DBT was initially developed to help alleviate suicidal thoughts and behaviors among individuals with borderline personality disorder. Small clinical trials and case studies have examined the use of DBT among older adults with comorbid depression and personality disorders. In DBT, therapists work with clients on skills to manage suicidal thoughts and behaviors including mindfulness, interpersonal effectiveness, emotion regulation, and distress tolerance (Linehan & Wilks, 2015). Lynch et al. (2007) concluded that DBT could be applied to older adults with personality disorder with minimal modifications. DBT among older adults appears to be effective in reducing interpersonal sensitivity and interpersonal aggression.

Schema therapy has been proposed to treat some types of personality disorders among older adults. Schema therapy is a structured treatment focused on skill-building and problem-solving. Specifically, schema therapy focuses on early maladaptive schemas that are considered core elements of personality disorders. In a multiple baseline study, Videler et al. (2018) found that schema therapy reduced dysfunctional core beliefs among older adults with personality disorders, though gains were not maintained following the active treatment phase.

Substance Use Disorders

There are a number of evidence-based treatments for unhealthy alcohol use, but few have been designed and tested specifically with older adults (Kuerbis et al., 2014). The most recent treatment improvement protocol (TIP) from the Substance Abuse and Mental Health Services Administration (SAMHSA) for substance use problems in older adults (2020) recommends that treatment for unhealthy alcohol use begin with a less intensive approach such as a brief intervention that integrates motivational interviewing (MI). For older adults with low-severity problems, treatment can be as short as one session focused on MI and a few CBT coping strategies focused on high-risk situations and antecedents and consequences of substance use.

Several brief treatment models for older adults have been developed and tested in primary care settings. Examples include Project GOAL (**G**uiding **O**lder **A**dult **L**ifestyles; Fleming et al., 1999), Healthy Living as You Age (Moore et al., 2011), and Project SHARE (**S**enior **H**ealth and **A**lcohol **R**isk **E**ducation; Ettner et al., 2014). These interventions commonly consist of an assessment followed by a few short sessions focused on MI, recognizing drinking triggers/antecedents and strategies for managing urges.

Older adults with moderate to severe substance use problems will likely need a longer treatment. CBT is appropriate for older adults with substance use problems and can be expanded to include skills related to mood management and other substance use triggers. For example, the Gerontology Alcohol Project (GAP; Center for Substance Abuse Treatment, 2005) is a longer term (16-session) treatment that is appropriate for clients who need a more intensive level of treatment. In this group treatment, clients work through nine modules after completing an assessment of alcohol use patterns and related problems. Sessions focus on analyzing alcohol behavior, managing social pressure, managing situations at home and alone, managing negative thoughts and emotions associated with alcohol use, managing anxiety and tension, managing anger and frustration, controlling alcohol use, coping with urges, and preventing a slip from becoming a return to use.

Schizophrenia

Older adults with schizophrenia may be treated with a combination of psychotherapy and antipsychotic medication. However, there are concerns about the long-term safety and effectiveness of antipsychotics among older adults. For example, Jin et al. (2012)

found that there was a high rate of discontinuation of medication among middle-aged and older patients with schizophrenia, with half of the patients discontinuing their prescribed antipsychotic medication within 6 months. Additionally, there was a high rate of side effects, with no improvements in the severity of symptoms as measured by the Brief Psychiatric Rating Scale. Practitioners suggest that older adults and their caregivers receive information about possible side effects of antipsychotics, as well as available psychosocial treatments, in order to make an informed decision about treatment options (Jeste & Maglione, 2013).

There are a few psychosocial treatments for older adults with schizophrenia that have support. Cognitive behavioral social skills training is effective for middle-aged and older adults with schizophrenia and involves a group treatment model that combines problem-solving skills, social skills, and CBT. In adults age 45 and older with schizophrenia, cognitive behavioral social skills training resulted in improvements in insight, social activities, and overall functioning, with gains maintained at a 1-year follow-up (Granholm et al., 2007). Another treatment for older patients with schizophrenia is functional adaptation skills training, which is a 24-week behavioral program that was found to improve everyday living skills and social skills, with gains maintained at a 3-month follow-up (Patterson et al., 2006). Topics in the treatment included many instrumental activities of daily living including medication management, social skills, communication skills, organization and planning, transportation, and financial management. As seen in the description of these treatments, many psychosocial treatments for schizophrenia focus on both symptom management and skills training for social skills and tasks of everyday living. This approach can also be seen in the treatment program Helping Older People Experience Success, which was designed for older adults with serious mental illness, some of whom had schizophrenia (Mueser et al., 2010). Treatment components focused on improving self-efficacy, reducing negative symptoms, and improving social skills and community functioning.

CONCLUSION

This chapter discussed several topics relevant to older adults' mental health including access and use of mental health services, prevalence of common mental health diagnoses, assessment of mental health symptoms, and empirically supported treatments for older adults. Although some topics presented in this chapter need additional research focused specifically on an older adult population, several conclusions can be drawn from the material. First, several studies have documented that older adults use mental health services less frequently than other age groups, although it is unclear why this is the case and likely involves a combination of stigma and barriers/access to treatment. Second, several of the mental health problems discussed in the chapter may present differently among older adults, such as the specific symptoms of depression that older adults endorse. Practitioners need to be cautious to separate physical from mental health symptoms to avoid underdiagnosing or overdiagnosing mental health problems among older adults. Third, assessment instruments for older adults need to be selected cautiously to ensure that adequate validity and reliability have been established for this population. Finally, empirically supported treatments are available for older adults for many types of mental health problems, and older adults benefit as much as or more from psychotherapy as compared to other age groups.

DISCUSSION QUESTIONS

1. What are the most common types of mental health conditions experienced by older adults?
2. How do beliefs about mental healthcare differ between younger and older adults?
3. What symptoms of depression would you look for among older adults versus younger adults?
4. What factors are associated with increased risk of suicide among older adults?
5. How is depression assessed among older adults who have dementia?
6. What evidence-based treatments are available for older adults for each of the diagnoses presented in the chapter?

A robust set of instructor resources designed to supplement this text is located at http://connect.springerpub.com/content/book/978-0-8261-6617-3. Qualifying instructors may request access by emailing textbook@springerpub.com.

REFERENCES

Administration on Aging. (2012). *A profile of older Americans: 2012*. https://www.acl.gov/sites/default/files/Aging%20and%20Disability%20in%20America/2012profile.pdf

Alexopoulos, G. S., Abrams, R. C., Young, R. C., & Shamoian, C. A. (1988). Cornell scale for depression in dementia. *Biological Psychiatry, 23*(3), 271–284. https://doi.org/10.1016/0006-3223(88)90038-8

American Psychiatric Association. (2022). *Diagnostic and statistical manual of mental disorders* (5th ed., text rev.). https://doi.org/10.1176/appi.books.9780890425787

Babitsch, B., Gohl, D., & Von Lengerke, T. (2012). Re-revisiting Andersen's Behavioral Model of Health Services use: A systematic review of studies from 1998–2011. *GMS Psycho-Social-Medicine, 9*, Doc11. https://doi.org/10.3205/psm000089

Bach, B., & First, M. B. (2018). Application of the ICD-11 classification of personality disorders. *BMC Psychiatry, 18*(1), 351. https://doi.org/10.1186/s12888-018-1908-3

Bae, J. N., & Cho, M. J. (2004). Development of the Korean version of the Geriatric Depression Scale and its short form among elderly psychiatric patients. *Journal of Psychosomatic Research, 57*(3), 297–305. https://doi.org/10.1016/j.jpsychores.2004.01.004

Barry, K. L., & Blow, F. C. (2016). Drinking over the lifespan: Focus on older adults. *Alcohol Research: Current Reviews, 38*(1), 115–120.

Blow, F. C., Brower, K. J., Schulenberg, J. E., Demo-Dananberg, L. M., Young, J. P., & Beresford, T. P. (1992). The Michigan Alcoholism Screening Test-Geriatric Version (MAST-G): A new elderly specific screening instrument. *Alcoholism: Clinical and Experimental Research, 16*(2), 372.

Blow, F. C., Gillespie, B. W., Barry, K. L., Mudd, S. A., & Hill, E. M. (1998). Brief screening for alcohol problems in elderly populations using the Short Michigan Alcoholism Screening Test-Geriatric Version (SMAST-G). *Alcoholism: Clinical and Experimental Research, 22* (Suppl.), 131A.

Böttche, M., Kuwert, P., & Knaevelsrud, C. (2012). Posttraumatic stress disorder in older adults: An overview of characteristics and treatment approaches. *International Journal of Geriatric Psychiatry, 27*(3), 230–239. https://doi.org/10.1002/gps.2725

Breslow, R. A., Castle, I.-J. P., Chen, C. M., & Graubard, B. I. (2017). Trends in alcohol consumption among older Americans: National health interview surveys, 1997–2014. *Alcohol: Clinical and Experimental Research, 41*(5), 976–986. https://doi.org/10.1111/acer.13365

Bush, K., Kivlahan, D. R., McDonell, M. B., Fihn, S. D., Bradley, K. A., & Ambulatory Care Quality Improvement Project. (1998). The AUDIT alcohol consumption questions (AUDIT-C): An effective brief screening test for problem drinking. *Archives of Internal Medicine, 158*(16), 1789–1795. https://doi.org/10.1001/archinte.158.16.1789

Byers, A. L., Arean, P. A., & Yaffe, K. (2012). Low use of mental health services among older Americans with mood and anxiety disorders. *Psychiatric Services, 63*(1), 66–72. https://doi.org/10.1176/appi.ps.201100121

Canuto, A., Weber, K., Baertschi, M., Andreas, S., Volkert, J., Dehoust, M. C., Sehner, S., Wegscheider, K., Ausín, B., Crawford, M. J., Da Ronch, C., Grassi, L., Hershkovitz, Y., Muñoz, M., Quirk, A., Rotenstein, O., Santos-Olmo, A. B., Shalev, A., Strehle, J., Wittchen, H.-U., Schultz, H., & Härter, M. (2018). Anxiety disorder in old age: Psychiatric comorbidities, quality of life, and prevalence according to age, gender, and country. *American Journal of Geriatric Psychiatry, 26*(2), 174–185. https://doi.org/j.jagp.2017.08.015

Center for Substance Abuse Treatment. (2005). *Substance abuse relapse prevention for older adults: A group treatment approach*. DHHS Publication No. (SMA) 05-4053. Substance Abuse and Mental Health Services Administration.

Centers for Disease Control and Prevention. (2014). *Fatal injury reports, national and regional, 1999–2014*. http://webappa.cdc.gov/sasweb/ncipc/mortrate10_us.html

Chao, Y. Y., Seo, J. Y., Katigbak, C., & Chang, Y. P. (2020). Utilization of mental health services among older Chinese immigrants in New York City. *Community Mental Health Journal, 56*(3), 1331–1343. https://doi.org/10.1007/s10597-020-00570-2

Chen, S., Chiu, H., Xu, B., Ma, Y., Jin, T., Wu, M., & Conwell, Y. (2010). Reliability and validity of the PHQ-9 for screening late-life depression in Chinese primary care. *International Journal of Geriatric Psychiatry, 25*(11), 1127–1133. https://doi.org/10.1002/gps.2442

Cohen, C. I., Meesters, P. D., & Zhao, J. (2015). New perspectives on schizophrenia in later life: Implications for treatment, policy, and research. *The Lancet Psychiatry, 2*(4), 340–350. https://doi.org/10.1016/S2215-0366(15)00003-6

Cole, M. G., Bellavance, F., & Mansour, A. (1999). Prognosis of depression in elderly community and primary care populations: a systematic review and meta-analysis. *American Journal of Psychiatry, 156*(8), 1182–1189. https://doi.org/10.1176/ajp.156.8.1182

Conwell, Y. (1997). Management of suicidal behavior in the elderly. *Psychiatric Clinics of North America, 20*(3), 667–683. https://doi.org/10.1016/S0193-953X(05)70336-1

Conwell, Y., Duberstein, P. R., & Caine, E. D. (2002). Risk factors for suicide in later life. *Biological Psychiatry, 52*(3), 193–204. https://doi.org/10.1016/S0006-3223(02)01347-1

Crocq, M. A., & Crocq, L. (2000). From shell shock and war neurosis to posttraumatic stress disorder: A history of psychotraumatology. *Dialogues in Clinical Neuroscience, 2*(1), 47–55. https://doi.org/10.31887/DCNS.2000.2.1/macrocq

Cuijpers, P., Geraedts, A. S., van Oppen, P., Andersson, G., Markowitz, J. C., & van Straten, A. (2011). Interpersonal psychotherapy for depression: A meta-analysis. *American Journal of Psychiatry, 168*(6), 581–592. https://doi.org/10.1176/appi.ajp.2010.10101411

Debast, I., Rossi, G., & Van Alphen, S. P. J. (2018). Age-neutrality of a brief assessment of the section III alternative model for personality disorders in older adults. *Assessment, 25*(3), 310–323. https://doi.org/10.1177/1073191118754706

Dingemans, P. M. A. J., Linszen, D. H., Lenior, M. E., & Smeets, R. M. W. (1995). Component structure of the expanded Brief Psychiatric Rating Scale (BPRS-E). *Psychopharmacology, 122*(3), 263–267. https://doi.org/10.1007/BF02246547

Edelstein, B. A., Heisel, M. J., McKee, D. R., Martin, R. R., Koven, L. P., Duberstein, P. R., & Britton, P. C. (2009). Development and psychometric evaluation of the reasons for living—Older adults scale: A suicide risk assessment inventory. *Gerontologist, 49*(6), 736–745. https://doi.org/10.1093/geront/gnp052

Ettner, S. L., Xu, H., Kenrik Duru, O., Ang, A., Tseng, C.-H., Tallen, L., Barnes, A., Mirkin, M., Ransohoff, K., & Moore, A. A. (2014). The effect of an educational intervention on alcohol consumption, at-risk drinking, and health care utilization in older adults: The Project SHARE study. *Journal of Studies on Alcohol and Drugs, 75*(3), 447–457. https://doi.org/10.15288/jsad.2014.75.447

Fiske, A., Wetherell, J. L., & Gatz, M. (2009). Depression in older adults. *Annual Review of Clinical Psychology, 5*, 363–389. https://doi.org/10.1146/annurev.clinpsy.032408.153621

Fleming, M. F., Manwell, L. B., Barry, K. L., Adams, W., & Stauffacher, E. A. (1999). Brief physician advice for alcohol problems in older adults: A randomized community-based trial. *Journal of Family Practice, 48*(5), 378–386.

Gellert, P., Lech, S., Kessler, E. M., Herrmann, W., Döpfmer, S., Balke, K., …, Schnitzer, S. (2021). Perceived need for treatment and non-utilization of outpatient psychotherapy in old age: Two cohorts of a nationwide survey. *BMC Health Services Research, 21*(1), 442. https://doi.org/10.1186/s12913-021-06384-6

Gould, C. E., Gerolimatos, L. A., Beaudreau, S. A., Mashal, N., & Edelstein, B. A. (2018). Older adults report more sadness and less jealousy than young adults in response to worry induction. *Aging & Mental Health, 22*(4), 512–518. https://doi.org/10.1080/13607863.2016.1277975

Granholm, E., McQuaid, J. R., McClure, F. S., Link, P. C., Perivoliotis, D., Gottlieb, J. D., . . ., Jeste, D. V. (2007). Randomised controlled trial of cognitive behavioural social skills training for older people with schizophrenia: 12-month follow-up. *Journal of Clinical Psychiatry, 68*(5), 730 – 737. https://doi.org/10.4088/jcp.v68n0510

Granier, K., Ingram, R., & Segal, D. (2020). The who and when of worry: The fading impact of gender on worry and anxiety severity among older adults. *Innovation in Aging, 4*(Suppl 1), 372. https://doi.org/10.1093/geroni/igaa057.1199

Gum, A. M., King-Kallimanis, B., & Kohn, R. (2009). Prevalence of mood, anxiety, and substance-abuse disorders for older Americans in the national comorbidity survey-replication. *American Journal of Geriatric Psychiatry, 17*(9), 769–781. https://doi.org/10.1097/JGP.0b013e3181ad4f5a

Haringsma, R., Engels, G. I., Beekman, A. T. F., & Spinhoven, P. (2004). The criterion validity of the Center for Epidemiological Studies Depression Scale (CES-D) in a sample of self-referred elders with depressive symptomatology. *International Journal of Geriatric Psychiatry, 19*(6), 558–563. https://doi.org/10.1002/gps.1130

Han, B. H., Moore, A. A., Sherman, S., Keyes, K. M., & Palamar, J. J. (2017). Demographic trends of binge alcohol use and alcohol use disorders among older adults in the United States, 2005–2014. *Drug and Alcohol Dependence, 170*, 198–207. https://doi.org/10.1016/j.drugalcdep.2016.11.003

Han, B. H., Brennan, J. J., Orozco, M. A., Moore, A. A., & Castillo, E. M. (2023). Trends in emergency department visits associated with cannabis use among older adults in California, 2005–2019. *Journal of the American Geriatrics Society, 71*(4), 1267–1274. https://doi.org/10.1111/jgs.18180

Heisel, M. J., & Flett, G. L. (2005). A psychometric analysis of the Geriatric Hopelessness Scale (GHS): Towards improving assessment of the construct. *Journal of Affective Disorders, 87*(2–3), 211–220. https://doi.org/10.1016/j.jad.2005.03.016

Heisel, M. J., & Flett, G. L. (2022). Screening for suicide risk among older adults: Assessing preliminary psychometric properties of the Brief Geriatric Suicide Ideation Scale (BGSIS) and the GSIS-Screen. *Aging & Mental Health, 26*(2), 392–406. https://doi.org/10.1080/13607863.2020.1857690

Heisel, M. J., Talbot, N. L., King, D. A., Tu, X. M., & Duberstein, P. R. (2015). Adapting interpersonal psychotherapy for older adults at risk for suicide. *The American Journal of Geriatric Psychiatry, 23*(1), 87–98. https://doi.org/10.1016/j.jagp.2014.03.010

Hinrichsen, G. A. (2008). Interpersonal psychotherapy as a treatment for depression in later life. *Professional Psychology: Research and Practice, 39*(3), 306–312. https://doi.org/10.1037/0735-7028.39.3.306

Horackova, K., Kopecek, M., Machů, V., Kagstrom, A., Aarsland, D., Motlova, L. B., & Cermakova, P. (2019). Prevalence of late-life depression and gap in mental health service use across European regions. *European Psychiatry, 57*, 19–25. https://doi.org/10.1016/j.eurpsy.2018.12.002

Institute of Medicine. (2012). *The mental health and substance use workforce for older adults: In whose hands?* National Academies Press.

Jacobs, M. L., & Bamonti, P. M. (2022). Clinical practice: A foundational geropsychology knowledge competency. *Clinical Psychology: Science and Practice, 29*(1), 28–42. https://doi.org/10.1037/cps0000046.

Jayasekara, R., Procter, N., Harrison, J., Skelton, K., Hampel, S., Draper, R., & Deuter, K. (2015). Cognitive behavioural therapy for older adults with depression: a review. *Journal of Mental Health, 24*(3), 168–171. https://doi.org/10.3109/09638237.2014.971143

Jeste, D. V., & Maglione, J. E. (2013). Treating older adults with schizophrenia: Challenges and opportunities. *Schizophrenia Bulletin, 39*(5), 966–968. https://doi.org/10.1093/schbul/sbt043

Jin, H., Shih, P. A. B., Golshan, S., Mudaliar, S., Henry, R., Glorioso, D. K., …, Jeste, D. V. (2012). Comparison of longer-term safety and effectiveness of 4 atypical antipsychotics in patients over age 40: A trial using equipoise-stratified randomization. *The Journal of Clinical Psychiatry, 73*(1), 10–18. https://doi.org/10.4088/JCP.12m08001

Karel, M. J., Gatz, M., & Smyer, M. A. (2012). Aging and mental health in the decade ahead: What psychologists need to know. *American Psychologist, 67*, 184–198. https://doi.org/10.1037/a0025393

Karim, J., Weisz, R., Bibi, Z., & ur Rehman, S. (2015). Validation of the eight-item Center for Epidemiologic Studies Depression Scale (CES-D) among older adults. *Current Psychology: A Journal for Diverse Perspectives on Diverse Psychological Issues, 34*(4), 681–692. https://doi.org/10.1007/s12144-014-9281-y

Kepner, W. E., Han, B. H., Nguyen, D., Han, S. S., Lopez, F. A., & Palamar, J. J. (2023). Past-month binge drinking and cannabis use among middle-aged and older adults in the United States, 2015–2019. *Alcohol, 107*, 32–37. https://doi.org/10.1016/j.alcohol.2022.07.006

Kirkham, J. G., Choi, N., & Seitz, D. P. (2016). Meta-analysis of problem solving therapy for the treatment of major depressive disorder in older adults. *International Journal of Geriatric Psychiatry, 31*(5), 526–535. https://doi.org/10.1002/gps.4358

Kok, R. M., & Reynolds, C. F. (2017). Management of depression in older adults: A review. *JAMA, 317*(20), 2114–2122. https://doi.org/10.1001/jama.2017.5706

Kook Lim, H. K., Hong, S. C., Won, W. Y., Hahn, C., & Lee, C. U. (2012). Reliability and validity of the Korean version of the Cornell Scale for Depression in Dementia. *Psychiatry Investigation, 9*(4), 332. https://doi.org/10.4306/pi.2012.9.4.332

Korte, J., Cappeliez, P., Bohlmeijer, E. T., & Westerhof, G. J. (2012). Meaning in life and mastery mediate the relationship of negative reminiscence with psychological distress among older adults with mild to moderate depressive symptoms. *European Journal of Ageing, 9*(4), 343–351. https://doi.org/10.1007/s10433-012-0239-3

Krishnamoorthy, Y., Rajaa, S., & Rehman, T. (2020). Diagnostic accuracy of various forms of geriatric depression scale for screening of depression among older adults: Systematic review and meta-analysis. *Archives of Gerontology and Geriatrics, 87*, 104002. https://doi.org/10.1016/j.archger.2019.104002

Kroenke, K., & Spitzer, R. L. (2002). The PHQ-9: A new depression diagnostic and severity measure. *Psychiatric Annals, 32*(9), 509–515. https://doi.org/10.3928/0048-5713-20020901-06

Kroenke, K., Spitzer, R. L., & Williams, J. B. W. (2001). The PHQ-9: Validity of a brief depression severity measure. *Journal of General Internal Medicine, 16*(9), 606–613. https://doi.org/10.1046/j.1525-1497.2001.016009606.x

Kuerbis, A. (2020). Substance use among older adults: Prevalence, etiology, assessment, and intervention. *Gerontology, 66*(3), 249–258. https://doi.org/10.1159/000504363

Kuerbis, A. N., Sacco, P., Blazer, D. G., & Moore, A. A. (2014). Substance abuse among older adults. *Clinics in Geriatric Medicine, 30*(3), 629–654. https://doi.org/10.1016/j.cger.2014.04.008

Lacey, C., Manuel, J., Schluter, P. J., Porter, R. J., Pitama, S., & Jamieson, H. A. (2019). Sociodemographic, environmental characteristics and comorbidities of older adults with schizophrenia who access community health service support: A national cross-sectional study. *Australian & New Zealand Journal of Psychiatry, 53*(6), 570–580. https://doi.org/10.1177/0004867419828480

Lamers, F., Jonkers, C. C. M., Bosma, H., Penninx, B. W. J. H., Knottnerus, J. A., & van Eijk, J. T. M. (2008). Summed score of the Patient Health Questionnaire-9 was a reliable and valid method for depression screening in chronically ill elderly patients. *Journal of Clinical Epidemiology, 61*(7), 679–687. https://doi.org/10.1016/j.jclinepi.2007.07.018

Lawrence, V., Murray, J., Banerjee, S., Turner, S., Sangha, K., Byng, R., . . ., Macdonald, A. (2006). Concepts and causation of depression: A cross-cultural study of the beliefs of older adults. *The Gerontologist, 46*(1), 23–32. https://doi.org/10.1093/geront/46.1.23

Legarreta, M., Graham, J., North, L., Bueler, C. E., McGlade, E., & Yurgelun-Todd, D. (2015). DSM-5 posttraumatic stress disorder symptoms associated with suicide behaviors in veterans. *Psychological Trauma: Theory, Research, Practice, and Policy, 7*(3), 277–285. https://doi.org/10.1037/tra0000026

Lenze, E. J., & Wetherell, J. L. (2011). Anxiety disorders: New developments in old age. *The American Journal of Geriatric Psychiatry, 19*(4), 301–304. https://doi.org/10.1097/JGP.0b013e31820db34f

Lenze, E. J., Rollman, B. L., Shear, M. K., Dew, M. A., Pollock, B. G., Ciliberti, C., …, Reynolds, C. F. (2009). Escitalopram for older adults with generalized anxiety disorder: A randomized controlled trial. *JAMA, 301*(3), 295–303. https://doi.org/10.1001/jama.2008.977

Lin, J. N., & Wang, J. J. (2008). Psychometric evaluation of the Chinese version of the Cornell Scale for Depression in Dementia. *Journal of Nursing Research, 16*(3), 202–210. https://doi.org/10.1097/01.JNR.0000387307.34741.39

Linehan, M. M., & Wilks, C. R. (2015). The course and evolution of dialectical behavior therapy. *American Journal of Psychotherapy, 69*(3), 97–110. https://doi.org/10.1176/appi.psychotherapy.2015.69.2.97

Ljubic, N., Ueberberg, B., Grunze, H., & Assion, H. J. (2021). Treatment of bipolar disorders in older adults: A review. *Annals of General Psychiatry, 20*(1), 45. https://doi.org/10.1186/s12991-021-00367-x

Lynch, T. R., Cheavens, J. S., Cukrowicz, K. C., Thorp, S. R., Bronner, L., & Beyer, J. (2007). Treatment of older adults with co-morbid personality disorder and depression: A dialectical behavior therapy approach. *International Journal of Geriatric Psychiatry, 22*(2), 131–143. https://doi.org/10.1002/gps.1703

Mackenzie, C. S., Pagura, J., & Sareen, J. (2010). Correlates of perceived need for and use of mental health services by older adults in the collaborative psychiatric epidemiological surveys. *American Journal of Geriatric Psychiatry, 18*(12), 1103–1115. https://doi.org/10.1097/JGP.0b013e3181dd1c06

Mackenzie, C. S., Heath, P. J., Vogel, D. L., & Chekay, R. (2019). Age differences in public stigma, self-stigma, and attitudes toward seeking help: A moderated mediation model. *Journal of Clinical Psychology, 75*(12), 2259–2272. https://doi.org/10.1002/jclp.22845

Mackenzie, C. S., & Pankratz, L. (2022). Perceived need, mental health literacy, neuroticism and self-stigma predict mental health service use among older adults. *Clinical Gerontologist*, 1–14. https://doi.org/10.1080/07317115.2022.2058440

Malakouti, S. K., Pachana, N. A., Naji, B., Kahani, S., & Saeedkhani, M. (2015). Reliability, validity and factor structure of the CES-D in Iranian elderly. *Asian Journal of Psychiatry, 18*, 86–90. https://doi.org/10.1016/j.ajp.2015.08.007

Meyer, T. J., Miller, M. L., Metzger, R. L., & Borkovec, T. D. (1990). Development and validation of the Penn State Worry Questionnaire. *Behaviour Research and Therapy, 28*(6), 487–495. https://doi.org/10.1016/0005-7967(90)90135-6

Moon, H., Lee, Y. S., Roh, S., & Burnette, C. E. (2018). Factors associated with American Indian mental health service use in comparison with white older adults. *Journal of Racial and Ethnic Health Disparities, 5*(4), 847–859. https://doi.org/10.1007/s40615-017-0430-5

Moore, A. A., Blow, F. C., Hoffing, M., Welgreen, S., Davis, J. W., Lin, J. C., Ramirez, K. D., Liao, D. H., Tang, L., Gould, R., Gill, M., Chen, O., & Barry, K. L. (2011). Primary care-based intervention to reduce at-risk drinking in older adults: A randomized controlled trial. *Addiction, 106*(1), 111–120. https://doi.org/10.1111/j.1360-0443.2010.03229.x

Moreno-Agostino, D., Chua, K. C., Peters, T. J., Scazufca, M., & Araya, R. (2022). Psychometric properties of the PHQ-9 measure of depression among Brazilian older adults. *Aging & Mental Health, 26*(11), 2285–2290. https://doi.org/10.1080/13607863.2021.1963951

Mueser, K. T., Pratt, S. I., Bartels, S. J., Swain, K., Forester, B., Cather, C., & Feldman, J. (2010). Randomized trial of social rehabilitation and integrated health care for older people with severe mental illness. *Journal of Consulting and Clinical Psychology, 78*(4), 561–573. https://doi.org/10.1037/a0019629

Murphy, D. J., Mackenzie, C. S., Dryden, R. P., & Hamm, J. M. (2024). Perceived control moderates the internalized stigma model of seeking mental health services in distressed older adults. *Journal of Counseling Psychology, 71*(5), 473–486. https://doi.org/10.1037/cou0000733

Nair, P., Bhanu, C., Frost, R., Buszewicz, M., & Walters, K. R. (2020). A systematic review of older adults' attitudes towards depression and its treatment. *The Gerontologist, 60*(1), e93–e104. https://doi.org/10.1093/geront/gnz048

National Institute on Aging. (2011). *Global health and aging*. http://www.who.int/ageing/publications/global_health.pdf

Nezu, C. M., Nezu, A. M., & Colosimo, M. M. (2015). Case formulation and the therapeutic alliance in contemporary problem-solving therapy (PST). *Journal of Clinical Psychology, 71*(5), 428–438. https://doi.org/10.1002/jclp.22179

Pachana, N., Byrne, G., Siddle, H., Koloski, N., Harley, E., & Arnold, E. (2007). Development and validation of the Geriatric Anxiety Inventory. *International Psychogeriatrics, 19*(1), 103–114. https://doi.org/10.1017/S1041610206003504

Park, S. H., & Kwak, M. J. (2021). Performance of the Geriatric Depression Scale-15 with older adults aged over 65 years: An updated review 2000–2019. *Clinical Gerontologist, 44*(2), 83–96. https://doi.org/10.1080/07317115.2020.1839992

Patterson, T. L., Mausbach, B. T., McKibbin, C., Goldman, S., Bucardo, J., & Jeste, D. V. (2006). Functional adaptation skills training (FAST): A randomized trial of a psychosocial intervention for middle-aged and older patients with chronic psychotic disorders. *Schizophrenia Research, 86*(1–3), 291–299. https://doi.org/10.1016/j.schres.2006.05.017

Penders, K. A., Peeters, I. G., Metsemakers, J. F., & Van Alphen, S. P. (2020). Personality disorders in older adults: A review of epidemiology, assessment, and treatment. *Current Psychiatry Reports, 22*(3), 14. https://doi.org/10.1007/s11920-020-1133-x

Phelan, E., Williams, B., Meeker, K., Bonn, K., Frederick, J., Logerfo, J., & Snowden, M. (2010). A study of the diagnostic accuracy of the PHQ-9 in primary care elderly. *BioMed Central Family Practice, 11*, 63. https://doi.org/10.1186/1471-2296-11-63

Pless Kaiser, A., Cook, J. M., Glick, D. M., & Moye, J. (2019). Posttraumatic stress disorder in older adults: A conceptual review. *Clinical Gerontologist, 42*(4), 359–376. https://doi.org/10.1080/07317115.2018.1539801

Posner, K., Brown, G. K., Stanley, B., Brent, D. A., Yershova, K. V., Oquendo, M. A., …, Mann, J. J. (2011). The Columbia–Suicide Severity Rating Scale: Initial validity and internal consistency findings from three multisite studies with adolescents and adults. *American Journal of Psychiatry, 168*(12), 1266–1277. https://doi.org/10.1176/appi.ajp.2011.10111704

Radloff, L. (1977). The CES-D scale: A self-report depression scale for research in the general population. *Applied Psychological Measurement, 1*(3), 385–401. https://doi.org/10.1177/014662167700100306

Reynolds, K., Pietrzak, R. H., El-Gabalawy, R., Mackenzie, C. S., & Sareen, J. (2015). Prevalence of psychiatric disorders in U.S. older adults: Findings from a nationally representative survey. *World Psychiatry, 14*(1), 74–81. https://doi.org/10.1002/wps.20193

Sajatovic, M., Strejilevich, S. A., Gildengers, A. G., Dols, A., Al Jurdi, R. K., Forester, B. P., …, Shulman, K. I. (2015). A report on older-age bipolar disorder from the International Society for Bipolar Disorders Task Force. *Bipolar Disorders, 17*(7), 689–704. https://doi.org/10.1111/bdi.12331

Saunders, R., Buckman, J. E., Stott, J., Leibowitz, J., Aguirre, E., John, A., …, Pilling, S. (2021). Older adults respond better to psychological therapy than working-age adults: Evidence from a large sample of mental health service attendees. *Journal of Affective Disorders, 294*, 85–93. https://doi.org/10.1016/j.jad.2021.06.084

Segal, D. L., June, A., Payne, M., Coolidge, F. L., & Yochim, B. (2010). Development and initial validation of a self-report assessment tool for anxiety among older adults: The Geriatric Anxiety Scale. *Journal of Anxiety Disorders, 24*(7), 709–714. https://doi.org/10.1016/j.janxdis.2010.05.002

Sharland, E., Rzepnicka, K., Schneider, D., Finning, K., Pawelek, P., Saunders, R., & Nafilyan, V. (2023). Socio-demographic differences in access to psychological treatment services: Evidence from a national cohort study. *Psychological Medicine, 53*(15), 7395–7406. https://doi.org/10.1017/S0033291723001010

Stroup, T. S., Olfson, M., Huang, C., Wall, M. M., Goldberg, T., Devanand, D. P., & Gerhard, T. (2021). Age-specific prevalence and incidence of dementia diagnoses among older US adults with schizophrenia. *JAMA Psychiatry, 78*(6), 632–641. https://doi.org/10.1001/jamapsychiatry.2021.0042

Sugishita, K., Sugishita, M., Hemmi, I., Asada, T., & Tanigawa, T. (2017). A validity and reliability study of the Japanese version of the geriatric depression scale 15 (GDS-15-J). *Clinical Gerontologist, 40*(4), 233–240. https://doi.org/10.1080/07317115.2016.1199452

Thomas, M. M., Harpaz-Rotem, I., Tsai, J., Southwick, S. M., & Pietrzak, R. H. (2017). Mental and physical health conditions in US combat veterans: Results from the National Health and Resilience in Veterans Study. *The Primary Care Companion for CNS Disorders, 19*(3), 27474. https://doi.org/10.4088/PCC.17m02118

Thompson, N. J., Fiorillo, D., Rothbaum, B. O., Ressler, K. J., & Michopoulos, V. (2018). Coping strategies as mediators in relation to resilience and posttraumatic stress disorder. *Journal of Affective Disorders, 225*, 153–159. https://doi.org/10.1016/j.jad.2017.08.049

Thorp, S. R., Ayers, C. R., Nuevo, R., Stoddard, J. A., Sorrell, J. T., & Wetherell, J. L. (2009). Meta-analysis comparing different behavioral treatments for late-life anxiety. *The American Journal of Geriatric Psychiatry, 17*(2), 105–115. https://doi.org/10.1097/JGP.0b013e31818b3f7e

Unützer, J., Katon, W., Callahan, C. M., Williams Jr, J. W., Hunkeler, E., Harpole, L., …, IMPACT Investigators. (2002). Collaborative care management of late-life depression in the primary care setting: A randomized controlled trial. *JAMA, 288*(22), 2836–2845. https://doi.org/10.1001/jama.288.22.2836

van Alphen, S. P. J., Engelen, G. J. J. A., Kuin, Y., Hoijtink, H. J. A., & Derksen, J. J. L. (2006). A preliminary study of the diagnostic accuracy of the Gerontological personality disorders Scale (GPS). *International Journal of Geriatric Psychiatry, 21*(9), 862–868. https://doi.org/10.1002/gps.1572

van der Veen, D. C., van Zelst, W. H., Schoevers, R. A., Comijs, H. C., & Voshaar, R. C. (2015). Comorbid anxiety disorders in late-life depression: Results of a cohort study. *International Psychogeriatrics, 27*, 1157–1165. https://doi.org/10.1017/S1041610214002312

van't Veer-Tazelaar, P. J., van Marwijk, H. W., van Oppen, P., van Hout, H. P., van der Horst, H. E., Cuijpers, P., ..., Beekman, A. T. (2009). Stepped-care prevention of anxiety and depression in late life: A randomized controlled trial. *Archives of General Psychiatry, 66*(3), 297–304. https://doi.org/10.1001/archgenpsychiatry.2008.555

Verheul, R., Andrea, H., Berghout, C. C., Dolan, C., Busschbach, J. J. V., van der Kroft, P. J. A., Bateman, A. W., & Fonagy, P. (2008). Severity Indices of Personality Problems (SIPP-118): Development, factor structure, reliability, and validity. *Psychological Assessment, 20*(1), 23–34. https://doi.org/10.1037/1040-3590.20.1.23

Videler, A. C., Hutsebaut, J., Schulkens, J. E., Sobczak, S., & Van Alphen, S. P. (2019). A life span perspective on borderline personality disorder. *Current Psychiatry Reports, 21*, 51. https://doi.org/10.1007/s11920-019-1040-1

Videler, A. C., van Alphen, S. P., van Royen, R. J., van der Feltz-Cornelis, C. M., Rossi, G., & Arntz, A. (2018). Schema therapy for personality disorders in older adults: A multiple-baseline study. *Aging & Mental Health, 22*(6), 738–747. https://doi.org/10.1080/13607863.2017.1318260

Vogel, D. L., Bitman, R. L., Hammer, J. H., & Wade, N. G. (2013). Is stigma internalized? The longitudinal impact of public stigma on self-stigma. *Journal of Counseling Psychology, 60*(2), 311–316. https://doi.org/10.1037/a0031889

Weathers, F. W., Litz, B. T., Keane, T. M., Palmieri, P. A., Marx, B. P., & Schnurr, P. P. (2013). *The PTSD checklist for DSM-5 (PCL-5)*. https://www.ptsd.va.gov/professional/assessment/adult-sr/ptsd-checklist.asp

Williams, J. R., & Marsh, L. (2009). Validity of the Cornell Scale for Depression in Dementia in Parkinson's disease with and without cognitive impairment. *Movement Disorders, 24*(3), 433–437. https://doi.org/10.1002/mds.22421

Wuthrich, V. M., Johnco, C. J., & Wetherell, J. L. (2015). Differences in anxiety and depression symptoms: Comparison between older and younger clinical samples. *International Psychogeriatrics, 27*, 1523–1532. https://doi.org/10.1017/S1041610215000526

Yang, K. H., Han, B. H., Moore, A. A., & Palamar, J. J. (2022). Trends in major depressive episodes and mental health treatment among older adults in the United States, 2010–2019. *Journal of Affective Disorders, 318*, 299–303. https://doi.org/10.1016/j.jad.2022.09.007

Yesavage, J., Brink, T. L., Rose, T. L., Lum, O., Huang, V., Adey, M., & Leirer, V. O. (1983). Development and validation of a geriatric depression screening scale: A preliminary report. *Journal of Psychiatric Research, 17*(1), 37–49. https://doi.org/10.1016/0022-3956(82)90033-4

Zhang, Y., Ting, R. Z., Lam, M. H., Lam, S. P., Yeung, R. O., Nan, H., ..., Chan, J. C. (2015). Measuring depression with CES-D in Chinese patients with type 2 diabetes: The validity and its comparison to PHQ-9. *BMC Psychiatry, 15*, 198. https://doi.org/10.1186/s12888-015-0580-0

9

Cognition and Aging

Kathrine Whitman, Talia Barrett, Jennifer H. Coane, and Sharda Umanath

LEARNING OBJECTIVES

- Describe the common age-related cognitive changes experienced by older adults regarding the major domains of cognition, including but not limited to perception, attention, memory, and language.
- Identify and describe underlying bases for the cognitive changes in aging, analyzing the relationship between behavioral outcomes and theoretical frameworks.
- Contextualize the pattern of findings examining cognitive aging with regard to both the methodological considerations outlined in this chapter and others raised in the study of psychology and aging more generally.
- Understand how common age-related changes in cognition broadly impact older adults' overall health and experiences in daily activities.

AGING: CHANGES IN COGNITIVE FUNCTIONING

Healthy aging is associated with changes in physical, emotional, and cognitive functioning. Many models of aging are framed as an accumulation of physical and cognitive deficits over time, which are assumed to lead to increased vulnerability and decreased function in late life. To date, the prevailing question in research has been "What goes wrong in aging?" rather than "What overall changes occur in aging?" Conflicting aging stereotypes are especially prevalent in cognitive aging, where older adults (OAs) are judged as simultaneously wiser and more forgetful relative to younger adults (YAs; Hummert, 2011). In reality, cognitive aging is rather nuanced. Whereas some cognitive functions, such as working memory, decline with age, other aspects of cognition, such as general knowledge, are maintained or even improve (Park & Schwarz, 1999). Importantly, changes in cognitive function are continuous throughout the life span, and OAs maintain and develop unique strengths and capabilities over time (Mergler & Goldstein, 1983). Alternative models of aging integrate both the limitations and distinct strengths of aging and emphasize critical, positive aspects of cognitive aging, such as areas of growth, resilience, and compensatory behavior. In this chapter, we provide an overview of the primary cognitive functions affected in healthy aging as well as major theories of cognitive aging. Our primary focus is on "healthy" or "normal" aging (i.e., aging in the absence of dementia or other significant neurological disease), which is characterized by gradual changes in cognitive abilities after age 60 on average (Schaie, 2008). We also discuss methodological concerns in the research on cognitive aging and the impacts of cognitive changes on OAs' everyday living. In each section, we strive to provide a balanced view of cognitive aging, addressing decline, maintenance, and improvement.

PRIMARY COGNITIVE FUNCTIONS AFFECTED IN AGING

Sensation and Perception

Sensory processing is the complex process by which the nervous system receives, integrates, interprets, and responds to sensory input from the environment. It is the foundation through which one perceives, remembers, and interacts with the world. In aging, declines in sensory processing, if uncorrected, can result in attentional, memory, and executive function impairments (Baltes & Lindenberger, 1997). If visual acuity declines, it can become more difficult to attend to relevant information, complicating everyday tasks such as reading and driving. Worsening eyesight can result in various memory impairments, including trouble describing scenes or recognizing faces. Spatial navigation and executive functioning are also impacted, as integrating information from the environment and making decisions based on this information becomes more challenging (Baltes & Lindenberger, 1997).

Similarly, uncorrected auditory deficits common in aging can harm OAs' cognitive health. Because more cognitive resources are needed to perceive auditory cues, effortful tasks involving divided attention, integration of information, or making judgments based on auditory information can be especially impaired (Peelle, 2018). For example, OAs performed significantly worse when answering survey questions that were read aloud compared with when the questions were written; no age-related differences were found in the written version of the survey (Park & Schwarz, 1999). Auditory declines also impact language and social cognition; impaired hearing can make it difficult to understand speech, participate in conversations, or perceive someone's emotional affect based on tone.

Degraded vision and hearing often coexist and exacerbate one another. For example, language interpretation depends on both auditory perception and visual cues like facial expressions and mouth movements. This was especially relevant for OAs during the COVID-19 pandemic, as mask-wearing muffled auditory output and eliminated visual lip-reading cues (Poon & Jenstad, 2022). Fortunately, sensory declines may be attenuated with environmental aids, including glasses and magnifying lenses, hearing aids, and tactile aids, such as vibrating alarms for hearing-impaired individuals. Moreover, a sensory-friendly environment—including minimal background noise, texts written in large fonts, and high-contrast imaging—can help counter sensory declines and support cognitive functioning.

Attention

This chapter focuses on attention in the form of attentional control, including sustained, selective, and divided attention (Kramer & Kray, 2006), all of which can change in older age. Sustained attention (i.e., vigilance; McDonough et al., 2019) is a person's ability to continually allocate attention toward something over time. The direction of a person's attention can be endogenous (i.e., goal driven; e.g., paying close attention to information because it will be on an exam) or exogenous (i.e., stimulus driven; e.g., perking up when you hear your name; Kramer & Kray, 2006). Data on age-related changes in sustained attention are mixed. Some research suggests OAs struggle more than YAs with initiating and sustaining attention unless prompted by an external stimulus (McDonough et al., 2019). Other findings indicate that OAs actually sustain their attention better than YAs, showing less mind wandering (Maillet & Schacter, 2016).

Selective attention is an individual's ability to focus on task-relevant information and ignore irrelevant stimuli. Attention is a finite resource; therefore, people must allocate attentional resources toward what is most necessary. Imagine you are reading in a coffee shop: Selective attention helps block conversations around you so you can focus on your book. In aging, there is a reduced ability to ignore distractors (Hasher & Zacks, 1988). Selective attention deficits depend on various individual and task-specific features though, such as motivation, practice, and task difficulty. When individuals are explicitly required or motivated to selectively attend to something, age differences can decrease; conversely, increased task difficulty exacerbates age differences (Kramer & Kray, 2006).

Divided attention refers to a person's ability to concurrently and effortfully process different types of information or perform two or more tasks. One example is cooking while talking: You must simultaneously focus on the recipe, the food on the stove, and the present conversation. Unsurprisingly, performance for all individuals, regardless of age, decreases under divided attention. Relative to YAs, OAs tend to struggle more with divided attention tasks when the cognitive demand exceeds a certain threshold. This depends on additional factors, however, such as the degree of response ambiguity, the presence of distractors, and memory load (Salthouse et al., 1995).

Many situations require a combination of these three aforementioned facets of attention. For example, while driving, a person needs to maintain focus on the road, inhibit distractions, and multitask by changing lanes. Whereas OAs might disproportionately struggle in certain situations requiring attention, the vast majority of individuals—no matter their age—are vulnerable to the harmful effects of multitasking (e.g., Strayer et al., 2011). Furthermore, attention influences other areas of cognition like memory and language. Retrieval from long-term memory takes attentional resources, and effectively encoding a long-term memory trace also requires attention (McDowd & Shaw, 2000).

Memory

Memory is defined as the ability to *encode, store, and retrieve* information. *Encoding* is the process by which a person takes in information, *storage* is the maintenance of that information, and *retrieval* is the ability to recall that information when necessary. Changes in memory are one of the most common concerns in OAs (Ponds & Jolles, 1996). Although age-related declines in memory are well documented, memory changes are *not* exclusively losses (Park & Schwarz, 1999). Like attention, memory is a rich, multifaceted construct in which various facets are differentially affected by the aging process.

Working memory is the system by which small amounts of information are kept in mind for very brief durations (less than 30 seconds). It entails an active process of maintaining, processing, or manipulating information (e.g., remembering several answer choices during a verbal survey; Engle et al., 1999). Declines in working memory begin in early adulthood and continue throughout the life span (Dobbs & Rule, 1989). Working memory is a crucial process for many other higher order cognitive functions (e.g., language and decision-making), and deficits in working memory are foundational to several theories of cognitive aging, as discussed later.

Long-term memory is the relatively permanent storage of information that can be remembered from several minutes to several decades later and includes explicit and implicit memories. It encompasses most aspects typically thought of as memory, including remembering how to write one's name, completing simple arithmetic, and retrieving cherished memories from one's life.

Explicit, or declarative, memories involve the conscious remembering of information. This type of memory can easily be put into words (i.e., explicitly declared) and traditionally includes both episodic and semantic memory (Rubin & Umanath, 2015; Tulving, 1972). Episodic memory pertains to remembering experienced events associated with a particular time and place, and deficits in this area are well established in cognitive aging research. In particular, OAs struggle with more effortful episodic memory tasks, such as *recalling* information with little environmental support, compared with *recognizing* previously learned information among several presented options (Light, 1992); additionally, OAs tend to do more gist-based processing (as opposed to item or verbatim processing; Abadie et al., 2021). Relative to YAs, OAs are more likely to omit information or include incorrect associations and may struggle with identifying when and where they learned something (i.e., source memory; Mitchell et al., 2003). Similarly, associative memory, or the ability to remember relationships between seemingly unrelated items (e.g., word–nonword pairs; Naveh-Benjamin, 2000), is particularly impacted in aging. These deficits can be mitigated at various stages of the memory process, from utilizing more effective encoding strategies (Coane, 2013) to relying on environmental support during retrieval (Craik et al., 1987).

Semantic memory—people's knowledge base (i.e., crystallized intelligence; Cattell, 1963)—is preserved and can even improve over the life span (Park & Schwarz, 1999), such that OAs often outperform YAs on general knowledge tests (Blazer et al., 2015). Furthermore, numerous studies have revealed that OAs show minimal age-related declines in their field of expertise (Salthouse, 1982). Relative to YAs, OAs also maintain and recover more marginal or previously inaccessible knowledge (Berger et al., 1999; Umanath et al., 2023). For example, in retaking a general knowledge test in which they did not receive correct answer feedback initially, OAs were more likely than YAs to successfully recall information that they had initially deemed inaccessible (i.e., stored in memory but not retrievable at the given moment; Umanath et al., 2023). OAs' reliance on prior knowledge can enhance their episodic memory performance and eliminate commonly observed age differences (Umanath & Marsh, 2014). Indeed, prior knowledge can offset deficits in real-world areas of functioning (e.g., driving and working) that depend on intact cognitive mechanisms (e.g., older adults' domain-specific knowledge may compensate for cognitive declines in job performance; Park & Gutchess, 2000).

Implicit memories are a type of long-term memory that pertains to information *outside of* conscious awareness or intent. Two types of implicit memory phenomena include priming effects (i.e., the phenomenon whereby exposure to one stimulus [e.g., a word such as *nurse*] facilitates a person's memory for a second stimulus [e.g., a separate, semantically related word, such as *doctor*; Balota et al., 1999]) and procedural memory. Procedural memory encompasses a wide variety of motor, cognitive, and intellectual functions, such as driving a car, playing a musical instrument, or writing. Automatically applied associations in procedural memory have been well documented in cognitive aging research through priming paradigms, with OAs demonstrating greater susceptibility to priming effects relative to YAs (Laver & Burke, 1993). The maintenance of implicit systems is double edged, as OAs may adapt more easily to deficits in declarative memory by relying on associations, but may also be more susceptible to false memories or struggle with integrating updated information (Dywan & Jacoby, 1990).

Lastly, prospective memory involves remembering to do something in the future, such as attending an appointment or taking medication at a certain time. Prospective memory begins with the intention to remember something later, usually in the context of relevant external cues (Einstein & McDaniel, 1996). Time-based memory tasks (e.g., "I will leave for my appointment at 2:30 p.m.") show greater declines with age compared with event-based tasks, at least in lab-based studies. For this reason, event-based reminders can help reduce age differences in completing prospective memory tasks (Henry et al., 2004). When studies are naturalistic, however, OAs often perform as well as or better than YAs in time-based prospective memory tasks (McBride et al., 2013).

Intelligence and Executive Functioning

One common conceptualization of intelligence includes the distinction between crystallized and fluid intelligence. As referenced earlier regarding semantic memory, crystallized intelligence pertains to knowledge that is gained through experience (e.g., verbal skills; Cattell, 1963) and is relatively well preserved in older adulthood (Blazer et al., 2015; Schaie, 2008). In contrast, fluid intelligence refers to individuals' dynamic, in-the-moment problem-solving and reasoning abilities and consistently demonstrates an inverse correlation with aging and is highly related to working memory. Interestingly, OAs' crystallized-fluid discrepancy might predict the onset of cognitive decline and could thus potentially facilitate early, and necessary, intervention (Bajpai et al., 2022).

Executive functioning includes a set of higher order cognitive skills that allow a person to self-regulate, plan ahead, and adapt behavior in response to environmental cues (Blazer et al., 2015). Executive functioning abilities decline over the course of the life span (Petok et al., 2022). Given the connection between executive functioning and routine activities of daily living (ADLs), related weaknesses pose problems for an individual's daily life. Executive functioning both depends on higher order cognitive processes and involves more basic processes, like working memory. Decision-making is a second example of this interconnectedness. Making a decision requires a range of cognitive and socioemotional factors, including but not limited to attention, memory, language, intelligence, executive functioning, emotional regulation, and motivation. Declines in areas like working memory and executive functioning worsen OAs' ability to make decisions; however, external support and use of prior knowledge can mitigate these deficits (Goh & Park, 2009; Umanath & Marsh, 2014).

Language

Language is a core cognitive function, critical for enabling communication among individuals and for the preservation and transmission of knowledge. Language use, broadly defined, includes the production of linguistic output, whether written, spoken, or signed, as well as the comprehension of linguistic input, through auditory, visual, or—in the case of Braille—tactile channels.

Language production entails the interaction of multiple cognitive and physiological processes (Levelt et al., 1999). For spoken language, the speaker must determine the message they wish to communicate including content, context, audience, time and space, and causality. Next, the speaker assembles a conceptual "frame" (determined by the goals and form of communication) and integrates relevant knowledge from semantic and episodic memory. For example, a speaker must account for previous points in the conversation and respond accordingly. Finally, the speaker must develop a speech plan, activate and retrieve the appropriate word form representations, and access the specific syllabic and phonological information. Thus, the act of language production requires the coordination of multiple cognitive processes: attention, working memory, long-term memory, executive functions, and inhibition (discussed later). Furthermore, the speaker must attend to the pragmatics (i.e., factors such as context and language conventions) and recognize any comprehension challenges in the audience.

In general, OAs have extensive vocabularies (Verhaeghen, 2003) as part of their preserved knowledge bases; however, they experience more word-finding difficulties than YAs (Albert et al., 2009). One of OAs' most common complaints is an increase in tip-of-the-tongue (TOT) states (Burke et al., 1991). TOTs occur when retrieval fails, such as trying to remember a person's name, with a core characteristic being the sense of imminent retrieval combined with retrieval of partial information (e.g., the initial letter; Brown & McNeil, 1966). In narrative production, like spontaneous speech, OAs are more likely to have less coherent and more verbose output compared with YAs (Gold & Arbuckle, 1995). Although relatively uncommon among OAs, decreased coherency and increased verbosity are more likely to occur in OAs relative to their younger counterparts (Arbuckle et al., 2004). Interestingly, when comparing a laboratory-based task (e.g., a picture-naming activity) to more naturalistic tasks (e.g., a discourse task assessing spontaneous naming), OAs performed better than YAs in the former. Conversely, in the naturalistic task, OAs made increased retrieval errors relative to YAs (Schmitter-Edgecombe et al., 2000), which suggests that task type is an important factor in language production. Regarding grammatical aspects of production (e.g., subject–verb agreement), OAs show gradual decline, due in part to declines in working memory (Marini & Andreetta, 2016).

Comprehension of spoken language is also a complex task. Speech unfolds rapidly over time, placing heavy demands on working and long-term memory. Many aspects of real-time comprehension are preserved in aging—even when complex syntactic structures are involved—whereas declines are more apparent in tasks that involve delayed probes (requiring judgments or memory; Shafto & Tyler, 2014). Other aspects of comprehension are affected by aging. Word recognition can be slower, and OAs are more sensitive to frequency and context effects (Rogers et al., 2012), but they have preserved access to meaning (DeDe & Flax, 2016). OAs show greater difficulty processing increasingly complex structures, largely due to changes in working memory capacity (Kemper et al., 2004). As mentioned earlier, changes in sensory acuity negatively impact language comprehension. However, OAs can and do rely on their expertise and linguistic knowledge to compensate for impoverished sensory signals, though such compensation may require different strategies, more processing time, or reallocation of resources (DeDe & Flax, 2016).

Emotional Processing

Compared with YAs, OAs show better emotional processing (Mather & Carstensen, 2005). For instance, OAs are better at positive reappraisal—the reconceptualization of a negative experience in a more positive way—than YAs, meaning they can more effectively change and suppress their negative emotions (Ikier & Duman, 2020). Enhanced emotional regulation over the life span is one theorized explanation for the *positivity effect*, or OAs' attentional and memory biases for positively valenced stimuli (Mather & Carstensen, 2005).

Wisdom

Wisdom is a positive stereotype frequently associated with aging (Hertzog et al., 2008). Sternberg (1985) found that wisdom is commonly associated with positive qualities such as reasoning skill, sagacity, perceptiveness, and the ability to learn from experience. Baltes and Staudinger (2000) defined wisdom as people's knowledge for "the fundamental pragmatics of life." This stereotype can serve to portray aging positively rather than as an inevitable cognitive decline. Mergler and Goldstein (1983) argue that OAs have certain adaptations (e.g., wisdom) due to developmental and experiential factors that make them better able to perform certain tasks than YAs (e.g., the transmission of cultural knowledge). There is currently limited research investigating the connection between wisdom and age, and existing studies have not yet revealed any clear correlation between the two constructs. However, one explanation for this might be the lack of standardization in how researchers have historically operationalized wisdom (Blazer et al., 2015; Jeste & Oswald, 2014).

THEORIES OF COGNITIVE AGING

Before discussing some of the major theories of cognitive aging, we provide a brief overview of two overarching principles that govern many, if not all, aspects of cognition.

Top-Down and Bottom-Up Processing

Processes can be characterized as *top-down* or *bottom-up*. *Top-down* refers to using prior knowledge, contextual information, or experience gained over time to interpret information from the environment. *Bottom-up* refers to using stimulus-driven information, such as sensory input. For example, when determining if an individual is someone we know, bottom-up information includes visual appearance (e.g., a person's face or clothing), whereas top-down information includes the present location and memories of prior encounters (Mandler, 1980). Cognitive tasks and everyday behaviors rely heavily on the interplay of these two modes of processing; when bottom-up information is scarce, top-down information can compensate and increase efficiency. As individuals age, they accumulate experience and knowledge; therefore, OAs often rely more heavily than YAs on top-down processing for supporting cognitive processes (Madden, 2007; see the "Memory" section). Moreover, some bottom-up processing declines with age (Madden, 2007; see "Sensation and Perception" section).

Controlled and Automatic Processing

The distinction between *automatic* and *controlled* processing (Posner & Snyder, 1975) provides an organizational structure characterizing resource allocation and requirements in ongoing cognitive processes. Automatic processes do not require mental resources; can occur outside of conscious awareness; and are fast acting, obligatory, stimulus driven, and effortless. Controlled processes, in contrast, are resource demanding, slow, volitional, effortful, and available for conscious report. The latter are generally required for complex or novel tasks, whereas automatic processes are involved in simple or well-practiced tasks. For a beginner, reading is effortful and attention demanding; with practice, extracting meaning from printed words is automatic and effortless (LaBerge & Samuels, 1974). Note that automatic and controlled cognitive processes operate along a continuum. As individuals age, automatic processes are typically well preserved; furthermore, the accumulation of experiences creates additional opportunities for complex tasks to be automatized or routinized. Controlled processes, conversely, are more susceptible to age-related declines (Blazer et al., 2015). Relatedly, the processing deficit model of cognitive aging (Craik & Byrd, 1982) proposes that effortful tasks, which require more processing resources and self-initiated behavior, are increasingly difficult with age. Importantly, the "environmental support hypothesis" suggests that age-related deficiencies can be attenuated through external cues that minimize the cognitive load required to complete a task. Written reminders, planners, and easily visible name badges can serve as environmental supports that relieve the controlled processing load required in daily life (Craik & Byrd, 1982).

Speed of Processing

An early and fundamental theory of cognitive aging is that speed of processing slows down as we age (Salthouse, 1996). That is, the ability to process information becomes less efficient and demands greater cognitive resources over time. Inefficiencies in core cognitive processes lead to deficits across a wide range of cognitive functions (Birren, 1965). Salthouse (1996) proposed a metaphor of a faulty assembly line to explain the limited time mechanism: The final product (cognitive function) is impaired, either because early steps of assembly took too long to complete, rushing the later processes, or because earlier assembly processes could only be somewhat completed in the time available, leading to finishing processes on a faulty "product." Slow processing speed also reduces the amount of *simultaneously* available information and functions needed for higher level processing. For example, this theory proposes that long-term memory deficits occur due to inefficiencies in transferring information from working memory.

Sensory Deficit and Common Cause Hypotheses

Although people's senses affect cognitive function throughout the life span, the association between cognitive and sensory functioning, particularly in visual and auditory systems, is amplified in OAs (Baltes & Mayer, 1999). The sensory deficit hypothesis proposes that changes in sensory function (described earlier) act as a driving cause of cognitive dysfunction. After all, if the quality of what is processed bottom-up is poor, it stands to reason that what comes after will be similarly degraded. For example, when given low-resolution images mimicking visual decline, people became significantly worse at solving complex visual tasks (Cronin-Golomb et al., 2007).

In the landmark Berlin Aging Study, Baltes and colleagues found that an array of cognitive functions, including differences in processing speed, general knowledge, reasoning, and memory, were mediated by visual and auditory acuity (Baltes & Mayer, 1999). Rather than relying on the sensory deficit hypothesis, they favor the "common cause" hypothesis, arguing that declines in sensory systems and cognition are caused by a shared, underlying mechanism inherent to aging (Baltes & Lindenberger, 1997).

Inhibitory Deficit Hypothesis

The inhibitory deficit hypothesis posits that OAs face increased challenges with facets of cognitive functioning not because they face difficulties in perceiving stimuli, but rather because they process *too much* information (Amer et al., 2022; Hasher et al., 2007). That is, OAs' ability to suppress unnecessary information deteriorates over time, leading to diffused attention, encoding of both relevant and irrelevant stimuli, and susceptibility to distraction (Hasher & Zacks, 1988). OAs also struggle to forget unwanted information and to suppress inappropriate responses. In other words, a decreasing ability to exclusively attend to and encode necessary information in the working memory stage results in overall cognitive deficits. In everyday life, failing to inhibit outdated or incorrect information in conversation may present as a person referring to someone by their former last name. Interestingly, when participants are presented with distracting stimuli in a lab setting, OAs' performance is more disrupted than YAs'; however, when previously distracting stimuli are later useful for completing a new task, OAs outperform YAs (Connelly et al., 1991).

Other Theories of Cognitive Aging

Numerous other theories address various aspects of cognitive aging, but describing each would extend beyond the scope of this chapter. Here, we briefly introduce a few additional theories. Changes in motivation and values in later life play an important role in explaining OAs' cognitive performance and are critical to consider (e.g., Castel et al., 2012; Hess, 2020). Findings regarding improved emotional processing are the foundation of the socioemotional selectivity theory of aging (Carstensen et al., 1999), which posits that whereas YAs are more focused on process-oriented goals, OAs' awareness of their shrinking time horizons causes them to prioritize activities, people, and memories that enhance their well-being.

The theory of cognitive reserve (Stern, 2009) posits that certain factors, such as education, occupation, and intellectually stimulating engagement, affect individuals' cognitive functioning by building reserves that can buffer against physiological changes associated with age. This theory was proposed to explain why cognitive abilities and outcomes can vary so greatly between individuals who have otherwise similar characteristics of aging, pathology, or even brain injury. For example, imagine two individuals who exhibit similar levels of amyloid plaques and tau tangles (two physiological hallmarks of Alzheimer disease): In this scenario, the individual with higher cognitive reserve would show lessened and even delayed symptoms of cognitive decline compared with their counterpart with similar physiological characteristics. One review examined the effects of reserve (operationalized by education, occupational complexity, and cognitively engaging activities) and found that higher reserve was associated with a lower risk of incident dementia (Valenzuela & Sachdev, 2006). Similarly, in a systematic review of 34 studies, Chapko et al. (2018) found consistent evidence for a protective effect of education on general cognition in participants with brain atrophy and/or cerebrovascular damage. However, critics of cognitive reserve theory highlight the potential for reverse-causality, as well as the heterogenous measurement and operationalization used in cognitive reserve research thus far. Recent work has sought to address these issues by defining operational cognitive resilience terms, including cognitive reserve, brain maintenance, and brain reserve (Stern et al., 2023). While these delineations are beyond the scope of this chapter, these definitions provide a framework to discuss potential explanations for differences in cognitive aging among individuals with otherwise similar cognitive vulnerability factors (e.g., behavioral and physiological risk factors).

Physiological, brain-based models of cognitive aging have become more prominent in recent decades, with popular theories addressing both increases *and* decreases in neural activation in cognitive aging. The hemispheric asymmetry reduction in older adults (HAROLD) model and the posterior-to-anterior shift in aging (PASA) model examine how changes in neural activation affect and potentially compensate for cognitive decline in aging (Dennis & Cabeza, 2008). The scaffolding theory of aging and cognition (STAC) model integrates both behavioral theories and neural network theories and posits that although cognitive declines occur, OAs can compensate by leveraging environmental supports or scaffolds (Reuter-Lorenz & Park, 2014). Integrative frameworks such as the biopsychosocial model and the successful aging model emphasize utilizing environmental support and facilitating an enriched lifestyle to best protect against cognitive decline (Park & Schwarz, 1999).

METHODOLOGICAL CONSIDERATIONS IN COGNITIVE AGING RESEARCH

Like all research, cognitive aging research is susceptible to methodological concerns. We focus on three issues affecting the external validity or generalizability of cognitive aging research: cohort effects, demographic effects, and stereotype threat.

Political events, educational influences, and sociocultural trends impact the cognitive health of people—a phenomenon known as a *cohort effect*. According to a co-constructive perspective of cohort effects in cognitive aging, the accumulation of cultural resources in modern times means that more recent generations' cognitive functioning will surpass that of older generations (Schaie, 2008). Researchers have coined the term *Flynn effect* to describe the way in which societal developments (e.g., improved healthcare and educational systems) have corresponded with enhancement in people's cognitive performance (Staudinger, 2020). Relative to earlier cohorts, a greater proportion of adults today hold professional occupations and reach higher levels of educational attainment. These occupational and educational changes serve as protective factors potentially buffering today's OAs against cognitive decline and should thus be taken into consideration by researchers (Stern, 2009).

As for demographic influences, race (and closely linked demographic characteristics, such as socioeconomic status and education) impacts the validity of cognitive aging assessments. For instance, dementia screening tools such as the Montreal Cognitive Assessment (MoCA; Nasreddine et al., 2005) regularly lead to incorrect diagnoses regarding cognitive impairment among non-White OAs (specifically, Black OAs; Manly, 2008; Milani et al., 2018). Predictors of cognitive ability in OAs also differ based on race. For example, Hamlin et al. (2022) found that social activity benefitted the episodic memory of White—but not Black—participants. The traditional focus on White OAs limits the generalizability of this research, thereby harming OAs of color and narrowing the scope of cognitive aging findings.

The activation of negative stereotypes can worsen OAs' performance of cognitive tasks. When individuals are aware of a stereotype about a group to which they belong, they become focused on avoiding confirmation of the stereotype. In turn, they experience *stereotype threat* and underperform on a given task in the stereotyped domain (Steele & Aronson, 1995). Relative to their nonthreatened OA counterparts, stereotype threat adversely impacts OAs' performance of real-world tasks (e.g., acquisition of motor skills and driving), and threatened older participants also report worse employment outcomes (e.g., lower occupational self-efficacy; Barber, 2020). Stereotype threat worsens OAs' episodic memory performance by potentially draining OAs of cognitive resources via negative mood, divided attention, and stress, resulting in fewer remaining resources to devote to successful retrieval (Fourquet et al., 2020). OAs often experience stereotype threat even when age-related stereotypes are not explicitly mentioned

(Bouazzaoui et al., 2015). Thus, stereotype threat can be activated explicitly (e.g., by blatantly mentioning that OAs are expected to perform worse than YAs), subtly (e.g., by simply referencing that the task is assessing memory), and implicitly (e.g., through priming tasks; Armstrong et al., 2017).

Other factors to consider that broadly affect OAs' cognitive performance include their increased conscientiousness (Jackson & Balota, 2012), the degree to which YAs are the appropriate "standard" against which OAs ought to be compared, and changes in circadian rhythms (i.e., time-of-day effects), which suggest that individuals perform better at their optimal time and that OAs are particularly sensitive to such effects (Yoon et al., 1999).

IMPACTS OF COGNITIVE AGING ON EVERYDAY LIVING

Activities of Daily Living

Three ADLs affected by age-related changes in cognition are driving, work, and sleep. Driving can serve as a potential proxy of cognitive health in OAs (Baudouin et al., 2023), given its reliance on intact cognitive abilities including visual attention and working memory (McDowd & Shaw, 2000). Concerns regarding older drivers are somewhat warranted, considering that OAs form the largest at-risk group for number of accidents per mile driven (Park & Gutchess, 2000). Additionally, older drivers' metacognitive assessment of their driving performance tends to be inaccurate (Horswill et al., 2013). Although driving requires a significant cognitive load, factors associated with older age—such as greater expertise and automaticity—are positively correlated with successful driving.

Data on the connection between age-based cognitive changes and work performance are mixed. Various factors impact, and can enhance, older workers' performance, including job experience (i.e., certain job tasks become automatic with practice), accumulated job-based knowledge, preserved tacit knowledge, and the use of environmental supports to compensate for age-based cognitive decline (Park & Gutchess, 2000). Moreover, willingness to use and familiarity with technology affects OAs' work performance. Albeit often integral to job completion, technologies are frequently novel and can thus be cognitively demanding for OA workers (Park & Gutchess, 2000; Rogers et al., 2020).

Lastly, data on the sleep–cognition connection in OAs are rather mixed. Both insufficient sleep and long sleep duration correlate with worse cognitive functioning in OAs, suggesting the importance of a moderate, "happy medium" quantity of sleep (Dzierzewski et al., 2018). Indeed, sleep deprivation, albeit unhealthy for all age groups, has more severe effects on OA cognition than on YA cognition (Dzierzewski et al., 2018). Beyond sleep quantity, sleep quality and disturbance impact OAs' cognitive health. However, in contrast to YA data, Scullin and Bliwise (2015) found mainly null effects of sleep on OA cognitive performance. The authors argue that (a) aging qualitatively changes the connection between sleep and cognition and (b) research into the effects of sleep on OA cognition should examine the impact of YAs' sleep patterns on cognitive health outcomes in later life.

Cognitive Training and Rehabilitation

Researchers have studied the effectiveness of cognitive training on OAs' cognitive health in an attempt to identify rehabilitative methods to buffer against cognitive decline. A primary goal of modern cognitive aging intervention research is to maintain or increase OAs' functional independence (Wu & Rebok, 2020). Successful training programs tend to include emphases on goal-setting and sustained motivation, cognitive activities that are sufficiently challenging, accessibility to information, large social networks, and recognition of participants' individual differences (e.g., baseline cognitive abilities and prior educational experiences; Wu & Rebok, 2020). Ideally, successful cognitive training programs teach older participants real-world skills (such as technology use) that are essential to OAs' autonomy and well-being in a dynamic environment.

Factors That Promote Healthy Cognitive Aging

ADLs and cognition are interdependent—just as a person's cognitive health influences their ADLs, a person's daily activities also impact their cognitive health. Physical activity is crucial for maintaining and even improving cognitive functioning throughout the life span. Various types of physical exercise, such as aerobic exercise and resistance training, are associated with better executive function (Colcombe & Kramer, 2003). Other studies show that nutritious diets high in fruits, vegetables, and healthy fats are inversely associated with cognitive decline (van de Rest et al., 2015). Social engagement, including leisure activities with others or involvement in local organizations, is positively associated with psychological well-being (Hertzog et al., 2008). Concordantly, poor social connections are predictive of cognitive decline. Engaging in intellectually stimulating activities, such as reading or playing an instrument, is associated with a reduced rate of cognitive decline in old age (Hertzog et al., 2008). Of course, the factors that promote healthy cognition in aging are not mutually exclusive and can be combined—a walking group may implement elements of socialization and fitness, whereas a book club may foster both intellectual and social engagement.

CONCLUSION

Like any other stage of development, late life is associated with a variety of age-related changes in cognition. Attitudes on cognitive aging range from concerns about empirically validated deficits in cognitive functions to ageist assumptions about unconditional, universal cognitive decline. In reality, aging is a highly individualized, diverse process in which some cognitive functions decline, some are maintained, and some even improve with age. Theories of cognitive aging attempt to explain these varied patterns of change. It is necessary to recognize and develop ways in which both YAs and OAs can best support cognitive function throughout the life span with compensatory behaviors, environmental aids, and enriched, well-balanced lifestyles. Healthy aging represents a developmental milestone with unique implications for cognitive functioning and overall well-being. As activist and scholar Ashton Applewhite reminds us, we are fortunate to be "old people in training" (Applewhite, 2016).

DISCUSSION QUESTIONS

1. Compare and contrast the ways in which the speed of processing hypothesis and inhibitory deficit hypothesis account for cognitive changes in healthy aging. In which ways could these hypotheses coexist? In which ways do these explanations contrast one another?
2. Given what you now know about the distinction between automatic and controlled processes, how do these processes impact older adults' performance in specific cognitive domains such as attention, memory, and language?
3. Memory is the cognitive function most associated with aging concerns. In what ways are working and long-term memory affected by the healthy aging process? Which areas of memory are maintained or improved with age?
4. What does it mean that cognitive functions are interdependent? Provide an example in the context of aging.
5. How might OAs' cognitive strengths and preserved cognitive functioning compensate for areas of decline? Provide two examples to support your argument.
6. Identify four activities of daily living that depend on intact cognitive functioning (at least two should be something that *was not* discussed in this chapter). How does healthy aging impact OAs' ability to perform these tasks?
7. How can researchers, practitioners, and policy makers in the field of cognitive aging combat stereotype threat and its detrimental effects on older adults' cognitive performance and well-being?
8. Older adults are the fastest-growing demographic; meanwhile, society increasingly relies on ever-changing technological innovation. In light of this, cognitive aging is especially pertinent. Describe ways in which older adults can both utilize and be challenged by technological progression in the context of everyday cognitive functioning.

A robust set of instructor resources designed to supplement this text is located at http://connect.springerpub.com/content/book/978-0-8261-6617-3. Qualifying instructors may request access by emailing textbook@springerpub.com.

REFERENCES

Abadie, M., Gavard, E., & Guillaume, F. (2021). Verbatim and gist memory in aging. *Psychology and Aging, 36*(8), 891–901. https://doi.org/10.1037/pag0000635

Albert, M. L., Spiro, A., Sayers, K. J., Cohen, J. A., Brady, C. B., Goral, M., & Obler, L. K. (2009). Effects of health status on word finding in aging. *Journal of the American Geriatrics Society, 57*(12), 2300–2305. https://doi.org/10.1111/j.1532-5415.2009.02559.x

Amer, T., Wynn, J. S., & Hasher, L. (2022). Cluttered memory representations shape cognition in old age. *Trends in Cognitive Sciences, 26*(3), 255–267. https://doi.org/10.1016/j.tics.2021.12.002

Applewhite, A. (2016). *This chair rocks: A manifesto against ageism* (1st Celadon ed.). Celadon Books.

Arbuckle, T. Y., Pushkar, D., Bourgeois, S., & Bonneville, L. (2004). Off-target verbosity, everyday competence, and subjective well-being. *Gerontology, 50*(5), 291–297. https://doi.org/10.1159/000079126

Armstrong, B., Gallant, S. N., Li, L., Patel, K., & Wong, B. I. (2017). Stereotype threat effects on older adults' episodic and working memory: A meta-analysis. *Gerontologist, 57*(S2), S193–S205. https://doi.org/10.1093/geront/gnx056

Bajpai, S., Upadhayay, A. D., Banerjee, J., Chakrawarthy, A., Chatterjee, P., Lee, J., & Dey, A. B. (2022). Discrepancy in fluid and crystallized intelligence: An early cognitive marker of dementia from the LASI-DAD cohort. *Dementia and Geriatric Cognitive Disorders Extra, 12*(1), 51–59. https://doi.org/10.1159/000520879

Balota, D. A., Cortese, M. J., Duchek, J. M., Adams, D., Roediger III, H. L., McDermott, K. B., & Yerys, B. E. (1999). Veridical and false memories in healthy older adults and in dementia of the Alzheimer's type. *Cognitive Neuropsychology, 16*(3–5), 361–384. https://doi.org/10.1080/026432999380834

Baltes, P. B., & Lindenberger, U. (1997). Emergence of a powerful connection between sensory and cognitive functions across the adult life span: A new window to the study of cognitive aging? *Psychology and Aging, 12*(1), 12–21. https://doi.org/10.1037/0882-7974.12.1.12

Baltes, P. B., & Mayer, K. U. (Eds.). (1999). *The Berlin aging study: Aging from 70 to 100.* Cambridge University Press.

Baltes, P. B., & Staudinger, U. M. (2000). Wisdom: A metaheuristic (pragmatic) to orchestrate mind and virtue toward excellence. *American Psychologist, 55*(1), 122–136. https://doi.org/10.1037//0003-066x.55.1.122

Barber, S. J. (2020). The applied implications of age-based stereotype threat for older adults. *Journal of Applied Research in Memory and Cognition, 9*(3), 274–285. https://doi.org/10.1016/j.jarmac.2020.05.002

Baudouin, E., Zitoun, S., Corruble, E., Vidal, J.-S., Becquemont, L., & Duron, E. 2023). Association between car driving and successful ageing. A cross sectional study on the "S.AGES" cohort. *PLoS One, 18*(5), e0285313. https://doi.org/10.1371/journal.pone.0285313

Berger, S. A., Hall, L. K., & Bahrick, H. P. (1999). Stabilizing access to marginal and submarginal knowledge. *Journal of Experimental Psychology: Applied, 5*(4), 438–447. https://doi.org/10.1037/1076-898X.5.4.438

Birren, J. E. (1965). Age changes in speed of behavior: Its central nature and physiological correlates. In A. T. Welford & J. E. Birren (Eds.), *Behavior, aging, and the nervous system*. Thomas.

Blazer, D. G., Yaffe, K., & Liverman, C. T. (2015). Characterizing and assessing cognitive aging. In D. G. Blazer, K. Yaffe, & C. T. Liverman (Eds.), *Cognitive aging: Progress in understanding and opportunities for action* (pp. 37–88). The National Academies Press. https://doi.org/10.17226/21693

Bouazzaoui, B., Follenfant, A., Ric, F., Fay, S., Croizet, J. C., Atzeni, T., & Taconnat, L. (2015). Ageing-related stereotypes in memory: When the beliefs come true. *Memory, 24*(5), 659–668. https://doi.org/10.1080/09658211.2015.10408

Brown, R., & McNeill, D. (1966). The "tip of the tongue" phenomenon. *Journal of Verbal Learning & Verbal Behavior, 5*(4), 325–337. https://doi.org/10.1016/S0022-5371(66)80040-3

Burke, D. M., MacKay, D. G., Worthley, J. S., & Wade, E. (1991). On the tip of the tongue: What causes word finding failures in young and older adults? *Journal of Memory and Language, 30*(5), 542–579. https://doi.org/10.1016/0749-596X(91)90026-G

Carstensen, L. L., Isaacowitz, D. M., & Charles, S. T. (1999). Taking time seriously: A theory of socioemotional selectivity. *American Psychologist, 54*(3), 165–181. https://doi.org/10.1037/0003-066X.54.3.165

Castel, A. D., McGillivray, S., & Friedman, M. C. (2012). Metamemory and memory efficiency in older adults: Learning about the benefits of priority processing and value-directed remembering. In M. Naveh-Benjamin & N. Ohta (Eds.), *Memory and aging: Current issues and future directions* (pp. 245–270). Psychology Press.

Cattell, R. B. (1963). Theory of fluid and crystallized intelligence: A critical experiment. *Journal of Educational Psychology, 54*(1), 1–22. https://doi.org/10.1037/h0046743

Chapko, D., McCormack, R., Black, C., Staff, R., & Murray, A. (2018). Life-course determinants of cognitive reserve (CR) in cognitive aging and dementia—A systematic literature review. *Aging & Mental Health, 22*(8), 915–926. https://doi.org/10.1080/13607863.2017.1348471

Coane, J. H. (2013). Retrieval practice and elaborative encoding benefit memory in younger and older adults. *Journal of Applied Research in Memory and Cognition, 2*(2), 95–100. https://doi.org/10.1016/j.jarmac.2013.04.001

Colcombe, S., & Kramer, A. F. (2003). Fitness effects on the cognitive function of older adults: A meta-analytic study. *Psychological Science, 14*(2), 125–130. https://doi.org/10.1111/1467-9280.t01-1-01430

Connelly, S. L., Hasher, L., & Zacks, R. T. (1991). Age and reading: The impact of distraction. *Psychology and Aging, 6*(4), 533–541. https://doi.org/10.1037/0882-7974.6.4.533

Craik, F. I. M., & Byrd, M. (1982). Aging and cognitive deficits: The role of attentional resources. In F. I. M. Craik & S. Trehub (Eds.), *Aging and cognitive processes (Advances in the study of communication and affect)* (Vol. 8, pp. 191–211). Plenum Press.

Craik, F. I. M., Byrd, M., & Swanson, J. M. (1987). Patterns of memory loss in three elderly samples. *Psychology and Aging, 2*(1), 79–86. https://doi.org/10.1037/0882-7974.2.1.79

Cronin-Golomb, A., Gilmore, G. C., Neargarder, S., Morrison, S. R., & Laudate, T. M. (2007). Enhanced stimulus strength improves visual cognition in aging and Alzheimer's disease. *Cortex, 43*(7), 952–966. https://doi.org/10.1016/s0010-9452(08)70693-2

DeDe, G., & Flax, J. N. (2016). Language comprehension in aging. In H. H. Wright (Ed.), *Cognition, language and aging* (pp. 107–135). John Benjamins Publishing Company. https://doi.org/10.1075/z.200

Dennis, N. A., & Cabeza, R. (2008). Neuroimaging of healthy cognitive aging. In F. I. M. Craik & T. A. Salthouse (Eds.), *The handbook of aging and cognition* (pp. 1–54). Psychology Press.

Dobbs, A. R., & Rule, B. G. (1989). Adult age differences in working memory. *Psychology and Aging, 4*(4), 500–503. https://doi.org/10.1037/0882-7974.4.4.500

Dywan, J., & Jacoby, L. (1990). Effects of aging on source monitoring: Differences in susceptibility to false fame. *Psychology and Aging, 5*(3), 379–387. https://doi.org/10.1037/0882-7974.5.3.379

Dzierzewski, J. M., Dautovich, N., & Ravyts, S. (2018). Sleep and cognition in older adults. *Sleep Medicine Clinics, 13*(1), 93–106. https://doi.org/10.1016/j.jsmc.2017.09.009

Einstein, G. O., & McDaniel, M. A. (1996). Retrieval processes in prospective memory: Theoretical approaches and some new empirical findings. In M. Brandimonte, G. O. Einstein, & M. A. McDaniel (Eds.), *Prospective memory: Theory and applications* (pp. 115–141). Lawrence Erlbaum Associates Publishers.

Engle, R. W., Tuholski, S. W., Laughlin, J. E., & Conway, A. R. A. (1999). Working memory, short-term memory, and general fluid intelligence: A latent-variable approach. *Journal of Experimental Psychology: General, 128*(3), 309–331. https://doi.org/10.1037//0096-3445.128.3.309

Fourquet, N. Y., Patterson, T. K., Li, C., Castel, A. D., & Knowlton, B. J. (2020). Effects of age-related stereotype threat on metacognition. *Frontiers in Psychology, 11*, 604978. https://doi.org/10.3389/fpsyg.2020.604978

Goh, J. O., & Park, D. C. (2009). Neuroplasticity and cognitive aging: The scaffolding theory of aging and cognition. *Restorative Neurology and Neuroscience, 27*(5), 391–403. https://doi.org/10.3233/RNN-2009-0493

Gold, D. P., & Arbuckle, T. Y. (1995). A longitudinal study of off-target verbosity. *Journal of Gerontology: Psychological Sciences, 50*(6), 307–315. https://doi.org/10.1093/geronb/50B.6.P307

Hamlin, A. M., Kraal, A. Z., Sol, K., Morris, E. P., Martino, A. G., Zaheed, A. B., & Zahodne, L. B. (2022). Social engagement and its links to cognition differ across non-Hispanic black and white older adults. *Neuropsychology, 36*(7), 640–650. https://doi.org/10.1037/neu0000844

Hasher, L., & Zacks, R. T. (1988). Working memory, comprehension, and aging: A review and a new view. In G. H. Bower (Ed.), *Psychology of learning and motivation* (Vol. 22, pp. 193–225). Academic Press.

Hasher, L., Lustig, C., & Zacks, R. (2007). Inhibitory mechanisms and the control of attention. In A. R. A. Conway, C. Jarrold, M. J. Kane, A. Miyake & J. N. Towse (Eds.), *Variation in working memory* (pp. 227–249). Oxford University Press.

Henry, J. D., MacLeod, M. S., Phillips, L. H., & Crawford, J. R. (2004). A meta-analytic review of prospective memory and aging. *Psychology and Aging, 19*(1), 27–39. https://doi.org/10.1037/0882-7974.19.1.27

Hertzog, C., Kramer, A. F., Wilson, R. S., & Lindenberger, U. (2008). Enrichment effects on adult cognitive development: Can the functional capacity of older adults be preserved and enhanced? *Psychological Science in the Public Interest, 9*(1), 1–65. https://doi.org/10.1111/j.1539-6053.2009.01034.x

Hess, T. M. (2020). Aging and cognitive functioning: The impact of goals and motivation. In A. K. Thomas & A. Gutchess (Eds.), *The Cambridge handbook of cognitive aging: A life course perspective* (pp. 332–349). Cambridge University Press. https://doi.org/10.1017/9781108552684.021

Horswill, M. S., Taylor, K., Newnam, S., Wetton, M., & Hill, A. (2013). Even highly experienced drivers benefit from a brief hazard perception training intervention. *Accident Analysis & Prevention, 52*, 100–110. https://doi.org/10.1016/j.aap.2012.12.014

Hummert, M. L. (2011). Age stereotypes and aging. In K. Warner Schaie & S. L. Willis (Eds.), *Handbook of the psychology of aging* (7th ed., pp. 249–262). Elsevier Academic Press. https://doi.org/10.1016/B978-0-12-380882-0.00016-4

Ikier, S., & Duman, Ç. (2020). The happiest and the saddest autobiographical memories and aging. *Current Psychology, 41*, 4907–4919. https://doi.org/10.1007/s12144-020-00993-w

Jackson, J. D., & Balota, D. A. (2012). Mind-wandering in younger and older adults: Converging evidence from the Sustained Attention to Response Task and reading for comprehension. *Psychology and Aging, 27*(1), 106–119. https://doi.org/10.1037/a0023933

Jeste, D. V., & Oswald, A. J. (2014). Individual and societal wisdom: Explaining the paradox of human aging and high well-being. *Psychiatry: Interpersonal & Biological Processes, 77*(4), 317–330. https://doi.org/10.1521/psyc.2014.77.4.317

Kemper, S., Crow, A., & Kemtes, K. (2004). Eye-fixation patterns of high- and low-span young and older adults: Down the garden path and back again. *Psychology and Aging, 19*(1), 157–170. https://doi.org/10.1037/0882-7974.19.1.157

Kramer, A. F., & Kray, J. (2006). Aging and attention. In E. Bialystok & F. I. M. Craik (Eds.), *Lifespan cognition: Mechanisms of change* (pp. 57–69). Oxford University Press. https://doi.org/10.1093/acprof:oso/9780195169539.003.0005

LaBerge, D., & Samuels, S. J. (1974). Toward a theory of automatic information processing in reading. *Cognitive Psychology, 6*(2), 293–323. https://doi.org/10.1016/0010-0285(74)90015-2

Laver, G. D., & Burke, D. M. (1993). Why do semantic priming effects increase in old age? A meta-analysis. *Psychology and Aging, 8*(1), 34–43. https://doi.org/10.1037/0882-7974.8.1.34

Levelt, W. J. M., Roelofs, A., & Meyer, A. S. (1999). A theory of lexical access in speech production. *Behavioral and Brain Sciences, 22*(1), 1–38. https://doi.org/10.1017/S0140525X99001776

Light, L. L. (1992). The organization of memory in old age. In F. I. M. Craik & T. A. Salthouse (Eds.), *The handbook of aging and cognition* (pp. 111–165). Lawrence Erlbaum Associates, Inc.

Madden, D. J. (2007). Aging and visual attention. *Current Directions in Psychological Science, 16*(2), 70–74. https://doi.org/10.1111/j.1467-8721.2007.00478.x

Maillet, D., & Schacter, D. L. (2016). When the mind wanders: Distinguishing stimulus-dependent from stimulus-independent thoughts during incidental encoding in young and older adults. *Psychology and Aging, 31*(4), 370–379. https://doi.org/10.1037/pag0000099

Mandler, G. (1980). Recognizing: The judgment of previous occurrence. *Psychological Review, 87*(3), 252–271. https://doi.org/10.1037/0033-295X.87.3.252

Manly, J. J. (2008). Race, culture, education, and cognitive test performance among older adults. In S. M. Hofer & D. F. Alwin (Eds.), *Handbook of cognitive aging: Interdisciplinary perspectives* (pp. 398–417). Sage Publications, Inc. https://doi.org/10.4135/9781412976589.n25

Marini, A., & Andreetta, S. (2016). Age-related effects on language production: A combined psycholinguistic and neurolinguistic perspective. In H. H. Wright (Ed.), *Cognition, language and aging* (pp. 55–81). John Benjamins Publishing Company. https://doi.org/10.1075/z.200

Mather, M., & Carstensen, L. L. (2005). Aging and motivated cognition: The positivity effect in attention and memory. *Trends in Cognitive Sciences, 9*(10), 496–502. https://doi.org/10.1016/j.tics.2005.08.005

McBride, D. M., Coane, J. H., Drwal, J., & LaRose, S. A. (2013). Differential effects of delay on time-based prospective memory in younger and older adults. *Aging, Neuropsychology, and Cognition, 20*(6), 700–721. https://doi.org/10.1080/13825585.2013.765937

McDonough, I. M., Wood, M. M., & Miller Jr., W. S. (2019). A review on the trajectory of attentional mechanisms in aging and the Alzheimer's disease continuum through the attention network test. *Yale Journal of Biology and Medicine, 92*(1), 37–51.

McDowd, J. M., & Shaw, R. J. (2000). Attention and aging: A functional perspective. In F. I. M. Craik & T. A. Salthouse (Eds.), *The handbook of aging and cognition* (pp. 221–292). Lawrence Erlbaum Associates Publishers.

Mergler, N. L., & Goldstein, M. D. (1983). Why are there old people? *Human Development, 26*(2), 72–90. https://doi.org/10.1159/000272872

Milani, S. A., Marsiske, M., Cottler, L. B., Chen, X., & Striley, C. W. (2018). Optimal cutoffs for the Montreal Cognitive Assessment vary by race and ethnicity. *Alzheimer's & Dementia: Diagnosis, Assessment & Disease Monitoring, 10*, 773–781. https://doi.org/10.1016/j.dadm.2018.09.003

Mitchell, K. J., Johnson, M. K., & Mather, M. (2003). Source monitoring and suggestibility to misinformation: Adult age-related differences. *Applied Cognitive Psychology, 17*(1), 107–119. https://doi.org/10.1002/acp.857

Nasreddine, Z. S., Phillips, N. A., Bédirian, V., Charbonneau, S., Whitehead, V., Collin, I., Cummings, J. L., & Chertkow, H. (2005). The Montreal cognitive assessment, MOCA: A brief screening tool for mild cognitive impairment. *Journal of the American Geriatrics Society, 53*(4), 695–699. https://doi.org/10.1111/j.1532-5415.2005.53221.x

Naveh-Benjamin, M. (2000). Adult age differences in memory performance: Tests of an associative deficit hypothesis. *Journal of Experimental Psychology: Learning, Memory, and Cognition, 26*(5), 1170–1187. https://doi.org/10.1037//0278-7393.26.5.1170

Park, D. C., & Gutchess, A. H. (2000). Cognitive aging and everyday life. In N. Charness, D. C. Park, & B. Sabel (Eds.), *Aging and communication* (pp. 217–232). Springer.

Park, D., & Schwarz, N. (Eds.). (1999). *Cognitive aging: A primer*. Psychology Press. https://doi.org/10.4324/9780203727027

Peelle, J. E. (2018). Language and aging. In G. I. de Zubicaray & N. O. Schiller (Eds.), *The Oxford handbook of neurolinguistics* (pp. 295–316). Oxford University Press.

Petok, J. R., Dang, L., & Hammel, B. (2022). Impaired executive functioning mediates the association between aging and deterministic sequence learning. *Aging, Neuropsychology, and Cognition, 31*(2), 323–339. https://doi.org/10.1080/13825585.2022.2153789

Ponds, R. W. H. M., & Jolles, J. (1996). Memory complaints in elderly people: The role of memory abilities, metamemory, depression, and personality. *Educational Gerontology, 22*(4), 341–357. https://doi.org/10.1080/0360127960220404

Poon, B. T., & Jenstad, L. M. (2022). Communication with face masks during the COVID-19 pandemic for adults with hearing loss. *Cognitive Research: Principles and Implications, 7*(1), 24. https://doi.org/10.1186/s41235-022-00376-8

Posner, M. I., & Snyder, C. R. R. (1975). Attention and cognitive control. In R. L. Solso (Ed.), *Information processing and cognition* (pp. 55–85). Erlbaum.

Reuter-Lorenz, P. A., & Park, D. C. (2014). How does it STAC Up? Revisiting the scaffolding theory of aging and cognition. *Neuropsychology Review, 24*(3), 355–370. https://doi.org/10.1007/s11065-014-9270-9

Rogers, C. S., Jacoby, L. L., & Sommers, M. S. (2012). Frequent false hearing by older adults: The role of age differences in metacognition. *Psychology and Aging, 27*(1), 33–45. https://doi.org/10.1037/a0026231

Rogers, W. A., Blocker, K. A., & Dupuy, L. (2020). Current and emerging technologies for supporting successful aging. In A. K. Thomas & A. Gutchess (Eds.), *The Cambridge handbook of cognitive aging: A life course perspective* (pp. 717–736). Cambridge University Press. https://doi.org/10.1017/9781108552684.044

Rubin, D. C., & Umanath, S. (2015). Event memory: A theory of memory for laboratory, autobiographical, and fictional events. *Psychological Review, 122*(1), 1–23. https://doi.org/10.1037/a0037907

Salthouse, T. A. (1982). *Adult cognition: An experimental psychology of human aging*. Springer New York, NY. https://doi.org/10.1007/978-1-4613-9484-6

Salthouse, T. A. (1996). The processing-speed theory of adult age differences in cognition. *Psychological Review, 103*(3), 403–428. https://doi.org/10.1037/0033-295X.103.3.403

Salthouse, T. A., Fristoe, N. M., Lineweaver, T. T., & Coon, V. E. (1995). Aging of attention: Does the ability to divide decline? *Memory & Cognition, 23*(1), 59–71. https://doi.org/10.3758/bf03210557

Schaie, K. W. (2008). Historical processes and patterns of cognitive aging. In S. M. Hofer & D. F. Alwin (Eds.), *Handbook of cognitive aging: Interdisciplinary perspectives* (pp. 368–383). Sage Publications, Inc. https://doi.org/10.4135/9781412976589.n23

Schmitter-Edgecombe, M., Vesneski, M., & Jones, D. W. (2000). Aging and word-finding: A comparison of spontaneous and constrained naming tests. *Archives of Clinical Neuropsychology, 15*(6), 479–493. https://doi.org/10.1016/S0887-6177(99)00039-6

Scullin, M. K., & Bliwise, D. L. (2015). Sleep, cognition, and normal aging: Integrating a half century of multidisciplinary research. *Perspectives on Psychological Science, 10*(1), 97–137. https://doi.org/10.1177/1745691614556680

Shafto, M. A., & Tyler, L. K. (2014). Language in the aging brain: The network dynamics of cognitive decline and preservation. *Science, 346*(6209), 583–587. https://doi.org/10.1126/science.1254404

Staudinger, U. M. (2020). The positive plasticity of adult development: Potential for the 21st century. *American Psychologist, 75*(4), 540–553. https://doi.org/10.1037/amp0000612

Steele, C. M., & Aronson, J. (1995). Stereotype threat and the intellectual test performance of African Americans. *Journal of Personality and Social Psychology, 69*(5), 797–811. https://doi.org/10.1037/0022-3514.69.5.797

Stern, Y. (2009). Cognitive reserve. *Neuropsychologia, 47*(10), 2015–2028. https://doi.org/10.1016/j.neuropsychologia.2009.03.004

Stern, Y., Albert, M., Barnes, C. A., Cabeza, R., Pascual-Leone, A., & Rapp, P. R. (2023). A framework for concepts of reserve and resilience in aging. *Neurobiology of Aging, 124*, 100–103. https://doi.org/10.1016/j.neurobiolaging.2022.10.015

Sternberg, R. J. (1985). Implicit theories of intelligence, creativity, and wisdom. *Journal of Personality and Social Psychology, 49*(3), 607–627. https://doi.org/10.1037/0022-3514.49.3.607

Strayer, D. L., Watson, J. M., & Drews, F. A. (2011). Cognitive distraction while multitasking in the automobile. In B. H. Ross (Ed.), *The psychology of learning and motivation* (Vol. 54, pp. 29–58). Academic Press.

Tulving, E. (1972). Episodic and semantic memory. In E. Tulving & W. Donaldson (Eds.), *Organization of memory* (pp. 381–402). Academic Press.

Umanath, S., Barrett, T. E., Kim, S., Walsh, C. A., & Coane, J. H. (2023). Older adults recover more marginal knowledge and use feedback more effectively than younger adults: Evidence using "I don't know" vs. "I don't remember" for general knowledge questions. *Frontiers in Psychology, 14*, 1145278. https://doi.org/10.3389/fpsyg.2023.1145278

Umanath, S., & Marsh, E. J. (2014). Understanding how prior knowledge influences memory in older adults. *Perspectives on Psychological Science, 9*(4), 408–426. https://doi.org/10.1177/1745691614535933

van de Rest, O., Berendsen, A. A., Haveman-Nies, A., & de Groot, L. C. (2015). Dietary patterns, cognitive decline, and dementia: A systematic review. *Advances in Nutrition, 6*(2), 154–168. https://doi.org/10.3945/an.114.007617

Valenzuela, M., & Sachdev, P. (2006). Brain reserve and cognitive decline: A non-parametric systematic review. *Psychological Medicine, 36*(8), 1065–1073. https://doi.org/10.1017/S0033291706007744

Verhaeghen, P. (2003). Aging and vocabulary score: A meta-analysis. *Psychology and Aging, 18*(2), 332–339. https://doi.org/10.1037/0882-7974.18.2.332

Wu, R., & Rebok, G. W. (2020). Maximizing the impact of cognitive engagement interventions for older adults. In A. K. Thomas & A. Gutchess (Eds.), *The Cambridge handbook of cognitive aging: A life course perspective* (pp. 685–700). Cambridge University Press. https://doi.org/10.1017/9781108552684.042

Yoon, C., May, C. P., & Hasher, L. (1999). Aging, circadian arousal patterns, and cognition. In N. Schwarz, D. C. Park, B. Knaüper, & S. Sudman (Eds.), *Cognition, aging, and self-reports* (pp. 117–143). Psychology Press/Erlbaum (UK) Taylor & Francis.

10

Neurocognitive Disorders in Late Life

Brian P. Yochim

LEARNING OBJECTIVES

- Use the diagnostic criteria for mild cognitive impairment, dementia, and mild and major neurocognitive disorder to classify symptoms of cognitive impairment among older adults.
- Recognize symptoms of Alzheimer disease, Lewy body disease, vascular dementia, and frontotemporal dementia among older adults.
- Match the underlying neuropathology of common neurocognitive disorders to the cognitive and behavioral symptoms of them.

Most people will retain intact cognitive functioning throughout their lifetimes, at least into the late stages of a terminal illness. Although the cognitive abilities of someone in their 90s are not as strong as they were in their 30s or 60s, most adults remain able to live independently. Extrapolating from worldwide prevalence data (Cao et al., 2020), 95% of people ages 71 to 79, 85% of people ages 80 to 89, and 64% of people age 90 or more years do not have dementia. A minority of people, however, develop impairment in their cognitive abilities that is severe enough to interfere with their abilities to live independently. Cognitive decline that is significant enough to interfere with independent living is known as dementia, and the *Diagnostic and Statistical Manual of Mental Disorders* (*DSM-5-TR*; American Psychiatric Association [APA], 2022) includes the term *major neurocognitive disorder* (NCD) to refer to this condition. This chapter explains these concepts, as well as mild cognitive impairment (MCI) or mild NCD and the transient condition of delirium.

NCDs are not unique to late life. Children can be born with neurological problems causing intellectual disability. Children and adults of all ages can also experience strokes and traumatic brain injuries (TBIs). However, strokes and TBIs occur most often among older adults, and conditions such as Alzheimer disease that cause neurocognitive impairment are also most common among older adults. Before we discuss chronic causes of NCDs such as Alzheimer disease, it is important to understand the more temporary and treatable condition of delirium.

DELIRIUM

A frequent occurrence among hospitalized older adults, which has also likely been experienced by any reader of this textbook at some point in life, is delirium. The nature of delirium (i.e., being delirious) is a rapid decline in cognitive functioning in response to a substantial change in one's physical condition. If you have had surgery with general anesthesia, you have likely been delirious upon awakening. The *DSM-5-TR* diagnostic criteria for delirium include an impairment in attention and awareness of the environment that develops rapidly and is caused by a medical condition (APA, 2022). Impairment is shown in at least one other area of cognitive functioning, such as memory, language, or perception. Symptoms fluctuate throughout the day; in an extreme example, a person can be extremely agitated and disoriented one hour and be pleasant and well oriented the next hour. Patients may drift in and out of sleep throughout a conversation. Common causes of delirium include infections, metabolic abnormalities, and changes in medications. While delirium can resolve by addressing the underlying condition, the effects of delirium can linger long after the cause has been established and treated.

Clinicians are often asked to determine whether a person's cognitive decline is due to dementia, delirium, or both. A useful thought process is to consider someone's cognitive decline as "delirium unless proven otherwise." Delirium tends to have a more rapid onset than dementia, occurring over the span of hours or days, whereas dementia tends to develop over months or years. Acute medical conditions (e.g., infections, changes in medications, acute withdrawal from excess use of alcohol or other drugs) lead to delirium, and thus the cognitive and behavioral state is closely associated with a change in medical condition, whereas dementia occurs more independently of changes in one's medical condition. Patients with delirium often experience hallucinations, usually of a visual nature. Patients can also experience illusions, which are misperceptions of actual visual stimuli, such as seeing characters move in a painting on the wall or misperceiving spots on the floor as bugs. Patients are frequently disoriented and benefit from frequent reminders of the current place and time. For example, patients may state that they are in the hospital when in fact they have been discharged to a rehabilitation facility. Deficits in orientation and language may lead patients to answer orientation questions incorrectly; for example, when asked what year it is, they may answer with the year they were born or their current age. Patients may show socially inappropriate behaviors they would not normally exhibit, such as aggression toward medical staff, rude statements, or removing clothing. Patients may also show emotional disturbances such as excessive anxiety or crying. The sleep–wake cycle is very often disrupted, such that patients wake up in the middle of the night ready to start the day and then may sleep throughout the daytime.

There is a strong relationship between urinary tract infections (UTIs) and the development of delirium (Krinitski et al., 2021). Chae and Miller (2015) found that 19.4% of patients with delirium had a UTI. They also found that 11.2% of patients with dementia had UTIs and suggested that UTIs can precipitate or exacerbate an onset of dementia. Chae and Miller suggested that one mechanism for this relationship could involve the immune system interfering with neurological functioning. Balogun and Philbrick (2014) found that patients with delirium had rates of UTI ranging from 25.9% to 32% compared with 13% of hospitalized patients without delirium. Among patients with UTIs, rates of delirium ranged from 30% to 35%, and among hospitalized patients without UTIs, rates ranged from 7.7% to 8%.

While it is important to rule out delirium when diagnosing dementia, it is also important to note that the weakened state of the brain that leads to dementia also increases one's risk of delirium (APA, 2022). Often, people who were starting to show mild cognitive deficits experience a steep decline in functioning after a major medical procedure such as surgery with general anesthesia. This is often experienced as delirium immediately after surgery, with decreased memory that is slow to improve or never improves. For example, 16% of patients undergoing surgery for a hip fracture developed delirium during their hospital stay, with factors such as dementia, pneumonia, blood loss, UTIs, and infections increasing the risk (de Haan et al., 2023). Lingehall et al. (2017) found that 26.3% of patients age 70 and older undergoing cardiac surgery developed dementia within 5 years after surgery. Among those who had developed dementia, 87% had experienced delirium after their surgeries. Lower cognitive functioning before surgery and delirium after surgery were highly associated with eventual development of dementia. This illustrates the close relationship between delirium and dementia. We turn now to discussion of NCDs, also known as dementia and MCI.

NEUROCOGNITIVE DISORDERS: DIAGNOSTIC TERMINOLOGY

The most recent terms used to describe these conditions have been major or mild NCD, dementia, and MCI. It is important to understand that all these terms refer to a constellation of cognitive and behavioral symptoms and that these symptoms have a variety of underlying causes. Unlike most other mental health disorders, a great deal is known about the underlying neurological causes of NCDs. Thus, a comprehensive evaluation and diagnosis includes an attempt to pinpoint the underlying cause. The *DSM-5-TR* includes specifiers of "probable" or "possible" to reflect the probabilistic nature of specifying likely causes.

The term "dementia" has classically referred to an impairment in one's cognitive functioning that is a decline from a prior level and is severe enough to interfere with one's ability to live independently. The term has typically been associated with Alzheimer disease, but it is important to understand that Alzheimer disease is only one of many conditions that can cause dementia. Formal diagnostic criteria were published in 2011 by the National Institute on Aging (NIA) and Alzheimer's Association (AA; McKhann et al., 2011). When the *DSM-5* was published in 2013, the term "neurocognitive disorder" was intended to replace the term "dementia" to acknowledge that conditions other than Alzheimer disease can cause this syndrome of cognitive impairment, and this terminology remains in the *DSM-5-TR*. The use of the term "neurocognitive disorder" in *DSM* also reflects how the disorder can occur in adults of all ages, whereas "dementia" has typically been associated only with older adults.

It is important to establish that a patient is indeed demonstrating a decline when diagnosing dementia or NCD. People with a history of intellectual developmental disorders, for example, may show impairment that interferes with their ability to live independently, but a NCD would not be diagnosed until decline is occurring. People with Down syndrome almost always develop Alzheimer disease if they live long enough, such that Down syndrome is considered a genetic form of Alzheimer disease (Fortea et al., 2021), and detection of cognitive decline suggestive of a neurocognitive disorder becomes challenging. Likewise, people with high levels of cognitive functioning sometimes show a decline (e.g., from a high-average to a low-average level of cognitive functioning) that resembles a pattern seen in Alzheimer disease, but dementia is not diagnosed until the impairment is severe enough to interfere with the ability to live independently. Decline and impairment are two different concepts, and a person can experience one without the other. Both must be present to be diagnosed with an NCD.

In the 1980s and 1990s it was realized that patients experience a mild cognitive decline before they have cognitive impairment severe enough to be called dementia. Various labels used to represent this state have included "MCI," "cognitive impairment, not dementia (CIND)," "mild neurocognitive disorder," and "cognitive disorder not otherwise specified (NOS)." The term MCI emerged as the preferred term, and in 2011 the NIA and AA published their diagnostic criteria for MCI due to Alzheimer disease (Albert et al., 2011). This set of criteria expanded awareness that (a) one can have Alzheimer disease but not have symptoms severe enough to be considered dementia and (b) other conditions in addition to Alzheimer disease can cause MCI as well as dementia. The criteria also make it known that, while memory decline is typically the first observable symptom, sometimes patients first show decline in other areas such as visuospatial ability or language (discussed later in the sections on Alzheimer disease and frontotemporal dementia). Amnestic MCI refers to the more typical condition of decline in memory, whereas nonamnestic MCI refers to decline in other cognitive domains. The cognitive decline may be in one domain ("single-domain MCI") or more than one cognitive domain ("multidomain MCI"). This also reflects the fact that one can have impairment in more than one cognitive domain, but it is not considered dementia until the cognitive impairment interferes with everyday living.

MCI continues to be a major focus of research. As treatments for Alzheimer disease or other causes of MCI become developed, they may be given as early as possible in the course of the disease, such as when one starts to show symptoms of MCI. Patients and their families also usually appreciate being informed about this condition and what it means. Over time the term MCI has become highly associated with Alzheimer disease, to the point that it was difficult to know what diagnosis to apply to someone who is showing mild cognitive decline due to a stroke, a TBI, or other conditions such as Parkinson disease. Recognizing this, the *DSM-5* incorporated the term "mild neurocognitive disorder" to refer to cognitive decline from any neurological problem that is not severe enough to interfere with daily functioning.

The *DSM-5-TR* criteria differentiate between major and mild NCD based on the degree to which the cognitive decline interferes with independence in everyday functioning, such as managing finances or medications. Note that impairment in only one domain may be sufficient for the disorder to be considered "major," unlike prior criteria (e.g., McKhann et al., 2011) that required impairment in two or more domains. The exception is that in order to be diagnosed with a major NCD due to probable Alzheimer disease, impairment must be demonstrated in two or more domains.

PREVALENCE OF DEMENTIA

Approximately 16% of Americans age 70 and over have dementia (Zhu et al., 2021). Rates of dementia increase with age and lower levels of education and are higher among Hispanic and Black older Americans than among White older Americans (Hudomiet et al., 2022) and higher among those with lower occupational complexity (Hyun et al., 2022). The prevalence rate of dementia among Indigenous populations in Australia, Brazil, Canada, and the United States was found to vary from 0.4% to 26.8% (Souza-Talarico et al., 2016). Souza-Talarico et al. found that decreased education level and increased numbers of health conditions were associated with increased risk of dementia. In the United States, midlife hypertension, midlife obesity, and late-life physical inactivity were the lifestyle factors most associated with the development of dementia (Lee et al., 2022). The prevalence of dementia in the world due to any cause increases with advancing age, from 0.27% among individuals age 50 to 59, to 1.8% in ages 60 to 69, to 5.1% in ages 70 to 79, to 15.1% in ages 80 to 89, to 35.7% in individuals ages 90 to 99 (Cao et al., 2020). Women aged 80 and over have rates of dementia (25%) significantly higher than men (12%; Cao et al., 2020), but this difference may be shrinking over time (Hudomiet et al., 2022).

There is evidence that the actual prevalence and incidence of dementia may be declining (Hudomiet et al., 2022; Wolters et al., 2020). This may be related to increasing levels of education in more recent cohorts of older adults; for example, the mean number of years of education for men age 65 and over was 11.8 in 2000 and 13.4 in 2016 (Hudomiet et al., 2022).

CAUSES OF NEUROCOGNITIVE DISORDERS

Many, if not most, patients with a major NCD have more than one etiology, as shown by autopsies of patients with a history of an NCD. For example, Nichols et al. (2023), in a large autopsy sample in the United States and United Kingdom, found that 91% of patients with dementia had more than one neuropathological cause and 41% had three or more causes. Schneider et al. (2007) found that more than half of individuals with dementia had multiple etiologies and only 30% had Alzheimer disease alone. Therefore, a diagnostic evaluation can be considered a way of ruling out various possible causes until two or more possibilities cannot be ruled out. Symptoms of a disease process may not emerge until a certain amount of brain tissue is lost, and it may take the additive effect of two or more diseases before symptoms become noticeable.

A discussion of etiologies of NCDs begins with TBIs, which can occur at any age but are particularly common among older adults.

TRAUMATIC BRAIN INJURIES

Although commonly associated with younger people, TBIs are also a common problem among older adults. Adults aged ≥75 years have the highest rates of TBI-related death (76.7 per 100,000 in 2019), followed by those aged 65 to 74 years (24.0 in 2019) and adults aged 55 to 64 years (19.0 in 2019); adults age 75 and older experience 32% of TBI-related hospitalizations and 28% of TBI-related deaths (Centers for Disease Control and Prevention, 2022). American Indian and Alaska Native adults have higher rates of TBIs than any other racial group (Daugherty et al., 2019). Women accounted for 62% of people age 65 and older hospitalized for TBI (Albrecht et al., 2015). The evaluation of older adults with cognitive changes should always incorporate gathering information about possible TBIs.

In addition, modern treatment for acute brain injuries has preserved the lives of many people with TBIs who would have perished at the time of injury in the past. This will result in more people who have suffered severe TBIs living into old age with the deficits that accompany the TBI. Often people had TBIs at younger ages, before our current knowledge about TBIs, and this history is not elicited until late life. The brain damage experienced by a person earlier in life may lead to particular areas of the brain being more susceptible than other areas to future insults. For example, a patient reported a vague history of injury to the left side of his head sometime in his early 20s, along with being hospitalized for 2 weeks afterward and being feverish and unable to speak for a few days. This patient, 60 years later, became severely delirious when given a strong painkiller medication and showed symptoms of aphasia, which can result from damage to the left hemisphere. The patient's left hemisphere may have been particularly susceptible to various insults to the brain because of an injury long ago.

Falls cause the majority of TBIs in all ages, followed by motor vehicle accidents (GBD, 2019; Traumatic Brain Injury and Spinal Cord Injury Collaborators, 2019). Falls cause the majority of TBIs among older adults, resulting in 69.7% of TBIs among adults age 65 to 74, 82.5% of TBIs among adults age 75 to 84, and 87.5% of TBIs among adults age 85 and older (Ghneim et al., 2022). When part of the head suddenly strikes something, the opposite side of the brain also can sustain damage. For example, if someone falls backwards off a ladder, their occipital lobe may suffer damage. Their brain will also recoil off the back of the skull, causing damage to the frontal lobes. This concept of damage to the opposite part of the brain from the part that was struck is known as contracoup damage.

TBIs also can occur in the context of other incidents; for example, a person may have a stroke and suddenly lose the ability to use their leg, causing them to fall down steps and strike their head. Likewise, older patients who suffer TBIs have a high rate of suffering intracranial hemorrhages or strokes while hospitalized and within a year after discharge (Albrecht et al., 2015; Ghneim et al., 2022). This rate decreases sharply within 4 months after the TBI and then continues to decrease over the year after the TBI, but the risk of stroke after TBI remains higher than before a TBI. Common nontraumatic causes of brain injury among older adults include brain tumors (the most common) and anoxia (deprivation of oxygen; Chan et al., 2013).

We turn now to causes of NCDs that are more unique to old age and that tend to develop more gradually.

ALZHEIMER DISEASE

Alzheimer disease is the most common cause of NCDs among older adults. The hallmark neuropathological features of Alzheimer disease include the development of plaques, composed mainly of amyloid beta, and neurofibrillary tangles, consisting mainly of tau. These lead to cerebral atrophy, or degeneration, and loss of synapses. Amyloid plaques occur between neurons as by-products of neuronal degeneration and hinder communication between neurons. Cognitive decline and impairment are more associated with the number of neurofibrillary tangles than plaques (Aschenbrenner et al., 2018). When the microtubules transporting substances from a neuronal cell body to the end of the axon become twisted, the twisted microtubules form into neurofibrillary tangles. Neurons lose their structural integrity as a result. The tangles occur in the hippocampus, entorhinal cortex, and other parts of the temporal lobe, before spreading to other parts of the brain, including the nucleus basalis of Meynert in the forebrain (Boller & Duykaerts, 2003). Amyloid beta might hasten tau accumulation and enable the spread of tau beyond the medial temporal lobe (Scheltens et al., 2021). The nucleus basalis of Meynert contributes to the production of acetylcholine and connects with the hippocampus, which is highly involved with memory (Blumenfeld, 2022).

Treatments for Alzheimer Disease

Because of this impact on acetylcholine, current pharmacological treatments attempt to prevent the breakdown of acetylcholine. Acetylcholinesterase, or cholinesterase, is an enzyme that breaks down acetylcholine. By inhibiting cholinesterase, the amount of acetylcholine is increased, which should improve memory functioning. Cholinesterase inhibitors such as donepezil, galantamine, and rivastigmine are commonly prescribed for patients suspected of having Alzheimer disease. Another medication, memantine, works as an *N*-methyl-*D*-aspartate (NMDA) receptor antagonist that is meant to decrease glutamate activity. Both these classes of medications may lead to small improvements in functioning in patients with dementia (Vaci et al., 2021), but cholinesterase inhibitors have side effects including nausea, diarrhea, and muscle weakness in older adults (Sharma, 2019). Lifestyle interventions have also been a focus of research. The Finnish Geriatric Intervention Study to Prevent Cognitive Impairment and Disability (FINGER) project found that a combination of nutritional consultation, physical exercise, cognitive training, social activities, and vascular and metabolic risk management led to improved neuropsychological test performance, compared with control participants, in a sample of older adults at increased risk of dementia (Ngandu et al., 2015).

Two primary outcome measures have been used to determine the effectiveness of medications for Alzheimer disease. One has been the Alzheimer's Disease Assessment Scale-Cognitive Subscale (ADAS-Cog; Rosen et al., 1984; see review by Kueper et al., 2018). Another has been the "Sum of Boxes" (SB) from the Clinical Dementia Rating (CDR-SB; Morris, 1993), a scale for rating dementia severity in which impairment is rated in six categories (Memory, Orientation, Judgment and Problem Solving, Community Affairs, Home and Hobbies, and Personal Care). Scores range from 1 to 18, with higher scores indicating greater impairment. (This is not to be confused with the Dementia Rating Scale, a cognitive test by Mattis, 1988.)

Medications that use antibodies to clear amyloid from the brain are being developed. In a study of 1,795 patients with mild cognitive impairment or mild dementia due to Alzheimer disease, scores on the CDR in patients who were given the medication lecanemab were found to change an average of 1.21 points over 18 months, whereas scores for those given a placebo changed 1.66 points (van Dyck et al., 2023). Likewise, there was a 1.44-point difference in the ADAS-Cog between the two groups. This medication involves biweekly drug infusions, and the mild improvement in functioning may not be clinically meaningful (The Lancet, 2022).

Neuropathological Ratings of Alzheimer Disease

The presence of Alzheimer disease cannot be established definitively until autopsy of the affected individual's brain because of the obvious risk in obtaining a biopsy of brain tissue in a living person. Therefore, clinicians make diagnoses such as "major NCD due to probable Alzheimer disease" or "dementia of the Alzheimer's type" when Alzheimer disease seems the most likely etiology. At least three sets of criteria gauge the severity of Alzheimer disease in a deceased person's brain. The Braak and Braak (1991) criteria track a progression of the disease from the transentorhinal cortex (stages I and II) to the hippocampus (stages III and IV) and ending with involvement throughout the neocortex (stages V and VI). The Consortium to Establish a Registry for Alzheimer's Disease (CERAD) also proposed criteria for staging the disease (Gearing et al., 1995). After Ronald Reagan developed complications related to Alzheimer disease, the NIA–Reagan Institute criteria (Newell et al., 1999) were developed. The NIA–Reagan criteria provide a high, intermediate, or low likelihood that a person's dementia was due to Alzheimer disease. Many people who are cognitively intact throughout life are nonetheless found to have the neuropathologic features of Alzheimer disease in their brains at autopsy (Nichols et al., 2023). One may have the disease while not having cognitive impairment. When working with patients, it can be difficult to determine how to answer the question: "So do I have Alzheimer disease or not?"

Amyloid plaques also develop in the arteries and capillaries of the brain, which is known as *amyloid angiopathy*. Amyloid angiopathy occurs in as many as 85% to 95% of people with Alzheimer disease (Vinters, 2015). Amyloid angiopathy can cause intracerebral hemorrhages to occur, and it can also cause cerebral microinfarctions (Chang Wong & Chang Chui, 2022).

Genetics of Alzheimer Disease

Genetic studies have identified several genes associated with familial risk of developing Alzheimer disease as early as one's 40s or 50s, which occur in less than 1% of the population: the amyloid precursor protein (*APP*) gene on chromosome 21, presenilin 1 (*PSEN1*) on chromosome 14, and presenilin 2 (*PSEN2*) on chromosome 1 (Scheltens et al., 2021). Other rare genetic mutations that increase the risk include *SORL1*, *TREM2*, and *ABCA7*. The ε4 form of apolipoprotein E (ApoE ε4) is associated with a three to four times increased risk and younger age of developing Alzheimer disease (Jansen et al., 2019). In contrast, the ε2 form and ε3 form (which occur in less than 1% of the population) are associated with a lower risk, as are other rare genes such as the Ala673Thr protective mutation of *APP* among Icelandic people and the Pro522Arg mutation in the *PLCG2* gene (Scheltens et al., 2021).

Biomarkers of Alzheimer Disease

A biomarker is anything that serves as a quantifiable representation or marker of a specific pathophysiological disease process. Biomarkers of Alzheimer disease are categorized into those for beta-amyloid (A), tau (T), and neurodegeneration (N); this is known as the ATN framework (Jack et al., 2018). Common examples include neuroimaging findings (e.g., MRI or PET scan results) or levels of a chemical in cerebrospinal fluid (CSF) samples. CSF levels of amyloid beta and tau are obtained through lumbar punctures (also known as spinal taps), in which a needle is inserted between two lumbar vertebrae. Amyloid biomarkers include CSF levels of amyloid beta and amyloid PET. Tau biomarkers include CSF levels of phosphorylated tau and tau PET. Neurodegeneration is indicated by biomarkers of structural MRI, fluoro-deoxyglucose (FDG)–PET, and CSF total tau (Jack et al., 2018). Neuropsychological tests are also considered a biomarker of Alzheimer disease (Vinters, 2015). The three most established biomarkers are atrophy in the medial temporal lobe as depicted on MRI, hypometabolism shown in the posterior cingulate and temporoparietal areas on 18 FDG-PET, and amyloid beta deposition shown on amyloid-PET (Scheltens et al., 2021). While not as established, tau biomarkers are more highly associated with cognitive functioning (Aschenbrenner et al., 2018). Biomarkers that can be obtained from blood instead of neuroimaging or CSF are being developed but are less established (Janelidze et al., 2016). Using these biomarkers to define Alzheimer disease among 85-year-olds, the prevalence of Alzheimer disease was found to be three times higher than Alzheimer disease suspected on clinical symptoms alone (Jack et al., 2019). In their exploration of the biomarkers of Alzheimer disease (Jack et al., 2018), the NIA/AA do not currently promote the use of biomarker tests in routine clinical care.

There are several reasons for this limitation: (a) the core clinical criteria provide very good diagnostic accuracy and utility in most patients; (b) more research needs to be done to ensure that criteria that include the use of biomarkers have been appropriately designed; (c) there is limited standardization of biomarkers from one locale to another; and (d) access to biomarkers is limited to varying degrees in community settings (McKhann et al., 2011, p. 266).

Progression of Alzheimer Disease

Declines in memory are usually the first symptom of Alzheimer disease, because the hippocampus is impacted early in the disease process. Patients or their caregivers will often report that the patient's "long-term" memory is intact but that their "short-term" memory is poor. They often will report that the patient can remember events from prior years without difficulty, but that they forget conversations within minutes. This parallels the neuropathology that is occurring in the patient's brain; as the hippocampus deteriorates, the brain's ability to form new memories declines. However, memories or knowledge already established years ago remains unaffected by the disease until late in its course. Likewise, procedural memory is preserved late into the disease course, so patients can still engage in activities involving this type of memory, such as using tools and kitchen utensils, playing musical instruments, or completing yardwork. Caregivers can capitalize on a patient's remaining skills while preventing deficits from interfering; for example, a patient may still be able to make an omelet but may need a reminder to turn the stove off when done. Social functioning often remains intact, so that relationships can continue to enrich one's life. Intact social functioning often enables the patient to compensate for memory loss (e.g., by talking around a question asked, rather than answering it when they do not know the answer), which can mask the symptoms of this and prevent loved ones or acquaintances from noticing a decline in the patient's memory.

Memory problems progress insidiously, and a concerning event may surprise the patient and/or their family members. They may travel out of town and find themselves unable to learn how to find their hotel room. Patients may find themselves becoming lost when driving in an unfamiliar area. They may go to an appointment and return home several hours later after receiving assistance in finding their way home. In this sense, their driving per se (i.e., the procedural memory of operating a motor vehicle) may be intact, but memory impairment interferes with their navigation. Their spouses may notice the patient frequently repeats questions and forgets recent events, such as a conversation or a movie from the prior day. They may be unable to learn how to operate a new appliance because of inability to remember instructions given to them. Neuropsychologists look for whether these symptoms are occurring by presenting patients with a set of information, such as a list of words, short stories, or simple diagrams, and then asking the patient to recall the stimuli immediately after presentation and then sometime later, usually 20 to 30 minutes after initial presentation.

After entering the medial temporal area, Alzheimer disease typically then spreads to nearby neuroanatomical areas, such as the lateral temporal lobes and frontal lobes. This leads to accompanying declines in language abilities, such as finding words in daily conversation. Patients often use *circumlocutions* when they cannot recall a word, using other words or phrases to convey the desired word. Patients can also make paraphasic errors in their speech, saying a word semantically (e.g., "rain cover") or phonologically (e.g., "umbilical") similar to the target word (e.g., "umbrella"). Impaired word-finding manifests in neuropsychological testing as poor performance on confrontation naming tests, in which individuals are "confronted" with a stimulus, usually a picture, and asked to name the item.

As the disease spreads to the frontal lobes, patients show behavioral changes in response to damage to this area, such as poor social comportment (e.g., swearing, rude statements they would not have said before), poor planning (e.g., difficulty planning a meal or a set of errands), poor decision-making (e.g., making poor financial decisions), or impulsivity (e.g., engaging in extramarital affairs). One patient described making impulsive online purchases and then forgetting that items had been purchased when they arrived at her doorstep. These abilities are typically considered elements of executive functioning. The NIA/AA criteria (McKhann et al., 2011), as well as the *DSM-5-TR*, place poor social behavior into its own domain of cognitive functioning (social cognition), whereas planning and decision-making are considered a part of executive functioning.

Alzheimer disease eventually intrudes into the posterior temporal lobes and parietal and occipital lobes. Patients may misperceive important visual stimuli, such as picking up a television remote when the phone is ringing or failing to notice the item they wanted to purchase in the grocery store. They may not be able to quickly process changes in their visual environment, such as when driving or walking. Reading may become laborious, and loved ones may wonder why the patient has "lost interest" in this activity. Decreased reading may also result from finding that they cannot remember what they have read. Visual perceptual problems may lead to difficulty entering information correctly in a checkbook or noticing that their bathroom is dirty.

Every person with Alzheimer disease has a different trajectory of the disease process and thus will experience a different set of symptoms at various points in time. If the pathology develops first in areas other than the medial temporal lobes, then symptoms resulting from damage to those parts of the brain are the first to manifest. This leads to syndromes that may be named after the area affected (e.g., *posterior cortical atrophy*) or the resulting symptoms (e.g., *primary progressive aphasia* [PPA]). PPA is most often caused by the same pathology that causes frontotemporal degeneration and is described in the section on frontotemporal dementia.

Occasionally Alzheimer disease develops first in places like the occipital lobe or posterior temporal lobe, causing posterior cortical atrophy. This atrophy is most often caused by Alzheimer disease (Crutch et al., 2017). Degeneration of the occipital lobes leads to deficits in visuospatial skills. Early symptoms can include difficulty recognizing faces; finding things in the kitchen, house, or grocery store; or difficulty assembling new furniture. One patient described an inability to associate the names and faces of new neighbors who moved in next door. Deficient visuospatial skills are also a common symptom of Lewy body disease, described next.

LEWY BODY DISEASE

Another common cause of neurocognitive disorders is Lewy body disease. Lewy body disease and Parkinson disease are intertwined; cognitive impairment in people with Parkinson disease results from the accumulation of Lewy bodies. While the two syndromes differ in their timing of motor symptoms and cognitive symptoms, both syndromes and their underlying pathologies become similar with time. If cognitive symptoms develop before the onset of motor symptoms, the condition is known as Lewy body disease.

In 1912, Frederick Lewy discovered small circular bodies found in the cells of the substantia nigra in patients with Parkinson disease. Eventually termed "Lewy bodies," these cell bodies may be the second or third most common neuropathological finding in patients with dementia (Nichols et al., 2023; Sezgin et al., 2019). Lewy bodies are found in the brains of patients with Parkinson disease, in patients with multiple system atrophy, and in those with dementia due to suspected Lewy bodies. Lewy bodies are composed of alpha-synuclein (Kon et al., 2020). This pathology is associated with loss of neurons. Whether Lewy bodies have a neuroprotective or neurotoxic role and the extent to which they cause the clinical symptoms of Lewy body disease are not yet known (Walker et al., 2015). Some people with no history of clinical symptoms nonetheless have significant alpha-synuclein pathology found at autopsy (Nichols et al., 2023).

Lewy bodies may develop first in the reticular formation of the medulla, followed by the brainstem, the limbic system, and then the neocortex (Braak et al., 2003), with other patterns of progression possible. They can accumulate in axons and dendrites, becoming known as Lewy neurites, which can also accumulate in the nucleus basalis of Meynert (an area in the basal forebrain) and the hippocampus, and approximately 80% of people with dementia with Lewy bodies also have the amyloid plaques and neurofibrillary tangles of Alzheimer disease (Kon et al., 2020). Structural neuroimaging, such as MRI, is limited in differentiating Lewy body disease from other causes of dementia. However, patients with Lewy body disease show less metabolism in the occipital area on perfusion single photon emission CT and metabolic PET compared with healthy control participants or patients with Alzheimer disease (Sezgin et al., 2019). This finding is listed as a supportive biomarker in the diagnostic criteria for dementia due to Lewy body disease (McKeith et al., 2017), and it has high sensitivity and specificity.

Patients with Lewy body disease often experience well-formed visual hallucinations of people or animals or sensations of the "presence" of someone nearby. Patients may also have a delusion that someone else is living in their home (Sezgin et al., 2019). Clinicians may address these symptoms by prescribing antipsychotic medications. However, patients with dementia with Lewy bodies can have problematic reactions to antipsychotic medications, known as neuroleptic sensitivity (Sezgin et al., 2019). Lewy body disease and Parkinson disease involve a reduced level of dopamine; thus, antipsychotic medications that are designed to reduce levels of dopamine would be expected to worsen symptoms caused by a shortage of dopamine. Clinicians must be aware that a new onset of visual hallucinations in older adults commonly results from Lewy body symptoms rather than a psychotic process.

People with Lewy body disease commonly have impairments in attention, visuospatial skills, and executive functioning (Sezgin et al., 2019). Tiraboschi et al. (2006) found that including visuospatial impairment as a core diagnostic criterion would improve sensitivity to the disease. Lewy body disease is also associated with fluctuations in cognition, and this is a core diagnostic feature. Ferman et al. (2004) specified this further, finding that daytime sleep of 2 or more hours, staring into space for long periods, daytime drowsiness and lethargy, and episodes of disorganized speech occurred much more often in people with Lewy body disease than in people with Alzheimer disease or participants with no neurological disorder.

Lewy body disease is associated with a specific sleep disorder. During REM sleep, the body is typically paralyzed, so that we do not move while we are dreaming. In contrast, people with REM sleep behavior disorder act out their dreams and may yell, scream, wave their limbs, punch, or kick during the REM sleep phase. The dreams in which this occurs often involve a perceived attacker such as a person, animal, or insect. Up to 70% to 90% of patients with REM sleep behavior disorder develop dementia, usually due to Lewy bodies, or Parkinson disease within 15 years of onset (Howell & Schenck, 2015). It is thought to develop from insults to the brainstem areas involved in the control of REM sleep, such as the reticular formation. These areas may be affected by Lewy body disease earlier than other parts of the brain, which would account for REM sleep behavior disorder occurring years before the manifestations of Lewy body disease (Walker et al., 2015).

Cholinesterase inhibitors and memantine have been found to have small but significant effects on cognitive functioning (e.g., 0.46-point difference on a 30-point measure) in patients with Lewy body disease (Meng et al., 2019). Patients with Lewy body disease have a high risk of problematic side effects of medications, which complicates pharmacological treatment. Medications that address hallucinations might worsen motor symptoms, and medications for motor symptoms might worsen hallucinations, also posing a challenge to treatment. Donepezil and rivastigmine, used for treating

Alzheimer disease, have also been shown to improve cognition and activities of daily living in patients with dementia due to Lewy body disease or Parkinson disease (Taylor et al., 2020). The digestive system contains many acetylcholine receptors, and acetylcholinesterase inhibitors increase the activity of acetylcholine in the digestive system, frequently resulting in unpleasant gastrointestinal side effects.

PARKINSON DISEASE

Neurocognitive disorders can occur in the late stages of Parkinson disease, with one study finding 46% of patients developed dementia within 10 years of diagnosis (Williams-Gray et al., 2013). The first symptoms of Parkinson's are typically a mild tremor while the hands are at rest, muscular rigidity, and slowing of movements. Eventually patients show poor balance, frequent falls, and difficulty walking. A person's gait may become characterized by short, shuffling steps without lifting the feet very much (a "magnetic gait"). Their face may show less expression, and they may appear to have a masked face. Handwriting becomes small and difficult to decipher. Parkinson disease is caused by the atrophy of neurons that produce dopamine in the substantia nigra of the brain. NCD due to Parkinson disease is diagnosed when the disease is clearly established, and the cognitive symptoms are similar to those found in Lewy body disease, with impairments in attention, executive functioning, visuospatial skills, and memory (Sezgin et al., 2019). If motor symptoms have not yet developed, then Lewy body disease is listed as the possible or probable cause. Litvan et al. (2012) published diagnostic criteria for MCI due to Parkinson disease. Although Parkinson disease is thought to result in a "subcortical" profile of neuropsychological test performance, as opposed to the "cortical" pattern found in Alzheimer disease, in reality both patient groups often show similar performance (Emre et al., 2007).

VASCULAR DISEASE

A buildup of vascular damage in the brain may interfere with cognitive functioning to the extent that a person may be diagnosed with NCD as a result. Vascular disease is considered the second or third most common cause of dementia. Risk factors for this condition include a history of cigarette smoking, type 2 diabetes, poorly controlled hypertension, atrial fibrillation, and high cholesterol (Chang Wong & Chang Chui, 2022). Rates of hypertension and diabetes have been found to be twice as common among older African Americans compared with White Americans (Gottesman et al., 2015). Vascular risk factors can lead to atherosclerotic plaques building up in the cerebral arteries, interfering with adequate blood supply. Eventually, arteries may become completely blocked, leading to a shortage or lack of blood supply to nearby areas of the brain, a condition called *ischemia*. Neuroimaging often shows multiple ischemic lesions in these patients, typically bordering the cerebral ventricles (i.e., "periventricular") and expanding outward from the ventricles. The arteries first to become blocked tend to be smaller arteries, followed by arteries of increasing size. One example of small arteries that are prone to narrowing are the lenticulostriate arteries, which supply the basal ganglia (Blumenfeld, 2022). Ischemia in this region can cause slower speed of processing. Hence, some of the first deficits seen in these patients are in processing speed.

Other patients may stay cognitively intact until a large *infarction* occurs. A cerebral infarction is the death of brain tissue due to sudden lack of blood supply. Infarctions most often are caused by an artery completely closing off, as in ischemia. Ischemic strokes can be caused by a *thrombus*, a blood clot that forms within a cerebral artery, or an *embolus*, which is a blood clot that breaks off from another artery in the body and becomes stuck in a cerebral artery, causing an *embolic* stroke. Embolic strokes can occur suddenly, whereas thrombotic strokes may take longer to become manifest. Approximately 10% to 15% of strokes are cerebral hemorrhages, or a breakage in an artery, with blood spilling out (Gil-Garcia et al., 2022). Strokes vary in size from large-vessel infarcts to small-vessel infarcts. Clinical descriptions of MRI or CT scans may refer to "small-vessel disease," which refers to evidence of ischemia in the small blood vessels of the brain. Tiny strokes found on imaging or autopsy are often called "lacunes," a French term originating from the Latin *lacuna*, meaning "cavity" (Regenhardt et al., 2019). The most common site of large infarctions is the left or right middle cerebral artery, which supplies a large part of the lateral cerebral cortex. Typically patients show some degree of recovery in the weeks after a stroke, but the stroke may have caused enough damage that the patient is left with a permanent NCD.

The cognitive presentation of cerebrovascular disease varies to a large extent, depending on the location of ischemic damage (Chang Wong & Chang Chui, 2022). If patients develop the disease slowly and gradually, they may show declines in processing speed and executive functioning. Significant strokes can cause sudden impairment in language, visual perception, attention, executive functioning, and/or processing speed. If an infarction occurs in the left middle cerebral artery, the patient may suddenly develop *aphasia*, or a disturbance in their ability to produce and/or understand language. Strokes in the areas fed by the right middle cerebral artery can cause left inattention, also known as left neglect or hemineglect, a condition in which patients fail to attend to any stimuli (e.g., visual, tactile, auditory) in the left side of space. Patients with right hemisphere damage may also develop anosognosia ("not knowing that one does not know"), a condition in which patients are not aware, or do not believe, that they have impairments. This condition interferes substantially with rehabilitation and recovery.

FRONTOTEMPORAL DEMENTIA

Frontotemporal dementia refers to several types of dementia that result from damage to the frontal and/or temporal lobes. The actual damage may result from several different neuropathologies. Most cases of frontotemporal lobar degeneration are caused by the development of pathological proteins including fused in sarcoma (FUS), Ewing sarcoma, and TATA-binding protein-associated factor 15 (the three of which are abbreviated "FET"); abnormal accumulation of tau ("tauopathies"); or the transactive response (TAR) DNA-binding protein with molecular weight 43 kDa (TDP-43; Mackenzie & Neumann, 2016). TDP-43 is basically a protein in the cell nucleus that helps regulate DNA and RNA activity, and when it builds up in the cytoplasm, it can cause neuropathology (Younes & Miller, 2020). The resulting syndromes may be called frontotemporal dementia or may be a description of the clinical syndrome, as in PPA. Symptoms can develop in one's 50s (Younes & Miller, 2020). A proportion of patients with this condition also develop motor neuron diseases such as amyotrophic lateral sclerosis (ALS), in which patients become unable to engage in any form of voluntary muscle movements. The most common genetic cause of frontotemporal dementia and ALS is the *C9orf72* expansion (Boeve et al., 2022).

Frontotemporal dementia typically occurs as the behavioral variant subtype (Box 10.1) or the language variant subtype. It is thought to be the third most common type of dementia among people younger than 65 (Vieira et al., 2013). The disorder is most common among ages 45 to 64, with 60% of cases diagnosed in this age group. It is often mistaken as a new-onset psychiatric disorder because of the significant behavioral changes and the assumption that neurodegenerative diseases start much later in life. Arnold Pick is thought to have been the first to describe a patient with frontotemporal dementia, in 1892. In 1911, Alois Alzheimer named the syndrome "Pick's disease," and "Pick's disease" and "frontotemporal dementia" have often been used interchangeably.

In the behavioral variant of frontotemporal dementia, patients gradually develop behavioral changes that interfere with social and occupational functioning, such as inability to inhibit socially inappropriate behaviors. They may say derogatory comments about strangers within hearing distance of them. They may start to purchase pornographic materials for the first time in their lives. Patients may engage in risky financial expenditures, and their partners may not learn about it until significant amounts of money have been lost. Patients may lose the initiative to complete basic activities of daily living such as bathing or brushing teeth and may need prompts to do so. People who have been faithful to their spouses throughout their lives may suddenly engage in extramarital affairs. Other abnormal behaviors have included leaving the house unclothed, completing tasks at odd times of the day (e.g., yard work in the middle of the night), or changing one's diet to an extreme. Possibly the most tragic component of this syndrome is that patients are usually unaware that their behavior has changed.

PPA is a progressive language disorder in which profound impairments in language are the first symptoms to manifest. The syndrome is currently categorized into three subtypes (Gorno-Tempini et al., 2011): the nonfluent/agrammatic, the semantic, and the logopenic subtypes.

One can think of the nonfluent/agrammatic variant of PPA as a slowly developing Broca aphasia, which is usually caused by strokes in Broca area. Agrammatism refers to impairment in grammar, including verb conjugation, appropriate word order in sentences, and the use of function words such as articles and prepositions.

BOX 10.1 Loss of Behavioral Initiative

Patients with the behavioral variant of frontotemporal dementia may show lack of initiative, such as needing prompting to bathe and put dirty clothes in the laundry, or to solve problems suddenly presented to them. For instance, one patient left a stove burner on, resulting in a small fire on the stovetop. His wife and grandchildren promptly extinguished the fire, and the patient went to take a nap rather than help clean up the resulting mess of burned food and fire extinguisher foam. The same patient would forget to feed his dog, despite the dog barking repeatedly near his food dish. He also showed an inability to choose his clothes to wear for the day, and his wife needed to choose his clothes in order to make it to an appointment on time.

The semantic variant, previously known as "semantic dementia," can be conceptualized as a loss of semantic knowledge. This loss of knowledge leads to impaired ability to name things and to describe objects when confronted with them (i.e., in "confrontation naming" tasks). This also leads to an inability to read or spell "irregularly" spelled words such as "people," "hour," "said," or "two." The deficit results from loss of the knowledge of that concept, as opposed to loss of ability to associate letters and sounds. The logopenic subtype is the most recently described and is usually caused by Alzheimer disease. Thus, a given syndrome (i.e., PPA) can be caused by different etiologies (e.g., Alzheimer disease or the forms of pathology that cause frontotemporal degeneration).

LIMBIC-PREDOMINANT AGE-RELATED TDP-43 ENCEPHALOPATHY

TDP-43 protein inclusions also can lead to a condition that causes memory deficits similar to, but often more severe than, those seen in Alzheimer disease: limbic-predominant age-related TDP-43 encephalopathy (LATE). This condition may be present in 20% to 50% of individuals over age 80 and often accompanies hippocampal sclerosis, which involves significant loss of neurons in the hippocampus (Nelson et al., 2019), though hippocampal sclerosis is not unique to this condition. Hippocampal sclerosis results from various disease processes such as epilepsy, oxygen deprivation, infections, and various neurodegenerative conditions.

ALCOHOL-RELATED DEMENTIA

Light to moderate use of alcohol may actually protect against development of Alzheimer disease and other causes of dementia. In a meta-analysis, Mewton et al. (2023) found that light to moderate alcohol use reduced the risk of dementia compared with abstainers. Light to moderate use was associated with decreased risk of dementia compared with abstainers or those who drank more than 14 drinks per week (Koch et al., 2019). Definitions of light and moderate vary across culture and time. In the United States, moderate use is considered to be up to one drink per day for women and up to two drinks per day for men, with a drink defined as 12 ounces of beer or 5 ounces of wine (U.S. Department of Agriculture & U.S. Department of Health and Human Services, 2020).

Heavy alcohol use (i.e., more than 21 drinks per week) and a history of alcohol-induced loss of consciousness significantly increase the risk of dementia (Kivimäki et al., 2020). Chronic heavy alcohol use is related to widespread cortical atrophy, especially in the frontal lobes, cerebellum, hippocampus, amygdala, and corpus callosum (Visontay et al., 2021). Diagnostic criteria for alcohol-related dementia were proposed by Oslin et al. (1998). While not yet clinically validated, they include:

1. A clinical diagnosis of dementia at least 60 days after the last exposure to alcohol. 2. Significant alcohol use as defined by a minimum average of 35 standard drinks per week for men (28 for women) for greater than a period of 5 years. The period of significant alcohol use must occur within 3 years of the initial onset of dementia (Oslin et al., 1998, p. 208).

The criteria note that cognitive impairment stabilizes or improves after 60 days of abstinence.

Alcohol-related dementia may account for 9% to 22% of cases of dementia (Rao & Topiwala, 2020). The *DSM-5-TR* includes the term alcohol-induced neurocognitive disorder to refer to this condition. It is unique compared with conditions like Alzheimer disease because it is thought to be less progressive than other causes of NCD. Patients may show improvements in their functioning after a year of sobriety (Stavro et al., 2013), although older age is related to poorer recovery (Ridley et al., 2013).

The damage to the brain that results in dementia might be due to direct toxic effects of ethanol (ETOH), to a deficiency of thiamine, or to a combination of both factors. Thiamine is also known as vitamin B_1, which is not to be confused with vitamin B_{12}. Alcohol interferes with thiamine metabolism, and excessive alcohol use is often associated with unhealthy diets, leading to inadequate thiamine intake. Ethanol may affect neuronal integrity directly through oxidative stress and glutamate excitotoxicity (Rao & Topiwala, 2020). Wernicke encephalopathy represents an acute condition caused by deficient thiamine levels and involves a combination of ophthalmoplegia (paralysis of an eye muscle), ataxia (uncoordinated movements), and confusion. Korsakoff syndrome is more of a long-term condition of severe memory impairment related to hippocampal damage. In addition to memory impairment, chronic alcohol use disorder is associated with deficits in visuoperception (Creupelandt et al., 2021). Alcohol use is also implicated in a large number of TBIs (Rao & Topiwala, 2020).

It is difficult to establish a clear relationship between specific levels of lifetime alcohol intake and development of cognitive impairment because of variability in types of alcoholic drinks, definitions of what a standard drink is, and definitions of normal intake and excessive intake. To add to this, lifetime patterns of excessive use, periods of no alcohol use, and periods of light use vary from person to person. People with a history of alcohol use disorders are also more likely to have histories of head injuries, use of other substances, and vascular risk factors, which complicate the establishment of a direct relationship. Alcohol-related dementia tends to have a younger age of onset, with its larger prevalence rates to be found among younger patients with dementia (Ridley et al., 2013).

OTHER CAUSES OF NEUROCOGNITIVE DISORDERS

Other, less common causes of NCDs in late life that are beyond the scope of this chapter include corticobasal degeneration, multiple system atrophy, and progressive supranuclear palsy. Adults of all ages can develop NCDs caused by Huntington disease, HIV infection, infection from other diseases such as hepatitis C, prion disease, and many other causes.

CONCLUSION

This chapter reviewed the most common causes of NCDs in older adults. We began with a discussion of delirium, which should be ruled out whenever an older adult is showing signs of cognitive decline. Next, an overview of the current diagnostic terminology was presented, including MCI, dementia, and the *DSM-5-TR* diagnoses of mild

NCD and major NCD. We next reviewed TBIs, Alzheimer disease, Lewy body disease, Parkinson disease, vascular disease, frontotemporal degeneration (which includes a behavioral variant and a language variant), LATE, and alcohol-related dementia.

As a final note, it can be helpful to conceptualize the symptoms of any NCD as what would be expected from damage to a specific part of the brain, whatever the cause of the damage. For example, both Alzheimer disease and herpes simplex encephalitis tend to strike the medial temporal area. Thus, the deficits one would expect from damage to the medial temporal area (i.e., memory deficits) occur with either disease. In the unusual circumstance that Alzheimer disease strikes the occipital lobes first, then the corresponding symptoms are profound visuospatial deficits. Likewise, sometimes strokes happen in the basal ganglia, leading to motor deficits that typically occur in Parkinson disease, which also involves degeneration of the basal ganglia. This condition is known as "vascular Parkinsonism" (Thanvi et al., 2005). We typically associate particular diseases with a constellation of symptoms, but these associations are based on what parts of the brain are most often affected by these disease processes. Neuropsychologists can evaluate the symptoms that would be expected from damage to particular parts of the brain, whatever the cause, and help patients and their families adjust to these profound changes in their lives.

DISCUSSION QUESTIONS

1. What might happen if someone is mistakenly diagnosed with major neurocognitive disorder when it is actually a delirium?
2. You are asked to determine whether an older adult is experiencing delirium or dementia. Describe how you would approach this.
3. If you could find out the genetic likelihood that you will develop Alzheimer disease, would you want to know? Is it possible to have Alzheimer disease without having dementia?
4. A patient of yours has been diagnosed with mild neurocognitive disorder possibly due to Alzheimer disease. They ask you, "So does this mean I have Alzheimer disease?" Describe how you might answer their question.
5. This same patient asks you, "So what's the difference between Alzheimer disease and dementia?" Describe how you would answer this.
6. Describe the biomarkers of Alzheimer disease, as put forth in the NIA/AA diagnostic criteria.
7. A patient has recently developed an impairment in their visuospatial skills. Describe two conditions this may be caused by and how you might distinguish between the two.
8. Describe the two variants of frontotemporal dementia.

A robust set of instructor resources designed to supplement this text is located at http://connect.springerpub.com/content/book/978-0-8261-6617-3. Qualifying instructors may request access by emailing textbook@springerpub.com.

REFERENCES

Albert, M. S., DeKosky, S. T., Dickson, D., Dubois, B., Feldman, H. H., Fox, N. C., . . ., Phelps, C. H. (2011). The diagnosis of mild cognitive impairment due to Alzheimer's disease: Recommendations from the National Institute on Aging–Alzheimer's Association workgroups on diagnostic guidelines for Alzheimer's disease. *Alzheimer's & Dementia, 7*(3), 270–279. https://doi.org/10.1016/j.jalz.2011.03.008

Albrecht, J. S., Liu, X., Smith, G. S., Baumgarten, M., Rattinger, G. B., Gambert, S. R., . . ., Zuckerman, I. H. (2015). Stroke incidence following traumatic brain injury in older adults. *Journal of Head Trauma Rehabilitation, 30*(2), E62–E67. https://doi.org/10.1097/HTR.0000000000000035

American Psychiatric Association. (2022). *Diagnostic and statistical manual of mental disorders* (5th ed., text rev.). https://doi.org/10.1176/appi.books.9780890425787

Aschenbrenner, A. J., Gordon, B. A., Benzinger, T. L. S., Morris, J. C., & Hassenstab, J. J. (2018). Influence of tau PET, amyloid PET, and hippocampal volume on cognition in Alzheimer disease. *Neurology, 91*(9), e859–e866. https://doi-org.ucsf.idm.oclc.org/10.1212/WNL.0000000000006075

Balogun, S. A., & Philbrick, J. T. (2014). Delirium, a symptom of UTI in the elderly: Fact or fable? A systematic review. *Canadian Geriatrics Journal, 17*(1), 22–26. https://doi.org/10.5770/cgj.17.90

Blumenfeld, H. (2022). *Neuroanatomy through clinical cases* (3rd ed.). Oxford University Press.

Boeve, B. F., Boxer, A. L., Kumfor, F., Pijnenburg, Y., & Rohrer, J. D. (2022). Advances and controversies in frontotemporal dementia: diagnosis, biomarkers, and therapeutic considerations. *The Lancet. Neurology, 21*(3), 258–272. https://doi-org.ucsf.idm.oclc.org/10.1016/S1474-4422(21)00341-0

Boller, F., & Duykaerts, C. (2003). Alzheimer's disease: Clinical and anatomic issues. In T. E. Feinberg & M. J. Farah (Eds.), *Behavioral neurology and neuropsychology* (2nd ed., pp. 515–544). McGraw-Hill.

Braak, H., & Braak, E. (1991). Neuropathological staging of Alzheimer-related changes. *Acta Neu-ropathology, 82*(4), 239–259. https://doi.org/10.1007/BF00308809

Braak, H., Del Tredici, K., Rüb, U., de Vos, R. A. I., Jansen Steur, E. N., & Braak, E. (2003). Staging of brain pathology related to sporadic Parkinson's disease. *Neurobiology of Aging, 24*(2), 197–211. https://doi.org/10.1016/s0197-4580(02)00065-9

Cao, Q., Tan, C. C., Xu, W., Hu, H., Cao, X. P., Dong, Q., Tan, L., & Yu, J. T. (2020). The prevalence of dementia: A systematic review and meta-analysis. *Journal of Alzheimer's Disease, 73*(3), 1157–1166. https://doi-org.ucsf.idm.oclc.org/10.3233/JAD-191092

Centers for Disease Control and Prevention. (2022). *Surveillance report of traumatic brain injury-related deaths by age group, sex, and mechanism of injury—United States, 2018 and 2019*. Centers for Disease Control and Prevention, U.S. Department of Health and Human Services.

Chae, J. H. J., & Miller, B. J. (2015). Beyond urinary tract infections (UTIs) and delirium: A systematic review of UTIs and neuropsychiatric disorders. *Journal of Psychiatric Practice, 21*(6), 402–411. https://doi.org/10.1097/PRA.0000000000000105

Chan, V., Zagorski, B., Parsons, D., & Colantonio, A. (2013). Older adults with acquired brain injury: A population based study. *BioMed Central Geriatrics, 13*, 97. https://doi.org/10.1186/1471-2318-13-97

Chang Wong, E., & Chang Chui, H. (2022). Vascular cognitive impairment and dementia. *Continuum (Minneapolis, Minnesota), 28*(3), 750–780. https://doi-org.ucsf.idm.oclc.org/10.1212/CON.0000000000001124

Creupelandt, C., Maurage, P., & D'Hondt, F. (2021). Visuoperceptive impairments in severe alcohol use disorder: A critical review of behavioral studies. *Neuropsychology Review, 31*(3), 361–384. https://doi-org.ucsf.idm.oclc.org/10.1007/s11065-020-09469-x

Crutch, S. J., Schott, J. M., Rabinovici, G. D., Murray, M., Snowden, J. S., van der Flier, W. M., . . ., Fox, N. C. (2017). Consensus classification of posterior cortical atrophy. *Alzheimer's & Dementia, 13*(8), 870–884. https://doi.org/10.1016/j.jalz.2017.01.014

Daugherty, J., Waltzman, D., Sarmiento, K., Xu, L. (2019). Traumatic brain injury–related deaths by race/ethnicity, sex, intent, and mechanism of injury—United States, 2000–2017. *MMWR Morbidity and Mortality Weekly Report, 68*(46), 1050–1056. http://dx.doi.org/10.15585/mmwr.mm6846a2

de Haan, E., van Rijckevorsel, V. A. J. I. M., Bod, P., Roukema, G. R., de Jong, L., & Dutch Hip Fracture Registry Collaboration. (2023). Delirium after surgery for proximal femoral fractures in the frail elderly patient: Risk factors and clinical outcomes. *Clinical Interventions in Aging, 18*, 193–203. https://doi-org.ucsf.idm.oclc.org/10.2147/CIA.S390906

Emre, M., Aarsland, D., Brown, R., Burn, D. J., Duyckaerts, C., Mizuno, Y., . . ., Dubois, B. (2007). Clinical diagnostic criteria for dementia associated with Parkinson's disease. *Movement Disorders, 22*(12), 1689–1707. https://doi.org/10.1002/mds.21507

Ferman, T. J., Smith, G. E., Boeve, B. F., Ivnik, R. J., Petersen, R. C., Knopman, D., . . ., Dickson, D. W. (2004). DLB fluctuations: Specific features that reliably differentiate DLB from AD and normal aging. *Neurology, 62*(2), 181–187. https://doi.org/10.1212/wnl.62.2.181

Fortea, J., Zaman, S. H., Hartley, S., Rafii, M. S., Head, E., & Carmona-Iragui, M. (2021). Alzheimer's disease associated with Down syndrome: A genetic form of dementia. *The Lancet. Neurology, 20*(11), 930–942. https://doi-org.ucsf.idm.oclc.org/10.1016/S1474-4422(21)00245-3

GBD 2016 Traumatic Brain Injury and Spinal Cord Injury Collaborators. (2019). Global, regional, and national burden of traumatic brain injury and spinal cord injury, 1990–2016: A systematic analysis for the Global Burden of Disease Study 2016. *The Lancet. Neurology, 18*(1), 56–87. https://doi-org.ucsf.idm.oclc.org/10.1016/S1474-4422(18)30415-0

Gearing, M., Mirra, S. S., Hedreen, J. C., Sumi, S. M., Hansen, L. A., & Heyman, A. (1995). The Consortium to Establish a Registry for Alzheimer's Disease (CERAD), Part X. Neuropathology confirmation of the clinical diagnosis of Alzheimer's disease. *Neurology, 45*(3 Pt 1), 461–466. https://doi.org/10.1212/wnl.45.3.461

Ghneim, M., Brasel, K., Vesselinov, R., Albrecht, J., Liveris, A., Watras, J., Michetti, C., Haan, J., Lightwine, K., Winfield, R., Adams, S., Podbielski, J., Armen, S., Zacko, J. C., Nasrallah, F., Schaffer, K., Dunn, J., Smoot, B., Schroeppel, T., Stillman, Z., …, Additional Study Group Members of The American Association for the Surgery of Trauma Geri-TBI Study. (2022). Traumatic brain injury in older adults: Characteristics, outcomes, and considerations. Results from the American Association for the Surgery of Trauma Geriatric Traumatic Brain Injury (GERI-TBI) multicenter trial. *Journal of the American Medical Directors Association, 23*(4), 568–575.e1. https://doi-org.ucsf.idm.oclc.org/10.1016/j.jamda.2022.01.085

Gil-Garcia, C. A., Flores-Alvarez, E., Cebrian-Garcia, R., Mendoza-Lopez, A. C., Gonzalez-Hermosillo, L. M., Garcia-Blanco, M. D., & Roldan-Valadez, E. (2022). Essential topics about the imaging diagnosis and treatment of hemorrhagic stroke: A comprehensive review of the 2022 AHA guidelines. *Current Problems in Cardiology, 47*(11), 101328. https://doi-org.ucsf.idm.oclc.org/10.1016/j.cpcardiol.2022.101328

Gorno-Tempini, M. L., Hillis, A. E., Weintraub, S., Kertesz, A., Mendez, M., Cappa, S. F., . . ., Grossman, M. (2011). Classification of primary progressive aphasia and its variants. *Neurology, 76*(11), 1006–1014. https://doi.org/10.1212/WNL.0b013e31821103e6

Gottesman, R. F., Fornage, M., Knopman, D. S., & Mosley, T. H. (2015). Brain aging in African-Americans: The Atherosclerosis Risk in Communities (ARIC) experience. *Current Alzheimer Research, 12*(7), 607–613. https://doi.org/10.2174/1567205012666150701102445

Howell, M. J., & Schenck, C. H. (2015). Rapid eye movement sleep behavior disorder and neurodegenerative disease. *Journal of the American Medical Association Neurology, 72*(6), 707–712. https://doi.org/10.1001/jamaneurol.2014.4563

Hudomiet, P., Hurd, M. D., & Rohwedder, S. (2022). Trends in inequalities in the prevalence of dementia in the United States. *Proceedings of the National Academy of Sciences of the United States of America, 119*(46), e2212205119. https://doi-org.ucsf.idm.oclc.org/10.1073/pnas.2212205119

Hyun, J., Hall, C. B., Katz, M. J., Derby, C. A., Lipnicki, D. M., Crawford, J. D., Guaita, A., Vaccaro, R., Davin, A., Kim, K. W., Han, J. W., Bae, J. B., Röhr, S., Riedel-Heller, S., Ganguli, M., Jacobsen, E., Hughes, T. F., Brodaty, H., Kochan, N. A., Trollor, J., …, for Cohort Studies of Memory in an International Consortium. (2022). Education, occupational complexity, and incident dementia: A COSMIC Collaborative Cohort Study. *Journal of Alzheimer's Disease, 85*(1), 179–196. https://doi-org.ucsf.idm.oclc.org/10.3233/JAD-210627

Jack, C. R., Jr, Bennett, D. A., Blennow, K., Carrillo, M. C., Dunn, B., Haeberlein, S. B., Holtzman, D. M., Jagust, W., Jessen, F., Karlawish, J., Liu, E., Molinuevo, J. L., Montine, T., Phelps, C., Rankin, K. P., Rowe, C. C., Scheltens, P., Siemers, E., Snyder, H. M., Sperling, R., …, Contributors.

(2018). NIA-AA Research Framework: Toward a biological definition of Alzheimer's disease. *Alzheimer's & Dementia: The Journal of the Alzheimer's Association, 14*(4), 535–562. https://doi-org.ucsf.idm.oclc.org/10.1016/j.jalz.2018.02.018

Jack, C. R., Jr, Therneau, T. M., Weigand, S. D., Wiste, H. J., Knopman, D. S., Vemuri, P., Lowe, V. J., Mielke, M. M., Roberts, R. O., Machulda, M. M., Graff-Radford, J., Jones, D. T., Schwarz, C. G., Gunter, J. L., Senjem, M. L., Rocca, W. A., & Petersen, R. C. (2019). Prevalence of biologically vs clinically defined Alzheimer spectrum entities using the National Institute on Aging–Alzheimer's Association Research Framework. *JAMA Neurology, 76*(10), 1174–1183. https://doi-org.ucsf.idm.oclc.org/10.1001/jamaneurol.2019.1971

Janelidze, S., Stomrud, E., Palmqvist, S., Zetterberg, H., van Westen, D., Jeromin, A., Song, L., Hanlon, D., Tan Hehir, C. A., Baker, D., Blennow, K., & Hansson, O. (2016). Plasma β-amyloid in Alzheimer's disease and vascular disease. *Scientific Reports, 6*, 26801. https://doi-org.ucsf.idm.oclc.org/10.1038/srep26801

Jansen, I. E., Savage, J. E., Watanabe, K., Bryois, J., Williams, D. M., Steinberg, S., Sealock, J., Karlsson, I. K., Hägg, S., Athanasiu, L., Voyle, N., Proitsi, P., Witoelar, A., Stringer, S., Aarsland, D., Almdahl, I. S., Andersen, F., Bergh, S., Bettella, F., Bjornsson, S., …, Posthuma, D. (2019). Genome-wide meta-analysis identifies new loci and functional pathways influencing Alzheimer's disease risk. *Nature Genetics, 51*(3), 404–413. https://doi-org.ucsf.idm.oclc.org/10.1038/s41588-018-0311-9

Kivimäki, M., Singh-Manoux, A., Batty, G. D., Sabia, S., Sommerlad, A., Floud, S., Jokela, M., Vahtera, J., Beydoun, M. A., Suominen, S. B., Koskinen, A., Väänänen, A., Goldberg, M., Zins, M., Alfredsson, L., Westerholm, P. J. M., Knutsson, A., Nyberg, S. T., Sipilä, P. N., Lindbohm, J. V., …, Strandberg, T. (2020). Association of alcohol-induced loss of consciousness and overall alcohol consumption with risk for dementia. *JAMA Network Open, 3*(9), e2016084. https://doi-org.ucsf.idm.oclc.org/10.1001/jamanetworkopen.2020.16084

Koch, M., Fitzpatrick, A. L., Rapp, S. R., Nahin, R. L., Williamson, J. D., Lopez, O. L., DeKosky, S. T., Kuller, L. H., Mackey, R. H., Mukamal, K. J., Jensen, M. K., & Sink, K. M. (2019). Alcohol consumption and risk of dementia and cognitive decline among older adults with or without mild cognitive impairment. *JAMA Network Open, 2*(9), e1910319. https://doi-org.ucsf.idm.oclc.org/10.1001/jamanetworkopen.2019.10319

Kon, T., Tomiyama, M., & Wakabayashi, K. (2020). Neuropathology of Lewy body disease: Clinicopathological crosstalk between typical and atypical cases. *Neuropathology: Official Journal of the Japanese Society of Neuropathology, 40*(1), 30–39. https://doi-org.ucsf.idm.oclc.org/10.1111/neup.12597

Krinitski, D., Kasina, R., Klöppel, S., & Lenouvel, E. (2021). Associations of delirium with urinary tract infections and asymptomatic bacteriuria in adults aged 65 and older: A systematic review and meta-analysis. *Journal of the American Geriatrics Society, 69*(11), 3312–3323. https://doi-org.ucsf.idm.oclc.org/10.1111/jgs.17418

Kueper, J. K., Speechley, M., & Montero-Odasso, M. (2018). The Alzheimer's Disease Assessment Scale-Cognitive Subscale (ADAS-Cog): Modifications and responsiveness in pre-dementia populations: A narrative review. *Journal of Alzheimer's Disease, 63*(2), 423–444. https://doi.org/10.3233/JAD-170991

The Lancet. (2022). Lecanemab for Alzheimer's disease: Tempering hype and hope. *Lancet (London, England), 400*(10367), 1899. https://doi.org/10.1016/S0140-6736(22)02480-1

Lee, M., Whitsel, E., Avery, C., Hughes, T. M., Griswold, M. E., Sedaghat, S., Gottesman, R. F., Mosley, T. H., Heiss, G., & Lutsey, P. L. (2022). Variation in population attributable fraction of dementia associated with potentially modifiable risk factors by race and ethnicity in the US. *JAMA Network Open, 5*(7), e2219672. https://doi-org.ucsf.idm.oclc.org/10.1001/jamanetworkopen.2022.19672

Lingehall, H. C., Smulter, N. S., Lindahl, E., Lindkvist, M., Engström, K. G., Gustafson, Y. G., & Olofsson, B. (2017). Preoperative cognitive performance and postoperative delirium are independently associated with future dementia in older people who have undergone cardiac surgery: A longitudinal cohort study. *Critical Care Medicine, 45*(8), 1295–1303. https://doi.org/10.1097/CCM.0000000000002483

Litvan, I., Goldman, J. G., Tröster, A. I., Schmand, B. A., Weintraub, D., Petersen, R. C., . . ., Emre, M. (2012). Diagnostic criteria for mild cognitive impairment in Parkinson's disease: Movement

Disorder Society task force guidelines. *Movement Disorders, 27*(3), 349–356. https://doi.org/10.1002/mds.24893

Mackenzie, I. R., & Neumann, M. (2016). Molecular neuropathology of frontotemporal dementia: Insights into disease mechanisms from postmortem studies. *Journal of Neurochemistry, 138*(Suppl 1), 54–70. https://doi-org.ucsf.idm.oclc.org/10.1111/jnc.13588

Mattis, S. (1988). *Dementia rating scale. Professional manual.* Psychological Assessment Resources.

McKeith, I. G., Boeve, B. F., Dickson, D. W., Halliday, G., Taylor, J.-P., Weintraub, D., . . ., Kosaka, K. (2017). Diagnosis and management of dementia with Lewy bodies: Fourth consensus report of the DLB Consortium. *Neurology, 89*(1), 88–100. https://doi.org/10.1212/WNL.0000000000004058

McKhann, G. M., Knopman, D. S., Chertkow, H., Hyman, B. T., Jack, C. R., Kawas, C. H., . . ., Phelps, C. H. (2011). The diagnosis of dementia due to Alzheimer's disease: Recommendations from the National Institute on Aging—Alzheimer's Association workgroups on di-agnostic guidelines for Alzheimer's disease. *Alzheimer's & Dementia, 7*(3), 263–269. https://doi.org/10.1016/j.jalz.2011.03.005

Meng, Y. H., Wang, P. P., Song, Y. X., & Wang, J. H. (2019). Cholinesterase inhibitors and memantine for Parkinson's disease dementia and Lewy body dementia: A meta-analysis. *Experimental and Therapeutic Medicine, 17*(3), 1611–1624. https://doi.org/10.3892/etm.2018.7129

Mewton, L., Visontay, R., Hoy, N., Lipnicki, D. M., Sunderland, M., Lipton, R. B., Guerchet, M., Ritchie, K., Najar, J., Scarmeas, N., Kim, K. W., Riedel Heller, S., van Boxtel, M., Jacobsen, E., Brodaty, H., Anstey, K. J., Haan, M., Scazufca, M., Lobo, E., Sachdev, P. S., …, Collaborators from the Cohort Studies of Memory in an International Consortium. (2023). The relationship between alcohol use and dementia in adults aged more than 60 years: A combined analysis of prospective, individual-participant data from 15 international studies. *Addiction (Abingdon, England), 118*(3), 412–424. https://doi-org.ucsf.idm.oclc.org/10.1111/add.16035

Morris J. C. (1993). The Clinical Dementia Rating (CDR): Current version and scoring rules. *Neurology, 43*(11), 2412–2414. https://doi-org.ucsf.idm.oclc.org/10.1212/wnl.43.11.2412-a

Nelson, P. T., Dickson, D. W., Trojanowski, J. Q., Jack, C. R., Boyle, P. A., Arfanakis, K., Rademakers, R., Alafuzoff, I., Attems, J., Brayne, C., Coyle-Gilchrist, I. T. S., Chui, H. C., Fardo, D. W., Flanagan, M. E., Halliday, G., Hokkanen, S. R. K., Hunter, S., Jicha, G. A., Katsumata, Y., Kawas, C. H., …, Schneider, J. A. (2019). Limbic-predominant age-related TDP-43 encephalopathy (LATE): Consensus working group report. *Brain: A Journal of Neurology, 142*(6), 1503–1527. https://doi-org.ucsf.idm.oclc.org/10.1093/brain/awz099

Newell, K. L., Hyman, B. T., Growdon, J. H., & Hedley-Whyte, E. T. (1999). Application of the National Institute on Aging (NIA)—Reagan Institute criteria for the neuropathological diagnosis of Alzheimer disease. *Journal of Neuropathology and Experimental Neurology, 58*(11), 1147–1155. https://doi.org/10.1097/00005072-199911000-00004

Ngandu, T., Lehtisalo, J., Solomon, A., Levälahti, E., Ahtiluoto, S., Antikainen, R., Bäckman, L., Hänninen, T., Jula, A., Laatikainen, T., Lindström, J., Mangialasche, F., Paajanen, T., Pajala, S., Peltonen, M., Rauramaa, R., Stigsdotter-Neely, A., Strandberg, T., Tuomilehto, J., Soininen, H., …, Kivipelto, M. (2015). A 2-year multidomain intervention of diet, exercise, cognitive training, and vascular risk monitoring versus control to prevent cognitive decline in at-risk elderly people (FINGER): A randomized controlled trial. *Lancet (London, England), 385*(9984), 2255–2263. https://doi-org.ucsf.idm.oclc.org/10.1016/S0140-6736(15)60461-5

Nichols, E., Merrick, R., Hay, S. I., Himali, D., Himali, J. J., Hunter, S., Keage, H. A. D., Latimer, C. S., Scott, M. R., Steinmetz, J. D., Walker, J. M., Wharton, S. B., Wiedner, C. D., Crane, P. K., Keene, C. D., Launer, L. J., Matthews, F. E., Schneider, J., Seshadri, S., White, L., …, Vos, T. (2023). The prevalence, correlation, and co-occurrence of neuropathology in old age: Harmonization of 12 measures across six community-based autopsy studies of dementia. *The Lancet. Healthy longevity, 4*(3), e115–e125. https://doi-org.ucsf.idm.oclc.org/10.1016/S2666-7568(23)00019-3

Oslin, D., Atkinson, R. M., Smith, D. M., & Hendrie, H. (1998). Alcohol related dementia: Proposed clinical criteria. *International Journal of Geriatric Psychiatry, 13*(4), 203–212. https://doi-org.ucsf.idm.oclc.org/10.1002/(sici)1099-1166(199804)13:4<203::aid-gps734>3.0.co;2-b

Rao, R., & Topiwala, A. (2020). Alcohol use disorders and the brain. *Addiction (Abingdon, England), 115*(8), 1580–1589. https://doi-org.ucsf.idm.oclc.org/10.1111/add.15023

Regenhardt, R. W., Das, A. S., Ohtomo, R., Lo, E. H., Ayata, C., & Gurol, M. E. (2019). Pathophysiology of lacunar stroke: History's mysteries and modern interpretations. *Journal of Stroke and Cerebrovascular Diseases: The Official Journal of National Stroke Association, 28*(8), 2079–2097. https://doi.org/10.1016/j.jstrokecerebrovasdis.2019.05.006

Ridley, N. J., Draper, B., & Withall, A. (2013). Alcohol-related dementia: An update of the evidence. *Alzheimer's Research and Therapy, 5*(1), 3. https://doi.org/10.1186/alzrt157

Rosen, W. G., Mohs, R. C., & Davis, K. L. (1984). A new rating scale for Alzheimer's disease. *The American Journal of Psychiatry, 141*(11), 1356–1364. https://doi.org/10.1176/ajp.141.11.1356

Scheltens, P., De Strooper, B., Kivipelto, M., Holstege, H., Chételat, G., Teunissen, C. E., Cummings, J., & van der Flier, W. M. (2021). Alzheimer's disease. *Lancet, 397*(10284), 1577–1590. https://doi-org.ucsf.idm.oclc.org/10.1016/S0140-6736(20)32205-4

Schneider, J. A., Arvanitakis, Z., Bang, W., & Bennett, D. A. (2007). Mixed brain pathologies account for most dementia cases in community-dwelling older persons. *Neurology, 69*(24), 2197–2204. https://doi.org/10.1212/01.wnl.0000271090.28148.24

Sezgin, M., Bilgic, B., Tinaz, S., & Emre, M. (2019). Parkinson's disease dementia and Lewy body disease. *Seminars in Neurology, 39*(2), 274–282. https://doi-org.ucsf.idm.oclc.org/10.1055/s-0039-1678579

Sharma, K. (2019). Cholinesterase inhibitors as Alzheimer's therapeutics (review). *Molecular Medicine Reports, 20*(2), 1479–1487. https://doi.org/10.3892/mmr.2019.10374

Souza-Talarico, J. N., Carvalho, A. P., Brucki, S. M. D., Nitrini, R., & Ferretti-Rebustini, R. E. L. (2016). Dementia and cognitive impairment prevalence and associated factors in indigenous populations: A systematic review. *Alzheimer's Disease and Associated Disorders, 30*(3), 281–287. https://doi.org/10.1097/WAD.0000000000000140

Stavro, K., Pelletier, J., & Potvin, S. (2013). Widespread and sustained cognitive deficits in alcoholism: A meta-analysis. *Addiction Biology, 18*(2), 203–213. https://doi-org.ucsf.idm.oclc.org/10.1111/j.1369-1600.2011.00418.x

Taylor, J. P., McKeith, I. G., Burn, D. J., Boeve, B. F., Weintraub, D., Bamford, C., Allan, L. M., Thomas, A. J., & O'Brien, J. T. (2020). New evidence on the management of Lewy body dementia. *The Lancet. Neurology, 19*(2), 157–169. https://doi-org.ucsf.idm.oclc.org/10.1016/S1474-4422(19)30153-X

Thanvi, B., Lo, N., & Robinson, T. (2005). Vascular Parkinsonism—An important cause of Parkinsonism in older people. *Age and Ageing, 34*(2), 114–119. https://doi.org/10.1093/ageing/afi025

Tiraboschi, P., Salmon, D. P., Hansen, L. A., Hofstetter, R. C., Thal, L. J., & Corey-Bloom, J. (2006). What best differentiates Lewy body from Alzheimer's disease in early-stage dementia? *Brain, 129*(Pt 3), 729–735. https://doi.org/10.1093/brain/awh725

U.S. Department of Agriculture & U.S. Department of Health and Human Services. (2020). *Dietary guidelines for Americans, 2020–2025* (9th ed). DietaryGuidelines.gov

Vaci, N., Koychev, I., Kim, C. H., Kormilitzin, A., Liu, Q., Lucas, C., Dehghan, A., Nenadic, G., & Nevado-Holgado, A. (2021). Real-world effectiveness, its predictors and onset of action of cholinesterase inhibitors and memantine in dementia: Retrospective health record study. *The British Journal of Psychiatry: The Journal of Mental Science, 218*(5), 261–267. https://doi.org/10.1192/bjp.2020.136

van Dyck, C. H., Swanson, C. J., Aisen, P., Bateman, R. J., Chen, C., Gee, M., Kanekiyo, M., Li, D., Reyderman, L., Cohen, S., Froelich, L., Katayama, S., Sabbagh, M., Vellas, B., Watson, D., Dhadda, S., Irizarry, M., Kramer, L. D., & Iwatsubo, T. (2023). Lecanemab in early Alzheimer's disease. *The New England Journal of Medicine, 388*(1), 9–21. https://doi.org/10.1056/NEJMoa2212948

Vieira, R. T., Caixeta, L., Machado, S., Silva, A. C., Nardi, A. E., Arias-Carrion, O., & Carta, M. G. (2013). Epidemiology of early-onset dementia: A review of the literature. *Clinical Practice & Epidemiology in Mental Health, 9*, 88–95. https://doi.org/10.2174/1745017901309010088

Vinters, H. V. (2015). Emerging concepts in Alzheimer's disease. *Annual Review of Pathology: Mechanisms of Disease, 10*, 291–319. https://doi.org/10.1146/annurev-pathol-020712-163927

Visontay, R., Rao, R. T., & Mewton, L. (2021). Alcohol use and dementia: New research directions. *Current Opinion in Psychiatry, 34*(2), 165–170. https://doi-org.ucsf.idm.oclc.org/10.1097/YCO.0000000000000679

Walker, Z., Possin, K. L., Boeve, B. F., & Aarsland, D. (2015). Lewy body dementias. *Lancet, 386*(10004), 1683–1697. https://doi.org/10.1016/S0140-6736(15)00462-6

Williams-Gray, C. H., Mason, S. L., Evans, J. R., Foltynie, T., Brayne, C., Robbins, T. W., & Barker, R. A. (2013). The CamPaIGN study of Parkinson's disease: 10-year outlook in an incident population-based cohort. *Journal of Neurology, Neurosurgery, and Psychiatry, 84*(11), 1258–1264. https://doi-org.ucsf.idm.oclc.org/10.1136/jnnp-2013-305277

Wolters, F. J., Chibnik, L. B., Waziry, R., Anderson, R., Berr, C., Beiser, A., Bis, J. C., Blacker, D., Bos, D., Brayne, C., Dartigues, J. F., Darweesh, S. K. L., Davis-Plourde, K. L., de Wolf, F., Debette, S., Dufouil, C., Fornage, M., Goudsmit, J., Grasset, L., Gudnason, V., …, Hofman, A. (2020). Twenty-seven-year time trends in dementia incidence in Europe and the United States: The Alzheimer Cohorts Consortium. *Neurology, 95*(5), e519–e531. https://doi-org.ucsf.idm.oclc.org/10.1212/WNL.0000000000010022

Younes, K., & Miller, B. L. (2020). Frontotemporal dementia: Neuropathology, genetics, neuroimaging, and treatments. *The Psychiatric Clinics of North America, 43*(2), 331–344. https://doi-org.ucsf.idm.oclc.org/10.1016/j.psc.2020.02.006

Zhu, Y., Chen, Y., Crimmins, E. M., & Zissimopoulos, J. M. (2021). Sex, race, and age differences in prevalence of dementia in medicare claims and survey data. *The Journals of Gerontology. Series B, Psychological Sciences and Social Sciences, 76*(3), 596–606. https://doi-org.ucsf.idm.oclc.org/10.1093/geronb/gbaa083

11

Death and the Dying Process, Bereavement, and Widowhood

Andrea June and Meghan A. Marty

> **LEARNING OBJECTIVES**
>
> - Describe recent U.S. trends in type and location of death.
> - Explain the role of advance planning and available healthcare options facing a terminal illness.
> - Compare and contrast the commonly interchanged words of grief, bereavement, and mourning.
> - Differentiate symptoms of bereavement and other clinical diagnoses.
> - Identify theoretical models and interventions for coping with bereavement.
> - Discuss the impact of sociodemographic variables on coping with bereavement.

The topic of death has tremendous biopsychosocial complexity. We discuss it under the social aspects of aging because familial, societal, and cultural norms provide the context for understanding the how, when, and where of our deaths as well as our experiences of bereavement and grief. And yet, near the end of life, it is important to note that each person prepares for and faces the challenges differently. The varying illnesses and physical conditions combined with the individual uniqueness that we bring to the dying and bereavement processes create this biopsychosocial complexity. The challenge of our legal, healthcare, and community systems is to meet these diverse individual needs while evolving with society's changing norms. These topics are globally relevant, as they impact all of humanity, and yet it is important to note that any discussion of these topics is also inherently bound by one's cultural perspective. As such, we acknowledge a primary and limited focus on the multicultural American society in our discussion of end-of-life issues in this chapter.

DYING IN AMERICA

Definition and Causes of Death

The legal and medical communities have long contended with how to determine when someone has died. Previously defined as the absence of heartbeat and respiration, advances in medical technology (e.g., ventilators and defibrillators) have blurred the definitive moment at which the transition from life to death takes place (Parent & Turi, 2020). The Uniform Declaration of Death Act of 1980 provided guidance to state law makers and offered an expansion to the definition. Approved by the American Medical Association and American Bar Association and still used today, the determination of death can also be made when the function of the circulatory and respiratory systems or the entire brain, including brainstem and neocortex, irreversibly ceases. Nonetheless, this well-established definition continues to be controversial among philosophers and scientists. Recent biomedical ethicists have recommended updating the law to reflect *permanent* cessation, rather than irreversible, and a focus on neurorespiratory criteria needed to regain consciousness (Omelianchuk et al., 2022; Parent & Turi, 2020). Omelianchuk et al. (2022) have proposed revising it to "brain injury leading to permanent loss of the capacity for consciousness, the ability to breathe spontaneously, and brainstem reflexes" (p. 532).

Life expectancy and the leading causes of death have shifted in the past 100 years due to medical advances, improved disease prevention, and health promotion. Without antibiotics, acute infections could not be cured; death occurred rapidly and throughout the life course in the early 1900s. Life expectancy at birth reached a peak of 78.8 years in 2019, but decreased to 77 years with the emergence of the COVID-19 pandemic in 2020 (Kochanek et al., 2020; Murphy et al., 2021). Indeed, 2021 saw the highest death rate since 2003 due to COVID-19 and additional increases in death rates due to unintentional injuries (i.e., drug overdose), chronic liver disease and cirrhosis, suicide, and homicide (Ahmad et al., 2022). The highest overall death rates by age occurred among persons aged ≥85 years, and the highest overall age-adjusted death rates at the intersections of sex, race, and ethnicity occurred among males of non-Hispanic American Indian or Alaska Native (AI/AN) and non-Hispanic Black or African American populations (Ahmad et al., 2022). Age-adjusted death rates differed by race and ethnicity and decreased for all groups from 2021 to 2022. Overall age-adjusted death rates were lowest among multiracial and Asian persons and highest among Black and AI/AN persons (Ahmad et al., 2023b). The three leading causes of death in 2022 were heart disease, cancer, and unintentional injury. COVID-19 fell to fourth place in 2022 due to a large decrease in COVID-19–associated deaths compared with those in 2021 (Xu et al., 2022). Although the overall and COVID-19–associated death rates decreased for persons aged ≥85 years from 2021 to 2022, rates remained higher for this group compared with all other age groups. In addition, although overall and COVID-19–associated death rates decreased among all racial and ethnic groups, age-adjusted total and COVID-19–associated death rates remained high for Black and AI/AN persons compared with other groups (Ahmad et al., 2023a).

Institutionalization of Death

Increased life expectancy and advances in medicine have not only changed the causes of death but also the context of death and dying. Prior to 1900, the multigenerational family assumed responsibility for all activities surrounding death, and the majority of people died at home (Corr et al., 2009). Over time, Americans have turned this responsibility over to paid professionals. By 1949, nearly 50% of deaths occurred in a healthcare institution (Corr et al., 2009). More recent data from 2018 show that approximately 35% of all U.S. deaths occurred in medical facilities (Centers for Disease Control and Prevention, National Center for Health Statistics, 2020). An additional 27% of U.S. deaths occurred in a nursing home or long-term care facility compared with the 31% who died at home. Between 2020 and 2022, the most common location of COVID-19 deaths was a hospital inpatient setting, with 59% reported in 2022 (Ahmad et al., 2023a).

Death Trajectories

Understanding the different trajectories of dying associated with the leading causes of death is important because of the impact of expected survival on quality of life, care decisions, and family concerns (Kwak et al., 2011). In *Time for Dying*, Glaser and Strauss (1968) proposed several common dying trajectories found in American hospitals based on their field observations: gradual slant, downward slope, peaks and valleys, and descending plateaus. Lunney et al. (2002) later modified the theory to four modal trajectories: sudden death, terminal illness, organ failure, and frailty. The terminal illness category is found among certain types of cancer and is characterized by individuals maintaining a high functional status that rapidly declines. Individuals with chronic obstructive pulmonary disease or congestive heart failure would be in the organ failure group, who experience gradually decreasing functional ability including periods of increased symptom intensity and disability. The frailty trajectory involves slow decline of functional ability with steadily progressive disability as a result of such illnesses as neurocognitive disorders. However, as with any research aggregated to a group level, these identified trajectories do not preclude individual variation of symptoms or functional decline within a given disease process (Gott et al., 2007).

ATTITUDES TOWARD DEATH

Research supports the notion that fear of death is a universal human phenomenon and that our awareness of the inevitability of death and dying creates apprehension and anxiety (Becker, 1973). Variables such as gender, age, race and ethnicity, religious beliefs, personality traits, health status, purpose, having children, and marital status are frequently studied and are variables that affect death anxiety, though the relationship is often complex and intertwined (Fortner et al., 2000; Jong, 2021; Kahraman & Erkent, 2023). Attitudes toward an individual's own impending death have also been an important subject of scientific inquiry. Although not the first effort to seek to understand the experience of dying individuals, Kübler-Ross's (1969) *On Death and Dying* resonated with the public and scientific communities when she posited that dying persons went through a series of five attitudes toward death: *denial, anger, bargaining, depression,* and *acceptance*. Evaluation of her theory of stages has revealed many criticisms and yet, the articulation of her theory served a pivotal role in the development of the field. Several contemporary theories merit mention, as they have evolved to reflect current trends in the illness experience. Building upon the work of his predecessors, Rando (2000) discussed the concept of *anticipatory mourning* as the diverse reactions and coping processes of individuals and families experienced during the course of a life-limiting illness, including the anticipation of future losses. Hong and Cagle (2019) also provide evidence of the general premise of terror management theory. Specifically, they note that increased exposure to reminders that you will die one day, and therefore addressing personal discomfort with death, may reduce death anxiety, improve comfort with talking about death, and then lead to better attitudes or better management of end-of-life care.

ADVANCE CARE PLANNING

Advance care planning is a broad term describing various processes by which an individual communicates choices about future end-of-life decisions (National Institute on Aging, 2022). These choices can be communicated informally through discussion and/or formally through documented advance directives to healthcare providers, biological or chosen family, friends, or spiritual guides. The most common advance care planning preparations include completion of a living will or a do-not-resuscitate order and appointment of a durable power of attorney. Physician orders for life-sustaining treatment (POLST) documents, also known as portable medical orders, are another mechanism for advance care planning increasingly used in many states (National POLST, 2022). Completed by a patient in consultation with healthcare providers during a medical appointment, POLSTs provide doctor's orders regarding the specific treatments to be administered or withheld in medical scenarios that are common at the end of life (Schmidt et al., 2014). Because most people nearing the end of life are not physically, mentally, or cognitively able to make their own decisions about care, advance care planning is essential to ensure that individuals receive care reflecting their values, goals, and preferences (Institute of Medicine [IOM], 2014). Advance care planning is considered an essential step for achieving a "good death" in which physical pain and emotional distress are minimized and the patient's and family members' treatment preferences are respected (Carr & Luth, 2016). It is also linked to practices that contribute to both superior patient and survivor well-being—reduced use of aggressive, costly, and futile treatments at the end of life and greater use of palliative care (IOM, 2014). Moreover, advance care planning is also associated with better outcomes for family members, including reduced decision-making burden, and fewer anxiety and depressive symptoms (Weathers et al., 2016).

Legislation requiring that individuals are educated about their choices was established by the Patient Self-Determination Act (PSDA; Omnibus Budget Reconciliation Act, 1990), which applies to all healthcare institutions receiving federal funds such as Medicare. Specifically, individuals have the right to facilitate their own healthcare decisions, accept or refuse medical treatments, and execute an advance directive. The PSDA also requires institutions to inquire about whether an individual has completed an advance directive and to document its presence in the medical record. Between 1990 and 2003, the number of advance directives completed more than doubled (Carr &

Luth, 2017). Despite the available provisions to make these choices known in advance, individuals and families in death-averse societies often wait until a medical crisis is imminent before considering preferences. It is a frequently cited statistic that although approximately 80% agree with the value of an advance directive, less than 40% of American adults have one documented (Genewick et al., 2018). Among older adults, completion rates are slightly higher. Zhu and Enguidanos (2022) found that among adults aged 50 years or older and their partners, 44% had completed an advance directive.

Predictors of advance directive completion are complex and involve patient, provider, societal and familial influence, and location factors (Genewick et al., 2018). Older age is associated with completion of advance directives across all health institutions (Lovell & Yates, 2014). Advance directives are more common among individuals receiving any type of long-term care (Jones et al., 2011). This is consistent with literature showing that patients with chronic or terminal disease have a higher rate of advance directive completion than those who do not (Rao et al., 2014). Although exact estimates vary across samples, and the disparity has narrowed over time, rates of advance care planning remain low among Black and Latin(x) populations compared with non-Hispanic Whites (Carr, 2011; Koss & Baker, 2017). This may reflect differences in a preference for more aggressive care, a historically based distrust in the healthcare system to provide quality care, a preference for family to communicate wishes rather than using a written document, a belief that one's God controls the timing and nature of death, a cultural taboo against openly discussing or planning for a death, or a lower level of health literacy among minority populations (Carr, 2011; Waite et al., 2013). Adults with lower levels of education and literacy also are less likely to do advance care planning, in part because they are reluctant to make decisions about treatments they do not fully understand (Porensky & Carpenter, 2008; Waite et al., 2013).

PALLIATIVE AND HOSPICE CARE

World Health Organization (WHO, 2023) offers a definition of palliative care as an approach that improves the quality of life of patients and their families by focusing on assessment and treatment of physical, psychosocial, and spiritual needs. However, this definition does not provide clarity as to the difference between hospice and palliative care with regard to treatment options. Indeed, these terms are so frequently referred to as one entity that many people do not realize there is a distinction in many countries. Palliative care is focused on treatment of any conditions that are life limiting at any point in the disease trajectory without limiting curative approaches, whereas hospice care refers to a special type of comprehensive palliative care provided during the last 6 months of life when an individual has chosen to forgo aggressive, life-prolonging treatments and focus on quality of life (National Institute on Aging, 2021). Figure 11.1 shows a representation of the proposed model of care for those with life-limiting illness that helps distinguish the two types of care.

Palliative care in hospital settings is most often provided by a consult team of healthcare workers composed of a physician, nurse, social worker, and chaplain. However, with increasing frequency, palliative care consult teams and hospice teams have expanded to include other professionals such as psychologists, pharmacists,

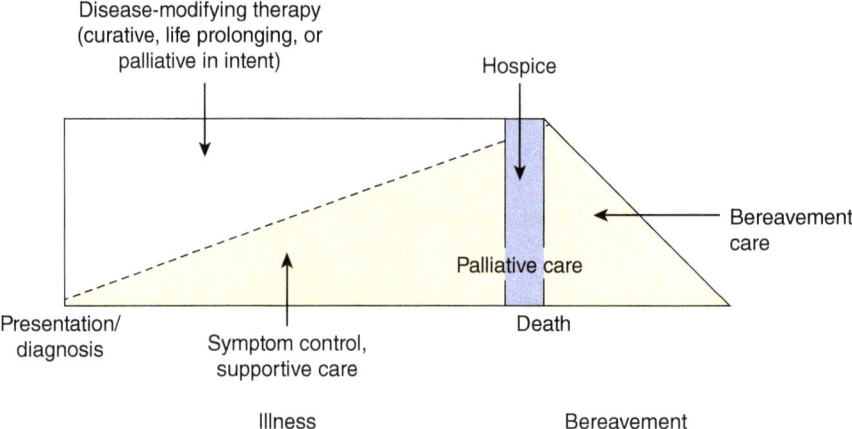

Figure 11.1 Continuum of care.
Source: EPEC (Education for Physicians on End-of-Life Care) Participant's Handbook. The Robert Wood Johnson Foundation/American Medical Association. © The EPEC Project, 1999. Reprinted with permission of Northwestern University.

dietitians, occupational or physical therapists, and volunteers (National Institute on Aging, 2021). Evidence suggests that when terminally ill individuals and their families are under the care of a palliative or hospice team, outcomes are improved. Utilization is associated with reduced symptom burden, higher well-being and dignity, decreased intensity of treatment nearing the end of life, and increased family satisfaction with care (Bükki et al., 2013; Connor et al., 2005; Miller et al., 2002). Despite the positive outcomes cited for these quality-of-life care options for terminally ill individuals and their families, hospice and palliative care services are underutilized. Providers and families may be reluctant to discuss it, believing that a referral to palliative or hospice care symbolizes "giving up" on the individual and that there is no hope (Le et al., 2014). Indeed, the underutilization of palliative care is often compounded by misinformation about how it differs from hospice. Other factors that may influence utilization include lower healthcare literacy, experience of discriminatory healthcare practices and behaviors (based on age, race, ethnicity, gender, or sexual orientation), beliefs that suffering in death is part of a divine plan, concerns about how it is paid for, and unequal or poor access to medical care (Addis et al., 2009; Shalev et al., 2018).

MENTAL HEALTH AT THE END OF LIFE

While not inevitable during the dying process, individuals at the end of life may experience a range of mental health disorders, including depression, anxiety, delirium, or dementia, along with emotional distress associated with loss of autonomy/control, loss of dignity, fear, grief, or existential and spiritual concerns (Werth et al., 2002). Among adults receiving palliative care, the estimated prevalence of depression ranges from 24% to 70% (Perusinghe et al., 2021). *Demoralization*, a common presentation of existential distress at the end of life, includes symptoms of hopelessness and helplessness, thought to be caused by a loss of purpose and meaning in life, and is clinically significant in an estimated 13% to 18% of individuals with progressive disease or cancer (Robinson et al., 2015). A number of psychotherapeutic individual and group interventions have been developed that aim to alleviate emotional distress and existential suffering in patients with life-threatening illness. Several meta-analytic studies suggest these interventions are generally effective and improvement is sustained over time (e.g., Bauereiß et al., 2018; Faller et al., 2013), while others are more equivocal (e.g., Perusinghe et al., 2021). Mounting empirical evidence suggests that people with advanced or terminal illness can benefit from psychedelic-assisted therapies for the management of a range of symptoms, including those of a physical, psychosocial, and spiritual nature (Maia et al., 2022). However, more research is needed to better understand the safety and efficacy of these agents among older adults, particularly those with comorbid conditions such as cardiovascular disease, as very few older adults have been included in existing clinical trials, and those who were included tended to be the "young old" (younger than 75) and relatively healthy (Johnston et al., 2023; Nigam et al., 2023).

MEDICAL AID IN DYING

In medical aid in dying (MAID), a physician provides the means to enable an individual to end their life. In contrast, euthanasia is the deliberate termination of life carried out by a physician. Globally, euthanasia is less likely to be legal or be socially supported than MAID. Euthanasia is not legal in the United States. MAID is legal or tolerated in many countries, and although there are no federal laws in the United States permitting it, several states have enacted laws allowing and regulating it.

Oregon voters passed the first MAID legislation in 1994 with the Death With Dignity Act that went into effect in 1997, and most current legislation is modeled after it. This legislation permits adult residents of the state to voluntarily end their lives with self-administration of lethal medication prescribed from a licensed physician, provided certain specifications are met. The patient must be deemed by two physicians, one prescribing and one consulting, to have a terminal illness and less than 6 months to live. The physicians must also determine that the resident is capable of making an informed healthcare decision and is acting voluntarily. The physicians are required to discuss all healthcare alternatives to MAID with the patient including hospice and palliative care. If either physician believes the patient's judgment is impaired by a mental disorder, the patient must be referred for a psychological evaluation. Finally, patients must request MAID twice verbally separated by at least 15 days and once in writing signed in the presence of two witnesses (www.oregon.gov/oha). According to the most recent report by the Death With Dignity National Center, 10 states plus the District of Columbia currently have laws in place to support medical aid in dying (Oregon [1994], Washington [2008], Montana [2009], Vermont [2013], California [2015], Colorado [2016], District of Columbia [2017], Hawaii [2019], Maine [2019], New Jersey [2019], and New Mexico [2021]). An additional six states are considering Death With Dignity legislation during the 2024 legislative session. Detailed history of political advocacy efforts for each state can be found on the website deathwithdignity.org/states/.

As required by law, each year, the Oregon Health Authority and Washington State Department of Health publish information about their residents' usage of these acts. Analyzing the data from 1998 to 2017 in Oregon and from 2009 to 2017 in Washington, Al Rabadi et al. (2019) reported that a combined 3,368 prescriptions were written, with 2,558 deaths from ingesting the lethal medication. Kozlov et al. (2022) examined available public records from 1998 to 2020 and summarized data from the nine U.S. jurisdictions with MAID laws at the time. They reported that 5,329 patients died by MAID, while 8,451 received a prescription. Although the specific percentages differ regarding those using MAID, the overall findings reported in these studies are similar. Individuals who die under MAID tend to be older, non-Hispanic White, educated, and diagnosed with cancer. Frequency by sex is split, with slightly more males having died by MAID. With increased age of the legislation, MAID use also increases in each jurisdiction. Kozlov et al. (2022) note it may become clearer with time whether these demographic differences are preferences or the result of systemic bias that has unintentionally limited access of MAID to certain populations who might desire the option.

Advocates of MAID laws argue that it should be respected as a healthcare choice among many others that Americans are currently afforded (Compassion & Choices, n.d.). Reasons patients report choosing to pursue MAID include loss of autonomy, impaired quality of life, and inadequate pain control (Al Rabadi et al., 2019). Available data suggest that the law has psychological benefits, as individuals with life-limiting illnesses take comfort in knowing that this option exists (Cerminara & Perez, 2000). Advocates argue that the meticulous record keeping by Oregon and Washington provide evidence that the safeguards in the law are effective (Al Rabadi et al., 2019; Brock, 2000). Despite opposition from some professional healthcare organizations, others at the national and state levels assert that the issue is complex and have remained neutral (e.g., American Psychological Association, Oregon Medical Association). One could argue that the oath to do no harm also applies to actively preventing capable individuals from executing a healthcare choice. Indeed, the current laws allow for physicians to participate or refer patients to another provider. Regarding the position that society should instead focus on building better access to hospice and palliative care, Wang et al. (2015) showed that Oregon residents had the highest quartile of hospice use of all the states, suggesting these are not mutually exclusive. Indeed, in the *2019 State-by-State Report Card on Access to Palliative Care in Our Nation's Hospitals*, the Center to Advance Palliative Care (CAPC) and the National Palliative Care Research Center (NPCRC) gave all jurisdictions with MAID laws a passing grade, giving more credence to the assertion that quality hospice care and MAID need not be mutually exclusive.

Regardless of how one dies, they leave loved ones who survive. We turn now to the topic of bereavement.

BEREAVEMENT

Definitions of Bereavement, Grief, and Mourning

Bereavement refers to the objective situation of having recently lost a significant person through death (Shear, 2012). The emotional reaction to bereavement is typically referred to as *grief* and includes a wide range of cognitive, social, behavioral, physiological, and somatic manifestations that vary in pattern and intensity over time (Shear, 2012). The term *mourning* typically refers to the outward expressions of grief (e.g., wearing black clothing) that are shaped by one's society or cultural group.

Common Reactions to Bereavement

As noted in the beginning of the chapter, any understanding of the reaction to bereavement will be entangled with culture. The social constructions of any culture will influence if, how, when, and where grief is expressed, felt, and understood. Cultural sensitivity and awareness are necessary in understanding common group reactions as well as within-group individual diversity to bereavement, making the "typical" experience elusive. Researchers are examining the connections between culture and grief to bring about a greater global awareness (see, for example, Eyetsemitan, 2021); readers are strongly encouraged to seek out such resources, particularly since the summary of the literature that follows is based on the Western perspective of reactions to bereavement.

Psychological reactions are typically most intense in early bereavement and may be identified by four dimensions: affective, behavioral, cognitive, and physiological (Stroebe et al., 2001). Affective reactions to bereavement may include depression, despair and dejection, anxiety, guilt, anger and hostility, anhedonia, and loneliness. Behavioral reactions to bereavement may include agitation, fatigue, crying, and social withdrawal. Cognitive reactions to bereavement may include preoccupation with thoughts of the deceased, lowered self-esteem, self-reproach, helplessness and hopelessness, a sense of unreality, and problems with memory and concentration. Finally, physical reactions to bereavement may include loss of appetite, sleep disturbance, energy loss and exhaustion, somatic complaints, physical complaints similar to those the deceased had endured, changes in drug intake, and susceptibility to illness and disease. Spiritual manifestations of grief may also exist, including a change in religious activity or a sense of anger or betrayal (Strada, 2011).

Bereavement and Mental Health Disorders

As indicated previously, common or "typical" reactions to bereavement may encompass a wide range of symptoms and experiences. These symptoms and experiences may also be criteria for the diagnosis of a variety of mental health disorders. One systematic review examining the incidence of mental health disorders in the first year of widowhood found approximately 22% of the widowed met diagnostic criteria for major depressive disorder (MDD), almost 12% met diagnostic criteria for posttraumatic stress disorder (PTSD), and this group was at higher risk for developing panic disorder and generalized anxiety disorder (Onrust & Cuijpers, 2006). Professionals working with bereaved older adults should carefully consider the presence of other mental health conditions in addition to a normative response to a significant loss that takes into account the bereaved individual's history and cultural norms for the expression of distress in the context of loss (American Psychiatric Association [APA], 2022). In addition to discussing several considerations for differential assessment in the text, core symptom differences are summarized in Table 11.1.

Grief and MDD share several common symptoms, such as intense feelings of sadness, rumination, insomnia, poor appetite, weight loss, and difficulties with concentration (APA, 2022). However, grief can be distinguished from MDD such that with grief the predominant effects are feelings of emptiness and loss, rather than depressed mood or anhedonia, and may be accompanied by positive emotions and

TABLE 11.1 DIFFERENTIATING SYMPTOMS OF BEREAVEMENT AND OTHER CLINICAL DIAGNOSES

	Uncomplicated Bereavement	Major Depressive Disorder	Posttraumatic Stress Disorder	Prolonged Grief Disorder
Affect	Sadness, emptiness, and loss; can experience positive emotions and humor	Depressed; inability to anticipate happiness or pleasure; pervasive guilt	Fear; anger; horror; shame; inability to experience positive emotions; guilt focused on the cause or consequences of the traumatic event	Sadness; intense emotional pain related to the death; emotional numbness; intense loneliness
Intensity	Decreases over days to weeks; occurs in waves, with increases often associated with reminders of the deceased	Persistent; not necessarily tied to specific triggers	Increases associated with reminders of the traumatic event; usually specific to the event; avoidance of stimuli related to the event	Increases are more pervasive and unexpected; severe symptoms >12 months; avoidance of reminders that the deceased is no longer present
Thought content	Preoccupation with thoughts and memories of the deceased	Self-critical; pessimistic rumination	Persistent and exaggerated negative beliefs about oneself, others, or the world	Intense yearning/longing for the deceased and/or preoccupation with thoughts of the deceased
Self-esteem	Typically preserved	Worthlessness; self-loathing	May worsen in response to negative beliefs and expectations about oneself	Confusion about one's role in life; diminished sense of identity
Thoughts of death	If present, generally focused on the deceased and joining the deceased	Focused on ending one's life because of feeling worthless, undeserving of life, unable to cope	May be associated with reckless or self-destructive behavior	Desire to die to be with the deceased; sense that life is meaningless or empty without the deceased

Source: From American Psychiatric Association. (2022). Diagnostic and statistical manual of mental disorders (5th ed., text rev.). https://doi.org/10.1176/appi.books.9780890425787

humor. The intensity of dysphoria in grief tends to decrease over days to weeks and often occurs in waves, typically triggered by thoughts or reminders of the deceased, whereas MDD is characterized by pervasive unhappiness and misery, with an inability to anticipate happiness or pleasure. Thought content in grief generally features a preoccupation with thoughts and memories of the deceased, self-esteem is generally preserved, and if self-derogatory ideation is present, it typically involves perceived failings with regard to the deceased (e.g., not telling the deceased how much they were loved). In grief, thoughts of death and dying are generally focused on the deceased and possibly about "joining" the deceased, rather than ending one's life because of feeling worthless, undeserving of life, or unable to cope with the pain of depression. Previous editions of the *Diagnostic and Statistical Manual of Mental Disorders* (*DSM*) advised clinicians to refrain from diagnosing MDD in individuals within the first 2 months following the death of a loved one. However, the current MDD diagnostic criteria indicate this condition may occur in the context of early bereavement and that clinicians should carefully consider the presence of both (APA, 2022).

The development of PTSD in a bereaved individual is more likely when the loss of life has been massive, such as in a natural disaster or war-related violence, or horrific in nature, such as in sudden, unexpected, and violent losses (e.g., suicide, homicide; Kristensen et al., 2012). In such cases, *prolonged grief disorder* (see the following additional information) should also be considered in the differential diagnosis. PTSD can be triggered by exposure to actual or threatened death, serious injury, or sexual violence; through direct experience; witnessing a traumatic event as it occurs to others; or learning that a traumatic event has happened to a close family member or friend (APA, 2022). The primary emotion is fear or horror, nightmares are common, painful reminders are linked to the specific traumatic event, and there is a persistent inability to experience positive emotions (APA, 2022). In contrast, bereavement is triggered by the loss of a significant person through death. Here, the primary emotion is sadness accompanied by yearning/longing for the deceased, nightmares are rare, painful reminders of the deceased and the relationship with the deceased are more pervasive and unexpected, and the ability to experience positive emotions typically remains intact.

Prolonged Grief Disorder

APA's (2022) *Diagnostic and Statistical Manual of Mental Disorders* (5th ed., text rev.; *DSM-5-TR*) and WHO's (2019) *International Statistical Classification of Diseases and Related Health Problems* (11th ed.; *ICD-11*) include an entry for *prolonged grief disorder* (PGD), also referred to as *complicated grief, pathological grief, prolonged grief,* or *traumatic grief* throughout the literature. This type of grief response deviates from the normative grief experience in time course and/or intensity of symptoms, taking into consideration the social, cultural, and religious norms of the individual, and results in clinically significant distress and/or functional impairment (APA, 2022). The current conceptualization of PGD is characterized by intense yearning or longing for the deceased and/or preoccupation with thoughts or memories of the deceased, either of which has occurred nearly every day for at least the last month (APA, 2022). Further, for a diagnosis of PGD to be made, an individual must experience at least three additional symptoms nearly every day for at least the last month as a result of the death, including identity disruption, marked sense of disbelief about the death, avoidance of reminders that the deceased is no longer present, intense emotional pain, difficulty reintegrating into relationships and activities, emotional numbness, feeling that life is meaningless, or intense loneliness (APA, 2022). Importantly, a diagnosis of PGD can only be made after at least 12 months have elapsed using *DSM-5-TR* criteria, whereas *ICD-11* criteria only require a minimum of 6 months since the death of a person who was close to the bereaved individual (APA, 2022; WHO, 2019). Individuals with symptoms of PGD are at heightened risk for suicidal ideation, harmful health behaviors (e.g., increased tobacco and alcohol use), serious medical conditions (e.g., cardiac disease, immunological deficiency), and reduced quality of life (APA, 2022).

Among adults of all ages, estimated rates of PGD range from 1.2% to 3.7% in the general population (Kersting et al., 2011; Rosner et al., 2021), to 9.8% in bereavement associated with natural (i.e., nonviolent) death (Lundorff et al., 2017), to 49% in bereavement associated with unnatural death (e.g., accident, suicide, homicide; Djelantik et al., 2020). Bereavement associated with a COVID-19 death has a higher potential risk of probable PGD than deaths from other natural causes (e.g., dementia) but lower potential risk of probable PGD than deaths from unnatural causes (e.g., homicide; Gang et al., 2022). Older age has emerged as one risk factor for developing PGD (Lundorff et al., 2017). Confirmed prospective risk factors for developing prolonged grief across all age groups include low social support, anxious/avoidant/insecure attachment style, discovering or identifying the body (in cases of violent death), being the spouse or parent of the deceased, high predeath marital dependence, and high neuroticism (Burke & Neimeyer, 2012). Other research indicates that lower level of education and higher level of cognitive impairment may be associated with higher prevalence of prolonged grief among older adults (Newson et al., 2011).

Theoretical Models of Adjustment to Bereavement

Traditional models of coping with bereavement stemmed from the psychoanalytic tradition and posited that confronting the reality of a loss and relinquishing the bond to the deceased were essential for overcoming bereavement (Stroebe & Schut, 2001). Also growing out of the psychoanalytic tradition was the concept of *grief work*, characterized by reviewing the past, including events that occurred before and at the time of death; focusing on memories; and working toward detachment from the deceased (Stroebe & Schut, 2001). This concept was also incorporated into the attachment theory perspective of coping with bereavement, which posited that working through grief takes place through a sequence of overlapping, flexibly occurring phases: shock, yearning and protest, despair, and recovery (Stroebe & Schut, 2001).

Despite the widely accepted notion that natural response to the death of a loved one involves discrete orderly stages that result in resolution, this concept has also received much critical examination among contemporary bereavement researchers, and there is surprisingly little empirical support for the concept. For example, in a sample of primarily non-Hispanic White older women who lost a loved one from natural causes, Maciejewski et al. (2007) found disbelief peaked at 1-month post-loss, yearning peaked at 4 months post-loss, anger peaked at 5 months post-loss, and depression peaked at 6 months post-loss. However, in contrast to stage model predictions, they also found that acceptance of the death was the most frequently endorsed experience initially and increased throughout the study period (1-24 months post-loss). Additionally, anger and denial occurred at relatively low levels throughout the first 2 years of adjustment. Thinking about the grieving process as phases or stages may be useful as a general orientation to which reactions are likely involved in the experience of grief; however, many variables including situational, personal, and environmental factors, are likely to determine the individual grieving process of older adults (Röcke & Cherry, 2002).

One contemporary model of coping with bereavement, the dual process model (DPM), proposes adaptive grieving is characterized by a dynamic process of both focusing on the loss ("loss orientation") and attending to the everyday consequences of the loss ("restoration orientation"; Stroebe & Schut, 2010). As shown in Figure 11.2, loss orientation entails engagement with stimuli that serve as reminders of the loss (e.g., looking through old photos or sharing stories of the deceased), whereas restoration orientation entails withdrawing from the loss and turning toward everyday life functions (e.g., finances, household tasks) and building a future without the deceased (e.g., finding new sources of social and emotional support). Central to the DPM is the notion that adaptive grieving involves a normative oscillation between these two orientations. The duration of time spent in either orientation may

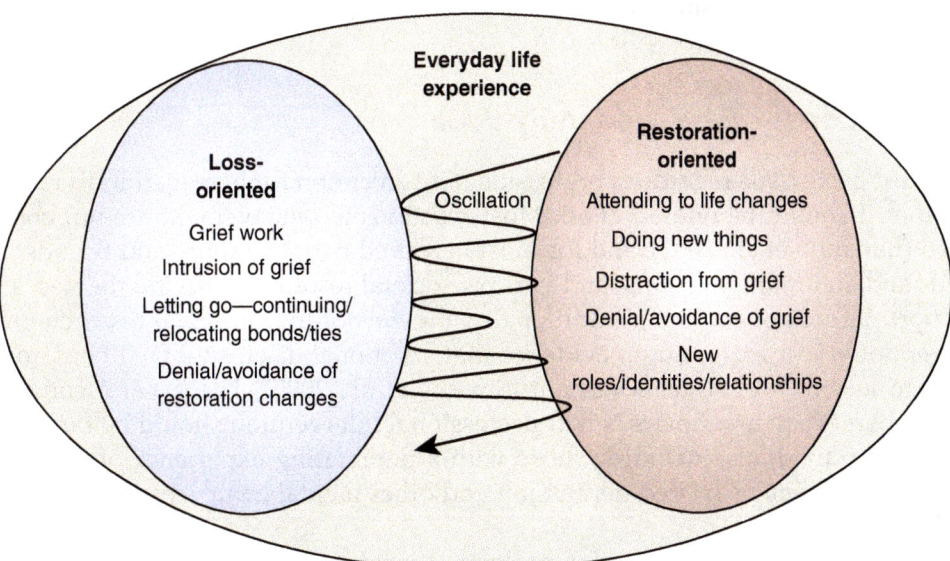

Figure 11.2 The dual process model of coping with bereavement.
Source: From Stroebe, M. S., & Schut, H. (2001). Models of coping with bereavement: A review. In M. S. Stroebe, R. O. Hansson, W. Stroebe, & H. Schut (Eds.), *Handbook of bereavement research: Consequences, coping, and care* (pp. 375–403). American Psychological Association.

vary, although difficulties may arise if the griever becomes "stuck" in either one. There is mounting empirical support for the tenets and clinical utility of the DPM (Stroebe & Schut, 2010).

Another contemporary approach to understanding coping with bereavement is the *continuing bonds* perspective, which is rooted in attachment theory (Field et al., 2005). This perspective highlights the ways in which a connection to the deceased following the death of a significant other may be maintained and, in contrast to the earlier notion of grief work, this continued connection to the deceased is seen as largely normative. Continuing bonds may be maintained through experiences such as imaginary conversations with the deceased; thinking of good memories of the deceased; or a sense that the deceased is guiding, watching over, or comforting the grieving individual. The current consensus among bereavement researchers is that it is not generally adaptive for bereaved people to continue their bonds with deceased loved ones or to relinquish them, and it is important to attend to individual differences as well as underlying processes in continuing or relinquishing bonds (Stroebe et al., 2010).

A final contemporary model for coping with bereavement focuses on the adaptive process of reaffirming or reconstructing a world of meaning that is challenged by the loss of a loved one (Neimeyer, 2001). This meaning-making, narrative approach to coping with bereavement emphasizes processing both the story of the death and the story of the relationship with the deceased, such that grief is integrated into a changed self-narrative. One study of older widowed individuals found those who struggled to find meaning in early bereavement showed greater grief and depression across the first few years of the loss (Coleman & Neimeyer, 2010). In contrast, the widowed individuals who succeeded in making sense of the loss in early bereavement demonstrated considerable resilience 4 years later, including higher levels of pride, joy, and well-being.

Intervention for Bereaved Individuals

The most basic issue regarding professional intervention for bereaved individuals is whether it should be offered at all. Most reactions to bereavement are not complicated (Bonanno et al., 2002), and for most bereaved people, family and friends, religious and community groups, and various societal resources provide the necessary support (Stroebe et al., 2007). Additionally, a review of the empirical research on the concept of *grief work* found no evidence that emotional disclosure facilitates adjustment to loss in normal bereavement (Stroebe et al., 2005). The general consensus among bereavement scholars is that professional intervention should be targeted at high-risk individuals, including those with a debilitating experience of prolonged grief or bereavement-related depression and other mental health disorders (Stroebe et al., 2007).

Evidence suggests therapy for prolonged grief or bereavement-related depression and stress disorders leads to substantial and lasting results (Stroebe et al., 2007). Intervention strategies borrowing from diverse theoretical psychotherapy models may be useful in the treatment of complex bereavement in later life, including behavioral activation, emotion regulation, challenging dysfunctional thinking, retelling the narrative of the death, reconstructing meaning, reworking the continuing bond, life review, goal work, and expressive arts approaches (Neimeyer & Holland, 2015). Developed specifically for individuals with complex bereavement reactions, prolonged grief disorder therapy (PGDT; previously called complicated grief therapy) involves a combination of modified in vivo and imaginal exposure focusing on processing traumatic symptoms related to the death and promotes a sense of connection with the deceased loved one and restoring life in the face of a changed reality. Randomized clinical trials have shown PGDT produces greater improvement in complex bereavement and depressive symptoms than grief-focused interpersonal psychotherapy among bereaved individuals across the life span (Shear et al., 2005) and older adults (Shear et al., 2014). There is very little empirical evidence supporting the use of psychotropic medication to treat grief-related symptoms, and critics of using a pharmacological treatment approach caution against the "medicalization" of grief (Neimeyer & Holland, 2015).

LATE-LIFE SPOUSAL LOSS

General Characteristics

The loss of a spouse or long-term partner is a common occurrence in later life. Much of the existing empirical knowledge of late-life spousal loss is based on the experiences of heterosexual couples, and because women are affected more often, at a younger age, and for longer time periods than men, we see even more of a focus in the literature on the experiences of older heterosexual women. The literature on the grieving process of same-sex partners in late life is sparse; much of the existing research is based on gay men who lost partners or close friends from HIV-related illness. Within the bereavement literature, it is often discussed under the heading of *disenfranchised grief*, although the term is not specific to the sexual minority community. Disenfranchised grief is a term used to describe when an individual's grief is not openly acknowledged, socially validated, or publicly mourned (Doka, 2008).

Common emotions after late-life spousal loss include shock, sadness, pain, numbness, turmoil, remorse, self-blame, regret, and feelings of betrayal and anger (Naef et al., 2013). Sleep disturbance, fatigue, lack of energy, loss of appetite, and nausea are common health concerns (Naef et al., 2013). As with other types of bereavement, most widow/ers find the intensity of grief decreases over time (Naef et al., 2013). A pervasive sense of loneliness in daily life following the loss of a life companion is common; studies show that older widowed persons experience times in a day or a year that are particularly difficult (e.g., mealtimes, bedtime, anniversaries; Naef et al., 2013). The extent of participation in leisure activities fluctuates; however, most older widow/ers keep or increase social contacts (Naef et al., 2013). Relationships with family, friends, neighbors, and other widow/ers are a resource in late-life spousal bereavement, and continued engagement with their lost partners may also serve as a source of comfort (e.g., through sensing the presence of the deceased, reliving the past through memories and dreams, by taking up an activity of the deceased; Naef et al., 2013). Some may have difficulty appearing in public alone and socializing as a single person, but some also find their new status to be a chance to experience self-growth, learn new skills, and assume new roles (Naef et al., 2013).

Impact of Spousal Loss on Partner Mortality

The premature or early death of a widowed person shortly after that individual is widowed is often referred to as the *widowhood effect*. Although the cause of this phenomenon is likely multifactorial, the findings of most longitudinal studies, which controlled for several confounding variables, indicate an excess risk of mortality in the first 6 months during bereavement (Ennis et al., 2021). As compared with married people, widow/ers have higher rates of accidental and violent causes of death, including completed suicide, and alcohol-related diseases, as well as a number of medical diagnoses, including cardiovascular disease and cancer (Ennis et al., 2021). Most research findings indicate that widowers are at relatively more excessive risk of mortality than widows (Ennis et al., 2021).

Bereavement After Caregiving

Late-life spousal bereavement is often preceded by an extended period of chronic illness or disability during which family members take on caregiving tasks. Research investigating the impact of the caregiving experience on bereavement indicates that most caregivers benefit from anticipation prior to the loss (e.g., thinking about the impending death and the caregiver's life afterwards). Additionally, caregivers experience stress relief following bereavement, with rapid decreases in depression and grief symptoms within a year after the death (Boerner & Schulz, 2009). However, a sizeable minority (up to 30%) do experience continued high levels of stress and mental health difficulties, as well as prolonged grief, after the death (Boerner & Schulz, 2009). Notably, some research indicates the positive, rewarding preloss aspects of the caregiving experience (which may provide the caregiver with a sense of meaning and/or achievement) may also be associated with postloss depression and grief, demonstrating the importance of attending to both positive and negative aspects of caregiving in prediction of caregivers' responses to the death of the person for whom they cared (Boerner et al., 2004).

CONCLUSION

This chapter aimed to introduce readers to the tremendous biopsychosocial complexity of understanding death and loss, in consideration of the diversity found among older adults. This review of the literature suggests our ever-evolving understanding of these concepts is both a product of and a reaction to societal norms and systems (i.e., medical, economic, family, technology). While advances in technology and health prevention have created longer life expectancies, it also helped shape a society with high death aversion. Our longer life spans have raised important questions about quality of life as we age and how a "good death" may be defined differently for each of us. Nevertheless, death and dying continue to remain negatively valenced events for individuals and their loved ones. The experience of grief is highly individualized, but differentiating common grief experiences from clinical manifestations allows us to provide additional support to those who need it.

DISCUSSION QUESTIONS

1. Consider preparing your own advance directives at this time. After researching this on your own, describe some of the decisions you need to make in this process.
2. How might you describe the differences between hospice and palliative care to a patient and family who is facing a terminal illness?
3. Compare euthanasia and medical aid in dying and describe some characteristics of people who have engaged in medical aid in dying.
4. Describe some of the common psychological reactions in early bereavement. Which of these have you noticed in yourself or others when faced with loss?
5. Describe some differences between uncomplicated bereavement and MDD.
6. Describe the dual process model of bereavement. Discuss what this means for someone trying to be supportive of a loved one who has recently lost someone.
7. What is disenfranchised grief? How can society be more inclusive to the grief of all individuals?

A robust set of instructor resources designed to supplement this text is located at http://connect.springerpub.com/content/book/978-0-8261-6617-3. Qualifying instructors may request access by emailing textbook@springerpub.com.

REFERENCES

Addis, S., Davies, M., Greene, G., MacBride-Stewart, S., & Sheperd, M. (2009). The health, social care and housing needs of lesbian, gay, bisexual, and transgender older people: A review of the literature. *Health and Social Care in the Community*, 17(6), 647–658. https://doi.org/10.1111/j.1365-2524.2009.00866.x

Ahmad, F. B., Cisewski, J. A., & Anderson, R. N. (2022). Provisional mortality data – United States, 2021. *MMWR. Morbidity and Mortality Weekly Report*, 71(17), 597–600. https://doi.org/10.15585/mmwr.mm7117e1

Ahmad, F. B., Cisewski, J. A., Xu, J., & Anderson, R. N. (2023a). COVID-19 mortality update – United States, 2022. *MMWR. Morbidity and Mortality Weekly Report*, 72(18), 493–496. https://doi.org/10.15585/mmwr.mm7218a4

Ahmad, F. B., Cisewski, J. A., Xu, J., & Anderson, R. N. (2023b). Provisional mortality data–United States, 2022. *MMWR. Morbidity and Mortality Weekly Report*, 72(18), 488–492. https://doi.org/10.15585/mmwr.mm7218a3

Al Rabadi, L., LeBlanc, M., Bucy, T., Ellis, L. M., Hershman, D. L., Meyskens, F. L., Jr, Taylor, L., & Blanke, C. D. (2019). Trends in medical aid in dying in Oregon and Washington. *JAMA Network Open*, 2(8), e198648. https://doi.org/10.1001/jamanetworkopen.2019.8648

American Psychiatric Association. (2022). *Diagnostic and statistical manual of mental disorders* (5th ed., text rev.). https://doi.org/10.1176/appi.books.9780890425787

Bauereiß, N., Obermaier, S., Özünal, S. E., & Baumeister, H. (2018). Effects of existential interventions on spiritual, psychological, and physical well-being in adult patients with cancer: Systematic review and meta-analysis of randomized controlled trials. *Psycho-Oncology*, 27(11), 2531–2545. https://doi.org/10.1002/pon.4829

Becker, E. (1973). *The denial of death*. Free Press.

Boerner, K., & Schulz, R. (2009). Caregiving, bereavement, and complicated grief. *Bereavement Care*, 28(3), 10–13. https://doi.org/10.1080/02682620903355382

Boerner, K., Schultz, R., & Horowitz, A. (2004). Positive aspects of caregiving and adaptation to bereavement. *Psychology and Aging*, 19(4), 668–675. https://doi.org/10.1037/0882-7974.19.4.668

Bonanno, G. A., Wortman, C. B., Lehman, D. R., Tweed, R. G., Haring, M., Sonnega, J., . . ., Nesse, R. M. (2002). Resilience to loss and chronic grief: A prospective study from preloss to 18-months postloss. *Journal of Personality and Social Psychology, 83*(5), 1150–1164. https://doi.org/10.1037//0022-3514.83.5.1150

Brock, D. W. (2000). Misconceived sources of opposition to physician-assisted suicide. *Psychology, Public Policy, and Law, 6*(2), 305–313. https://doi.org/10.1037/1076-8971.6.2.305

Bükki, J., Scherbel, J., Stiel, S., Klein, C., Meidenbauer, N., & Ostgathe, C. (2013). Palliative care needs, symptoms, and treatment intensity along the disease trajectory in medical oncology outpatients: A retrospective chart review. *Supportive Care in Cancer, 21*(6), 1743–1750. https://doi.org/10.1007/s00520-013-1721-y

Burke, L. A., & Neimeyer, R. A. (2012) Prospective risk factors for complicated grief: A review of the empirical literature. In M. S. Stroebe, H. Schut, J. van der Bout, & P. Boelen (Eds.), *Complicated grief: Scientific foundations for healthcare professionals* (pp. 145–161). Routledge.

Carr, D. (2011). Racial differences in end-of-life planning: Why don't Blacks and Latinos prepare for the inevitable? *Omega: Journal of Death and Dying, 63*(1), 1–20. https://doi.org/10.2190/OM.63.1.a

Carr, D., & Luth, E. (2016). End of life planning and health care. In L. K. George & K. Ferraro (Eds.), *Handbook of aging and the social sciences* (8th ed., pp. 375–394). Academic Press.

Carr, D., & Luth, E. A. (2017). Advance care planning: Contemporary issues and future directions. *Innovation in Aging, 1*(1), igx012. https://doi.org/10.1093/geroni/igx012

Centers for Disease Control and Prevention, National Center for Health Statistics. (2020). *Underlying cause of death 2000–2018.* http://wonder.cdc.gov/ucd-icd10.html

Center to Advance Palliative Care. (2019). *A state-by-state report card on access to palliative care in our nation's hospitals.* https://reportcard.capc.org/

Cerminara, K. L., & Perez, A. (2000). Therapeutic death: A look at Oregon's' law. *Psychology, Public Policy, and Law, 6*, 503–525. https://doi.org/10.1037/1076-8971.6.2.503

Coleman, R. A., & Neimeyer, R. A. (2010). Measuring meaning: Searching for and making sense of spousal loss in late-life. *Death Studies, 34*(9), 804–834. https://doi.org/10.1080/07481181003761625

Compassion & Choices. (n.d.). *Death with dignity.* https://www.compassionandchoices.org/death-with-dignity

Connor, S. R., Teno, J., Spence, C., & Smith, N. (2005). Family evaluation of hospice care: Results from voluntary submission of data via website. *Journal of Pain and Symptom Management, 30*(1), 9–17. https://doi.org/10.1016/j.jpainsymman.2005.04.001

Corr, C. A., Nabe, C. M., & Corr, D. M. (2009). *Death and dying, life and living* (6th ed.). Wadsworth.

Djelantik, A. A. A. M. J., Smid, G. E., Mroz, A., Kleber, R. J., & Boelen, P. A. (2020). The prevalence of prolonged grief disorder in bereaved individuals following unnatural losses: Systematic review and meta regression analysis. *Journal of Affective Disorders, 265*, 146–156. https://doi.org/10.1016/j.jad.2020.01.034.

Doka, K. J. (2008). Disenfranchised grief in historical and cultural perspective. In M. S. Stroebe, R. O. Hansson, H. Schut, & W. Stroebe (Eds.), *Handbook of bereavement research and practice: Advances in theory and intervention* (pp. 223–240). American Psychological Association. https://doi.org/10.1037/14498-011

Ennis, J., & Majid, U. (2021). "Death from a broken heart": A systematic review of the relationship between spousal bereavement and physical and physiological health outcomes. *Death Studies, 45*(7), 538–551. https://doi.org/10.1080/07481187.2019.1661884

Eyetsemitan, F. E. (2021). *Death, dying, and bereavement around the world: Theories, varied views, and customs.* Charles C. Thomas Publisher, Ltd.

Faller, H., Schuler, M., Richard, M., Heckl, U., Weiss, J., & Küffner, R. (2013). Effects of psycho-oncologic interventions on emotional distress and quality of life in adult patients with cancer: Systematic review and meta-analysis. *Journal of Clinical Oncology, 31*(6), 782–793. https://doi.org/10.1200/JCO.2011.40.8922

Field, N. P., Gao, B., & Paderna, L. (2005). Continuing bonds in bereavement: An attachment theory based perspective. *Death Studies, 29*(4), 277–299. https://doi.org/10.1080/07481180590923689

Fortner, B. V., Neimeyer, R. A., & Rybarczeck, B. (2000). Correlates of death anxiety in older adults: A comprehensive review. In A. Tomer (Ed.), *Death attitudes and the older adult* (pp. 95–108). Brunner Routledge.

Gang, J., Falzarano, F., She, W. J., Winoker, H., & Prigerson, H. G. (2022). Are deaths from COVID-19 associated with higher rates of prolonged grief disorder (PGD) than deaths from other causes? *Death Studies, 46*(6), 1287–1296. https://doi.org/10.1080/07481187.2022.2039326

Genewick, J. E., Lipski, D. M., Schupack, K. M., & Buffington, A. L. H. (2018). Characteristics of patients with existing advance directives: Evaluating motivations around advance care planning. *American Journal of Hospice & Palliative Medicine, 35*(4), 664–668. https://doi.org/10.1177/1049909117731738

Glaser, B. G., & Strauss, A L. (1968). *Time for dying*. Aldine Publishing.

Gott, M., Barnes, S., Parker, C., Payne, S., Seamark, D., Gariballa, S., & Small, N. (2007). Dying trajectories in heart failure. *Palliative Medicine, 21*(2), 95–99. https://doi.org/10.1177/0269216307076348

Hong, S., & Cagle, J. G. (2019). Comfort with discussions about death, religiosity, and attitudes about end-of-life care. *Asian Social Work & Policy Review, 13*(2), 141–145. https://doi.org/10.1111/aswp.12164

Institute of Medicine. (2014). *Dying in America: Improving quality and honoring individual preferences near the end of life*. National Academies Press.

Johnston, C. B., Mangini, M., Grob, C., & Anderson, B. (2023). The safety and efficacy of psychedelic-assisted therapies for older adults: Knowns and unknowns. *The American Journal of Geriatric Psychiatry, 31*(1), 44–53. https://doi.org/10.1016/j.jagp.2022.08.007

Jones, A. L., Moss, A. J., & Harris-Kojetin, L. D. (2011). *Use of advance directives in long-term care populations* (NCHS Data Brief No. 54). National Center for Health Statistics.

Jong, J. (2021). Death anxiety and religion. *Current Opinion in Psychology, 40*, 40–44. https://doi.org/10.1016/j.copsyc.2020.08.004

Kahraman, S., & Erkent, D. (2023). The mediator role of attitude towards aging and elderliness in the effect of the meaning and purpose of life on death anxiety. *Current Psychology, 42*, 19518–19525. https://doi.org/10.1007/s12144-022-03087-x

Kersting, A., Brahler, E., Glaesmer, H., & Wagner, B. (2011). Prevalence of complicated grief in a representative population-based sample. *Journal of Affective Disorders, 131*, 339–343. https://doi.org/10.1016/j.jad.2010.11.032

Kochanek, K. D., Xu, J., & Arias, E. (2020). *Mortality in the United States, 2019* (NCHS data brief No. 395, pp. 1–8).

Koss, C. S., & Baker T. A. (2017). Race differences in advance directive completion: The narrowing gap between white and African American older adults. *Journal of Aging and Health, 292*(2), 324–342. https://doi.org/10.1177/0898264316635568

Kozlov, E., Nowels, M., Gusmano, M., Habib, M., & Duberstein, P. (2022). Aggregating 23 years of data on medical aid in dying in the United States. *Journal of the American Geriatrics Society, 70*(10), 3040–3044. https://doi.org/10.1111/jgs.17925

Kristensen, P., Weisaeth, L, & Heir, T. (2012). Bereavement and mental health after sudden and violent losses: A review. *Psychiatry, 75*(1), 76–97. https://doi.org/10.1521/psyc.2012.75.1.76

Kübler-Ross, E. (1969). *On death and dying*. Macmillan.

Kwak, J., Allen, J. Y., & Haley, W. E. (2011). Advance care planning and end-of-life decision making. In P. Dilworth-Anderson & M. H. Palmer (Eds.), *Annual review of gerontology and geriatrics: Pathways through the transitions of care for older adults* (Vol. 31, pp. 143–165). Springer Publishing.

Le, B. C., Mileshkin, L., Doan, K., Saward, D., Spruyt, O., Yoong, J., . . ., Philip, J. (2014). Acceptability of early integration of palliative care in patients with incurable lung cancer. *Journal of Palliative Medicine, 17*(5), 553–558. https://doi.org/10.1089/jpm.2013.047

Lovell, A., & Yates, P. (2014). Advance care planning in palliative care: A systematic literature review of the contextual factors influencing its uptake 2008–2012. *Palliative Medicine, 28*(8), 1026–1035. https://doi.org/10.1177/026921631453131

Lundorff, M., Holmgren, H., Zachariae, R., Farver-Vestergaard, I., & O'Connor, M. (2017). Prevalence of prolonged grief disorder in adult bereavement: A systematic review and meta-analysis. *Journal of Affective Disorders, 212*, 138–149. https://doi.org/10.1016/j.jad.2017.01.030

Lunney, J. R., Lynn, J., & Hogan, C. (2002). Profiles of older Medicare decedents. *Journal of the American Geriatrics Society, 50*(6), 1108–1112. https://doi.org/10.1046/j.1532-5415.2002.50268.x

Maciejewski, P. K., Zhang, B., Block, S. D., & Prigerson, H. G. (2007). An empirical examination of the stage theory of grief. *Journal of the American Medical Association, 297*(7), 716–723. https://doi.org/10.1001/jama.297.7.716

Maia, L.O, Beaussant, Y., & Garcia, A. C. M. (2022). The therapeutic potential of psychedelic-assisted therapies for symptom control in patients diagnosed with serious illness: A systematic review. *Journal of Pain Symptom Management, 63*(6), 725–738. https://doi.org/10.1016/j.jpainsymman.2022.01.024.

Miller, S. C., Mor, V., Wu, N., Gozalo, P., & Lapane, K. (2002). Does receipt of hospice care in nursing homes improve the management of pain at the end of life? *Journal of the American Geriatrics Society, 50*(3), 507–515. https://doi.org/10.1046/j.1532-5415.2002.50118.x

Murphy, S. L., Kochanek, K. D., Xu, J., & Arias, E. (2021). *Mortality in the United States, 2020* (NCHS data brief, No. 427, pp. 1–8).

Naef, R., Ward, R., Mahrer-Imhof, R., & Grande, G. (2013). Characteristics of the bereavement experience of older persons after spousal loss: An integrative review. *International Journal of Nursing Studies, 50*(8), 1108–1121. https://doi.org/10.1016/j.ijnurstu.2012.11.026

National Institute on Aging. (2022). Advance care planning: Advance directives for health care. https://www.nia.nih.gov/health/advance-care-planning-advance-directives-health-care

National Institute on Aging (2021). *What are palliative care and hospice care?* https://www.nia.nih.gov/health/what-are-palliative-care-and-hospice-care

National POLST Paradigm. (2022). *About POLST.* https://polst.org/about/

Neimeyer, R. A. (Ed.). (2001). *Meaning reconstruction and the experience of loss.* American Psychological Association.

Neimeyer, R. A., & Holland, J. M. (2015). Bereavement in later life: Theory, assessment, and intervention. In P. A. Lichtenberg & B. T. Mast (Eds.), *APA handbook of clinical geropsychology: Vol. 2. Assessment, treatment, and issues of later life* (pp. 645–666). American Psychological Association.

Newson, R. S., Boelen, P. A., Hek, K., Hofman, A., & Tiemeier, H. (2011). The prevalence and characteristics of complicated grief in older adults. *Journal of Affective Disorders, 132*(1–2), 231–238. https://doi.org/10.1016/j.jad.2011.02.021

Nigam, K., Curseen, K., & Beaussant, Y. (2023). Psychedelics and related pharmacotherapies as integrative medicine for older adults in palliative care. *Clinics in Geriatric Medicine, 39*(3), 423–436. https://doi.org/10.1016/j.cger.2023.04.004

Omelianchuk, A., Bernat, J., Caplan, A., Greer, D., Lazaridis, C., Lewis, A., Pope, T., Ross, L. F., & Magnus, D. (2022). Revise the Uniform Determination of Death Act to align the law with practice through neurorespiratory criteria. *Neurology, 98*(13), 532–536. https://doi.org/10.1212/WNL.00000000002000

Omnibus Budget Reconciliation Act, Pub. L. 101–508, 104 Stat. 143 (1990).

Onrust, S. A., & Cuijpers, P. (2006). Mood and anxiety disorders in widowhood: A systematic review. *Aging and Mental Health, 10*(4), 327–334. https://doi.org/10.1080/13607860600638529

Perusinghe, M., Chen, K. Y., & McDermott, B. (2021). Evidence-based management of depression in palliative care: A systematic review. *Journal of Palliative Medicine, 24*(5), 767–782. https://doi.org/10.1089/jpm.2020.0659

Porensky, E. K., & Carpenter, B. D. (2008). Knowledge and perceptions in advance care planning. *Journal of Aging and Health, 20*(1), 89–106. https://doi.org/10.1177/0898264307309963

Parent, B., & Turi, A. (2020). Death's troubled relationship with the law. *AMA Journal of Ethics, 22*(12), E1055–E1061. https://doi.org/10.1001/amajethics.2020.1055

Rando, T. A. (Ed.). (2000). *Clinical dimensions of anticipatory mourning: Theory and practice in working with the dying, their loved ones, and their caregivers.* Research Press.

Rao, J. K., Anderson, L. A., Lin, F., & Laux, J. P. (2014). Completion of advance directives among U.S. consumers. *American Journal of Preventive Medicine, 46*(1), 65–70. https://doi.org/10.1016/j.amepre.2013.09.008

Robinson, S., Kissane, D. W., Brooker, J., & Burney, S. (2015). A systematic review of the demoralization syndrome in individuals with progressive disease and cancer: A decade of research. *Journal of Pain and Symptom Management, 49*(3), 595–610, https://doi.org/10.1016/j.jpainsymman.2014.07.008.

Röcke, C., & Cherry, K. E. (2002). Death at the end of the 20th century: Individual processes and developmental tasks in old age. *International Journal of Aging and Human Development, 54*(4). https://doi.org/10.2190/L9FW-GD24-GC5H-DXHW

Rosner, R., Comtesse, H., Vogel, A., & Doering, B. K. (2021). Prevalence of prolonged grief disorder. *Journal of Affective Disorders, 287*, 301–307. https://doi.org/10.1016/j.jad.2021.03.058.

Schmidt, T. A., Zive, D., Fromme, E. K., Cook, J. N., & Tolle, S. W. (2014). Physician orders for life-sustaining treatment (POLST): Lessons learned from analysis of the Oregon POLST Registry. *Resuscitation, 85*(4), 480–485. https://doi.org/10.1016/j.resuscitation.2013.11.027

Shalev, A., Phongtankuel, V., Kozlov, E., Shen, M. J., Adelman, R. D., & Reid, M. C. (2018). Awareness and misperceptions of hospice and palliative care: A population-based survey study. *The American Journal of Hospice & Palliative Care, 35*(3), 431–439. https://doi.org/10.1177/1049909117715215

Shear, M. K. (2012). Getting straight about grief. *Depression and Anxiety, 29*, 461–464. https://doi.org/10.1002/da.21963

Shear, M. K., Frank, E., Houck, P. R., & Reynolds, C. F., 3rd. (2005). Treatment of complicated grief: A randomized controlled trial. *Journal of the American Medical Association, 293*(21), 2601–2608. https://doi.org/10.1001/jama.293.21.2601

Shear, M. K., Wang, Y., Skritskaya, N., Duan, N., Mauro, C., & Ghesquiere, A. (2014). Treatment of complicated grief in elderly persons: A randomized clinical trial. *Journal of the American Medical Association Psychiatry, 71*(11), 1287–1295. https://doi.org/10.1001/jamapsychiatry.2014.1242

Strada, E. A. (2011). Health-care teams. In S. H. Qualls & J. E. Kasl-Godley (Eds.), *End-of-life issues, grief, and bereavement: What clinicians need to know* (pp. 43–63). John Wiley.

Stroebe, M. S., Hansson, R. O., Stroebe, W, & Schut, H. (2001). Introduction: Concepts and issues in contemporary research on bereavement. In M. S. Stroebe, R. O. Hannson, W. Stroebe, & H. Schut (Eds.), *Handbook of bereavement research: Consequences, coping, and care* (pp. 3–22). American Psychological Association.

Stroebe, M. S., & Schut, H. (2001). Models of coping with bereavement: A review. In M. S. Stroebe, R. O. Hansson, W. Stroebe, & H. Schut (Eds.), *Handbook of bereavement research: Consequences, coping, and care* (pp. 375–403). American Psychological Association.

Stroebe, M. S., & Schut, H. (2010). The dual process model of coping with bereavement: A decade on. *Omega: Journal of Death and Dying, 61*(4), 273–289. https://doi.org/10.2190/OM.61.4.b

Stroebe, M. S., Schut, H., & Boerner, K. (2010). Continuing bonds in adaptation to bereavement: Toward theoretical integration. *Clinical Psychology Review, 30*(2), 259–268. https://doi.org/10.1016/j.cpr.2009.11.007

Stroebe, W., Schut, H., & Stroebe, M. S. (2005). Grief work, disclosure and counseling: Do they help the bereaved? *Clinical Psychology Review, 25*(4), 395–414. https://doi.org/10.1016/j.cpr.2005.01.004

Stroebe, M. S., Schut, H., & Stroebe, W. (2007). Health outcomes of bereavement. *Lancet, 370*(9603), 1960–1973. https://doi.org/10.1016/S0140-6736(07)61816-9

Waite, K. R., Federman, A. D., McCarthy, D. M., Sudore, R., Curtis, L. M., Baker, D. W., ..., Paasche-Orlow, M. K. (2013). Literacy and race as risk factors for low rates of advance directives in older adults. *Journal of the American Geriatrics Society, 61*(3), 403–406. https://doi.org/10.1111/jgs.12134

Wang, S., Aldridge, M. D., Gross, C. P., Canavan, M., Cherlin, E., Johnson-Hurzeler, R., & Bradley, E. (2015). Geographic variation of hospice use patterns at the end of life. *Journal of Palliative Medicine, 18*(9), 771–780. https://doi.org/10.1089/jpm.2014.0425

Weathers, E., O'Caoimh, R., Cornally, N., Fitzgerald, C., Kearns, T., Coffey, A., ..., Molloy, D. W. (2016). Advance care planning: A systematic review of randomised controlled trials conducted with older adults. *Maturitas, 91*, 101–109. https://doi.org/10.1016/j.maturitas.2016.06.016

Werth, J. L., Gordon, J. R., & Johnson, R. R. (2002). Psychosocial issues near the end of life. *Aging & Mental Health, 6*(4), 402–412. https://doi.org/10.1080/13607860210000007027

World Health Organization. (2019). *International statistical classification of diseases and related health problems* (11th ed.). https://icd.who.int/

World Health Organization. (2023). *Constitution*. https://www.who.int/about/governance/constitution

Xu, J., Murphy, S. L., Kochanek, K. D., & Arias, E. (2022). *Mortality in the United States, 2021* (NCHS Data Brief, No. 456, pp. 1–8).

Zhu, Y., & Enguidanos, S. (2022). Advance directives completion and hospital out-of-pocket expenditures. *Journal of Hospital Medicine, 17*(6), 437–444. https://doi.org/10.1002/jhm.12839

12

Relationships, Families, and Aging: Changes in Roles With Aging

Rachel L. Rodriguez, J. W. Terri Huh, and Susan Ryan

> **LEARNING OBJECTIVES**
>
> - Describe trends in the marital and relationship statuses of older adults.
> - Apply their knowledge of the (a) social, (b) biological/physiological, and (c) social selection theories of how marital quality affects physical and mental health to everyday life.
> - Describe the frequency of current living arrangements for older adults and contrast these findings from developed and less developed countries.
> - Describe protective factors that are associated with better mental health among caregivers of parents and spouses.

Along with the global population aging phenomenon, there has been an increase in the diversity of family structures and households across the world. Several additional factors contribute to the shifting family structures and households, such as improvements in medicine and life expectancy; decreasing rates of fertility; later-life marriages; and increasing rates of divorce, remarriage, cohabitation, lone parenthood, and stepfamily formation. Such growth in the diversity of family structure has also led to changes in the manner in which intergenerational, spousal, sibling, and other kinship relationships function. This in turn affects the way in which older adults receive care and support. Emerging late-life care networks recognize the blend among older adults' care needs, available and actual family care networks, and outcomes for older adults and their support networks (Freedman et al., 2023). This framework also delineates the alternative options for meeting care needs, such as residential care, paid home care, other community-based long-term services and supports, and assistive technologies.

The importance of social factors and relationships on health status has strong support in the literature. Furthermore, the impact of social support for positive health outcomes or providing a buffer from poor health indicates that understanding social networks and relationship status is essential to determining how to promote health in the aging population. This chapter seeks to delve into these societal trends and examine how they are affecting the physical health and well-being of the globally aging population. The first section explores trends in nuptial and relationship status and the impact this has on physical and psychological health of older adults. This is followed by a discussion of the impact of living arrangements for older adults. The next section examines the caregiving relationship in late life, which serves to illustrate the chronic challenges and opportunities that relationships can support across the life span and across different roles. The chapter concludes with an examination of the impact of COVID and the pandemic on the psychological well-being of older adults, with particular attention to the role of relationships.

NUPTIAL AND RELATIONSHIP STATUS: PREVALENCE AND DEMOGRAPHICS

According to the United Nations' *World Population Ageing* report (United Nations, Department of Economic and Social Affairs, Population Division, 2015), the marital status of older persons varies little across development region (more developed to least developed). The overall proportion of married individuals for both genders among individuals ages 60 and older in less developed regions is 64% and approximately 60% in the more developed regions. Regardless of development region, the proportion of married men is much higher (approximately 80%) than for women (slightly below 50%) in this age demographic. A number of factors contribute to this gender difference in marital status, including the fact that older male spouses are more likely to die before their wives and that men tend to marry younger women (United Nations, Department of Economic and Social Affairs, Population Division, 2015). This then translates into lower remarriage probabilities for older women than for older men, partly because of the reduced availability of men in similar or older age ranges (United Nations, Department of Economic and Social Affairs, Population Division, 2015).

If approximately 60% of the older population is married, then there is a significant portion (~40%) of older adults over the age of 60 across the world that are not married. The group of unmarried older individuals includes those who are widowed, divorced, or never married. According to U.S. Census data, in 2015 a higher percentage of women aged 65 and older were widowed (34%) compared with their male counterparts (12%). Moreover, 5% of women and 5% of men in this age group fell into the never married category. Divorced and separated (including married/spouse absent) older persons represented only 15% of Americans more than the age of 65 in 2015. However, this percentage has increased since 1980, when approximately 5.3% of the older population were divorced or separated/spouse absent.

Divorce rates—the number of persons divorced per 1,000 married persons—among older men and women have been noticeably increasing over the past decades, especially in the United States. For the more than 50 age group, this is due in part to the aging of the Baby Boomer population (those individuals born between 1946 and 1964). Baby Boomers were the first cohort to divorce and remarry in large numbers during young adulthood. This phenomenon, known as the "Gray Divorce," has persisted since 1990, with recent data showing that 36% of U.S. adults getting divorced are aged 50 or older (Brown & Lin, 2022). Moreover, the only age group with an increasing divorce rate is adults aged 65 and older.

Another interesting trend among today's unmarried aging population is the increasing rates of dating and cohabitation (a state in which unmarried couples live together in a long-term relationship resembling marriage) among this group. Using data from the 2005 to 2006 National Social Life, Health, and Aging Project, Brown and Shinohara (2013) found that roughly 15% of older single Americans were currently dating. Looking at these rates further, there are significant gender differences in how men and women approach dating relationships later in life. Older men tend to be more interested in formalizing these relationships through marriage than older women (McWilliams & Barrett, 2014; Stevens, 2002). However, both genders report that remarriage can be stressful (de Jong Gierveld, 2002). Older women tend to prefer the companionship of dating as opposed to remarriage, as it allows them to avoid the potential burden of caregiving that marriage can entail in old age (Dickson et al., 2005). Maintaining autonomy is also a reason many older women cite for the choice of not entering into a cohabiting relationship or marriage (Dickson et al., 2005; Stevens, 2002). Although older widowed women's interest in remarriage declines with age, the likelihood of having a male companion does not seem to decline (Moorman et al., 2006).

Rates of older cohabitors have increased dramatically over the past 3 decades. While the global prevalence rate of cohabitation among older adults is not known, Brown and Wright (2017) estimated that 14% of persons aged 50 and older in the United States are in a cohabitating union. A portrait of cohabitating older adults in the United States suggests that more men tend to enter into a cohabitating relationship, and those who choose to cohabitate have lower incomes (particularly women) and are less likely to own their homes than are remarried persons (Brown et al., 2012). Cohabitation is also more common among Blacks and Hispanics than among non-Hispanic Whites (Raley, 1996; Wherry & Finegold, 2004). As the proportion of Black and Hispanic older adults continues to increase, it is logical to assume that rates of cohabitation among older adults will continue to rise in kind.

EFFECTS OF NUPTIAL AND RELATIONSHIP STATUS ON PHYSICAL AND PSYCHOLOGICAL HEALTH

A large research literature shows that relationships, especially marriage, have an important protective role in supporting physical and psychological health (Umberson & Thomeer, 2020). Moreover, for older adults, relationships and social support promote health, reduce mortality, maintain functional ability, and promote psychological well-being. This section examines the quality of different relationships as a determinant of health and mental health outcomes. The first section reviews marital relationships, on which much research endeavors have focused. This section also includes a review of the role that dissolution of marital unions and other union-level characteristics may play in physical and psychological well-being in late life. The remaining sections include a discussion of other types of relationships, that is, cohabitated unions, sibling relationships, and friendships, and how these relationships may impact physical and psychological health.

Marital Quality and the Effects of Marriage on Physical and Psychological Health

The protective effects of marriage for physical and emotional well-being are widely documented (Carr & Springer, 2010). Research repeatedly finds lower rates of chronic illness, physical limitations, disability, and mortality in married individuals when compared with nonmarried counterparts. Studies have often looked to the role of marital quality to determine the protective effects of marriage. Marital quality refers to a married person's assessment of their marriage in terms of marital happiness and satisfaction, marital conflict and disagreement, marital interactions, attitudes, and behaviors.

Marriages reporting higher marital happiness and overall better quality are associated with fewer psychological and physical health problems (Liu & Waite, 2014; Thomas et al., 2017). However, a long research archive demonstrates that marriage is not always beneficial, and for older adults, a poor marital relationship may be more harmful for health than being single (Birmingham et al., 2015; Liu & Upenieks, 2021; Zhang et al., 2016). Data from the 20-year *Marital Instability Over the Life Course* study (Booth et al., 2003) found that respondents in relationships with a low marital quality trajectory had the lowest levels of psychological well-being over time (Dush et al., 2008).

A meta-analysis of 126 published empirical articles over the past 50 years in 11 countries examined the association between marital relationship quality and physical health in over 72,000 individuals and found that greater marital quality was related to better physical health regardless of study design, marital quality measure, and publication year (Robles et al., 2014). Objective health measures included markers of cardiovascular disease and blood pressure, among others. Greater marital quality was associated with better subjective health ratings and better self-rated health and/or lower self-rated symptoms (excluding pain). Moreover, the effects of this meta-analysis demonstrated that poorer marital quality is a risk factor for poorer health outcomes.

This same meta-analysis showed similar effects for the relationship between marital quality and psychological health (Robles et al., 2014). Indeed, greater marital quality was related to greater psychological well-being on a number of indicators including depressive and/or anxiety symptoms, self-esteem, life satisfaction, and happiness. Additionally, diagnosed depression was related to lower marital satisfaction.

There are three main accepted explanations of "how" and "why" marital quality affects health: (a) social, (b) biological/physiological, and (c) social selection. First, social explanations highlight the emotional support and health-enhancing support exchanged in high-quality marriages (e.g., Umberson et al., 2006). For example, spouses in high-quality, happy marriages are more likely to encourage each other in engaging in positive healthy behaviors and the avoidance of unhealthy behaviors. They may encourage better eating habits, physical exercise, compliance with medication, and reduction of smoking and alcohol consumption. On the other hand, those in poorer-quality, unhappy marriages exhibit poorer eating habits, erratic sleep patterns, and higher rates of smoking and substance use (Miller et al., 2013). Higher-quality marriages may also buffer the potential negative health effects of life stressors such as work strains, unemployment, and illness (Zhang et al., 2016). This is especially important as couples face the physical challenges of aging.

A second explanation focuses on the responses of biological/physiological pathways to close and nurturing relationships. These pathways often affect multiple physiological systems, including cardiovascular, endocrine, immune, metabolic, and sympathetic nervous systems (Robles et al., 2014). For example, negative interactions, such as marital strain and hostility, have been linked with elevated blood pressure, elevated heart rate, and excretion of stress hormones, compromising both the cardiovascular and immune systems (Birmingham et al., 2015; Liu & Waite, 2014).

Finally, social selection explanations posit that marital quality and health may be mutually influential and that poor physical and mental health may color both one's own and one's spouse's assessment of marital quality (Carr & Pudrovska, 2015). For example, physical or mental health problems may affect one's ability to contribute to the household financially due to inability to maintain employment and/or contribute effectively in the form of completing household chores. Similarly, physical or mental health problems may also inhibit one's ability to provide emotional support central to a good marriage. Indeed, several studies have demonstrated an elevated risk of divorce in couples where one or both spouses have a serious physical or mental health condition (Idstad et al., 2015; Mojtabai et al., 2017).

While it is clear that marital quality impacts physical and psychological health, it is less clear if these effects vary by gender or race and ethnicity. Research is equivocal in terms of gender, with clinical and laboratory-based studies showing greater female vulnerability to marital strain; however, larger population-based studies detect few, if any, gender differences (Umberson & Williams, 2005). Surprisingly, not only are there few studies examining racial and ethnic differences in marital quality, there is also little research examining the impact of race and ethnicity on marital quality and health. While some scholars have proposed that the well-documented racial health disparities gap can be partly explained by the fact that Blacks are less likely than Whites to be married, little is known about the impact that marital quality has on these outcomes (Carr & Pudrovska, 2015).

On the other hand, there is growing evidence that the protective effects of marital quality on health vary over the life course. In particular, the deleterious effects of marital stress on health have been shown to intensify with age (Umberson et al., 2006). Henry et al. (2007) hypothesized that unlike other social relationships in which older adults may minimize or leave negative interactions, they are less likely to leave their long-term marital partners. This finding suggests that because older adults are more likely to stay in marriages even with high degrees of marital stress, they remain in a pattern of negative emotions and stressful interactions, which then can create or intensify already-existing health problems.

When Marriage Ends: Impact on Health and Psychological Outcomes

The literature consistently shows that divorced and widowed persons have poorer physical and mental health than their married counterparts. These effects have been documented for a range of outcomes including self-rated health, mortality, cardiovascular disease, chronic illness, smoking-related cancers, functional limitations, depression, and substance use (Hughes & Waite, 2009; Zhang & Hayward, 2006). Moreover, it has been shown that the transition out of marriage, be it through divorce or widowhood, undermines the health of men more than women (Williams & Umberson, 2004). However, the negative health outcomes for marital dissolution are impacted by the quality of the marriage that has ended. Several studies examining the long-term impact of dissolved troubled marriages found gains for physical health and psychological well-being and health decrements for those who remained married (Hawkins & Booth, 2005; Williams & Umberson, 2004). Similarly, research on widowhood shows that the emotional toll varies based on the quality of the marriage. Those with higher-quality marriages, as measured by warmth, conflict, and dependence, experienced worse grief symptoms (Carr et al., 2000). In addition, a recent study looking at the role of marital status and physical function found that large social networks (i.e., having three or more individuals in one's family network) may be enough to offset some of the negative physical consequences of being single, although this study did not differentiate this effect on those who were single due to divorce, becoming widowed, or never married (Clouston et al., 2014).

Cohabitation

Though cohabitation is becoming more common among single adults aged 60 and older, the research into its effects on health and well-being is just beginning. At present, the predominant view is that cohabitation is associated with greater advantages for overall well-being relative to being nonpartnered but provides fewer economic, psychological, and health benefits relative to being married (Brown et al., 2012; Carr & Springer, 2010; Liu & Reczek, 2012). This finding appears to be especially true for women (Brown et al., 2012). The mechanisms through which this occurs has not yet been fully investigated; however, the underlying theoretical framework is thought to be similar to that proposed for marital unions and described previously. Interestingly, international comparisons suggest that the benefits of cohabitation are comparable to marriage in nations where it is a culturally normative and legally protected institution (Stavrova et al., 2012). For example, registered cohabitators living in the Netherlands have the same rights as married couples when it comes to inheritance and pension receipt following a partner's death (Perelli-Harris & Gassen, 2012). Cultural norms and social policies such as this may lessen financial and other anxieties associated with being single and heighten the desirability of cohabitation.

Other Significant Relationships in Late Life

Marital and romantic partnerships are not the only important relationships during adulthood. Sibling relationships and friendships are also important to physical and psychological well-being, especially in middle and late life. However, unlike marital and romantic relationships that are readily measured in census and other national surveys, investigations of the prevalence and interaction patterns in these relationships are reserved for specialized studies.

SIBLING RELATIONSHIPS

Perhaps the longest-lasting relationship of an individual's life is the one with their surviving siblings. It is one of the few adult relationships that can last from childhood to late adulthood and involves a shared cultural, family, and biological history. Research has shown that many older adults do have contact with their siblings and report these relationships to be meaningful (Bedford & Aviolo, 2012; Connidis, 2010; Connidis & Campbell, 2001). Additionally, the literature states that relationships with siblings can contribute to life satisfaction, higher morale, fewer depressive symptoms, psychological well-being, and a greater sense of emotional security in old age (Cicirelli, 1995; Stocker et al., 2020).

Though considered second in priority to marital and parent–child relationships, sibling networks are important, and a dramatic increase in sibling exchange is often seen in later life (Stocker et al., 2020). Factors influencing the extent of sibling contact and the importance of the relationship include geographic proximity, being without a partner, and a decrease in contemporaries who can share life review activities. Additionally, the literature suggests that siblings offer more psychological support (companionship, advice, or encouragement) than instrumental support (household assistance, shopping, or financial assistance) in late life. Moreover, relatively few individuals report depending on a sibling for day-to-day needs in old age, although they list them as a source of social and emotional support. Cicirelli (1995) found that 60% of respondents said they would help a sibling if their sibling needed their assistance, yet only 7% had actually turned to a sibling as a primary source of assistance during their own time of crisis. Indeed, siblings should be considered important members of social networks of older adults, especially those who do not have partners and/or adult children available as immediate sources of support.

Research has shown that the gender of siblings significantly impacts the emotional closeness of sibling pairs and the extent of contact between siblings. Sister-to-sister and sister-to-brother relationships show greater emotional closeness and more frequency of contact than brother-to-brother relationships (Connidis & Campbell, 2001; Stocker et al., 2020). Moreover, the closeness of the bond to a sister (by both men and women) was related to reports of fewer depressive symptoms (Cicirelli, 1989). At the same time, however, more conflict is reported between sister-to-sister relationships than other sibling combinations, which is also related to increased reports of depressive symptoms.

FRIENDSHIPS

Research on friendship in late life is growing both in size and sophistication. Research indicates that although the number of close friendships tends to decrease with age, friendships provide multiple and key sources of support to older adults, including instrumental and emotional support (Blieszner & Roberto, 2004; Blieszner et al., 2019). Friendships across the life span are often characterized by caring; self-disclosure; trust; loyalty; and shared interests, values, and pleasant events (Adams et al., 2000). Furthermore, while there is variation in the patterns of support received across the life span, strains in friendships tend to decrease over time and levels of positive support tend to remain stable or increase (Birditt et al., 2009; Newsom et al., 2005). This finding is likely due to the greater tendency among older adults to end nonfamily relationships that are overly negative (Henry et al., 2007).

Close friendships may also evolve into fictive kinship (i.e., considered to be "like family" even though there are no blood or legal ties). When viewed in this way, emotional bonds may be tighter than in other friendships and expectations and obligations greater. These fictive kin friendships play important roles for many older adults who may not have blood relations available to provide support. For example, Chatters et al. (1994) note that fictive kin play important roles for older African Americans by extending their family networks. Fictive kin are also of vital importance to gay, lesbian, bisexual, and transgender persons, as well as never-married heterosexual women, all of whom must depend more on friends than relatives for providing social, psychological, and instrumental support (Blando, 2001; Grossman et al., 2000; McDill et al., 2006).

Whether considered fictive kin or not, friend relationships contribute to physical and psychological well-being in adulthood and old age. This is achieved through multiple pathways such as provision of emotional and instrumental support, socialization, and engagement in shared interests and activities (Chen & Feeley, 2014; de Vries, 2018; Santini et al., 2015). Friendships and relational closeness are also important for maintaining cognitive functioning later in life (Blieszner et al., 2019; Cohn-Schwartz et al., 2021; Zahodne et al., 2021).

CAREGIVING RELATIONSHIPS

The caregiving relationship is a critical one to examine within our dynamically shifting society, and provides many opportunities to understand the impacts of relationships under significant and chronic physical, emotional, and societal strain. With the increasing numbers of older adults living well into their 80s and 90s, the number of health-related challenges they face also increases, many of them impairing the individual's ability to independently care for themselves. This has subsequently given rise to informal caregiving as part of the healthcare landscape for many older adults. Informal caregiving is defined as the act of providing unpaid assistance and support to family members or acquaintances who may have physical, psychological, or developmental needs. Two general functional domains of caregiving that been identified: instrumental and emotional. Caregiving is defined by assistance with activities of daily living (ADLs) such as bathing, toileting, and transporting from one place to another, as well as assistance with instrumental ADLs such as managing finances, medications, and appointments, shopping, preparing meals, and accessing different services. Caregiving also involves significant emotional support such as listening, counseling, and companionship and providing behavioral support such as managing challenging behaviors.

While in many cases, particularly when the caregiver is a family member, caregiving is considered "unpaid," the true cost as calculated in terms of hours of care provided is estimated to be $470 billion (Reinhard et al., 2015). According to the Alzheimer's Association, the annual cost of care provided for patients with major neurocognitive disorders was $340 billion on average, or 72% of all unpaid costs for 17.9 billion hours of care provided (Alzheimer's Association, 2023). However, there are other costs in terms of both physical and mental health outcomes of caregivers, who themselves need significant support to maintain their abilities to provide care to older adults. This section focuses on the caregiving relationship, which may serve as a model for a developmental relationship that can carry across the life span, and introduces various theoretical frameworks for the impact of this important relationship on health and well-being in older adults.

The impact of caregiving has been studied using a foundational theory developed by Pearlin et al. (1990), or Pearlin's stress process theory. This theory proposes that caregivers' characteristics such as gender, race/ethnicity, age, and social roles are important components that influence the caregivers' experience of stress and burden, which may then result in depression, anxiety, and declining physical health. An updated model proposed by Moss et al. (2020) and sociocultural theory (SCT; Dilworth-Anderson et al., 2002) provide further determinant moderators and mediators to explain differential contributions to caregiving stress, mental health, and quality of life.

Moss et al. (2020) proposed a model to better understand the specific needs of caregivers. Their model expands on Pearlin's model by including environmental, psychological, social, and health-related factors, as well as those related to the care and functioning of the care recipient. This model also provides a nice complement to Dilworth-Anderson et al.'s (2002) SCT, which emphasizes the complex sociocultural and historically under-researched caregiving pathways experienced by communities of color, individuals from nonconforming gender or sexual orientation communities, immigrants, those living in underserved geographic locations, and those with non-dominant religious affiliations. The SCT also attends to the exponential impacts that intersectionality may have on not just the caregiving relationship but also the well-being of the caregiver, care recipient, and society as a whole. While the theoretical roots of these models are wel-established, empirical data have yet to catch up to substantiate support, and the models require further study. Nonetheless, these models provide alternative pathways to determine more inclusive, expansive, and comprehensive care for families in general and particularly those that include caregivers.

General Trends in Caregiving

While the number of caregivers in the United States who provide care to individuals of all ages has not changed since 2015, the number of caregivers providing care to an adult aged 50 and over has risen from 34.2 million (14.3% of all caregivers) to 41.8 million (16.8% of all caregivers; AARP and National Alliance for Caregiving, 2020). More recent surveys indicate some reduction in the number of caregivers who provide care to an individual with a neurocognitive disorder (Alzheimer's Association, 2023). Although the rate of caregiving for individuals with dementia is a relatively minor proportion compared with those providing care to an adult or child with only physical impairments, the duration (as amounts of years and numbers of hours per week) of providing care is significantly higher for caregivers of individuals with major neurocognitive disorders. Caregivers of individuals with major neurocognitive disorders provide more extensive support and help across the range of ADLs compared with caregivers of other diseases, with the greatest gaps in bathing/showering (34% vs. 20%), feeding (33% vs. 20%), and dealing with incontinence (32% vs. 12%; Alzheimer's Association, 2023). In terms of hours of care provided per week, one study found that caregivers of patients with dementia provided on average 27 more hours per month (92 hours vs. 65 hours) than caregivers of people with other medical problems (Kasper et al., 2015). Individuals with major neurocognitive disorders require significantly more care of all types, which may vary through the course of the disease, but generally, the degree of care increases exponentially as the care recipient declines in all aspects of their functioning.

Women tend to provide care more often than men (AARP and National Alliance for Caregiving, 2020). Data from the 2018 National Health and Wellness Survey of seven countries (Japan, the United States, and five European nations) suggest some differences in the gender gap, with the United States (61.5%) showing significantly more women caregivers compared with Japan (51.9%) and the five European countries (56.4%; Ohno et al., 2021). The majority of caregivers tend to be female spouses and daughters (61%; Kasper et al., 2015). Spouses tended to provide significantly more hours of caregiving per week (56.4 hours) compared with adult children (27.3 hours; Pinquart & Sörensen, 2011). Caregivers from nondominant racial and ethnic backgrounds tend to be younger, are less likely to be a spouse, and are more likely to have lower levels of education and income (Pinquart & Sörensen, 2005). As noted by Dilworth-Anderson et al. (2002), any research on caregiving by diverse ethnic groups is limited and needs to be understood with that background. When non-White populations are studied, rates of caregiving by ethnicity show differences in number of hours of care provided per week, with Black caregivers more likely to provide more than 40 hours of care per week (54.3%) than White caregivers (38.6%; Alzheimer's Association, 2023). However, Black caregivers were 69% less likely than their White counterparts to use respite services (Ejem et al., 2022; Parker & Fabius, 2020). These differences are important to note since they demonstrate healthcare disparities in care needs and access for individuals from diverse nondominant communities. There continue to be significant disparities in health and healthcare across racially and ethnically diverse populations of caregivers (Alzheimer's Association, 2023). Caregivers across different non-White communities report greater care demands, less help from and use of formal services, and differential levels of depression compared with White caregivers (Pinquart & Sörensen, 2005; Rote et al., 2019).

Physical, Psychological, and Emotional Impacts of Caregiving

There are high rates of reported emotional stress in caregivers, which tend to be highest when providing care for a close relative, such as a spouse or parent (45% and 44%, respectively; AARP & National Alliance for Caregiving, 2020). Approximately 17% of all caregivers report fair or poor health, which is higher than that reported by the general public in the Centers for Disease Control and Prevention/National Center for Health Statistics (CDC/NCHS), National Health Interview Survey (Clarke et al., 2015). Providing more hours of care, caring for someone with mental health issues, coresiding with care recipients, and providing medical/nursing tasks were noted to elevate risk for negative health (AARP & National Alliance for Caregiving, 2020). It is therefore not surprising that individuals caring for someone with a major neurocognitive disorder may be particularly at risk for negative health and mental health outcomes (Alzheimer's Association, 2023)

Studies demonstrate that caregivers of individuals with major neurocognitive disorders experience more stress, and worse physical and mental health effects compared with other caregivers of individuals with other care needs or non caregivers of the same age. These studies also support the finding that caregivers experience more burden due to behavior problems compared with physical and cognitive impairments (Pinquart & Sörensen, 2003). There have been many studies comparing spouses to adult children as caregivers with results suggesting that spouses might experience higher rates of burden (Ott et al., 2007; Rinaldi et al., 2005) and other studies showing that adult child caregivers may experience more burden (Andren & Elmstahl,

2007; Chappell et al., 2014). However, rates of mental health issues when they develop may be similar regardless of the relationship between caregivers and care recipients (Pinquart & Sörensen, 2003). Caregivers seem to be more likely to develop depression or anxiety when the care recipient is younger in age with greater disease severity, which encompasses ADL function and behavioral symptoms. Caregiver characteristics that seem to predict development of depression or anxiety were being female (Ma et al., 2018), being a spouse or adult child, perceived poor health of the caregiver, low levels of financial resources, more hours caregiving, and functional impairment of the caregiver (Alzheimer's Association, 2023).

Adult Children as Caregivers

Caregivers who are adult children often have compounded family and nonfamily responsibilities, which may often conflict and therefore affect their health over time. Two theories, primarily informed by Pearlin's stress models, have been developed referring to the possible impact of having multiple roles on the mental health of middle-aged caregivers. The first refers to the role strain or role conflict perspective, which posits that multiple roles (e.g., employee, caregiver, spouse) may result in more challenges with restricted time and resources of the individual (Burke, 2017) and therefore the adult child caregiver may experience more depressive symptoms. The second theory is the role enhancement perspective, which posits that there may be positive consequences from holding multiple roles, such as status security and status enhancement, which may be protective against depression. This second theory posits that different roles may give purpose, meaning, and direction in the adult child caregiver's life (Thoits, 1983).

In general, studies support the finding that adult child caregivers tend to have more depression compared with similar-aged individuals who are not caregivers (Alzheimer's Association, 2023; Barnett, 2015). However, based on the theories described previously, there may be different pathways toward developing depression in adult child caregivers based on the types of additional roles ascribed. Children reporting secure attachment style may experience less depression when entering into the caregiving role (Atkins, 2021). There have been mixed findings of employment and being a caregiver, with some studies suggesting that such a combination could lead to higher levels of depression (Stoller & Pugliesi, 1989), supporting the role conflict theory, and others reporting lower levels of depression (measured as emotional strain related to caregiving; Williams et al., 2008) for those who were employed, supporting the role enhancement theory. It is possible that gender may play a moderating role between employment and caregiving, in that female caregivers spend more hours on care and are more likely to provide personal assistance (Kasper et al., 2015; Pinquart & Sörensen, 2006), and therefore the balance between caregiving and employment may become more strained for women. However, one study looking at the relationship between employment status and caregiving suggests better psychological and physical health for married and employed caregivers (Barnett, 2015) regardless of gender. Adult child caregivers seemed to experience more depression when they were caring for their father or father-in-law (Chumbler et al., 2004). Chumbler et al. (2004) also showed that being employed and married decreased depressive symptoms, supporting the protective role of marriage in depression. As a whole, these studies seem to provide more support for role enhancement theory and that marriage and employment may mitigate the strain of caregiving.

The updated model proposed by Moss et al. (2020) suggests that there are greater needs that Pearlin's stress model does not take into account, which may provide further avenues to understanding the relationship between depression and various categories of needs. Moss et al.'s (2020) model may also inform how to tailor services according to the care needs along the five categories they propose of environmental, psychological, social, healthcare related, and care recipient needs and functioning. Moss et al.'s (2020) framework, which they developed out of semi-structured in-depth interviews with a small sample of caregivers, with unclear racial and ethnic makeup, go beyond the different relationships between the caregiver and care recipient to the larger systems in which this relationship must navigate to receive supports and potentially influence perceptions of burden and experience of depression. This is a relatively new model, and it is unclear how these factors relate to the development of depression or other mental health concerns among caregivers.

According to *Caregiving in the United States 2020* (AARP & National Alliance for Caregiving, 2020), there has been an increase in the number of caregivers reporting providing care for two or more people in 2020 (24%) compared with 2015 (15%). A popular view in U.S. culture is that of the "sandwich generation." This is the idea that adult child caregivers are experiencing further stress due to their dual caregiving roles of caring for children and parents. Recent studies are inconclusive as to whether having coresiding children relates to lower mental health of caregivers (Barnett, 2015; Owsiany et al., 2023; Penning & Wu, 2016). Within the United States, Owsiany et al. (2023) suggest higher burnout in sandwich generation caregivers but similar rates of depression across groups (caregivers of parents, caregivers of children only, non-caregivers, and sandwich generation caregivers). Older studies suggest that the more influential factor regardless of whether there was a coresiding child seems to be employment and marital status (Chumbler et al., 2004; Martin 2000), in that being employed and married seem to confer better mental health.

Given the dearth of early research conducted on culturally and ethnically diverse caregivers, there is a great need for theory and research involving non-White caregiving groups to better capture and explain the complexities of the caregiving experience (Dilworth-Anderson et al., 2002). While there may be higher resilience and positive attitudes toward caregiving in non-White caregivers, more recent research points to higher rates of depression in Hispanic, Black, and Asian American caregivers (Gilmore-Bykovskyi et al., 2018; Rote et al., 2019). One study suggests that these rates are partially explained by higher levels of poor physical health prior to becoming caregivers in Black and Hispanic communities (Chen et al., 2020). One theory that allows greater accommodation for the cultural context is SCT (Dilworth-Anderson et al., 2002), which emphasizes cultural norms, beliefs, attitudes, and values in terms of how individuals accommodate and learn to adapt to life's challenges. Taken from this lens, Dilworth-Anderson et al. (2002) refer to the ways in which Black caregivers' experiences are filtered through the prism of institutional, structural, and cultural factors (i.e., mistrust, lack of resources, lack of access to care, and family reciprocity), which would result in higher dependence on family and informal networks for receiving care or support (Dilworth-Anderson et al., 2002; Haley et al., 1987).

Older Adults as Caregivers

More than two thirds of caregivers of people with dementia are spouses or longtime partners (Alzheimer's Association, 2023). Spouses may experience more caregiving burden but similar rates of depression as adult child caregivers (Pinquart & Sörensen, 2003). Burden is typically defined as perceived stress related to caregiving that can lead to many negative physical and emotional consequences, whereas depression is defined as significant clinical symptoms that lead to functional impairment. Spouses themselves are older and have their own health problems and related functional impairments, which may impact their abilities to provide care and lead to the perception of more burden. A meta-analysis on caregivers' stress showed that the care recipients' impairments and caregivers' involvement had stronger effects on burden than on depression (Pinquart & Sörensen, 2003). This seems to suggest that although spouse caregivers are impacted by caregiving responsibilities, other characteristics may serve as protective factors against depression in spouse caregivers, such as relationship closeness (Fauth et al., 2012).

Studies suggest that despite high rates of stress and feelings of burden, rates of mental health problems in caregivers (while still higher than in average community-dwelling older adult populations) are relatively low. These studies indicate a range of 16% to 35% of caregivers in their samples reporting symptoms of depression (Alzheimer's Association, 2023; Jennings et al., 2015). Pinquart and Sörensen (2003) report caregivers who perceived positive aspects of caregiving, such as feeling useful or experiencing closeness to the care recipient, had lower levels of burden and depression. Given the minority of caregivers with depression and anxiety, these findings suggest that many caregivers also perceive positive benefits to being in a caregiving role such as improvements in problem-solving abilities, self-understanding, and self-efficacy. These reports also show support for the role enhancement and sociocultural theories.

IMPACT OF THE COVID-19 PANDEMIC ON OLDER ADULT RELATIONSHIPS

Older adults weathered the upheaval and isolation brought about by lockdowns and social distancing better than younger people, showing less pandemic-related stress, less social isolation, fewer negative effects of social isolation, greater financial stability, and better relationship quality than younger people (Birditt et al., 2021; Klaiber et al., 2021). Overall, adults over 65 tended to report less social isolation than other groups, but the oldest old (those 85 and older), along with young adults, reported the highest levels of perceived isolation and loneliness (Birditt et al., 2021). Quality of relationships remained stable for older adults over a 6-month period early in the pandemic, but perceptions of social support varied, which was notable because the two are usually positively correlated. Researchers posited that the heightened stress of the pandemic meant that even when older adult relationships were strong, family members and friends had less to give in the way of support (Lin et al., 2022). Heightened stress, job loss, and isolation among caregivers contributed to a global increase in the prevalence and severity of elder abuse by family members during the COVID-19 pandemic, with older adults with dementia being at the greatest risk (Du & Chen, 2021; Makaroun et al., 2021).

However, older adults showed resilience and adaptability. A study of 776 adults in Canada and the United States found that in the early months of the COVID-19 pandemic, older adults coped with stressors better than younger adults and enjoyed greater overall well-being, particularly when compared with young adults, many of whom had to return home from college or lost jobs, and with parents of young children, who faced the stress of parenting and working from home at the same time (Birditt et al., 2021; Klaiber et al., 2021). Older adults seemed better able to maintain a positive view of their romantic partners under the stress of the pandemic (Shavit et al., 2023). A study of Korean older adults found that although contact with friends and neighbors went down, contact with family members increased for older adults. Older women experienced a greater decline in extrafamilial contact and a greater increase in contact with family members than men (Ryu et al., 2022). Access to technology was a protective factor for maintaining contact with family members, but groups varied in their access to technology, with minority, low-income, and physically disabled older adults less likely to have access. Those who had access to technology were able to maintain family rituals and traditions by hosting celebrations over video or car parades (Gilligan et al., 2020). The overall amount of social interaction decreased for older adults, but was partially made up for by time on the phone and writing letters.

In sum, older adults enjoyed resilience factors that protected them from relationship distress and deterioration during the COVID-19 pandemic, but for the more vulnerable among them, including those 85 and older, minority, low-income, and physically disabled older adults, outcomes were poorer.

CONCLUSION

Today's older adults experience much more diversity in terms of relationships, roles, and living arrangements than past cohorts. Studies from multiple sources point to strong associations between familial and other relationships with health, well-being, and mental health for all ages.

Relationships can provide a protective role toward well-being and mental health in late life; married or cohabitating individuals, having sibling relationships, or development of fictive kin relationships all show protection from depression or minimize effects of depression. The rising rates of dating and cohabitation among single older adults suggest more promising health and mental health outcomes for some single older adults. Furthermore, studies indicate that the quality of these relationships is a decisive factor resulting in better health and mental health outcome. The caregiving relationship serves as a compelling model for weathering a multitude of stressors within the social and interpersonal relationship framework. By examining this relationship more closely, we can gain valuable insights into how individuals, families, and communities cope with challenges. A comprehensive study of the caregiving relationship, with more inclusion of diverse communities, has the potential to illuminate effective strategies for resilience and adaptation. Moreover, these insights can contribute significantly to the improvement of current healthcare systems, offering valuable lessons on support structures, interpersonal and family dynamics, and how to promote well-being in caregivers and care recipients. Understanding the intricacies of this relationship may help with advancing not only individual health outcomes but also the overall efficacy of healthcare delivery.

The impact of the COVID-19 global pandemic on the family and support structure is still emerging. Without doubt, at the beginning of the pandemic, older adults faced increased risk of the effects of social isolation, illness, stress, and mortality. However, as time passed the resilience of this age group shone through, with many recent studies showing that older adults coped and adapted better to the stresses of pandemic lockdown and isolation than younger adults.

In conclusion, this chapter identified multiple exciting and interesting movements in the shifts in family structure, households, and caregiving arrangements. These changes in turn have been impacting the way relationships, family structure, and social networks may alter mental and physical health, particularly later in life. The primary take-home message from this chapter is that high-quality relationships are important factors in maintaining physical and mental health and function later in life. These findings further implicate the need to bolster the social networks that exist, and particularly to find adequate means to support similar functions when social networks are in short supply or nonexistent.

DISCUSSION QUESTIONS

1. Provide three possible explanations of how marital quality affects health.
2. Describe three theories about the mental health of caregivers who are adult children.
3. Describe trends in nuptial and relationship status among older adults.
4. Discuss how the dissolution of marriage, through either divorce or widowhood, impacts the physical and emotional well-being of the older adult.
5. Compare two specific ways that caregiving burden might differ for caregivers of patients with major neurocognitive disorders versus caregivers of patients with other conditions.
6. Identify three culture-specific factors that may impact caregiving stress or depression.
7. Describe the difficulties that older adults faced in maintaining relationships during the COVID-19 pandemic as well as protective factors.

A robust set of instructor resources designed to supplement this text is located at http://connect.springerpub.com/content/book/978-0-8261-6617-3. Qualifying instructors may request access by emailing textbook@springerpub.com.

REFERENCES

AARP and National Alliance for Caregiving. (2020). *Caregiving in the United States 2020*. https://doi.org/10.26419/ppi.00103.001.

Adams, R. G., Blieszner, R., & De Vries, B. (2000). Definitions of friendship in the third age: Age, gender, and study location effects. *Journal of Aging Studies, 14*(1), 117–133. https://doi.org/10.1016/s0890-4065(00)80019-5

Alzheimer's Association. (2023). Alzheimer's disease facts and figures. *Alzheimer's & Dementia, 19*(4), 1598–1695. https://doi.org/10.1002/alz13016.

Andren, S., & Elmstahl, S. (2007). Relationships between income, subjective health and caregiver burden in caregivers of people with dementia in group living care: A cross-sectional community-based study. *International Journal of Nursing Studies, 44*(3), 435–446. https://doi.org/10.1016/j.ijnurstu.2006.08.016

Atkins, G. C. (2021). *A stress process approach to assessing caregiver burden, depressive symptoms, and quality of life: The role of attachment in adult relationships* (Publication No. 28712762) [Doctoral dissertation, University of Alabama at Birmingham]. ProQuest Dissertations & Theses Global.

Barnett, A. E. (2015). Adult child caregiver health trajectories and the impact of multiple roles over time. *Research on Aging, 37*(3), 227–252. https://doi.org/10.1177/0164027514527834

Bedford, V. H., & Avioli, P. S. (2012). Siblings in middle and late adulthood In R. Blieszner & V. H. Bedford (Eds.), *Handbook of families and aging* (2nd ed., pp. 125–153). Praeger.

Birditt, K. S., Jackey, L. M. H., & Antonucci, T. C. (2009). Longitudinal patterns of negative relationship quality across adulthood. *Journals of Gerontology Series B: Psychological Sciences & Social Sciences, 64B*(1), 55–64. https://doi.org/10.1093/geronb/gbn031

Birditt, K. S., Turkelson, A., Fingerman, K. L., Polenick, C. A., & Oya, A. (2021). Age differences in stress, life changes, and social ties during the COVID-19 pandemic: Implications for psychological well-being. *The Gerontologist, 61*(2), 205–216. https://doi.org/10.1093/geront/gnaa204

Birmingham, W. C., Uchino, B. N., Smith, T. W., Light, K. C., & Butner J. (2015). It's complicated: Marital ambivalence on ambulatory blood pressure and daily interpersonal functioning. *Annals of Behavioral Medicine, 49*(5), 743–753. https://doi.org/10.1007/s12160-015-9709-0

Blando, J. A. (2001). Twice hidden: Older gay and lesbian couples, friends, and intimacy. *Generations, 25*(2), 87–89. https://www.jstor.org/stable/44877611

Blieszner, R., & Roberto, K. A. (2004). Friendship across the life span: Reciprocity in individual and relationship development. In F. R. Lang & K. L. Fingerman (Eds.), *Growing together: Personal relationships across the lifespan* (pp. 159–182). Cambridge University Press.

Blieszner, R., Ogletree, A. M., & Adams, R. G. (2019). Friendship in later life: A research agenda. *Innovation in Aging, 3*(1), igz005. https://doi.org/10.1093/geroni/igz00

Booth, A., Johnson, D., Amato, P., & Rogers, S. (2003). *Marital instability over the life course: A six-wave panel study, 1980, 1983, 1988, 1992–1994, 1997, 2000* (Version 1) [Data file]. Interuniversity Consortium for Political and Social Research.

Brown, S. L., Bulanda, J. R., & Lee, G. R. (2012). Transitions into and out of cohabitation in later life. *Journal of Marriage and Family, 74*(4), 774–793. https://doi.org/10.1111/j.1741-3737.2012.00994.x

Brown, S. L., & Lin, I. F. (2022). The graying of divorce: A half century of change. *The Journals of Gerontology. Series B, Psychological Sciences and Social Sciences, 77*(9), 1710–1720. https://doi.org/10.1093/geronb/gbac057

Brown, S. L., & Shinohara, S. K. (2013). Dating relationships in older adulthood: A national portrait. *Journal of Marriage and Family, 75*(5), 1194–1202. https://doi.org/10.1111/jomf.12065

Brown, S. L., & Wright, M. R. (2017). Marriage, cohabitation, and divorce in later life. *Innovation in Aging, 1*(2), igx015. https://doi.org/10.1093/geroni/igx015

Burke, R. J. (2017). The sandwich generation: Individual, family, organizational, and societal challenges and opportunities. In R. J. Burke & L. M. Calvano (Eds.), *The sandwich generation: Caring for oneself and others at home and at work* (pp. 3–39). Edward Elgar Publishing, Inc.

Carr, D., House, J. S., Kessler, R. C., Nesse, R. M., Sonnega, J., & Wortman, C. (2000). Marital quality and psychological adjustment to widowhood among older adults: A longitudinal analysis. *Journals of Gerontology Series B: Psychological Sciences and Social Sciences, 55*(4), S197–S207. https://doi.org/10.1093/geronb/55.4.s197

Carr, D., & Pudrovska, T. (2015). Marital quality & health. In J. D. Wright (Ed.), *International encyclopedia of the social & behavioral sciences* (2nd ed., Vol. 14, pp. 512–517). Elsevier.

Carr, D., & Springer, K. W. (2010). Advances in families and health research in the 21st century. *Journal of Marriage and Family, 72*(3), 743–761. https://doi.org/10.1111/j.1741-3737.2010.00728

Chappell, N. L., Dujela, C., & Smith, A. (2014). Spouse and adult child differences in caregiving burden. *Canadian Journal on Aging, 33*(4), 462–472. https://doi.org/10.1017/S0714980814000336

Chatters, L. M., Taylor, R. J., & Jayakody, R. (1994). Fictive kinship relations in black extended families. *Journal of Comparative Family Studies, 25*(3), 297–312. https://doi.org/10.3138/jcfs.25.3.297

Chen, Y., & Feeley, T. H. (2014). Social support, social strain, loneliness, and well-being among older adults: An analysis of the health and retirement study. *Journal of Social and Personal Relationships, 32*(2), 141–161. https://doi.org/10.1177/0265407513488728

Chen, C., Thunell, J., & Zissimopoulos, J. (2020). Changes in physical and mental health of Black, Hispanic, and White caregivers and noncaregivers associated with onset of spousal dementia. *Alzheimer's Dementia (NY), 6*(1), e12082. https://doi.org/10.1002/trc2.12082.

Chumbler, N. R., Pienta, A. M., & Dwyer, J. W. (2004). The depressive symptomatology of parent care among the near elderly. The influence of multiple role commitments. *Research on Aging, 26*(3), 330–351.

Cicirelli, V. G. (1989). Feelings of attachment to siblings and well-being in later life. *Psychology and Aging, 4*(2), 211–218. https://doi.org/10.1037//0882-7974.4.2.211

Cicirelli, V. G. (1995). *Sibling relationships across the life span*. Plenum Press.

Clarke, T. C., Ward, B. W., Freeman, G., & Schiller, J. S. (2015, September). *Early release of selected estimates based on data from the January–March 2015 National Health Interview Survey*. https://www.cdc.gov/nchs/data/nhis/earlyrelease/earlyrelease201509.pdf

Clouston, S., Lawlor, A., & Verdery, A. (2014). The role of partnership status on late-life physical function. *Canadian Journal on Aging, 33*(4), 413–425. https://doi.org/10.1017/S0714980814000282

Cohn-Schwartz, E., Levinsky, M., & Litwin, H. (2021). Social network type and subsequent cognitive health among older Europeans. *International Psychogeriatrics, 33*(5), 495–504. https://doi.org/10.1017/S1041610220003439

Connidis, I. A. (2010). *Family ties and aging* (2nd ed). Pine Forge Press.

Connidis, I. A., & Campbell, L. D. (2001). Closeness, confiding, and contact among siblings in middle and late adulthood. In A. Walker, M. Manoogian-O'Dell, L. McGraw, & D. L. White (Eds.), *Families in later life* (pp. 149–155). Pine Forge Press.

de Jong Gierveld, J. (2002). The dilemma of repartnering: Considerations of older men and women entering new intimate relationships in later life. *Ageing International, 27*, 61–78. https://doi.org/10.1007/s12126-002-1015-z

de Vries, B. (2018). The unsung bonds of friendship—and caring—among older adults. *Generations, 42*(3), 77–81. https://www.jstor.org/stable/e26591693

Dickson, F. C., Hughes, P. C., & Walker, K. L. (2005). An exploratory investigation into dating among later-life women. *Western Journal of Communication, 69*(1), 67–82. https://doi.org/10.1080/10570310500034196

Dilworth-Anderson, P., Williams I. C., & Gibson B. E (2002). Issues of race, ethnicity, and culture in caregiving research: A 20-year review (1980–2000). *The Gerontologist, 42*(2), 237–272. https://doi.org/10.1093/geront/42.2.237

Du, P., & Chen, Y. (2021). Prevalence of elder abuse and victim-related risk factors during the COVID-19 pandemic in China. *BMC Public Health, 21*(1), 1096. https://doi.org/10.1186/s12889-021-11175-z

Dush, C. M. K., Taylor, M. G., & Kroeger, R. A. (2008). Marital happiness and psychological well-being across the life course. *Family Relations, 57*(2), 211–226. https://doi.org/10.1111/j.1741-3729.2008.00495.x

Ejem, D., Atkins, G. C., Perkins, M., Morhardt, D. J., Williams, I. C., & Cothran, F. A. (2022). Stressors and acceptability of services among black caregivers of persons with memory problems. *Journal of Gerontological Nursing, 48*(6), 13–18. https://doi.org/10.3928/00989134-20220505-01

Fauth, E. B., Gerstorf, D., Ram, N., & Malmberg, B. (2012). Changes in depressive symptoms in the context of disablement processes: Role of demographic characteristics, cognitive function, health, and social support. *The Journals of Gerontology, Series B, 67B*(2), 167–177. https://doi.org/10.1093/geronb/gbr078

Freedman, V. A., Agree, E. M., Seltzer, J. A., Birditt, K. S., Fingerman, K. L., Friedman, E. M., Lin, I. F., Margolis, R., Park, S. S., Patterson, S. E., Polenick, C. A., Reczek, R., Reyes, A. M., Truskinovsky, Y., Wiemers, E. E., Wu, H., Wolf, D. A., Wolff, J. L., & Zarit, S. H. (2023). The changing demography of late-life family caregiving: A research agenda to understand future care networks for an aging U.S. population. *The Gerontologist, 64*(2), gnad036. https://doi.org/10.1093/geront/gnad036

Gilligan, M., Suitor, J. J., Rurka, M., & Silverstein, M. (2020). Multigenerational social support in the face of the COVID-19 pandemic. *Journal of Family Theory & Review, 12*(4), 431–447. https://doi.org/10.1111/jftr.12397

Gilmore-Bykovskyi, A., Johnson, R., Walljasper, L., Block, L., & Werner, N. (2018). Underreporting of gender and race/ethnicity differences in NIH-funded dementia caregiver support interventions. *American Journal of Alzheimer's Disease and Other Dementias, 33*(3), 145–152. https://doi.org/10.1177/1533317517749465

Grossman, A. H., D'Augelli, A. R., & Hershberger, S. L. (2000). Social support networks of lesbian, gay, and bisexual, adults 60 years of age and older. *Journal of Gerontology: Psychological Sciences, 55*(3), P171–P179. https://doi.org/10.1093/geronb/55.3.p171.

Hawkins, D., & Booth, A. (2005). Unhappily ever after: Effects of long-term, low-quality marriages on well-being. *Social Forces, 84*(1), 451–471. https://doi.org/10.1353/sof.2005.0103

Haley, W. E., Levine, E. G., Brown, S. L., & Bartolucci, A. A. (1987). Stress, appraisal, coping, and social support as predictors of adaptational outcome among dementia caregivers. *Psychology and Aging, 2*(4), 323–330. https://doi.org/10.1037//0882-7974.2.4.323

Henry, N. J. M., Berg, C. A., Smith, T. W., & Florsheim, P. (2007). Positive and negative characteristics of marital interaction and their association with marital satisfaction in middle-aged and older couples. *Psychology and Aging, 22*(3), 428–441. https://doi.org/10.1037/0882-7974.22.3.428

Hughes, M. E., & Waite, L. J. (2009). Marital biography and health at midlife. *Journal of Health and Social Behavior, 50*(3), 344–358. https://doi.org/10.1177/002214650905000307

Idstad, M., Torvik, F. A., Borren, I., Rognmo, K., Røysamb, E., & Tambs, K. (2015). Mental distress predicts divorce over 16 years: The HUNT study. *BMC Public Health, 15*, 320. https://doi.org/10.1186/s12889-015-1662-0

Jennings, L. A., Reuben, D. B., Evertson, L. C., Serrano, K. S., Ercoli, L., Grill, J., . . ., Wenger, N. S. (2015). Unmet needs of caregivers of individuals referred to a dementia care program. *Journal of the American Geriatrics Society, 63*(2), 282–289. https://doi.org/10.1111/jgs.13251

Kasper, J. D., Freedman, V. A., Spillman, B. C., & Wolff, J. L. (2015). The disproportionate impact of dementia on family and unpaid caregiving to older adults. *Health Affairs, 34*(10), 1642–1649. https://doi.org/10.1377/hlthaff.2015.0536

Klaiber, P., Wen, J. H., DeLongis, A., & Sin, N. L. (2021). The ups and downs of daily life during COVID-19: Age differences in affect, stress, and positive events. *The Journals of Gerontology. Series B, Psychological Sciences and Social Sciences, 76*(2), e30–e37. https://doi.org/10.1093/geronb/gbaa096

Lin, J., Zajdel, M., Keller, K. R., Gilpin Macfoy, F. O., Shaw, P., Curtis, B., Ungar, L., & Koehly, L. (2022). Life under stay-at-home orders: A panel study of change in social interaction and emotional wellbeing among older Americans during COVID-19 pandemic. *BMC Public Health, 22*(1), 1777. https://doi.org/10.1186/s12889-022-14103-x

Liu, H., & Reczek, C. (2012). Cohabitation and U.S. adult mortality: An examination by gender and race. *Journal of Marriage and Family, 74*(4), 794–811. https://doi.org/10.1111/j.1741-3737.2012.00983.x

Liu, Y., & Upenieks, L. (2021). Marital quality and well-being among older adults: A typology of supportive, aversive, indifferent, and ambivalent marriages. *Research on Aging, 43*(9–10), 428–439. https://doi.org/10.1177/0164027520969149

Liu, H., & Waite, L. (2014). Bad marriage, broken heart? Age and gender differences in the link between marital quality and cardiovascular risks among older adults. *Journal of Health and Social Behavior, 55*(4), 403–423. https://doi.org/10.1177/0022146514556893

Ma, M., Dorstyn, D., Ward, L., & Prentice, S. (2018). Alzheimers' disease and caregiving: A meta-analytic review comparing the mental health of primary carers to controls. *Aging and Mental Health, 22*(11), 1395–1405. https://doi.org/10.1080/13607863.2017.1370689

Makaroun, L. K., Beach, S., Rosen, T., & Rosland, A.-M. (2021). Changes in elder abuse risk factors reported by caregivers of older adults during the COVID-19 pandemic. *Journal of the American Geriatrics Society, 69*(3), 602–603. https://doi.org/10.1111/jgs.17009

Martin, C. D. (2000). More than the work: Race and gender differences in caregiving burden. *Journal of Family Issues, 21*(8), 981–1005. https://doi.org/10.1177/019251300021008003

McDill, T., Hall, S. K., & Turell, S. C. (2006). Aging and creating families: Never-married heterosexual women over forty. *Journal of Women & Aging, 18*(3), 37–50. https://doi.org/10.1300/J074v18n03_04

McWilliams, S., & Barrett, A. E. (2014). Online dating in middle and later life: Gendered expectations and experiences. *Journal of Family Issues, 35*(3), 411–436. https://doi.org/10.1177/0192513X12468437

McWilliams, S., & Barrett, A. E. (2014). Online dating in middle and later life: Gendered expectations and experiences. *Journal of Family Issues, 35*(3), 411–436. https://doi.org/10.1177/0192513X12468437

Miller, R. B., Hollist, C. S., Olson, J., & Law, D. (2013). Marital quality and health over 20 years: A growth curve analysis. *Journal of Marriage and Family, 75*(3), 667–680. https://doi.org/10.1111/jomf.12025

Mojtabai, R., Stuart, E. A., Hwang, I., Eaton, W. W., Sampson, N., & Kessler, R. C. (2017). Long-term effects of mental disorders on marital outcomes in the National Comorbidity Survey ten-year follow-up. *Social Psychiatry and Psychiatric Epidemiology, 52*(10), 1217–1226. https://doi.org/10.1007/s00127-017-1373-1

Moorman, S. M., Booth, A., & Fingerman, K. L. (2006). Women's romantic relationships after widowhood. *Journal of Family Issues, 27*(9), 1281–1304. https://doi.org/10.1177/0192513X06289096

Moss, S. A., Gebhardt-Kram, L. E., Dabelko-Schoeny, H., & Cheavens, J. (2020). Identifying the needs of family caregivers of people with dementia to improve service delivery: Bridging a research-practice gap. *Journal of Clinical and Translational Science, 4* (Suppl. 1), 135–136. https://doi.org/10.1017/cts.2020.401

Newsom, J. T., Rook, K. S., Nishishiba, M., Sorkin, D. H., & Mahan, T. L. (2005). Understanding the relative importance of positive and negative social exchanges: Examining specific domains and appraisals. *Journal of Gerontology: Psychology Science, 60*(6), P304–P312. https://doi.org/10.1093/geronb/60.6.P304

Ohno, S., Chen, Y., Sakamaki, H., Matsumaru, N., Yoshino, M., Tsukamoto, K. (2021). Burden of caring for Alzheimer's disease or dementia patients in Japan, the U.S., and EU: Results from the National Health and Wellness Survey: A cross-sectional survey. *Journal of Medical Economics, 24*(1), 266–278. https://doi.org/10.1080/13696998.2021.1880801

Ott, C. H., Sanders, S., & Kelber, S. T. (2007). Grief and personal growth experience of spouses and adult–child caregivers of individuals with Alzheimer's disease and related dementias. *Gerontologist, 47*(6), 798–809. https://doi.or/10.1093/geront/47.6.798

Owsiany, M. T., Fenstermacher, E. A., & Edelstein, B. A. (2023). Burnout and depression among sandwich generation caregivers: A brief report. *The International Journal of Aging and Human Development, 97*(4), 425–434. https://doi.org/10.1177/00914150231183137

Parker, L. J., & Fabius, C. D. (2020). Racial differences in respite use among black and white caregivers for people living with dementia. *Journal of Aging and Health, 32*(10), 1667–1675. https://doi.org/10.1177/0898264320951379

Pearlin, L. I., Mullan, J. T., Semple, S. J., & Skaff, M. M. (1990). Caregiving and the stress process: An overview of concepts and their measures. *Gerontologist, 30*(5), 583–594. https://doi.org/10.1093/geront/30.5.583

Penning, M. J., & Wu, Z. (2016). Caregiver stress and mental health: Impact of caregiving relationship and gender. *The Gerontologist, 56*(6), 1102–1113. https://doi.org/10.1093/geront/gnv038

Perelli-Harris, B., & Gassen, N. S. (2012). How similar are cohabitation and marriage? Legal approaches to cohabitation across Western Europe. *Population and Development Review, 38*(3), 435–467. https://doi.org/10.1111/j.1728-4457.2012.00511.x

Pinquart, M., & Sörensen, S. (2003) Differences between caregivers and noncaregivers in psychological health and physical health: A meta-analysis. *Psychology and Aging, 18*(2), 250–267. https://doi.org/10.1037/0882-7974.18.2.250

Pinquart, M., & Sörensen, S. (2005). Ethnic differences in stressors, resources, and psychological outcomes of family caregiving: A meta-analysis. *Gerontologist, 45*(1), 90–106. https://doi.org/10.1093/geront/45.1.90

Pinquart, M., & Sörensen, S. (2006). Gender differences in caregivers stressors, social resources, and health: An updated meta-analysis. *The Journals of Gerontology. Series B, Psychological Sciences and Social Sciences, 61*(1), P33–P45. https://doi.org/10.1093/geronb/61.1.p33

Pinquart, M., & Sörensen, S. (2011). Spouses, adult children, and children-in-law as caregivers of older adults: A meta-analytic comparison. *Psychology and Aging, 26*(1), 1–14. https://doi.org/10.1037/a0021863

Raley, R. K. (1996). A shortage of marriageable men? A note on the role of cohabitation in black–white differences in marriage rates. *American Sociological Review, 61*(6), 973–983. https://doi.org/10.2307/2096303

Reinhard, S. C., Feinberg, L. F., Choula, R., & Houser, A. (2015). Valuing the invaluable. *Insight on the Issues, 104*, 1–25.

Rinaldi, P., Spazzafumo, L., Mastriforti, R., Mattioli, P., Marvardi, M., Polidori, M. C., . . ., Mecocci, P. (2005). Predictors of high level of burden and distress in caregivers of demented patients: Results of an Italian multicenter study. *International Journal of Geriatric Psychiatry, 20*(2), 168–174. https://doi.org/10.1002/gps.1267

Robles, T. F., Slatcher, R. B., Trombello, J. M., & McGinn, M. M, (2014). Marital quality and health: A meta-analytic review. *Psychological Bulletin, 140*(1), 140–187. https://doi.org/10.1037/a0031859

Rote, S. M., Angel, J. L., Moon, H., & Markides, K. (2019). Caregiving across diverse populations: New evidence from the national study of caregiving and Hispanic EPESE. *Innovation in Aging, 3*(2), igz033. https://doi.org/10.1093/geroni/igz033

Ryu, S. I., Park, Y.-H., Kim, J., Huh, I., Chang, S. J., Jang, S.-N., & Noh, E.-Y. (2022). Impact of COVID-19 on the social relationships and mental health of older adults living alone: A two-year prospective cohort study. *PLoS One, 17*(7), e0270260. https://doi.org/10.1371/journal.pone.0270260

Santini, Z. I., Koyanagi, A., Tyrovolas, S., Mason, C., & Haro, J. M. (2015). The association between social relationships and depression: A systematic review. *Journal of Affective Disorders, 175*, 53–65. https://doi.org/10.1016/j.jad.2014.12.049

Shavit, Y. Z., Estlein, R., Elran-Barak, R., & Segel-Karpas, D. (2023). Positive relationships have shades of gray: Age is associated with more complex perceptions of relationship quality during the COVID-19 lockdown. *Journal of Adult Development, 30*(2), 224–235. https://doi.org/10.1007/s10804-022-09431-6

Stavrova, O., Fetchenhauer, D., & Schlosser, T. (2012). Cohabitation, gender, and happiness: A cross cultural study in thirty countries. *Journal of Cross-Cultural Psychology, 43*(7), 1063–1081. https://doi.org/10.1177/0022022111419030

Stevens, N. (2002). Re-engaging: New partnerships in late-life widowhood. *Ageing International, 27*, 27–42. https://doi.org/10.1007/s12126-002-1013-1

Stocker, C. M., Gilligan, M., Klopack, E. T., Conger, K. J., Lanthier, R. P., Neppl, T. K., O'Neal, C. W., & Wickrama, K. A. S. (2020). Sibling relationships in older adulthood: Links with loneliness and well-being. *Journal of Family Psychology, 34*(2), 175–185. https://doi.org/10.1037/fam0000586

Stoller, E. P., & Pugliesi, K. L. (1989). Other roles of caregivers: Competing responsibilities or supportive resources. *The Journals of Gerontology: Series B, 44*(6), S231–S238. https://doi.org/10.1093/geronj/44.6.s231

Thoits, P. A. (1983). Multiple identities and psychological well-being: A reformulation and test of the social isolation hypothesis. *American Sociological Review, 48*(2), 174–187. https://doi.org/10.2307/2095103

Thomas, P. A., & Liu, H., Umberson, D. (2017). Family relationships and well-being. *Innovation in Aging, 1*(3), igx025. https://doi.org/10.1093/geroni/igx025

Umberson, D., & Thomeer, M. B. (2020). Family matters: Research on family ties and health, 2010–2020. *Journal of Marriage and the Family, 82*(1), 404–419. https://doi.org/10.1111/jomf.12640

Umberson, D., & Williams, K. (2005). Marital quality, health, and aging: Gender equity? [Special Issue II]. *Journal of Gerontology Series B: Psychological Sciences and Social Sciences, 60B*, 109–113. https://doi.org/10.1093/geronb/60.special_issue_2.s109

Umberson, D., Williams, K., Powers, D. A., Liu, H., & Needham, B. (2006). You make me sick: Marital quality and health over the life course. *Journal of Health and Social Behavior, 47*(1), 1–16. https://doi.org/10.1177/002214650604700101

United Nations, Department of Economic and Social Affairs, Population Division. (2015). *World population ageing 2015* (ST/ESA/SER.A/390). http://www.un.org/en/development/desa/population/publications/pdf/ageing/WPA2015_Report.pdf

Wherry, L., & Finegold, K. (2004). *Marriage promotion and the living arrangements of black, Hispanic, and white children*. The Urban Institute. https://www.urban.org/sites/default/files/publication/57786/311064-Marriage-Promotion-and-the-Living-Arrangements-of-Black-Hispanic-and-White-Children.PDF

Williams, K., & Umberson, D., (2004). Marital status, marital transitions, and health: A gendered life course perspective. *Journal of Health and Social Behavior, 45*(1), 81–98. https://doi.org/10.1177/002214650404500106

Williams, S. W., Williams, C. S., Zimmerman, S., Munn, J., Dobbs, D., & Sloane, P. D. (2008). Emotional and physical health of informal caregivers of residents at the end of life: The role of social support. *Journals of Gerontology, Series B, Psychological Sciences and Social Sciences, 63*(3), S171–S183. https://doi.org/10.1093/geronb/63.3.s171

Zahodne, L. B., Sharifian, N., Kraal, A. Z., Sol, K., Zaheed, A. B., Manly, J. J., & Brickman, A. M. (2021). Positive psychosocial factors and cognitive decline in ethnically diverse older adults. *Journal of the International Neuropsychological Society, 27*(1), 69–78. https://doi.org/10.1017/S1355617720000648

Zhang, Z., & Hayward, M. (2006). Gender, the marital life course, and cardiovascular disease in late midlife. *Journal of Marriage and Family, 68*(3), 639–657. https://doi.org/10.1111/j.1741-3737.2006.00280.x

Zhang, Z., Liu, H., & Yu, Y.-L. (2016). Marital biography and health in middle and late life. In J. Bookwala (Ed.), *Couple relationships in the middle and later years: Their nature, complexity, and role in health and illness* (pp. 199–218). American Psychological Association.

13

Aging, Work, and Retirement

Christina Matz and Jacquelyn James

> **LEARNING OBJECTIVES**
> - Summarize how ageism may impact work and retirement trajectories and the role of the Age Discrimination in Employment Act in attempting to mitigate that effect.
> - Discuss several ways to define older workers beyond chronological age.
> - Name several reasons for the trend toward working beyond conventional retirement ages.
> - Describe different patterns and trends in later-life work engagement presented in this chapter.
> - Appreciate the various push–pull factors affecting retirement timing and patterns.
> - Summarize how the notion of retirement has changed over the years.
> - Explain the issues surrounding the working longer debate in the context of marginalization.

The intersection of aging, work, and retirement presents a complex landscape that demands attention from researchers, policy makers, and society as a whole. In this chapter, we will explore the intricate dynamics of aging, work in later life, ageism, retirement trends and patterns, historical context, and relevant policies. Moreover, we will highlight the challenges posed by the aging workforce, including the need to address work longevity, early retirement, career patterns, financial concerns, and health and disability issues. Throughout, we emphasize the importance of adopting an intersectional lens to ensure equitable treatment for marginalized older workers.

THE INTERSECTION OF AGING, WORK, AND RETIREMENT

Work refers to activities performed for the purpose of earning a living or contributing to society. It is a multifaceted and complex concept that influences and is influenced by all aspects of a person's development, including intellectual, emotional, social, and physical elements (Matz et al., 2020). A job can be any activity performed for pay and may be temporary or transient, whereas an occupation may refer to a regular or relatively permanent field of work or means of livelihood. A profession typically refers to an occupation that requires college or postgraduate training, usually comprising a life's work at its end (Papalia et al., 2007). In other words, work life can encompass a series of jobs or careers, extending beyond paid roles to include volunteer work and familial and community responsibilities.

Retirement has traditionally been seen as a clear-cut withdrawal from the paid workforce. However, in recent decades it has evolved into a gradual, complex, and multifaceted process; it is no longer a single event, but a series of transitions, involving multiple exits from and re-entries into paid and unpaid work (Calvo et al., 2018; Hedge & Borman, 2012; Maestas, 2010). This change reflects longer life expectancies and varied individual and societal factors, leading many to extend their working years past traditional retirement ages (Czaja et al., 2020; Rothwell et al., 2008). The late 1980s marked a shift toward later retirement, reversing the trend of early retirement (see Figure 13.1; Cahill, et al., 2006; Morrissey et al., 2022). Today, workers age 55 or older make up just under a quarter of the overall labor force, and we have more age diversity than ever in the workplace (Morrissey et al., 2022). It is important to note that various definitions of "older workers" exist in the research, one of which categorizes workers aged 55 or older as such; definitions will be discussed later in this chapter.

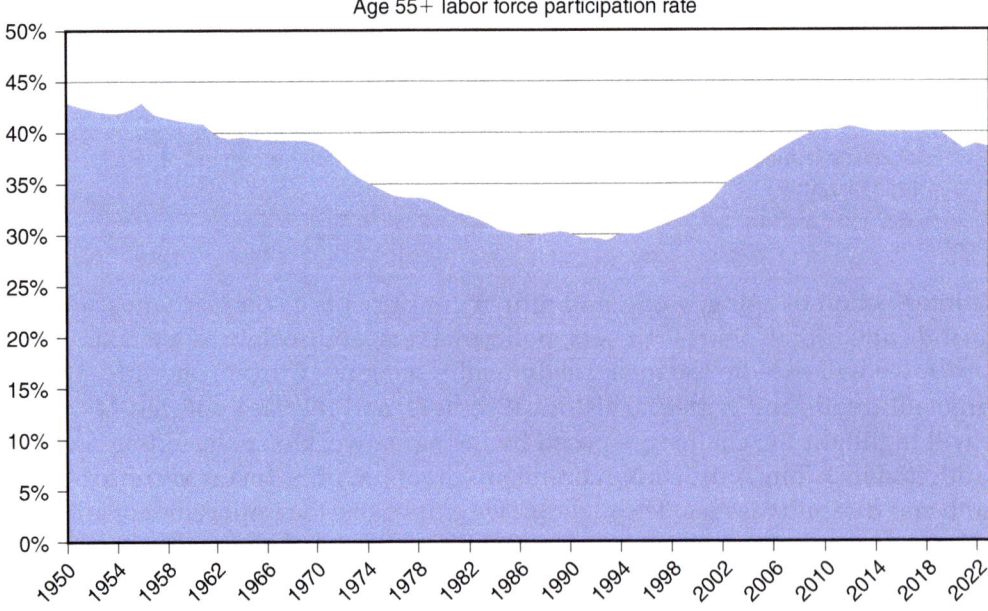

Figure 13.1 Participation rate at older ages levels off and begins to rise.

Source: From U.S. Bureau of Labor Statistics. (2021). *Number of people 75 and older in the labor force is expected to grow 96.5 percent by 2030.* TED: The Economics Daily. https://www.bls.gov/opub/ted/2021/

Decisions regarding work at older ages extend beyond financial necessity, encompassing aspects of personal identity, meaning, social status, health, and well-being (Paul et al., 2023). Consequently, the choices of when, how, and whether to work or retire have become more and more multifaceted and individualized. Additionally, it is increasingly acknowledged that the ability of older adults to engage in work that aligns with their preferences is influenced not only by personal choices but also by wider socioeconomic, structural, historical, and cultural elements. These factors contribute to social disparities in the trajectories of work and retirement (Matz & Brown, 2021; National Academies of Science Engineering, & Medicine [NASEM], 2022).

Given these wide-reaching changes, it is imperative that employers have a clear understanding of the age-biased norms and assumptions that constrain their ability to respond to their older employees' needs and preferences, as well as their capacity to draw on the talent of the aging workforce (Moen et al., 2017). Surveys estimate that only about one third of employers (36%) are actively evaluating their policies and practices in response to demographic shifts in the workforce and just 6% have enacted specific policies to adapt to an aging workforce (Society for Human Resource Management, 2014). Addressing ageism and other forms of marginalization and promoting inclusive, quality work environments are crucial steps toward equitable outcomes. Policies and programs that support work flexibility, financial preparedness, health and well-being, and lifelong learning can facilitate a smooth transition into retirement while optimizing the potential and contributions of older adults in the workforce. In the coming sections we expand on some of these issues and trends.

AGEISM AND MARGINALIZATION

Ageist attitudes and beliefs create a major source of inequality for older adults in the workplace. At the individual level, ageism is evident in feelings one has toward older adults (including oneself), beliefs about older people, and discrimination against them. These beliefs are rooted in culture-based age stereotypes and have a negative effect on the health of older persons (Chang et al., 2020). They may be unintentional/implicit or intentional/explicit (James et al., 2013). Ageism in the context of the labor market can manifest as being denied a job based on age, being treated as less capable, being passed over for a work role, receiving less social support, or being blamed for failures or problems due to age, among other examples (Gonzales et al., 2015). A recent consensus study published by NASEM (2022) reveals that the most common stereotype is ambivalence, with older adults being viewed as "well intentioned but incompetent." That is, older adults are seen as kind and well meaning on one hand and incompetent on the other; "doddering but dear" (Cuddy et al., 2005; NASEM, 2022).

Ageism is deeply ingrained and operates at the institutional or structural level as well. Structural ageism occurs when societal institutions promote bias against older persons. Chang et al. (2020), in a systematic review, reported that employers were significantly less likely to hire older than younger job applicants, that older workers had less access to training, and that those who faced ageism in the workplace were more likely to retire early. A recent study by AARP found that 61% of employees age 45 and older say that they have experienced or seen age discrimination at work (Terrell, 2018), and another survey found that more than 75% of older workers said that their age was a barrier to getting a job (Lipnic, 2018). Derous and Decoster's research (2017) demonstrated that even implicit age cues on anonymous resumes (e.g., older-sounding names, old-fashioned extracurricular activities) can lead to worse ratings of applicant hireability.

Thus, any examination of aging and work must address the role of ageism. One of the most pervasive types of ageism is through use of "othering" language and viewing older adults as a monolith. The Frameworks Institute has recently reframed aging and ageism (Sweetland et al., 2017) to shift these stigmatizing societal perceptions. For instance, they recommend moving away from terms such as "seniors," "elderly," "the aged," and similar "othering" terms because they connote a stereotype and suggest that members of the group are not part of society, but rather a group apart (Sweetland et al., 2017). Further, they note the importance of avoiding negativistic and fatalistic attitudes toward aging, such as age being an obstacle to overcome. Instead, language that emphasizes personhood such as "older adult" and "older worker" is more appropriate. These adaptations have a bearing on the world of work because the way in which managers and younger coworkers communicate with older adult workers, and the words they use, may have the potential of being demeaning, stigmatizing, and ultimately harmful to older workers' opportunities at work and their health (Levy et al., 2020).

Another problematic practice is seen in workplace discussions about different generations in the workplace and how to overcome or bridge generational differences and tensions. The research evidence has largely rejected the idea that generations have distinct attitudes and values (Rudolph et al., 2021). Further, relying on generational stereotypes can be harmful to individuals of all ages and can add tension to workplace interactions and exchanges across age groups. Instead, employers should focus on taking a more nuanced, theoretically driven view of individual differences that influence outcomes like motivation, retention, and organizational commitment (Costanza & Finkelstein, 2015; NASEM, 2022; Rudolph et al., 2021).

Finally, attention must be paid to the intersections of age/ageism and other marginalized social identities such as race/ethnicity, gender, disability, sexual orientation, religion, or socioeconomic status, as individual identities are not mutually exclusive; they shape choice and opportunity when it comes to work and the labor market and often result in divergent work and retirement trajectories (Matz & Brown, 2021). It is imperative that when thinking about aging and work, an intersectional lens is used to understand where inequities lie and to better inform solutions (Jason & Matz, 2024). For instance, ageism is intimately entangled with ableism—the privileging of the "normal" or able body (Reynolds, 2018). Workplaces may be inadvertently uplifting older workers who fit a "preferred way of being old . . ." which "is to not be old at all, but rather to maintain some image of middle-age functionality and appearance" (Berridge & Martinson, 2018, p. 83.) Further, White-centered professionalism (i.e., implicit/unconscious bias favoring White and Western culture, race-based standards coded as a "cultural" workplace fit) is reinforced in various ways in the workplace, and those who do not or cannot conform to the culture are open to prejudice, ostracism, and other negative outcomes (Hebl et al., 2020). When multiple marginalized identities (e.g., being chronically disabled and Black) intersect with ageism, untold numbers of constrained choices accumulate over a lifetime, driving increasing distance between the privileged and the marginalized on a variety of employment and retirement outcomes, health, and life expectancy (Jason & Matz, 2024; NASEM, 2022).

WHO IS AN OLDER WORKER?

Chronological age, or the number of years lived since birth, is the earliest and most common approach to defining older workers. The Age Discrimination in Employment Act (ADEA, 1967) defines an older worker as any individual 40 and older who is still an active worker (Sterns et al., 2005). Other frequently used cutoffs include 45, 50, or 55 years, yet these cutoffs are often arbitrary (Zacher & Rudolph, 2023). Chronological age has been favored by courts in the assessment of individual performance capacity. It has consistently been used as a way to evaluate job performance when it is believed that there are no other specific means of accurately measuring performance. Commercial airline pilots, for example, are still subject to mandatory retirement, now at 65 raised from 60, based on their chronological age.

However, chronological age is typically a poor proxy for the processes of maturation, development, status, or other key changes that may be of interest in defining older workers. Most typical age-related biological and cultural changes, such as declines in cognitive abilities, improvements in knowledge and experience, changes in health status, personality, and motivations, tend to happen gradually throughout a person's life, and there is a great deal of variation from person to person (Zacher & Rudolph, 2023). When participants in a recent study by Zacher and Rudolph (2023) were asked at what age a worker becomes an "older worker," responses ranged from 30 to 75 years, with a mean value of approximately 55 years. Qualitative responses indicated that a variety of factors may go into one's perception of who is an "older worker." Researchers have identified a variety of ways to think about age in relation to work that go beyond chronological age, for instance, functional, psychosocial, organizational, life span, and psychology of work approaches (Pitt-Castouphes, et al., 2012; Schalk et al., 2010; Sterns & Doverspike, 1988; Zacher & Rudolph, 2023).

Functional age focuses on how a person performs compared with the average person of a given age. Rather than the actual number of lived years, functional age uses people's state of health/performance capacity to determine whether someone is young or old (Schalk et al., 2010). For example, a 50-year-old individual who can run a mile as fast as the average 25-year-old has a functional age of 25. This approach is based on biological and psychological changes, and it considers the range of abilities as well as the changes in skill, wisdom, and experience (Birren & Stafford, 1986). Two examples of functional age approaches are physical abilities analysis and functional capacity assessment.

According to Sterns and Doverspike (1988), psychosocial definitions of older workers focus on three issues, all of which are fluid: (a) the age at which society perceives an individual to be older, (b) the social attitudes regarding older workers, and (c) possible implications in employment settings when labeling a worker as "older." How a worker is viewed may be a function of their longevity in the organization and changes within the organization that no longer use the older worker's skill set or render the worker's skill set as irrelevant. These views may shift over time and in response to certain events. For instance, societal views toward older adults seemed to have shifted significantly during the COVID-19 pandemic, with older workers being perceived as more vulnerable health wise and less competent with technology, which may have resulted in some employers being discriminatory in their employment decision-making and older adults being discouraged from seeking certain employment opportunities (Hollis-Sawyer, 2021).

The organizational approach focuses on understanding the roles of individuals in an organization and the impact of the mix of ages of personnel. This perspective emphasizes expertise, tenure, and career stage rather than age. While tenure (the length of the employee's service to the organization) and career stage are concepts often confounded with age (Schalk et al., 2010), modern-day career paradigms seldom involve a single career in a single organization. Thus, people in their 50s and 60s can be new to an organization or they may have been working there for quite a long time. They may be early career (starting a new adventure), mid-career (gaining experience), or late career (making use of credentials; Pitt-Catsouphes et al., 2012). For example, a football player in his late 30s can be in "late career" and a career changer in her mid-50s can be in "early career." Likewise, a professor may have spent many years in education and postdoctoral training and only be starting their career at age 40.

The life-span orientation (Sterns & Doverspike, 1988) combines each of the aforementioned approaches with an understanding that people are dynamic and that behavioral change occurs over the entire working life of individuals. The emphasis in this approach is the recognition of substantial individual differences as people age (Bowen et al., 2011; Moen, 2016). Individuals are influenced by normative age-graded, biological, and environmental influences (physical and cognitive changes as one ages), normative history-graded factors (generational events), and nonnormative influences unique to every individual. These normative and nonnormative influences interact to influence and steer an individual's career path. Over time, they determine the strengths and limitations and the skills and experience that individuals bring to their organizational role.

Finally, the psychology of work perspective (Blustein et al., 2016) goes beyond the traditional approaches of industrial/organizational and vocational psychology by formally considering the impact of social barriers that prevent individuals from fully achieving their potential. It focuses on the realities of individual working lives as they are experienced. This perspective is particularly helpful for understanding those individuals who are challenged by a poor regional economy; disability or addictions; or work limitations due to care of children, a spouse, or older loved ones. Individuals with more education have better resources to adapt and succeed financially over their working lifetimes. This view aligns with other social justice–focused theoretical applications to understanding the intersection of aging and work that call attention to the variety of socioeconomic, structural, historical, and cultural factors contributing to unfair workplace practices, lack of care structures, poor health, heightened stress, early retirement, and employment/retirement insecurity (Jason & Matz, 2024; Matz & Brown, 2021), such as intersectionality theory, life course theory (Dannefer, 2011), and constrained choice theory (Bird & Riecker, 2008).

Considering these different ways of defining older workers that acknowledge age as a social construction moves us away from conceptualizations that turn age into a flattened, one-dimensional experience toward a dynamic, multilevel, and multidimensional system of stratification. A more expansive conceptualization increases our understanding of how issues at the intersection of aging, work, and retirement are understood and interpreted and move us toward identifying comprehensive and equitable solutions.

A variety of key pieces of legislation have aimed to address discrimination in the workplace. The ADEA of 1967, amended in 1978 and 1986, marked the beginning of legally protecting workers older than 40 in the United States from discrimination in the workplace and afforded most workers the ability to decide when to exit the workforce by eliminating mandatory retirement. There are several exceptions, however. The ADEA prohibits age-based employment discrimination against persons 40 years of age or older unless the organization can establish that the age limitation is a bona fide occupational qualification (BFOQ) necessary to the performance of the duties of the position. However, the scope of the BFOQ allowance is very narrow and applies to a limited range of jobs, such as airline pilots and bus drivers who are assigned a mandatory retirement age or for models or actors who need to show authenticity in a given role. Also, smaller businesses with fewer employees (fewer than 20) are not covered under the federal law, and it generally does not protect independent contractors, only employees.

Although the ADEA and other antidiscriminatory legislation such as the Civil Rights Act of 1964 and the American with Disabilities Act of 1990 made more overt discrimination in organizations (e.g., with hiring, firing, promotions, layoffs, compensation, benefits, job assignments, training, harassment) illegal, they do not easily address more subtle or covert forms of discrimination. This type of discrimination tends to be more ambiguous and harder to detect since it's not inscribed in the legal system per se and tends to occur predominantly in the interpersonal sphere (e.g., perpetuating stereotypes about older workers or excluding older employees from training programs or professional development opportunities based on age-related assumptions). However, covert types of discrimination can have equally negative effects on work and health outcomes as legally protected types of discrimination. Ageist work environments provide a foundation for more overt discrimination practices (Stypinska & Turek, 2017).

THE AGING WORKFORCE

Historical and Demographic Changes

The phenomenon of the increasing numbers of older individuals in the U.S. workforce has been forecast for decades. For a summary of changes in labor force participation rates see Table 13.1 (U.S. Bureau of Labor Statistics [BLS], 2023). There was an upward trend in participation rates of those age 55 and older from 29.4% in 1993 to 39.4% in 2008 (Copeland, 2010). During the economic recovery that followed the Great Recession of 2007/2008, approximately 40% of those ages 55 or older were in the labor force, and these older workers made up 23.6% of the overall labor force in 2020 (Morrissey et al., 2022). Despite dips in the labor force participation rate of older adults during the COVID-19 pandemic in 2021, it is expected that prior upward trends will continue (Morrissey et al., 2022). Projections suggest that by 2030, 9.5% of the civilian labor force will be older than 65; further, the labor force age 75 years and older is expected to grow by 96.5% (BLS, 2021).

Many factors have contributed to a growing number of Americans continuing to work later in life. First, life expectancy has increased. Although recent years have seen a decline due to the COVID-19 pandemic and the opioid crisis, life expectancy in the United States has risen by over 30 years between 1900 and 2020, partly thanks to various public health initiatives (O'Connell-Domenech, 2023). Thus, increasing numbers of older adults are faced with perhaps 15, 20, or 30 years of life beyond the typical retirement age

TABLE 13.1 CIVILIAN LABOR FORCE PARTICIPATION RATE BY AGE

Group	Participation Rate				Percentage Point Change		
	2002	2012	2022	2032	2002–12	2012–22	2022–32
Total, 16 years and older	66.6	63.7	62.2	60.4	-2.9	-1.5	-1.8
16–19	47.4	34.3	36.8	30.9	-13.1	2.5	-5.9
20–24	76.4	70.9	71.0	67.8	-5.5	0.0	-3.2
25–34	83.7	81.7	83.2	82.1	-2.0	1.5	-1.0
35–44	84.1	82.6	83.0	81.9	-1.6	0.4	-1.0
45–54	82.1	80.2	81.1	80.9	-1.9	0.9	-0.2
55–64	61.9	64.5	65.2	68.4	2.6	0.7	3.2
65–74	20.4	26.8	26.6	29.9	6.5	-0.3	3.3
75 and older	5.1	7.6	8.2	9.9	2.5	0.6	1.7

Source: From U.S. Bureau of Labor Statistics. (2023). *Civilian labor force participation rate by age, sex, race, and ethnicity.* https://www.bls.gov/emp/tables/civilian-labor-force-participation-rate.htm

of 65. For many, this prolonged life expectancy has been accompanied by good overall health, which allows workers to continue to perform the same work at much older ages. It is important to note, however, that there are substantial racial disparities in life expectancy and health due to social and economic disparities (Hill & Artiga, 2023).

Second, the U.S. labor force has become increasingly educated over the last two decades. From 1992 to 2016, the share of the labor force made up of people with a bachelor's degree and advanced degrees (master's, professional, and doctoral degrees) has grown consistently, rising by 7 percentage points and 5 percentage points, respectively (Brundage, 2017). Higher levels of education correlate with longer workforce participation.

Third, many older adults find themselves working beyond traditional retirement age due to insufficient savings, rising living costs, and the need to finance a longer life span and maintain health insurance. A prominent change contributing to this rise in financial insufficiency for retirement has been the shift from defined benefit (DB) plans to defined contribution (DC) plans in the private sector. DB plans, traditionally known as pensions, offer a guaranteed monthly benefit at retirement, usually based on salary and tenure. In contrast, DC plans, like 401(k)s (an option to set aside tax-deferred money from one's salary) in the United States place the onus on individuals to contribute a portion of their salary, often matched by employers, with the retirement benefit dependent on the performance of these investments. This shift underscores a broader trend toward greater individual responsibility to finance retirement. As traditional pensions decline, individuals now face the task of determining contribution levels and investment choices and managing retirement funds. This change raises concerns about the preparedness and financial literacy of individuals to make these complex decisions and often means a later retirement (Khan et al., 2014). Further, while employer-sponsored plans cover 64.6% of non-Hispanic White workers, only 55.7%

of Black workers and 38.4% of Hispanic workers are covered, due primarily to ethno-racial differences in employer size, proportion of employees in full-time and part-time jobs, and occupational segregation (see NASEM, 2022).

Changes in the age at which individuals are eligible for certain benefits are another factor affecting work longevity. In 1983 the Social Security Act was amended to gradually increase the "full retirement age" from 65 years of age if born in 1937 or earlier in annual increments to age 67 for those born in 1960 or later. Under current law, individuals can choose to retire as early as age 62 and receive 70% of their full benefit to offset the longer time they will receive payments, while those who claim at age 67 receive 100%. Individuals can delay retirement after their "full retirement age" and receive increased payments, up to 124% if they claim at age 70 (see Social Security website: www.ssa.gov; Romig, 2023). These changes in Social Security's benefit calculation rules now allow workers to delay receiving benefits, with the incentive of receiving more benefits if they wait (Wheaton & Crimmins, 2013). However, the age for signing up for Medicare remains 65, and waiting longer may lead to higher costs for Part B and Part D. Even if a person is still employed and has health insurance, they must sign up at 65 to lock in their benefits. In other words, the world of work has evolved from one that incentivized early retirement (by providing secure pensions) to one that, in many cases, discourages it. Presently, the future of Social Security has become a national concern. Worries about the ability of this entitlement to sustain future generations is a matter of evolving changes within government policy.

Equally important is the perspective of the worker who is now fully responsible for self-managing both career and retirement. Since the 1970s, organizations have moved away from paternalism and maternalism, and workers are increasingly responsible for themselves (Sterns & Kaplan, 2003). That means that issues such as career updating, training to maintain expertise, and decisions to change careers are individual decisions alone. How a person experiences their work role (i.e., socially and emotionally) and how their work evolves over the life span can have profound impacts on financial, emotional, and physical health outcomes (Carstensen, 2009; Matz et al., 2020). On the one hand, a job can provide people with financial and social resources, a valued social status, stability, and occupational health and safety; conversely, jobs can also be marked by a devastating absence of these qualities (Paul et al., 2023). The rise in levels of burnout and languishing during the COVID-19 pandemic and related discussions around "quiet quitting" and "the great resignation" only highlighted the importance of individual experiences in work life as important in understanding decisions about work (Grant, 2021; Newport, 2022; O'Connell-Domenech, 2022; Sterns & Chang, 2010).

Job Performance and Age

Not only are workers having to self-manage their work and retirement, older workers also have to overcome various age-related challenges in order to successfully remain in a workforce that oftentimes is not designed with health- or disability-related challenges in mind (Rothwell et al., 2008). Some of these adverse stressors include changes in cognitive capacity, sensory decline, musculoskeletal decline, and motor deficits. Research on job performance and age reveals a complex relationship influenced by various factors. When it comes to cognitive abilities, for instance, older workers may experience age-related declines in processing speed and memory, but they also have a wealth of experience, knowledge, and skills accumulated over their careers that can compensate for these deficits, leading to sustained or even improved job performance in some cases (NASEM, 2022). In fact, age is rarely linked to lower real-world functioning (Salthouse, 2012). Findings of cognitive decline with age are further complicated by individual differences in the extent to which these declines are manifest, especially among educated older adults (Bosma et al., 2003), and knowledge of the ways that older adults adapt to such changes by optimizing strengths and minimizing weaknesses (Baltes & Lindenberger, 1997; Niessen et al., 2010). Noteworthy also is the impact of organizational context and efforts to minimize the impact of declines with supervisor support, flexible work arrangements, and other inclusive efforts (Veth et al., 2019). In addition, it seems that different types of declines affect jobs in various ways and at multiple junctures, for example, earlier in life for baseball players, later for air traffic controllers, and still later for professors and judges (Ackerman & Kanfer, 2020). Finally, as Ackerman and Kanfer (2020) point out, many job-dependent cognitive skills related to job performance are not assessed by any of the current cognitive tests, for example, employees' domain knowledge of job requirements, critical thinking skills, reading and writing skills, and importantly, individual motivation for engaging in the work.

For jobs that require physical labor, older workers might face challenges due to a decline in physical strength and endurance (Sterns & Miklos, 1995), which is less of an issue in roles that have fewer physical demands. There is a perception that older workers may struggle with adapting to new technologies. However, research indicates that with proper training and support, older workers can effectively adapt to technological changes (Chang et al., 2023). Moreover, while older workers may take somewhat longer to learn new skills, they are more than capable of learning and can bring a depth of understanding to new information based on their experience (Beier & Ackerman, 2005).

Age is associated with many positive performance measures as well. Older workers often exhibit a strong work ethic, reliability, engagement, and commitment to their jobs (Ng & Feldman, 2012) as well as better emotional stability and mental health than their younger counterparts (Grossmann et al., 2010). They tend to have lower absenteeism rates and can be more motivated by intrinsic rewards like satisfaction from a job well done, rather than extrinsic rewards like promotions (Ng & Feldman, 2012). With age often comes better interpersonal skills too; older workers are generally better at handling social situations in the workplace, which includes conflict resolution, mentoring, and teamwork (Grossmann et al., 2010).

In sum, while aging can bring some challenges, many of these can be mitigated or offset by experience, knowledge, and other positive attributes that older workers bring to the workplace. The relationship between age and job performance is not linear or straightforward and is influenced by a multitude of individual, occupational, and contextual factors. For example, jobs that rely heavily on accumulated knowledge and expertise might see improved performance with age, while those that require intensive physical labor or rapid cognitive processing might see some decline (Posthuma & Campion, 2009).

Even so, older workers do have to contend with their changing roles in the workforce as well as potentially confounding roles at home, such as caregiver. Changes in the work environment may also increase levels of adversity for the older worker.

Not only can the physical environment pose stressors, but attitudes of supervisors and coworkers also have an effect. Negative attitudes can be reflected in offering updating and training only to younger staff, not considering older workers for new assignments, or allowing stereotypes about older workers to influence management decisions instead of valid assessment relevant to the work to be performed.

CHANGING NATURE OF RETIREMENT

Historical Changes

A number of scholars have explored evolution and trends in career, work, and retirement, highlighting significant historical changes in the nature of retirement (Blustein, 2013; Hedge & Borman, 2012; Quinn, 2010; Wang, 2013; Wang et al., 2013; Zickar, 2013). The concept of retirement was introduced in the late 19th and early 20th centuries in Germany. Initially, due to low life expectancy and lack of pension systems, workers typically remained employed until death. In the United States, retirement was rare through the 1700s and 1800s, with older adults valued for their wisdom (Sterns & Kaplan, 2003).

The late 19th century saw the rise of labor unions advocating for worker privileges, leading to the perception of older workers as less capable and more expensive. This period marked the beginning of policies promoting retirement to create job opportunities for younger workers. The 1930s Great Depression and the introduction of the Social Security system, along with company-sponsored pension plans, established the norm of retiring at age 65 (Papalia et al., 2007; Richardson, 1993).

World War II further solidified retirement practices with the development of healthcare and pension plans as part of benefits packages (Stabilization Act of 1942). Over the decades, retirement ideologies have evolved, influenced by advancements in lifespan development and gerontology. Legislative changes like the ADEA in 1986 and the Americans with Disabilities Act (ADA) in 1990 have altered retirement norms, focusing on performance-based evaluations rather than age. This shift emphasizes direct assessment of job-relevant skills and the relevance of standard tests to actual job performance.

Retirement Patterns and Options

As discussed earlier, multiple exit patterns have replaced the traditional, one-time transition out of work (Mutchler et al. 1997). Mutchler et al. (1997) conducted a seminal study categorizing retirement exits into "crisp" and "blurred" patterns. Crisp exits refer to a one-time, definitive departure from full-time work, while blurred transitions involve multiple shifts between work and nonwork statuses, including periods of unemployment and re-entry into the workforce. These patterns reflect diverse retirement experiences influenced by age, financial stability, and health.

"Bridge employment" has emerged as a popular option, where retirees leave their primary careers but continue working in different capacities (Cahill et al., 2006). This approach allows retirees to remain active and financially stable. It often involves a shift from full-time to part-time work or a change in career fields. "Encore careers" offer a chance to pursue work that is personally meaningful or socially significant later in life (Freedman, 2007, 2017). These careers may be shorter but are often deeply fulfilling and driven by a desire to contribute positively to society. Further, the rise of "blended working" models, which combine on-site and remote work, offers flexibility that can be particularly appealing to older workers (Van Yperen & Wortler, 2016). This arrangement allows retirees to balance work with other interests or responsibilities, tailoring their engagement level to personal preferences and needs.

Carr et al. (2021) identified typologies focused on an individual's engagement in post-retirement paid work in the years following the Great Recession of 2007/2008. They found that five typologies emerged: (a) transitioning from part-time back to full-time work, (b) shifting to part-time work, (c) moving to partial retirement, (d) phased retirement, and (e) full retirement. Over half (58%) of the older workers studied engaged in some form of paid work after leaving their full-time jobs in 2008. Those who continued working post-retirement were more likely to have a working spouse and better health compared with those who fully retired. Key factors such as age, race, gender, and wealth varied across these typologies.

Factors Related to Retirement Transitions

As retirement has evolved into a process rather than an event, it has become harder to examine why people retire and what factors may influence the process. For example, recent economic recessions have led some individuals to continue to delay retirement, while others sought work without success, and still others, the so-called "discouraged workers," stopped searching and retired by default. Further complicating matters are multiple overlapping criteria by which someone might be called retired, including career cessation, reduced work effort, pension receipt, or self-report (Ekerdt, 2010). Nonetheless, researchers have identified various *push* factors and *pull* factors that shape the timing of and pathways through the retirement transition (Topa et al., 2018), and these may well operate in different ways for individuals depending on their social positions.

Pull factors are those that draw individuals toward retirement. The most frequently discussed pull factor is financial readiness. The decision to exit the workforce, continue working, or engage in a different manner of workforce participation is often driven by financial needs and a worker's preparedness for the cost of exiting the workforce. While many employees approach retirement having accumulated significant wealth and assets over the course of their lives, enabling them to be financially ready for retirement, a significant and growing number do not experience such financial readiness (Papadopoulos et al., 2020). Pre-retirees are often not adequately prepared to maintain the lifestyle to which they are accustomed, nor are they prepared for how to manage medical uncertainties and the costs that could accompany them. Sixty-five percent of Americans expect that they will have to work past the Social Security normal retirement age (66–67) to have enough money to retire (Oakley & Kenneally, 2019). Brown et al. (2018) report that the typical (median) American worker has nothing ($0) saved for retirement, with only 40% of Americans having any savings at all in retirement accounts. Among those who do, the typical account balance is $40,000—far short of the industry-recommended savings target of six times current income at age 50. Most workers have savings that are less than what they earn in a year and are at high risk of being unable to maintain their standard of living in retirement. Further, financial shocks caused by factors like an economic recession, divorce, catastrophic medical expenses, natural disaster, disability, care for an ailing family member, or loss of an income source experienced in the years leading up to retirement can lead to significant downward mobility even for those who are middle or upper class (Papadopoulos et al., 2020).

To address the challenges of retirement financial insecurity, various strategies have been proposed (Hoagland, 2016; Munnell, 2016; Pew Charitable Trusts, 2017; Polivka, 2012), including enhancing Social Security, making retirement plans like 401(k)s automatic, and ensuring all workers have access to employer-based retirement plans. Notably, "working longer," or delaying retirement, has become a commonly proposed solution, with advocates arguing that extended labor force participation could cut the cost of Social Security for an aging population, provide a bigger pool of experienced labor, and shore up individuals' financial security (Munnell, 2019). What this solution has failed to consider, however, is that there is a large segment of older adults for whom choosing to work longer is not an option (Berkman & Truesdale, 2022; NASEM, 2022). In recent years, we have seen shifts in our collective understanding of how structural factors and multiple sources of oppression (e.g., ageism, ableism, racism, and other "isms" based on marginalized social identities) intersect to constrain choice and opportunity over the life course, resulting in health and economic inequities. Yet discourse on work and retirement in later life has not always captured (and has sometimes mischaracterized) the variety and complexity of lived experiences—in particular for low-income workers, workers of color, women, and others marginalized due to their social positions (Jason & Matz, 2024; Matz & Brown, 2021).

Recent research has pointed to a variety of issues that may affect low-income and marginalized workers during the retirement transition, including financial vulnerability, limited work prospects, significant caregiving responsibilities, health complications, cultural and familial factors, and perceptions of control (Blanco et al., 2016; Carr et al., 2020; Calvo et al., 2019; Diaz-Valdes et al., 2024; Gatta, 2018; Ruggiano et al., 2017). Thus, solutions focused on increasing work longevity must also move beyond ideas rooted in individual agency and choice (i.e., those that assume that all people are able to make "good choices" to secure their health and well-being, employment security, and pension and welfare provision in later life) and toward broader approaches that identify and address the socioeconomic, structural, historical, and cultural factors that limit agency and contribute to disparate work trajectories over the life span.

Other pull factors that have been identified include things like desire for leisure and personal pursuits, family and social factors, and opportunity for an "encore" career or volunteering. The attraction of leisure time and the opportunity to engage in personal interests can pull individuals toward retirement. The prospect of having free time to travel, pursue hobbies, or spend time with family can be a strong motivator (Wang et al., 2013). Family commitments, such as the desire to spend time with grandchildren or care for a family member, can also be a significant pull factor. Although family commitments can be seen as a pull factor, they can also be seen as a push factor, as described later. Social relationships and the desire to have a more flexible schedule to engage in social activities also influence the decision (Cahill et al., 2006). Finally, some individuals are pulled toward retirement by the prospect of an "encore" career or the opportunity to volunteer for a cause important to them. This involves pursuing work that is often more fulfilling and aligned with personal values (Freedman, 2007, 2017; Matz-Costa et al., 2019).

Conversely, push factors are those that compel individuals to leave the workforce earlier than anticipated. Health is one of the most commonly discussed push factors. Health factors have been widely investigated as predictors of retirement (Olesen et al.,

2012; Scharn et al., 2018). Poor health, both physical and mental, can limit an individual's capacity to work, making retirement a necessity rather than a choice, especially in physically demanding jobs. However, as Hasselhorn et al. (2022) point out, poor health is often linked with early retirement, but evidence suggests that good health can also lead to early retirement. Conversely, both good and poor health can result in delayed retirement. These mixed findings emphasize the complexity of this relationship and the interplay of various factors at the individual, organizational, and national levels.

Nevertheless, supporting provisions for worker health and safety at the workplace can prevent workplace-related illness and disability that could cause workers to have to leave or reduce their work hours before they are ready (Pitt-Catsouphes et al., 2015). Presenteeism, or the reduction in productivity that occurs when people work when in suboptimal health, has been on the rise due to worsening mental health, financial well-being, and sleep that many employees experienced during the COVID-19 pandemic, as well as fears over job security, social isolation, and increasingly blurred boundaries between work and home lives (Ferreira et al., 2022).

Other push factors include family caregiving responsibilities, job dissatisfaction and work environment, and involuntary job loss. Family caregiving responsibilities often force older workers to choose between their jobs and caregiving roles. This has led to increased job turnover and early retirement (Stokes et al., 2023). Lahaie et al. (2013) found that for women and first-generation immigrants, providing care for older family members may result in early retirement and involuntary reduction of work hours to meet the demands of caregiving. Moreover, Hispanic and first-generation immigrant older caregivers had less access to paid leave, had less schedule flexibility, and faced an unsupportive work culture. Those forced into reducing their hours or permanently exiting the workplace due to care responsibilities are at greater risk of poverty in later life, due to reduced earnings, lower Social Security benefits, and loss of employer-sponsored health insurance (Feinberg & Choula, 2012). Overall, there are poor supports for working caregivers, and these workers end up being pushed to the brink financially, emotionally, and health wise. This makes policies and programs that provide paid family leave and that financially support caregivers who transition in and out of caregiving and the workforce by counting time dedicated to caregiving toward employment history for Social Security extremely important (Carr et al., 2021).

Negative aspects of the work environment, such as high stress, low job satisfaction, or perceived age discrimination, can push individuals toward early retirement as well. These factors contribute to a less engaging and rewarding work life, leading to a decision to retire (Brooke & Taylor, 2005; Judge et al., 2001). Policies and programs that protect employees from covert discriminatory practices based on age and other vulnerable identities have been proposed to address this issue in part (e.g., Fair Employment Protection Act of 2014). As mentioned prior, there is a large body of work examining various aspects of work environments and how they impact employment outcomes. Findings from this research provide insights as to what employers can do to enhance workplace culture and retain older workers.

Finally, economic downturns or organizational restructuring often result in involuntary job loss, which can prematurely push older workers into retirement. This is particularly relevant for older workers who face ageism and may find it challenging to secure new employment (Mandal & Roe, 2008). These factors, or any of the push factors for that matter, may also force workers into part-time work rather than completely out of the workforce. While part-time work is often upheld as an attractive option for older adults who want or need to continue working but do not want to continue at the same pace that they had been, for many, part-time work may be a form of underemployment. Those with less marketable skills may be "stuck" with part-time work when what they really need is full-time work. Further, part-time workers typically do not qualify for critical benefits, including health insurance. Lowering the eligibility age for Medicare to 60 may partially address this issue, as would legislation that incentivizes firms to develop benefit programs for regular, non-full-time employees and specific investment and saving options for part-time workers.

Finally, there are factors that are neither push nor pull factors per se but that can, if properly supported, help to facilitate a range of desired pathways to retirement (Carr et al., 2021). For instance, informal work and "gig" employment is of increasing significance as more older workers and underemployed workers seek out such work as a means to supplement their incomes (i.e., a "side hustle") or as a primary source of income (Nutsubidze & Nutsubidze, 2019). These types of positions provide many older workers flexibility and control that are greatly appreciated by those preferring to work on their own terms (Blumberg, 2020; Webb et al., 2020) and may lead to a delay of full retirement. However, this type of work does not provide individuals with legal or social protection, exposing them to more economic risk than other workers (Webb et al., 2020). Further, typical employee benefits are rarely available in these types of positions. Advocating for legislation requiring companies that hire independent contractors to classify them as employees, such as Uber, Lyft, and DoorDash, can allow workers to access benefits and worker protections (Carr et al., 2021).

Flexible arrangements like remote work, flexible scheduling, or shift working could make continued engagement in work feasible for older workers who might otherwise fully retire due to caregiving responsibilities, certain health conditions, or a significant commute. The COVID-19 pandemic tested the efficacy of a range of flexible work arrangements in a variety of jobs. In a randomized controlled trial, Cahill et al. (2015) found that older workers who perceived increased organizational support for flexible work options increased their expected retirement age over the course of 2 years. In addition, a greater sense of schedule control shaped employee satisfaction with work–family balance even under conditions of high work unit pressure (James et al., 2015).

Finally, there is the importance of job retraining, particularly around technology, to enable older workers to stay engaged in the workforce longer (Carr et al., 2021). Providing opportunities for older workers to receive training in new skills allows for greater choice about the timing of their departure from work and can lead to increased opportunities for new types of jobs or upward mobility in later phases of one's career. Technology changes certainly play a role in shaping the degree to which individuals feel like they can engage in the work force longer.

Retirement Planning

Effective retirement planning is increasingly recognized as vital for a fulfilling retirement phase. This preparation should begin early, yet studies show a lack of proactive retirement planning among many individuals (Dennis & Fike, 2012). Retirement education programs encompass a wide range of issues including financial planning, health considerations, and psychosocial aspects of retirement (Hunter, 1976).

The changing nature of retirement income sources necessitates a shift in planning strategies. Individuals must consider a mix of income sources including state and private pensions, personal savings, investments, and potential earnings from continued work (Ellis et al., 2015). The landscape of retirement income has been altered by factors like the increase in the full retirement age for Social Security benefits and the rising cost of Medicare premiums. These changes mean individuals must plan more comprehensively for their financial future, considering the potential for longer life spans and the variability of income sources in retirement.

Retirement planning now involves not only financial preparation but also adapting to the psychosocial aspects of transitioning from a work-centric life (James et al., 2016). This includes managing changes in daily routines and identity shifts from being a "worker" to a retiree as well as finding ways to stay physically, cognitively, and socially active. Retirement education and planning programs thus play a crucial role in preparing individuals for this significant life transition.

It is important to note that an emerging body of research suggests that there are considerable ethno-racial disparities in retirement planning behaviors that we do not yet fully understand. For instance, the Economic Policy Institute estimates that only 4 out of 10 Hispanic workers have a retirement plan in their current jobs, compared with 63% of White and 64% of Black workers age 55 or older (Morrissey et al., 2022). The participation rate for Black workers, however, is lower than for White workers, at 50.3% and 54.4%, respectively. While there are varied reasons behind this, both qualitative (Blanco, 2015; Gatta, 2018) and quantitative research (Carr et al., 2020; Diaz-Valdes et al., 2024) has shown that among Hispanic individuals in particular, cultural and familial factors may be at play when it comes to planning for retirement. Lytle et al. (2015) point out that ethno-racial and cultural variables are some of the most understudied variables in the retirement planning literature and call for an increased focus on this area moving forward.

CONCLUSION

As the population ages, the nature of work and retirement needs to adjust accordingly. There is a greater need than in times past for nations to develop policies and workplaces to identify strategies to maximize the value of an aging workforce and for individuals to plan for what work, life, and retirement pathways best suit their needs. Everyone should have the right to choice and opportunity when it comes to paid and unpaid work as they age. We know, however, that social position impacts the extent to which this is true or not. Rising levels of inequality mean wealthier and more privileged older adults can work and/or retire as they see fit, while those with lower incomes and additional layers of being "othered" often experience a variety of constraints that affect their ability to realize their preferred work relationships (Berkman & Truesdale, 2022; Matz & Brown, 2021; NASEM, 2022).

The combination of changing demographics and an increasingly technology-driven/sophisticated workplace puts greater emphasis on ergonomic and technological interventions in workspaces' design to extend the work life of older adults who desire to participate in the work force. Programs that facilitate planning for one's work life across the life span would aid in individual preparation for the various options available to extend one's work life and to determine one's retirement course. Planning will continue to be instrumental in preparing individuals for the financial and care needs that exist with changes in one's work life. More empirical research in this area is greatly needed in order to understand and meet the needs of an aging workforce, especially research that centers the experiences of those most proximal to the inequity—older workers who occupy marginalized social identities—when developing solutions.

ACKNOWLEDGMENTS

Special gratitude is extended to Harvey L. Sterns and Cynthia McQuown, the original authors of the first edition of this chapter. Their valuable contributions have laid the groundwork for this section edition.

DISCUSSION QUESTIONS

1. How do the six ways of defining older workers (chronological, functional, psychosocial, organizational, life-span developmental, and psychology of work) differ from each other? Discuss examples of how each definition might apply in a workplace setting.

2. What are some key characteristics of older workers? Discuss how these characteristics might influence their work performance and workplace dynamics.

3. Summarize the Age Discrimination in Employment Act and discuss its impact on older adult workers. How effective do you think this act is in protecting older workers from discrimination?

4. The chapter describes various patterns of retirement. Discuss these different patterns and how they reflect changes in societal and economic trends.

5. What are the different financial strategies adults can use to plan for retirement? Discuss the importance of each strategy in the context of current economic trends.

6. How does health influence decisions about retirement? Discuss the interplay between physical and mental health and the decision to retire or continue working.

7. How has the notion of retirement changed over the years? Discuss the factors that have contributed to this change and how it impacts today's workforce.

8. Discuss how ageism in the workplace might impact older workers and their retirement plans. What measures can be taken to mitigate the effects of ageism on retirement planning?

A robust set of instructor resources designed to supplement this text is located at http://connect.springerpub.com/content/book/978-0-8261-6617-3. Qualifying instructors may request access by emailing textbook@springerpub.com.

REFERENCES

Ackerman, P. L., & Kanfer, R. (2020). Work in the 21st century: New directions for aging and adult development. *American Psychologist, 75*(4), 486–498. https://doi.org/10.1037/amp0000615

Berkman, L. F., & Truesdale, B. C. (2022). Is working longer in jeopardy? In L. F. Berkman & B. C. Truesdale (Eds.), *Overtime: America's aging workforce and the future of working longer.* Oxford Academic.

Baltes, P. B., & Lindenberger, U. (1997). Emergence of a powerful connection between sensory and cognitive functions across the adult life span: A new window to the study of cognitive aging? *Psychology and Aging, 12*(1), 12–21. https://doi.org/10.1037//0882-7974.12.1.12

Beier, M. E., & Ackerman, P. L. (2005). Age, ability, and the role of prior knowledge on the acquisition of new domain knowledge: Promising results in a real-world learning environment. *Psychology and Aging, 20*(2), 341–355. https://doi.org/10.1037/0882-7974.20.2.341

Berridge, C. W., & Martinson, M. (2018). Valuing old age without leveraging ableism. *Generations, 41*(4), 83–91. https://depts.washington.edu/uwmedptn/wp-content/uploads/Valuing-Old-Age-Without-Leveraging-Ableism-Feb-2019.pdf

Bird, C. E., & Riecker, P. P. (2008). *Gender and health: The effects of constrained choices and social policies*. Cambridge University Press.

Birren, J. E., & Stafford, J. I. (1986). Changes in the organization of behavior with age. In J. E. Birren & J. Livingston (Eds.), *Age, health, and employment* (pp. 93–113). Prentice-Hall.

Blanco, L.R., Aguila, E., Gongora, A., & Duru, K. (2016). Retirement planning among Hispanics: In God's hands? *Journal of Aging & Social Policy, 29*(4), 311–331. https://doi.org/10.1080/08959420.2016.1272161

Blanco, L.R., Ponce, M., Gongora, A., & Duru, O.K (2015). A qualitative analysis of the use of financial services and saving behavior among older African Americans and Latinos in the Los Angeles area. *SAGE Open, 5*(1), 1–14. https://doi.org/10.1177/2158244014562388

Blumberg, D. L. (2020, March 17). Could new gig economy laws prevent you from working? *Forbes*. https://www.forbes.com/sites/nextavenue/2020/03/17/could-new-gig-economylaws-

Blustein, D. L. (2013). *The Oxford handbook of the psychology of working*. Oxford University Press.

Blustein, D. L., Olle, C., Connors-Kellgren, A., & Diamonti, A. J. (2016). Decent work: A psychological perspective. *Frontiers in Psychology, 7*, 407. https://doi.org/10.3389/fpsyg.2016.00407

Age Discrimination in Employment Act, 29 U.S.C. Sec. 621 et seq. (1967 & Supp V. 1978 & 1986).

Americans With Disabilities Act of 1990, Pub.L. No. 101-336, Sec.1211, 9 (1990).

Bosma, H., van Boxtel, M. P. J., Ponds, R. W. H. M., Houx, P. J. H., & Jolles, J. (2003). Education and age-related decline: The contribution of mental workload. *Educational Gerontology, 29*(2), 165–173. https://doi.org/10.1080/10715769800300191

Bowen, C. E., Noack, M. G., & Staudinger, U. M. (2011). Aging in the work context. In K. W. Schaie & S. L. Willis (Eds.), *Handbook of psychology of aging* (7th ed., pp. 263–277). Academic Press.

Brooke, L., & Taylor, P. (2005). Older workers and employment: Managing age relations. *Ageing & Society, 25*(3), 415–429. https://doi.org/10.1017/S0144686X05003466

Brown, S., Saad-Lessler, J., & Oakley, D. (2018). *Retirement in America: Out of reach for working Americans?* National Institute on Retirement Security. https://www.nirsonline.org/wp-content/uploads/2018/09/FINAL-Report-.pdf

Brundage, V. (2017). *Profile of the labor force by educational attainment*. U.S. Bureau of Labor Statistics. https://www.bls.gov/spotlight/2017/educational-attainment-of-the-labor-force/home.htm

Cahill, K. E., Giandrea, M. D., & Quinn, J. F. (2006). Retirement patterns from career employment. *The Gerontologist, 46*(4), 514–523. https://doi.org/10.1093/geront/46.4.514

Cahill, K. E., James, J. B., & Pitt-Catsouphes, M. (2015). The impact of a randomly-assigned time and place management initiative on work and retirement expectations. *Work, Aging and Retirement, 1*(4), 350–368. https://doi.org/10.1093/workar/wav012

Calvo, E., Madero-Cabib, I., & Staudinger, U. M. (2018). Retirement sequences of older Americans: Moderately destandardized and highly stratified across gender, class, and race. *Gerontologist, 58*(6), 1166–1176. https://doi.org/10.1093/geront/gnx052

Calvo, R., Carr, D. C., & Matz-Costa, C. (2019). Expanding the happiness paradox: Ethnoracial disparities in life satisfaction among older immigrants in the United States. *Journal of Aging and Health, 31*(2), 231–255. https://doi.org/10.1177/0898264317726608

Carr, D. C., Matz, C., Taylor, M., & Gonzales, E. (2021). Retirement transitions in the US: Patterns and pathways from full-time work. *Public Policy & Aging Report, 31*(3), 71–77. https://doi.org/10.1093/ppar/prab013

Carr, D. C., Moen, P., Perry Jenkins, M., & Smyer, M. (2020). Postretirement life satisfaction and financial vulnerability: The moderating role of control. *The Journals of Gerontology: Series B, 75*(4), 849–860. https://doi.org/10.1093/geronb/gby105

Carstensen, L. (2009). *A long bright future*. Broadway Books.

Chang, C., Xu, H., & Xie, B. (2023). Aging workforce in the context of technological advancements: Toward a socio-ecological model, *Work, Aging and Retirement, 9*(4), 323–328. https://doi.org/10.1093/workar/waad025

Chang, E. S., Kannoth, S., Levy, S., Wang, S.-Y., Lee, J. E., & Levy, B. R. (2020). Global reach of ageism on older persons' health: A systematic review. *PLoS One, 15*(1), e0220857. https://doi.org/10.1371/journal.pone.0220857

Copeland, C. (2010). *Labor force participation rates: The population age 55 and older, 2008* (Vol. 31, No. 2). Employees Benefits Research Institute (EBRI).

Costanza, D. P., & Finkelstein, L. M. (2015). Generationally based differences in the workplace: Is there a *there* there? *Industrial and Organizational Psychology: Perspectives on Science and Practice, 8*(3), 308–323. https://doi.org/10.1017/iop.2015.15

Cuddy, A. J. C., Norton, M. I., & Fiske, S. T. (2005). This old stereotype: The pervasive and persistence of the elderly stereotype. *Journal of Social Issues, 61*(2), 267–285. https://doi.org/10.1111/j.1540-4560.00405.x

Czaja, S. J., Sharit, J., & James, J. (Eds). (2020). *Current and emerging trends in aging and work.* Springer.

Dannefer, D. (2011). The life course, aging, and the sociological imagination: New prospects for theory. In R. Binstock & L. George (Eds.), *Handbook of aging and social sciences* (pp. 3–16). Academic Press.

Dennis, H., & Fike, A. T. (2012). Retirement planning: New context, process, language, and players. In J. W. Hedge & W. C. Borman (Eds.), *The Oxford handbook work and aging* (pp. 538–548). Oxford University Press.

Derous, E., & Decoster, J. (2017). Implicit age cues in resumes: Subtle effects on hiring discrimination. *Frontiers in Psychology, 8*, 1321. https://doi.org/10.3389/fpsyg.2017.01321

Diaz-Valdes, A., Matz-Costa, C., Rutledge, M. S., & Calvo, E. (2024). Determinants of Hispanic and non-Hispanic workers' intent to work past age 65: An analysis from the life course perspective. *The International Journal of Aging and Human Development, 98*(3), 300–328. https://doi.org/10.1177/00914150231196095

Ekerdt, D. J. (2010). Frontiers of research on work and retirement. *The Journals of Gerontology: Series B, 65B*(1), 69–80. https://doi.org/10.1093/geronb/gbp109

Ellis, C., Munnell, A., & Eschtruth, A. (2015). *Falling short: The coming retirement crisis and what to do about it.* Oxford University Press.

Feinberg, L., & Choula, R. (2012). Fact sheet: *Understanding the impact of family caregiving on work.* http://www.aarp.org/content/dam/aarp/research/public_policy_institute/ltc/2012/understanding-impact-family-caregiving-work-AARP-ppi-ltc.pdf

Ferreira, A. I., Mach, M., Martinez, L. F., & Miraglia, M. (2022). Sickness presenteeism in the aftermath of COVID-19: Is presenteeism remote-work behavior the new (ab)normal? *Frontiers in Psychology, 12*, 748053. https://doi.org/10.3389/fpsyg.2021.748053

Freedman, M. (2007). The social-purpose encore career: Baby boomers, civic engagement, and the next stage of work. *Generations, 4*, 43–46. https://www.jstor.org/stable/26555479

Freedman, M. (2017). The encore life: A generation of experienced workers is ready to serve. *Generations, 40*(4), 74–78.

Gatta, M. (2018). *Waiting on retirement: Aging and economic insecurity in low-wage work.* Stanford University Press.

Gonzales, E., Marchiondo, L., Ran, S., Brown, C., & Goettge, K. (2015). *Age discrimination in the workplace and its association with health and work: Implications for social policy* (Research Brief 201502). Boston University.

Grant, A. (2021, April 19). *There's a name for the blah you're feeling: It's called languishing.* The New York Times. https://www.nytimes.com/2021/04/19/well/mind/covid-mental-health-languishing.html

Grossmann, I., Na, J., Varnum, M. E. W., & Nisbett, R. E. (2010). Reasoning about social conflicts improves into old age. *Proceedings of the National Academy of Sciences of the United States of America, 107*(16), 7246–7250. https://doi.org/10.1073/pnas.10017151

Hasselhorn, H. M., Leinonen, T., Bültmann, U., Mehlum, I. S., du Prel, J. B., Kiran, S., Majery, N., Solovieva, S., & de Wind, A. (2022). The differentiated roles of health in the transition from work to retirement—Conceptual and methodological challenges and avenues for future research. *Scandinavian Journal of Work, Environment & Health, 48*(4), 312–321. https://doi.org/10.5271/sjweh.4017

Hebl, M., Cheng, S. K., & Ng, L. C. (2020). Modern discrimination in organizations. *Annual Review of Organizational Psychology and Organizational Behavior, 7*, 257–282. https://doi.org/10.1146/annurev-orgpsych-012119-044948

Hedge, J. W., & Borman, W. C. (2012). *The Oxford handbook of work and aging*. Oxford University Press.

Hill, L., & Artiga, S. (2023, May 23). *What is driving widening racial disparities in life expectancy?* Kaiser Family Foundation. https://www.kff.org/racial-equity-and-health-policy/issue-brief/what-is-driving-widening-racial-disparities-in-life-expectancy

Hoagland, G. W. (2016). The economic, fiscal, and financial, implications, of an aging society. *Generations, 40*(4), 16–22. https://www.jstor.org/stable/26556242

Hollis-Sawyer, L. (2021). Differential treatment of older workers due to COVID-19 accommodations: Potential issues of ageism and age discrimination. *Journal of Elder Policy, 1*(3), 441. https://doi.org/10.18278/jep.1.3.6

Hunter, W. W. (1976). *Preparation for retirement* (3rd ed.). Institute of Gerontology, University of Michigan–Wayne State University.

James, J. B., Matz-Costa, C., & Smyer, M. (2016). Retirement security: It's not just about the money. *American Psychologist, 71*(4), 334–344. https://doi.org/10.1037/a0040220

James, J. B., McKechnie, S., Swanberg, J., & Besen, E. (2013). Exploring the workplace impact of intentional/unintentional age discrimination. *Journal of Managerial Psychology, 28*(7/8), 907–927. https://doi.org/10.1108/JMP-06-2013-0179

James, J. B, Pitt-Catsouphes, M., McNamara, T. K., Snow, D. L., & Johnson, P. L. (2015). The relationship of work unit pressure to satisfaction with work–family balance: A new twist on negative spillover? In S. K. Ammons & E. L. Kelly (Eds.), *Work and family in the new economy* (pp. 219–258). Emerald Group Publishing Limited.

Jason, K., & Matz, C. (2024, February 14). Intersectional perspectives to health and work in later life. *Generations, 47*(4). https://generations.asaging.org/intersectional-perspectives-health-work

Judge, T. A., Thoresen, C. J., Bono, J. E., & Patton, G. K. (2001). The job satisfaction–job performance relationship: A qualitative and quantitative review. *Psychological Bulletin, 127*(3), 376–407. https://doi.org/10.1037/0033-2909.127.3.376

Khan, M. R., Rutledge, M. S., & Wu, A. Y. (2014). *Do longevity expectations influence retirement plans?* (Working Paper WP#2014-1). Center for Retirement Research at Boston College. http://crr.bc.edu/briefs/do-longevity-expectations-influence-retirement-plans/

Lahaie, C., Earle, A., & Heymann, J. (2013). An uneven burden: Social disparities in adult caregiving responsibilities, working conditions, and caregiver outcomes. *Research on Aging, 35*(3), 243–274. https://doi.org/10.1177/0164027512446028

Levy, R., Slade, M. D., Chang, E. S., Kannoth, S., & Wang, S. Y. (2020). Ageism amplifies cost and prevalence of health conditions. *The Gerontologist, 60*(1), 174–181. https://doi.org/10.1093/geront/gny131

Lipnic, V. A. (2018). *The state of age discrimination and older workers in the U.S. 50 years after the Age Discrimination in Employment Act (ADEA)*. U.S. Equal Employment Opportunity Commission Report.

Lytle, M. C., Clancy, M. E., Foley, P. F., & Cotter, E. W. (2015). Current trends in retirement: Implications for career counseling and vocational psychology. *Journal of Career Development, 42*(3), 170–184. https://doi.org/10.1177/0894845314545785

Maestas, N. (2010). Back to work: Expectations and realizations of work after retirement. *Journal of Human Resources, 45*(3), 718–748. https://doi.org/10.1353/jhr.2010.0011

Mandal, B., & Roe, B. (2008). Job loss, retirement and the mental health of older Americans. *Journal of Mental Health Policy Economics, 11*, 167–176. PMID: 19096091

Matz, C., & Brown, M. (2021). The choices of (low-income) aging workers on the margins: Expanding the narrative. In E. F. Fideler (Ed.), *Handbook on aging and work*. Rowman & Littlefield.

Matz, C., Sabbath, E., & James, J. (2020). An integrative conceptual framework of engagement in socially-productive activity in later life: Implications for clinical and mezzo social work practice. *Clinical Social Work Journal, 48*, 156–168. https://doi.org/10.1007/s10615-020-00756-x

Matz-Costa, C., Berzin, S., Pitt-Catsouphes, M., & Halvorsen, C. (2019). Perceptions of the meaningfulness of work among older social purpose workers: An ecological momentary Assessment study. *Journal of Applied Gerontology, 38*(8), 1121–1146. https://doi.org/10.1177/0733464817727109

Moen, P. (2016). Work over the gendered life course. In M. Shanahan, J. Mortimer, & M. Kirkpatrick Johnson (Eds.), *Handbook of the life course*. Springer.

Moen, P., Kojola, E., & Schaefers, K. (2017). Organizational change around an older workforce. *The Gerontologist, 57*(5), 847–856. https://doi.org/10.1093/geront/gnw048

Morrissey, M., Radpour, S., & Schuster, B. (2022, November 16). *The older workers and retirement chartbook*. Economic and Policy Institute.

Munnell, A. H. (2016). Restoring public confidence in retirement income. *Generations, 40*(4), 23–29. https://www.jstor.org/stable/26556243

Munnell, A. H. (2019). Socioeconomic barriers to working longer. *Generations, 43*(3), 42–50. https://www.jstor.org/stable/26841731

Mutchler, J. E., Burr, J. A., Pienta, A. M., & Massagli, M. P. (1997). Pathways to labor force exit: Work transitions and work instability. *Journal of Gerontology: Social Sciences, 52B*(1), S4–S12. https://doi.org/10.1093/geronb/52b.1.s4

National Academies of Sciences, Engineering, and Medicine. (2022). *Understanding the aging workforce: Defining a research agenda*. The National Academies Press.

Newport, C. (2022, December 29). *The year in quiet quitting*. The New Yorker. https://www.newyorker.com/culture/2022-in-review/the-year-in-quiet-quitting

Ng, T. W. H., & Feldman, D. C. (2012). Evaluating six common stereotypes about older workers with meta-analytical data. *Personnel Psychology, 65*(4), 821–858. https://doi.org/10.1111/peps.12003

Niessen, C., Swarrowsky, A., & Leiz, M. (2010). Age and adaptation: Strategies of coping with stigmatization among elderly workers. *Journal of Managerial Psychology, 25*(4), 356–383. https://doi.org/10.1108/02683941011035287

Nutsubidze, T., & Nutsubidze, K. (2019). *Informal and non-standard employment: A look at the impact on social protection policy* (Working Paper 2019-11). Center for Retirement Research at Boston College.

O'Connell-Domenech, A. (2022, August 31). Pandemic burnout helped cause 'quiet quitting' trend. *The Hill: Changing America*. https://thehill.com/changing-america/respect/equality/3621512-pandemic-burnout-helped-cause-quiet-quitting-trend-experts-say

O'Connell-Domenech, A. (2023, February 7). *More people are living to be 100: Here's why*. The Hill. https://thehill.com/changing-america/well-being/longevity/3847532-more-people-are-living-to-be-100-heres-why/

Oakley, D., & Kenneally, K. (2019). *Retirement insecurity 2019: Americans' views of the retirement crisis*. National Institute on Retirement Security. https://www.nirsonline.org/wp-content/uploads/2019/02/OpinionResearch_final-1.pdf

Olesen, S. C., Butterworth, P., & Rodgers, B. (2012). Is poor mental health a risk factor for retirement? Findings from a longitudinal population survey. *Social Psychiatry and Psychiatric Epidemiology, 47*(5), 735–744. https://doi.org/10.1007/s00127-011-0375-7

Papadopoulos, M., Fisher, B., Ghilarducci, T., & Radpour, S. (2020). *Recession increases downward mobility in retirement: Middle earners hit from both sides*. Schwartz Center for Economic Policy Analysis at the New School for Social Research.

Papalia, D. E., Sterns, H. L., Feldman, R. D., & Camp, C. J. (2007). *Adult development and aging* (3rd ed.). McGraw-Hill.

Paul, K. I., Scholl, H., Moser, K., Zechmann, A., & Batinic, B. (2023). Employment status, psychological needs, and mental health: Meta-analytic findings concerning the latent deprivation model. *Frontiers in Psychology, 14*, 1017358. https://doi.org/10.3389/fpsyg.2023.1017358

Pew Charitable Trusts. (2017). *Retirement plan access and participation across generations*. Issue Brief. http://www.pewtrusts.org/en/research-and-analysis/issue-briefs/2017/02/retirement-plan-access-and-participation-across-generations

Pitt-Catsouphes, M., James, J. B., & Matz-Costa, C. (2015). Workplace-based health and wellness programs: The intersection of aging, work, and health. *The Gerontologist, 55*(2), 262–270. https://doi.org/10.1093/geront/gnu114

Pitt-Catsouphes, M., Matz-Costa, C., James, J. (2012). *Through a different looking glass: The prism of age*. Sloan Center on Aging & Work, Boston College.

Polivka, L. J. (2012). A future out of reach? The growing risk in the U.S. retirement security system. *Generations, 2*, 12–17. https://www.jstor.org/stable/26555905

Posthuma, R. A., & Campion, M. A. (2009). Age stereotypes in the workplace: Common stereotypes, moderators, and future research directions. *Journal of Management, 35*(1), 158–188. https://doi.org/10.1177/0149206308318617

Quinn, J. F. (2010). Work, retirement, and the encore career: Elders and the future of the American workforce. *Generations, 34*, 45–55. https://www.jstor.org/stable/44877647

Reynolds, J. M. (2018). The extended body: On aging, disability, and well-being. *Hastings Center Report, 48*(Suppl 3), S31–S36. https://doi.org/10.1002/hast.910

Richardson, V. E. (1993). *Retirement counseling: A handbook for gerontology practitioners*. Springer Publishing.

Romig, K. (2023, April 25). *Raising social security's retirement age would cut benefits for all new retirees. Harm would fall disproportionately on seniors with low incomes*. Center on Budget and Policy Priorities. https://www.cbpp.org/research/social-security/raising-social-securitys-retirement-age-would-cut-benefits-for-all-new

Rothwell, W. J., Sterns, H. L., Spokus, D., & Reaser, J. M. (2008). *Working longer: New strategies for managing, training, and retaining older workers*. American Management Association.

Rudolph, C. W., Rauvola, R. S., Costanza, D. P., & Zacher, H. (2021). Generations and generational differences: Debunking myths in organizational science and practice and paving new paths forward. *Journal of Business Psychology, 36*(6), 945–967. https://doi.org/10.1007/s10869-020-09715-2

Ruggiano, N., O'Driscoll, J., Lukic, A., & Schotthoefer, L. (2017). Work is like a therapy that prevents aging: Perceptions of retirement, productivity, and health among minorities and immigrants. *SAGE Open, 7*(1), 215824401668723. https://doi.org/10.1177/2158244016687234

Salthouse, T. (2012). Consequences of age-related cognitive declines. *Annual Review of Psychology, 63*, 201–226. https://doi.org/10.1146/annurev-psych-120710-100328

Schalk, R., Van Veldhoven, M., de Lange, A. H., de Witte, H., Kraus, K., Stamov-Roßnagel, C., ..., Zacher, H. (2010). Moving European research on work and ageing forward: Overview and agenda. *European Journal of Work and Organizational Psychology, 19*(1), 76–101. https://doi.org/10.1080/13594320802674629

Scharn, M., Sewdas, R., Boot, C. R. L., Huisman, M., Lindeboom, M., & van der Beek, A. J. (2018). Domains and determinants of retirement timing: A systematic review of longitudinal studies. *BMC Public Health, 18*(1), 1083. https://doi.org/10.1186/s12889-018-5983-7

Society for Human Resource Management. (2014). *Executive summary: Preparing for an aging workforce*. http://www.workcompprofessionals.com/advisory/2015L5/february/AgingWorkforce.pdf

Sterns, H. L., & Chang, B. (2010). Workforce issue and retirement. In J. C. Cavanaugh & C. K. Cavanaugh (Eds.), *Aging in America* (Vol. 3, pp. 81–105). Praeger.

Sterns, H. L., & Doverspike, D. (1988). Training and developing the older worker: Implications for human resource management. In H. Dennis (Ed.), *Fourteen steps in managing an aging workforce* (pp. 97–110). Lexington.

Sterns, H. L., Doverspike, D., & Lax, G. (2005). The age discrimination in employment act. In F. S. Landy (Ed.), *Employment discrimination litigation: Behavioral, quantitative, and legal perspectives* (pp. 256–293). Josey-Bass.

Sterns, H. L., & Miklos, S. (1995). The aging worker in a changing environment: Organizational and individual issues. *Journal of Vocational Behavior, 47*(3), 248–268. https://doi.org/10.1006/jvbe.1995.0003

Sterns, H. L., & Kaplan, J. (2003). Self-management of career and retirement. In G. A. Adams & T. A. Beehr (Eds.), *Retirement: Reasons, processes, and results* (1st ed., pp. 188–213). Springer Publishing Company.

Stokes, J. E., Kindratt, T. B., Antonucci, T. C., Cox, C. G., & Choi, H. (2023). Employment dynamics among adult children at the onset of parental dementia: Variation by sociodemographic characteristics. *Journal of Aging and Health, 0*(0). https://doi.org/10.1177/08982643231201547

Stypinska, J., & Turek, K. (2017). Hard and soft age discrimination: The dual nature of workplace discrimination. *European Journal of Ageing, 14*(1), 49–61. https://doi.org/10.1007/s10433-016-0407-y

Sweetland, J., Volmert, A. E., & O'Neil, M. (2017). *Finding the frame: An empirical approach to reframing aging and ageism*. FrameWorks Institute.

Terrell, K. (2018, August). *Age discrimination is common at work*. AARP. https://www.aarp.org/work/age-discrimination/common-at-work/

Topa, G., Depolo, M., & Alcover, C.-M. (2018). Early retirement: A meta-analysis of its antecedent and subsequent correlates. *Frontiers in Psychology, 8*, 2157. https://doi.org/10.3389/fpsyg.2017.02157

U.S. Bureau of Labor Statistics. (2021). *Number of people 75 and older in the labor force is expected to grow 96.5 percent by 2030*. TED: The Economics Daily. https://www.bls.gov/opub/ted/2021/

U.S. Bureau of Labor Statistics. (2023). *Civilian labor force participation rate by age, sex, race, and ethnicity*. https://www.bls.gov/emp/tables/civilian-labor-force-participation-rate.htm

Van Yperen, N. W., & Wortler, B. (2016). Blended working and the employability of older workers, retirement timing, and bridge employment. *Work, Aging, and Retirement, 3*(1), 102–108. https://doi.org/10.1093/workar/waw036

Veth, K. N., Kozillus, H. P. L. M., Vander Heijden. B. I. J. M., Mean, B. J. M., & DeLange, A. H. (2019). Which HRM practices enhance employee outcomes at work across the life-span? *Journal of Human Resource Management, 30*, 2777–2808. https://doi.org/10.1080/09585192.2017.1340322

Wang, M. (2013). *The Oxford handbook of retirement*. Oxford University Press.

Wang, M., Olson, D. A., & Shultz, K. S. (2013). *Mid and later career issues: An integrative perspective*. Routledge.

Webb, A., McQuaid, R., & Rand, S. (2020). Employment in the informal economy: Implications of the COVID-19 pandemic. *International Journal of Sociology and Social Policy, 40*(9/10), 1005–1019. https://doi.org/10.1108/IJSSP-08-2020-0371

Wheaton, F., & Crimmins, E. M. (2013). The demography of aging and retirement. In M. Wang (Ed.), *The Oxford handbook of retirement* (pp. 22–41). Oxford University Press.

Zacher, H., & Rudolph, C. W. (2023). The construction of the "older worker." *Merits, 3*(1), 115–130. https://doi.org/10.3390/merits3010007

Zickar, M. J. (2013). The evolving history of retirement within the United States. In M. Wang (Ed.), *The Oxford handbook of retirement* (pp. 10–21). Oxford University Press.

Aging and the Legal System

Sheri Gibson and Rachel Weiskittle

LEARNING OBJECTIVES

- Differentiate among advance directives, living wills, power of attorney, durable power of attorney, guardianship, and conservatorship (Bloom's level 4).
- Identify ethical principles at play in common ethical dilemmas healthcare professionals and researchers face when working with older adults (Bloom's level 4).
- Identify risk factors and signs of elder abuse (Bloom's level 3).
- Use a lens of multiculturalism when determining if behaviors toward older adults represent abuse (Bloom's level 3).

ETHICAL COMPETENCIES IN GEROPSYCHOLOGY

Psychologists make decisions every day involving fundamental beliefs and values about what is most appropriate in working with older adults, families, and healthcare professionals and within clinical or academic settings. A psychologist's comprehensive understanding of treatment is grounded in the ethical guidelines and principles of the American Psychological Association's (APA's) Ethics Code (APA, 2017; www.apa.org/ethicscode/). The APA Ethics Code serves as a standard to direct the actions and decision-making of psychologists in their work with clients, families, communities, and colleagues, with an emphasis on promoting advocacy for social change.

Within clinical geropsychology practice, the Geropsychology Knowledge and Skills Assessment Tool (Karel et al., 2010) captures the foundational competencies of geropsychology involving legal and ethical standards in four specific areas. Competencies include one's ability to

> ... identify complex ethical and legal issues that arise in the care of older adults, analyze them accurately, and proactively address them, including: (a) tension between sometimes competing goals of promoting autonomy and protecting safety of at-risk older adults; (b) decision making capacity and strategies for optimizing older adults' participation in informed consent regarding a wide range of medical, residential, financial, and other life decisions; (c) surrogate decision making as indicated regarding a wide range of medical, residential, financial, end of life, and other life decisions; and (d) state and organizational laws and policies covering elder abuse, advance directives, conservatorship, guardianship, multiple relationships, and confidentiality. (Karel et al., 2010, p. 117)

ADVANCE CARE PLANNING FOR OLDER ADULTS

Many of the ethical issues that psychologists face when working with older adults revolve around healthcare decisions and whether the older adult is capable of making their own healthcare decisions. Several terms are commonly used when discussing healthcare decision-making. Advance directives, also known as living wills, are documents that specify a person's wishes for end-of-life care. Hospitals are typically required to present information on advance directives prior to admission in accordance with the Patient Self-Determination Act of 1990. Any individual older than the age of 18 can complete an advance directive, though research suggests that only about a quarter of U.S. adults have completed advance directives (Yadav et al., 2017). Lack of awareness of advance directives is typically the most common reason for not completing one.

Several pieces of information are typically included in an advance directive. For the purposes for planning in the event of becoming unable to make decisions secondary to a disabling circumstance, individuals can specify their preference for medical treatment (full treatment vs. comfort-focused treatment), extraordinary measures (tube feeding, ventilator, etc.), and preferences for CPR, also known as a do-not-resuscitate (DNR) order. Individuals can also designate a healthcare surrogate to make decisions for them if they are unable to; this information may also be included in a medical power of attorney (POA) document, which is discussed in the next section. This person is sometimes referred to as a healthcare agent or healthcare proxy. If no surrogate is designated, the default surrogate is the next of kin, typically in the order of spouse/domestic partner, adult child, parent, sibling, or other relative. If no one is available to serve as the healthcare surrogate, the court may appoint a guardian to make the decisions. A guardian may also need to be appointed if the family is in conflict about the patient's wishes, though this is an ethical gray area. We revisit these issues later in the chapter when we discuss potential ethical problems around surrogate decision-making.

Some advance directives include POA documents. A POA is a legal document that designates someone to make decisions on your behalf if you are deemed unable to make or express such decisions. With regard to older adults, a POA is typically designated for healthcare and/or financial matters. A financial POA is typically called a general POA, whereas a healthcare POA is typically called a medical POA. Individuals can choose whether a POA goes into effect immediately once it is signed (called a "durable POA") or whether it only goes into effect once the person is unable to make decisions, as verified by a healthcare professional (called a "springing POA"). Springing POAs can be difficult due to the specificity of incapacity that would trigger an agent's power to use their authority. In most cases, certification of incapacity by at least one doctor is needed to trigger a springing POA. If a specific threshold for incapacity is not explicitly outlined in the springing POA, families can find themselves spending extra time in court determining whether the conditions of incapacity have been met and whether the agent is prepared to assume their duties. Clinicians may be asked to help an older adult complete a living will or POA. It may be beneficial to choose a different person for the medical versus financial POA depending on who is most familiar with the older adult's views on life and death versus their financial affairs. Table 14.1 lists some example options that are typically included in forms that document treatment preferences. One example of this type of form that is used in California is the Physician Orders for Life-Sustaining Treatment (POLST). On the POLST, the patient can list their healthcare agent, though the POLST does not include the level of detail regarding healthcare decisions that may be present in a

TABLE 14.1 SAMPLE QUESTIONS TYPICALLY USED WHEN DOCUMENTING TREATMENT PREFERENCES

Decision	Description and Options
CPR	If the patient has no pulse and is not breathing: ■ Administer CPR or not (DNR order)
Medical interventions	If patient has a pulse and/or is breathing: ■ Full treatment—Prolong life using all medically effective means (for example, intubation, ventilation). ■ Selective treatment—Treat medical conditions but do not intubate (for example, intravenous fluids or antibiotics). Avoid intensive care. ■ Comfort-focused treatment—Maximize comfort. Do not use full and selective treatments unless consistent with comfort goals. Examples include oxygen or oral suctioning.
Artificially administered nutrition	Whether to offer food by mouth is feasible or desired: ■ Long-term artificial nutrition, including feeding tubes ■ Trial period of artificial nutrition, including feeding tubes ■ No artificial means of nutrition, including feeding tubes
Healthcare proxy	■ Specify name and contact information of someone who can make decisions for you if you are unable to.

DNR, do not resuscitate.

medical POA or advance directive. The POLST is freely available at www.capolst.org/polst-for-healthcare-providers/forms.

While the POLST is the form used in California, most states have similar forms that capture treatment preferences. For example, Colorado uses the Medical Orders for Scope of Treatment (MOST) form, which is freely available at www.coloradoadvancedirectives.com/most-in-colorado.

ETHICS IN LONG-TERM CARE

While the majority of older adults receive care from family members, approximately 11% of adults older than the age of 65 receive services in nursing home or long-term care settings, assisted living, or retirement communities (National Alliance for Caregiving [NAC], 2020). Ethical challenges can first emerge from the initial transition from independent living to a higher level of residential care.

For many of us, regardless of age, change can be difficult and typically requires time to adapt to any new circumstance or environment. You might recall events in your life which required changes that were anxiety provoking: the first day of high school, leaving home for college, starting a new job, moving to a new city, or immigrating to a different country. Similar anxieties and fears are present for the older individual who may be faced with leaving a home and condensing a lifelong accumulation of sentimental possessions into a small room or apartment. Let us consider the following scenario:

> Ms. Bartman, an 84-year-old widowed woman, was sent to the emergency department (ED) after she tripped on her oxygen tubing and fell in the living area of her single-family home. At the ED, she reported lying on the floor for 3 hours until her next-door neighbor came over for a routine visit. She suffered bruises on her left arm and leg but did not sustain a head injury. Prior to this injury, Ms. Bartman had experienced two additional falls in the last 3 months and had undergone a left hip replacement for a fracture. She has lived alone for the past 10 years following the death of her husband for whom she was the primary caregiver. Ms. Bartman was treated for multiple medical conditions including congestive heart failure (CHF), atrial fibrillation, hypertension, diabetes, and chronic obstructive pulmonary disease (COPD). Ms. Bartman has a stepdaughter who resides in another state. Prior to the COVID-19 pandemic, her stepdaughter would visit twice a year, but she had only traveled once to see Ms. Bartman in the past 3 years. Ms. Bartman has a close relationship with her neighbor of 30 years. Her neighbor has shared her concerns with Ms. Bartman's stepdaughter about her recent falls, and when suggesting that Ms. Bartman consider moving to a higher level of care, Ms. Bartman declined the offer. Ms. Bartman's stepdaughter did not offer for her to move to her home because she knew that Ms. Bartman would miss her neighbor and would not have enough support in another state.
>
> On examination at the ED, Ms. Bartman was found to have severe leg edema and an ulcerated sore on her coccyx. She presented as poorly nourished with a weight of

(continued)

125 pounds, down from 152 pounds the previous year. Her mental status deteriorated rapidly on the second day of admission with delirium, but the agitation had resolved by the end of the week. A cognitive screen a week later indicated problems with immediate memory and orientation, but Ms. Bartman denied any difficulties managing things on her own, including her medications. On the day of the hospital discharge, Ms. Bartman declined home-health services and stated she would be sure to call her neighbor for help when needed. She denied feeling depressed and expressed excitement at the thought of returning to the comfort of her own home. Ms. Bartman's stepdaughter had spoken to the attending physician and committed to calling Ms. Bartman by phone each day. While in the hospital, Ms. Bartman signed a medical POA designating her neighbor as her primary agent and her stepdaughter as a secondary agent given their respective proximities to Ms. Bartman.

Three days after discharge, Ms. Bartman fell again in her home. This time, she fell outside on the back porch and was found 9 hours later by paramedics with blood on her forehead. She was lying semiconscious close to her back door. Although she did not seem to have sustained any major injury, she was hospitalized and given intravenous fluids. The clinical team and Ms. Bartman agreed that in the interest of maintaining her safety, she should be discharged to a subacute rehabilitation stay in a nursing home. Ms. Bartman's neighbor and stepdaughter believed that she would be safer to transition into long-term care. Ms. Bartman reluctantly agreed and restated her preference to return to her own home. After 20 days in the rehabilitation facility, her physician determined that she lacked capacity for medical decision-making and the medical durable POA was activated. Ms. Bartman was transferred to permanent long-term skilled nursing care. Her physical and cognitive abilities worsened over the next 5 months, and she appeared depressed to both her neighbor and stepdaughter. The advance directive documents had not been completed, and Ms. Bartman was placed on a feeding tube. In the days that followed, she had multiple episodes of breathlessness that required several resuscitation attempts that finally failed. Ms. Bartman died after living 5 months in the nursing home. On review of the admission chart record, she was noted as "depressed and disoriented."

In Ms. Bartman's case, several ethical and legal questions arise for psychologists and other healthcare professionals:

- To what extent does the healthcare team promote Ms. Bartman's autonomy and independence versus implementing protective interventions to maintain her personal safety?
- What more do we need to know about familial and nonfamilial dynamics and the strength of the relationship between Ms. Bartman and her neighbor and Ms. Bartman and her stepdaughter? Did her neighbor have the capacity to serve as surrogate decision maker? To what extent is it our role to ascertain this? If not the neighbor, then who? Did she and the stepdaughter know Ms. Bartman's values, preferences, and wishes for her care and end-of-life decisions?

- How much weight do we place on Ms. Bartman's preference to return home in the face of declined physical functioning? What information do we need to gather to appreciate her refusal to receive care in a rehabilitation or skilled nursing setting?
- And finally, who on the healthcare team is responsible for gathering relevant familial and psychosocial information and how is it shared with the neighbor and stepdaughter and the rest of the care team? Most importantly, how is the plan of care communicated with Ms. Bartman? Who should be involved in those discussions?

FOUNDATIONAL ETHICS OF DECISION-MAKING

To appreciate the underpinnings of ethical dilemmas, clinicians must be familiar with the complexity and range of life events and decisions encountered by older adults, family members, and other healthcare professionals. Specific decisions have been identified (American Bar Association [ABA] & APA, 2021) and include the following: (a) medical decision-making that can range from simple decisions—such as medication management—to complex decisions such as end of life or choosing a medical treatment (Sjöberg et al., 2021); (b) financial decision-making ranging from balancing one's checkbook to managing investments and assets (Gignac et al., 2023; Yu et al., 2022); (c) independent living decisions regarding the level of supervision or independence needed in one's living situation (Okabe et al., 2021; Usher & Stapleton, 2022); (d) driving ability—for example, at what point does a person discontinue driving?; (e) decision-making around sexual consent and relationships, particularly in situations where either one or both individuals have cognitive impairment; and finally, (f) the ability to make a will (referred to as *testamentary capacity*; Brenkel et al., 2018; Martin et al., 2022; Voskou et al., 2018). In addition, a psychologist may be called upon to evaluate the capacity to make a wide range of other decisions (e.g., capacity to marry, capacity to refuse or accept visitors in a hospice setting).

At the center of developing ethical competencies is the tension between autonomy, protection, and beneficence—the intention to do good and no harm on behalf of the patient (APA, 2017)—all of which must include appreciation for an individual's right to make life decisions and choices that are consistent with their beliefs and values. In most situations, those principles can be a guiding force in treatment planning, provision of education, and discussion with patients and families about interventions and the best course of action for the patient. However, in some situations, conflict arises between what the patient wants and what the provider or family believes is best for the patient. A common challenge for professionals is discerning whether or not an older individual can be their own decision maker, particularly in situations where they are engaging in seemingly poor decision-making. Such situations include neglecting one's healthcare needs (i.e., taking psychiatric or other chronic disease medications as prescribed, attending healthcare appointments, and general hygiene care), changing directives in a last will and testament, entering intimate partnerships or new relationships, or engaging in risky behaviors such as alcohol or substance use and cigarette smoking.

AUTONOMY AND SURROGATE DECISION-MAKING

In situations where others (healthcare professionals, friends, family, coworkers) question the type of decisions made by an older adult, concerns may be raised about whether the individual has the ability to make decisions and, if not, what should be done to protect that individual from endangering themselves or others. Two core principles—autonomy and protection—are maximized when responding to these issues. Clinicians and physicians are often called to assess whether an individual has the cognitive capacity to function in any particular domain of decision-making. Eight domains of capacity specific to older adults have been identified by Moye and Marson (2007): (a) independent living, (b) financial management, (c) consent to treatment, (d) testamentary capacity, (e) consent to participate in research, (f) sexual consent, (g) voting, and (h) driving.

Capacity is delineated into either clinical capacity or legal capacity (also called competency).

Clinical Decisional Capacity

Clinical capacity is based on the judgment of healthcare professionals and usually revolves around whether the patient has the ability to express a choice, understand the risks and benefits of the decision, appreciate the significance of the decision, and state rational explanations for their decision (ABA & APA, 2021). Clinical capacity forms the basis for clinical action but does not determine an individual's legal right to perform certain tasks or make certain decisions. Clinical capacity determinations are domain specific. As outlined in the eight domains of capacity, an older adult may lack capacity for financial decisions but capacity may be intact for medical decisions/consent to treatment. The assumption behind a capacity assessment is that the individual could eventually regain capacity to make decisions in that area. For example, if the older adult is experiencing delirium due to various medications, the effects of this would be expected to clear over time.

Judgments about clinical decisional capacity are commonly made through informal information-gathering processes that involve interviewing persons within the familial and psychosocial network such as caregivers, family members, clinicians, attorneys, adult protective service caseworkers, and law enforcement. Neuropsychologists, psychologists, and physicians use various formal assessment measures for determining multiple domains of clinical capacity. If a patient is found to lack clinical capacity in a specific domain, the healthcare team may turn to the surrogate decision maker to provide insight into the person's wishes. The decisions made by a surrogate should be guided by two standards: (a) *substituted judgment* and (b) *best interests*. *Substituted judgment* involves the surrogate's understanding and appreciation for the individual's preferences, values, and wishes to inform their decision-making based on what the individual would have decided if they had the capacity to do so (Bush et al., 2017). In cases where there is insufficient information to make a substituted judgment, the surrogate's decision-making should be guided by the *best interest* standard. In other words, the surrogate's decision would be considered in the best interest of the incapacitated person. Courts may become involved if the surrogate objects to a recommended treatment or if there is conflict within the family about what the patient would want.

The decision of clinical capacity is usually done through clinical interview without a formal measure. However, formal measures are available that may assist in the interview process, although the ultimate decision about capacity should involve multiple informants and methods and not rely solely on one source of information. Formal measures of decisional capacity are typically domain specific and focus on areas such as the capacity to make medical and/or financial decisions (Wood & Lichtenburg, 2016). Instruments can include hypothetical vignettes, which allow the clinician to understand the individual's reasoning process in how they approach the vignette. Examples of these types of instruments for capacity to make medical decisions that have been validated in multiple populations and contexts include the MacArthur Competence Assessment Tool for Treatment (MacCAT; Grisso & Appelbaum, 1998; Grover et al., 2022; Ries et al., 2020), the Hopemont Capacity Assessment Interview (Edelstein, 2000; Kepper et al., 2023), and the Capacity to Consent to Treatment Instrument (Marson et al.,1995). More information about these and other capacity assessment instruments is available in a handbook designed for psychologists, *Assessment of Older Adults with Diminished Capacity*, written jointly by the American Bar Association Commission on Law and Aging and the APA (ABA & APA, 2021). This handbook, as well as handbooks designed for lawyers and judges, is freely available at www.apa.org/pi/aging/programs/assessment. A case-based follow-up to the APA and ABA handbook, *Assessing Capacities of Older Adults: A Casebook to Guide Difficult Decisions*, provides additional context and guidance for navigating the varied challenges of assessing capacity through clinically oriented case examples (Moye, 2020).

Guardianship, Conservatorship, and Other Protective Arrangements

When older adults can no longer manage their affairs and there is no one available to act as surrogates, or the surrogates are in conflict, the court may need to appoint guardians or conservators. This decision is made by magistrates and judges. The judge decides on the level of supervision that may be needed to support or protect the older individual or their assets (Catlin et al., 2022; Johns et al., 2022). Although it varies by state, the following requirements are typically needed to file for a competency hearing: (a) a disabling condition (dementia, mental, or medical disorder), (b) a lack of cognitive ability to evaluate information and communicate preferences, (c) an inability to care for oneself without intervention, and (d) a determination that guardianship is the only feasible way to protect the person. Two forms of legal protections commonly used by courts are guardianship and conservatorship.

The responsibilities and duties associated with designated guardians or conservators vary from state to state. In most states, a guardian is a person who is legally responsible for someone who is unable to manage their own affairs, which can include domains of healthcare, personal affairs, and financial management. They are typically responsible for making sure that the individual receives appropriate services. A conservator is typically and primarily responsible for protecting and handling financial affairs for a person who is deemed incompetent. Federal laws do not govern guardianship practices; thus, duties or responsibilities associated with a guardianship role are left to individual states and jurisdictions to outline and uphold. Most determinations are made in probate court. Probate court is part of the state court system where cases involving wills and estates are presented to and ruled by a magistrate. In contrast, criminal courts are designated for criminal cases that typically involve a juried trial.

When a guardian or conservator is designated by the court, the older adult loses their right to make independent and autonomous decisions about living arrangements, medical treatment, selling or purchasing property, changing a will, driving, entering marriage or getting a divorce. Surrogate decisions can even be made and upheld despite objections from the incapacitated adult (Weiss et al., 2012). That said, the guardian or conservator is encouraged to always keep the older adult's preferences and values at the forefront of their decision-making. Consider the following case example:

Mrs. Maria Rodriguez, an 86-year-old Hispanic woman, has been widowed for 10 years. She has two adult children—a son, Carlos, and a daughter, Elena—both of whom live out of state. Mrs. Rodriguez has been diagnosed with late-stage ovarian cancer. Due to cognitive decline, she has a legal guardian appointed by the court, Ms. Emily Martinez, a close friend and social worker.

Medical History

Mrs. Rodriguez has a history of hypertension and type 2 diabetes, which are currently managed with medication. She has experienced a significant decline in her overall physical and cognitive functioning over the past year, resulting in increased dependency on her guardian for daily care and decision-making. Her diagnosis of ovarian cancer was at an advanced stage, with limited treatment options and a prognosis of less than 1 year with treatment.

Values and Preferences

Mrs. Rodriguez has always valued her independence and quality of life. She expressed her wish to live at home for as long as possible and avoid invasive medical interventions. She is deeply rooted in her Hispanic heritage and values family traditions, religious beliefs, and close-knit family bonds. Mrs. Rodriguez has consistently expressed a desire to maintain her dignity and avoid prolonged suffering.

Clinical Assessment

Oncologists have recommended a combination of aggressive chemotherapy and surgical procedures to treat the ovarian cancer. The treatment could extend Mrs. Rodriguez's life but may cause significant discomfort and side effects. Without treatment, Mrs. Rodriguez's life expectancy is estimated to be less than 6 months.

Guardian's Dilemma

Ms. Martinez, as the court-appointed guardian, faces a challenging decision. She must weigh Mrs. Rodriguez's values and preferences and her doctor's medical recommendations to determine the most appropriate course of action. The options are:

- *Aggressive treatment:* Proceed with chemotherapy and surgery, with the hope of extending Mrs. Rodriguez's life, but potentially causing discomfort and side effects.

(continued)

- *Palliative care:* Opt for palliative care and symptom management, focusing on maximizing Mrs. Rodriguez's comfort and quality of life in her remaining time.
- *Family input:* Consult with Mrs. Rodriguez's adult children, Carlos and Elena, to involve them in the decision-making process and consider their perspectives.

Ethical Considerations

The ethical considerations include balancing the principles of autonomy, beneficence, and nonmaleficence in decision-making while respecting Mrs. Rodriguez's values and cultural background when making the best medical choices and, finally, ensuring that open and transparent communication occurs among all parties involved.

Resolution

Ms. Martinez arranges a family meeting that includes Mrs. Rodriguez, Carlos, and Elena. They discuss the medical options, considering Mrs. Rodriguez's values and the opinions of her children. After much deliberation, they collectively decide on a palliative care approach to prioritize Mrs. Rodriguez's comfort, dignity, and the preservation of her cultural values during her remaining time.

This case highlights the complex and delicate nature of decision-making in end-of-life situations, especially when an individual is unable to make decisions independently. Furthermore, it underscores the importance of involving family members and guardians in discussions that respect the individual's values and wishes.

The previous paragraphs focus mostly on a person's capacity to make medical decisions. As noted in the beginning of this section, there are other domains of capacity, some of which are encountered more often in working with older adults. The following sections highlight the unique clinical considerations, approaches, and support resources for assessing some of the most common domains of capacity outside of medical decision-making.

Assessing Financial Capacity

If an older adult is giving money to someone or spending a lot of money in a potentially irresponsible way (i.e., gambling), a provider may begin to question the person's capacity to make financial decisions. As discussed earlier, a financial POA may need to be appointed if the person is found to lack capacity to make financial decisions. One formal measure of financial capacity, the Financial Capacity Instrument (Marson et al., 2000), enables a clinician to obtain more detailed information about an older adult's ability to understand financial activities such as cash transactions, checkbook management, and financial judgment. Other capacity assessment instruments such as the Hopemont Capacity Assessment Interview (Edelstein, 2000) or the Independent Living Scales (Loeb, 1996) include a section on financial decision-making, which can be used to inform a decision about financial capacity. The Lichtenberg Financial Decision Rating and Screening Scales (Lichtenberg et al., 2016) provide a structured interview to assess an older adult's ability to make a significant financial decision, such as making a large donation or entering into an annuity.

Assessing Sexual Consent Capacity

Other areas of decisional capacity include whether an older adult has the capacity to enter into a sexual relationship. These types of decisions are often challenging for family and healthcare professionals. Most of the concerns around capacity to enter into sexual relationships center on patients with dementia (Srinivasan et al., 2019; Wilkins, 2015). Consider a situation where two older adults are living in a long-term care setting and want to initiate a sexual relationship. There may be concern that one or both of the individuals are unable to understand the pros and cons of this type of relationship due to dementia (Graf & Johnson, 2021; Syme & Steele, 2016;). Alternatively, consider a situation in which a person with dementia lives in a long-term care setting and their long-term partner lives in the community and does not have dementia. Would you have concerns about them continuing to have sexual intercourse, even as the person with dementia continues to experience cognitive decline?

Although sexual consent decisions are rarely a legal concern, it can become complicated due to balancing the principles of autonomy and do no harm, while also considering the negative attitudes that exist regarding older adults' sexuality (Syme & Cohn 2021; Traeen et al., 2021). Srinivasan et al. (2019) suggest that an assessment of sexual consent capacity should include the patient's awareness of the relationship, the patient's ability to avoid exploitation, and the patient's awareness of potential risks such as sexually transmitted diseases. Any assessment of sexual consent capacity should include a review of medical records (including an assessment of conditions that may impact sexual functioning); a clinical interview to assess values around sex as well as understanding, reasoning, and choice; collateral interviews (i.e., family or nursing home staff); neuropsychological testing; and discussion with other team members at the facility (ABA & APA, 2021, Syme & Steele, 2016). Even if the older adult is found to lack capacity to consent to sex, some researchers advocate that certain sexual behaviors may still be allowable based on a committee decision that includes nursing home staff and family members (Hillman, 2017; Wilkins, 2015). This approach is suggested to avoid a condescending attitude toward sexual expression among older adults with dementia.

Assessing Driving Capacity

Determining an older adult's capacity to continue driving is also complex. For many individuals, the decision to stop driving has a major impact on perceived independence. However, family members may become concerned that an older adult with dementia lacks the judgment to continue driving, depending on the severity of the condition. In a longitudinal study of men with dementia, the decision to stop driving was often made abruptly after a physician recommendation (Stasiulis et al., 2020). Follow-up interviews 2 years later indicated that approximately half of the participants had stopped driving but the other half continued to drive up to 5 days per week.

Psychologists are often asked to assist with the decision to stop driving, either in terms of assessing the older adult's functioning with regard to skills involved in driving or by initiating a discussion with the older adult around their views about driving and whether the individual has any concerns or motivation to reduce or stop driving. There are several components of a driving evaluation, including a medical exam, psychological exam, and evaluation by a driving specialist (ABA & APA, 2021). Although the core part of the psychological exam should focus on cognitive functioning, it should also include assessment of symptoms of depression and anxiety, as these conditions can impair reaction time and lead to distraction when driving (ABA & APA, 2021). The evaluation by a driver specialist is critical because impairments observed in psychological testing may or may not impact driving skills (Bahrampouri et al., 2021; Carr et al., 2019; Wolfe & Lehockey, 2016). Although this varies across jurisdictions, there are steps that healthcare professionals and family members can take if they are concerned about an older adult's ability to drive safely. In California, for example, physicians are required to report a medical condition, such as dementia, to the Department of Motor Vehicles (DMV), which will trigger a reexamination of driving ability. In some cases, based on the physician's report, the DMV may decide that the diagnosis is not severe enough yet to require a reexamination. Therefore, when a physician provides this information to the DMV, it does not necessarily mean that the person's license will be revoked. In some states, certain healthcare professionals are required to notify the DMV when certain conditions are diagnosed, whereas in other states, healthcare professionals are not allowed to share this type of private health information. In most states, family members can file a report with the DMV that will trigger a reexamination of driving ability.

ELDER MISTREATMENT, NEGLECT, AND EXPLOITATION

An important area where ethical and legal tensions arise is in cases of suspected or identified elder abuse and exploitation. According to the Centers for Disease Control and Prevention, elder abuse is defined as "an intentional act or failure to act by a caregiver or another person in a relationship involving an expectation of trust that causes or creates a risk of harm to an older adult" (Hall et al., 2016, p. 25). Various forms of elder abuse have been identified and include physical, sexual, emotional, caregiver and self-neglect, and financial exploitation. Important to note is that most states vary in their definitions of the various forms of abuse to older or at-risk adults, thus creating barriers for collecting and analyzing national data to describe the prevalence and incidence rates of elder mistreatment and exploitation. Some scholars have attempted to provide empirical evidence for the prevalence of elder abuse. A widely cited and landmark prevalence study published by Acierno et al. (2010) used a randomized telephone dialing methodology to survey 5,777 older adults. Results suggested that 1 in 10 respondents reported experiencing some form of abuse in the past year. The highest prevalence rate reported was financial abuse by a family member (5.2%), followed by potential neglect (5.1%), emotional abuse (4.6%), physical abuse (1.6%), and finally, sexual abuse (0.6%). The authors concluded that the most consistent correlates with abuse were low social support and previous exposure to a traumatic event.

Risk and Protective Factors for Elder Abuse

Several risk factors increase older adults' vulnerability to mistreatment, neglect, and exploitation. Risk factors pertaining to the older adult on an individual level include physical, cognitive, and sensory deficits; emotional instability (i.e., mental illness); physical and psychosocial isolation; a recent major life transition (i.e., widowhood); relocation; and/or poor access to resources such as medical care, mental health treatment, or spiritual/social activities. Several studies have investigated the association between dementia and older adult victimization (McCausland et al., 2016; Ramsey-Klawsnik, 2017). Aggregated findings suggest a higher prevalence of abuse among older individuals with a diagnosis of dementia (Cooper et al., 2009; Cooper & Livingston, 2020), with upward of 50% of persons with dementia experiencing some form of abuse (Cooper & Livingston, 2020). Another study that surveyed caregivers of older adults with dementia reported that 47% of care recipients had been mistreated by their caregivers (Wigglesworth et al., 2010).

Several factors increase an individual's risk for perpetrating elder abuse. These include inadequate preparation or training for caregiving responsibilities, poor emotion regulation skills, current or history of substance misuse, high stress levels, poor physical health, and social isolation (e.g., Storey, 2020). Characteristics of one's relationship with a vulnerable older adult can also increase risk of perpetrating abuse, such as having a high financial or emotional dependence on the older adult and longstanding familial conflict (Pillemer et al., 2016). Environmental and societal contexts also influence risk for perpetuating abuse toward older adults. When institutional settings, such as assisted living and long-term care facilities, are understaffed or mismanaged, older adult residents are at increased risk for mistreatment and neglect (Yon et al., 2019). This may take the form of direct, targeted abuse, but may also surface in more diffuse ways, such as through diminished quality or oversight of direct patient care provision. Staff burnout and poor working environments have also been found to increase risk of resident mistreatment and neglect.

Knowledge and understanding of protective factors can inform efforts to reduce the risk of elder mistreatment and prevent recurrence. Strong social support and community connections are among the most salient protective factors against elder mistreatment (Yon et al., 2019). While the literature indicates that families are by and large perpetrators of abuse, families also serve as a protective factor. Families often identify abusive situations and can intervene to prevent further abuse from happening. Approximately 14% of nonmandatory reports to adult protective services are made by family members of the vulnerable adult (Lachs & Berman, 2011), indicating that family member outreach is an important and frequent catalyst for support in addition to social service groups. Family members can support the older loved one in seeking additional resources or connecting that person to community resources.

Ethical Considerations in Cases of Elder Abuse

The ethical dilemmas in most cases of elder mistreatment, neglect, and exploitation return to the principles of autonomy and beneficence. As discussed earlier in the chapter, all persons are viewed to be competent unless determined otherwise by a physician or psychologist. Law enforcement and adult protective services—the human services agency commonly involved in investigating and intervening in cases of elder abuse—are sometimes confronted with an older adult's right to refuse services, particularly if the older person appears capable of understanding the consequences of doing so. Self-determination is an important component in intervention and can be a limitation to implementing services and resources. For example, a caseworker may determine that an at-risk adult may benefit from meal preparation services and home healthcare. The at-risk individual has the right to accept meal services yet refuse home healthcare. Unless there is a law, code, or ordinance prohibiting or limiting a person's choice, the at-risk adult has the right to make lifestyle choices that others may feel is objectionable or even dangerous, such as:

- refusing medical treatment,
- refusing to take necessary medication,
- using alcohol or illicit substances,
- living in a dirty or cluttered home,
- continuing to live with a perpetrator,
- keeping a large number of pets, and
- engaging in other behaviors that may not be safe (i.e., gambling, having multiple intimate partners).

Regardless of mental capacity, most states mandate healthcare professionals report suspected or confirmed maltreatment; still, several states do not legally mandate professionals to report, and each state may have a different definition or criteria to identify an "at-risk adult." Healthcare professionals, including psychologists, need to be familiar with state laws guiding the reporting of mistreatment of older adults in their jurisdiction. A list of national resources for information about elder rights and protections can be found in Table 14.2. Familiarization can help psychologists

TABLE 14.2 RESOURCES FOR INFORMATION ABOUT ELDER RIGHTS AND PROTECTIONS

Organization	Website
Administration on Aging	www.acl.gov/about-acl/administration-aging
American Bar Association Commission on Law & Aging	www.americanbar.org/aba.html
Gerontological Society of America	www.geron.org
National Adult Protective Services Network	www.apsnetwork.org
National Center on Elder Abuse	www.ncea.acl.gov/home
National Clearinghouse on Abuse in Later Life	www.ncall.us
National Committee for the Prevention of Elder Abuse	www.preventelderabuse.org
Psychologists in Long-Term Care (PLTC)	www.pltcweb.org/index.php

identify a course of action to either protect or prevent abuse of an at-risk older adult (Bush et al., 2017).

Respecting Cultural Differences in Cases of Elder Abuse

Cultural competence and respect for normative practices among all individuals from diverse backgrounds must be the first guiding principle when caring for older adults and when determining whether elder abuse has occurred. Introspection around biases or lack of knowledge of the relevant culture might be a helpful start in determining the course of action necessary to be a competent clinician. Culture and diversity in this context are not limited to understanding different racial and ethnic practices, but includes knowledge of how different groups may embrace the meaning of their identity. This may include but is not limited to those who identify as a person with a disability, as a person who is a sexual or gender minority (SGM), as a person without housing, or a person who has been incarcerated. These identities may intersect with psychosocial factors relevant to aging, such as loyalty to family, caregiving, financial dependence, intergenerational communication, and perception of age or illness-related burden. This is not an exhaustive list, as every microsystem and macrosystem of function brings with it different complexities as well as creativity for problem resolution and life celebrations. As in all clinical work, there are several ways to ensure that a reasonable amount of consideration has been made not to cause any additional harm to the older adult identified for protection. Any underestimation of the needs and efforts to clarify the situation from which elder abuse is suspected could be detrimental. Not only could it hurt the well-being of the identified older adult, it could also likely place a tremendous amount of emotional burden on that individual due to feelings of shame for being the cause of the family's additional hardship during investigations (Roberto, 2023).

It is prudent for clinicians to refer to the APA Ethics Code (2017) that clearly states under the general principles that psychologists "do no harm" (Principle A: Beneficence and Nonmaleficence); "exercise reasonable judgment and take precautions to ensure that their potential biases, the boundaries of their competence . . . do not lead to . . . unjust practices" (Principle D: Justice); and "respect the dignity and worth of all people, and the rights of individuals to . . . self-determination . . . are aware of and respect culture, individual and role differences" (Principle E: Respect for People's Rights and Dignity). Unless the older adult is determined through assessment to be clinically or legally incapacitated and therefore unable to self-protect or self-determine the desirable treatment from others, professionals who are often mandated to report elder abuse (psychologists and others) are encouraged to carefully navigate the terrain of varied and even conflicting information before taking any action.

Lewis and Mackie (2020) highlighted the tendency of elder abuse legislators to ignore the wishes of older adults, specifically those living in rural areas, by reporting elder abuse that would consequently subject the older adult to increased emotional turmoil such as shame and also fear of being further abused. They pointed to the possibility of achieving a more successful intervention outcome by attending to the specific culture of older adults living in rural settings. Additional empirical studies, including recommendations for legislative change, have focused on prevention and response efforts for rural-dwelling older adults (Warren & Blundell, 2019; Zhang et al., 2022).

Older LGBT adults are also underserved and marginalized in both legal and healthcare settings, particularly in long-term care. LGBT older adults are more likely to live alone, be socially isolated, and have less family support than their straight-identifying counterparts (Koller, 2019), which can lead to greater reliance on formal caregivers (Henning-Smith & Shippee, 2015) and place them at increased risk for mistreatment or neglect. This disparity in social connection can also make older LGBT adults more reliant on long-term care facilities. In a recent survey of mental health providers who work in long-term care, 61% reported working with at least one older LGBT resident in the past year (Smith et al., 2019). However, this figure is likely an underestimate due to older adults' nondisclosure of SGM identity for fear of discrimination or stigma.

These fears, unfortunately, are well founded. Older LGBT adults are likely to face suboptimal care in long-term care facilities due to prejudice and discrimination based on their SGM identity. In a national community-based study of transgender older adults, approximately 14% reported they were denied equal treatment or service and experienced verbal harassment and physical attacks from staff in long-term care facilities for being perceived as transgender (James et al., 2016). Long-term care has been described in the health equity literature as heteronormative and cisnormative, in that care recipients are assumed to identify as heterosexual and cisgender. Even when long-term care providers report personal comfort in providing care to older LGBT adults, the vast majority list educational and training barriers to providing adequate care, such as a lack of training in LGBT issues (85%) and a lack of familiarity with evidence-based treatments for this population (76%; Smith et al., 2019). This experience is widespread: A recent systematic review of providers' and LGBT individuals' perspectives on long-term care emphasized an urgent need for research that identifies effective evidence-based interventions for older LGBT adults in this setting (Caceres et al., 2020).

There are implications for professionals to more thoughtfully and collaboratively work with victims of elder abuse. In so doing, mandated reporters and legislators could better help balance older adults' rights and wishes with what seems to be in the best interest of the victims. Other research involving different ethnic groups and individuals from diverse cultures also lends support to the need for an in-depth understanding of the context from which such important decisions pertaining to claims of elder abuse are usually made. Consider the following examples:

- Financial/material exploitation:
  - A 75-year-old male veteran with a diagnosis of schizophrenia and a recent above-knee amputation due to unmanaged diabetes resides in a supportive group home with other veterans. He is able to ambulate with his new prosthesis, although he relies mostly on a manual wheelchair for ease and convenience. During a recent outing, one of the veteran residents asked to use his debit card and drained all of his monthly allowance. When the veteran was unable to purchase personal hygiene necessities and stopped going out on his usual outings to the nearby convenience store, the group home care aide learned of the exploitation and filed a report with adult protective services.
  - Cultural/ethical query: How would knowing the cultural background make a difference when understanding whether or not elder abuse had occurred?

- Emotional abuse:
  - A 94-year-old man lives in his own home with his youngest son. Most friends and family are aware that he has an enmeshed relationship with his son. This enmeshment has been known to involve occasional arguments followed by reconciliations and mutual overprotection from the criticism of others. Unhealthy alcohol use within the family has been a norm, and altercations are frequent among male siblings and relatives after an evening of binge drinking together at the older adult's home. Such behaviors affect the older adult emotionally, as his son yells vulgarities when intoxicated and then apologizes the next morning when sober. When interviewed, the older adult, denied any evidence of abuse despite noticeable bruises on his forearm.
  - Cultural/ethical query: Are there any specific ethnic groups that might tolerate such a pattern of coexistence whereby a report of elder abuse would bring more hardship to the older adult?

Although elder abuse is largely defined to include seven different types, mainly physical abuse, sexual abuse, emotional abuse, financial/material exploitation, neglect, abandonment, and self-neglect (Hall et al., 2016), the definition of "abuse" could be different for older adults in minority ethnic groups, especially when the concept could only be translated to mean "violence" or when disrespect could be considered "a major form of abuse" such as within the Chinese community (Bowes et al., 2012). Lee et al. (2012) argue that the existing definition of financial abuse may be inaccurate because it is based on perceptions of supposedly highly educated professionals and policy makers, but not from older adults. In their study, for example, they found that Korean immigrants defined financial abuse as adult children either taking (stealing) possessions and/or assets from their parents or failing to financially support their parents.

Similarly, in an attempt to define elder abuse in culturally relevant terms, Sanchez (2021) sought to identify the "ecological framework" that could be at play for sustaining elder abuse and neglect among Latino older adults. They noted that acculturation status and differences in cultural beliefs and identity between the family caregiver and the older adult care recipient may be viewed as important factors for understanding elder abuse in Latino families. For example, U.S.-born Hispanic children are perceived to value traditional cultures less than their foreign-born parents. This might explain their lack of awareness and also their likely different definition of elder abuse. Similarly, the family's financial standing and beliefs about aging should be considered when determining whether elder abuse or neglect has occurred because multiple ecological stressors could have been responsible for the outcome. Consequently, attending to these factors might help in the development of interventions that would avoid placing blame solely on the abuser.

Many controversies remain regarding the meaning and definition of elder abuse, and it is therefore not surprising that there is a lack of consensus, and even confusion, among healthcare professionals. Elder abuse is further made difficult to define due to the lack of training in geropsychology across healthcare professions, which would otherwise allow a greater appreciation of diversity issues in the competent care of older adults (Scheiderer, 2012). Koocher and Kieth-Spiegel (2016) proposed a six-item self-assessment as part of training in diversity to reflect upon one's biases and cultural competence. One item relevant for decision-making in reporting elder abuse involves the question: "As I seek to protect myself, what are my ethical obligations when I notice a cultural incongruity in values between my professional association, my employer, legal obligations, and the people I serve?" (p. 132).

A review of the prevalence and risk factors for elder abuse in Asia (China, India, Singapore, Japan, and Korea) emphasized the need for sensitivity to the different normative definitions of elder abuse. They stressed the importance of establishing rapport with suspected older adult victims due to their unwillingness to share their experience of abuse that they likely perceive to be shameful or determine as a family affair to be kept private (Yan et al., 2015). Hence, elder abuse might not simply be a matter of whether reporting is warranted, but rather, a term to be sensitively considered in the context of culture, diversity, and socioeconomic status. It is important to be mindful of different perceptions of older adults from minority groups and their sociocultural barriers to seeking help, such as lack of dominant language proficiency and isolation (Adib et al., 2019; Wydall & Zerk, 2017; Zannettino et al., 2015).

ETHICS IN RESEARCH

Adhering to ethical standards when recruiting prospective research participants should be the standard practice of every researcher. Specifically, researchers are responsible for ensuring that best efforts are made to help participants understand as fully as possible the information depicted on informed consent forms. Older adults and individuals with lower education can be more vulnerable to inadequately understanding informed consent (Aguila et al., 2016). With the projected exponential increase in the older adult population in the coming decades (Ortman et al., 2014), it is expected that research using older adults as participants will also increase accordingly. There have been concerns and fears over the unethical inclusion of older adults with cognitive impairment in research, but the exclusion could deprive them of the opportunity to benefit from research where their well-being and quality of life could otherwise be improved.

These considerations give rise to an important question of participants' varying levels of cognitive functioning. How might researchers ethically obtain consent from older adults who may present with impaired cognition without violating the ethical code to protect individuals from any potential harm as a research participant? As mentioned earlier, education level could also impact the understanding of informed consent information, but if cognition is also impaired, the challenge is much greater to warrant additional attention. One other important question is: Should the participants or the authorized representative consent to research when prospective participants are cognitively impaired? Several studies have attempted to provide guidance, which is summarized as follows.

Capacity to consent or decisions about who should provide consent on behalf of the older adult participant undoubtedly require careful consideration. Specifically, it has been noted that ethical dilemmas begin at the level of capacity evaluation, where the full range of contextual biopsychosocial information, including medical conditions, family relation, social function, and financial situation, need to be considered for accuracy of capacity judgment (Aguila et al., 2016; Jimenez et al., 2015). Prusaczyk et al. (2017) explained how the capacity to consent for research participation is dependent on the older adult's cognitive ability and the study's complexity. They discussed the "principle of proportionality of the capacity to consent" wherein the amount of risk, time, and benefit involved in the study would determine how stringent the "standards of capacity to consent" should be (p. 477). That is, if a study involves more risk and time, the greater the importance to show adequate capacity to consent, whereas if benefits are involved, the lesser the need to prove adequate capacity. Ries et al. (2017) found in their survey of older adults, informal caregivers, researchers, and institutional review board members a unanimous opinion that for older adults with dementia, the need for a legal guardian's consent to participate in research becomes greater as the risks of the study increase. Despite the consensus, it was highlighted that many cognitively impaired older adults do not have a legal guardian. In a survey of older adults, informal caregivers, physicians, researchers, and research ethics board members, the level of comfort with using proxy consent increased when risks to participants with dementia was lower (Dubois et al., 2011).

Some brief screening tools can assist a researcher in evaluating capacity to consent to research participation. Resnick et al. (2007) validated a five-item Evaluation to Sign Consent (ESC) measure in a randomized controlled trial using mainly European American nursing home residents aged 79 to 93 with a mean Mini Mental Status Examination (MMSE) score of 18. They found 63% of residents did not pass the ESC. As a comparison, a similar four-item capacity-to-consent screen was also validated for older adults in Korea using culturally and educationally appropriate questions (Lee, 2010). The majority (72%) had either no education or completed only elementary school. Lee demonstrated sensitivity to demographic backgrounds of participants by asking, "If you don't want to, do you have to be in the study?" versus Resnick et al.'s directive: "Explain what they would do if they were experiencing distress or discomfort," which was more suitable for the study's predominantly White participants. Such attention to language when designing capacity measures is essential for protecting the rights and interests of research participants. While thoughtful planning is required when working with older adults with cognitive impairment, Gatz (2006) reminded researchers of the complexities of evaluating older adults' abilities to consent to participate in research or medical treatment. Gatz cautioned against the assumption that normal cognition equates to sound decision-making capacity because of the potential for cognitive changes in the older population and the existence of "a range of statuses between cognitive competence and decisional incapacity" (p. 468). Hence, it is important that researchers carefully weigh the risks and benefits of their study as well as attend to the nuances of capacity to consent that might not depend only on cognitive status at the time of recruitment. Researchers are also encouraged to observe legislative guidelines for research in their practice jurisdiction to ensure that prospective participants with impaired decision-making capacity are protected accordingly, such as whether proxy consent is absolutely required for research regardless of risks (Ries et al., 2019).

CONCLUSION

As the U.S. older adult population grows, a number of ethical issues—only a few of which were discussed in this chapter—are increasingly coming into view for clinicians and healthcare providers. The microsystems and macrosystems in which older adults live and thrive require a level of cultural sensitivity, an understanding of aging processes, and knowledge about professional ethics and legal standards involved in decision-making. We have discussed the complexities of elder abuse and victimization, which involve complex judgments about capacity and potential surrogate decision-making for an older adult. At the heart of ethical principles and guidelines is the challenge between autonomy and protection. We have also documented some of the real-world dilemmas faced by practitioners and families navigating long-term care placement and information sharing that occurs between providers, older adults, and the family. And finally, we addressed the ethical standards required for older adults to consent to participate in research—an important component to furthering the science and thus expanding our knowledge and understanding of aging adults and families and the communities in which we flourish together.

DISCUSSION QUESTIONS

1. Define the following terms and provide an example of when it would be useful to have each document: advance directive, power of attorney, and healthcare surrogate.
2. Describe the difference between clinical capacity and legal capacity (competence) and discuss instruments used to assess capacity in older adults.
3. Define the domains of capacity discussed in the chapter and provide examples of ethical challenges that may be encountered in each domain.
4. Describe the concern when working with older adults about balancing the principles of autonomy and beneficence.
5. Discuss the prevalence of elder abuse and the cultural issues that are important to consider when determining the severity of elder abuse.
6. In the context of research with older adults, describe proxy consent and the ethical concerns with it.

ACKNOWLEDGMENTS

Special thanks to Dr. Magdalene Lim and Paige Klein for their contributions to this chapter.

A robust set of instructor resources designed to supplement this text is located at http://connect.springerpub.com/content/book/978-0-8261-6617-3. Qualifying instructors may request access by emailing textbook@springerpub.com.

REFERENCES

Acierno, R., Hernandez, M., Amstadter, A., Resnick, H., Steve, K., Muzzy, W., & Kilpatrick, D. G. (2010). Prevalence and correlates of emotional, physical, sexual, and financial abuse and potential neglect in the United States: The National Elder Mistreatment Study. *American Journal of Public Health, 100*(2), 292–297. https://doi.org/10.2105/AJPH.2009.163089

Adib, M., Esmaeili, M., Zakerimoghadam, M., & Nayeri, N. D. (2019). Barriers to help-seeking for elder abuse: A qualitative study of older adults. *Geriatric Nursing, 40*(6), 565–571. https://doi.org/10.1016/j.gerinurse.2019.04.003

Aguila, E., Weidmer, B. A., Rivera Illingworth, A., & Martinez, H. (2016). Culturally competent informed-consent process to evaluate a social policy for older persons with low literacy: The Mexican case. *SAGE Open, 6*(3), 2158244016665886. https://doi.org/10.1177/2158244016665886

American Bar Association & American Psychological Association Assessment of Capacity in Older Adults Project Working Group. (2021). *Assessment of older adults with diminished capacity: A handbook for psychologists*. https://www.apa.org/pi/aging/programs/assessment/capacity-psychologist-handbook.pdf

American Psychological Association. (2017). *Ethical principles of psychologists and code of conduct: Including 2017 amendments*. http://www.apa.org/ethics/code

Bahrampouri, S., Khankeh, H. R., Hosseini, S. A., Mehmandar, M., & Ebadi, A. (2021). Components of driving competency measurement in the elderly: A scoping review. *Medical Journal of the Islamic Republic of Iran, 35*, 2. https://doi.org/10.47176/mjiri.35.2

Bowes, A., Avan, G., & Macintosh, S. B. (2012). Cultural diversity and the mistreatment of older people in Black and minority ethnic communities: Some implications for service provision. *Journal of Elder Abuse & Neglect, 24*(3), 251–274. https://doi.org/10.1080/08946566.2011.653319

Brenkel, M., Whaley, K., Herrmann, N., Crawford, K., Hazan, E., Cardiff, L., Owen, A. M., & Shulman, K. (2018). A case for the standardized assessment of testamentary capacity. *Canadian Geriatrics Journal, 21*(1), 26–31. https://doi.org/10.5770/cgj.21.283

Bush, S. S., Allen, R. S., & Molinari, V. A. (2017). Ethical issues and decision making in geropsychology. In S. S. Bush, R. S. Allen, & V. A. Molinari (Eds.), *Ethical practice in geropsychology* (pp. 35–56). American Psychological Association.

Caceres, B. A., Travers, J., Primiano, J. E., Luscombe, R. E., & Dorsen, C. (2020). Provider and LGBT individuals' perspectives on LGBT issues in long-term care: A systematic review. *The Gerontologist, 60*(3), e169–e183. https://doi.org/10.1093/geront/gnz012

Carr, D. B., Stowe, J. D., & Morris, J. C. (2019). Driving in the elderly in health and disease. *Handbook of Clinical Neurology, 167*, 563–573. https://doi.org/10.1016/B978-0-12-804766-8.00031-5

Catlin, C. C., Connors, H. L., Teaster, P. B., Wood, E., Sager, Z. S., & Moye, J (2022). Unrepresented adults face adverse healthcare consequences: The role of guardians, public guardianship reform, and alternative policy solutions. *Journal of Aging & Social Policy, 34*(3), 418–437. https://doi.org/10.1080/08959420.2020.1851433

Cooper, C., & Livingston, G. (2020). Elder abuse and dementia. In A. Phelan (Ed.), *Advances in elder abuse research: Practice, legislation and policy* (pp. 137–147). Springer.

Cooper, C., Selwood, A., Blanchard, M., Walker, Z., Blizard, R., & Livingston, G. (2009). Abuse of people with dementia by family carers: Representative cross sectional survey. *British Medical Journal, 338*, b155. https://doi.org/10.1136/bmj.b155

Dubois, M. F., Bravo, G., Graham, J., Wildeman, S., Cohen, C., Painter, K., & Bellemare, S. (2011). Comfort with proxy consent to research involving decisionally impaired older adults: Do type of proxy and risk-benefit profile matter? *International Psychogeriatrics, 23*(9), 1479–1488. https://doi.org/10.1017/S1041610211000433

Edelstein, B. (2000). Challenges in the assessment of decision-making capacity. *Journal of Aging Studies, 14*(4), 423–437. https://doi.org/10.1016/S0890-4065(00)80006-7

Gatz, M. (2006). Cognitive capacities of older adults who are asked to consent to medical treatment or to clinical research. *Behavioral Sciences & the Law, 24*(4), 465–468. https://doi.org/10.1002/bsl.694

Gignac, G. E., Gerrans, P., & Andersen, C. B. (2023). Financial literacy mediates the effect between verbal intelligence and financial anxiety. *Personality and Individual Differences, 203*, 112025. https://doi.org/10.1016/j.paid.2022.112025

Graf, A. S., & Johnson, V. (2021). Describing the "Gray" area of consent: A comparison of sexual consent understanding across the adult lifespan. *The Journal of Sex Research, 58*(4), 448–461. https://doi.org/10.1080/00224499.2020.1765953

Grisso, T., & Applebaum, P. S. (1998). *MacArthur competence assessment tool for treatment (MacCATT)*. Professional Resource Press/Professional Resource Exchange.

Grover, D., Tekkalaki, B., Yadawad, V., Patil, N. M., Chate, S. S., & Patil, S. (2022). Capacity to consent for treatment in patients with psychotic disorder: A cross-sectional study from North Karnataka. *Indian Journal of Psychological Medicine, 44*(6), 592–597. https://doi.org/10.1177/02537176221100272

Hall, J. E., Karch, D. L., & Crosby, A. E. (2016). *Elder abuse surveillance: Uniform definitions and recommended core data elements for use in elder abuse surveillance* (Version 1.0). https://www.cdc.gov/violenceprevention/pdf/ea_book_revised_2016.pdf

Henning-Smith, C. E., & Shippee, T. P. (2015). Expectations about future use of long-term services and supports vary by current living arrangement. *Health Affairs, 34*(1), 39–47. https://doi.org/10.1377/hlthaff.2014.0556

Hillman, J. (2017). Sexual consent capacity: Ethical issues and challenges in long-term care. *Clinical Gerontologist, 40*(1), 43–50. https://doi.org/10.1080/07317115.2016.1185488

James, S. E., Herman, J. L., Rankin, S., Keisling, M., Mottet, L., & Anafi, M. (2016). *The report of the 2015 U.S. Transgender Survey.* https://www.transequality.org/sites/default/files/docs/USTS-Full-Report-FINAL.PDF

Jimenez, X. F., Esplin, B. S., & Hernandez, J. O. (2015). Capacity consultation and contextual complexities: Depression, decisions, and deliberation. *Psychosomatics, 56*(5), 592–597. https://doi.org/10.1016/j.psym.2015.06.002

Johns, A. F., Dinerstein, R. D., & Dudek, P. E. K (2022). Guardianships vs. special needs trusts, and other protective arrangements: Ensuring judicial accountability and beneficiary autonomy. *Syracuse Law Review, 72*(1), 423–468.

Karel, M., Emery, E., Molinari, V., & the CoPGTP Task Force on the Assessment of Geropsychology Competencies. (2010). Development of a tool to evaluate geropsychology knowledge and skill competencies. *International Psychiatrics, 22*(6), 886–896. https://doi.org/10.1017/S1041610209991736

Kepper, P. J., Hardi, A., Holden, S., & Holden, T. (2023). Cognition, capacity, and consent for elective surgery in older adult populations. *Journal of the American College of Surgeons, 237*(3), 578–580. https://doi.org/10.1097/XCS.0000000000000774

Koller, J. (2019). *LGBT+ older adults: At-risk for inadequate support and social isolation.* American Society on Aging. https://www.asaging.org/blog/lgbt-older-adults-risk-inadequate-support-and-social-isolation

Koocher, G. P., & Keith-Spiegel, P. (2016). *Ethics in psychology and the mental health professions: Standards and cases.* Oxford University Press.

Lachs, M., & Berman, J. (2011). *Under the radar: New York State elder abuse prevalence study.* Lifespan of Greater Rochester, Inc., Weill Cornell Medical Center of Cornell University, and New York City Department for the Aging. https://ocfs.ny.gov/reports/aps/Under-the-Radar-2011May12.pdf

Lee, M. (2010). The capacity to consent to research among older adults. *Educational Gerontology, 36,* 592–603. https://doi.org/10.1080/03601270903324461

Lee, H. Y., Lee, S. E., & Eaton, C. K. (2012). Exploring definitions of financial abuse in elderly Korean immigrants: The contribution of traditional cultural values. *Journal of Elder Abuse & Neglect, 24*(4), 293–311. https://doi.org/10.1080/08946566.2012.661672

Lewis, B., Purser, K., & Mackie, K. (2020). *The human rights of older persons. A human rights-based approach to elder law.* Springer. https://doi.org/10.1007/978-981-15-6735-3

Lichtenberg, P. A., Ficker, L., Rahman-Filipiak, A., Tatro, R., Farrell, C., Speir, J. J., . . ., Jackman Jr., J. D. (2016). The Lichtenberg Financial Decision Screening Scale (LFDSS): A new tool for assessing financial decision making and preventing financial exploitation. *Journal of Elder Abuse & Neglect, 28*(3), 134–151. https://doi.org/10.1080/08946566.2016.1168333

Loeb, P. A. (1996). *ILS: Independent living scales manual.* Psychological Corporation.

Marson, D. C., Ingram, K. K., Cody, H. A., & Harrell, L. E. (1995). Assessing the competency of patients with Alzheimer's disease under different legal standards: A prototype instrument. *Archives of Neurology, 52*(10), 949–954. https://doi.org/10.1001/archneur.1995.00540340029010

Marson, D. C., Sawrie, S. M., Snyder, S., McInturff, B., Stalvey, T., Boothe, A., . . ., Harrell, L. E. (2000). Assessing financial capacity in patients with Alzheimer disease: A conceptual model and prototype instrument. *Archives of Neurology, 57*(6), 877–884. https://doi.org/10.1001/archneur.57.6.877

Martin, R. C., Gerstenecker, A., Hebert, K., Triebel, K., & Marson, D. (2022). Assessment of testamentary capacity in older adults: Description and initial validation of a standardized interview instrument. *Archives of Clinical Neuropsychology, 27*(6), 1133–1147. https://doi.org/10.1093/arclin/acac028

McCausland, B., Knight, L., Page, L., & Trevillion, K. (2016). A systematic review of the prevalence and odds of domestic abuse victimization among people with dementia. *International Review of Psychiatry, 28*(5), 475–484. https://doi.org/10.1080/09540261.2016.1215296

Moye, J. E. (2020). *Assessing capacities of older adults: A casebook to guide difficult decisions.* American Psychological Association.

Moye, J., & Marson, D. C. (2007). Assessment of decision-making capacity in older adults: An emerging area of practice and research. *Journal of Gerontology: Psychological Sciences, 62B,* 3–11. https://doi.org/10.1093/geronb/62.1.p3

National Alliance for Caregiving. (2020). *Caregiving in the U.S. 2020.* National Alliance for Caregiving and AARP. http://www.caregiving.org/caregiving2020

Okabe, T., Suzuki, M., Iso, N., Tanaka, K., Sagari, A., Miyata, H., Han, G., Maruta, M., Tabira., & Kawagoe, M. (2021). Long-term changes in older adults' independence levels for performing activities of daily living in care settings: A nine-year follow-up study. *International Journal of Environmental Research and Public Health, 18*(18), 9641. https://doi.org/10.3390/ijerph18189641

Ortman, J. M., Velkoff, V. A., & Hogan, H. (2014). *An aging nation: The older population in the United States, current population reports.* U.S. Census Bureau. https://pdfs.semanticscholar.org/9e8d/9dc95a5130fa4fd0eb808b5c888e628c2023.pdf

Pillemer, K., Burnes, D., Riffin, C., & Lachs, M. S. (2016). Elder abuse: Global situation, risk factors, and prevention strategies. *The Gerontologist, 56*(Suppl_2), S194–S205. https://doi.org/10.1093/geront/gnw004

Prusaczyk, B., Cherney, S. M., Carpenter, C. R., & DuBois, J. M. (2017). Informed consent to research with cognitively impaired adults: transdisciplinary challenges and opportunities. *Clinical Gerontologist, 40*(1), 63–73. https://doi.org/10.1080/07317115.2016.1201714

Ramsey-Klawsnik, H. (2017). Older adults affected by polyvictimization: A review of early research. *Journal of Elder Abuse & Neglect, 29*(5), 299–312. https://doi.org/10.1093/geront/gnw004

Resnick, B., Gruber-Baldini, A. L., Pretzer-Aboff, I., Galik, E., Buie, V. C., Russ, K., & Zimmerman, S. (2007). Reliability and validity of the evaluation to sign consent measure. *The Gerontologist, 47*(1), 69–77. https://doi.org/10.1093/geront/47.1.69

Ries, N. M., Thompson, K. A., & Lowe, M. (2017). Including people with dementia in research: An analysis of Australian ethical and legal rules and recommendations for reform. *Bioethical Inquiry, 14*(3), 359–374. https://doi.org/10.1007/s11673-017-9794-9

Ries, N. M., Mansfield, E., & Sanson-Fisher, R. (2019). Planning ahead for dementia research participation: Insights from a survey of older Australians and implications for ethics, law and practice. *Bioethical Inquiry, 16*(3), 415-429. https://doi.org/10.1007/s11673-019-09929-x

Ries, N. M., Mansfield, E., & Sanson-Fisher, R. (2020). Ethical and legal aspects of research involving older people with cognitive impairment: A survey of dementia researchers in Australia. *International Journal of Law and Psychiatry, 68,* 101534. htps://doi.org/10.1016/j.ijlp.2019.101534

Roberto, K. A. (2023). Older family members: Victims and perpetrators of elder abuse and violence. In Sturmey, P. (Eds.), *Violence in families: Advances in preventing and treating violence and aggression.* Springer. https://doi.org/10.1007/978-3-031-31549-7_6

Sanchez, Y. M. (2021). *Elder mistreatment in Mexican American communities: The Nevada and Michigan experiences. Understanding elder abuse in minority populations* (pp. 66–67). Routledge.

Scheiderer, E. M. (2012). Elder abuse: Ethical and related considerations for professionals in psychology. *Ethics & Behavior, 22*(1), 75–87. https://doi.org/10.1080/10508422.2012.638828

Sjöberg, M., Edberg, A. K., Rasmussen, B. H., & Beck, I. (2021). Documentation of older people's end-of-life-care in the context of specialized palliative care: A retrospective review of patient records. *BMC Palliative Care, 20*(1), 91. https://doi.org/10.1186/s12904-021-00771-w

Smith, R. W., Altman, J. K., Meeks, S., & Hinrichs, K. L. (2019). Mental health care for LGBT older adults in long-term care settings: Competency, training, and barriers for mental health providers. *Clinical Gerontologist, 42*(2), 198–203. https://doi.org/10.1080/07317115.2018.1485197

Srinivasan, S., Glover, J., Tampi, R. R., Tampi, D. J., & Sewell, D. D. (2019). Sexuality and the older adult. *Current Psychiatry Reports, 21*(10), 97. https://doi.org/10.1007/s11920-019-1090-4

Stasiulis, E., Rapoport, M. J., Sivajohan, B., & Naglie, G. (2020). The paradox of dementia and driving cessation: "It's a Hot Topic," "Always on the Back Burner." *The Gerontologist, 60*(7), 1261–1272. https://doi.org/10.1093/geront/gnaa034

Storey, J. E. (2020). Risk factors for elder abuse and neglect: A review of the literature. *Aggression and Violent Behavior, 50,* 101339. https://doi.org/10.1016/j.avb.2019.101339

Syme, M. L., & Cohn, T. J. (2021). Aging sexual stereotypes and sexual expression in mid-and later life: Examining the stereotype matching effect. *Aging & Mental Health, 25*(8), 1507–1514. https://doi.org/10.1080/13607863.2020.1758909

Syme, M. L., & Steele, D. (2016). Sexual consent capacity assessment with older adults. *Archives of Clinical Neuropsychology, 31*(6), 495–505. https://doi.org/10.1093/arclin/acw046

Traeen, B., Fischer, N., & Kvalem, I. L. (2021). Sexual intercourse activity and activities associated with sexual interaction in Norwegians of different sexual orientations and ages. *Sexual and Relationship Therapy, 38*(4), 715–731. https://doi.org/10.1080/14681994.2021.1912316

Usher, R., & Stapleton, T. (2022). Assessment of older adults' decision-making capacity in relation to independent living: A scoping review. *Health & Social Care in the Community, 30*(2), e255–e277. https://doi.org/10.1111/hsc.13487

Voskou, P., Douzenis, A., Economou, A., & Papageorgiou, S. G. (2018). Testamentary capacity assessment: Legal, medical, and neuropsychological issues. *Journal of Geriatric Psychiatry and Neurology, 31*(1), 3–12. https://doi.org/10.1177/0891988717746508

Warren, A., & Blundell, B. (2019). Addressing elder abuse in rural and remote communities: Social policy, prevention and responses. *Journal of Elder Abuse & Neglect, 31*(4–5), 424–436. https://doi.org/10.1080/08946566.2019.1663333

Weiss, B., Berman, E., Howe, C., & Fleming, R. B. (2012). Medical decision making for older adults without family. *Journal of American Geriatrics Society, 60*(11), 2144–2150. https://doi.org/10.1111/j.1532-5415.2012.04212.x

Wigglesworth, A., Mosqueda, L., Mulnard, R., Liao, S., Gibbs, L., & Fitzgerald, W. (2010). Screening for abuse and neglect of people with dementia. *Journal of the American Geriatrics Society, 58*(3), 493–500. https://doi.org/10.1111/j.1532-5415.2010.02737.x

Wilkins, J. M. (2015). More than capacity: Alternatives for sexual decision making for individuals with dementia. *Gerontologist, 55*(5), 716–723. https://doi.org/10.1093/geront/gnv098

Wolfe, P. L., & Lehockey, K. A. (2016). Neuropsychological assessment of driving capacity. *Archives of Clinical Neuropsychology, 31*(6), 517–529. https://doi.org/10.1093/arclin/acw050

Wood, S., & Lichtenburg, P. A., (2016). Financial capacity and financial exploitation of older adults: Research findings, policy recommendations and clinical implications. *Clinical Geropsychologist, 40*(1), 3–13. https://doi.org/10.1080/07317115.2016.1203382

Wydall, S., & Zerk, R. (2017). Domestic abuse and older people: Factors influencing help-seeking. *The Journal of Adult Protection, 19*(5), 247–260. https://doi.org/10.1108/JAP-03-2017-0010

Yadav, K.N., Gabler, N. B., Cooney, E., Kent, S., Kim, J., Herbst, N., Mante, A., Halpern, S. S., & Courtright, K. R. (2017). Approximately one in three US adults completes any type of advance directive for end-of-life care. *Health Affairs, 36*(7), 1244–1251. https://doi.org/10.1377/hlthaff.2017.0175

Yan, E., Chan, K.-L., & Tiwari, A. (2015). A systematic review of prevalence and risk factors for elder abuse in Asia. *Trauma, Violence & Abuse, 16*(2), 199–219. https://doi.org/10.1177/1524838014555033

Yon, Y., Ramiro-Gonzalez, M., Mikton, C. R., Huber, M., & Sethi, D. (2019). The prevalence of elder abuse in institutional settings: A systematic review and meta-analysis. *European Journal of Public Health, 29*(1), 58–67. https://doi.org/10.1093/eurpub/cky093

Yu, L., Mottola, G., Wilson, R. S., Valdes, O., Bennett, D. A., & Boyle, P. A. (2022). Metamemory and financial decision making in older adults without dementia. *Neuropsychology, 36*(1), 35–43. https://doi.org/10.1037/neu0000773

Zannettino, L., Bagshaw, D., Wendt, S., & Adams, V. (2015). The role of emotional vulnerability and abuse in the financial exploitation of older people from culturally and linguistically diverse communities in Australia. *Journal of Elder Abuse & Neglect, 27*(1), 74–89. https://doi.org/10.1080/08946566.2014.976895

Zhang, L. P., Du, Y. G., Dou, H. Y., & Liu, J. (2022). The prevalence of elder abuse and neglect in rural areas: a systematic review and meta-analysis. *European Geriatric Medicine, 13*(3), 585–596. https://doi.org/10.1007/s41999-022-00628-2

15

The Social Context of Aging

Nancy A. Pachana and Sophie Griffiths

LEARNING OBJECTIVES

- Define functional ability in later life and how it contributes to healthy aging.
- Explain the relationship between social determinants and health outcomes, particularly among historically marginalized groups.
- Outline key strategies individuals can employ to maintain physical and mental well-being in later life.
- Describe the deleterious effects of ageism on well-being at any age.
- Identify how individuals, communities, and even universities can contribute to an age-inclusive society.

The social context of aging considers the influence of various societal factors in shaping individuals' experiences, perceptions, and behaviors as they grow older. Societal norms, values, institutional structures, environments, and individual relationships influence health, well-being, and quality of life as we age.

Cultural values, traditions, and practices shape the expectations and behaviors of people with respect to aging. In addition, matters of equity, diversity, and inclusion are increasingly the subjects of aging research. Furthermore, global demographic trends, including longer life spans and increasing rates of population aging, significantly impact the way aging is perceived and governed, leading to transformations in the societal context surrounding aging.

In this chapter, we will broadly consider the following key contributing factors to the social context of aging, along with relevant theories and models, to illustrate the pathways and impacts of the social context on aging within a global context:

- Models of healthy aging
- The social determinants of health in later life
- Strategies to maintain physical and mental well-being in later life
    - Physical activity
    - Mental engagement
    - Social engagement
- Stereotypes and ageism
- Strategies for an age-inclusive society

MODELS OF HEALTHY AGING

The World Health Organization (WHO) defines healthy aging as affording people the conditions under which they are able to be and do what they find personally meaningful (WHO, 2020, 2021). The goal of the United Nations Decade of Healthy Ageing (2021–2030), in which we find ourselves, is to maximize functional ability so that healthy aging becomes a reality. Functional aging refers to a person's ability to meet basic needs, learn and grow, build and maintain relationships, and be mobile and actively contribute to their communities. It is important to note that the aforementioned list of goals and activities can be achieved even in the face of health or mental health concerns; thus, we are moving ever further from equating healthy aging solely with health itself. Functional ability depends on the intrinsic capacities of a person—their ability to undertake quotidian tasks in service of their goals and needs as and how they can. Functional ability also depends on the environment in which people find themselves. It is important to remember that environments are not just about physical structures but also about interpersonal interactions occurring within environments, instrumental and emotional supports required to navigate environments, and technologies or design elements that might enable or detract from functionality. Services, systems, and policies are also a key feature of environments.

The Pathway to Optimize Functional Ability

A critical goal of the Decade of Healthy Ageing is to see measurable improvements in the lives of older adults, wherever they might be in the world. In its *Decade of Healthy Ageing: Baseline Report* (WHO, 2020), the WHO sets out a pathway of action to optimize functional ability. Such actions should be informed by the views of, and in partnership with, older adults themselves. A key element influencing the success of such an action pathway is the breadth and strength of data, research, and innovation to support and accelerate implementations to improve functionality.

There are a wide variety of models of healthy aging (for a review, see Menassa et al., 2023), and most adopt a life span approach to the topic. One of the earliest models of note is that by Rowe and Kahn (1997), subsequently updated and adapted numerous times. In its original conceptualization, and for its time, it represented an advance, as it posited a multifactorial approach to healthy aging, part of which involved continued engagement with life.

The WHO itself has moved progressively through both definitions and models of healthy aging. This has tended to follow successive moves away from a purely biological or health-based view of well-being. Indeed, in 1948 the WHO offered that health is a state of physical, mental, and social well-being, not simply the absence of disease; in his overview of progressive definitions of well-being, Larsen (2022) cites both the movement toward a holistic view of well-being and pushback against this trend. The Active Ageing model (WHO, 2002) was both a model and a policy framework; strictly speaking, it was not empirically tested. Research by Paúl et al. (2012) tested the model in a sample of community-dwelling older adults and found that many of the determinants listed within the model (e.g., behavioral, personal, and social determinants) were either not independent or not significant (see Figure 15.1). In addition, some factors, such as psychological factors, exerted an outsized influence. Their work points to the need for testing models with empirical data and the importance of objective and subjective variables contributing to healthy aging. They also point out that the nature and influence of specific variables and determinants of healthy aging may vary across cultures and contexts.

A final overarching model for consideration is that of Wahl et al. (2012) and, most recently, Pachana and Wahl (2022). The model (see Figure 15.2) attempts to give a holistic understanding of health in later life. It offers an integrative contextual

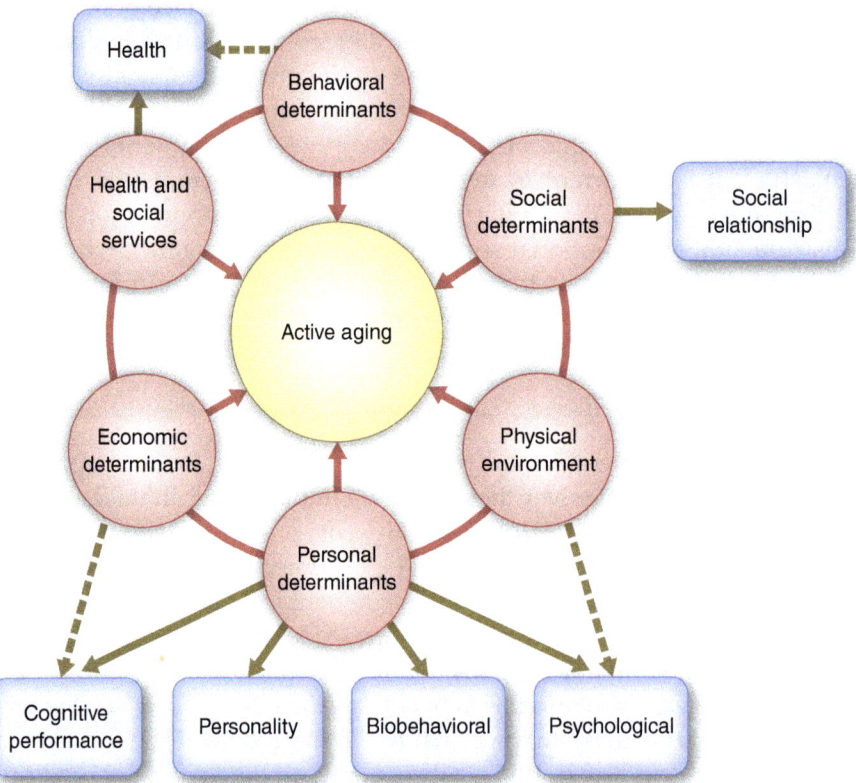

Figure 15.1 World Health Organization model of active aging.
Source: From Paúl, C., Ribeiro, O., & Teixeira, L. (2012). Active ageing: An empirical approach to the WHO model. *Current Gerontology and Geriatric Research*, 2012, 382972–382910. https://doi.org/10.1155/2012/382972.

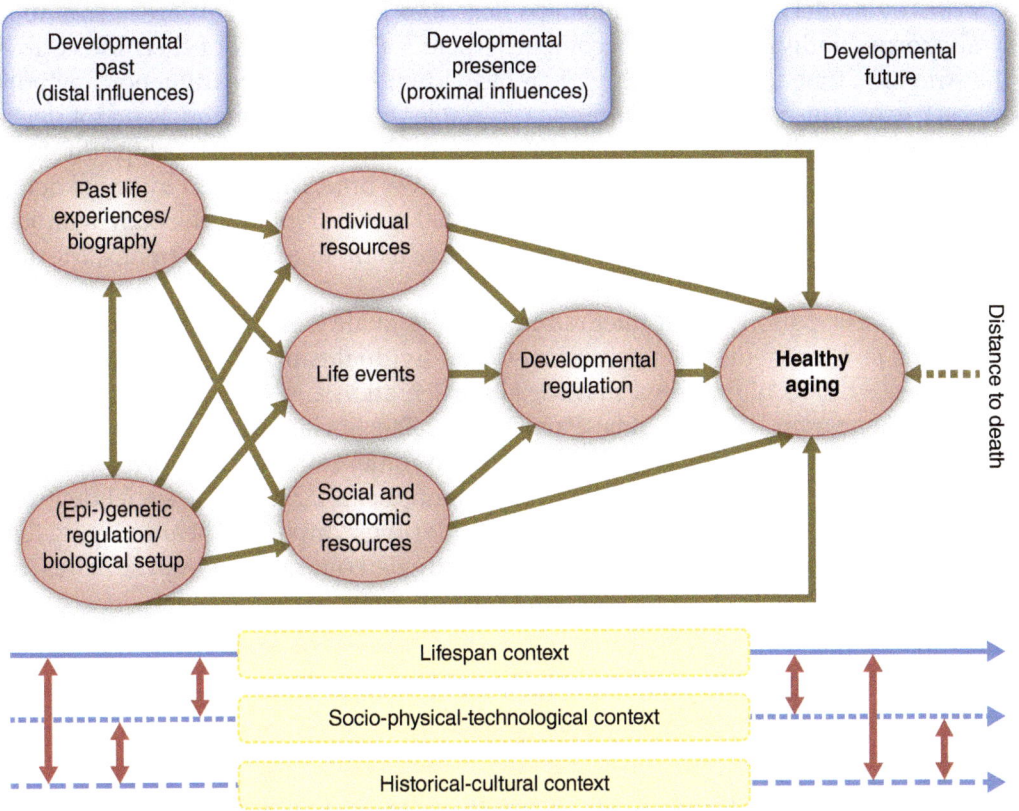

Figure 15.2 Model of health in later life.
Source: From Pachana, N., & Wahl, H.-W. (2022). *Healthy aging: Current and future frameworks and developments*. https://doi.org/10.1016/B978-0-12-818697-8.00054-6

framework applicable in research, prevention, and intervention work. It adopts a life-span perspective and moves fluidly across the familiar terrain of biopsychosocial models while being cognizant of the individual's context. Important contemporary features of this contextual backdrop include technological, historical, and cultural contexts. Distal, proximal, and future timelines of developmental perspectives are included. Elements of the basic formula of environmental factors and individual capacity are present, but factors such as life events are also given space; this is particularly important, as such events can often shape mental health trajectories, and responses to such events may differ between individuals with dissimilar biological genetic or epigenetic loads.

Many of the models noted here and in Menassa et al. (2023) highlight the importance of the social context of an individual, including social relationships, in promoting overall well-being as we age. Two key theories, social identity theory and the social identity model of identity change, help us understand the mechanisms through which life transitions impact our social context.

In addition to work, one's friends and family form an integral part of one's social network throughout life. Antonucci et al. (2014) developed a life span theory of how social relationships, and particularly emotional closeness, developed across the life span and how these relationships were tied to the life course of individuals. The notion of a convoy model of social relationships describes how individuals are surrounded by supportive individuals who accompany them for parts or all of their life course. The structure, function, and quality of an individual's convoy are influenced by both personal (e.g., age, gender) and situational variables (e.g., role demands) and influence health and well-being. The convoy model expanded how social relationships throughout life were viewed: as more complex, evolving over time, influenced by social determinants (such as socioeconomic status), and social norms. Notably, the convoy model has found very broad applicability across cultures as divergent as Germany, Mexico, and Lebanon (Antonucci et al., 2014).

Social participation, social integration, and the quality of social relationships are part of the environment and a component of individual capacity crucial for healthy aging. Research has highlighted that social participation and interactions are critical protective factors for healthy aging (Paiva et al., 2023). Social isolation and loneliness, as well as deficiencies in a person's environmental context, are risk factors for illnesses, including dementia (Gale et al., 2018; Penninkilampi et al., 2018). The social determinants of aging are increasingly recognized both for their impact on healthy aging and for these being modifiable risk factors that individuals, communities, and societies can address; this is the subject of the following section.

SOCIAL DETERMINANTS OF HEALTH IN LATER LIFE

The Social Determinants of Health

The concept of social determinants of health emerged in the late 20th century as researchers and policy makers recognized that individual health outcomes are not solely determined by medical care or genetics. The WHO report on social determinants of health noted that "systemic differences in health between social groups, that are avoidable by reasonable means, are unfair" (Marmot et al., 2012). Social, economic, and environmental factors are now recognized as critical determinants shaping such health disparities, which can lead to different health outcomes across populations. This concept firmly roots itself in public health and social epidemiology, emphasizing how people's health and well-being are significantly affected by the circumstances in which they are born, live, and grow.

These circumstances include income and social protection, education, job security/insecurity, housing and environment, social inclusion, discrimination, and access to affordable healthcare. These factors directly impact people's intrinsic capacity to meet basic needs, build and maintain relationships, learn, grow, be mobile, and contribute to society. These social determinants are the primary domains the WHO highlights as critical to healthy aging (WHO, 2021). Understanding the impact of social determinants on health is particularly important for historically excluded minority groups, such as First Nations people (Richmond & Ross, 2009), so that public health policy across the life span is relevant to the contexts and experiences of these groups.

Understanding the connections between social factors and health outcomes is vital in addressing health disparities and promoting health equity among older adults. For example, individuals with lower socioeconomic status generally experience poorer health than those with greater wealth, facing higher risks of chronic conditions such as heart disease and diabetes (McMaughan et al., 2020). Conversely, older adults with stronger social networks may enjoy improved mental well-being and experience lower rates of anxiety and depression (Newman & Zainal, 2020). By understanding the impact of social determinants, policy makers can develop targeted strategies to address the root causes of health inequalities and help foster a healthier aging population.

The Importance of Social Relationships and Group Membership

Social relationships are an essential buffer to health and well-being for older adults, as they are for all people throughout their life span; their importance as a determinant of health in the social context is crucial. Early theoretical stances in gerontology, such as disengagement theory (Coleman, 1991; Cumming & Henry, 1961), posited that the quantity of social relationships declined with advancing age and assumed that this was a natural function of loss and withdrawal from society. Such theoretical models were superseded by the active aging and successful aging models discussed in the previous section. Later studies supported the idea that while the number of relationships declines in later life, the quality of social relationships generally improves and becomes more positive with age (Luong et al., 2011). Many older adults express higher satisfaction levels and fewer negative experiences in their social interactions than younger adults. Older adults frequently recall experiencing stronger positive and milder negative emotions, reporting less conflict when interacting with their close social partners than younger adults (see Chapter 5, "Age-Related Illnesses," for more details). Overall, research shows that the style of social and intimate relationships transforms in later life such that older adults perceive their relationships more positively.

Finally, membership of groups is a powerful protective factor in later life in terms of well-being. In general, having a more extensive social network of family, friends, and social groups positively impacts physical and mental health (e.g., Jetten et al., 2009). Stronger social relationships positively impact longevity, as shown in a large meta-analysis across nearly 150 studies and more than 300,000 participants (Holt-Lunstad et al., 2010). Membership in social groups with a shared sense of identity is posited to provide protective psychological resources to maintain health and well-being (Jetten et al., 2014). The power of social connection and social groups to alleviate loneliness and improve health, and at a relatively low cost, is an important consideration in terms of public health initiatives (Jetten et al., 2014).

STRATEGIES TO MAINTAIN PHYSICAL AND MENTAL WELL-BEING IN LATER LIFE

Maintaining health in later life requires active strategies for best outcomes. Ensuring good levels of physical activity, mental stimulation, and meaningful social interactions have been found in a wide variety of studies, across cultures and levels of socioeconomic and health status, to lead to better health outcomes in later life. Maintaining good health also reduces risk of events that limit both life span and quality of life, such as falls. There are many steps older adults can take to be proactive with respect to maintaining physical and mental well-being, some of which are discussed next.

Physical Activity

PHYSICAL INACTIVITY AND SEDENTARY BEHAVIORS

A growing number of systematic reviews have demonstrated the benefits of physical activity on physical and mental well-being, as well as quality of life. The aspects of physical activity that hold the greatest promise of improving or maintaining physical health in later life are aerobic activities, muscle-strengthening activities, and reducing sedentary behaviors (Macera et al., 2017). Guidelines differ across populations, countries, and contexts, and so rather than agreement on a particular amount of activity that is optimal, increasing activity levels as much as possible, engaging in strength and balance-enhancing exercises, and reducing time sitting are key health messages. Every time someone takes the stairs instead of the elevator or limits the amount of time spent watching TV, they can contribute to increased activity and well-being.

A systematic review by Marquez et al. (2020) found strong evidence (primarily from randomized controlled trials [RCTs]) that physical activity increases the quality of life for older adults aged over 65 years. Interestingly, the evidence was somewhat weaker in younger cohorts. The exception from the populations examined were people living with dementia, for whom insufficient high-quality trials were found. However, physical activity has been shown to benefit older adults' cognitive performance more generally (Domingos et al., 2021). Physical activity can be incredibly beneficial to older adults living with chronic disease. This is critical as, in the United States, over 90% of people age 65+ have one or more chronic illnesses (Hung et al., 2011). Regular physical activity can slow the progression of disease and reduce complications in this group, but having a chronic illness may also pose barriers to engaging in physical activity.

RISKS POSED BY LACK OF PHYSICAL ACTIVITY

The major health risks posed by physical inactivity include coronary heart disease, hypertension, stroke, and type 2 diabetes; all-cause mortality is also greater in physically inactive groups (Macera et al., 2016). Physical inactivity can also lead to falls, the risks of which increase significantly in later life (Dellinger, 2017). Falls have substantial negative health implications later in life, leading to increased morbidity and mortality and decreased quality of life. Falls also result in cost-intensive interventions (such as hip replacements) and are the single most significant cause of traumatic brain injury in later life (Ambrose et al., 2013).

WHAT CAN BE DONE?

Effective communication of the benefits of physical activity, or strength and balance exercises, and avoiding sedentary behaviors, are key to increasing well-being in later life. For example, although the impact of sitting for excessive periods during the day is perhaps easily related to physical health status, the negative effects of sedentary behavior go beyond the physical. A recent systematic review showed a link between sedentary behavior and increased risk of cognitive declines in later life (Falck et al., 2017). Also, older persons may have different ideas of what "physical activity" and "sedentary behaviors" mean in relation to their own lives. A recent qualitative study (Palmer et al., 2021) was interesting in that it found that some older persons equated "sitting around" as a less moral behavior than "being busy," while others said they felt the need to rest or have more quiet time as they got older, but perhaps felt stigmatized because of this. Striking the right tone and clarity of messaging in communications

> **BOX 15.1 Pickleball**
>
> Leisure activities are a great way of increasing physical activity and minimizing sedentary behaviors in later life. Certain activities may be terrific for people with specific limitations, such as swimming for those with joint complications or tai chi or Pilates for those looking to improve flexibility. Leisure activities have the added benefit of the chance for social engagement.
>
> Pickleball is an activity that has recently become popular with older adults in the United States as well as places such as Australia. Pickleball is a combination of tennis, table tennis, and badminton. The general conditions of the sport are familiar to many older people, and the underhanded strokes and lower ball speed make it accessible to those with a wide range of abilities (Ryu et al., 2018). There is some suggestion from empirical work that pickleball is viewed favorably among older persons and may help with retirement transitions (Ryu et al., 2018), as well as physical, emotional, and sociocognitive fitness (Buzzelli & Draper, 2020). Regular engagement in organized sports such as pickleball may contribute to better mental health, particularly lower rates of depression (Heo et al., 2018).

about public health is critical. Recognizing the degree to which social determinants such as poverty or dwelling in unsafe neighborhoods are contributing factors to lower physical activity and poorer nutrition is also important.

Barriers and motivators to engagement in physical activity later in life are also critical to understand from a public health perspective. A recent systematic review showed that such barriers and facilitators in later life were relatively similar in those ages 50 to 64 and those 65+ (Spiteri et al., 2019), but more age differences emerged with respect to motivators. Environmental and social factors as barriers and facilitators were consistently reported by all age groups. Regarding barriers, increasing safety concerns were reported more by older age groups and work constraints by younger groups. Interestingly, ageist stereotypes were more frequently reported by relatively younger versus older participants. In addition, the same attribute could be identified by subgroups as sometimes a barrier, sometimes a motivator (for example, prior experience of being physically active).

Mental Stimulation

MENTAL STIMULATION AND COGNITIVELY CHALLENGING ACTIVITIES

Lack of mental stimulation in older populations can contribute to cognitive declines, particularly in memory functioning, in later life (Ye, 2023). Engaging in mentally challenging activities stimulates building and maintaining neuronal connections in the brain. Such activities promote cognitive reserve or cognitive resilience. Higher cognitive reserves allow people to perform a wide variety of mental tasks more efficiently. Increased cognitive reserve can protect against cognitive declines and dementia (Stern, 2012). Participating in cognitively stimulating activities helps improve brain structure and function (Arenaza-Urquijo et al., 2017). Various types of cognitively stimulating activities may have differing effects on specific cognitive skills; in one study, for example, cognitively challenging activities appeared to have a greater effect on speed of processing than did socially stimulating activities (Vujic et al., 2022).

RISKS POSED BY LACK OF COGNITIVE STIMULATION

Unaddressed hearing loss represents one of the most prominent potentially modifiable risk factors for dementia (Livingston et al., 2020). Hearing loss leads to decreases in mental stimulation, as well as declines in social interactions and often a withdrawal from activities, ultimately negatively impacting brain structure and function (Slade et al., 2020). The impact of hearing loss on health is true even if only one ear is affected (Pierzycki et al., 2020). Hearing loss interventions, such as hearing aids, have been shown to be effective in treating hearing loss, and the subsequent gains in social activity and mental stimulation through participation in a wider range of everyday activities may be the means by which cognitive functioning is bolstered in older people (Dawes & Völter, 2023).

The COVID-19 pandemic offered lessons in how social isolation led to decreased well-being, not solely through loneliness but also through lack of mental stimulation. Confinement to a restricted, often impoverished environment was the fate of many older adults in residential aged care settings who experienced lockdowns. This led to a chronic lack of social, cognitive, and sensorimotor stimulation that is critical for physical, mental, and social well-being later in life (Plagg et al., 2020). Changes to the ability to interact with others during social and leisure activities led to secondary effects in terms of physical activity, nutrition, negative lifestyle activities such as smoking and drinking, and decreased mental stimulation (Di Santo et al., 2020).

WHAT CAN BE DONE?

A wide range of activities can promote cognitive stimulation. Everything from swing dancing, to mahjong, to birdwatching can prove mentally challenging (as well as potentially providing social engagement and physical activity). The key is to have meaningful and enjoyable activities so that participation is sustained over time. Learning activities also engage the brain; there is much accumulated evidence that activities such as learning a language or learning to play a musical instrument have cognitive benefits in later life (e.g., Klimova, 2018; Mansky et al., 2020). Learning how to use computers or other such devices, as well as engaging in formal computer-based cognitive training programs or engaging in more informal computer game-playing, has also been shown to improve cognitive functioning and possibly reduce risk of cognitive decline (e.g., Djabelkhir et al., 2017; Giladi et al., 2011). Such games also have the potential to improve emotional functioning and reduce stress in people across the life span (Pallavicini et al., 2021).

Having dedicated spaces to pursue hobbies or activities is also vital; these should be accessible to public transportation and inclusive of those with physical and sensory limitations. Many community centers and retirement villages offer such activities.

Arts and other cultural activities are important for maintaining mental well-being and may help prevent depression (Noguchi et al., 2022). Access must be ensured for those with limited mobility. For those who identify with a particular ethnic or cultural background, engaging in such activities not only promotes well-being but also intergenerational connections (Warburton & McLaughlin, 2007).

 **BOX 15.2 Museum Programs for Persons Living With Dementia**

Many people greatly enjoy going to art museums; some may feel that such activities would not be beneficial or desired by those living with dementia, but this is a false assumption. Museums have been recognized as cultural institutions that contribute to well-being and flourishing, and museum visitation is often an activity deemed health enhancing in social prescribing programs, which direct healthcare consumers toward community activities to enhance well-being (Bild & Pachana, 2022). This has been particularly studied for people at risk of or who have been diagnosed with dementia. Using data from the English Longitudinal Study of Ageing, and after controlling for a range of sociodemographic and health-related variables, Fancourt et al. (2018) showed that for adults over 50, regular museum attendance was correlated with a decrease in risk of dementia over a 10-year period compared with less frequent attendance. Improved mood and cognitive functioning were observed in people living with dementia after a 6-week art museum–based program of activities; while the emotional gains dissipated after completion of the program, the cognitive gains persisted at 6-week follow-up (D'Cunha et al., 2019). Participants in this study also reported greater quality of life resulting from taking part in the program. Art museums worldwide are creating stimulating programs for people living with dementia to improve well-being across physical, emotional, and social domains (e.g., the Meet Me at MOMA program in New York City; Rosenberg, 2009). Many of the programs designed for people living with dementia involve making art as well as viewing art; many times, spouses and care partners are actively involved, and the often group-based activities provide for social engagement in a nonmedical setting (Cotter & Pawelski, 2022). Such programs have also demonstrated positive effects in terms of greater self-esteem and reduction in social isolation (Rosenberg, 2009).

Social Engagement

SOCIAL ISOLATION

Human beings are social creatures, and high-quality relationships are vital for health and well-being at all stages of life. Social isolation is an objective state of being apart from others and is defined as having few social relationships and minimal interaction with others, whereas loneliness is a subjective, unwelcome feeling of sadness that occurs when there is a mismatch between the quality and quantity of social relationships that we have and those that we want (Mansfield et al., 2021). Loneliness is further conceptualized into multiple subtypes, as described later. Social isolation and loneliness are two related but conceptually different states that are highly detrimental to health and well-being, and older adults are extremely vulnerable to both.

Social isolation is the objective lack of (or limited) social contact with others; it is a serious health risk that is associated with negative physical and mental health outcomes (Blazer, 2020). Older adults may be more susceptible to social isolation because of health conditions such as hearing impairments, mobility challenges (which can constrain social contacts), and other functional limitations. Historically marginalized groups such as migrants, First Nations people, LGBTQI+, people living in homeless or domestic violence contexts, and geographically isolated populations are at increased risk of social isolation; the risk is increased in such groups with increasing age and greater physical comorbidities.

RISKS POSED BY SOCIAL ISOLATION

Social isolation poses significant health risks, with studies linking it to a 29% increased risk of premature mortality from all causes (National Academies of Sciences & Medicine, 2020) and a 50% higher risk of developing dementia (Penninkilampi et al., 2018). In a longitudinal study examining the impact of social isolation on the brain, individuals experiencing social isolation exhibited negative structural and functional brain changes, including decreases in memory functioning (Lammer et al., 2023). Social isolation has emerged as a concerning risk factor for compromised health and serious cognitive decline in older adults.

WHAT CAN BE DONE?

The antidote to social isolation is social connection, an umbrella term that encompasses the factors of *structural* (the opportunities one has to interact with others physically), *functional* (a perceived sense of having support available that serves one's needs), and *quality* (the level of positive valence of relationships) of social relationships (Suragarn et al., 2021). Numerous strategies and interventions aim to increase social connectedness and can be applied at different scales. For example, the WHO advocates for structural change through age-friendly environments at a global and population scale, which this chapter covers in a later section. At a smaller scale, the key driver is to increase social contact opportunities in groups or between individuals. This can be done in myriad ways, including social participation in purposeful activities, hobbies, therapies, and recreational activities (O'Rourke et al., 2018). The social partner does not always have to be human, as evidenced by studies of animal contact that demonstrate the strength of meaningful connection with pets. Lifelong learning and skill acquisition programs are another avenue of social connection. Educational programs have further significant benefits and foster cognitive vitality, sense of purpose, and a connection to the wider world that aid an individual's sense of psychological well-being (Narushima et al., 2018).

Loneliness

Loneliness is often linked to social isolation, but it is not the same. A meta-analysis (Mansfield et al., 2021) of the loneliness literature further conceptualizes that there are quantitively different types of loneliness that include:

- *Emotional loneliness:* the absence of meaningful relationships
- *Social loneliness:* a perceived deficit in the quality of social connections
- *Existential loneliness:* a feeling of fundamental separateness from others and the wider world

Other types of loneliness can include:

- *Transient loneliness:* a feeling that comes and goes
- *Situational loneliness:* occurring only at certain times and events like holidays
- *Chronic loneliness:* an enduring feeling of sadness

Social neuroscientist John Cacioppo is a leading researcher in loneliness and describes it as contagious, heritable, and affecting one in four people, with a 20% increased risk of early death, akin to smoking 15 cigarettes per day (Cacioppo & Cacioppo, 2018). He describes loneliness as social pain, likening it to physical pain. Physical pain alerts you to withdraw from the painful stimuli, and social pain, or loneliness, signals a human to cease being solitary and connect with other humans to increase health, safety, and well-being (Cacioppo & Patrick, 2008).

The WHO advocacy brief on social isolation and loneliness in older people outlines individual, community, and societal interventions (WHO, 2021c). Among them are psychoeducation to equip individuals with coping skills, peer support and social activity groups, volunteer befriending services, and social prescribing activities (such as the museum as a prescribed activity, described earlier). Three levels of interventions are proposed, from individual- and relationship-level interventions, such as one-on-one and group activities along with digital and face-to-face interactions; to the community level, including improved infrastructure to support interaction (see also the section on age-friendly environments later in the chapter); to societal-level strategies such as addressing laws and policies to facilitate social cohesion and integration.

STEREOTYPES AND AGEISM

Stereotypes are assumptions and attributions about specific characteristics or behaviors of people based on their group membership. Stereotypes often fail to consider individual variations or complexities within the group, leading to a tendency to perceive diversity within "in-groups" while perceiving a homogeneity among members of out-groups (Haslam et al., 1993). Stereotypes are based on many factors, including race, gender, ethnicity, sexual orientation, occupation, and age. Stereotypes based on age intersect with all other stereotypes, and age-based stereotypes apply to all ages, as

BOX 15.3 Examples of Global Campaigns to End Loneliness

Loneliness is a significant public health issue for all ages and countries and is often referred to as an epidemic. Many government-supported and not-for-profit social campaigns are active globally to try to build awareness of the harms and to act to reduce loneliness. Two programs with global reach are the Campaign to End Loneliness (2023) and the Global Initiative on Loneliness and Connection (www.gilc.global); these programs seek to address broad groups of people who are vulnerable to loneliness. In the United States, AARP is a national interest group representing older Americans. Their research showed that about one third of adults over 45 years feel lonely, with those with low incomes especially vulnerable (AARP, 2018).

seen in different generational stereotyping. Stereotypes of older people are, concerningly, frequently negative, highlighting perceptions of diminished physical and cognitive abilities, increased frailty, and dependence on others.

The Stereotype Content Model

The stereotype content model (SCM; Cuddy et al., 2009) offers a framework for understanding how stereotypes and interpersonal impressions are formed and perceived. The model suggests two primary dimensions of social perception: warmth and competency. Varying combinations of high and low competence on these dimensions results in four categories of stereotypes (e.g., high warmth and high competence are reflective of "admiration"; low warmth and low competence are reflective of "contempt"). A congruent impression such as a high-competence and high-warmth stereotype is typically the domain of close in-group allies, while a low-competence, low-warmth stereotype is often reserved for out-group members. Ambivalent stereotypes are envious (a combination of high competence and low warmth) or paternalistic (a combination of low competence and highwarmth). Warmth refers to perceptions of friendliness, kindness, and sincerity, and older people are generally perceived as warm due to their association with positive traits such as wisdom, experience, and nurturing. This dimension reflects the idea that older individuals are perceived as approachable, caring, and deserving of respect.

Competency relates to perceptions of capability, efficiency, and effectiveness. Older people are often stereotyped as less competent, particularly in areas that require cognitive abilities or technological skills. This dimension reflects the assumption that all older individuals experience cognitive decline, problems with memory, and difficulty adapting to new technologies.

Stereotype Embodiment

Stereotype embodiment occurs when individuals internalize and display stereotypes about their social group. Becca Levy is a prominent researcher on stereotype embodiment in the context of aging and its effects on older adults. Her research has demonstrated how negative age stereotypes can significantly influence physical and mental well-being (Levy, 2009, 2022). For example, if a person believes the stereotype that aging leads to cognitive decline and reduced functioning, they may become more susceptible to these effects. Levy has demonstrated that internalized ageist stereotypes increase risk of dementia, reduce well-being and physical functioning, and may result in the loss of an average of 7.5 years of life span (Levy, 2022).

Both negative and positive age stereotypes exist, and each has the potential to enhance or detract from longevity. Some examples of positive age stereotypes include:

- *Wisdom and experience*: Older individuals are depicted as possessing knowledge and valuable life experience, allowing them to offer guidance and insights to younger generations.
- *Resilience and emotional well-being*: Positive age stereotypes recognize that life experience has cultivated resilience and effective coping skills in older adults.

- *Active and engaged in the community*: Positive age stereotypes highlight the active and meaningful contributions made by older adults to their communities, including unpaid volunteering and caregiving roles.

Examples of negative age stereotypes include:

- *Cognitive decline*: an assumption that aging inevitably leads to reduced cognitive functioning and difficulties in learning new things
- *Frailty and physical weakness*: an assumption that all older adults are fragile, dependent, and vulnerable to illness
- *Technological ineptitude*: an assumption that older adults struggle to adapt to technology and possess only limited digital literacy

AGEISM

The WHO defines ageism as "the stereotyping, prejudice, and discrimination against individuals or groups based on their age" (WHO, 2021a). Ageist attitudes can be directed toward any age group; however, evidence shows that ageism disproportionately disadvantages older adults, and just over half of all people worldwide hold moderate to severe ageist attitudes, with rates being much higher in lower-income countries and among younger people (Mikton et al., 2021). This has detrimental consequences for individuals and societies in many domains. Two crucial domains are:

- *Health and well-being*: Ageism significantly negatively impacts the physical and mental health of older adults and leads to disparities in access to healthcare, social exclusion, and quality of life.
- *Economic and social implications*: Ageism perpetuates age-based stereotypes and discrimination, which limits opportunities for older adults in employment and social participation, hindering social and economic prosperity.

Ageism intersects with all other forms of prejudice and stereotyping, and it is unique in that holding ageist beliefs is prejudice against our future selves (Nelson, 2005). Unlike most other prejudices such as racism and sexism, ageism remains for the most part a socially condoned prejudice.

Hostile and Benevolent Ageism

Similar to the two dimensions of age stereotypes, there are two dimensions of ageism known as hostile and benevolent:

- Hostile ageism refers to negative and prejudiced attitudes, beliefs, and behavior toward older adults. It involves the devaluation, stereotyping, and discrimination against individuals based on age. Hostile ageism portrays older adults as incompetent, burdensome, and lacking in worth.

- Benevolent ageism involves seemingly positive yet patronizing attitudes and stereotypes of older adults. It includes beliefs that older adults are warm, wise, and kind but in need of protection and aid. While benevolent ageism may appear well intentioned, it has a sinister side of reinforcing frail age stereotypes that restrict an individual's autonomy.

Research has shown that older White males are the most frequent recipients of hostile ageism, whereas older women and people with intersecting identities of race are more frequently subject to benevolent ageism (Gans et al., 2023). However, both forms of ageism have detrimental effects on older adults' well-being and contribute to social exclusion, limited opportunities, and unequal treatment.

The Financial and Social Costs of Ageism and Negative Age Stereotypes

A 2018 study identified the economic burden of negative age stereotypes and ageism within the American healthcare system. The study considered three variables: (a) ageism measured as discrimination toward older adults by others, (b) negative age stereotypes, and (c) negative self-perceptions of aging. The study reported that the 1-year cost of these variables to the healthcare system was $63 billion (Levy et al., 2018). Similar impacts are assumed on a global scale.

An Australian study estimated that if an additional 5% of adults over 55 years were employed, there would be a positive impact of $48 billion on the national economy. Ageism in the workplace is a key factor limiting the opportunities for people in this age bracket, with most hiring managers reporting 55 years as their cutoff for candidate selection (Billett et al., 2011). This is particularly strong in Australia, with one of the lowest labor force participation rates of people over 55 years in all Organisation for Economic Co-operation and Development (OECD) countries.

WHO Framework for Action Against Ageism

The WHO released a Global Report on Ageism in 2021 (WHO, 2021b) to raise awareness about the pervasive issue of ageism and its detrimental impact on older adults as individuals of all nations and cultures and on society as a whole. The report provides evidence-based insights into the nature, prevalence, and consequences of ageism worldwide, highlighting the urgent need for action to combat ageism and promote age-friendly societies. As well as raising awareness, the report proposes key action areas to help reduce ageism.

Policies and laws can be used to reduce ageism against any age group. Policies that address age discrimination can be strengthened at all levels by enhancing enforcement mechanisms and increasing monitoring. Examples of policies and laws include employment laws to protect from discrimination of workers based on their age. The Inter-American Convention on Protecting the Human Rights of Older Persons is a treaty that prohibits age discrimination and further encourages positive attitudes toward and dignified, respectful, and considerate treatment of older adults. Countries that adopt this convention express their commitment to addressing ageism and recognize that legally binding, explicit standards and accountability mechanisms are essential to the success of this convention.

Educational activities help enhance empathy, dispel misconceptions, and reduce prejudice and discrimination by providing accurate information and counter-stereotypical examples. Interventions may include specific modules on aspects of aging and often include components of intergenerational contact. Programs exist for all age groups, from schools, through universities, and into professional development contexts. Some programs seek to dispel ignorant and stereotypical attitudes by presenting accurate information; others focus on building empathy, often through perspective-taking activities, to counter prejudice by generating greater identification. To date the research and evaluation of these programs have occurred only in high-income countries, with encouraging results. Expanding programs to low-income countries is an important next step (WHO, 2021b).

Fostering contact between generations is one of the most robust methods to reduce intergroup prejudice and stereotypes; age-integrated societies, events, and programs are to be encouraged to reduce ageism against all ages. Interventions can be direct (in-person) or indirect (vicariously), including orchestrated contact leading to friendships. Intergroup contact theory (Brown & Hewstone, 2005) posits that positive interactions between individuals from different social groups can reduce prejudice and improve intergroup relations when certain conditions, such as equal status, common goals, intergroup cooperation, and positive contact experiences, are met.

Finally, the WHO (2015) recognizes that although aging is universal, different cultural factors shape individuals' perceptions, actions, and experiences. Cultural norms and expectations of aging can impact how people are perceived, the roles they can assume, and the support systems that are available to them. More cross-cultural research is required to address ageism in such settings.

An Age-Friendly World

"A WORLD IN WHICH YOU WOULD WANT TO GROW OLDER" (WHO, 2023)

In 2002, to respond to the needs of an aging society, the WHO introduced the "Age-Friendly" construct in the Active Ageing Policy Framework (Fulmer et al., 2020; WHO, 2002). This global initiative promotes active and healthy aging by creating inclusive and accessible environments for older adults. It comprises eight interconnected domains that address older people's societal needs to optimize opportunities to enhance the quality of life in later years (see Figure 15.3).

The eight interconnected domains of the Age-Friendly ecosystem reflect the ideals of a strengths-based approach to aging that aims to foster inclusion and participation in all aspects of society.

The eight domains include transportation, housing, social participation, respect and social inclusion, civic participation and employment, communication and information, community support and health services, and outdoor spaces and buildings.

This framework serves as a collaborative roadmap to involve various stakeholders who have a role in shaping the societies in which older adults live. Stakeholders include governments, policy makers, urban planners and architects, healthcare and social service providers, community organizations, businesses and employers, and older adults and their families. This collective effort aims to create environments

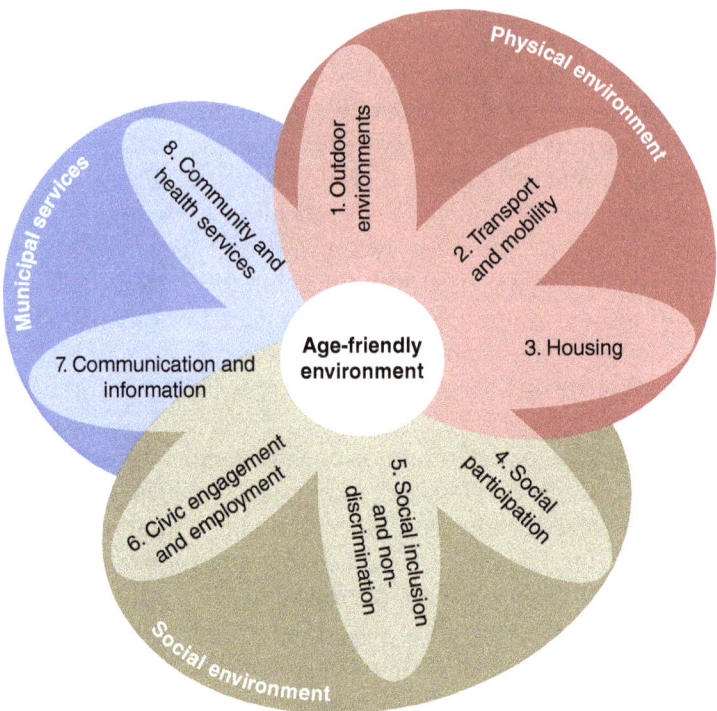

Figure 15.3 The eight domains of age-friendly environments.
Source: From Ronzi, S., Orton, L., Buckner, S., Bruce, N., & Pope, D. (2020). How is respect and social inclusion conceptualised by older adults in an aspiring age-friendly city? A photovoice study in the North-West of England. *International Journal of Environmental Research and Public Health, 17*(24), 9246. https://doi.org/10.3390/ijerph17249246

that promote healthy and positive aging. Age-friendly environments enable older people to age safely in a place that is right for them; live free from poverty; engage in continuous personal development; retain autonomy, health, and dignity; and actively contribute to their communities. The central premise is that older people know best what they need and are at the center of all efforts to create a more age-friendly world (WHO, 2023).

Each of the eight domains is tailored to address the barriers older individuals face. Social participation, respect and social inclusion, and civic participation and employment specifically focus on overcoming challenges that result in the social exclusion of older adults. Social exclusion refers to the barriers within a society that restrict opportunities relevant to livelihood (Chung et al., 2021). Socially excluded individuals and groups experience harm through lack of opportunity to participate in society, leading to a lack of access to resources, goods and services, rights, and participation opportunities, eventually leading to separation from mainstream society. For older adults, this can significantly contribute to detrimental health outcomes (Donovan & Blazer, 2020).

The Age-Friendly framework is adapted to suit different environments and is applied in numerous contexts as part of an ecosystem. For example, the WHO Global Network for Age-Friendly Cities and Communities (WHO, 2022) was established in 2010 to connect cities, communities, and organizations worldwide with the shared vision of making their communities great places to grow old. This network provides resources and support for collaboration and currently has a membership of approximately 1,445 cities and communities in 51 countries, covering over 300 million people worldwide.

Having age-friendly structures within society—age-friendly hospitals, cities, universities, and communities—gives people the best chance to maximize their intrinsic capacity in a supportive environment. Barriers to participation are lowered when societal institutions are age inclusive in their approach. Older adults themselves are more likely to utilize services when they feel included, listened to, and accepted (WHO, 2022).

CONCLUSION

In summary, our understanding of healthy aging has evolved significantly, moving past the simple "absence of illnesses" to encompass holistic well-being that requires consideration of social, personal, and environmental factors. We have introduced some fundamental theories of how older adults build social connections, such as social identity theory and socioemotional selectivity theory, as well as outlining the nature and importance of the social determinants of health, which are the social, economic, and environmental conditions that shape our lives and influence our health outcomes. We have examined some strategies that may help overcome barriers that older people face, as well as activities and behaviors that may increase health and well-being. The WHO's *Decade of Healthy Ageing* (2021–2030) underscores the importance of combatting ageism, nurturing social connections, and building environments where people of all ages can thrive. The crisis of social isolation and loneliness resulting in part from the COVID-19 pandemic has emerged as a significant public health issue, and the antidote lies in solutions that address the social contexts in which people live. The shifts in global demographics drive the importance of addressing the social context of older adults, and we hope to have highlighted the areas of potential opportunities for change that benefits all of society.

DISCUSSION QUESTIONS

1. How have definitions and models of healthy aging evolved over time?
2. What are some of the social determinants of healthy aging?
3. What is cognitive reserve, and how can it be enhanced?
4. What are some of the differences between loneliness and social isolation?
5. What are some examples of positive and negative age stereotypes?
6. What are some strategies, on an individual and societal level for combatting ageism?

A robust set of instructor resources designed to supplement this text is located at http://connect.springerpub.com/content/book/978-0-8261-6617-3. Qualifying instructors may request access by emailing textbook@springerpub.com.

REFERENCES

AARP. (2018). *AARP 2018 loneliness and social connections: A national survey of adults 45 and older*. Roper Center for Public Opinion Research. https://doi.org/10.25940/ROPER-31118687

Ambrose, A. F., Paul, G., & Hausdorff, J. M. (2013). Risk factors for falls among older adults: A review of the literature. *Maturitas, 75*(1), 51–61. https://doi.org/10.1016/j.maturitas.2013.02.009

Antonucci, T. C., Ajrouch, K. J., & Birditt, K. S. (2014). The convoy model: Explaining social relations from a multidisciplinary perspective. *Gerontologist, 54*(1), 82–92. https://doi.org/10.1093/geront/gnt118

Arenaza-Urquijo, E. M., De Flores, R., Gonneaud, J., Wirth, M., Ourry, V., Callewaert, W., Landeau, B., Egret, S., Mézenge, F., Desgranges, B., & Chételat, G. (2017). Distinct effects of late adulthood cognitive and physical activities on gray matter volume. *Brain Imaging and Behavior, 11*(2), 346–356. https://doi.org/10.1007/s11682-016-9617-3

Bild, E., & Pachana, N. A. (2022). Social prescribing: A narrative review of how community engagement can improve wellbeing in later life. *Journal of Community & Applied Social Psychology, 32*(6), 1148–1215. https://doi.org/10.1002/casp.2631

Billett, S., Dymock, D., Johnson, G., & Martin, G. (2011). Overcoming the paradox of employers' views about older workers. *The International Journal of Human Resource Management, 22*(6), 1248–1261. https://doi.org/10.1080/09585192.2011.559097

Blazer, D. (2020). Social isolation and loneliness in older adults—A mental health/public health challenge. *JAMA Psychiatry, 77*(10), 990. https://doi.org/10.1001/jamapsychiatry.2020.1054

Brown, R., & Hewstone, M. (2005). An integrative theory of intergroup contact. In B. Gawronski (Ed.), *Advances in experimental social psychology* (Vol. 37, pp. 255–343). Elsevier Academic Press. https://doi.org/10.1016/S0065-2601(05)37005-5

Buzzelli, A. A., & Draper, J. A. (2020). Examining the motivation and perceived benefits of pickleball participation in older adults. *Journal of Aging and Physical Activity, 28*(2), 180–186. https://doi.org/10.1123/JAPA.2018-0413

Cacioppo, J. T., & Cacioppo, S. (2018). The growing problem of loneliness. *The Lancet, 391*(10119), 426. https://doi.org/10.1016/s0140-6736(18)30142-9

Cacioppo, J. T., & Patrick, W. (2008). *Loneliness: Human nature and the need for social connection*. WW Norton & Company.

Campaign to End Loneliness. (2023). *The campaign to end loneliness*. https://www.campaigntoendloneliness.org/

Chung, S., Kim, M., Auh, E. Y., & Park, N. S. (2021). WHO's global age-friendly cities guide: Its implications of a discussion on social exclusion among older adults. *International Journal of Environmental Research and Public Health, 18*(15), 8027. https://doi.org/10.3390/ijerph18158027

Coleman, P. (1991). In E. Cumming & W. Henry (Eds.), Growing old: The process of disengagement. Basic Books, New York, 1961. (Reprint: Arno, New York, 1979, ISBN 0405 118147.). *Ageing and Society, 11*(2), 217–220. https://doi.org/10.1017/S0144686X00004025

Cotter, K. N., & Pawelski, J. O. (2022). Art museums as institutions for human flourishing. *The Journal of Positive Psychology, 17*(2), 288–302. https://doi.org/10.1080/17439760.2021.2016911

Cuddy, A. J. C., Fiske, S. T., Kwan, V. S. Y., Glick, P., Demoulin, S., Leyens, J.-P., Bond, M. H., Croizet, J.-C., Ellemers, N., Sleebos, E., Htun, T. T., Kim, H.-J., Maio, G., Perry, J., Petkova, K., Todorov, V., Rodríguez-Bailón, R., Morales, E., Moya, M.,. . ., Ziegler, R. (2009). Stereotype content model across cultures: Towards universal similarities and some differences. *British Journal of Social Psychology, 48*(1), 1–33. https://doi.org/10.1348/014466608x314935

Cumming E., & Henry, W. (1961). Growing Old: The Process of Disengagement. Basic Books.

D'Cunha, N. M., McKune, A. J., Isbel, S., Kellett, J., Georgousopoulou, E. N., & Naumovski, N. (2019). Psychophysiological responses in people living with dementia after an art gallery intervention: An exploratory study. *Journal of Alzheimer's Disease, 72*(2), 549–562. https://doi.org/10.3233/jad-190784

Dawes, P., & Völter, C. (2023). Do hearing loss interventions prevent dementia? *Zeitschrift für Gerontologie und Geriatrie, 56*(4), 261–268. https://doi.org/10.1007/s00391-023-02178-z

Dellinger, A. (2017). Older adult falls: Effective approaches to prevention. *Current Trauma Reports, 3*(2), 118–123. https://doi.org/10.1007/s40719-017-0087-x

Di Santo, S. G., Franchini, F., Filiputti, B., Martone, A., & Sannino, S. (2020). The effects of COVID-19 and quarantine measures on the lifestyles and mental health of people over 60 at increased risk of dementia. *Frontiers in Psychiatry, 11*, 578628. https://doi.org/10.3389/fpsyt.2020.578628

Djabelkhir, L., Wu, Y.-H., Vidal, J.-S., Cristancho-Lacroix, V., Marlats, F., Lenoir, H., Carno, A., & Rigaud, A.-S. (2017). Computerized cognitive stimulation and engagement programs in older adults with mild cognitive impairment: Comparing feasibility, acceptability, and cognitive and psychosocial effects. *Clinical Interventions in Aging, 12*, 1967–1975. https://doi.org/10.2147/CIA.S145769

Domingos, C., Pêgo, J. M., & Santos, N. C. (2021). Effects of physical activity on brain function and structure in older adults: A systematic review. *Behavioural Brain Research, 402*, 113061. https://doi.org/10.1016/j.bbr.2020.113061

Donovan, N. J., & Blazer, D. (2020). Social isolation and loneliness in older adults: Review and commentary of a national academies report. *The American Journal of Geriatric Psychiatry, 28*(12), 1233–1244. https://doi.org/10.1016/j.jagp.2020.08.005

Falck, R. S., Davis, J. C., & Liu-Ambrose, T. (2017). What is the association between sedentary behaviour and cognitive function? A systematic review. *British Journal of Sports Medicine, 51*(10), 800–811. https://doi.org/10.1136/bjsports-2015-095551

Fancourt, D., Steptoe, A., & Cadar, D. (2018). Cultural engagement and cognitive reserve: Museum attendance and dementia incidence over a 10-year period. *British Journal of Psychiatry, 213*(5), 661–663. https://doi.org/10.1192/bjp.2018.129

Fulmer, T., Patel, P., Levy, N., Mate, K., Berman, A., Pelton, L., Beard, J., Kalache, A., & Auerbach, J. (2020). Moving toward a global age-friendly ecosystem. *Journal of the American Geriatrics Society, 68*(9), 1936–1940. https://doi.org/10.1111/jgs.16675

Gale, C. R., Westbury, L., & Cooper, C. (2018). Social isolation and loneliness as risk factors for the progression of frailty: The English Longitudinal Study of Ageing. *Age and Ageing, 47*(3), 392–397. https://doi.org/10.1093/ageing/afx188

Gans, H. M., Horhota, M., & Chasteen, A. L. (2023). Ageism against older adults: How do intersecting identities influence perceptions of ageist behaviors? *Journal of Applied Gerontology, 42*(6), 1191–1199. https://doi.org/10.1177/07334648231161937

Giladi, N., Shatil, E., Korczyn, A. D., Peretz, C., Aharonson, V., & Birnboim, S. (2011). Computer-based, personalized cognitive training versus classical computer games: A randomized double-blind prospective trial of cognitive stimulation. *Neuroepidemiology, 36*(2), 91–99. https://doi.org/10.1159/000323950

Haslam, S. A., McGarty, C., Oakes, P. J., & Turner, J. C. (1993). Social comparative context and illusory correlation: Testing between ingroup bias and social identity models of stereotype formation. *Australian Journal of Psychology, 45*(2), 97–101. https://doi.org/10.1080/00049539308259125

Heo, J., Ryu, J., Yang, H., & Kim, K. M. (2018). Serious leisure and depression in older adults: A study of pickleball players. *Leisure Studies, 37*(5), 561–573. https://doi.org/10.1080/02614367.2018.1477977

Holt-Lunstad, J., Smith, T. B., & Layton, J. B. (2010). Social relationships and mortality risk: A meta-analytic review. *PLOS Medicine, 7*(7), e1000316. https://doi.org/10.1371/journal.pmed.1000316

Hung, W. W., Ross, J. S., Boockvar, K. S., & Siu, A. L. (2011). Recent trends in chronic disease, impairment and disability among older adults in the United States. *BMC Geriatrics, 11*(1), p. 47. https://bmcgeriatr.biomedcentral.com/articles/10.1186/1471-2318-11-47

Jetten, J., Haslam, C., Haslam, S. A., & Branscombe, N. R. (2009). The social cure. *Scientific American Mind, 20*(5), 26–33. https://doi.org/10.1038/scientificamericanmind0909-26

Jetten, J., Haslam, C., Haslam, S. A., Dingle, G., & Jones, J. M. (2014). How groups affect our health and well-being: The path from theory to policy. *Social Issues and Policy Review, 8*(1), 103–130. https://doi.org/10.1111/sipr.12003

Klimova, B. (2018). Learning a foreign language: A review on recent findings about its effect on the enhancement of cognitive functions among healthy older individuals. *Frontiers in Human Neuroscience, 12*, 305–305. https://doi.org/10.3389/fnhum.2018.00305

Lammer, L., Beyer, F., Luppa, M., Sanders, C., Baber, R., Engel, C., Wirkner, K., Loffler, M., Riedel-Heller, S. G., Villringer, A., & Witte, A. V. (2023). Impact of social isolation on grey matter structure and cognitive functions: A population-based longitudinal neuroimaging study. *Elife, 12*, e83660. https://doi.org/10.7554/eLife.83660

Larsen, L. T. (2022). Not merely the absence of disease: A genealogy of the WHO's positive health definition. *History of the Human Sciences, 35*(1), 111–131. https://doi.org/10.1177/0952695121995355

Levy, B. (2009). Stereotype embodiment: A psychosocial approach to aging. *Current Directions in Psychological Science, 18*(6), 332–336. https://doi.org/10.1111/j.1467-8721.2009.01662.x

Levy, B. (2022). *Breaking the age code: How your beliefs about aging determine how long & well you live* (1st ed.). William Morrow, an imprint of HarperCollinsPublishers.

Levy, B. R., Slade, M. D., Chang, E.-S., Kannoth, S., & Wang, S.-Y. (2018). Ageism amplifies cost and prevalence of health conditions. *The Gerontologist, 60*(1), 174–181. https://doi.org/10.1093/geront/gny131

Livingston, G., Huntley, J., Sommerlad, A., Ames, D., Ballard, C., Banerjee, S., Brayne, C., Burns, A., Cohen-Mansfield, J., Cooper, C., Costafreda, S. G., Dias, A., Fox, N., Gitlin, L. N., Howard, R., Kales, H. C., Kivimäki, M., Larson, E. B., Ogunniyi, A.,, . . ., Mukadam, N. (2020). Dementia prevention, intervention, and care: 2020 report of the Lancet Commission. *Lancet, 396*(10248), 413–446. https://doi.org/10.1016/S0140-6736(20)30367-6

Luong, G., Charles, S. T., & Fingerman, K. L. (2011). Better with age: Social relationships across adulthood. *Journal of Social and Personal Relationships, 28*(1), 9–23. https://doi.org/10.1177/0265407510391362

Macera, C. A., Cavanaugh, A., & Bellettiere, J. (2016). State of the art review: Physical activity and older adults. *American Journal of Lifestyle Medicine, 11*(1), 42–57. https://doi.org/10.1177/1559827615571897

Mansfield, L., Victor, C., Meads, C., Daykin, N., Tomlinson, A., Lane, J., Gray, K., & Golding, A. (2021). A conceptual review of loneliness in adults: Qualitative evidence synthesis. *International Journal of Environmental Research and Public Health, 18*(21), 11522. https://doi.org/10.3390/ijerph182111522

Mansky, R., Marzel, A., Orav, E. J., Chocano-Bedoya, P. O., Grünheid, P., Mattle, M., Freystätter, G., Stähelin, H. B., Egli, A., & Bischoff-Ferrari, H. A. (2020). Playing a musical instrument is associated with slower cognitive decline in community-dwelling older adults. *Aging Clinical and Experimental Research, 32*(8), 1577–1584. https://doi.org/10.1007/s40520-020-01472-9

Marmot, M., Allen, J., Bell, R., Bloomer, E., & Goldblatt, P. (2012). WHO European review of social determinants of health and the health divide. *Lancet, 380*(9846), 1011–1029. https://doi.org/10.1016/S0140-6736(12)61228-8

Marquez, D. X., Aguiñaga, S., Vásquez, P. M., Conroy, D. E., Erickson, K. I., Hillman, C., Stillman, C. M., Ballard, R. M., Sheppard, B. B., Petruzzello, S. J., King, A. C., & Powell, K. E. (2020). A systematic review of physical activity and quality of life and well-being. *Translational Behavioral Medicine, 10*(5), 1098–1109. https://doi.org/10.1093/tbm/ibz198

McMaughan, D. J., Oloruntoba, O., & Smith, M. L. (2020). Socioeconomic status and access to healthcare: Interrelated drivers for healthy aging. *Frontiers in Public Health, 8*, 231. https://doi.org/10.3389/fpubh.2020.00231

Menassa, M., Stronks, K., Khatmi, F., Roa Díaz, Z. M., Espinola, O. P., Gamba, M., Itodo, O. A., Buttia, C., Wehrli, F., Minder, B., Velarde, M. R., & Franco, O. H. (2023). Concepts and definitions of healthy ageing: A systematic review and synthesis of theoretical models. *eClinicalMedicine, 56*, 101821. https://doi.org/10.1016/j.eclinm.2022.101821

Mikton, C., de la Fuente-Núñez, V., Officer, A., & Krug, E. (2021). Ageism: A social determinant of health that has come of age. *Lancet, 397*(10282), 1333–1334. https://doi.org/10.1016/S0140-6736(21)00524-9

Narushima, M., Liu, J., & Diestelkamp, N. (2018). Lifelong learning in active ageing discourse: Its conserving effect on wellbeing, health and vulnerability. *Ageing and Society, 38*(4), 651–675. https://doi.org/10.1017/s0144686x16001136

National Academies of Sciences & Medicine. (2020). *Social isolation and loneliness in older adults: Opportunities for the health care system*. The National Academies Press. https://doi.org/10.17226/25663

Nelson, T. D. (2005). Ageism: Prejudice against our feared future self. *Journal of Social Issues, 61*(2), 207–221. https://doi.org/10.1111/j.1540-4560.2005.00402.x

Newman, M. G., & Zainal, N. H. (2020). The value of maintaining social connections for mental health in older people. *The Lancet Public Health, 5*(1), e12–e13. https://doi.org/10.1016/s2468-2667(19)30253-1

Noguchi, T., Ishihara, M., Murata, C., Nakagawa, T., Komatsu, A., Kondo, K., & Saito, T. (2022). Art and cultural activity engagement and depressive symptom onset among older adults: A longitudinal study from the Japanese Gerontological Evaluation Study. *International Journal of Geriatric Psychiatry, 37*(3), n/a. https://doi.org/10.1002/gps.5685

O'Rourke, H. M., Collins, L., & Sidani, S. (2018). Interventions to address social connectedness and loneliness for older adults: A scoping review. *BMC Geriatrics, 18*(1), 214. https://doi.org/10.1186/s12877-018-0897-x

Pachana, N., & Wahl, H.-W. (2022). *Healthy aging: Current and future frameworks and developments*. https://doi.org/10.1016/B978-0-12-818697-8.00054-6

Paiva, A. F., Cunha, C., Voss, G., & Delerue Matos, A. (2023). The interrelationship between social connectedness and social engagement and its relation with cognition: A study using SHARE data. *Ageing and Society, 43*(8), 1735–1753. https://doi.org/10.1017/S0144686X2100129X

Pallavicini, F., Pepe, A., & Mantovani, F. (2021). Commercial off-the-shelf video games for reducing stress and anxiety: Systematic review. *JMIR Mental Health, 8*(8), e28150. https://doi.org/10.2196/28150

Palmer, V. J., Gray, C. M., Fitzsimons, C., Mutrie, N., Wyke, S., Der, G., Chastin, S. F. M., Skelton, D. A., Cox, S., Coulter, E., Čukić, I., Dall, P., Deary, I., Dontje, M., Gale, C., Gill, J., Granat, M., Greig, C., Hindle, E., ..., Stewart, S. (2021). Sitting as a moral practice: Older adults' accounts from qualitative interviews on sedentary behaviours. *Sociol Health & Illness, 43*(9), 2102–2120. https://doi.org/10.1111/1467-9566.13383

Paúl, C., Ribeiro, O., & Teixeira, L. (2012). Active ageing: An empirical approach to the WHO model. *Current Gerontology and Geriatric Research, 2012*, 382972–382910. https://doi.org/10.1155/2012/382972

Penninkilampi, R., Casey, A. N., Singh, M. F., & Brodaty, H. (2018). The association between social engagement, loneliness, and risk of dementia: A systematic review and meta-analysis. *Journal of Alzheimers Disease, 66*(4), 1619–1633. https://doi.org/10.3233/jad-180439

Pierzycki, R. H., Edmondson-Jones, M., Dawes, P., Munro, K. J., Moore, D. R., & Kitterick, P. T. (2020). Associations between hearing health and well-being in unilateral hearing impairment. *Ear & Hearing, 42*(3), 520–530. https://doi.org/10.1097/aud.0000000000000969

Plagg, B., Engl, A., Piccoliori, G., & Eisendle, K. (2020). Prolonged social isolation of the elderly during COVID-19: Between benefit and damage. *Archives of Gerontology and Geriatrics, 89*, 104086. https://doi.org/10.1016/j.archger.2020.104086

Richmond, C. A. M., & Ross, N. A. (2009). The determinants of First Nation and Inuit health: A critical population health approach. *Health Place, 15*(2), 403–411. https://doi.org/10.1016/j.healthplace.2008.07.004

Rosenberg, F. (2009). The MoMA Alzheimer's Project: Programming and resources for making art accessible to people with Alzheimer's disease and their caregivers. *Arts & Health, 1*(1), 93–97.

Rowe, J. W., & Kahn, R. L. (1997). Successful aging. *The Gerontologist, 37*(4), 433–440. https://doi.org/10.1093/geront/37.4.433

Slade, K., Plack, C. J., & Nuttall, H. E. (2020). The effects of age-related hearing loss on the brain and cognitive function. *Trends in Neurosciences, 43*(10), 810–821. https://doi.org/10.1016/j.tins.2020.07.005

Spiteri, K., Broom, D., Bekhet, A. H., de Caro, J. X., Laventure, B., & Grafton, K. (2019). Barriers and motivators of physical activity participation in middle-aged and older-adults—A systematic review. *Journal of Aging and Physical Activity, 27*(4), 929–944. https://doi.org/10.1123/japa.2018-0343

Stern, Y. (2012). Cognitive reserve in ageing and Alzheimer's disease. *The Lancet Neurology, 11*(11), 1006–1012. https://doi.org/10.1016/s1474-4422(12)70191-6

Suragarn, U., Hain, D., & Pfaff, G. (2021). Approaches to enhance social connection in older adults: An integrative review of literature. *Aging and Health Research, 1*(3), 100029. https://doi.org/10.1016/j.ahr.2021.100029

Vujic, A., Mowszowski, L., Meares, S., Batchelor, J., & Naismith, S. L. (2022). Not all mentally stimulating activities are alike: Insights from a 4-factor model and implications for late-life cognition. *Aging Neuropsychology and Cognition, 30(5)*, 822–836. https://doi.org/10.1080/13825585.2022.2094878

Wahl, H.-W., Iwarsson, S., & Oswald, F. (2012). Aging well and the environment: Toward an integrative model and research agenda for the future. *Gerontologist, 52*(3), 306-316. https://doi.org/10.1093/geront/gnr154

Warburton, J., & McLaughlin, D. (2007). Passing on our culture: How older Australians from diverse cultural backgrounds contribute to civil society. *Journal of Cross-Cultural Gerontology, 22*(1), 47–60. https://doi.org/10.1007/s10823-006-9012-4

World Health Organization. (2002). *Active ageing: A policy framework.*

World Health Organization. (2020). *Decade of healthy ageing: Baseline report.* https://www.who.int/initiatives/decade-of-healthy-ageing

World Health Organization. (2021a). *Global report on ageism.* https://www.who.int/publications/i/item/9789240016866

World Health Organization. (2021b). *Global report on ageism.* https://apps.who.int/iris/handle/10665/340208

World Health Organization. (2021c). *Social isolation and loneliness among older people: Advocacy brief.* https://apps.who.int/iris/handle/10665/343206

World Health Organization. (2022). *About the global network for age-friendly cities and communities.* https://extranet.who.int/agefriendlyworld/who-network/

World Health Organization. (2023). *Age-friendly world.* https://extranet.who.int/agefriendlyworld/about-us/

Ye, Z. (2023). Factors influencing memory decline in older adults: A comprehensive review. *Studies in Psychological Science, 1*(1), 27–41.

Index

acceptance versus denial, 118
activities of daily living (ADLs), 237
activity theory, 48–49
ADLs. *See* activities of daily living
African American LGB women, 28
age-friendly environments, domains of, 314
age-friendly world, 313
ageism, 311. *See also* aging
   benevolent and hostile, 311–312
   domains, 311
   financial and social costs of, 312
   and marginalization, 253–254
   stereotypes and, 309–310
   strategies to counteract, 18–19
   WHO define as, 311
   WHO framework for action against, 312–313
aging, 2. *See also specific entries*
   biological models of, 36
   genetics of, 41–43
   internationally, 5–9
   population, meeting needs of, 9, 10
   psychological models of, 43–44
   research methods in psychology of, 11–14
   social models of, 47–48
   views of, 18
aging workforce, 257–259. *See also* retirement
   COVID-19 pandemic, 258
      quiet quitting, 258
   defined benefit (DB), 258
   defined contribution (DC) plans, 258
   historical and demographic changes, 257–259
alcohol-related dementia, 200–201
Alzheimer disease, 103, 191
   biomarkers of, 193–195
      NIA/AA criteria, 193, 194
   genetics of, 192–193
   neuropathological ratings of, 192
   treatments for, 191–192

American Psychological Association (APA), 24
American with Disabilities Act of 1990, 257
amyloid angiopathy, 192
amyotrophic lateral sclerosis (ALS), 199
anabolic resistance, 58
anemia, 62
antagonistic pleiotropy, 38
antioxidants, 40
anxiety disorders, 145–147, 156
APA. *See* American Psychological Association
aphasia, 198
apolipoprotein E (APOE), 43
apoptosis, 38
arrhythmia, 62
asthma, 81
atrophy, hair follicles, 60
autoimmune responses, 63

Baby Boomer population, 10, 232
balance/gait, 61
B cells, 63
behavioral initiative, loss of, 199
bereavement, 216
   after caregiving, 224
   bereaved individuals, intervention for, 222–223
      grief work, concept of, 222
   clinical diagnoses, 218
   common reactions to, 217
   definitions of, 216
   differentiating symptoms of, 218
   dual process model of coping with, 221
   and mental health disorders, 217, 219
   theoretical models of adjustment to, 220–222
BFOQ. *See* bona fide occupational qualification
binge drinking among adults, 149
BMI. *See* body mass index
body mass index (BMI), 58

bona fide occupational qualification (BFOQ), 257
brain, 76, 83. *See also specific entries*
 brain regions of interest (ROIs), 94, 96
 CT image, 93–94
 diffusion imaging, 96
 diffusion MRI, 94
 diffusion-weighted imaging (DWI), 94
 event-related brain potential (ERP), 98
 functional MRI (fMRI), 99, 100
 magnetic resonance spectroscopy (MRS), 94
 MRI image, 93–94, 100
 MRI slices in axial plane, 94
 PET scanning, 98, 99
 resting-state fMRI (rs-fMRI), 99
 single-photon emission computed tomography (SPECT), 98, 99
 voxel-based morphometry (VBM), 96 map, 97
brain, age-related changes in, 93
 changes with typical aging, 100–103
 investigation, methods of, 93–100
brain-derived neurotrophic factor (BDNF), 108
brain volume loss, 103
Broca aphasia, 199

calcium reduction, 58
caloric restriction, 40–41
cannabis, use trends in, 149
CAPC. *See* Center to Advance Palliative Care
cardiovascular disorders (CVDs), disorders of, 78
 cerebral arteriosclerosis, 79
 congestive heart failure, 79
 hypertension, 79
 strokes, 79
cardiovascular system, 62
 age-related changes, to physiology, 62–63
care, continuum of, 214
caregiving relationships, 237–238
 caregivers, adult children as, 240–241
 caregivers, older adults as, 242
 caregiving, general trends in, 238–239
 physical, psychological, and emotional impacts of, 239–240
 sociocultural theory (SCT), 238
cartilage, 59
cataracts, 77
CDC. *See* Centers for Disease Control and Prevention
cell senescence, 38
Center for Epidemiologic Studies Depression Scale (CES-D), 151

Centers for Disease Control and Prevention (CDC), 9
Center to Advance Palliative Care (CAPC), 216
cerebral arteriosclerosis, 79
CES-D. *See* Center for Epidemiologic Studies Depression Scale
Chinese Exclusion Act, 19
chronic kidney disease, 85
chronic obstructive pulmonary disease (COPD), 81
chronological age, 3, 255
circumlocutions, 194
Civil Rights Act of 1964, 257
clinical decisional capacity, 280–281
cognitive abilities, 2
cognitive aging, 166. *See also specific entries*
cognitive aging on everyday living, impacts of, 177
 cognitive training, 178
 daily living, activities of, 177
 healthy cognitive aging, factors promote, 178
 rehabilitation, 178
cognitive aging research, 176–177
 activation of negative stereotypes, 176
 cohort effect, 176
 demographic influences, 176
 Flynn effect, 176
 stereotype threat, 176
 stereotype threat and underperform task, 176
cognitive aging, theories of, 173
 controlled and automatic processing, 173
 inhibitory deficit hypothesis, 174–175
 physiological, brain-based models, 175
  HAROLD model, 175
  STAC model, 175
 sensory deficit and common cause hypotheses, 174
 speed of processing, 174
 theory of cognitive reserve, 175
 top-down and bottom-up processing, 173
cognitive behavioral therapy (CBT) for depression, 155, 156
cognitive decline, 185, 191. *See also* cognitive aging
 APA criteria, 185
 DSM-5-TR criteria, 185
cognitive functioning, changes in, 167–168
 attention, 168
 emotional processing, 172
 intelligence and executive functioning, 170–171

language, 171–172
memory, 169–170
perception, 167
sensory processing, 167
wisdom, 172
cognitive impairment, 150
cognitive impairment, not dementia (CIND), 188
cognitively challenging activities, 305
cognitive stimulation
 risks posed by lack of, 306
cohabitation, 232, 235
cohort effects, 17–18, 23–25.
communication, 304
Compensation-Related Utilization of Neural Circuits Hypothesis (CRUNCH), 103
conflicting aging stereotypes, 166
congestive heart failure, 79
conscientiousness, 122
conservatorship, 281
constipation, 86–87
continuity theory, 49
COPD. See chronic obstructive pulmonary disease
coping strategies
 adept at managing stressors, 125
 approach versus avoidance strategies, 124
 behavioral versus cognitive strategies, 124
 COVID-19 pandemic as significant stressor, 125
 problem-focused versus emotion-focused strategies, 124
Cornell Scale for Depression in Dementia (CSDD), 152–154
coronavirus disease-19 (COVID-19), 80
corpus callosum, 102
critical gerontology, 49–50
cultural stressors, 19–20, 25–27
culture hypothesis, 18

DBT. See dialectical behavior therapy
death
 advance care planning, 212–213
 attitudes toward, 211–212
 causes of, 210
 COVID-19–associated, 210
 definition of, 210
 institutionalization of, 211
 medical aid in dying (MAID), 215–216
  legislation, 215
 palliative and hospice care, 213–214
 trajectories, 211
default-mode network (DMN), 99

defense mechanisms, 121, 122
Defense of Marriage Act, 24
delirium, 186–187
 APA, 2022 criteria, 187
 DSM-5-TR diagnostic criteria, 186
dementia, 121, 189
 museum programs for persons living with, 307
demoralization, 214
dermatitis, 75
diabetes mellitus, 82
diabetes mellitus, long-term problems associated with, 83
dialectical behavior therapy (DBT), 156, 157
digestive system, 69
 age-related changes to physiology, 69–70
digestive system, disorders of, 86–87
 constipation, 86–87
 gastritis, 87
disabling hearing loss, 60
disenfranchised grief, 223
disengagement theory, 49
divorce rates, 232
DMN. See default-mode network
DNA damage, 57
driving capacity, assessment, 284–285

early secure attachment, proposed model of, 121
ego integrity, 119
ego integrity versus despair, 118
elder abuse
 ethical considerations in cases, 286–288
 respecting cultural differences in cases of, 288–291
 risk and protective factors for, 286
elder mistreatment, 285
elder rights and protections, resources, 287
embolic stroke, 198
embolus, 198
emotional functioning, in late life, 125
 age and emotional well-being, 126
 age-related differences in emotion regulation, 133–135
  emotion-regulation strategies, 134
  SOC-ER model, 134
 changes in older adulthood, 128–131
  COVID-19 pandemic, 131
 happy aging, keys to, 135
 models of, 126–128
 positive and negative stimuli, attention to, 131–133
  age-related positivity effect, 131

emotional reactivity, 130
emotion regulation skills, 130
endocrine system, 65
    age-related changes to physiology, 65–66
    disorders of, 82–84
        diabetes mellitus, 82
        hyperthyroidism, 82–83
        hypothyroidism, 84
        thyroid cancer, 84
end of life. *See also* death
    advance care planning about, 212–213
    legislation, 212
        Patient Self-Determination Act, 212
    mental health at, 214–215
    POLST documents, 212
    predictors of, 213
epigenetics, 43
Erik Erikson's theory of psychosocial development, 118–120
ethanol (ETOH), 201
ethics
    in long-term care, 277–279
    in research, 291–292

felt age, 3
financial capacity, assessment, 283–284
foundational ethics of decision-making, 279
free radicals, 39–40
frontotemporal dementia, 198–200
functional ability, pathway to optimize, 299–302
functional age, 3, 255

gait speed, 4
gastritis, 87
GDS. *See* Geriatric Depression Scale
generational influences, 10
Generation X, 10, 46
Generation Z, 10
generativity, concept of, 21
genetics of aging, 41–43
genome-wide association studies (GWAS), 42
Geriatric Depression Scale (GDS), 151, 152, 156
gerotranscendence, 118, 119
glare, 60
glaucoma, 77
gray divorce, 232
gray matter, 101, 104
    plasticity, 105
grief, 216. *See also* bereavement
grip strength, 4
group membership, importance of, 303

growth, 20–21, 27
guardianship, 281
    case example, 282–283
gut–brain axis, 109
GWAS. *See* genome-wide association studies

happiness, definitions of, 126
happiness ratings, 126
HAROLD model, of brain, 103
Hayflick limit, 37
health disparities, 19–20, 25–27
Health Equity Promotion Model, 28
health in later life, model of, 301
health, social determinants of, 302–303
healthy aging, models of, 299
healthy brain aging, 100
hearing, 60–61
    loss, 60
Helicobacter pylori, 87
hepatitis C, 201
hippocampus, 102
HIV infection, 201
hormesis, 40
Huntington disease, 201
hypertension, 79, 102
hyperthyroidism, 82–83
hypothalamic-pituitary-adrenal (HPA) axis, 121
hypothyroidism, 84

identity crisis, 44
immune system, 63
    age-related changes to physiology, 63–64
IMPACT, clinical trials for primary care, 155
infarction, 198
insulin-like growth factor 1 (IGF-1), 108
insulin resistance, 66
integumentary system, 56
    age-related changes, physiology of, 56–57
    disorders of, 74–75
        dermatitis, 75
        pruritus, 75
        shingles, 75
        skin cancer, 75
interpersonal psychotherapy (IPT), 155
intersectionality, 27–29
ischemia, 197

Japan Geriatrics Society, 3
job performance, and age, 259–261

lacuna, 198
LATE. *See* limbic-predominant age-related TDP-43 encephalopathy
late life, significant relationships in, 235. *See also* caregiving relationships
   friendship, 236–237
   sibling relationships, 235–236
late-life spousal loss, 255
   characteristics, general, 223–224
leisure activities, 305
Lewy body disease, 195–197
LGBTQ+
   adults, 21, 24, 29
   aging, 28
      communities, 21, 24, 28
   health, 26, 27
   older adults, 22–27
   population, 23
   protagonists, 24
   rights movement, 23
life course perspective, 47
ligaments, 59
limbic-predominant age-related TDP-43 encephalopathy (LATE), 200
loneliness, 308–309
lung cancer, 81-82

macular degeneration, 77
major depressive disorder (MDD), 217
major neurocognitive disorder (NCD), 185
marital quality, 233
   affects health, 233
   biological/physiological pathways, responses of, 234
   deleterious effects of, 234
   impacts physical and psychological health, 234
   social selection, 234
marriage ends, 234
   dissolved troubled marriages, long-term impact of, 235
   divorce/widowhood, 235
   health and psychological outcomes, impact on, 234–235
   negative physical consequences, 235
MCI. *See* mild cognitive impairment
MDD. *See* major depressive disorder
menopause, 68
mental health, 141, 142, 151
   conditions, among adults 65 and older, 146
   conditions among older adults, assessment of, 151, 153. *See also specific depression scales and tools*
   conditions other than depression, assessment instruments for, 153
   stigma, 143–144
mental healthcare. *See* mental health
mental stimulation, 305
mild cognitive impairment (MCI), 109, 185, 188
mitochondrial DNA, 39
mood disorders, 144–145, 154
   DSM criteria, 145
mourning, 216
multimorbidity, 74, 80
muscle–to–body fat ratio shifts, 69
musculoskeletal system, 57–59
   age-related changes, to physiology, 58–59
   disorders of, 75–76
      osteoarthritis, 76
      osteoporosis, 76
      sarcopenia, 76

National Institute on Minority Health and Health Disparities (NIMHD), 26
National Palliative Care Research Center (NPCRC), 216
NCD. *See* major neurocognitive disorder
negative age stereotypes, 312
nervous system, 59
   age-related changes, to physiology, 59–60
   disorders of, 76–78
      cataracts, 77
      glaucoma, 77
      macular degeneration, 77
      peripheral neuropathy, 78
      presbycusis, 77–78
      tinnitus, 77–78
neurocognitive disorder, 188
   DSM criteria, 188
neurocognitive disorders (NCD), 2, 185–189
   causes of, 189
neuroplasticity, 103–109
   drivers of, 105
   individual and combined influences of exercise, diet, and sleep on, 108
   principles of, 106
neutrophils, 63
NIMHD. *See* National Institute on Minority Health and Health Disparities
normalcy–pathology homology, 103
NPCRC. *See* National Palliative Care Research Center
nucleotide polymorphism, 42
nuptial and relationship status, 231
   physical and psychological health, effects on, 232–233

OAs. *See* older adults
occipital lobes, 102
older adults (OAs)
    advance care planning for, 275–277
        do-not-resuscitate (DNR) order, 275
        Physician Orders for Life-Sustaining Treatment (POLST), 276
        power of attorney (POA) document, 275, 276
        sample questions, documenting treatment preferences, 276
    defining, 3–5
    empirically supported treatments for, 154
        anxiety disorders, 156
        mood disorders, 154
        personality disorders, 156–157
        posttraumatic stress disorder, 156
        schizophrenia, 157–158
        substance use disorders, 157
        suicide, 154
    ethnically minoritized, 17
        cohort effects, 17–18
        cultural stressors, 19–20
        growth, 20–21
        health disparities, 19–20
        resilience, 20–21
        strategies to counteract ageism, 18–19
        views of aging, 18
    relationships
        impact of COVID-19 pandemic on, 242–243
    sexually and gender-diverse, 21–23
older worker, 255–257
oldest old, 4
olfactory impairment, 61
    risk, 61
osteoarthritis, 76
osteoporosis, 76
oxidative stress, 70

Parkinson disease, 197
Patient Health Questionnaire-9 (PHQ-9), 152
Patient Self-Determination Act (PSDA), 212
peripheral neuropathy, 78
periventricular WMHs, 101
personality development, 117
personality disorders, 147–148, 156–157
personality theories, 118
    coping perspective, 124–125
    model, proposed, 121
    personality change in adulthood, longitudinal studies of, 123–124
        mean-level stability, 123
        rank-order stability, 123
    psychodynamic perspectives, 118–122
    trait perspectives, 122–123
PGDT. *See* prolonged grief disorder therapy
p53 gene, 43
pharmacotherapy interventions for anxiety disorders, 156
PHN. *See* postherpetic neuralgia
PHQ-9. *See* Patient Health Questionnaire-9
physical disabilities, 2
physical inactivity, 304
    risks posed by lack of, 304
pickleball activity, 305
Pick's disease, 199
plasticity, 104
platelets, 63
pneumonia, 80
posterior cortical atrophy, 195
postherpetic neuralgia (PHN), 75
posttraumatic stress disorder (PTSD), 147, 156, 217
PPA. *See* primary progressive aphasia
pre–old age, 4
presbycusis, 77–78
primary cognitive functions, affected in aging, 171–172
    attention, 168
    emotional processing, 172
    intelligence and executive functioning, 170–171
    language, 171–172
        comprehension, 172
        tip-of-the-tongue (TOT) states, 171
    memory, 169–170
    perception, 167–168
    sensation, 167–168
    wisdom, 172
primary progressive aphasia (PPA), 195, 199, 200
prion disease, 201
problem-solving therapy, 155
prolonged grief disorder, 219–220
prolonged grief disorder therapy (PGDT), 223
prostate cancer, 86
protective arrangements, 281
pruritus, 75
PSDA. *See* Patient Self-Determination Act
psychological models, of aging, 43–44
psychological treatment options, by diagnosis, 154
psychology of aging, research methods in, 11–14
    age effects, 11
    cohort effects, 11
    cohort-sequential design, 13
    cross-sectional research, 13

longitudinal research, 11
measurement invariance, 12
missing at random (MAR), 12
missing completely at random (MCAR), 12
not missing at random (NMAR), 12
sequential designs, 13
time-of-measurement effects, 11
time-sequential study, 13
psychosocial development, Erikson's stages of, 44
identity crisis, 44
stage crisis between "integrity" and "despair," 44
PTSD. See posttraumatic stress disorder

questionnaire. See Patient Health Questionnaire-9 (PHQ-9)

racism, 2
Railroad Retirement System, 3
reactive oxygen species (ROS), 39, 40
red blood cells, 63
REM sleep duration, 109
reproductive system, 68
age-related changes, to physiology, 68–69
disorders of, 85–86
prostate cancer, 85–86
uterine and ovarian cancer, 85–86
resilience, 20–21, 27
respiratory system, 64
age-related changes to physiology, 64–65
disorders of, 80–82
asthma, 81
chronic obstructive pulmonary disease (COPD), 81
coronavirus disease-19 (COVID-19), 80
lung cancer, 81–82
pneumonia, 80
resveratrol, 40
retirement, 6
changing nature of, 261
France raised age of, 6
historical changes, 261
patterns and options, 261–262
bridge employment, 261
encore careers, 261
typologies focused on, 262
planning, 10, 265–266
transitions, factors related to, 262–265
flexible arrangements, 265
"gig" employment, 265
part-time work, 265
push factors and pull factors, 262–264

role theory, 48
ROS. See reactive oxygen species

sarcopenia, 76
SAVI. See Strength and Vulnerability Integration model
Scaffolding Theory of Aging and Cognition (STAC), 103
schizophrenia, 150, 157–158
Brief Psychiatric Rating Scale, 158
cognitive behavioral social skills training, 158
psychosocial treatments, 158
seborrheic dermatitis, 75
sedentary behaviors, 304
selective optimization with compensation (SOC), 44–46
Baltes's model of human development, 45–46
cultural shifts, 46
fourth age, 46
nonnormative influences, 46
normative history-graded influences, 46
social influences, 46
selective serotonin reuptake inhibitors (SSRIs), 156
self-esteem, 48
self-neglect, 285
self-sustaining system, 3
senescence-associated secretory phenotype (SASP), 38
SES. See socioeconomic status
sexual consent capacity, assessment, 284
shingles, 75
single nucleotide polymorphism (SNP), 42
sirtuin, 43
skin cancer, 75
small vessel disease, 101
smell, 61
smoking cessation, 101
SNP. See single nucleotide polymorphism
SOC. See selective optimization with compensation
social determinants of health, 50
social engagement, 307
social environment, 121
social isolation, 307
risks posed by, 308
social models of aging, 47–48
social relationships, importance of, 303
social security, 3
socioeconomic status (SES), 19–20
socioemotional selectivity theory (SST), 46, 126–130

Soskin, Betty Reid, 2
spleen, 63
spousal loss on partner mortality, impact of, 224
    widowhood effect, 224
SSRIs. *See* selective serotonin reuptake inhibitors
SST. *See* socioemotional selectivity theory
STAC. *See* Scaffolding Theory of Aging and Cognition
stereotype content model, 310
stereotype embodiment, 310–311
    positive age stereotypes, examples of, 310–311
Strength and Vulnerability Integration (SAVI) model, 127, 128
stress reactivity, 129
strokes, 79. *See also* embolic stroke
subjective age, 3
substance use disorders, 148–150, 157
    diagnostic orphans, 150
    DSM criteria, 150
    Gerontology Alcohol Project (GAP), 157
    Project GOAL, 157
    SAMHSA recommendation, 157
    treatment improvement protocol (TIP), 157
suicide, 148, 154
super aging, 100
super old, 4
surrogate decision-making, 280
sweat output, 61

taste, age-related changes in, 61
taste buds, 61
TBIs. *See* traumatic brain injuries
T cells, 63, 64
tDCS. *See* transcranial direct current stimulation
telomeres, 36–39
TGGD older adults, 23, 24
thrombus, 198
thyroid, 66
thyroid cancer, 84
tinnitus, 77–78
trait theories, 122
    Five-Factor Model, 122
    OCEAN traits, 122
    personality traits, 122

transcranial direct current stimulation (tDCS), 109
translation, 42
traumatic brain injuries (TBIs), 186, 188, 190
typical brain aging, 100

unfinished architecture, 45
Uniform Declaration of Death Act of 1980, 210
unmarried aging population, 232
urinary system, 66–67
    age-related changes, to physiology, 67–68
    disorders of, 84–85
        chronic kidney disease, 85
        urinary tract infections (UTIs), 67, 84–85, 187
urinary tract infections (UTIs), 67, 84–85, 187
U-shaped curve, to happiness, 126
U.S. population by age group, as of 2023, 8
uterine and ovarian cancer, 85–86
UTIs. *See* urinary tract infections
UV light, 57

vascular disease, 197–198
vascular endothelial growth factor (VEGF), 108
VEGF. *See* vascular endothelial growth factor
vestibular receptors, 61, 62
vision, 60
visual difficulties, 60

waking hours, 109
weathering hypothesis, 50
white matter hyperintensities (WMHs), 101, 102
white matter plasticity, 105
WHO. *See* World Health Organization
WMHs. *See* white matter hyperintensities
World Health Organization (WHO), 213
    framework for action against ageism, 312–313
    model of active aging, 300

xerosis, 75

yeast *silent information regulator 2* (Sir2), 41